Lecture Notes in Computer Science

Lecture Notes in Computer Science

Vol. 23: Programming Methodology. 4th Informatik Symposium, IBM Germany Wildbad, September 25–27, 1974. Edited by C. E. Hackl. VI, 501 pages. 1975.

Vol. 24: Parallel Processing. Proceedings 1974. Edited by T. Feng. VI, 433 pages. 1975.

Vol. 25: Category Theory Applied to Computation and Control. Proceedings 1974. Edited by E. G. Manes. X, 245 pages. 1975.

Vol. 26: GI-4. Jahrestagung, Berlin, 9.–12. Oktober 1974. Herausgegeben im Auftrag der GI von D. Siefkes. IX, 748 Seiten. 1975.

Vol. 27: Optimization Techniques. IFIP Technical Conference. Novosibirsk, July 1–7, 1974. (Series: I.F.I.P. TC7 Optimization Conferences.) Edited by G. I. Marchuk. VIII, 507 pages. 1975.

Vol. 28: Mathematical Foundations of Computer Science. 3rd Symposium at Jadwisin near Warsaw, June 17–22, 1974. Edited by A. Blikle. VII, 484 pages. 1975.

Vol. 29: Interval Mathematics. Procedings 1975. Edited by K. Nickel. VI, 331 pages. 1975.

Vol. 30: Software Engineering. An Advanced Course. Edited by F. L. Bauer. (Formerly published 1973 as Lecture Notes in Economics and Mathematical Systems, Vol. 81) XII, 545 pages. 1975.

Vol. 31: S. H. Fuller, Analysis of Drum and Disk Storage Units. IX, 283 pages. 1975.

Vol. 32: Mathematical Foundations of Computer Science 1975. Proceedings 1975. Edited by J. Bečvář. X, 476 pages. 1975.

Vol. 33: Automata Theory and Formal Languages, Kaiserslautern, May 20–23, 1975. Edited by H. Brakhage on behalf of GI. VIII, 292 Seiten. 1975.

Vol. 34: GI – 5. Jahrestagung, Dortmund 8.–10. Oktober 1975. Herausgegeben im Auftrag der GI von J. Mühlbacher. X, 755 Seiten. 1975.

Vol. 35: W. Everling, Exercises in Computer Systems Analysis. (Formerly published 1972 as Lecture Notes in Economics and Mathematical Systems, Vol. 65) VIII, 184 pages. 1975.

Vol. 36: S. A. Greibach, Theory of Program Structures: Schemes, Semantics, Verification. XV, 364 pages. 1975.

Vol. 37: C. Böhm, λ-Calculus and Computer Science Theory. Proceedings 1975. XII, 370 pages. 1975.

Vol. 38: P. Branquart, J.-P. Cardinael, J. Lewi, J.-P. Delescaille, M. Vanbegin. An Optimized Translation Process and Its Application to ALGOL 68. IX, 334 pages. 1976.

Vol. 39: Data Base Systems. Proceedings 1975. Edited by H. Hasselmeier and W. Spruth. VI, 386 pages. 1976.

Vol. 40: Optimization Techniques. Modeling and Optimization in the Service of Man. Part 1. Proceedings 1975. Edited by J. Cea. XIV, 854 pages. 1976.

Vol. 41: Optimization Techniques. Modeling and Optimization in the Service of Man. Part 2. Proceedings 1975. Edited by J. Cea. XIII, 852 pages. 1976.

Vol. 42: James E. Donahue, Complementary Definitions of Programming Language Semantics. VII, 172 pages. 1976.

Vol. 43: E. Specker und V. Strassen, Komplexität von Entscheidungsproblemen. Ein Seminar. V, 217 Seiten. 1976.

Vol. 44: ECI Conference 1976. Proceedings 1976. Edited by K. Samelson. VIII, 322 pages. 1976.

Vol. 45: Mathematical Foundations of Computer Science 1976. Proceedings 1976. Edited by A. Mazurkiewicz. XI, 601 pages. 1976.

Vol. 46: Language Hierarchies and Interfaces. Edited by F. L. Bauer and K. Samelson. X, 428 pages. 1976.

Vol. 47: Methods of Algorithmic Language Implementation. Edited by A. Ershov and C. H. A. Koster. VIII, 351 pages. 1977.

Vol. 48: Theoretical Computer Science, Darmstadt, March 1977. Edited by H. Tzschach, H. Waldschmidt and H. K.-G. Walter on behalf of GI. VIII, 418 pages. 1977.

Vol. 49: Interactive Systems. Proceedings 1976. Edited by A. Blaser and C. Hackl. VI, 380 pages. 1976.

Vol. 50: A. C. Hartmann, A Concurrent Pascal Compiler for Minicomputers. VI, 119 pages. 1977.

Vol. 51: B. S. Garbow, Matrix Eigensystem Routines – Eispack Guide Extension. VIII, 343 pages. 1977.

Vol. 52: Automata, Languages and Programming. Fourth Colloquium, University of Turku, July 1977. Edited by A. Salomaa and M. Steinby. X, 569 pages. 1977.

Vol. 53: Mathematical Foundations of Computer Science. Proceedings 1977. Edited by J. Gruska. XII, 608 pages. 1977.

Vol. 54: Design and Implementation of Programming Languages. Proceedings 1976. Edited by J. H. Williams and D. A. Fisher. X, 496 pages. 1977.

Vol. 55: A. Gerbier, Mes premières constructions de programmes. XII, 256 pages. 1977.

Vol. 56: Fundamentals of Computation Theory. Proceedings 1977. Edited by M. Karpiński. XII, 542 pages. 1977.

Vol. 57: Portability of Numerical Software. Proceedings 1976. Edited by W. Cowell. VIII, 539 pages. 1977.

Vol. 58: M. J. O'Donnell, Computing in Systems Described by Equations. XIV, 111 pages. 1977.

Vol. 59: E. Hill, Jr., A Comparative Study of Very Large Data Bases. X, 140 pages. 1978.

Vol. 60: Operating Systems, An Advanced Course. Edited by R. Bayer, R. M. Graham, and G. Seegmüller. X, 593 pages. 1978.

Vol. 61: The Vienna Development Method: The Meta-Language. Edited by D. Bjørner and C. B. Jones. XVIII, 382 pages. 1978.

Vol. 62: Automata, Languages and Programming. Proceedings 1978. Edited by G. Ausiello and C. Böhm. VIII, 508 pages. 1978.

Vol. 63: Natural Language Communication with Computers. Edited by Leonard Bolc. VI, 292 pages. 1978.

Vol. 64: Mathematical Foundations of Computer Science. Proceedings 1978. Edited by J. Winkowski. X, 551 pages. 1978.

Vol. 65: Information Systems Methodology, Proceedings, 1978. Edited by G. Bracchi and P. C. Lockemann. XII, 696 pages. 1978.

Vol. 66: N. D. Jones and S. S. Muchnick, TEMPO: A Unified Treatment of Binding Time and Parameter Passing Concepts in Programming Languages. IX, 118 pages. 1978.

Vol. 67: Theoretical Computer Science, 4th GI Conference, Aachen, March 1979. Edited by K. Weihrauch. VII, 324 pages. 1979.

Vol. 68: D. Harel, First-Order Dynamic Logic. X, 133 pages. 1979.

Vol. 69: Program Construction. International Summer School. Edited by F. L. Bauer and M. Broy. VII, 651 pages. 1979.

Vol. 70: Semantics of Concurrent Computation. Proceedings 1979. Edited by G. Kahn. VI, 368 pages. 1979.

Vol. 71: Automata, Languages and Programming. Proceedings 1979. Edited by H. A. Maurer. IX, 684 pages. 1979.

Vol. 72: Symbolic and Algebraic Computation. Proceedings 1979. Edited by E. W. Ng. XV, 557 pages. 1979.

Vol. 73: Graph-Grammars and Their Application to Computer Science and Biology. Proceedings 1978. Edited by V. Claus, H. Ehrig and G. Rozenberg. VII, 477 pages. 1979.

Vol. 74: Mathematical Foundations of Computer Science. Proceedings 1979. Edited by J. Bečvář. IX, 580 pages. 1979.

Vol. 75: Mathematical Studies of Information Processing. Proceedings 1978. Edited by E. K. Blum, M. Paul and S. Takasu. VIII, 629 pages. 1979.

Vol. 76: Codes for Boundary-Value Problems in Ordinary Differential Equations. Proceedings 1978. Edited by B. Childs et al. VIII, 388 pages. 1979.

Lecture Notes in Computer Science

Edited by G. Goos and J. Hartmanis

131

Logics of Programs

Workshop, Yorktown Heights, New York, May 1981

Edited by Dexter Kozen

Springer-Verlag
Berlin Heidelberg New York 1982

Editor
Dexter Kozen
IBM Research
Yorktown Heights, NY 10598, USA

CR Subject Classifications (1979): 5.21, 5.24

ISBN 3-540-11212-X Springer-Verlag Berlin Heidelberg New York
ISBN 0-387-11212-X Springer-Verlag New York Heidelberg Berlin

Printing and binding: Beltz Offsetdruck, Hemsbach/Bergstr.
2145/3140-543210

FOREWORD

It is almost twenty years since the foundations of programming logic were laid, and the field is as active now as ever. Current interest ranges all the way from practical program verification and specification to model theory and complexity. With such a broad field, it was inevitable that distinct schools would develop, each with its own language and philosophy, leading at times to duplicated effort and misunderstanding. The Logics of Programs Workshop was conceived as a way to bring the various schools together to air new ideas and old grudges, share results and techniques, and perhaps reach some consensus about where the field should be heading.

The workshop was held at the IBM Thomas J. Watson Research Center in Yorktown Heights, New York on May 4, 5, and 6, 1981. Fifty-five participants from nine countries took part in two and a half days of technical presentations and a half day of round-table discussion. The technical papers which appear in Part I of this volume have not been refereed and are to be considered working papers. Part II contains an edited transcript of the discussion.

The workshop was made possible through the generous support of the National Science Foundation[1] and IBM Corporation. I sincerely thank everyone who helped make the workshop a success, especially Leonard Berman, Celeste Bertin, Meera Blattner, John Cherniavsky, Jeanne Ferrante, Steve Fortune, Albert Meyer, Karen Møller, Rohit Parikh, Vaughan Pratt, Dana Waering, and Mark Wegman. Special thanks go to Michelle Cofer for her expert handling of minor crises, Jim Thatcher and Diana Seidel for providing accommodations and organizing a superb party, and Frances Kozen for general support in ways too numerous to mention.

Dexter Kozen
Yorktown Heights, New York
September 1, 1981

---

[1]Grant MCS8019346.

CONTENTS

PROOF RULES DEALING WITH FAIRNESS

- Extended Abstract - *)

Krzysztof R. Apt
University of Rotterdam

Ernst-Rüdiger Olderog
University of Kiel

Abstract. We provide proof rules allowing to deal with two fairness assumptions in the context of Dijkstra's do-od programs. These proof rules are obtained by considering a translated version of the original program which uses random assignment x:=? and admits only fair runs. The proof rules use infinite ordinals and deal with the original programs and not their translated versions.

1. Introduction

One of the troublesome issues concerning non-deterministic and parallel programs is that of fairness. This assumption states roughly speaking that each possible continuation is scheduled for execution sufficiently often. The meaning of a continuation depends on the language considered. For example, in the case of Dijkstra's guarded commands a possible continuation is a branch guarded by a guard evaluating to true. "Sufficiently often" can be interpreted here in a variety of ways the simplest of them being "eventually".

The aim of this paper is to develop a simple proof theoretic approach to the issue of fairness. This approach was originally suggested in APT & PLOTKIN [1].

We restrict our attention to Dijkstra's do-od-programs whose components are simple while-programs. Each fairness assumption (we study here two of them) can be incorporated here by providing an appropriate equivalent version of the original program which uses the random assignment x:=? (set x to an arbitrary non-negative integer) for scheduling purposes

---

Author's addresses: K.R. Apt, Faculty of Economics, University of Rotterdam, P.O. Box 1738, 3000 DR Rotterdam, The Netherlands;
E.-R. Olderog, Institut für Informatik und Praktische Mathematik, Christian-Albrechts-Universität Kiel, Olshausenstr. 40-60, D-2300 Kiel 1, West Germany.

*) The full version of this paper is available as Bericht Nr. 8104, Institut für Informatik und Praktische Mathematik, University of Kiel, March 1981, and has been submitted for publication.

and admits only fair computations. By applying to this version of program Hoare-style proof-rules considered in APT & PLOTKIN [1] we arrive at proof rules dealing with fairness. It should be stressed that these proof rules deal with the original program - the applied transformations are "absorbed" into the assertions leaving the program in question intact. Using these proof rules total correctness of do-od-programs under the assumption of (weak and strong) fairness can be proved. The proof rules use infinite ordinals.

The use of such infinitistic methods seems to be needed in view of the results of EMERSON & CLARKE [3] who show that termination under fairness assumption is not first order definable. The results of APT & PLOTKIN [1] imply soundness and relative completeness of our system for a special type of assertion languages - those which allow the use of the least fixed point operator and ordinals.

2. Definitions

We consider programs of the form

$$S = \underline{do}\ B_1 \longrightarrow S_1 \ [] \ldots [] \ B_n \longrightarrow S_n\ \underline{od}$$

where the B_i are quantifier-free formulas and the S_i are deterministic while-programs. We have a simple model of state in mind, viz. $\sigma: \mathcal{V}ar \rightarrow \mathcal{D}$. $\mathcal{V}ar$ denotes here the set of program variables and $\mathcal{D}$ is a domain of an interpretation. Thus the meaning of a subprogram S_i is a partially defined mapping $\mathcal{M}(S_i)$ from states to states. To state the notions of fairness and total correctness properly we employ so-called computation sequences of S defined as follows: For $i \in \{1,\ldots,n\}$ and states σ, σ' we write

$\sigma \xrightarrow{i} \sigma'$ iff $\models B_i(\sigma)$ and $\mathcal{M}(S_i)(\sigma) = \sigma'$ and

$\sigma \xrightarrow{i}$ iff $\models B_i(\sigma)$ and $\mathcal{M}(S_i)(\sigma)$ is undefined.

Computation sequences of S are now exactly those sequences ξ of states which fall into one of the following cases:

1° $\xi = \sigma_1 \xrightarrow{i_1} \sigma_2 \xrightarrow{i_2} \ldots \xrightarrow{i_{m-1}} \sigma_m$

where $i_j \in \{1,\ldots,n\}$ and $\models (\neg B_1 \wedge \ldots \wedge \neg B_n)(\sigma_m)$.

Then ξ is said to properly terminate.

2° $\xi = \sigma_1 \xrightarrow{i_1} \sigma_2 \xrightarrow{i_2} \ldots \xrightarrow{i_{m-1}}$

where $i_j \in \{1,\ldots,n\}$.

Then ξ is said to fail.

3° $\xi = \sigma_1 \xrightarrow{i_1} \sigma_2 \xrightarrow{i_2} \dots \xrightarrow{i_{j-1}} \sigma_j \xrightarrow{i_j} \dots$

where $i_j \in \{1,\dots,n\}$ and ξ is infinite.

Then ξ is said to diverge.

(Note that all finite sequences ξ of maximal length must fall into the cases 1° or 2° because $B_i(\sigma)$ is always defined, i.e. $\models B_i(\sigma)$ or $\models \neg B_i(\sigma)$ holds.)

A computation sequence ξ of S is said to be weakly fair iff ξ is either finite (i.e. properly terminates or fails) or infinite, i.e. of the form

$$\xi = \sigma_1 \xrightarrow{i_1} \sigma_2 \xrightarrow{i_2} \dots \sigma_j \xrightarrow{i_j} \dots$$

with $i_j \in \{1,\dots,n\}$, but then fulfils the following condition

$$\forall i \in \{1,\dots,n\} \; ((\overset{\infty}{\forall} j \in \mathbb{N} \models B_i(\sigma_j)) \rightarrow (\overset{\infty}{\exists} j \in \mathbb{N} \; i_j = i)) \; ^{*)}$$

i.e. if B_i is almost always true then the i-th component is infinitely often chosen. In other words we explicitly disallow infinite sequences ξ with

$$\exists i \in \{1,\dots,n\} \; (\overset{\infty}{\forall} j \in \mathbb{N} \models B_i(\sigma_j) \wedge \overset{\infty}{\forall} j \in \mathbb{N} \; i_j \neq i) .$$

A computation sequence ξ of S is said to be strongly fair iff ξ is either finite or infinite, i.e. of the form

$$\xi = \sigma_1 \xrightarrow{i_1} \sigma_2 \xrightarrow{i_2} \dots \sigma_j \xrightarrow{i_j} \dots$$

with $i_j \in \{1,\dots,n\}$, but then fulfils the following condition

$$\forall i \in \{1,\dots,n\} \; ((\overset{\infty}{\exists} j \in \mathbb{N} \models B_i(\sigma_j)) \rightarrow (\overset{\infty}{\exists} j \in \mathbb{N} \; i_j = i))$$

i.e. if B_i is infinitely often true then the i-th component is infinitely often chosen. In other words we explicitly disallow infinite sequences ξ with

$$\exists i \in \{1,\dots,n\} \; (\overset{\infty}{\exists} j \in \mathbb{N} \models B_i(\sigma_j) \wedge \overset{\infty}{\forall} j \in \mathbb{N} \; i_j \neq i) .$$

Now we can state precisely what we understand by total correctness of programs with or without fairness assumptions. For arbitrary first order formulas P and Q we define:

*) The quantifier $\overset{\infty}{\forall}$ means "for all, but finitely may" and $\overset{\infty}{\exists}$ means "there exist infinitely many".

$\models \{P\}\ S\ \{Q\}$ [under weak (strong) fairness assumption]

iff every [weakly (strongly) fair] computation sequence of S starting in a state σ with $\models P(\sigma)$ is properly terminating, i.e. is of the form

$$\sigma \xrightarrow{i_1} \ldots \xrightarrow{i_m} \sigma', \text{ and } \sigma' \text{ fulfils } \models Q(\sigma').$$

Thus under fairness assumption we need not bother about unfair computation sequences.

3. The Transformations

Let

$S = \underline{do}\ B_1 \rightarrow S_1 \,[]\, \ldots \,[]\, B_n \rightarrow S_n\ \underline{od}.$

We consider the weak fairness assumption first. We use the following transformation

```
T*weak(S) = if B1 → turn:=1 [] ... [] Bn → turn:=n [] ¬(B1 ∨ ... ∨ Bn)→skip fi;
            for i:= 1 to n do z[i]:=? od;
            do
              ...
            [] Bi ∧ turn=i →
                 Si;
                 if ¬Bi ∨ mini ≤ 0 then turn:=indexi;
                                        z[turn]:=? fi;
                 for j:=1 to n do
                   if j≠turn then if Bj then z[j]:=z[j] -1
                                        else z[j]:=?     fi fi
                 od
              ...
            od
```

where i ranges from 1 to n.

The random assignment $z[i]:=?$ means "Set $z[i]$ to an arbitrary non-negative integer". min_i and $index_i$ are shorthands defined as follows

$$min_i = \begin{cases} \min\{z[j] \mid j \neq i \wedge B_j\} & \text{if } \bigvee_{j \neq i} B_j \\ +\infty & \text{otherwise} \end{cases}$$

$$index_i = \begin{cases} \min\{j \mid j \neq i \wedge B_j \wedge z[j] = min_i\} & \text{if } \bigvee_{j \neq i} B_j \\ i & \text{otherwise} \end{cases}$$

We require that turn and $z[1],\ldots,z[n]$ are variables of sort $\{1,\ldots,n\}$ resp. integer which do not occur in S.

Some informal explanations may help to understand why $T^*_{weak}(S)$ admits only weakly fair runs: If $z[j]>0$ holds, $z[j]$ is equal to the number of times B_j is still to be continuously true before control is switched to S_j (via turn:=j). Since more than one $z[j]$ can become 0 at the same time, we allow $z[j]$ to be negative. Each time when B_j is true but S_j is not executed $z[j]$ gets decreased by 1. If B_j is not true, $z[j]$is reset to an arbitrary non-negative value. turn=i means that the i-th component has the control. Control is transferred to another component if $\neg B_i$ holds or there exists a $j \neq i$ with B_j and $z[j] \leq 0$. In both cases control gets transferred to the least component j with the minimal $z[j]$ for which at this moment B_j holds. If no such j exists, then all guards $B_1,\ldots,B_n$ are false and the program terminates.

We now pass to the issue of <u>strong fairness</u>. As basis for our proof rule we take the following transformation

$T^*_{strong}(S)$ = <u>if</u> $B_1 \rightarrow$ turn:=1 $\square \ldots \square$ $B_n \rightarrow$ turn:=n $\square$ $\neg(B_1 \vee \ldots \vee B_n) \rightarrow$ skip <u>fi</u>;
<u>for</u> i:= 1 <u>to</u> n <u>do</u> z[i]:=? <u>od</u>;
<u>do</u>
...
$\square$ $B_i \wedge$ turn=i $\rightarrow$
S_i; <u>do</u> $B_i \wedge \neg \bigvee_{j \neq i} B_j \rightarrow S_i$ <u>od</u>;
<u>if</u> $\neg B_i \vee min_i \leq 0$ <u>then</u> turn:=$index_i$;
z[turn]:=? <u>fi</u>;
<u>for</u> j:=1 <u>to</u> n <u>do</u>
<u>if</u> $j \neq turn \wedge B_j$ <u>then</u> z[j]:= z[j]-1 <u>fi</u>
<u>od</u>
...
od

where i ranges from 1 to n.

This transformation is very similar to the one used for the case of weak fairness. The main difference is that the value of $z[j]$ is not reset in the case when B_j is false.

The following lemma relates $T^*_{weak}(S)$ and $T^*_{strong}(S)$ to S and is of independent interest.

Lemma 1 (a) If ξ is a weakly (strongly) fair computation sequence of S then an element-wise extension ξ' of ξ is a computation sequence of $T^*_{weak}(S)$ $(T^*_{strong}(S))$.

(b) If ξ' is a computation sequence of $T^*_{weak}(S)$ $(T^*_{strong}(S))$ then its element-wise restriction ξ to the variables of S is a weakly (strongly) fair computation sequence of S.

Intuitively this lemma states that $T^*_{weak}(S)$ $(T^*_{strong}(S))$ admits exactly all weakly (strongly) fair computation sequences of S.

4. The Proof Rules

The transformed programs use random assignments. In APT & PLOTKIN [1] proof rules have been developed which allow to prove total correctness of such programs. The relevant proof rule is the following

$$\frac{\begin{array}{l} P_0 \longrightarrow \exists \alpha\, p(\alpha) \\ p(0) \longrightarrow \neg(B_1 \vee \dots \vee B_n) \wedge Q_0 \\ p(\alpha) \wedge \alpha > 0 \quad \longrightarrow \quad B_1 \vee \dots \vee B_n \\ \{p(\alpha) \wedge \alpha > 0 \wedge B_i\} \quad S_i \quad \{\exists \beta < \alpha\ p(\beta)\} \quad i=1,\dots,n \end{array}}{\{P_0\}\ \underline{do}\ B_1 \rightarrow S_1 \,\square\, \dots \,\square\, B_n \rightarrow S_n\ \underline{od}\ \{Q_0\}}$$

where S_i are while-programs allowing random assignments and where α and β are ordinals.

Below we use the following notation

$\bar{z} = (z[1],\dots,z[n])$, $\underset{\sim}{z} = (\underset{\sim}{z}[1], \dots, \underset{\sim}{z}[n])$

$\bar{z} -_i 1 = (y_1, \dots, y_n)$

$$\text{where } y_j = \begin{cases} z[j]-1 & \text{if } j \neq i \text{ and } B_j \\ z[j] & \text{otherwise} \end{cases}$$

$[\bar{z} \cdot \underset{\sim}{z}] = (y_1,\dots,y_n)$

$$\text{where } y_j = \begin{cases} z[j] & \text{if } B_j \\ \underset{\sim}{z}[j] & \text{otherwise} \end{cases}$$

Applying the above proof rule to $T^*_{weak}(S)$ we derive the following

Proof rule for weak fairness $(n \geq 2)$

1^0 $P_0 \wedge \bigvee_i (B_i \rightarrow turn=i) \rightarrow \forall \bar{z} \geq 0 \; \exists \alpha \; p(\alpha, turn, \bar{z})$

2^0 $p(0, turn, \bar{z}) \rightarrow \bigwedge_i \neg (B_i \wedge turn=i) \wedge Q_0$

3^0 $p(\alpha, turn, \bar{z}) \wedge \alpha > 0 \rightarrow \bigvee_i (B_i \wedge turn=i)$

$4i^0$ $(i=1,\ldots,n)$

$$\{p(\alpha, i, \bar{z}) \wedge \alpha > 0 \wedge B_i\}$$

$$S_i$$

$$\{((\neg B_i \vee min_i \leq 0) \wedge index_i = k \longrightarrow$$

$$\forall \underset{\sim}{z} \geq 0 \; \forall \bar{z}[k] \geq 0 \; \exists \beta < \alpha \; p(\beta, k, [\bar{z}-_k 1 \cdot \underset{\sim}{z}]))$$

$$(B_i \wedge min_i > 0 \longrightarrow \forall \underset{\sim}{z} \geq 0 \; p(\alpha, i, [\bar{z}-_i 1 \cdot \underset{\sim}{z}]))$$

$\{P_0\}$ do $B_1 \rightarrow S_1 \; [] \; \ldots \; [] \; B_n \rightarrow S_n$ od $\{Q_0\}$
under weak fairness assumption

where α, β are ordinals and turn, $z[1], \ldots, z[n]$ variables not occurring freely in P_0, Q_0 or $B_1, \ldots, B_n, S_1, \ldots, S_n$.

An analogous rule for strong fairness can be derived from $T^*_{strong}(S)$. These proof rules can be considerably simplified in the case of two guards.

Corollary (to Lemma 1). For all formulas P and Q without free variables turn, $z[1], \ldots, z[n]$ the following holds

$\models \{P\} \; S \; \{Q\}$ under weak fairness assumption

iff $\models \{P\} \; T^*_{weak}(S) \; \{Q\}$ (under no assumption)

and similarly for the strong fairness assumption.

5. An Example

We provide here a natural example for fairness suggested by P. Cousot. Let L be a complete lattice (with ordering $\sqsubseteq$ and least element $\perp$) which fulfils the finite chain property, i.e. every strictly increasing $\sqsubseteq$-chain in L is finite. Further on, let $f_i : L^n \rightarrow L$ be monotone for $i=1,\ldots,n$ and $A, \bar{x}, \bar{I}, lfp(f_1,\ldots,f_n)$ be the following abbreviations:

$A = x_1 \neq f_1(\bar{x}) \vee \ldots \vee x_n \neq f_n(\bar{x})$.

$\bar{x} = (x_1,\ldots,x_n)$ and $\bar{\bot} = (\bot,\ldots,\bot)$ (n times).

$lfp(f_1,\ldots,f_n)$ denotes the least fixed point of the monotone operator $(f_1,\ldots,f_n): L^n \rightarrow L^n$.

Then using our proof rules we can prove

$\models \{\bar{x}=\bar{\bot}\}$

$\underline{do}\ A \rightarrow x_1:=f_1(\bar{x})\ \square \ldots \square\ A \rightarrow x_n:=f_n(\bar{x})\ \underline{od}$

$\{\bar{x}=lfp(f_1,\ldots,f_n)\}$

under weak (resp. strong) fairness assumption

where $\models$ refers to validity in L. (This correctness result is a special case of a more general theorem proved in COUSOT[2] .) The full proof can be found in the full version of the paper.

References

[1] APT, K.R. & G.D. PLOTKIN, A Cook's Tour of countable nondeterminism, Technical Report, Department of Computer Science, University of Edinburgh, 1980 (to appear in Proc. ICALP 81).

[2] COUSOT, P., Asynchronous iterative methods for solving a fixed point system of monotone equations in a complete lattice, Rapport de Recherche No 88, L.A.7, Université Scientifique et Medicale de Grenoble, 1977.

[3] EMERSON, E.A. & E.M. CLARKE, Characterizing correctness properties of parallel programs using fixpoints, in: Proc. ICALP 80, Lecture Notes in Computer Science 85, Springer Verlag, pp. 169-181, 1980.

Hoare's Logic Is Incomplete When It Does Not Have To Be

J. Bergstra[†]

A. Chmielinska[††]

J. Tiuryn[†††]

Abstract:

If Hoare's Logic, HL($\underline{A}$), is complete on a structure $\underline{A}$, then the set PC($\underline{A}$) of all asserted programs true over $\underline{A}$ is recursive in the first order theory of $\underline{A}$, Th($\underline{A}$). We show that this implication cannot be reversed.

Introduction

It is known (cf. [5]) that for a given first order language $\mathcal{L}$, the set of Floyd-Hoare partial correctness assertions $PC_{\mathcal{L}} = \{\{P\}\ \alpha\ \{Q\} \mid P,Q$ are first order formulae over $\mathcal{L}$, α is a *while*-program over $\mathcal{L}$, and $\models \{P\}\ \alpha\ \{Q\}\}$ is a Π^0_2-complete set. In particular $PC_{\mathcal{L}}$ is not r.e., and therefore it cannot possess a finitary sound and (absolutely) complete proof system.

Let HL denote the standard Hoare's proof system for proving partial correctness of *while*-programs. Cook's [4] idea to repair incompleteness of HL was to take the first order

† University of Leiden, Department of Computer Science, The Netherlands
†† University of Torun, Department of Mathematics, Poland
††† M.I.T., Laboratory for Computer Science, USA
††† Boston University, Department of Mathematics, USA
††† University of Warsaw, Department of Mathematics, Poland.

This work was supported in part by The National Science Foundation, Grant No. MCS 8010707, and by a grant to the M.I.T. Laboratory for Computer Science by the IBM Corporation.

theory of an $\mathcal{L}$- structure $\underline{A}$, abbreviated Th($\underline{A}$), as additional axioms, obtaining in this way an enlarged proof system HL($\underline{A}$). In general for a given $\mathcal{L}$-structure $\underline{A}$, the set PC($\underline{A}$) = $\{\{P\}\ \alpha\ \{Q\} \mid A \models \{P\}\ \alpha\ \{Q\}\}$ is Π_1^0 in Th($\underline{A}$) (cf. [1]), and hence still is not r.e. even in Th($\underline{A}$). Thus HL($\underline{A}$) cannot be complete for all $\underline{A}$'s.

For some structures $\underline{A}$, however, HL($\underline{A}$) is complete. Cook's theorem [4] says that for every structure $\underline{A}$ for which $\mathcal{L}$ is expressive for *while*-programs, HL($\underline{A}$) is complete. However, expressiveness is not necessary for completeness of the HL system: any non standard model of arithmetic possess a complete HL, but the first order language of arithmetic is **never** expressive for *while*-programs over such model (cf. [2]). Moreover, expressiveness represents what amounts to a degenerate case: when expressiveness holds, programming logic (e.g. regular Dynamic Logic) collapses to first order logic, and in particular partial correctness assertions reduce to first order formulae.

From the above it follows that if for a given structure $\underline{A}$, HL($\underline{A}$) is complete, then PC($\underline{A}$) is recursive in Th($\underline{A}$). This paper is motivated by the following question: **is** HL($\underline{A}$) **complete for every structure $\underline{A}$ such that** PC($\underline{A}$) **is recursive in** Th($\underline{A}$)? It is our aim to show that the answer to the above question is negative. We will present a general construction of counterexamples for this situation.As a corollary of our results we obtain an example of a structure which shows that ability of coding finite sequences cannot be removed from assumptions of Harel's theorem on arithmetic universes (cf. [5]).

Suppose now for a while that HL($\underline{A}$) is incomplete but PC($\underline{A}$) is recursive in Th($\underline{A}$).What can be done to make HL complete? For this question it is meaningful to consider HL($\mathcal{L}$, E) as a proof system over a first order theory E in language $\mathcal{L}$.HL($\underline{A}$) may be then identified with HL($\mathcal{L}$, Th($\underline{A}$)), where $\underline{A}$ is an $\mathcal{L}$-structure. It follows from [3] that $\underline{A}$ can be expanded to an $\mathcal{L}^*$-structure $\underline{A}^*$ with $\mathcal{L}^*-\mathcal{L}$ being finite, such that for some decidable theory T $\subseteq$ Th($\underline{A}^*$), PC($\underline{A}$) $\subseteq$ HL($\mathcal{L}^*$, Th($\underline{A}$) $\cup$ T).Thus Th($\underline{A}$) $\cup$ T, where T is decidable but formulated in an extended language contains enough information to derive all of PC($\underline{A}$).

1. Preliminaries

1.1 For completeness sale we start with a formulation of HL that suits our purposes best. There are four rules of inference.

1.1.1 Assignment rule

$$\frac{P \Rightarrow Q[t/x]}{\{P\}\ x := t\ \{Q\}}$$

where P,Q are first order formulae, x is a variable, t is a term, and Q[t/x] denotes a formula obtained from Q by uniformly substituting t for all free occurences of x in Q.

1.1.2 Composition rule

$$\frac{\{P\}\ \alpha\ \{Q\},\ \{Q\}\ \beta\ \{R\}}{\{P\}\ \alpha; \beta\ \{R\}}$$

where P,Q,R are first order formulae, and α, β are *while*-programs.

1.1.3 Conditional rule

$$\frac{\{P \wedge B\}\ \alpha\ \{Q\},\ \{P \wedge \neg B\}\ \beta\ \{Q\}}{\{P\}\ \mathit{if}\ B\ \mathit{then}\ \alpha\ \mathit{else}\ \beta\ \mathit{fi}\ \{Q\}}$$

where P,Q,B are first order formulae, B is quantifier free, and α, β are *while*-programs.

1.1.4 Iteration rule

$$\frac{P \Rightarrow R,\ \{R \wedge B\}\ \alpha\ \{R\},\ R \wedge \neg B \Rightarrow Q}{\{P\}\ \mathit{while}\ B\ \mathit{do}\ \alpha\ \mathit{od}\ \{Q\}}$$

where P,R,Q,B are first order formulae, B is quantifier free, and α is a *while*-program.

1.1.5 **Oracle axiom** (for a given structure $\underline{A}$). Every $P \in Th(\underline{A})$ is an axiom.

Given a structure $\underline{A}$, HL($\underline{A}$) denotes the set of all asserted programs $\{P\}\ \alpha\ \{Q\}$ provable by using rules (1.1.1 - 1.1.4) and oracle axiom for $\underline{A}$.

The reader can easily check that the following rule

Consequence rule

$$\frac{P \Rightarrow P_1,\ \{P_1\}\ \alpha\ \{Q_1\},\ Q_1 \Rightarrow Q}{\{P\}\ \alpha\ \{Q\}}$$

where P, P_1, Q, Q_1 are first order formulae, and α is a *while*-program; is derivable in HL.

Another rule easily derivable in HL is the following:

$$\frac{\{P\}\ \alpha\ \{Q\}}{\{\exists xP\}\ \alpha\ \{\exists xQ\}}$$

where P,Q are first order formulae, α is a *while*-program and x does not occur in α.

We will need a slightly stronger statement. Let a proof of $\{P\}\ \alpha\ \{Q\}$ in HL(A) be given and let x does not occur in α. This proof can be transforwarded into another one by putting $\{\exists xP\}\ \alpha\ \{\exists xQ\}$. Repeated application of this procedure yields the following lemma.

1.1.6 **Lemma**

Let X be the set of all variables occuring free in P,Q, or α. If HL(A) proves $\{P\}\ \alpha\ \{Q\}$, then there exists a proof of $\{P\}\ \alpha\ \{Q\}$ in HL(A) using only invariants and intermediate assertions with free variables in X.

1.2 As the next step in this technical introduction we will explain a construction of a structure $\underline{A} \oplus \underline{B}$ on which our paper is technically based.

Let $\mathcal{L}_1$, and $\mathcal{L}_2$ be two disjoint similarity types. Let A,B,$\perp$ be new symbols not belong to $\mathcal{L}_1 \cup \mathcal{L}_2$. A and B are unavy predicate symbols, and $\perp$ is a constant symbol. Let $\underline{A}$, $\underline{B}$ be $\mathcal{L}_1$-, $\mathcal{L}_2$-structures, respectively. Assume that carriers of $\underline{A}$ and $\underline{B}$ (denoted by $|\underline{A}|$ and $|\underline{B}|$, respectively) are disjoint. Let $\mathcal{L} = \mathcal{L}_1 \cup \mathcal{L}_2 \cup \{A,B,\perp\}$. $\underline{A} \oplus$ B is an $\mathcal{L}$-structure with carrier $|\underline{A} \oplus \underline{B}| = |\underline{A}| \cup |\underline{B}| \cup \{\perp\}$, where $\perp$ is a new element, not in $|\underline{A}| \cup |\underline{B}|$. A is a characteristic predicate of $|\underline{A}|$, and B is a characteristic predicate of $|\underline{B}|$. $\mathcal{L}_1$ (respectively $\mathcal{L}_2$) function symbols are defined the same as in $\underline{A}$ (as in $\underline{B}$, respectively), provided all arguments are taken from $|\underline{A}|$ (from $|\underline{B}|$, resp.) getting value $\perp$ otherwise. $\mathcal{L}_1$ (respectively $\mathcal{L}_2$) predicate symbols are defined the same as in A (as in B, resp.), provided all arguments are taken from |A| (from |B|, resp.), and set to be false elsewhere.

A ⊕ B is a kind of disjoint union of A and B. Clearly a meaningful alternative to this definition would be a two-sorted structure. We will not do so mainly with the purpose in mind to keep as close as possible to the standard Hoare formalism.

We are now in position to formulate a general theorem which has the claim in the introduction as a corollary.

1.2.1 **Theorem**

(i) For every A there is a structure B such that PC(A⊕B) is recursive in Th(A⊕B).

(ii) For arbitrary A and B, if HL(A) is incomplete, then so is HL(A⊕B).

It follows from the above result that if we take A such that HL(A) is incomplete (e.g. A can be chosen to be $\langle \omega, s, o \rangle$, where s is a successor function on nonnegative integers, or A can be the field of complex numbers, cf. [1] for proofs of incompleteness of HL(A) for these A's), and choose B such that PC(A⊕B) is recursive in Th(A⊕B), then HL(A⊕B) is also incomplete, and A ⊕ B is the kind of structure we looked for.

Let N stand for the standard model of arithmetic. By 1.2.1(ii) we have that for any A with incomplete HL(A), HL(A⊕N) is incomplete. Harel's theorem on arithmetical universes (cf. [5]) says that if B is a structure which contains the standard model of arithmetic (as a first order definable part of B) and if B has "ability" to code finite sequences of elements from |B|, then the first order language is expressive for *while*-programs over B, and therefore HL(B) is complete. Since obviously N is a first order definable part of A ⊕ N, this shows that quite technical assumption of being able to code finite sequences cannot be removed from Harel's theorem.

The proofs of (i) and (ii) are quite independent and are subjects of sections 2 and 3.

2. Adding an expressive structure (proof of (i))

Let A be a structure of signature $\mathcal{L}_1$. If A is finite, then choose any finite B. In that case A⊕B is finite as well and PC(A⊕B) is recursive in Th(A⊕B). This rerifies theorem 1.2.1(i) in that case.

Assume now that A is infinite. B is constructed as follows. Let A^* be an isomorphic copy of A such that $|A| \cap |A^*| = \emptyset$. Let $\mathcal{L}_1{}^*$ be a similarity type of A^*, such that $\mathcal{L}_1{}^*$ is an isomorphic copy of $\mathcal{L}_1$ and disjoint with $\mathcal{L}_1$. Then we expand A^* to an arithmetic universe in the sense of [5] (i.e. we add a definning predicate for "non negative integers" N, arithmetic operations, a relation for coding finite sequences, and in addition, for technical reasons, we add pairing and unpairing functions). We also expand the language of A^* by three new constants a, b, ⊥ denoting different elements. The resulting structure is B. It has the same domain as A^*, but it has got a richer similarity type which we will denote by $\mathcal{L}_2$.

It is clear that

2.1 Th(B) is recursive in Th(A⊕B).

It follows immediately from the definition of ⊕-construction.

Because B is expressive (being an arithmetical universe), HL(B) is complete. Therefore

2.2 PC(B) is recursive in Th(B). By (2.1) and (2.2) it is enough to prove that

2.3 PC(A⊕B) is many-one reducible to PC(B).

We will outline the proof of (2.3) by showing an effective simulation of computations on A⊕B by those on B. The details of this simulation are slightly messy but completely harmless and we take the liberty to skip some of them.

Let M: $|A| \Rightarrow |B|$ be a bijective mapping which corresponds to the isomorphism $A \simeq A^*$. First we code A ⊕ B in B × B as follows:

$$\mathrm{Code}(x) = \begin{cases} (a, M(x)), & \text{if } x \in |A| \\ (b, x), & \text{if } x \in |B| \\ (\bot, \bot), & \text{if } x = \bot \end{cases}$$

In order to describe a smooth translation of assertions and programs we introduce two infinite families of new variables: $y_0, y_1, \ldots, z_0, z_1, \ldots$

As a next step we show an effective translation **Tr** of first order formulae over the language of $\underline{A} \oplus \underline{B}$ which use individual variables: $x_0, x_1, \ldots$ to first order formulae over $\mathcal{L}_2$ with variables $y_0, y_1, \ldots, z_0, z_1, \ldots$ The translation will have the following property:
for every $P(x_0,\ldots, x_{n-1})$ over the language of $\underline{A}\oplus \underline{B}$, and for all $c_0,\ldots, c_{n-1} \in |\underline{A}\oplus\underline{B}|$,
$\underline{A} \oplus \underline{B} \models P(x_0,\ldots, x_{n-1}) [c_0,\ldots,c_{n-1}]$ iff $\underline{B} \models$ **tr** $(P)(y_0, z_0,\ldots,y_{n-1},z_{n-1})[\mathbf{code}(c_0),\ldots,\mathbf{code}(c_{n-1})]$.

Because the formal definition of **Tr** is slightly cumbersome we present its details. We first introduce some notations. For a term t and for $i \in \{1,2\}$, $\mathcal{L}_i(t)$ is a truth value equal to **true** iff t is a term over language $\mathcal{L}_i$.

Moreover, if t is a term over $\mathcal{L}_1$, then $\tilde{t}$ denotes the corresponding term over $\mathcal{L}_1{}^* \subseteq \mathcal{L}_2$.

We define **Tr** inductively. Let P be $t = t'$, where t contains the variables $X = \{x_{i_1},\ldots, x_{i_k}\}$, and t' contains the variables $X' = \{x_{j_1},\ldots, x_{j_m}\}$. Then **Tr**(P) is

2.4 "t in $\underline{A}$, and t' in $\underline{A}$, and $t=t'$" $\vee$

2.5 "t in $\underline{B}$, and t' in $\underline{B}$, and $t=t'$" $\vee$

2.6 "t is $\perp$, and t' is $\perp$"

Fomulae (2.4) - (2.6) can formally be written as follows:

(2.4') $$\bigwedge_{x_i \in X \cup X'} (y_i = \underline{a}) \wedge \mathcal{L}_1(t) \wedge \mathcal{L}_2(t') \quad \wedge$$
$$\tilde{t}[z_{i_1}/x_{i_1}, \ldots, z_{i_k}/x_{i_k}] = \tilde{t}'[z_{j_1}/x_{j_1}, \ldots, z_{j_m}/x_{j_m}].$$

(2.5') $$\bigwedge_{x_i \in X \cup X'} (y_i = \underline{b}) \wedge \mathcal{L}_2(t) \wedge \mathcal{L}_2(t') \quad \wedge$$
$$t[z_{i_1}/x_{i_1},\ldots,z_{i_k}/x_{i_k}] = t'[z_{j_1}/x_{j_1},\ldots,z_{j_m}/x_{j_m}]$$

(2.6') $$[\bigvee_{x_i \in X} (y_i = \perp) \quad \vee \quad (\neg \mathcal{L}_1(t) \wedge \neg \mathcal{L}_2(t)) \quad \vee$$
$$(\mathcal{L}_1(t) \wedge \bigvee_{x_i \in X} (y_i = \underline{b})) \quad \vee \quad (\mathcal{L}_2(t) \wedge \bigvee_{x_i \in X'} (y_i = \underline{a}))] \quad \wedge$$

$$[\bigvee_{x_i \in X'} y_1 = \bot \quad \vee \quad (\neg \ell_1(t') \wedge \neg \ell_2(t')) \quad \vee$$

$$(\ell_1(t') \wedge \bigvee_{x_i \in X'} (y_i = \underline{b})) \quad \vee \quad (\ell_2(t') \wedge \bigvee_{x_i \in X'} (y_i = \underline{a}))].$$

If P is $R(t_0,...,t_{n-1})$ with $R \in \ell_1$ and $X = \{x_{i_1},...,x_{i_k}\}$ are all variables occuring in P then Tr(P) is:

$$\bigwedge_{x_i \in X} (y_i = \underline{a}) \quad \wedge \quad \bigwedge_{j=0}^{n-1} \ell_1(t_j) \quad \wedge$$

$$\tilde{R}(\tilde{t}_0(z_{i_1}/x_{i_1}, ..., z_{i_k}/x_{i_k}), ..., \tilde{t}_{n-1}(z_{i_k}/x_{i_k}, ..., z_{i_k}/x_{i_k})).$$, where $\tilde{R} \in \ell_1{}^*$ is a

symbol which corresponds to R.

If P is A(t), then Tr(P) is:

$$\bigwedge_{x_i \in X} (y_i = \underline{a}) \quad \wedge \quad \ell_1(t).$$

The cases P is B(t) or P is $R(t_0, ..., t_{n-1})$ with $R \in \ell_2$ are dealt similarly and are left for the reader.

If P is $P_1 \vee P_2$, then Tr(P) is $Tr(P_1) \vee Tr(P_2)$.

If P has free variables $X = \{x_{i_1}, ..., x_{i_m}\}$, then $Tr(\neg P)$ is

$$\bigwedge_{x_i \in X} (y_i = \underline{a} \quad \vee \quad y_i = \underline{b} \quad \vee \quad y_i = \underline{\bot}) \quad \wedge \quad \neg Tr(P).$$

And finally $Tr(\exists x_i\, P)$ is

$$\exists y_i\, \exists z_i\, ((y_i = \underline{a} \quad \vee \quad y_i = \underline{b} \quad \vee \quad y_i = \underline{\bot}) \quad \wedge \quad Tr(P)).$$

This describes Tr in detail.

The next step is to extend Tr to programs α over the language of $\underline{A} \oplus \underline{B}$ in order to have this property for all first order formulae P, Q over the language of $\underline{A} \oplus \underline{B}$:

2.7 $\quad \underline{A} \oplus \underline{B} \models \{P\}\alpha\{Q\} \quad$ iff $\underline{B} \models \{Tr(P)\}\, Tr(\alpha)\{Tr(Q)\}$.

Given a program α and let $\{x_0, ..., x_{n-1}\}$ be all variables occuring in α. $Tr(\alpha)$ will be using variables $y_0, z_0, ..., y_{n-1}, z_{n-1}$ in such a way that the following diagram commutes

$$\begin{array}{ccc} |\underline{A}\oplus\underline{B}|^n & \xrightarrow{\alpha} & |\underline{A}\oplus\underline{B}|^n \\ \text{Code}^n \downarrow & & \downarrow \text{Code}^n \\ |\underline{B}\times\underline{B}|^n & \xrightarrow{Tr\alpha} & |\underline{B}\times\underline{B}|^n \end{array}$$

To achieve this every assignment statement $x_i := t$ in α is replaced by an assignment statement to both y_i and z_i, depending on $\mathcal{L}_1(t)$, $\mathcal{L}_2(t)$, and the values of y_j's corresponding to x_j's occuring in t. Every test P in α is replaced by Tr(P). The details of this construction can safely be left for the reader.

By (2.7), PC($\underline{A}\oplus\underline{B}$) is many-one reducible to PC($\underline{B}$). This completes the proof of part (i) of Theorem 1.2.1.

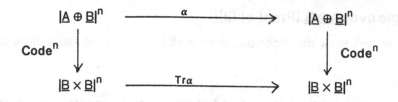

3. Hoare's Logic over $\underline{A} \oplus \underline{B}$ (Proof of (ii))

In this section we will show that incompleteness of HL($\underline{A}$) implies incompleteness of HL($\underline{A} \oplus \underline{B}$).

First we introduce some notations. Let P be a first order formula over the language of $\underline{A} \oplus \underline{B}$. $(P)_A$, a relativization of P to $|\underline{A}|$ is defined inductively as follows:

if P is atomic, then $(P)_A$ is P

$(\neg P)_A$ is $\neg(P)_A$

$(P_1 \vee P_2)_A$ is $(P_1)_A \vee (P_2)_A$

$(\exists x\, P)_A$ is $\exists x\, (A(x) \wedge (P)_A)$.

If X is a finite set of variables, then A(X) will always denote $\bigwedge_{x \in X} A(x)$. $(P)_B$ and B(X) are defined similarily.

We can now formulate on important lemma connecting PC(A) and PC($\underline{A} \oplus \underline{B}$).

3.1 **Lemma**

Let P,Q be first order formulae over $\mathcal{L}_1$, and let α be a *while*-program over $\mathcal{L}_1$. Let X be the set of all variables occuring free in P or Q or α.

(i) $\underline{A} \models \{P\}\ \alpha\ \{Q\}$ iff $\underline{A} \oplus \underline{B} \models \{A(X) \wedge (P)_A\}\ \alpha\ \{A(X) \wedge (Q)_A\}$.

(ii) If HL($\underline{A} \oplus \underline{B}$) proves $\{A(X) \wedge (P)_A\}\ \alpha\ \{A(x) \wedge (Q)_A\}$ using only invariants and inter-mediate assertions with free variables in X and of the form $A(X) \wedge (R)_A$, then HL($\underline{A}$) proves $\{P\}\ \alpha\ \{Q\}$.

Both parts of the above lemma are obvious and the proof is omitted. The result at this stage can be proved using the following proposition.

3.2 **Proposition**

Let P be a first order formula over the language of $\underline{A} \oplus \underline{B}$. Let X be the set of all variables occuring free in P. there exists a first order formula Q over $\mathcal{L}_1$ such that

$$\underline{A} \oplus \underline{B} \models (A(X) \wedge P) \leftrightarrow (A(X) \wedge (Q)_A).$$

Before we start proving Proposition 3.2 we show how to complete the proof of Theorem 1.2.1. Assume that HL($\underline{A}$) is incomplete. Choose $\{P\}\ \alpha\ \{Q\}$ true in $\underline{A}$ but not derivable in HL($\underline{A}$). Let X be the set of all variables occuring free in P, Q, or α. By Lemma 3.1.(i), $\{A(X) \wedge (P)_A\}\ \alpha\ \{A(X) \wedge (Q)_A\}$ is true in $\underline{A}\oplus\underline{B}$, and therefore if HL($\underline{A}\oplus\underline{B}$) $\vdash \{A(X) \wedge (P)_A\}\ \alpha\ \{A(X) \wedge (Q)_A\}$.

We derive a contradiction from this fact. Choose a proof of this asserted program in HL($\underline{A}\oplus\underline{B}$) and use Lemma 1.1.1 to transform it into a proof in which all intermediate assertions and invariants have their free variables in X. Conjuncting A(X) to all of these will not disburb the proof. Then, using Proposition 3.2, all invariants and intermediate assertions can be written in the form $A(X) \wedge (R)_A$ with R a first order formula over $\mathcal{L}_1$. By Lemma 3.1(ii), HL($\underline{A}$) proves $\{P\}\ \alpha\ \{Q\}$ in contrast to our assumptions.

The proof of Proposition 3.2 follows from a series of auxiliary lemmas stated below.

3.3 Lemma ($\perp$ - elimination)

For every first order formula P over $\mathcal{L}_1 \cup \{A, B, \perp\}$ there is a formula $P^\perp$ over $\mathcal{L}_1 \cup \{A, B\}$ such that

(i) $\underline{A}\oplus\underline{B} \models (P) \leftrightarrow P^\perp$

(ii) $\underline{A}\oplus\underline{B} \models (P^\perp)_A \leftrightarrow ((P)_A)^\perp$.

Proof: The proof is by induction on structure of P. The basis step is long due to a large number of cases to be considered. We show only one - the other cases for the basis step are dealt similarly.

Let P be $t_1 = t_2$ where t_1, t_2 are terms, and assume that $\perp$ occurs in t_1. It is easy to see that over $\underline{A}\oplus\underline{B}$ t_1 assumes constantly value $\perp$. Consider the following three sub-cases for t_2:

3.3.1 $\perp$ occurs in t_2

3.3.2 t_2 is a variable, say x

3.3.3 remaining cases.

For (3.3.1) we define $P^{\perp}$ as *true*. For (3.3.2) $P^{\perp}$ is $\neg A(x) \wedge \neg B(x)$. Finally for (3.3.3), if X is the set of all variables occuring in t_2, then we set $P^{\perp}$ to be $\neg A(X)$, i.e. $\bigvee_{x_i \in X} \neg A(x_i)$. Observe that if $X = \emptyset$ then $P^{\perp}$ becomes *false*. It is easy to check that $P^{\perp}$ defined above satisfies (i) and (ii). The inductive step is straightforward.

$(P \wedge Q)^{\perp}$ is $P^{\perp} \wedge Q^{\perp}$

$(\neg P)^{\perp}$ is $\neg(P^{\perp})$

$(\forall x\, P)^{\perp}$ is $\forall x\, (P^{\perp})$.

Again it is very easy to check that $P^{\perp}$ has the desired properties.

3.4 <u>Lemma</u>

Let P be a first order formula over $\mathcal{L}_1 \cup \{A,B\}$, and assume that x occurs free in P. There exists a formula $P^{(x)}$ over $\mathcal{L}_1 \cup \{A,B\}$ such that x is not free in $P^{(x)}$, and

(i) $\underline{A} \oplus \underline{B} \models B(x) \Rightarrow (P \leftrightarrow P^{(x)})$

(ii) $\underline{A} \oplus \underline{B} \models B(x) \Rightarrow \{(P^{(x)})_A \leftrightarrow ((P)_A)^{(x)}\}$.

<u>Proof</u>. The proof is by induction on P. Again, the basis step is quite long due to a large number of cases to be considered, and as in the previous proof we will discuss here only one case in detail leaving for the reader the remaining one.

Suppose P is $t_1 = t_2$ and consider the following possibilities.

3.4.1 Both t_1 and t_2 are x

3.4.2 x occurs in t_1 and in t_2 and neither t_1 nor t_2 is x

3.4.3 t_1 is x, t_2 is not x and x occurs in t_2

3.4.4 t_1 is x, and x does not occur in t_2

3.4.5 t_1 is not x, x occurs in t_1, and it does not occur in t_2.

Symmetrical cases to these from (3.4.1) - (3.4.5) are omitted in the above list.

It is easy to check that in case (3.4.1), (3.4.2) P is constantly true when x gets any value from $|\underline{B}|$. Therefore we set in these cases $P^{(x)}$ to be *true*.

In case (3.4.3) - (3.4.5) P is constantly false for every value of x in $|\underline{B}|$, and we set $P^{(x)}$ to be *false*.

The reader can easily check that (i) and (ii) are satisfied. Inductive step being obvious is omitted.

Before proceeding to the last auxiliary result let us observe that due to symmetry of construction of $\underline{A}\oplus\underline{B}$ Lemmas 3.3 and 3.4 remain true when $\mathcal{L}_1$ is interchanged with $\mathcal{L}_2$ and A with B.

3.5 Lemma

For every first order formula P over the language of $\underline{A}\oplus\underline{B}$ there exist a nonnegative integer n, formulae $F_1, ..., F_n$ over $\mathcal{L}_1 \cup \{A,B\}$, and formulae $G_1, ..., G_n$ over $\mathcal{L}_2 \cup \{A,B\}$ such that

$$\underline{A} \oplus \underline{B} \models \bigwedge_{i=1}^{n} ((F_i)_A \vee (G_i)_B)$$

Proof: We prove the statement of Lemma 3.5 by induction on P.

Let P be of the form $t_1 = t_2$. Consider the following cases.

3.5.1 t_1 is a variable, say x. In t_2 there occur symbols from $\mathcal{L}_1$, and $\mathcal{L}_2$.

3.5.2 t_1 is over $\mathcal{L}_1$, t_2 is over $\mathcal{L}_2$, and both t_1 and t_2 are not variables.

3.5.3 t_1 is over $\mathcal{L}_1$, in t_2 there are symbols from $\mathcal{L}_1$ and $\mathcal{L}_2$.

3.5.4 t_1 and t_2 are over $\mathcal{L}_i \cup \{A,B,\perp\}$, where i = 1 or i = 2.

Cases symmetric to these listed above are omitted. Observe that if t_1 and t_2 satisfy (3.5.1), then $\underline{A}\oplus\underline{B} \models x = \perp \leftrightarrow P$. For (3.5.2) we have $\underline{A}\oplus\underline{B} \models P$

Suppose P satisfies (3.5.3), let X_i for i = 1.2 be the set of all variables which occur in t_i. If $X_1 = \emptyset$ or $X_2 = \emptyset$, then obviously $\underline{A}\oplus\underline{B} \models \neg P$, otherwise it is easy to see that $\underline{A}\oplus\underline{B} \models P \leftrightarrow [(\bigvee_{x_i \in X_1} x_i = \perp) \wedge (\bigvee_{x_i \in X_2} x_i = \perp)]$.

In case (3.5.4) obviously $\underline{A} \oplus \underline{B} \models P \leftrightarrow t_1 = \perp$ holds.

Observe now that in cases (3.5.1) - (3.5.5) P is equivalent over $\underline{A} \oplus \underline{B}$ to a formula over $\mathcal{L}_i \cup \{A,B,\perp\}$, where i = 1 or i = 2. Using Lemma 3.3 we obtain a desired decomposition of P.

Other cases of P being an atomic formula are dealt similarly and we omit them.

The only nontrivial case in the inductive step is P being of the form $\forall x\, Q$, where $\underline{A} \oplus \underline{B} \models Q \leftrightarrow \bigwedge_{i=1}^{n} ((F_i)_A \vee (G_i)_B)$ for certain F_i's over $\mathcal{L}_1 \cup \{A,B\}$ and G_i's over $\mathcal{L}_2 \cup \{A,B\}$.

Since $\underline{A} \oplus \underline{B} \models (\forall x\, P) \leftrightarrow \bigwedge_{i=1}^{n} \forall x((F_i)_A \vee (G_i)_B)$,
it is enough to show a transformation of every formula $\forall x((F_i)_A \vee (G_i)_B)$ for i = 1, ..., n into a formula of desired form. First we observe that such a formula is equivalent over $\underline{A} \oplus \underline{B}$ to the disjunction of these formulae

3.5.5 $((F_i)_A (\perp/x) \vee (G_i)_A (\perp/x)) \quad \wedge$

3.5.6 $\forall x\, [A(x) \Rightarrow ((F_i)_A \vee (G_i)_B)] \quad \wedge$

3.5.7 $\forall x\, [B(x) \Rightarrow ((F_i)_A \vee (G_i)_B)]$

Using Lemma 3.3 we transform formula (3.5.6) into an equivalent one which has a desired form. transformations of (3.5.7) and (3.5.8) are similar and we present here only a transformation of (3.5.7).

By Lemma 3.4 (3.5.7) is equivalent over $\underline{A} \oplus \underline{B}$ to

3.5.8 $\forall x\, [A(x) \Rightarrow ((F_i)_A \vee (G_i^{(x)})_B)]$

Since in $(G_i^{(x)})_B$ x does not occur free, (3.5.9) is equivalent over $\underline{A} \oplus \underline{B}$ to

$(\forall x\, F_i)_A \vee (G_i^{(x)})_B$.

This completes the proof of Lemma 3.5.

3.6 Proof of Proposition 3.2

Let P be a first order formula over the language of $\underline{A} \oplus \underline{B}$. By Lemma 3.5 it is equivalent over $\underline{A} \oplus \underline{B}$ to $\bigwedge_{i=1}^{n} [(F_i)_A \vee (G_i)_B]$, where F_i's are over $\mathcal{L}_1 \cup \{A,B\}$ and G_i's are over $\mathcal{L}_2 \cup \{A,B\}$.

Let X be the set of all variables which occur free in P. By Lemma 3.4 for every $1 \leq i \leq n$, $A(X) \wedge (G_i)_B$ has a constant true value over $\underline{A}\oplus\underline{B}$ (i.e. it is equivalent over $\underline{A}\oplus\underline{B}$ to a sentence. Let ϵ_i be *true* if $\underline{A}\oplus\underline{B} \models A(X) \wedge (G_i)_B$, and *false* otherwise obviously.

3.6.1 $$\underline{A}\oplus\underline{B} \models (A(X) \wedge P) \quad \leftrightarrow \quad A(X) \wedge \bigwedge_{i=1}^{n} ((F_i)_A \vee \epsilon_i).$$

Let F_i^* be obtained from F_i by replacing in F_i every subformula of the form A(t) by *true*, and every subformula of the form B(t) by *false*. It follows easily from (3.6.1) that we can take as the sought Q: $\bigwedge_{i=1}^{n} (F_i^* \vee \epsilon_i)$. This completes the proof of proposition 3.2.

References

1. Bergstra, J.A., & J.V. Tucker, "Some natural structures which fail to possess a sound and decidable Hoare-like logic for their *while*-programs" (to appear in TCS. An earlier edition of this paper is registered at the Mathematical Centre as report IW 136/80).

2. Bergstra, J.A. & J.F. Tucker, "Expressiveness and the completeness of Hoare's logic", Mathematical Centre Report IW 143/80.

3. Bergstra, J.A., & J.V. Tucker, "Two theorems on the completeness of Hoare's Logic", Mathematical Centre Report IW?/81.

4. Cook, S.A., "Soundness and completeness of an axiom system for program verification", SIAM J. Computing ? (1978) 70-90.

5. Harel, D., "First order dynamic logic", Lecture notes in Computer Science 68, Springer 1978.

6. Wand, M., "A new incompleteness result for Hoare's system", JACM 25(1978) 168-175.

THE REFINEMENT OF SPECIFICATIONS AND THE STABILITY OF HOARE'S LOGIC*

J A BERGSTRA

Department of Computer Science
University of Leiden
2300 RA LEIDEN
The Netherlands

J V TUCKER

Department of Computer Studies
University of Leeds
LEEDS LS2 9JT
England

INTRODUCTION

Consider a programming environment with a program language, and a facility to define a data type as a set of primitive operators Σ which satisfy a set of axiomatic properties E. In the construction and maintenance of programs in such an environment one can easily be faced with the problem of "matching" a data type specification (Σ,E) to a proof that a particular program S, based upon Σ, is correct relative to particular input-output conditions p,q. *Implicitly or explicitly, the verification of* {p}S{q} *acts as a proof-theoretic criterion for the correctness of the axiomatisation* E. In order to prove the asserted program, it may be necessary, or convenient, to refine a specification E into another specification E' because {p}S{q} is true in an intended semantics, but the axioms E are too general (read: too weak!) to prove the appropriate information about the underlying data types.

For example, this activity of refining specifications to obtain correctness proofs will be part and parcel of any verification system whose design conforms, even superficially, to that used by Igarashi, London and Luckham in their pioneering work [12] on the Stanford PASCAL verifier. And, of course, refinement will assume prominence in systems supporting data abstraction. This is evident in the development of the PASCAL verifier [13], but in a system such as AFFIRM one finds the refinement of specifications and program verification placed on an equal footing [14].

Whatever the environment, one can enquire: *To what extent are the infinitely many ways of refining a specification independent of the required program verification? Given that a selection of specifications individually "encode" enough information to prove an asserted program* {p}S{q}, *surely the asserted program can be verified from the information about its data types which is common to all members of the family?* We shall formalise this question

*An earlier edition of this paper was prepared while the second author was at the Mathematical Centre, Amsterdam, and was registered as MC Report IW 155/80 .

and give it an answer.

For simplicity, let us assume that the assignment and control constructs available in the language of the environment are those of while-programs, and that a data type is specified by a set of primitive operators Σ satisfying a collection of first-order axioms E. The partial correctness of a program belonging to such an environment can be naturally analysed by the familiar axioms and proof rules first described in HOARE [11] *providing* one allows only assertions *provable* from the specification E to govern the Rule of Consequence. The resulting formal system, based upon the first-order assertion language L over Σ, we term *Hoare's logic for the specification E* and we denote it $HL(E)$. It is worth noticing that our simple environment and its associated Hoare logic represents the theoretical foundation of the Stanford VCG for the little fragment of PASCAL determined by the while-construct.

A specification E' is said to refine a specification E if any assertion provable from E is provable from E'. For a family of refinements $R_E = \{E_i : i \in I\}$ of a speification E we define the core of R_E by

$$CORE(R_E) = \{p \in L: E_i \vdash p, \text{ for each } i \in I\}.$$

Obviously, $E \subset CORE(R_E)$. A rather straightforward formal interpretation of our question reads thus: *Given an asserted program* $\{p\}S\{q\}$ *and a specification E, if for each choice* E_i *from a family of refinements* R_E *we know* $HL(E_i) \vdash \{p\}S\{q\}$ *then does this guarantee* $HL(CORE(R_E)) \vdash \{p\}S\{q\}$ *?*

Here is the answer.

THEOREM. *Let E be a first-order specification and* $\{p\}S\{q\}$ *an asserted program. Let* $R_E = \{E_i : i \in I\}$ *be a family of refinements of E such that* $HL(E_i) \vdash \{p\}S\{q\}$ *for each* $i \in I$. *If I is finite then the family is stable in the sense that*

$$HL(CORE(R_E)) \vdash \{p\}S\{q\}.$$

However, if I is infinite then the family may well be unstable: there is a specification E and an asserted program $\{p\}S\{q\}$, *and a countably infinite family* $R_E = \{E_i : i \in I\}$ *of refinements of E such that* $HL(E_i) \vdash \{p\}S\{q\}$ *but* $HL(CORE(R_E)) \nvdash \{p\}S\{q\}$.

Once one has carefully thought through the basic proof theory of Hoare's logic, the stability of finite families of refinements is quite easy to prove. But the instability of infinite families is harder to demonstrate because the computation-theoretic ideas involved carry a number of exercises in first-order model theory as overheads.

The instability result here should be compared with a theorem about arithmetical computation which was proved in our [7]: *for any asserted program* $\{p\}S\{q\}$ *and any infinite family* $R = \{E_i : i \in I\}$ *of refinements of Peano Arith-*

metic, if $HL(E_i) \vdash \{p\}S\{q\}$ *for each* $i \in I$ *then* $HL(CORE(R)) \vdash \{p\}S\{Q\}$. This is a particularly pleasing result since Peano Arithmetic is merely a refinement of the standard algebraic specification for arithmetic, designed to generate those assertions provable by induction.

After some preliminaries, we define Hoare's logic for a specification and look at its proof theory in which the basic tool is our Deduction Lemma 2.7. In Section 3 we prove the theorem. It should be noticed that the theorem does not concern semantical questions and that this gives it a certain novelty in the theoretical literature on program correctness. Most theoretical investigations and applications of Hoare's ideas about axiomatisation have contained a strong semantic bias since COOK [8]; see, for example, DE BAKKER [2] and the invaluable survey APT [1]. Practice, on the other hand, seems to have been preoccupied with proof theory.

This note is part of a series of articles about Hoare's logic and data type specifications: various incompleteness and completeness properties of the logic are re-examined in [4, 6]; algebraic speifications are studied in [5]; and the proof theory of the logic over arithmetic is the subject of [7]. All these articles recall [3], written in collaboration with J. Tiuryn, about the use of correctness formulae in defining the semantics of a programming system with first-order specified data types; but strictly speaking, none are required reading for the present paper.

We gratefully acknowledge conversations about verification with our colleagues R. J. R. Back and A. de Bruin.

1 ASSERTIONS, SPECIFICATIONS AND PROGRAMS

Prerequisite to any study of Hoare's logic are the primary sources HOARE [11] and COOK [8], but the reader would do well to consult the survey article APT [1].

The first-order language $L = L(\Sigma)$ of some signature Σ is based upon a set of variables $x_1, x_2, \ldots$ and its constant, function and relational symbols are those of Σ together with the boolean constants <u>true</u>, <u>false</u> and the equality relation. We assume L possesses the usual logical connectives and quantifiers; and the set of all algebraic expressions of L we denote $T(\Sigma)$.

If E is a set of assertions of L then the set of all formal theorems of E is denoted $Thm(E)$; we write $E \vdash p$ for $p \in Thm(E)$. Such a set E of formulae is usually called a theory, but in the present context we obviously need the more suggestive term *specification,* for L will serve as both an assertion/program specification language and a data type specification language.

1.1 <u>DEDUCTION THEOREM</u>. *Let* E *be a specification and let* p, q *be assertions. Then the following are equivalent:*

(1) $E \cup \{\hat{p}\} \vdash q$

(2) $E \vdash \hat{p} \rightarrow q$.

where $\hat{p}$ *is the universal closure of* p.

A specification E' is a refinement of a specification E if $Thm(E) \subset Thm(E')$. And two specifications E, E' are (logically) equivalent if $Thm(E) = Thm(E')$. If E is a specification and $R_E = \{E_i : i \in I\}$ is a family of refinements of E then we define the core of R_E by

$$CORE(R_E) = \bigcap_{i \in I} Thm(E_i) .$$

Using the syntax of L, the set $WP = WP(\Sigma)$ of all <u>while</u>-programs over Σ is defined in the customary way.

By a specified or asserted program we mean a triple of the form $\{p\}S\{q\}$ where $S \in WP$ and $p, q \in L$.

Such are the ingredients of Hoare's logic for a specification, but we also need their semantics in the proof of the theorem. Let us summarize the meanings for the various components and remark on the use of L as a data type specification language.

The semantics of a signature is a structure. For any structure A of signature Σ, the semantics of the first-order language L over Σ as determined by A has its standard definition in model theory and this we assume to be understood. The validity of $p \in L$ over structure A we write $A \models p$. The class of all models of a specification E is denoted $Mod(E)$; we write $Mod(E) \models p$ to mean that for every A, $Mod(E)$, $A \models p$. Gödel's Completeness Theorem says this about specifications:

$$E \vdash p \text{ if, and only if, } Mod(E) \models p .$$

As far as the proof theory of a data type axiomatisation E is concerned, the semantics of the specification is $Mod(E)$.

So consider the algebraic specification methods for data types where one invariably has a particular semantic model in mind for a specification. Following ADJ[9], it is usual to settle on the initial model $I(E)$ of $Mod(E)$ as the unique meaning for an algebraic axiomatisation E. The logic of E is oblivious of this (or any other) particular choice because it yields only those facts true in all models of E. Refinements are a natural accessory of algebraic specifications: one starts with a simple algebraic specification (Σ, E) to establish the correctness of the desired data type semantics A and then adds to E various assertions true in A as the need arises in program correctness proofs (say). Peano arithmetic illustrates this perfectly. Refinements are also a necessary accessory of algebraic specifications for although the algebraic methods can define virtually any data type one wants, the kinds of assertion provable from algebraic formulae are rather restricted; see [5] for a thorough discussion of this problem.

For the semantics of *WP* as determined by a structure A, we leave the reader free to choose any sensible account of while-program computations which applies to an arbitrary structure: COOK [8]; the graph-theoretic semantics in GREIBACH [10]; the denotational semantics described in DE BAKKER [2]. What constraint must be placed on this choice is merely the necessity of verifying the soundness of Hoare's logic (Theorem 2.9).

To the asserted programs we assign *partial correctness semantics:* the asserted program $\{p\}S\{q\}$ is *valid on a structure* A (in symbols: $A \models \{p\}S\{q\}$) if for each initial state $a \in$ states (A), $A \models p(a)$ implies either $S(a)$ terminates and $A \models q(S(a))$ or $S(a)$ diverges. And the asserted program $\{p\}S\{q\}$ is *valid for a specification* E if it is valid on every model of E; in symbols, $E \models \{p\}S\{q\}$ or $Mod(E) \models \{p\}S\{q\}$.

The *partial correctness theory of a structure* A is the set

$$PC(A) = \{\{p\}S\{q\}: A \models \{p\}S\{Q\}\} ;$$

and the *partial correctness theory of a specification* E is the set

$$PC(E) = \{\{p\}S\{q\}: Mod(E) \models \{p\}S\{q\}\} .$$

Clearly,

$$PC(E) = \cap_{A \in Mod(E)} PC(A) .$$

2 HOARE'S LOGIC

Hoare's logic for $WP = WP(\Sigma)$ with assertion language $L = L(\Sigma)$ and specification $E \subset L$, has the following axioms and proof rules for manipulating asserted programs: let $S, S_1, S_2 \in WP$; $p,q,p_1,q_1,r \in L$; $b \in L$, a quantifier-free formula.

1 Assignment axiom scheme: for $e \in T(\Sigma)$ and x a variable of L, the asserted program.

$$\{p[e/x]\}x := e\{p\}$$

is an axiom, where $p[e/x]$ stands for the result of substituting e for free occurrences of x in p.

2 Composition rule:

$$\frac{\{p\}S_1\{r\},\{r\}S_2\{q\}}{\{p\}S_1;\ S_2\{q\}}$$

3 Conditional rule:

$$\frac{\{p \wedge b\}S_1\{q\},\ \{p \wedge \neg b\}S_2\{q\}}{\{p\}\ \underline{\text{if}}\ b\ \underline{\text{then}}\ S_1\ \underline{\text{else}}\ S_2\ \underline{\text{fi}}\ \{q\}}$$

4 Iteration rule:

$$\frac{\{p\wedge b\}S\{p\}}{\{p\}\ \underline{\text{while}}\ b\ \underline{\text{do}}\ S\ \underline{\text{od}}\ \{p\wedge \neg b\}}$$

5 Consequence rule:

$$\frac{p\to p_1,\ \{p_1\}S\{q_1\},\ q_1\to q}{\{p\}S\{q\}}$$

And, in connection with 5,

6 Specification axiom scheme: Each member of Thm(E) is an axiom.

The set of asserted programs derivable from these axioms by the proof rules we denote HL(E), but if $E = \{t\}$ for some $t \in L$ then we use HL(t). As usual we write $HL(E) \vdash \{p\}S\{q\}$ in place of $\{p\}S\{q\} \in HL(E)$.

2.1 **REFINEMENT LEMMA.** *Let E and E' be specifications. If E' is a refinement of E then $HL(E) \subset HL(E')$. Thus, if E and E' are equivalent specifications then $HL(E) = HL(E')$.*

Actually, it is this first lemma which authorises our use of the term refinement in the present context for our interest in the logic of specifications and assertions is shaped by the logic of partial correctness it must support. Lemma 2.1 is obviously true as, indeed, are the next two proof-theoretical facts:

2.2 **FINITENESS LEMMA.** *Let E be a specification and $\{p\}S\{q\}$ an asserted program. If $HL(E) \vdash \{p\}S\{q\}$ then there is a finite set $F = \{t_i : i \in I\}$ of assertions such that $E \vdash t_i$ for each $i \in I$ and $HL(F) \vdash \{p\}S\{q\}$; in particular, there is a single assertion $t = \wedge_{i\in I} t_i$ such that $E \vdash t$ and $HL(t) \vdash \{p\}S\{q\}$.*

2.3 **PROOF DECOMPOSITION LEMMA.** *Let E be a specification and let p, q be assertions. Then*

(1) Assignment: $HL(E) \vdash \{p\}x := e\{q\}$ *if, and only if,* $E \vdash p \to q[e/x]$

(2) Composition: $HL(E) \vdash \{p\}S_1;S_2\{q\}$ *if, and only if, for some assertion* r, $HL(E) \vdash \{p\}S_1\{r\}$ *and* $HL(E) \vdash \{r\}S_2\{q\}$

(3) Conditional: $HL(E) \vdash \{p\}$ <u>if</u> b <u>then</u> S_1 <u>else</u> S_2 <u>fi</u>$\{q\}$ *if, and only if* $HL(E) \vdash \{p\wedge b\}S_1\{q\}$ *and* $HL(E) \vdash \{p\wedge\neg b\}S_2\{q\}$

(4) Iteration: $HL(E) \vdash \{p\}$ <u>while</u> b <u>do</u> S_0 <u>od</u> $\{q\}$ *if, and only if, for some assertion* r,
$E \vdash p \to r$, $HL(E) \vdash \{r\wedge b\}S\{r\}$, *and* $E \vdash r\wedge\neg b \to q$.

The ease with which one can calculate in a formal system is decided by its derived rules. Hoare's logic enjoys many derived rules which turn natural semantical properties into formal proof-theoretical laws with few syntactical concessions:

2.4 LEMMA. *Let* E *be a specification and* $\{\{p_i\}S\{q_i\}: i \in I\}$ *a finite set of asserted programs. Then the following is a derived rule of* $HL(E)$

$$\frac{\{p_i\}S\{q_i\} \quad \text{for each} \quad i \in I}{\{\bigvee_{i\in I} p_i\}S\{\bigvee_{i\in I} q_i\}}$$

2.5 LEMMA. *Let* E *be a specification and* $\{\{p_i\}S\{q_i\}: i \in I\}$ *be a finite set of asserted programs. Then the following is a derived rule of* $HL(E)$

$$\frac{\{p_i\}S\{q_i\} \quad \text{for each} \quad i \in I}{\{\bigwedge_{i\in I} p_i\}S\{\bigwedge_{i\in I} q_i\}} .$$

2.6 LEMMA. *Let* E *be a specification and* $\{p\}S\{q\}$ *an asserted program. Then the following is a derived rule of* $HL(E)$

$$\frac{\{p\}S\{q\}}{\{\exists y.p\}S\{q\}}$$

where y *is not a variable of* S *and not a free variable of* q.

The following theorem is fundamental for any reasoning about Hoare's logic for a specification.

2.7 DEDUCTION LEMMA. *Let* E *be a specification, let* t *be (the universal closure of) an assertion and let* $\{p\}S\{q\}$ *be an asserted program. Then the following are equivalent*

(1) $HL(E \cup \{t\}) \vdash \{p\}S\{q\}$

(2) $HL(E) \vdash \{t \wedge p\}S\{q\}$.

PROOF. That (2) implies (1) is obvious: clearly, $E \vdash t \to (p \to t \wedge p)$ and so by the Deduction Theorem 1.1 for first-order logic $E \cup \{t\} \vdash p \to t \wedge p$. From (2) and the Refinement Lemma 2.1 we know that $HL(E \cup \{t\}) \vdash \{t \wedge p\}S\{q\}$; thus by the Rule of Consequence it follows that $HL(E \cup \{t\}) \vdash \{p\}S\{q\}$. The reverse implication is proved by induction on the structure of S for which the basis is the assignment statement.

Assignment: $S ::= x := e$. Assume $HL(E \cup \{t\}) \vdash \{p\}x := e\{q\}$. Then $E \cup \{t\} \vdash p \to q[e/x]$ by Lemma 2.3 and $E \vdash t \to (p \to q[e/x])$ by the Deduction Theorem 1.1 for first order logic. But $E \vdash t \wedge p \to q[e/x]$ and so $HL(E) \vdash \{t \wedge p\}x := e\{q\}$ by Lemma 2.3.

The induction step divides into 3 cases.

Composition: $S ::= S_1;S_2$. Assume $HL(E \cup \{t\}) \vdash \{p\}S_1; S_2\{q\}$. By Lemma 2.3, there is some assertion r such that

$$HL(E \cup \{t\}) \vdash \{p\}S_1\{r\} \quad \text{and} \quad HL(E \cup \{t\}) \vdash \{r\}S_2\{q\}.$$

Now $E \cup \{t\} \vdash r \to (t \wedge r)$ and so $HL(E \cup \{t\}) \vdash \{p\}S_1\{t \wedge r\}$ by the Rule of Consequence. By the induction hypothesis,

$$HL(E) \vdash \{t \wedge p\}S_1\{t \wedge r\} \quad \text{and} \quad HL(E) \vdash \{t \wedge r\}S_2\{q\}$$

and hence $HL(E) \vdash \{t \wedge p\}S_1;\ S_2\{q\}$ by the Composition Rule.

Conditional: $S ::=$ if b then S_1 else S_2 fi. Assume $HL(E \cup \{t\}) \vdash \{p\}S\{q\}$. By Lemma 2.3, we know that

$$HL(E \cup \{t\}) \vdash \{p \wedge b\}S_1\{q\} \quad \text{and} \quad HL(E \cup \{t\}) \vdash \{p \wedge \neg b\}S_2\{q\}.$$

By the induction hypothesis,

$$HL(E) \vdash \{(t \wedge p) \wedge b\}S_1\{q\} \quad \text{and} \quad HL(E) \vdash \{(t \wedge p) \wedge \neg b\}S_2\{q\}$$

and hence $HL(E) \vdash \{t \wedge p\}S\{q\}$ by the Conditional Rule.

Iteration: $S ::=$ while b do S_0 od. Assume $HL(E \cup \{t\}) \vdash \{p\}S\{q\}$
By Lemma 2.3, there is some assertion r such that

$$E \cup \{t\} \vdash p \to r,\ HL(E \cup \{t\}) \vdash \{r \wedge b\}S_0\{r\} \text{ and } E \cup \{t\} \vdash r \wedge \neg b \to q.$$

Now $E \cup \{t\} \vdash r \to t \wedge r$ so applying the Rule of Consequence to the asserted program, and the Deduction Theorem 1.1 for first order logic to the logical theorems, we obtain

$$E \vdash t \to (p \to r) \quad HL(E \cup \{t\}) \vdash \{r \wedge b\}S_0\{t \wedge r\} \quad \text{and} \quad H \vdash t \to (r \wedge \neg b \to q)$$

and with some further logical rewriting and the induction hypothesis applied to S_0 we get

$$E \vdash t \wedge p \to t \wedge r \quad HL(E) \vdash \{(t \wedge r) \wedge b\}S_0\{t \wedge r\} \quad \text{and} \quad E \vdash (t \wedge r) \wedge \neg b \to q.$$

By the iteration clause of Lemma 2.3, $HL(E) \vdash \{t \wedge p\}S\{q\}$.

QED

The following fact has an essential role to play in the proof of our theorem.

2.8 LEMMA. *Let E be a specification and let $\{t_i : i \in I\}$ be a finite set of assertions. If $HL(E \cup \{t_i\}) \vdash \{p\}S\{q\}$ for each $i \in I$ then $HL(E \cup \{\vee_{i \in I} t_i\}) \vdash \{p\}S\{q\}$.*

PROOF. Assume $HL(E \cup \{t_i\}) \vdash \{p\}S\{q\}$ for each $i \in I$. Then by the Deduction Lemma 2.7, $HL(E) \vdash \{t_i \wedge p\}S\{q\}$ for each $i \in I$. By the derived rule Lemma 2.4, we have $HL(E) \vdash \{(\vee_{i \in I} t_i)\}S\{q\}$ and so the result follows by the Deduction Lemma 2.7.

QED

And finally we record this well known theorem which will be needed for technical reasons in the next section.

2.9 SOUNDNESS THEOREM. *Let E be a specification. Then HL(E) ⊂ PC(E).*

This is what is said in the corollary to Theorem 1 in COOK [8].

3 PROOF OF THE THEOREM

Let $R_E = \{E_i : i \in I\}$ be a finite family of refinements of the specification E and assume that $HL(E_i) \vdash \{p\}S\{q\}$ for each $i \in I$. By the Finiteness Lemma 2.2, we can choose assertions t_i such that $E_i \vdash t_i$ and $HL(t_i) \vdash \{p\}S\{q\}$ for each $i \in I$. By Lemma 2.8, we know $HL(\bigvee_{i\in I} t_i) \vdash \{p\}S\{q\}$, but $\bigvee_{i\in I} t_i \in CORE(R_E)$ and so we are done.

Now consider the case of an infinite family of refinements. Our counter example is combinatorially related to two-way unbounded lists and arrays and it could be described exclusively in terms of such structures. For technical clarity, however, we have found that our argument is better served by the example's looser relationship with arithmetic.

The basic specification is (Σ, E) where $\Sigma = \{a,b,N,L\}$ and a,b are constants and N,L are unary operator symbols; and E contains two algebraic axioms

$$NL(X) = X \quad \text{and} \quad LN(X) = X .$$

The models of E are precisely those structures composed of a set equipped with a permutation, its inverse and two distinguished points. But for the moment one may think of N,L as the next and last operators on two lists with roots a,b. For example, the initial algebra of Mod(E) picks out the model depicted in Figure 3.1 which we identify with two copies of integer arithmetic $\mathbb{Z} \wedge \mathbb{Z}$.

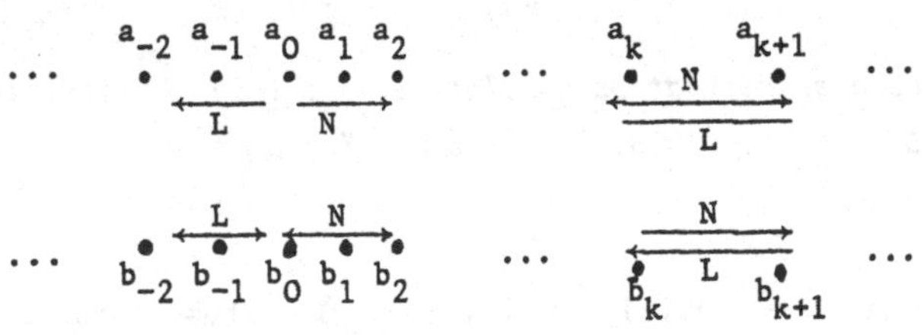

Figure 3.1

The asserted program {p}S{q} we shall study is defined by

$$S ::= \underline{\text{while}}\ x \neq b\ \underline{\text{do}}\ x := N(x)\ \underline{\text{od}}$$

$$p \equiv x = a \quad \text{and} \quad q \equiv \underline{\text{false}}.$$

If {p}S{q} were provable then this would guarantee that a,b are the roots of distinct lists, or arithmetics, as one can neither move, or count up, from a to b nor down from b to a. Notice that {p}S{q} is valid on the initial model $\mathbb{Z} \wedge \mathbb{Z}$ because $S(a_0)$ diverges, but it is not provable in HL(E) because it is not valid in a model of E such as

$$k - \mathbb{Z} = (\{\ldots,-2,-1,0,1,2,\ldots\};\ 0,k,x+1,x-1)$$

where a names 0, and b names k and $k \geq 0$ (by the Soundness Theorem 2.9).

Let $E_i = E \cup \{N^j(a) \neq b: 0 \leq j < i\} \cup \{N^i(a) = a\}$ for $i \in \omega$. The axioms of E_i are intended to force S to diverge on any input named by a because they introduce a cycle of length i generated by N applied to a from which b is procluded. Notice E_i is not valid in $\mathbb{Z} \wedge \mathbb{Z}$ but it is valid in $\mathbb{Z}_i \wedge \mathbb{Z}$ where $\mathbb{Z}_i$ is integer arithmetic modulo i.

3.1 LEMMA. *For each* $i \in \omega$, $HL(E_i) \vdash \{p\}S\{q\}$.

PROOF. Now S : : = while $x \neq b$ do x : = N(x) od so consider the body x : = N(x). By the Assignment Axiom Scheme, we know that for $j < i$

$$HL(E_i) \vdash \{(x = N^{j+1}(a))[N(x)/x]\}\ x := N(x)\{x = N^{j+1}(a)\}.$$

But the precondition is just $N(x) = N^{j+1}(a)$ and trivially $E_i \vdash x = N^j(a) \rightarrow N(x) = N^{j+1}(a)$. By the Rule of Consequence, we know that for $j < i$

$$HL(E_i) \vdash \{x = N^j(a)\}\ x := N(x)\{x = N^{j+1}(a)\}$$

and by Lemma 2.4

$$HL(E_i) \vdash \{\textstyle\bigvee_{j=0}^{i-1} x = N^j(a)\}\ x := N(x)\ \{\textstyle\bigvee_{j=0}^{i-1} x = N^{j+1}(a)\}\ .$$

Because $E_i \vdash N^i(a) = a$ and $E_i \vdash \bigvee_{j=0}^{i-1} x = N^{j+1}(a) \rightarrow \bigvee_{j=0}^{i-1} x = N^j(a)$ we can apply the Rule of Consequence to obtain

$$HL(E_i) \vdash \{r \wedge x \neq a\}x := N(x)\{r\}$$

wherein $r \equiv \bigvee_{j=0}^{i-1} x = N^j(a)$. By the Iteration Rule, we derive

$$HL(E_i) \vdash \{r\}\ \underline{\text{while}}\ x \neq a\ \underline{\text{do}}\ x := N(x)\ \underline{\text{od}}\ \{r \wedge \neg(x \neq a)\}$$

and since $E_i \vdash p \rightarrow r$ and $E_i \vdash (r \wedge \neg(x \neq a)) \rightarrow q$, the Rule of Consequence yields

$$HL(E_i) \vdash \{p\}S\{q\}$$

QED

To complete the proof of the theorem we have to demonstrate this next fact:

3.2 LEMMA. *If* $R_E = \{E_i: i \in \omega\}$ *then* $HL(CORE(R_E)) \not\vdash \{p\}S\{q\}$.

PROOF. Assume for a contradiction that $HL(CORE(R_E)) \vdash \{p\}S\{q\}$. Then by the Finiteness Lemma 2.2 we may choose an assertion $t \in CORE(R_E)$ such that

(1) $HL(t) \vdash \{p\}S\{q\}$.

For this statement (1) we shall find a contradiction.

Let D be the following set of assertions which are intended to rule out finite cycles in the operator N and to ensure a and b are mutually in-

$$D = \{N^i(X) \neq X\colon i \in \omega\} \cup \{N^i(a) \neq b,\ N^i(b) \neq a\colon i \in \omega\}.$$

For example, D is valid in $\mathbb{Z} \wedge \mathbb{Z}$, but we wish to show that the specification $E \cup \{t\} \cup D$ has a model in order to guarantee the consistency of (1) with the special requirements on the operator N.

3.3 LEMMA. *The specification* $E \cup \{t\} \cup D$ *has a model.*

PROOF. We use the Compactness Theorem. Any finite subset of $T = E \cup \{t\} \cup D$ is included in a finite initial segment $T_K = E \cup \{t\} \cup D_K$ where

$$D_K = \{N^i(X) \neq X\colon 0 \leq i < K\} \cup \{N^i(a) \neq b,\ N^i(b) \neq a\colon 0 \leq i < K\}$$

and K is sufficiently large. Consider the structure $\mathbb{Z}_K \wedge \mathbb{Z}_K$ made from two copies of integer arithmetic mod K and depicted in Figure 3.2

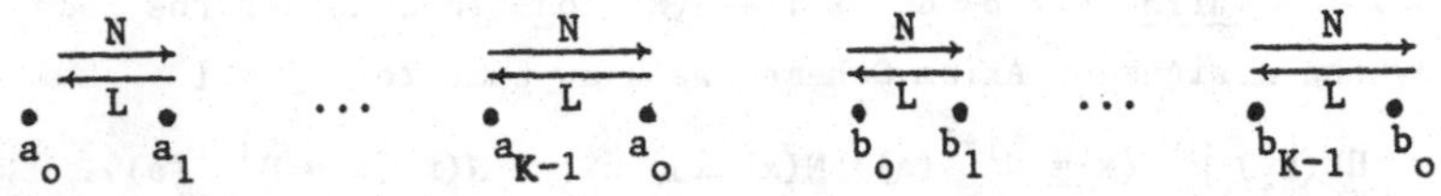

Figure 3.2

Clearly, $A \models D_K$ but, in addition, $A \models E_K$ and hence $A \models E \cup \{t\}$. Thus T_K has a model. Since every finite subset of T has a model, T has a model by the Compactness Theorem. QED

We now need a technical fact about the relationship between t and $E \cup D$.

3.4 LEMMA. *The specification* $E \cup D$ *admits quantifier elimination: for each assertion* $r \in L$ *there is a quantifier-free assertion* r^* *such that* $E \cup D \vdash r \leftrightarrow r^*$.

PROOF. Let $T = E \cup D$. Now T is a universally axiomatised first-order theory so, by a theorem of Robinson, if T is model-complete then T admits quantifier elimination (see SACKS [15, p67]). Another theorem of Robinson says that T is model complete if, and only if, for each model A of T, T DIAGRAM(A) is complete (SACKS [15, p36]). It is a routine matter to prove that for any model A of T, the set of formulae $T \cup$ DIAGRAM(A) is ω_1-categorical. Thus, by the Los-Vaught Test (SACKS [15, p34]) this set of assertions is complete. QED

Using Lemma 3.4 we can choose a quantifier-free assertion t^* such that $E \cup D \vdash t \leftrightarrow t^*$ and then choose a finite subset D^* of D such that $E \cup D^* \vdash t \leftrightarrow t^*$.

We shall construct a structure A which is a model for $E \cup \{t^*\} \cup D^*$ and in which for some $\ell \in \omega$, $A \models N^\ell(a) = b$. Assuming this is done, the contradiction to statement (1) is soon found:

Clearly $A \not\models \{p\}S\{q\}$ because S can terminate in ℓ steps from $x = a$ in A. Since $E \cup D^* \vdash t \leftrightarrow t^*$, we have that $A \models t \leftrightarrow t^*$ and $A \models t^*$ and so $A \models t$. Thus, $\{p\}S\{q\}$ is invalid on a model of $E \cup \{t\}$. By the Soundness Theorem 2.9

$$HL(E \cup \{t\}) \not\vdash \{p\}S\{q\}$$

and so obviously $HL(t) \not\vdash \{p\}S\{q\}$ which is the required contradiction.

3.5 <u>LEMMA</u>. *The specification* $E \cup \{t^*\} \cup D^*$ *has a model in which for some* $\ell \in \omega$, $F^{\ell}(a) = b$.

PROOF. By Lemma 3.3, $E \cup \{t\} \cup D$ has a model B and since $E \cup D \vdash t \leftrightarrow t^*$ we know $E \cup \{t^*\} \cup D$ is valid in B. Now it is straightforward to check that the substructure of B generated by the constants a, b is isomorphic to $\mathbb{Z} \wedge \mathbb{Z}$; and since $E \cup \{t^*\} \cup D$ consists of universal axioms only it is the case that

$$\mathbb{Z} \wedge \mathbb{Z} \models E \cup \{t^*\} \cup D.$$

(Here we need the simplification of t to t^*, of course.)

Consider the map ϕ_k: $\mathbb{Z} \wedge \mathbb{Z} \to \mathbb{Z} \wedge \mathbb{Z}$ defined by

$$\phi_k(a_i) = a_i \quad \text{and} \quad \phi_k(b_i) = a_{i+k} .$$

Each ϕ_k is an endomorphism of $\mathbb{Z} \wedge \mathbb{Z}$ and obviously

$$\phi_k(\mathbb{Z} \wedge \mathbb{Z}) \models F^k(a) = b.$$

By inspection, we can choose some k sufficiently large to guarantee that

$$\phi_k(\mathbb{Z} \wedge \mathbb{Z}) \models E \cup \{t^*\} \cup D^*.$$

To see that these extra axioms can be satisfied we consider each of the three sets in turn. First, $\phi_k(\mathbb{Z} \wedge \mathbb{Z}) \models E$ for any k because E contains only equations and ϕ_k is a homomorphism. Next, consider the quantifier-free assertion t^*. If one chooses $k > L = \|t^*\|$, the length of t^*, then ϕ_k cannot identify any of the inequalities making up t^*. It is easy to see in this case that for $k > L$, $\phi_k(\mathbb{Z} \wedge \mathbb{Z}) = t^*$. Thirdly, since D^* is finite it is included in some finite segment D_K of D as defined in the proof of Lemma 3.3. If one chooses $k > K$ then $\phi_k(\mathbb{Z} \wedge \mathbb{Z}) = D^*$ because no loops are introduced "below" k in the sense that

$$\phi_k(\mathbb{Z} \wedge \mathbb{Z}) \models \{F^i(a) \neq b,\ F^i(b) \neq a: 0 \leq i < k\}.$$

Therefore, choosing some $\ell > \max(L, K)$ leads to a model $A = \phi_{\ell}(\mathbb{Z} \wedge \mathbb{Z})$ such that

$$A \models E \cup \{t^*\} \cup D^* \cup \{F^{\ell}(a) = b\} .$$

QED

REFERENCES

[1] APT, K.R., *Ten years of Hoare's logic, a survey* in F.V. JENSEN, B.H. MAYOH and K.K. MØLLER (eds), *Proceedings from 5th Scandinavian Logic Symposium*, Aalborg University Press, Aalborg, 1979, 1-44. (A second edition of this paper will appear in ACM Transactions on Programming Languages and Systems).

[2] DE BAKER, J.W., *Mathematical theory of program correctness*, Prentice-Hall International, London, 1980.

[3] BERGSTRA, J.A., J. TIURYN & J.V. TUCKER, *Floyd's principle, correctness theories and program equivalence* (To appear in Theoretical Computer Science.)

[4] BERGSTRA, J.A. & J.V. TUCKER, *Some natural structures which fail to possess a sound and decidable Hoare-like logic for their* while-*programs* (To appear in Theoretical Computer Science.)

[5] BERGSTRA, J.A. & J.V. TUCKER, *Algebraically specified programming systems and Hoare's logic*, in S. EVEN & O. KARIV (eds), *Automata, languages and programming*, 8th Colloquium, Springer-Verlag, Berlin, 1981, 348-362.

[6] BERGSTRA, J.A. & J.V. TUCKER, *Expressiveness and the completeness of Hoare's logic*, Mathematical Centre, Department of Computer Science Research Report IW 149, Amsterdam, 1980.

[7] BERGSTRA, J.A. & J.V. TUCKER, *Hoare's logic and Peano's arithmetic*, Mathematical Centre, Department of Computer Science Research Report, Amsterdam, 1980.

[8] COOK, S.A., *Soundness and completeness of an axiom system for program verification*, SIAM J. Computing 7 (1978) 70-90.

[9] GOGUEN, J.A., J.W. THATCHER & E.G. WAGNER, *An initial algebra approach to the specification, correctness and implementation of abstract data types*, in R.T. YEH (ed.), *Current trends in programming methodology* IV, Data structuring, Prentice-Hall, Engelwood Cliffs, New Jersey, 1978, 80-149.

[10] GREIBACH, S.A., *Theory of program structures: schemes, semantics, verification*, Springer-Verlag, Berlin, 1975.

[11] HOARE, C.A.R., *An axiomatic basis for computer programming*, Communications Association Computing Machinery 12 (1969) 576-580.

[12] IGARASHI, S., R.L. LONDON & D.C. LUCKHAM, *Automatic program verification I: a logical basis and its implementation*, Acta Informatica 4 (1975) 145-182.

[13] LUCKHAM, D.C. & N. SUZUKI, *Verification of array, record and pointer operations in PASCAL*, ACM-Transactions on Programming Languages and Systems 1 (1979) 226-244.

[14] MUSSER, D.R., *Abstract data type specification in the AFFIRM system*, IEEE Transactions on Software Engineering 6(1) (1980) 24-32.

[15] SACKS, G.E., *Saturated model theory*, W.A. Benjamin, Inc., Reading, Massachusetts, 1972.

Toward a Logical Theory of Program Data

Robert Cartwright

Department of Mathematical Sciences
Rice University
Houston, Texas 77001

1. Introduction

Theoretical computer scientists have vigorously attacked the problem of developing theories of program execution -- creating an impressive array of formal systems such as Floyd-Hoare logic [Floyd 67, Hoare 69], Dynamic Logic [Pratt 76], Logic for Computable Functions [Milner 72], and first order programming logic [Cartwright and McCarthy 79]. All of these formalisms assume that a complementary theory of the program data domain -- the data values and operations manipulated by the program -- already exists. Yet relatively little attention has been focused on the problem of developing satisfactory theories of program data. The objective of this paper is to dispel some common misconceptions about the adequacy of existing ad hoc axiomatic approaches to data specification and and to kindle interest in data specification methods relying on explicit, constructive definitions.

A simple theory of primitive types supported by most conventional programming languages is too inexpressive to serve as the basis for a practical programming logic. To be intelligible, program specifications must expressed at a much higher level of abstraction than machine-oriented primitives such as pointers, records, fixed length arrays, and bit-strings. Unfortunately, most researchers in the area of data specification and abstraction have ignored the problem of generating suitable logical theories for reasoning about data domains. The most widely publicized data specification method, algebraic specification [ADJ 76,77] [Guttag 76,77], semantically characterizes data domains without providing a tractable formal theory in which to establish their properties. Unless theoretical computer scientists develop data specification methods that produce simple yet powerful logical theories, formal approaches to program documentation and correctness (e.g. formal testing systems [Carwright 81]) will never realize their potential as practical programming tools.

This paper addresses three major issues. First, it establishes a framework for formalizing and evaluating data specification methods and the logical theories that they generate. Second, it reviews the data specification methods proposed in the literature and evaluates how well they support formal reasoning about program data. Finally, it suggests some possible approaches to improving and extending existing data specification systems.

2. Mathematical Preliminaries

Before we can intelligently discuss data specifications, we must establish a common mathematical framework in which we can formalize the various approaches to the subject. For this purpose, I will use standard first order predicate logic with equality, because it is the most widely accepted formal system for describing mathematical domains and it is the most frequently cited logic in the literature on data specification. Moreover, it is well known that statements in higher order logics can be translated into equivalent statements in first order logic.

In the sequel, we will generally assume that a data specification is expressed within a <u>first order logical language</u> L including equality (=), and set of function symbols F, and a set of predicate symbols P. A type function ρ_L mapping F ∪ P into the natural numbers specifies the arity of each symbol. Constants are treated as 0-ary function symbols. A <u>structure</u> **M** corresponding to L is a triple <|**M**|,**F**,**P**> where |**M**| (called the <u>universe</u>) is a set of values, **F** is a map assigning to each function symbol in F a function on |**M**| (of the appropriate arity) and **P** is a map assigning to each predicate symbol in P a relation on |**M**| (of the appropriate arity). The reader who finds this terminology unfamiliar is encouraged to consult [Enderton 72].

A first order language L includes both a set of terms, constructed from variables and function symbols, and a set of formulas constructed from logical connectives and predicate symbols applied to terms. Given a structure **M** corresponding to L and an interpretation function **I** mapping the variables of L into |**M**|, every term in L denotes an object in |**M**| and every formula denotes a truth value **TRUE** or **FALSE** (which are distinct from all objects in the universe). The meaning of terms and formulas of L is defined by structural induction in the obvious way (See [Enderton 72] for the details). Terms and formulas containing no free variables are called <u>ground terms</u> and <u>sentences</u>, respectively. Their meanings are independent of the particular choice of interpretation function **I**. We will denote the set of ground terms corresponding to **M** by Ground(**M**). Given a set of sentences T in a first order language L, a <u>model</u> for T is a structure **M** corresponding to L such that every sentence of T is **TRUE** in M. A <u>term model</u> (sometimes called a syntactic model) for T is a model with a universe consisting of equivalence classes of ground terms in the language L.

A <u>theory</u> T is a collection of sentences in a language L with the following two properties:

(1) <u>Semantic consistency</u>: there exists a model for T.

(2) <u>Closure under logical implication</u>: every sentence that is **TRUE** in all models of T is a member of T.

A theory T is <u>axiomatizable</u> iff there exists a recursive set of sentences $A \subseteq T$ such that the closure of A under logical implication equals T. The set of sentences A is called an <u>axiomatization</u> of T.

In most cases, a theory T has an intended model called the <u>standard model</u>. Any model that is not isomorphic to the standard model is called a <u>non-standard model</u>. Two structures corresponding to the same logical language L are <u>elementarily distinct</u> iff there exists a sentence S in L such that S is true in one structure but not the other. A theory with elementarily distinct models is called <u>incomplete</u>.

A <u>logical definition</u> within a theory T is a collection of logical sentences D that introduces a set of new function and predicate symbols to the formal language L such that any model for T can be uniquely extended -- by adding interpretations for the new function and predicate symbols -- to a model for $T \cup D$.[1] A logical definition is <u>eliminable</u> iff for every sentence S in the extended language there exists an <u>equivalent</u> sentence S' in the original language. S' is <u>equivalent</u> to S when every model **M** of T has the property that **M** is a model for $T \cup \{S'\}$ iff the unique extension of **M** is a model for $T \cup D \cup \{S\}$.

3. Data Domains, Specifications, and Logical Theories

In the literature on data specification, there is little consensus on what a data domain is. In the context of the first order logic, I will use the following definition. A <u>data domain</u> **D** is a structure that satisfies the following constraints:

(1) (Enumerability) Every object in the universe must be denotable by a ground term. Furthermore, the set of function symbols in the language must be countable.

(2) (Existence of an abstract implementation) The structure has a corresponding <u>abstract implementation</u> consisting of a designated subset of ground terms called <u>canonical forms</u> and a (partially) computable evaluation function mapping ground terms into canonical forms that preserves the meaning of terms. More formally, an <u>abstract implementation</u> is a pair <Canon,Eval> consisting of a set Canon of ground terms and a partial recursive function Eval mapping Ground(**D**) into Canon, such that:

   (a) Eval is the identity on Canon. Canonical forms evaluate to themselves.

   (b) If two ground terms reduce to the same canonical form or their evaluations both diverge, then they have the same meaning in **D**. The converse does not necessarily hold; the structure is not required to map distinct canonical

---

[1]The uniqueness requirement can be relaxed at the expense of a more complex definition of eliminability.

forms into distinct elements of the universe.

(c) In **D**, no canonical form can have the same meaning as a divergent ground term.

The obvious intuition underlying this definition of data domain is that data domains are structures that have corresponding machine implementations. Canonical forms denote the "answers" that machine computations can generate. An implementation for a data domain evaluates expressions (ground terms) to produce answers (or divergence) with the same meanings as the original expressions.

In data domains including the divergent object (which must be unique by (2b)), it is standard practice to include a constant, usually written ⊥ ("bottom"), denoting the divergent object. Since expressions with divergent evaluations do not reduce to ⊥ (or any other ground term), ⊥ is not a canonical form. Nevertheless, ⊥ serves as the standard name for the divergent object, just as canonical forms serve as standard names for ordinary data objects.

A data specification method typically consists of a formal specification language L and a semantic definition mapping specifications written in L into data domains . Given any particular data specification, the method defines a corresponding mathematical structure. If the method is constructive, it also specifies the corresponding abstract implementation.

To support formal reasoning about program data, a data specification method must generate an axiomatizable theory with the following properties:

(1) The generated theory must be extensible. In other words, adding new types or operations to a data domain specification should simply add new sentences to the theory, preserving the truth of all statements in the original theory.

(2) The corresponding theory should be both powerful and intuitively "natural". Virtally any interesting property of the data domain should be expressible and provable within the theory.

While the second criterion is highly subjective, it is extremely important in practice. From Godel's first incompleteness theorem we know that any axiomatizable theory for a non-trivial data domain must be incomplete. Nevertheless, a well-crafted theory (like first order Peano arithmetic) can establish virtually every expressible true statement of practical interest. The few exceptions are statements (such as the consistency of arithmetic) whose proofs require transfinite induction up to large ordinal numbers (ϵ_0 or greater). A data specification system should be designed to generate simple, powerful theories like first order Peano arithmetic.

Three basic approaches to specifying data domains have been proposed in the literature:

(1) **Axiomatic specification** (e.g. algebraic specification [ADJ 76,77], [Guttag 76,77]). The programmer is responsible for devising a list of axioms that accurately and completely describe his data domain.

(2) **Domain identification**. (e.g. defining retracts within Scott's theory of Pw [Scott 76]). The programmer explicitly defines his data domain by writing logical definitions within a fixed, comprehensive theory of data objects. The definitions identify the program data domain with a subspace of the universe described by the theory.

(3) **Domain construction** (e.g. constructive data type definitions [Cartwright 76,80]). The programmer implicitly develops an axiomatization for his data domain by explicitly constructing the domain using a small collection of domain constructors. Additional primitive operations may be defined by using conventional logical definitions.

Of the three approaches, axiomatic specification has been the most thoroughly investigated and publicized. In fact, a special form of axiomatic specification, called "algebraic specification" has apparently won widespread acceptance among computer scientists as a viable system for specifying data domains. Nevertheless, on the basis of the technical and pragmatic criteria enumerated above, algebraic specification does not provide an adequate formal system for reasoning about the program data domain.

In the remainder of the paper, we will demonstrate that the two constructive approaches to data specification -- domain identification and domain construction -- provide a much sounder basis for reasoning about program data.

4. Axiomatic Data Specifications

An axomatic data domain specification consists of a list of axioms and axiom schemes formulated by the programmer that ostensibly capture the essential properties of the program data domain. The axioms are typically expressed in sorted first order predicate calculus with equality. As a specification method, the most significant weakness of the axiomatic approach is that axiomatic definitions are deceptively difficult to write and to understand. A programmer trying to devise an axiomatic specification for his program data domain is more likely to generate inconsistent nonsense than a correct specification. Axiomatizing a non-trivial mathematical structure is a tedious, error-prone process. A single clerical or conceptual error can transform an otherwise correct axiomatization into an inconsistent or blatantly incomplete system.

Unfortunately, there are no viable methods for determining whether an arbitrary axiomatization is inconsistent or blatantly incomplete. Axiomatic definitions are notoriously hard to debug. The quality of an axiomatic specification critically depends on the programmer's skill as a logician.

In response to the obvious lack of discipline in conventional axiomatic specifications, several researchers [ADJ 76,77] [Guttag 76,77] have proposed a disciplined form of axiomatic definition called "algebraic specification". An algebraic specification is an axiomatic specification consisting of a finite set of equations (or, in a generalization investigated by the ADJ group, a finite set of implications between equations). This restriction on the form of axioms guarantees that an axiomatic specification has a term model. In fact, it is easy to show that the set of all term models for an arbitrary algebraic specification forms a lattice ordered by the natural partial ordering induced by set inclusion. In every case, the top element of the lattice, called the final algebra, is the trivial term model containing a single object of each sort. The bottom element of the lattice, called the initial algebra, equates two ground terms u and v iff there is a derivation $u \equiv \gamma_0 = \ldots = \gamma_n \equiv v$ from the specification. In the ADJ formulation of algebraic specification, a data specification consisting of a set of equations defines the corresponding initial algebra.

At first glance, the initial algebra approach to algebraic specification appears to solve the major technical problems plaguing unconstrained axiomatic specification. In fact, an arbitrary initial algebra satisfies all the constraints listed in Section 3 necessary to qualify as a data domain -- assuming we are willing to accept an abstract implementation where the the evaluation algorithm for ground terms is the identity function.

If we examine algebraic specification more closely, however, it becomes clear that the initial algebra approach to axiomatic definitions does not solve the technical problems associated with the axiomatic method, but merely casts them in a different form. In addition, it does not accomodate data domains including computable functions as extensional data objects, because logical equality is a recursively enumerable relation in any initial algebra.

The most serious defect in the initial algebra approach to data specification is the inadequacy of algebraic specifications as first order axiomatizations for the correponding initial algebras. Since every algebraic specification admits the trivial algebra as a model, the corresponding theory does not contain any interesting theorems. In order to establish the properties of the specified initial algebra, the programmer is forced to work in a metatheory where algebras, homomorphisms, equations, and logical derivations are all legitimate objects in the domain of the theory. Presumably, the programmer is supposed to use some formulation of axiomatic set theory if he wishes to formally prove properties of the defined domain. As a practical matter, this approach to reasoning about program data domains is excessively complex and indirect.

For a definition of sorted first order predicate logic see [Enderton 72].

Another significant weakness of algebraic specification as a logical formalism is its lack of extensibility. Adding new axioms to an existing data specification (e.g. axiomatizing a new type) can easily modify the structure of the existing domain by coallescing previously distinct equivalence classes of ground terms. For example, assume that a programmer is given a correct specification for the primitive types supported by the programming language, and he extends the specification by writing equations describing a new abstract type. If he makes a mistake and (directly or indirectly asserts) that two previously distinct ground terms are equal (e.g. the Boolean values **true** and **false**) then the augmented specification is internally consistent, but describes a data domain that is inconsistent with the one implemented by the programming language. Algebraic specification retains consistency at the cost of modifying the structure of the data domain and potentially invalidating all prior reasoning every time a new type is specified.

The same phenomenom can occur if the programmer tries to define new (derived) functions by recursion equations. The equations may not be consistent with the existing structure of the domain either because the defined functions map equivalent ground terms into distinct objects or because the defined functions do not always terminate (using call-by-name computation rules). A simple example of the latter phenomenon is the attempted extension of the Boolean domain {**true**,**false**} by the recursively defined operation:

contra[x:Boolean] = **not** contra[x] .

In contrast to the ADJ group, Guttag has developed a formulation of algebraic specification that interprets algebraic specifications as logical theories. Instead of focusing on the initial algebra as the data domain corresponding to an algebraic specification, Guttag adopts the convention that every algebraic specification implicitly includes the inequation **true** $\neq$ **false**. If the resulting set of axioms is consistent and <u>sufficiently complete</u>, then the set of term models for the specification forms a lattice under the natural ordered based on set inclusion. Within this lattice, Guttag designates the final algebra as the specified domain.[2]

A set A of equations and inequations is sufficiently complete iff the <u>indistinguishable relation</u> **I** on ground terms defined by

I(x,y) $\equiv$ x$\neq$y is not provable from A by first order deduction

is an equivalence relation. Note that sufficient completeness implies consistency; otherwise **I** must be empty. In a sufficiently complete algebraic specification (a finite set of equations and inequations), the elements of the corresponding final algebra are the equivalence classes of the indistinguishable equivalence relation. In contrast to initial algebra specifications, the inequality relation rather than the equality relation is recursively enumerable, but not necessarily recursive. Still, final algebra specifications, like their initial counterparts, cannot define data domains with computable functions as extensional data objects.

In comparison to the initial algebra formulation, the advantage of Guttag's approach is that a <u>sufficiently complete</u> algebraic specification can be augmented by a collection of implicitly generated axioms to form a usable first order axiomatization for the specified domain. In addition to the inequation **true** = **false**, the set of implicitly generated axioms must include an induction axiom scheme (called <u>generator induction</u>) asserting that induction on the structure of ground terms holds for any first order definable formula. These implicit axioms are true in every term model in the lattice corresponding to the specification.

The resulting axiomatization is awkward in one important respect: the generator induction rule almost always includes several irrelevant premises corresponding to redundant ways to denote objects by ground terms. For example, in the data domain consisting of LISP S-expressions together with the usual operations Cons: S-expr × S-expr

---

[2]Guttag equivocates on this issue. In some contexts, he seems to imply that the specification is ambiguous and any algebra in the lattice is an acceptable data domain. This interpretation does not support domain extensibility, since a consistent extension of a specification may not be consistent with all algebras in the original lattice.

-> S-expr, Car: S-expr -> S-expr, and Cdr: S-expr -> S-expr, generator induction includes the extra premises

$$P(x) \Rightarrow P(Car(x)),\ P(x) \Rightarrow P(Cdr(x))$$

in addition to the usual

$$P(x) \wedge P(y) \Rightarrow P(Cons(x,y)).$$

Consequently, proofs tend to be unnecessarily long and complex.

In addition to generating an awkward induction rule, Guttag's first order axiomatization has a serious completeness problem. Every term model in the lattice corresponding to a sufficiently complete algebraic specification satisfies the corresponding first order axiomatization, implying that the axiomatization is blatantly incomplete if the lattice is non-trivial.

From a technical viewpoint, the most serious weakness in Guttag's version of algebraic specification is that the programmer is responsible for proving the consistency and sufficient completeness of his specifications. In addition, if he extends an existing domain by adding either new value spaces or operations, he must not only prove that augmented algebraic specification is sufficiently complete, but also prove that it is a consistent with the original domain (the axioms in the extension may distinguish ground terms that were indistinguishable in the original domain).

Ironically, the only straightforward way to prove the consistency of an algebraic specification (implicitly including the inequation **true ≠ false**) is to first construct an abstract domain within some established theory of program data (either by domain identification or domain construction) and prove that each equation (and the inequation) holds in the constructed domain. At this point, the obvious question arises: since complementary constructive definitions provide the only tractable way to prove the consistency of algebraic specifications, why bother writing algebraic specifications at all? Why not simply define the desired algebra by a constructive specification in the first place[3], and eliminate the need to prove consistency and sufficient completeness? One possible explanation is that the proponents of algebraic specification would like to use a practical machine implementation as the constructive model, so that proving the correctness of the implementation proves consistency as well. In this case, the programmer never develops an abstract constructive definition for the domain. Unfortunately, proving the correctness of practical data domain implementations is a very hard problem, particularly if the implementation involves pointers and shared representations (e.g. the standard implementation of LISP S-expressions).

Assuming the programmer manages to prove his specification is consistent, he still must prove that it is sufficiently complete to guarantee the existence of a final algebra. However, proving sufficient completeness is a much more subtle metamathematical problem than proving consistency. Except for a few special cases where heuristic checks (such as the one described in [Guttag and Horning 78]) are applicable, the programmer is forced to work in a complex metatheory in which equations and proofs are objects in the universe.

In summary, the axiomatic approach to data specification, regardless of its exact formulation, does not support a practical formal theory of program data, because it forces the programmer to develop the metamathematics (construction of models, proofs of completeness and consistency) corresponding to every data specification that he writes. In practice, programmers have neither the time nor the resources to shoulder this burden. A more promising approach to the general problem of data specification is to develop a system of domain construction mechanisms and work out the metamathematics for the entire system in advance -- relieving the programmer of this responsibility. Constructive data specification systems follow precisely this course.

---

[3]The model used to prove consistency may be some algebra in the set of term models other than the final one (which exists if the specification is sufficiently complete). However, the final algebra can be defined as a quotient over the original construction. Under reasonable assumptions, the required quotient is always definable. Classifying the power of specification methods is an interesting mathematical question that lies outside the scope of this paper.

5. Constructive Data Specifications

Philosophically, the two constructive approaches to data domain specification are very similar. Neither approach entrusts the programmer with the responsibility of metamathematically justifying his data specifications. Instead, the programmer works within a formal framework that lets him systematically define the domain that he wants. There is no possibility of generating either an inconsistent or blatantly incomplete specification.

5.1 Domain Identification

The "domain identification" approach uses essentially the same strategy to formalize program data domains that logicians employ to formalize conventional mathematics within axiomatic set theory. The basis of the approach is a comprehensive theory of computable objects, analogous to set theory, together with a methodology for introducing explicit domain definitions. In Dana Scott's theory of computable functions, the programmer defines data domains by identifying them with subspaces of the universal space Pw, the set of all subsets of the natural numbers viewed as a partial ordering under set inclusion. Subspaces are identified by recursively defined idempotent functions called retracts; the range of the function is the defined subspace. Every retract is denoted by a term (composed from combinators) in a logical theory for the universal space. Retracts can be combined using standard functionals to define retracts describing Cartesian products, unions, function spaces over the input spaces. Since the least fixed point operator is definable by a term within the theory of Pw, the definition of domains may be recursive. For example, the domain of LISP S-expressions over the arbitrary atom type ATOM (with corresponding retract is_ATOM) can be defined by the domain equation: by

$$SEXPR = ATOM \oplus SEXPR \times SEXPR$$

which corresponds to the retract:

$$is\_SEXPR = \mathbf{Y}\, [\lambda f\ .\ union(is\_ATOM, cart\_prod(f,f))$$

where $\mathbf{Y}$ is the least fixed point operator and union and cart_prod are functions mapping retracts to retracts that build discriminated unions and cartestian products respectively.[4] The interested reader is encouraged to consult [Scott 76] and [Stoy 77] for details.

A theory of Pw can be formalized either in a higher order logic incorporating the lambda calculus (similar to Milner's Logic for Computable Functions [Milner 72]) or in first order logic (see [Cartwright and Donahue 81]). In either case, retracts are simply particular ground terms in the logic (the least fixed point operator is a primitive function in Pw). Defining a new type simply involves introducing a new constant symbol as an abbreviation for the appropriate retract. Such type definitions are obviously eliminable.

Despite the obvious mathematical beauty of Scott's Pw model, the corresponding theory is not completely satisfactory as a logical theory of program data for several technical and methodological reasons. The major technical problem is that it is impossible to define a reasonable abstract implementation for Pw. The source of the problem is that Pw makes no distinction between terminating and non-terminating enumerations of the same set.

In Pw, natural numbers are represented by the corresponding singleton sets. Any reasonable abstract implementation of Pw should reduce expressions denoting integers to the appropriate canonical form (repeated applications of the successor function to 0). Yet the corresponding evaluation function is not computable; otherwise, we could construct a procedure to recursively enumerate the set of expressions equivalent to $\perp$ (identified as the empty set in Pw) -- solving the halting problem. The enumeration

---

[4] Several different forms of discriminated unions and cartesian products are definable within Scott's theory of Pw; they differ with regard to how they treat the divergent object $\perp$. Depending on which ones are used in the example, SEXPR may consist of ordinary S-expressions or some "lazy" variant. For an extensive discussion of this issue, see [Cartwright and Donahue 81].

procedure is trivial to construct. Consider expressions of the form 0 ∪ t where t is an arbitrary ground term. The expression means 0 iff t means ⊥. Dovetailing the evaluation of all expressions of the form 0 ∪ t provides the enumeration.

From a methodological viewpoint, there is another serious drawback to defining data domains as subspaces of a domain like Pw: the values in the universe are mathematical codes (analogous to Godel numbers) for the corresponding abstract data objects. A universe consisting of ground terms in canonical form is much more intuitively appealing. In the latter case, the denotation for an object describes a simple, natural way to construct it. Imagine an interactive formal program testing system that evaluates verification conditions on sample abstract test data. To interact with the user, the testing system must output the values of abstract data objects. However, a system based on Pw could not generate meaningful output, unless it converted the values to a more readable form based on extensive information about declared types of the test variables. At this point, interpreting abstract data values as elements of Pw seems pointless except as a metamathematical exercise. The symbolic values output by the testing system form a more natural universe for the defined domain.

This observation suggests that a data domain universe should consist simply of set of meaningful canonical forms with an explicitly defined equivalence relation describing the equality relation among them. The domain construction approach to data specitication develops exactly this point of view.

5.2 Domain Construction

The idea of domain construction has its roots in the symbolic view of data pioneered by John McCarthy [McCarthy 63] and embodied in the programming language LISP. To the author's knowlege, the first formal treatment of domain construction appears in [Cartwright 76]. A more recent paper [Cartwright 80] significantly expands the class of domains definable by method. A different formulation of the domain construction method formalized within LCF (Logic for Computable Functions) rather than first order logic appears in [Loeckx 80].

The domain construction approach to data specification is based on the premise that a data domain is set of of symbolic objects and associated operations satisfying the following three constraints:

[1] (Finite constructibility). Every data object is a canonical form constructed by composing operations taken from a fixed collection of primitive functions called <u>constructors</u>.

[2] (Unique constructibility). No two (syntactically distinct) canonical forms denote identical elements of the domain universe.

[3] (Explicit definability) Every operation -- excluding a small set of primitive functions and predicates serving as building blocks -- is explicitly defined by either a recursive function definition or an explicit predicate definition (see [Enderton 72]). In any non-trivial domain, these definitions are always eliminable (see [Cartwright and McCarthy 79]).

A simple example of a constructive data domain definition is the construction of the natural numbers from the 0-ary constructor 0 and the unary constructor suc:

0, suc(0), suc(suc(0)), ...

A useful constructive definition of the natural numbers would also include other operations such as predecessor, addition, multiplication. However, none of these operations can be designated as constructors, since that would violate the property of unique constructibility. In contrast, algebraic specification does not distinguish constructors from other operations in the data domain; the extra premises in the corresponding generator induction rule reflect this fact.

To support the recursive definition of arbitrary computable functions, a data domain must include a small set of basic operations -- besides constructors -- for manipulating the constructed objects. For this reason, every constructed domain includes: the 0-ary constructors **true** and **false**, the selector functions corresponding to each constructor, the equality function **equal**, and the standard conditional function **if-then-else**.

Since recursive definitions over a constructive domain can diverge on particular inputs, every domain includes the divergent object ⊥. Except for the primitive operation **if-then-else**, every domain operation is strict, i.e. the result is ⊥ if any argument has the value ⊥. The function **if-then-else** is strict only in its first argument. This definition corresponds to the standard protocol for evaluating conditional expressions.

Given a constructive data domain definition, it is straightforward to mechanically generate a Peano-like first order axiomatization for the defined domain augmented by ⊥. The construction is described in detail in [Cartwright 80]. Recursive function definitions always describe consistent extensions to the theory. Moreover, in non-trivial data domains, they are eliminable [Cartwright and McCarthy 79].

5.2.1 Partitioning the Domain into Types

A typical program data domain includes several different kinds of objects, e.g. natural numbers, strings of characters, and sequences of natural numbers. If no constraints are placed on the arguments accepted by constructors, the resulting "typeless" data domain will inevitably contain a multitude of irrelevant objects which have no intuitive significance. For example, a data domain including constructors both for the natural numbers and for LISP S-expressions would include objects like suc(cons(A,B)).

The obvious solution to this problem is to impose a type structure on the data domain and constrain the arguments of each constructor to belong to a particular type. In this context, a type simply defines a "meaningful" subset of the data domain. If we let each constructor c designate a distinct elementary type containing every object with outermost constructor c, then we exclude many irrelevant objects from the domain by constraining constructor arguments to belong to declared types formed from unions of elementary constructor types. The data specification system described in [Cartwright 76] uses precisely this notion of type. With such a facility, we can obviously eliminate objects like suc(cons(A,B)) from the data domain by declaring 0 ∪ suc as the argument type for suc.

Besides eliminating irrelevant objects, a data type definition facility gives the programmer a formal way to identify intuitively meaningful subsets of the data domain. Even in "typeless" languages like PURE LISP, virtually all functions and variables appearing in programs have intended domains which are "small" subsets of the entire data domain (e.g lists of dotted pairs, non-repeating lists of atoms). If a programming or specification language includes a rich data type definition facility, then the programmer can explicitly declare the exact domain and range of virtually every function that he defines, providing extra information to the program reader and to formal program tools.

To achieve this objective, the expanded data specification system described in [Cartwright 80] adds two new type definition mechanisms -- subset definition and quotient definition -- to the constructor definition and union definition schemes provided in the original system. With these four type construction mechanisms, a programmer can define any abstract type that programmers commonly use: integers, sequences, trees, balanced trees, LISP programs, finite sets, computable functions, etc. Moreover, the quotient definition mechanism supports a limited form of non-determinism -- without compromsing the constructive character of the method.

5.2.2 Four Type Construction Mechanisms

A brief description of the four type construction mechanisms follows.

Constructor Definition

A constructor type definition

constructor <id> (<selector-list>)

declares <id> to be a constructor taking an argument list described by <selector-list>, which is a sequence of selector definitions

<selector-id> : <type-id>

separated by commas where <type-id> declares the type of the argument and <selector-id> is the corresponding selector function. For example the constructor type definitions

constructor 0();
constructor suc(pred: natnum)

define the 0 and suc constructors for the natural numbers (assuming we subsequently define natnum as the union of 0 and suc).

Union Definition

A union type definition

union <id> = <type-list>

declares <id> as the union of the list of previously defined types appearing <type-list>. The ∪ symbol serves as a separator. For example, the type definition

union natnum = 0 ∪ suc

defines natnum as the union of the types 0 and suc. For the sake of more readable notation, constructor definitions may appear within the <type-list> defining a union. For example, the types natnum, 0, and suc can be defined in the single line:

union natnum = 0() ∪ suc(pred: natnum)

Subset Definition

The data types definable by constructor definition and union definition are nearly identical to the recursive types described in [Hoare 73]. A major limitation of recursive type definitions is that they can only define "context-free" types, precluding the definition of types like height-balanced binary trees or non-repeating sequences of integers. To accommodate data type definitions that are not context-free, subset definition lets the programmer designate an arbitrary first order definable subset of a previously defined type as a new type. The type definition:

subset <id> = { <var-id> ≺ <type-id> | <formula> }

declares <id> to be the subset of type <type-id> satisfying the first order formula <formula> with the single free variable <var-id>.[7] For example, we can define the type non-repeating sequence of natural numbers (nonrep) as follows:

union nat_seq = nil() ∪ cons(first: natnum, rest: nat_seq);
subset nonrep = {x ≺ nat_seq | nodup(x)}

where the function nodup is defined by the recursive definitions:

```
function nodup(x: nat_seq): Boolean ≡
  if x equal nil then true
  else if member(first(x), rest(x)) then false
  else nodup(rest(x))

function member(e: natnum, s: nat_seq): Boolean ≡
  if s equal nil then false
  else if e equal first(s) then true
  else member(e, rest(s))  .
```

Quotient Definition

While the ability to identify arbitrary recursive subsets of the domain as types greatly expands the collection of definable types, it still does not let the programmer define types containing objects that are not uniquely constructible -- such as finite sets, computable functions (viewed extensionally) and finite maps. In the case of finite sets, for example, it is possible to construct a set by accumulating it elements in any order. Although we can obviously represent finite sets by the constructive type

[7]We allow the Boolean expression <expr> to abbreviate the logical formula <expr> = **true**

consisting of non-repeating sequences, this formulation is much less appealing than one in which the order of accumulation is irrelevant.

At first glance, we appear to be in a quandary. The domain construction approach to data domain definition relies heavily on the principle of unique constructibility, yet some important abstract types -- such as finite sets -- contain objects that violate this principle. The solution to the problem is to add a type construction mechanism that generates types whose members are equivalence classes of conventional constructible objects. An abstract object that is not uniquely constructible is treated as the equivalence class of different constructions corresponding to the object. For example, each distinct way to construct a finite set is naturally represented by a distinct sequence of elements. The finite set $\{x_1, x_2, \ldots, x_n\}$ is formally defined as the equivalence class of sequences containing precisely the elements $x_1, x_2, \ldots, x_n$.

To preserve the principle of unique constructibility, we treat equivalence classes intensionally in the formal definition of data domain. The domain assigns distinct interpretations to distinct descriptions of the same equivalence class. Nevertheless, from the programmer's viewpoint, equivalence class data objects behave extensionally -- unless he specifically chooses to exploit the underlying intensional semantics.

The syntax for a quotient type definition is:

quotient <id> = <type-id> **under** <equiv-id>

where <id> is the name of the defined quotient type, <type-id> is the type on which the equivalence relation is being defined, and <equiv-id> is either the name of a binary function (mapping <type-id> × <type-id> into Boolean) or a binary predicate (over <type-id> × <type-id>) defining the equivalence relation on <type-id>.

In the formal semantic definition, the quotient type name <id> is simply a unary constructor with <type-id> as its declared domain. Applying the constructor <id> to an object x of type <type-id> constructs the object denoting the equivalence class containing x under the equivalence relation <equiv-id>. The reserved identifier **intension** is the name of the selector corresponding to all quotient constructors. Given an equivalence class object y, **intension** extracts the particular element of <type-id> used to denote the class.

In order to support equivalence classes as legitimate objects, we define the meaning of the primitive equality predicate = and function **equal** over quotient types as follows. If t_1 and t_2 are both objects of type <id>, then the atomic formula $t_1 = t_2$ is interpreted as an abbreviation for t_1 <equiv-id> t_2.[8] Furthermore, if <equiv-id> is a function name, then t_1 **equal** t_2 is interpreted as an abbreviation for t_1 <equiv-id> t_2. Since **equal** and = correspond to the computable and logical notions of extensional equality, the data domain also includes the equality function **eq** and predicate ≡ that capture the corresponding intensional notions (see [Cartwright 80]).

To guarantee the integrity of the informal interpretation of quotient type definitions, the programmer must prove that <equiv-id> defines an equivalence relation on the parent type <type-id>. The property is easily formalized within the logical theory of the data domain. If the programmer defines a quotient using a relation that is not in fact an equivalence relation, the extensional notions of equality do not have the usual properties of equality, but the theory of data domain is still consistent.

As an illustration of quotient definition, let us define the quotient type consisting of finite sets of natural numbers.

quotient nat_set = nonrep **under** set_equal;

where the function set_equal is defined by the recursive definitions:

function set_equal(x: nat_set, y: nat_set): Boolean ≡
  seq_equal(**intension**(x), **intension**(y))

[8] Recall that we allow an expession <expr> to abbreviate the logical formula <expr> = **true**

```
function seq_equal(u: nat_seq, v: nat_seq): Boolean ≡
    if u equal nil then v equal nil
    else member(first(u), v) and seq_equal(rest(u), delete(first(u), v))

function delete(e: natnum, s: nat_seq): nat_seq ≡
    if s equal nil then nil
    else if e equal first(s) then rest(s)
    else cons(first(s), delete(e, rest(s)))
```

where x **and** y abbreviates **if** x **then** y **else false**.

The function set_equal is formally defined as a function on ground terms belonging to the quotient type nat_set. However, since the answer does not depend on which intension (ground term) is used to denote a set, it is also a function on the extensional set objects denoted by ground terms. To define the primitive extensional operations corresponding to a quotient type q, the programmer frequently needs to access the intensional descriptions embedded in objects of type q by using the selector function **intension**. In these cases, the programmer is responsible for ascertaining that the function is well-defined on the quotient type.

If he makes a mistake and defines a function which is not well-defined from an extensional viewpoint, the function still has a precise meaning in the corresponding formal theory. In many cases, an operation which is not extensionally well-defined has a clear extensional interpretation as a non-deterministic operation. For example, the primitive operation **intension** selects an arbitrary element of the equivalence class denoted by the input object. A more useful example occurs in the context of the quotient type nat_set. In this case, the operation

λ q . first(**intension**(q))

selects an arbitrary element from the nat_set q -- the first element of the particular intension describing q.

To accommodate non-deterministic operations, the domain construction method allows programmers to define non-deterministic operations on quotient types as well as functions. For the sake of clarity, however, it forces programmers label non-deterministic function definitions differently from deterministic ones. Non-deterministic function definitions must use the keyword **multifunction** instead of **function**. For example, the definition of the choose operation described above has the following form:

multifunction choose(s: set): natnum ≡ first(**intension**(s))

In the formal semantic definition, there is absolutely no distinction between functions and multifunctions, since they are both ordinary functions at the intensional level. Consequently, the abstract implementation of the domain treats multifunctions and functions identically. The difference between non-deterministic operations and functions lies solely in what they implicitly assert. Consequently, a sophisticated formal testing system (or program verifier) would treat functions and multifunctions quite differently. A function definition would automatically generate a well-definedness lemma to be tested (or proven in some cases); a multifunction would not. Similarly, a verifier could apply special derived rules (concerning extensional equality) to formulas composed from extensional functions.

5.2.3 Supporting Parameterized Types

An annoying deficiency in the the domain construction system described in [Cartwright 80] is the lack of a parameterized type facility. Fortunately, the most common form of type parameterization can be handled merely by adding syntactic sugar to the system. In most programs, the most useful form of type parameterization is a type scheme with free variables denoting arbitrary types. The canonical examples of this form of parameterization are schemes such as **stack of** T, **set of** T, and **array** T_1 **of** T_2. Since the domain construction method views types as arbitrary recursive subsets of the data domain, a specific instance of a type scheme such as **set of** T is simply a subset of the more general type set of any where **any** the type consisting of the entire domain (except $\perp$).

As a result, a schematic type definition can be formalized simply as a general type definition where every type parameter is replaced by the universal type **any**, and a set of Boolean characteristic function definitions -- one for corresponding to every possible instance of the type parameters. Similarly, a function definition containing parameterized types in its signature has exactly the same meaning as the same definition with the type parameters replaced by **any**. However, a parameterized function definition with type parameters appearing in its declared range also implicitly asserts a set of lemmas (one for every possible instantiation of the type parameters) each stating that the function produces output of a particular instantiated type when given inputs of the corresponding instantiated types. The programmer presumably can informally prove the correctness of his range declaration independent of the values of the type parameters. Consequently, in the corresponding formal theory the proofs of all the lemmas will be identical (except for the bindings of the type parameters), eliminating the need to do the proof more than once.

Supporting a more general notion of type parameterization (such as that developed in the programming language RUSSELL [Demers and Donahue 79]) requires passing types as data objects and allowing functions to interrogate them. The domain construction method could be extended to accomodate this form of parameterization (by treating type parameters as sequences of functions), but it is questionable whether the additional power is worth the extra notational and conceptual complexity.

6. Toward Better Data Specification Systems

Data specification systems are still in the early stages of development. There are a number of interesting research directions that I believe are worth seriously investigating.

First, I would like to see a domain identification method similar Scott's system for defining retracts over Pw, but based on a domain consisting of lazy lists [Henderson and Morris 76] of atoms (including characters and integers) instead of Pw. As in Pw, functions are identified with their graphs (on finite elements); the same graph has many different intensional descriptions consisting of all possible ways to effectively enumerate it. As a universal domain, lazy lists have two advantages over Pw. First, the the domain distinguishes non-terminating sequence evaluations from terminating ones. Cons(0,⊥) and Cons(0,nil) are distinct objects. Second, lists form a much more satisfactory domain than Pw for naturally representing common data objects; anyone with much experience programming in LISP should appreciate this issue. Of course, the set of lazy lists has a more tenuous relationship with the classical lambda calculus than does Pw, but that does not seem particularly important in a system designed for practical use.

The second avenue I would like to see explored is the extension of domain construction to support a more "abstract" treatment of computable functions than a quotient type on an abstract syntax of programs. One way to accomplish this objective is to generalize the notion of constructor types to allow lazy constructors [Henderson and Morris 76]. As in the lazy list alternative to Pw, a computable function could be identified with the equivalence class of all lazy sequences enumerating its graph. The major technical obstacles are two-fold. First, developing intuitively satisfying representations for all finite elements of lazy types is a frustrating problem. The objects themselves will not work because it is impossible to determine when a lazy object containing an embedded ⊥ approximates another object. In Pw, Scott represents the finite set of natural numbers $\{i_1, \ldots, i_n\}$ (where i_n is the largest number) by the natural number corresponding to an i_n bit string with ones appearing in bit positions $i_1, \ldots, i_n$. This approach is much too grubby for my taste. An attractive alternative is to introduce a special constant ⊥⊥ ("pseudo-bottom") and create an extension of the lazy type consisting of finite objects containing ⊥⊥ instead of ⊥ elements.

The second technical obstacle is developing a natural first order axiomatization for lazy spaces. A recent paper by [Cartwright and Donahue 81] suggests an axiomatization containing three first order axiom schemes: 1) ordinary structural induction for finite objects, 2) the existence of least upper bounds for directed sets, and 3) the continuity of all functions. The utility of such an approach, however, remains to be proven.

A more conservative approach to accomodating an abstract treatment of functions as data objects would be to develop an intuitively natural collection of function combinators and identify functions with equivalence classes of terms composed of combinators. This approach does not really require any extension of the domain construction method described in this paper. It would merely include a standard collection of type and function definitions in every domain definition. The challenge is to develop a reasonable collection of combinators.

It would be interesting to know which formulations produce easier proofs of interesting data domain properties (as required by a program verification system).

References

ADJ (J. Goguen, J. Thatcher, E. Wagner) (1976) An Initial Algebra Approach to the Specification, Correctness, and Implementation of Abstract Data Types, IBM Research Report RC 6487.

ADJ (J. Goguen, J. Thatcher, E. Wagner, J. Wright) (1977) Initial Algebra Semantics and Continuous Algebras, Jour. ACM 24, 68-95.

Boyer, R. and J Moore. (1975): Proving Theorems about LISP Functions, Jour. ACM 22(1), 129-144 (January).

Cartwright, R. (1976): User-Defined Data Types as Aid to Verifying LISP Programs, in S. Michaelson and R. Milner (eds.), Automata Languages, and Programming, pp. 228-256, Edinburgh Press, Edinburgh.

Cartwright, R. (1980): A Constructive Alternative to Axiomatic Data Type Definitions. Proc. of 1980 LISP Conference, Stanford, California, August, 1980, pp. 46-55.

Cartwright, R. (1981): Formal Program Testing, Proc. Eighth Annual ACM Symposium on Principles of Programming Languages, January 1981, pp. 125-132.

Cartwright, R. and J. Donahue (1981): The Semantics of Lazy Evaluation, Technical Report, Department of Mathematical Sciences, Rice University, Houston, Texas.

Cartwright, R. and J. McCarthy (1979): First Order Programming Logic, Proc. Sixth Annual ACM Symposium on Principles of Programming Languages, January 1979, pp. 68-80.

Constable, R. and M. O'Donnell (1978): A Programming Logic, Winthrop Publishers, Cambridge.

Floyd, R. W. (1967): Assigning Meaning to Programs, Proc. of a Symposium in Applied Mathematics, American Mathematical Society, pp. 19-32.

Guttag, J. V. et. al. (1976): Abstract Data Types and Software Validation, USC Information Sciences Institute Technical Report ISI/RR-76-48.

Guttag, J. V. (1977): Abstract Data Types and the Development of of Data Types, Acta Informatica 10, 27-52.

Guttag, J. V. and J. J. Horning (1978): The Algebraic Specification Data Structures, Comm. ACM 20, 396-404.

Henderson, P. and J. Morris (1976): A Lazy Evaluator, Proc. of the 3rd Annual ACM Symposium on Principles of Programming Languages, January 1976, pp. 95-103.

von Henke, F. and D. C. Luckham (1974): Automatic Program Verification III: A Methodology for Verifying Programs, Stanford Artificial Intelligence Project Memo AIM-256.

Hoare, C. A. R. (1969): "An Axiomatic Basis for Computer Programming", Comm. ACM 12, 576-580.

Hoare, C. A. R. (1973): Recursive Data Types, Stanford Artificial Intelligence Project Memo AIM-223.

Loeckx, J. (1980): Algorithmic Specifications of Abstract Data Types, Technical Report, Informatik, Universitat des Saarlandes, Saarbrucken, West Germany.

McCarthy, J. (1963): A Basis for a Mathematical Theory of Computation, in P. Braffort and D. Hirschberg (eds.), Computer Programming and Formal Systems), pp. 33-70. North-Holland Publishing Company, Amsterdam.

Milner, R., Implementation and Application of Scott's Logic for Computable Functions. Proc. ACM Conf. on Proving Assertions about Programs, SIGPLAN Notices 7,1, January, 1972, pp. 1-6.

Pratt, V. (1976): Semantical Considerations of Floyd-Hoare Logic, 17th Annual IEEE Symposium on the Foundations of Computer Science, October, 1976, pp. 109-121.

DESIGN AND SYNTHESIS OF SYNCHRONIZATION SKELETONS USING BRANCHING TIME TEMPORAL LOGIC

Edmund M. Clarke
E. Allen Emerson
Aiken Computation Laboratory
Harvard University
Cambridge, Mass. 02138, USA

1. INTRODUCTION

We propose a method of constructing concurrent programs in which the *synchronization skeleton* of the program is automatically synthesized from a high-level (branching time) Temporal Logic specification. The synchronization skeleton is an abstraction of the actual program where detail irrelevant to synchronization is suppressed. For example, in the synchronization skeleton for a solution to the critical section problem each process's critical section may be viewed as a single node since the internal structure of the critical section is unimportant. Most solutions to synchronization problems in the literature are in fact given as synchronization skeletons. Because synchronization skeletons are in general finite state, the propositional version of Temporal Logic can be used to specify their properties.

Our synthesis method exploits the (bounded) *finite model property* for an appropriate propositional Temporal Logic which asserts that if a formula of the logic is satisfiable, it is satisfiable in a finite model (of size bounded by a function of the length of the formula). Decision procedures have been devised which, given a formula of Temporal Logic, f, will decide whether f is satisfiable or unsatisfiable. If f is satisfiable, a finite model of f is constructed. In our application, unsatisfiability of f means that the specification is inconsistent (and must be reformulated). If the formula f is satisfiable, then the specification it expresses is consistent. A model for f with a finite number of states is constructed by the decision procedure. The synchronization skeleton of a program meeting the specification can be read from this model. The finite model property ensures that any program whose synchronization properties can be expressed in propositional Temporal Logic can be realized by a system of concurrently running processes, each of which is a finite state machine.

Initially, the synchronization skeletons we synthesize will be for concurrent programs running in a shared-memory environment and for monitors. However, we believe that it is also possible to extend these techniques to synthesize distributed programs. One such application would be the automatic synthesis of network communication protocols from propositional Temporal Logic specifications.

Previous efforts toward parallel program synthesis can be found in the work of [LA78] and [RK80]. [LA78] uses a specification language that is essentially predicate

This work was partially supported by NSF Grant MCS-7908365.

calculus augmented with a special predicate to define the relative order of events in time. [RK80] uses an applied linear time Temporal Logic. Both [LA80] and [RK80] use *ad hoc* techniques to construct a monitor that meets the specification. We have recently learned that [WO81] has independently developed model-theoretic synthesis techniques similar to our own. However, he uses a linear time logic for specification and generates CSP-like programs.

We also discuss how a Model Checker for Temporal Logic formulae can be used to verify the correctness of *a priori* existing programs. In the traditional approach to concurrent program verification, the proof that a program meets its specification is constructed using various axioms and rules of inference in a deductive system such as Temporal Logic. The task of proof construction can be quite tedious, and a good deal of ingenuity may be required. We believe that this task may be unnecessary in the case of finite state concurrent systems, and can be replaced by a mechanical check that the system meets a specification expressed in a propositional temporal logic. The global system flowgraph of a finite state concurrent system may be viewed as defining a finite structure. We describe an efficient algorithm (a model checker) to decide whether a given finite structure is a model of a particular formula. We also discuss extended logics for which it is not possible to construct efficient model checkers.

The paper is organized as follows: Section 2 discusses the model of parallel computation. Section 3 presents the branching time logic that is used to specify synchronization skeletons. Sections 4 and 5 describe the model checker and the decision procedure, respectively. Finally, Section 6 shows how the synthesis method can be used to construct a solution to the starvation free mutual exclusion problem.

2. MODEL OF PARALLEL COMPUTATION

We discuss concurrent systems consisting of a finite number of fixed processes $P_1,\dots,P_m$ running in parallel. The treatment of parallelism is the usual one: nondeterministic interleaving of the sequential "atomic" actions of the individual processes P_i. Each time an atomic action is executed, the system "execution" state is updated. This state may be thought of as containing the location counters and the data values for all processes. The behavior of a system starting in a particular state may be described by a computation tree. Each node of the tree is labelled with the state it represents, and each arc out of a node is labelled with a process index indicating which nondeterministic choice is made, i.e., which process's atomic action is executed next. The root is labelled with the start state. Thus, a path from the root through the tree represents a possible computation sequence of the system beginning in a given start state. Our temporal logic specifications may then be thought of as making statements about patterns of behavior in the computation trees.

Each process P_i is represented as a flowgraph. Each node represents a region or a block of code and is identified by a unique label. For example there may be a node labelled CS_i the i representing "the critical section of code of process P_i." Such a region of code is uninterpreted in that its internal structure and intended application are unspecified. While in CS_i, the process P_i may simply increment variable x or it may perform an extensive series of updates on a large database. The underlying semantics of the computation performed in the various code regions are irrelevant to the synchronization skeleton. The arcs between nodes represent possible transitions between code regions. The labels on the arcs indicate under what conditions P_i can make a transition to a neighboring node. Our job is to supply the enabling conditions on the arcs so that the global system of processes $P_1,\ldots,P_k$ meets a given Temporal Logic specification.

3. THE SPECIFICATION LANGUAGE

Our specification language is a (propositional) branching time Temporal Logic called Computation Tree Logic (CTL) and is based on the language presented in [EC80]. Our current notation is inspired by the language of "Unified Branching Time" (UB) discussed in [BM81]. UB is roughly equivalent to that subset of the language presented in [EC80] obtained by deleting the infinitary quantifiers and the arc conditions and adding an explicit next-time operator. For example, in [EC80] we write $\forall$ path $\exists$ node P to express the inevitability of predicate P. The corresponding formula in our UB-like notation is AFP. The language presented in [EC80] is more expressive than UB as evidenced by the formula $\forall$ path $\overset{\infty}{\forall}$ node P (which is not equivalent to any formula in UB or in the language of [EC80] without infinitary quantifiers). However, the UB-like notation is more concise and is sufficiently expressive for the purposes of program synthesis.

We use the following syntax (where p denotes an atomic proposition and f_i denotes a (sub-)formula):

1. Each of p, $f_1 \wedge f_2$, and $\sim f_1$ is a formula (where the latter two constructs indicate conjunction and negation, respectively).
2. $EX_j f_1$ is a formula which intuitively means that there is an immediate successor state reachable by executing one step of process P_j in which formula f_1 holds.
3. $A[f_1 U f_2]$ is a formula which intuitively means that for every computation path, there exists an initial prefix of the path such that f_2 holds at the last state of the prefix and f_1 holds at all other states along the prefix.
4. $E[f_1 U f_2]$ is a formula which intuitively means that for some computation path, there exists an initial prefix of the path such that f_2 holds at the last state of the prefix and f_1 holds at all other states along the prefix.

Formally, we define the semantics of CTL formulae with respect to a structure $M = (S, A_1, \ldots, A_k, L)$ which consists of

S - a countable set of states,

A_i - $\subset S \times S$, a binary relation on S giving the possible transitions by process i, and

L - an assignment of atomic propositions true in each state.

Let $A = A_1 \cup \ldots \cup A_k$. We require that A be total, i.e., that $\forall x \in S\ \exists y (x,y) \in A$. A *path* is an infinite sequence of states $(s_0, s_1, s_2 \ldots) \in S^\omega$ such that $\forall i (s_i, s_{i+1}) \in A$. To any structure M and state $s \in S$ of M, there corresponds a computation tree with root labelled s_0 such that $s \xrightarrow{i} t$ is an arc in the tree iff $(s,t) \in A_i$.

We use the usual notation to indicate truth in a structure: $M, s_0 \models f$ means that at state s_0 in structure M formula f holds true. When the structure M is understood, we write $s_0 \models f$. We define $\models$ inductively:

$s_0 \models p$ iff $p \in L(s_0)$

$s_0 \models \sim f$ iff not $(s_0 \models f)$

$s_0 \models f_1 \wedge f_2$ iff $s_0 \models f_1$ and $s_0 \models f_2$

$s_0 \models EX_j f$ iff for some state t such that $(s_0, t) \in A_j$, $t \models f$

$s_0 \models A[f_1 U f_2]$ iff for all paths $(s_0, s_1, \ldots)$, $\exists i [i \geqslant 0 \wedge s_i \models f_2 \wedge \forall j (0 \leqslant j \wedge j < i \rightarrow s_j \models f_1)]$

$s_0 \models E[f_1 U f_2]$ iff for some path $(s_0, s_1, \ldots)$, $\exists i [i \geqslant 0 \wedge s_i \models f_2 \wedge \forall j (0 \leqslant j \wedge j < i \rightarrow s_j \models f_1)]$

We write $\models f$ to indicate that f is universally valid, i.e., true at all states in all structures. Similarly, we write $\dashv f$ to indicate that f is satisfiable, i.e., f is true in some state of some structure.

We introduce some abbreviations:

$f_1 \vee f_2 \equiv \sim(\sim f_1 \wedge \sim f_2)$, $f_1 \rightarrow f_2 \equiv \sim f_1 \vee f_2$, and $f_1 \leftrightarrow f_2 \equiv (f_1 \rightarrow f_2) \wedge (f_2 \rightarrow f_1)$ for logical disjunction, implication, and equivalence, respectively.

$A[f_1 V f_2] \equiv \sim E[\sim f_1 U \sim f_2]$ which means for every path, for every state s on the path, if f_1 is false at all states on the path prior to s, then f_2 holds at s.

$E[f_1 V f_2] \equiv \sim A[\sim f_1 U \sim f_2]$ which means for some path, for every state s on the path, if f_1 is false at all states on the path prior to s, then f_2 holds at s.

$AFf_1 \equiv A[\text{true } U f_1]$ which means for every path, there exists a state on the path at which f_1 holds.

$EFf_1 \equiv E[\text{true } U f_1]$ which means for some path, there exists a state on the path at which f_1 holds.

$AGf_1 \equiv \sim EF\sim f_1$ which means for every path, at every node on the path f_1 holds.

$EGf_1 \equiv \sim AF\sim f_1$ which means for some path, at every node on the path f_1 holds.

$AX_i f \equiv \sim EX_i \sim f$ which means at all successor states reachable by an atomic step of process P_i, f holds.

$EXf \equiv EX_1 f \vee \ldots \vee EX_k f$ which means at some successor state f holds.

$AXf \equiv \sim EX \sim f$ which means at all successor states f holds.

4. MODEL CHECKER

Assume that we wish to determine whether formula f is true in the finite structure $M = (S, A_1, \ldots, A_k, L)$. Let $sub^+(f_0)$ denote the set subformulae of f_0 with main connective other than $\sim$. We label each state $s \in S$ with the set of positive/negative formulae f in $sub^+(f_0)$ so that

$$f \in label(s) \text{ iff } M, s \models f$$

$$\sim f \in label(s) \text{ iff } M, s \models \sim f .$$

The algorithm makes $n+1$ passes where $n = length(f_0)$. On pass i every state $s \in S$ is labelled with f or $\sim f$ for each formula $f \in sub^+(f_0)$ of length i. Information gathered in earlier passes about formulae of length less than i is used to perform the labelling. For example, if $f = f_1 \wedge f_2$, then f should be placed in the set for s precisely when f_1 and f_2 are already present in the set for s. For modalities such as $A[f_1 U f_2]$ information from the successor states of s (as well as from s itself) is used. Since $A[f_1 U f_2] = f_2 \vee (f_1 \wedge AXA[f_1 U f_2])$, $A[f_1 U f_2]$ should be placed in the set for s when f_2 is already in the set for s or when f_1 is in the set for s and $A[f_1 U f_2]$ is in the set of each immediate successor state of s.

Satisfaction of $A[f_1 U f_2]$ may be seen to "radiate" outward from states where it holds immediately by virtue of f_2 holding:

Let

$$(A[f_1 U f_2])^0 = f_2$$

$$(A[f_1 U f_2])^{k+1} = f_2 \vee AX(A[f_1 U f_2])^k .$$

It can be shown that $M,s \models (A[f_1 U f_2])^k$ iff $M,s \models A[f_1 U f_2]$ and along every path starting at s, f_2 holds by the k-th state following s. Thus, states where $(A[f_1 U f_2])^0$ holds are found first, then states where $(A[f_1 U f_2])^1$ holds, etc. If $A[f_1 U f_2]$ holds, then $(A[f_1 U f_2])^{card(S)}$ must hold since all loop-free paths in M are of length $\leq card(S)$: Thus, if after card(S) steps of radiating outward, $A[f_1 U f_2]$ has still not been found to hold at state s, then put $\sim A[f_1 U f_2]$ in the set for s.

The algorithm for pass i is listed below in an Algol-like syntax:

```
    for every state s ∈ S do
      for every f ∈ sub⁺(f0) of length i do
        if f = A[f1 U f2] and f2 ∈ set(s) or
           f = E[f1 U f2] and f2 ∈ set(s) or
           f = EXj f1 and ∃t((s,t) ∈ Aj and f1 ∈ set(t)) or
           f = f1 ∧ f2 and f1 ∈ set(s) and f2 ∈ set(s)
        then add f to set(s)
      end
    end;
  A: for j = 1 to card(S) do
      for every state s ∈ S do
        for every f ∈ sub⁺(f0) of length i do
          if f = A[f1 U f2] and f1 ∈ set(s) and ∀t((s,t) ∈ A → f ∈ set(t)) or
             f = E[f1 U f2] and f1 ∈ set(s) and ∃t((s,t) ∈ A ∧ f ∈ set(t))
          then add f to set(s)
        end
    B: end
    end;
    for every state s ∈ S do
      for every f ∈ sub⁺(f0) of length i do
        then add ~f to set(s)
      end
  C: end
```

Figures 4.1-4.4 give snapshots of the algorithm in operation on the structure shown for the formula $AFb \wedge EGa$ (which abbreviates $AFb \wedge \sim AF\sim a$).

Suppose we extend the logic to permit $\forall$path $\overset{\infty}{\forall}$ node p or, equivalently, its dual $\exists$ path $\overset{\infty}{\exists}$ node p which we write $E\overset{\infty}{F}p$. We can generalize the model checker to handle this case by using the following proposition:

PROPOSITION 4.1. *Let* $M = (S, A_1, \ldots, A_k, L)$ *be a structure and* $s \in S$. *Then* $M,s \models E\overset{\infty}{F}p$ *iff there exists a path from* s *to a node* s' *such that* $M,s' \models p$ *and either* s' *is a successor of itself or the strongly connected component of* M *containing* s' *has cardinality greater than* 1. ■

Proof. (Only if:) Suppose $M,s \models E\overset{\infty}{F}p$. Then there is an infinite path $(s_0, s_1, s_2, \ldots)$ through M and a state $s' \in S$ such that

(1) $s_0 = s$,

(2) $s' = s_i$ for infinitely many distinct i, and

(3) $M,s' \models p$.

If s' is a successor of itself, we are done. Otherwise, there is a finite path $(s', \ldots, s'', \ldots s')$ from s' back to itself (because of (2)) which contains a state $s'' \neq s$. So, s'' is reachable from s' and s' is reachable from s'', and s' is in a strongly connected component of M of cardinality greater than 1.

(If:) If s' is a successor of itself, then p is true infinitely often along the path $(s', s', \ldots)$. Since s' is reachable from s, $M,s \models E\overset{\infty}{F}p$. If the

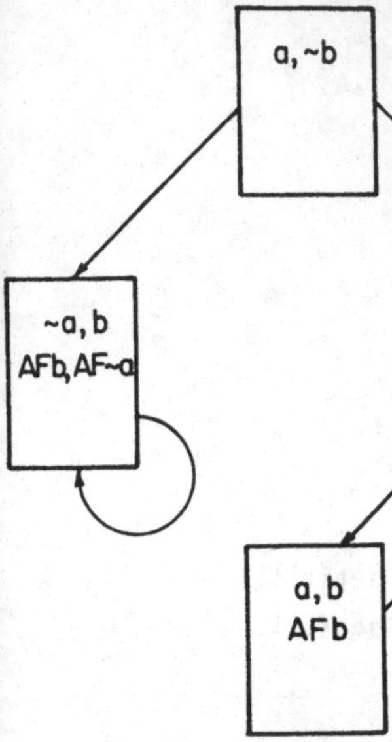

1st time at label A in pass 1

Figure 4.1

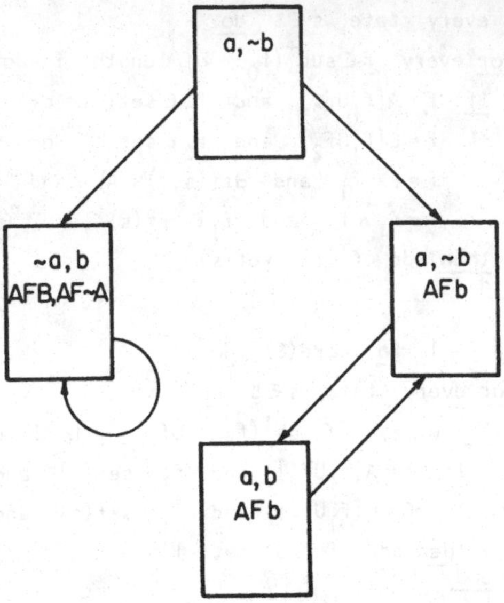

1st time at label B in pass 1

Figure 4.2

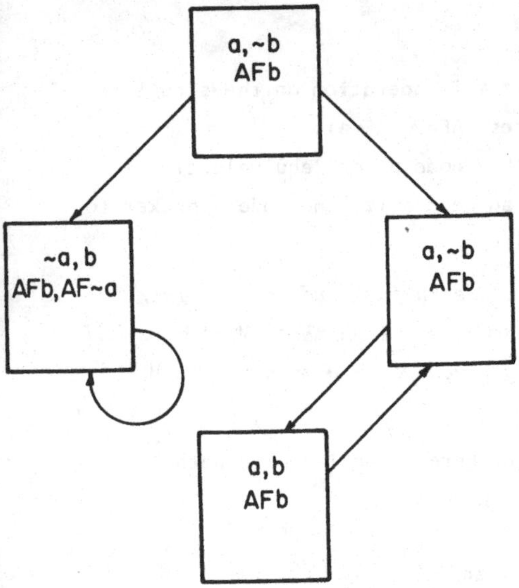

2nd time at label B in pass 1

Figure 4.3

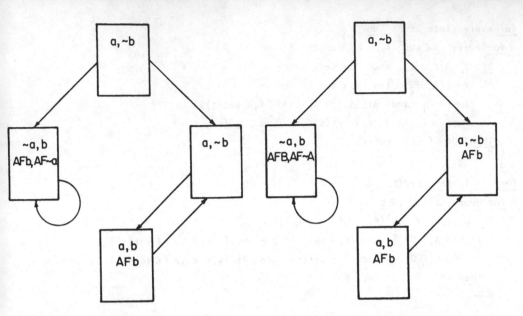

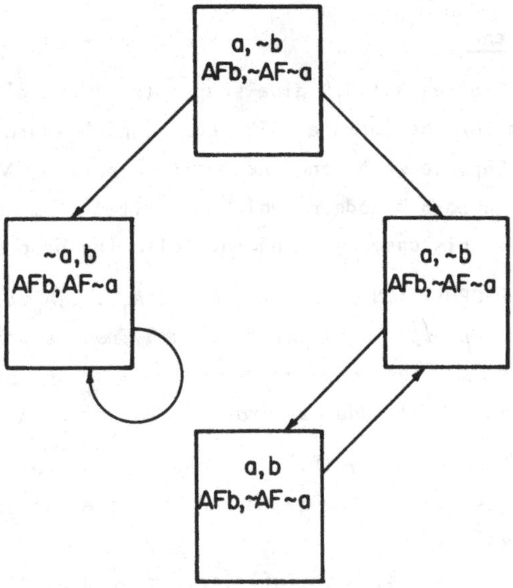

1st time at label C in pass 1

Figure 4.4

strongly connected component of M containing s' is of cardinality greater than 1, then there is a state $s''\neq s'$ such that s' is reachable from s'' and s'' is reachable from s''. Hence there is a finite path from s' back to itself, and an infinite path starting at s' which goes through s' infinitely often. Since s' is reachable from s, $M,s \models E\overset{\infty}{F}p$. ■

Notice that all algorithms discussed so far run in time polynomial in the size of the candidate model and formula. The algorithm for basic CTL presented above runs in time $\text{length}(f)\cdot(\text{card}(S))^2$. Since there is a linear time algorithm for finding the strongly connected components of a graph [TA72], we can also achieve the $\text{length}(f)\cdot(\text{card}(S))^2$ time bound when we include the infinitary quantifiers.

Finally, we show that it is not always possible to obtain polynomial time algorithms for model checking. Suppose we extend our language to allow either an existential or a universal path quantifier to prefix an arbitrary assertion from linear time logic as in [LA80] and [GP80]. Thus, we can write assertions such as

$$E[Fg_1 \wedge \ldots \wedge Fg_n \wedge Gh_1 \wedge \ldots \wedge Gh_n]$$

meaning

"there exists a computation path ρ such that, along ρ
sometimes g_1 and ... and sometimes g_n and
always h_1 and ... and always h_n."

We claim that the problem of determining whether a given formula f holds in a given finite structure M is NP-hard.

PROPOSITION 4.2. *Directed Hamiltonian Path is reducible to the problem of determining whether* $M,s \models f$ *where*

M *is a finite structure,*

s *is a state in* M *and*

f *is the assertion (using atomic propositions* $p_1,\ldots,p_n$*):*

$E[Fp_1 \wedge \ldots \wedge Fp_n \wedge G(p_1 \to XG\sim p_1) \wedge \ldots \wedge G(p_n \to XG\sim p_n))$. ■

Proof. Consider an arbitrary directed graph $G=(V,A)$ where $V=\{v_1,\ldots,v_n\}$. We obtain a structure from G by making proposition p_i hold at node v_i and false at all other nodes (for $1\leq i\leq n$), and by adding a source node u_1 from which all v_i are accessible (but not *vice versa*) and a sink node u_2 which is accessible from all v_i (but not *vice versa*).

Formally, let the structure $M=(U,B,L)$ consist of

$U = V\cup\{u_1,u_2\}$ where $u_1,u_2\notin V$

L, on assignment of states to propositions such that

$v_i \models p_i,\ \ v_i \not\models p_j,\ \ (1\leq i,\ j\leq n,\ i\neq j)$

$u_1 \not\models p_i,\ \ u_2 \not\models p_i\ \ (1\leq i\leq n)$ and

$$B = A \cup \{(u_1,v_i):v_i \in V\} \cup \{(v_i,u_2):v_i \in V\} \cup \{(u_2,u_2)\}.$$

It follows that

$M,u_1 \models f$ iff there is a directed infinite path in M starting at u_1 which goes through all $v_i \in V$ exactly once and ends in the self-loop through u_2;
iff there is a directed Hamiltonian path in G. ■

We believe that the model checker may turn out to be of considerable value in the verification of certain finite state concurrent systems such as network protocols. We have developed an experimental implementation of the model checker at Harvard which is written in C and runs on the DEC 11-70.

5. THE DECISION PROCEDURE

In this section we outline a tableau-based decision procedure for satisfiability of CTL formulae. Our algorithm is similar to one proposed for UB in [BM81].* Tableau-based decision procedures for simpler program logics such as PDL and DPDL are given in [PR77] and [BH81]. The reader should consult [HC68] for a discussion of tableau-based decision procedures for classical modal logics and [SM68] for a discussion of tableau-based decision procedures for propositional logic.

We now briefly describe our decision procedure for CTL and illustrate it with a simple example. The decision procedure is described in detail in the full paper. To simplify the notation in the present discussion, we omit the labels on arcs which are normally used to distinguish between transitions by different processes.

The decision procedure takes as input a formula f_0 and returns either "YES, f_0 is satisfiable," or "NO, f_0 is unsatisfiable." If f_0 is satisfiable, a finite model is constructed. The decision procedure performs the following steps:

1. Build the initial tableau T which encodes potential models of f_0. If f_0 is satisfiable, it has a finite model that can be "embedded" in T.
2. Test the tableau for consistency by deleting inconsistent portions. If the "root" of the tableau is deleted, f_0 is unsatisfiable. Otherwise, f_0 is satisfiable.
3. Unravel the tableau into a model of f_0.

The decision procedure begins by building a tableau T which is a finite directed AND/OR graph. Each node of T is either an AND-node or an OR-node and is labelled by a set of formulae. We use $G_1,G_2,\ldots$ to denote the labels of OR-nodes, $H_1,H_2,\ldots$ to denote the labels of AND-nodes, and $F_1,F_2,\ldots$ to denote the labels of arbitrary nodes of either type. No two AND-nodes have the same label, and no two

---

*The [BM81] algorithm is incorrect and will erroneously claim that certain satisfiable formulae are unsatisfiable. Correct tableau-based and filtration-based decision procedures for UB are given in [EH81]. In addition, Ben-Ari [BA81] states that a corrected version of [BM81] based on different techniques is forthcoming.

OR-nodes have the same label. The intended meaning is that, when node F is considered as a state in an appropriate structure, $F \models f$ for all $f \in F$. The tableau T has a "root" node $G_0 = \{f_0\}$ from which all other nodes in T are accessible.

The set of successors of an OR-node G, $\mathrm{Blocks}(G) = \{H_1, H_2, \ldots, H_k\}$ has the property that

$$\dashv G \text{ iff } \dashv H_1 \text{ or } \ldots \text{ or } \dashv H_k \ .$$

We can explain the construction of $\mathrm{Blocks}(G)$ as follows: Each formula in G may be viewed as a conjunctive formula $\alpha \equiv \alpha_1 \wedge \alpha_2$ or a disjunctive formula $\beta \equiv \beta_1 \vee \beta_2$. Clearly, $f \wedge g$ is an α formula and $f \vee g$ is a β formula. A modal formula may be classified as α or β based on its fixpoint characterization; thus, $\mathrm{EFp} = p \vee \mathrm{EXEFp}$ is a β formula and $\mathrm{AGp} = p \wedge \mathrm{AXAGp}$ is an α formula. A formula that involves no modalities or has main connective one of EX or AX is both α and β and is called an *elementary* formula. Any other formula is *nonelementary*. We say that a set of formulae F is *downward closed* provided that (i) if $\alpha \in F$ then $\alpha_1, \alpha_2 \in F$, and (ii) if $\beta \in F$ then $\beta_1 \in F$ or $\beta_2 \in F$. We construct the members H_i of $\mathrm{Blocks}(G)$ by repeatedly expanding each nonelementary formula in G into its α or β components. Each β expansion yields two blocks, one with β_1 and one with β_2. Expansion stops when all H_i are downward closed.

The set of successors of an AND-node H, $\mathrm{Tiles}(H) = \{G_1, G_2, \ldots, G_k\}$ has the property that, if H contains no propositional inconsistencies, then

$$\dashv H \text{ iff } \dashv G_1 \text{ and } \ldots \text{ and } \dashv G_k \ .$$

To construct $\mathrm{Tiles}(H)$ we use the information supplied by the elementary formulae in H. For example, if $\{\mathrm{AXh}_1, \mathrm{AXh}_2, \mathrm{EXg}_1, \mathrm{EXg}_2, \mathrm{EXg}_3\}$ is the set of all elementary formulae in H, then $\mathrm{Tiles}(H) = \{\{h_1, h_2, g_1\}, \{h_1, h_2, g_2\}, \{h_1, h_2, g_3\}\}$.

To build T, we start out by letting $G_0 = \{f_0\}$ be the root node. Then we create $\mathrm{Blocks}(G_0) = \{H_1, H_2, \ldots, H_k\}$ and attach each H_i as a successor of G_0. For each H_i we create $\mathrm{Tiles}(H_i)$ and attach its members as the successors of H_i. For each $G_j \in \mathrm{Tiles}(H_i)$ we create $\mathrm{Blocks}(G_j)$, etc. Whenever we encounter two nodes of the same type with identical labels we identify them. This ensures that no two AND-nodes will have the same label and that no two OR-nodes will have the same label. The tableau construction will eventually terminate since there are only $2^{\mathrm{length}(f_0)}$ possible labels, each of which can occur at most twice.

Suppose, for example, that we want to determine whether $\mathrm{EFp} \wedge \mathrm{EF{\sim}p}$ is satisfiable. We build the tableau T starting with root node $G_0 = \{\mathrm{EFp} \wedge \mathrm{EF{\sim}p}\}$. We construct $\mathrm{Blocks}(G_0) = \{H_0, H_1, H_2, H_3\}$. Each H_i is attached as a successor of G_0. Next, $\mathrm{Tiles}(H_i)$ is determined for each H_i (except H_1 which is immediately seen to contain a propositional inconsistency) and its members are attached as successors of H_i. (Note that two copies of $G_1 = \{\mathrm{EF{\sim}p}\}$ are created, one in $\mathrm{Tiles}(H_0)$ and the other in $\mathrm{Tiles}(H_2)$; but they are then merged into a single node.) Similarly, $G_2 \in \mathrm{Tiles}(H_2) \cap \mathrm{Tiles}(H_3)$. Continuing in this fashion we obtain the complete tableau shown in Fig. 5.1.

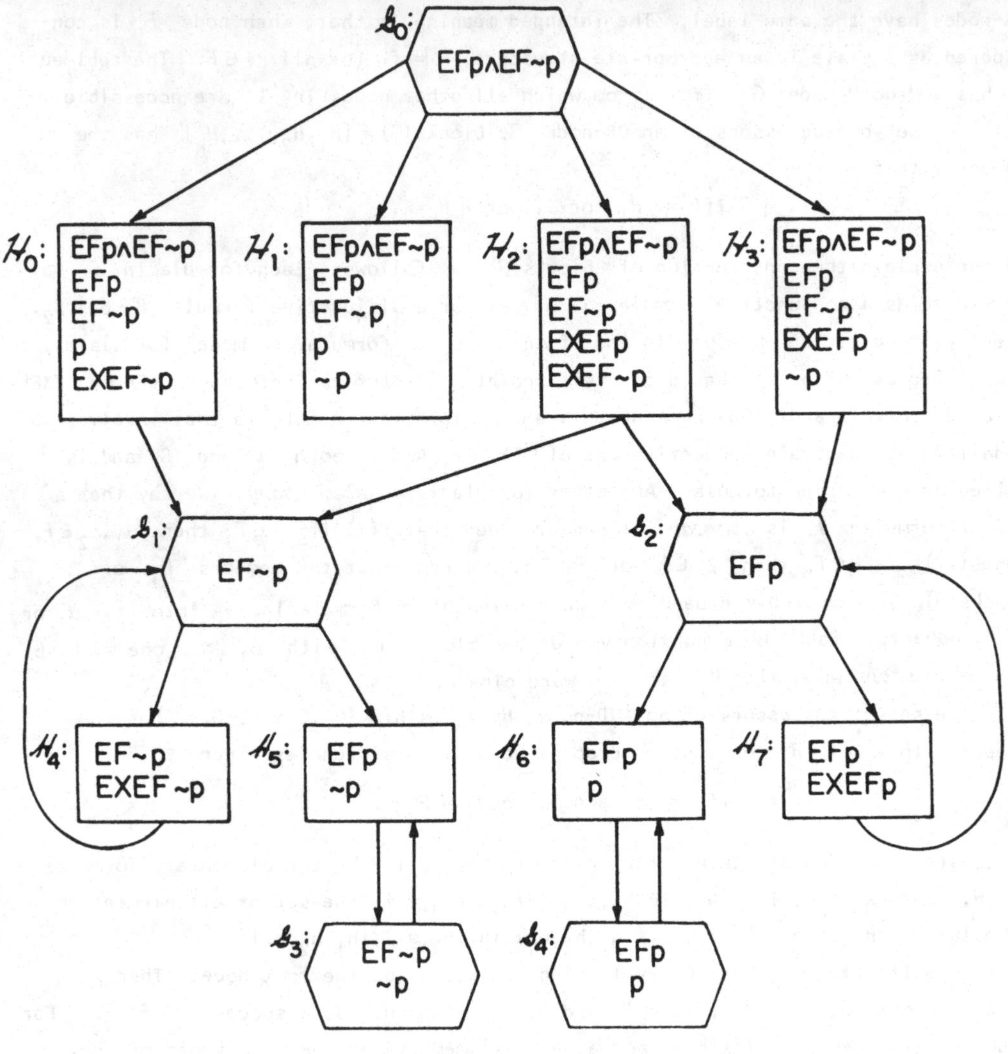
𝒮0:
EFp∧EF~p
ℋ0:
EFp∧EF~p
EFp
EF~p
p
EXEF~p
ℋ1:
EFp∧EF~p
EFp
EF~p
p
~p
ℋ2:
EFp∧EF~p
EFp
EF~p
EXEFp
EXEF~p
ℋ3:
EFp∧EF~p
EFp
EF~p
EXEFp
~p
𝒮1:
EF~p
𝒮2:
EFp
ℋ4:
EF~p
EXEF~p
ℋ5:
EFp
~p
ℋ6:
EFp
p
ℋ7:
EFp
EXEFp
𝒮3:
EF~p
~p
𝒮4:
EFp
p

Figure 5.1

Next we must test the tableau for consistency. Note that H_1 is inconsistent because it contains both p and ~p. We must also check that is possible for eventuality formulae such as AFh or EFh to be *fulfilled*: e.g., if $EFh \in F$, then there must be some node F' reachable from F such that $h \in F'$. If any node fails to pass this test, it is marked inconsistent. In this example, all nodes pass the test. Since the root is not marked inconsistent, $EFp \wedge EF{\sim}p$ is satisfiable.

Finally, we construct a model M of $EFp \wedge EF{\sim}p$. The states in M will be (copies of) the AND-nodes in the tableau. The model will have the property that for each state H, $M,H \models f$ for all $f \in H$. The root of M can be any consistent state $H_i \in \mathrm{Blocks}(G_0)$. We choose H_0. Now H_0 contains the eventualities EFp and EF~p. We must ensure that they are actually fulfilled in M. EFp is immediately fulfilled in H_0, but EF~p is not. So when we choose a successor state to H_0, which must be one of H_4 or H_5, we want to ensure that EF~p is fulfilled. Thus, we choose H_5. Finally, the only possible successor state of H_5 is H_5 itself.

6. SYNTHESIS ALGORITHM

We now present our method of synthesizing synchronization skeletons from a CTL description of their intended behavior. We identify the following steps:

1. Specify the desired behavior of the concurrent system using CTL.
2. Apply the decision procedure to the resulting CTL formula in order to obtain a finite model of the formula.
3. Factor out the synchronization skeletons of the individual processes from the global system flowgraph defined by the model.

We illustrate the method by solving a mutual exclusion problem for processes P_1 and P_2. Each process is always in one of three regions of code:

NCS_i	the NonCritical Section
TRY_i	the TRYing Section
CS_i	the Critical Section

which it moves through as suggested in Fig. 6.1.

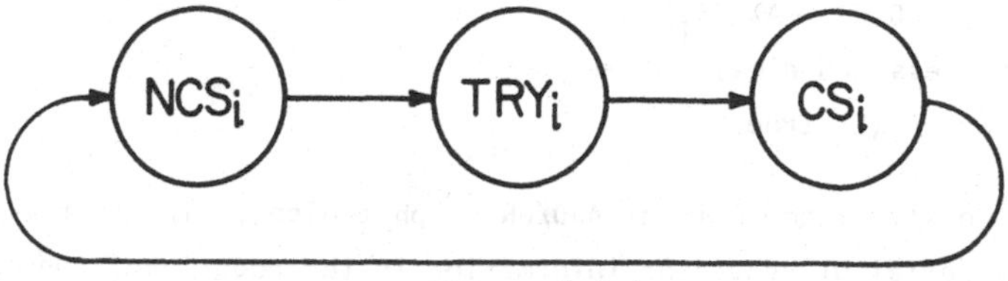

Figure 6.1

When it is in region NCS_i, process P_i performs "noncritical" computations which can proceed in parallel with computations by the other process P_j. At certain times, however, P_i may need to perform certain "critical" computations in the region CS_i. Thus, P_i remains in NCS_i as long as it has not yet decided to attempt critical section entry. When and if it decides to make this attempt, it moves into the region TRY_i. From there it enters CS_i as soon as possible, provided that the mutual exclusion constraint $\sim(CS_1 \wedge CS_2)$ is not violated. It remains in CS_i as long as necessary to perform its "critical" computations and then re-enters NCS_i. Note that in the synchronization skeleton described, we only record transitions between different regions of code. Moves entirely within the same region are not considered in specifying synchronization. Listed below are the CTL formulae whose conjunction specifies the mutual exclusion system:

1. start state

   $NCS_1 \wedge NCS_2$

2. mutual exclusion

   $AG(\sim(CS_1 \wedge CS_2))$

3. absence of starvation for P_i

   $AG(TRY_i \rightarrow AF\ CS_i)$

4. each process P_i is always in exactly one of the three code regions

   $AG(NCS_i \vee TRY_i \vee CS_i)$

   $AG(NCS_i \rightarrow \sim(TRY_i \vee CS_i))$

   $AG(TRY_i \rightarrow \sim(NCS_i \vee CS_i))$

   $AG(CS_i \rightarrow \sim(NCS_i \vee TRY_i))$

5. it is always possible for P_i to enter its trying region from its noncritical region

   $AG(NCS_i \rightarrow EX_i TRY_i)$

6. it is always the case that any move P_i makes from its trying region is into the critical region

   $AG(TRY_i \wedge EX_i True \rightarrow AX_i CS_i)$

7. it is always possible for P_i to re-enter its noncritical region from its critical region

   $AG(CS_i \rightarrow EX_i NCS_i)$

8. a transition by one process cannot cause a move by the other

   $AG(NCS_i \rightarrow AX_j NCS_i)$

   $AG(TRY_i \rightarrow AX_j TRY_i)$

   $AG(CS_i \rightarrow AX_j CS_i)$

9. some process can always move

   $AG(EX\ true)$

We must now construct the initial AND/OR graph tableau. In order to reduce the recording of inessential or redundant information in the node labels we observe the following rules:

(1) Automatically convert a formula of the form $f_1 \wedge \ldots \wedge f_n$ to the set of formulae $\{f_1,\ldots,f_n\}$. (Recall that the set of formulae $\{f_1,\ldots,f_n\}$ is satisfiable iff $f_1 \wedge \ldots \wedge f_n$ is satisfiable.)

(2) Do not physically write down an invariance assertion of the form AGf because it holds everywhere as do its consequences f and AXAGf (obtained by

α-expansion). The consequence AXAGf serves only to propagate forward the truth of AGf to any "descendent" nodes in the tableau. Do that propagation automatically but without writing down AGf in any of the descendent nodes. The consequence f may be written down if needed.

(3) An assertion of the form $f \vee g$ need not be recorded when f is already present. Since any state which satisfies f must also satisfy $f \vee g$, $f \vee g$ is redundant.

(4) If we have TRY_i present, there is no need to record $\sim NCS_i$ and $\sim CS_i$. If we have NCS_i present, there is no need to record $\sim TRY_i$ and $\sim CS_i$. If we have CS_i present, there is no need to record $\sim NCS_i$ and $\sim TRY_i$.

By the above conventions, the root node of the tableau will have the two formulae NCS_1 and NCS_2 recorded in its label which we now write as $\langle NCS_1\ NCS_2 \rangle$. In building the tableau, it will be helpful to have constructed Blocks(G) for the following OR-nodes: $\langle NCS_1\ NCS_2 \rangle$, $\langle TRY_1\ NCS_2 \rangle$, $\langle CS_1\ NCS_2 \rangle$, $\langle TRY_1\ TRY_2 \rangle$, and $\langle CS_1\ TRY_2 \rangle$. For all other OR-nodes G' appearing in the tableau, Blocks(G') will be identical to or can be obtained by symmetry from Blocks(G) for some G in the above list. We then build the tableau using the information about Blocks and Tiles contained in the list. Next we apply the marking rules to delete inconsistent nodes. Note that the OR-node $\langle CS_1\ CS_2\ AFCS_2 \rangle$ is marked as deleted because of a propositional inconsistency (with $\sim(CS_1 \wedge CS_2)$, a consequence of the unwritten invariance $AG(\sim(CS_1\ CS_2))$. This, in turn, causes the AND-node that is the predecessor of $\langle CS_1\ CS_2\ AFCS_2 \rangle$ to be marked. The resulting tableau is shown in Fig. 6.2. Each node in Fig. 6.2 is labelled with a minimal set of formulae sufficient to distinguish it from any other node.

We construct a model M from T by pasting together model fragments for the AND-nodes using local structure information provided by T. Intuitively, a fragment is a rooted dag of AND-nodes embeddable in T such that all eventuality formulae in the label of the root node are fulfilled in the fragment.

The root node of the model is H_0, the unique successor of G_0. From the tableau we see that H_0 must have two successors, one of H_1 or H_2 and one of H_3 or H_4. Each candidate successor state contains an eventuality to fulfill, so we must construct and attach its fragment. Using the method described, we choose the fragement rooted at H_1 to be the left successor and the fragment rooted at H_4 to be the right successor (see Fig. 6.3). This yields the portion of the model shown in Fig. 6.4.

We continue the construction by finding successors for each of the leaves: H_5, H_9, H_{10} and H_8. We start with H_5. By inspection of T, we see that the only successors H_5 can have are H_0 and H_9. Since H_0 and H_9 already occur in the structure built so far, we add the arcs $H_5 \xrightarrow{1} H_0$ and $H_5 \xrightarrow{2} H_9$ to the structure. Note that this introduces a cycle $(H_0 \xrightarrow{1} H_1 \xrightarrow{1} H_5 \xrightarrow{1} H_0)$. In general, a cycle can be dangerous because it might form a path along which some eventuality is never fulfilled; however, there is no problem this time because the root of a

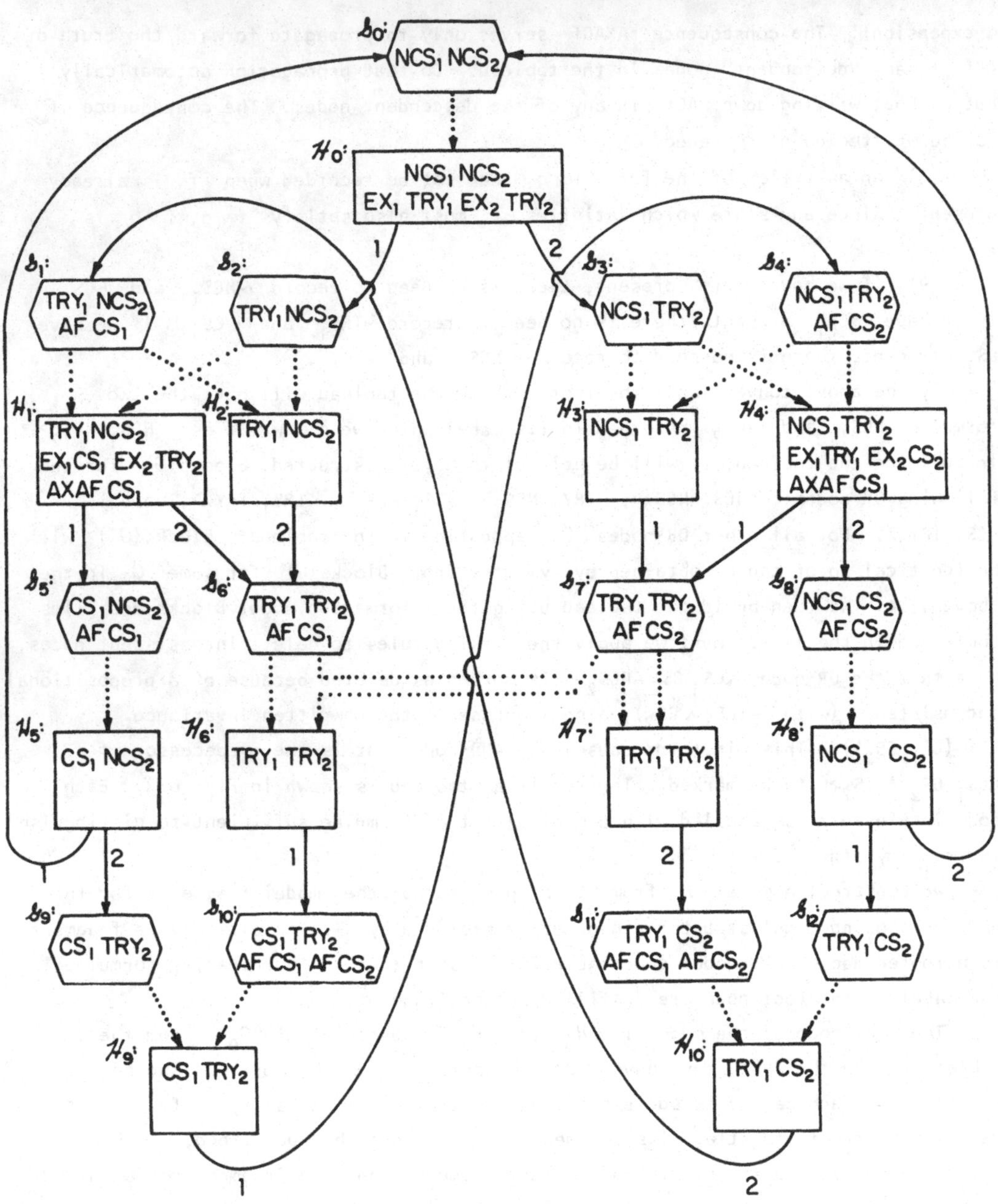

$\mathcal{S}_0$: NCS1 NCS2
$\mathcal{H}_0$: NCS1 NCS2 EX1 TRY1 EX2 TRY2
1
2
$\mathcal{S}_1$: TRY1 NCS2 AF CS1
$\mathcal{S}_2$: TRY1 NCS2
$\mathcal{S}_3$: NCS1 TRY2
$\mathcal{S}_4$: NCS1 TRY2 AF CS2
$\mathcal{H}_1$: TRY1 NCS2 EX1 CS1 EX2 TRY2 AXAF CS1
$\mathcal{H}_2$: TRY1 NCS2
$\mathcal{H}_3$: NCS1 TRY2
$\mathcal{H}_4$: NCS1 TRY2 EX1 TRY1 EX2 CS2 AXAF CS1
$\mathcal{S}_5$: CS1 NCS2 AF CS1
$\mathcal{S}_6$: TRY1 TRY2 AF CS1
$\mathcal{S}_7$: TRY1 TRY2 AF CS2
$\mathcal{S}_8$: NCS1 CS2 AF CS2
$\mathcal{H}_5$: CS1 NCS2
$\mathcal{H}_6$: TRY1 TRY2
$\mathcal{H}_7$: TRY1 TRY2
$\mathcal{H}_8$: NCS1 CS2
$\mathcal{S}_9$: CS1 TRY2
$\mathcal{S}_{10}$: CS1 TRY2 AF CS1 AF CS2
$\mathcal{S}_{11}$: TRY1 CS2 AF CS1 AF CS2
$\mathcal{S}_{12}$: TRY1 CS2
$\mathcal{H}_9$: CS1 TRY2
$\mathcal{H}_{10}$: TRY1 CS2

Figure 6.2

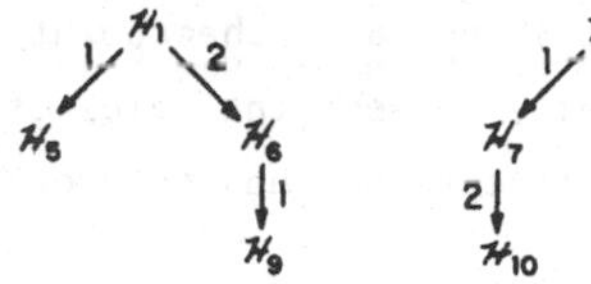

Figure 6.3

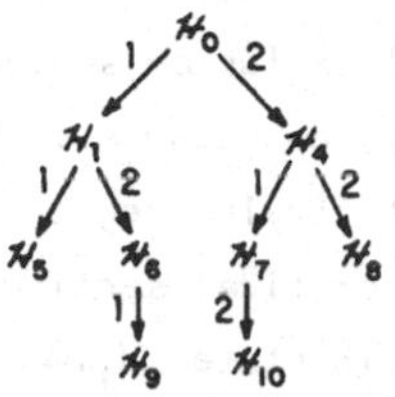

Figure 6.4

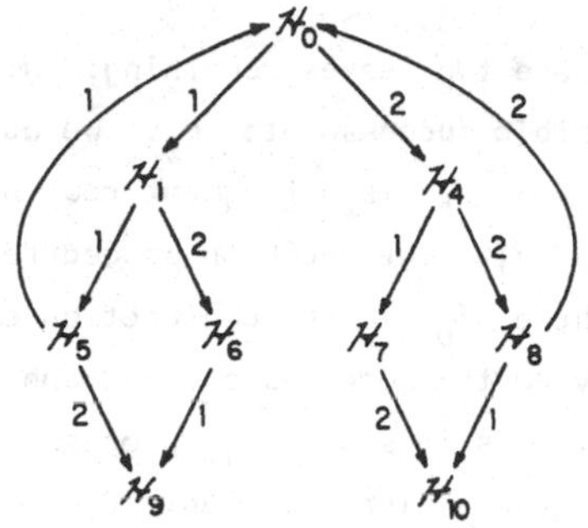

Figure 6.5

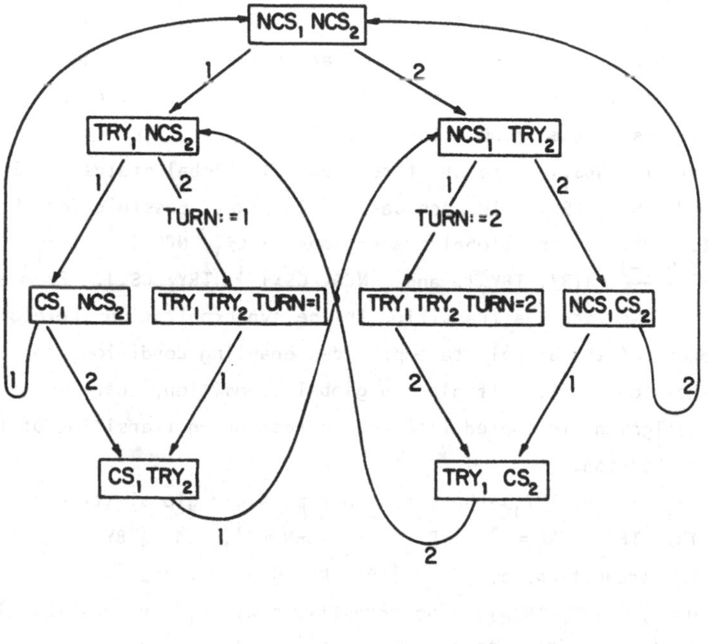

Figure 6.6

fragment, H_1, occurs along the cycle. A fragment root serves as a checkpoint to ensure that all eventualities are fulfilled. By symmetry between the roles of 1 and 2, we add in the arcs $H_8 \overset{1}{\rightarrow} H_{10}$ and $H_8 \overset{2}{\rightarrow} H_0$. The structure now has the form shown in Fig. 6.5.

We now have two leaves remaining: H_9 and H_{10}. We see from the tableau that H_4 is a possible successor to H_9. We add in the arc $H_9 \overset{1}{\rightarrow} H_4$. Again a cycle is formed but since H_4 is a fragment root no problems arise. Similarly, we add in the arc $H_{10} \overset{2}{\rightarrow} H_1$. The decision procedure thus yields a model M such that $M,s_0 \models f_0$ where f_0 is the conjunction of the mutual exclusion system specifications.

We may view the model as a flowgraph of global system behavior. For example, when the system is in state H_1, process P_1 is in its trying region and process P_2 is in its noncritical section. P_1 may enter its critical section or P_2 may enter its trying region. No other moves are possible in state H_1. Note that all states except H_6 and H_7 are distinguished by their propositional labels. In order to distinguish H_6 from H_7, we introduce a variable TURN which is set to 1 upon entry to H_6 and to 2 upon entry to H_7. If we introduce TURN's value into the labels of H_6 and H_7 then, the labels uniquely identify each node in the global system flowgraph. See Fig. 6.6.

We describe how to obtain the synchronization skeletons of the individual processes from the global system flowgraph. In the sequel we will refer to these global system states by the prcpositional labels.

When P_1 is in NCS_1, there are three possible global states $[NCS_1\ NCS_2]$, $[NCS_1\ TRY_2]$, and $[NCS_1\ CS_2]$. In each case it is always possible for P_1 to make a transition into TRY_1 by the global transitions $[NCS_1\ NCS_2] \overset{1}{\rightarrow} [TRY_1\ NCS_2]$, $[NCS_1\ TRY_2] \xrightarrow{1,TURN:=2} [TRY_1\ TRY_2]$, and $[NCS_1\ CS_2] \overset{1}{\rightarrow} [TRY_1\ CS_2]$. From each global transition by P_1, we obtain a transition in the synchronization skeleton of P_1. The P_2 component of the global state provides enabling conditions for the transitions in the skeleton of P_1. If along a global transition, there is an assignment to **TURN**, the assignment is copied into the corresponding transition of the synchronization skeleton.

Now when P_1 is in TRY_1, there are four possible global states: $[TRY_1\ NCS_2]$, $[TRY_1\ NCS_2]$, $[TRY_1\ TRY_2\ TURN=1]$, $[TRY_1\ TRY_2\ TURN=2]$, and $[TRY_1\ CS_2]$ and their associated global transitions by P_1: $[TRY_1\ NCS_2] \overset{1}{\rightarrow} [CS_1\ NCS_2]$ and $[TRY_1\ TRY_2\ TURN=1] \overset{1}{\rightarrow} [CS_1\ TRY_2]$. (No transitions by P_1 are possible in $[TRY_1\ TRY_2\ TURN=2]$ or $[TRY_1\ CS_2]$.) When P_1 is in CS_1 the associated global states and transitions are: $[CS_1\ NCS_2]$, $[CS_1\ TRY_2]$, $[CS_1\ NCS_2] \overset{1}{\rightarrow} [NCS_1\ NCS_2]$, and $[CS_1\ TRY_2] \overset{1}{\rightarrow} [NCS_1\ TRY_2]$. Altogether, the synchronization skeleton for P_1 is shown in Fig. 6.7(a). By symmetry in the global state diagram we obtain the synchronization skeleton for P_2 as shown in Fig. 6.7(b).

The general method of factoring out the synchronization skeletons of the individual processes may be described as follows: Take the model of the specification formula and retain only the propositional formulae in the labels of each node.

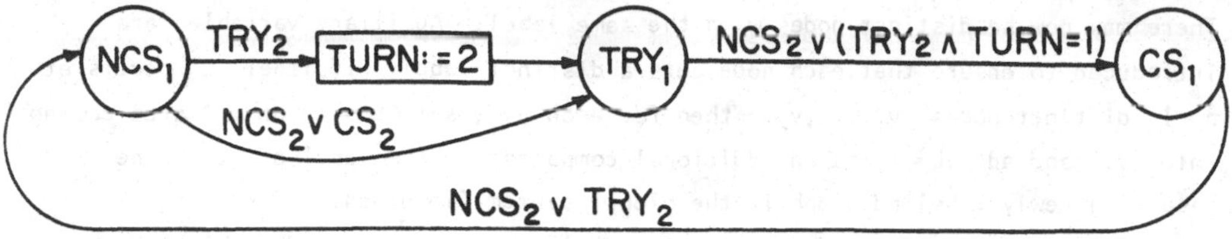

Figure 6.7 (a)

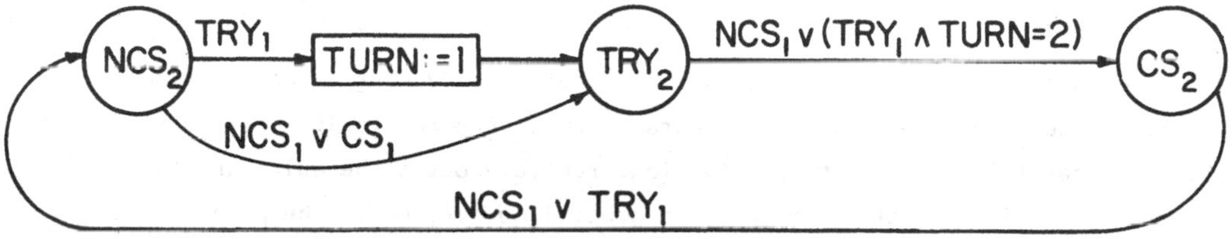

Figure 6.7 (b)

There may now be distinct nodes with the same label. Auxiliary variables are introduced to ensure that each node gets a distinct label: if label L occurs at $n>1$ distinct nodes $v_1,\ldots,v_n$, then for each v_i, set $L:=i$ on all arcs coming into v_i and add $L=i$ as an additional component to the label of v_i. The resulting newly labelled graph is the global system flowgraph.

We now construct the synchronization skeleton for process P_i which has m distinct code regions $R_1,\ldots,R_m$. Initially, the synchronization skeleton for P_i is a graph with m distinct nodes $R_1,\ldots,R_m$ and no arcs. Draw an arc from R_j to R_k if there is at least one arc of the form $L_j \to L_k$ in the global system flowgraph where R_j is a component of the label L_j and R_k is a component of the label L_k. The arc $R_j \to R_k$ is a transition in the synchronization skeleton and is labelled with the enabling condition

$$\vee\{(S_1 \wedge \ldots \wedge S_p) : [R_j\ S_1 \ldots S_p] \xrightarrow{i} [R_k\ S_1 \ldots S_p] \text{ is an arc in the global system flowgraph}\}.$$

Add $L:=n$ to the label of $R_j \to R_k$ if some arc $[R_j\ S_1 \ldots S_p] \xrightarrow{i,L:=n} [R_k\ S_1 \ldots S_p]$ also occurs in the flowgraph.

7. CONCLUSION

We have shown that it is possible to automatically synthesize the synchronization skeleton of a concurrent program from a Temporal Logic specification. We believe that this approach may in the long run turn out to be quite practical. Since synchronization skeletons are, in general, quite small, the potentially exponential behavior of our algorithm need not be an insurmountable obstacle. Much additional research will be needed, however, to make the approach feasible in practice.

We have also described a model checking algorithm which can be applied to mechanically verify that a finite state concurrent program meets a particular Temporal Logic specification. We believe that practical software tools based on this technique could be developed in the near future. Indeed, we have already programmed an experimental implementation of the model checker on the DEC 11/70 at Harvard.* Certain applications seem particularly suited to the model checker approach to verification: One example is the problem of verifying the correctness of existing network protocols many of which are coded as finite state machines. We encourage additional work in this area.

*We would like to acknowledge Marshall Brinn who did the actual programming for our implementation of the model checker.

8. BIBLIOGRAPHY

[BA81] Ben-Ari, M., personal communication, 1981.

[BH81] Ben-Ari, M., Halpern, J., and Pnueli, A., Finite Models for Deterministic Propositional Logic. Proceedings 8th Int. Colloquium on Automata, Languages, and Programming, to appear, 1981.

[BM81] Ben-Ari, M., Manna, Z., and Pnueli, A., The Temporal Logic of Branching Time. 8th Annual ACM Symp. on Principles of Programming Languages, 1981.

[CL77] Clarke, E.M., Program Invariants as Fixpoints. 18th Annual Symp. on Foundations of Computer Science, 1977.

[EC80] Emerson, E.A., and Clarke, E.M., Characterizing Correctness Properties of Parallel Programs as Fixpoints. Proceedings 7th Int. Colloquium on Automata, Languages, and Programming, Lecture Notes in Computer Science #85, Springer-Verlag, 1981.

[EH81] Emerson, E.A., and Halpern, J., A New Decision Procedure for the Temporal Logic of Branching Time, unpublished manuscript, Harvard Univ., 1981.

[FS81] Flon, L., and Suzuki, N., The Total Correctness of Parallel Programs. SIAM J. Comp., to appear, 1981.

[GP80] Gabbay, D., Pnueli, A., *et al.*, The Temporal Analysis of Fairness. 7th Annual ACM Symp. on Principles of Programming Languages, 1980.

[HC68] Hughes, G., and Cresswell, M., *An Introduction to Modal Logic*. Methuen, London, 1968.

[LA80] Lamport, L., "Sometime" is Sometimes "Not Never." 7th Annual ACM Symp. on Principles of Prgramming Languages, 1980.

[LA78] Laventhal, M., Synthesis of Synchronization Code for Data Abstractions, Ph.D. Thesis, M.I.T., June 1978.

[PA69] Park, D., Fixpoint Induction and Proofs of Program Properties, in *Machine Intelligence 5* (D. Mitchie, ed.), Edinburgh University Press, 1970.

[PR77] Pratt, V., A Practical Decision Method for Propositional Dynamic Logic. 10th ACM Symp. on Theory of Computing, 1977.

[RK80] Ramamritham, K., and Keller, R., Specification and Synthesis of Synchronizers. 9th International Conference on Parallel Processing, 1980.

[SM68] Smullyan, R.M., *First Order Logic*. Springer-Verlag, Berlin, 1968.

[TA55] Tarski, A., A Lattice-Theoretical Fixpoint Theorem and Its Applications. Pacific J. Math., 5, pp. 285-309 (1955).

[TA72] Tarjan, R., Depth First Search and Linear Graph Algorithms. SIAM J. Comp. 1:2, pp. 146-160, 1972.

[WO81] Wolper, P. Synthesis of Communicating Processes From Temporal Logic Specifications, unpublished manuscript, Stanford Univ., 1981.

The Type Theory of PL/CV3*

Robert L. Constable
Daniel R. Zlatin

Cornell University

Abstract

This paper presents the core of the type theory of the programming logic PL/CV3. From this core the full theory can be derived. Whereas the full theory was designed to be useable, the core theory was selected to be analyzable. This presentation strives to be succinct yet thorough. The last section consists of an extended example, but the approach here is not tutorial.

1. Introduction

1.1. Logic of programming versus logic of mathematics

We investigate the logic of programming because it will help us understand the programming process and enable us to be better at it. This "self-improvement" motive is not the typical reason that people study the logic of mathematics; and mathematical logic is not always a good role model for programming logic. Why is there this difference, and does it matter?

The chief reason for the difference is the computer. Programming is a formal activity unlike the "doing" of any other mathematics. It requires communication with unintelligent machines which do not understand wonderful mathematical solutions to problems. A solution must be programmed, and this means formalized. Such a situation stimulates us to seek computer aid in the preparation of solutions. But computer aid again requires us to formalize in a useful way; this time we must formalize the explanation of our mathematical solutions. Not everyone is interested in this recursive use of the computer to use the computer. Not everyone wants to use an automated logic for programming (and indeed it is a rare problem which is critical enough to require a completely machine verified solution). But every programmer is interested in knowing how to reason correctly about all stages of the programming process, including, especially, the final stages during which the activity is formal.

Why does this difference matter? In general it matters because programming logics are meant to be used and the logical theories of mathematics are meant to be studied. So they serve very different purposes. But since this paper is concerned with presenting only the core of a programming logic, that difference is not critical here, but, for example, is the driving force in [Constable, O'Donnell 78]. Another more subtle difference arises from the law of parsimony. We can see the issue plainly if we ask why none of the automated programming logics (such as LCF, PL/CV, Affirm, Gypsy, etc.) are based on Zermelo-Fraenkel set theory, one of the standard

*Research supported in part by NSF grant MCS-78-00953.

mathematical theories thought to be adequate to express most of modern mathematics. Notice that in Z-F set theory there is a concept of function and a concept of data type (namely set). There are also such concepts in programming, but they are quite different. A program is like a function, but is computable. A data type is like a set, but can be concretely represented and describes the objects of computations. From this similarity one suspects that a logic dealing with programs and data types may be nearly as rich as the logic of functions and sets. So there is no point in building two parallel theories where one might suffice.

1.2. Constructive mathematics and programming

There is, of course, a rather compelling reason to consider two theories, namely we need to express the mathematics as well as the programming. But in fact Z-F set theory is not all of mathematics. There are many kinds of "mathematics". In particular, the kind of mathematics that we would develop in a programming logic would look rather computational. Indeed, as the first author discovered [Constable 80], it would look rather like constructive mathematics. The similarity is so compelling that the programming logic PL/CV3 is based on an intuitionistic theory of types, in particular on ITT in [Martin-Löf 75]. The type theory ITT was designed for mathematics, so it needed some modification. In particular, the PL/CV3 theory treats operations intensionally while ITT does not; PL/CV3 uses quotient types but ITT does not; and PL/CV3 provides an explicit representation for recursive data types a la [Hoare 75] and [Scott 76] from which the integers can be defined. In ITT the integers are basic and can be used to encode data types. The latest presentation of ITT [Martin-Löf 79] includes well-orderings (which can be used to define ordinals). The version of PL/CV3 presented here adopts these well-orderings and uses them to encode recursive data types somewhat as before.

1.3. Type theory as a programming logic

The principal advantage of using constructive type theory in an automated programming logic is that any mathematical argument can be directly expressed. Thus by attending to such pragmatic issues as succinct notation, automatic deduction of immediate steps of inference, and proper organization of theories, it should be possible to express informal arguments in the theory by formal arguments which are no more than three to five times as long. This empirical claim will be explored in the experimental work at Cornell on the PL/CV3 and PRL systems; if it is correct, then such full-powered logics will find ample use in applications where reliability is critical. They will also form the basis for a systematic use of automated mathematics.

2. Type Theory

2.1. Primitive Concepts

To understand the concept of a small type and the type of all small types, one must understand the concept of an inductive definition, the notion of an algorithm, and the notion that the range type of an algorithm can depend on its argument.

First one defines a finite number of primitive types which are familiar from informal mathematical experience. From these examples, one understands a more abstract concept of type and the notion of what it means to specify a new primitive type. To specify a type, one tells how to construct the canonical objects of the type, and one gives a condition (in the form of an equivalence relation) telling when two such constructions are to be considered equal. The canonical objects are specified linguistically in terms of collections of signs, but the signs are understood to name mental objects in such a way that the properties of the object can be determined from the arrangement of the signs. The possibility of adding new primitive types is left open, but a fixed finite number (three, to be exact) are specified in advance.

Second, the concept of an operation which assigns to the elements of a type, say A, objects of another type, say B, is assumed. In particular, it is possible to assign to elements of a previously specified type small types which have already been built. At the intuitive level, these algorithms or operations will be presented by a typed λ-notation, e.g. $\lambda x \in A.x$ is the identity operation on type A.

Third, one of the important notions used to describe operations in the theory is the intuitive function space operation, $\rightarrow$. The notation $x \in A \rightarrow B(x)$ denotes the type of all functions which, on input of an element of A, say x, return an element of the type given by evaluating the function B on x. This is the informal idea of what it means for an algorithm to have a range that depends on its argument.

2.2. The Type Hierarchy

With these preliminary concepts understood, we are ready to specify precisely the type of small types. This is done by defining first the primitive types, then individuals of these types, then the basic type constructors, finally a method of building individuals (canonical objects) of each constructed type. Thus the type of small types has an inductive character, and the definition of the type of small types (denoted V) is to be understood as an open-ended inductive definition. It is summarized in figure 1.

In this core theory, the primitive types are chosen to be the types with, respectively, zero, one and two elements. The type with zero elements, denoted $\mathbb{0}$, is called the void type. It is a contradiction to construct any object whose type is $\mathbb{0}$. The type with one element is denoted **1**, and has as its only element $0_{\mathbf{1}}$. The type with two elements is denoted $\mathbb{B}$, and has as its elements $0_{\mathbb{B}}$ and $1_{\mathbb{B}}$.

__Product Creation__

Product types are built with the Π operation, which takes as arguments a type T from V, and an operation F which maps elements of T to elements of V. Elements of a product type are operations which map elements x of T to elements of F(x).

__Union Creation__

Union types are created by the Σ operator, which takes arguments with the same type specifications as the Π operator. Union types, however, are a generalization of binary disjoint union in that the union can be indexed by any arbitrary type, including one with an infinite number of elements.

__Well-ordering Creation__

The $\mathbb{W}$ operator creates a well-ordering type upon application to a type A in V and a function B from A to types in V. An element of a well-ordering can be thought of as a tree formed so that each branch has finite length, but the number of descendants from any node in the tree may be infinite. The nodes of one of these trees have values associated with them, taken from the type A. The fan-out from a node labelled with a value a in A can be put in one to one correspondence with the elements of B(a). More formally, an element of a well-ordering type is represented by an element a of A, and a function, which on application to an element b of B(a) gives the element of the well-ordering type at the end of the edge labelled with b that comes out of the node labelled with a. This function is a generalized predecessor function, as an element of a well-ordering has as many predecessors as there are elements in the type specified by applying B to the label on the root node.

__Quotient Creation__

A quotient type is created from a type A in V and an operation E of type $A \to A \to V$. The elements of a quotient type are equivalence classes of elements of A, under the equivalence relation formed by taking the reflexive, symmetric, transitive closure of E treated as a relation.

The process of defining types continues at a higher level by taking the entire collection of small types as an object, called a large type, and by defining various operations which analyze the structure of small types and then closing under the type forming operations. This process can be repeated indefinitely to produce an open hierarchy of universes, V_1 (small types), V_2 (large types), V_3 (very large types), etc. We will use V and V_1 synonomously.

Equality Creation

Now that we have the hierarchy to use, we can define generalized equality types. For elements x and y of a type T which is itself of type V_i (note that T may be V_{i-1}, and x and y may thus be types), the equality operation on type T produces a type that is empty if and only if x is the same object as y. The type expressed by =(T)(x)(y) is an element of V_i.

2.3. Introduction and Elimination

Having described the primitive types and their elements, and how to construct new types from pre-existing types, it remains to show how to build elements of composite types. This will be done separately for each type constructor. For each type formation method, there are operations for building elements of the type, and operations which, given an element of the type, produce different elements, possibly of other types. We refer to these two types of operations as "introduction" and "elimination" operations.

For every type T, we will specify the equality operation =(T), written $=_T$, with the intuitive type $=_T$: $x \in T \to (y \in T \to V)$. For each method of defining new types, we will give conditions under which elements of that type are equal. (Note that on quotient types, equality is not always decidable.)

Most of the functions introduced here are parameterized with respect to the types they will take as arguments when finally applied. Thus the equality operation described above actually has the type =: $T \in V \to (T \to (T \to V))$. Operations will be described without the extra parameters and will be used in examples without explicitly giving these parameters, but their full proper typing will be given in the

---

Primitive small types:

Φ	called the void or empty type	$\Phi \in V$
$\mathbf{1}$	the unit type with exactly one element	$\mathbf{1} \in V$
$\mathbf{B}$	the Boolean type with exactly two elements	$\mathbf{B} \in V$

Individuals:

$0_{\mathbf{1}} \in \mathbf{1}$
$0_{\mathbf{B}} \in \mathbf{B}$
$1_{\mathbf{B}} \in \mathbf{B}$

Type constructors:

Π: $A \in V \to (A \to V) \to V$	the product constructor
Σ: $A \in V \to (A \to V) \to V$	the union constructor
$\mathbf{W}$: $A \in V \to (A \to V) \to V$	the well-ordering constructor
$/$: $A \in V \to (A \to A \to V) \to V$	the quotient constructor

Figure 1

---

table that follows.

__Primitive Type Introduction__

There are no functions which introduce elements of our primitive types. The elements of the primitive types are assumed to exist.

__Primitive Type Elimination__

We need functions which operate on (eliminate) elements of our primitive types. For any choice of type T, there is a function **z** which maps elements of $\mathbf{\Phi}$ into an element of T. (Since there are no elements of $\mathbf{\Phi}$, this corresponds to being able to construct an element of any type from the contradiction that an element of the empty type was supplied.) For any choice of a function T: $\mathbf{B} \rightarrow \mathbf{V}$, there is a function **if** which given elements t1 and t2 of type $T(0_{\mathbf{B}})$ and $T(1_{\mathbf{B}})$, repectively, maps an element b of **B** to t1 if $b=0_{\mathbf{B}}$ and to t2 if $b=1_{\mathbf{B}}$. (Note that **1** elimination falls under the **K** combinator discussed below.) This gives us the intuitive types

$$\mathbf{z}: \mathbf{\Phi} \rightarrow T$$
$$\mathbf{if}: x \in T(0_{\mathbf{B}}) \rightarrow (T(1_{\mathbf{B}}) \rightarrow (x \in \mathbf{B} \rightarrow T(x)))$$

__Product Introduction__

To construct objects of types built with the "product constructor" **Π**, we must have operations which construct functions and manipulate functions. The most primitive set of such functions, borrowed from the (untyped) combinatory calculus, are the **S** and **K** functions. Intuitively, we have the relations

$$\mathbf{K}(x)(y) = x \qquad \text{or} \qquad \mathbf{K} = \lambda x.\lambda y.x$$
$$\mathbf{S}(f)(g)(x) = f(x)(g(x)) \qquad \mathbf{S} = \lambda f.\lambda g.\lambda x.f(x)(g(x))$$

A strict composition rule for typed combinators would require that the domain of the first operation be exactly that of the range of the second operation. In a system with operations whose range type can depend on the argument to the function, such a strict rule impedes the building of generalized operations. For specific terms of the argument type we would be able to compose the operations, but it would be impossible to build the general composition. Therefore, we allow a more liberal form of composition by modifying the **S** combinator. It can compose two functions provided that a proof is supplied that demonstrates that the composition is type correct on all elements of the intended range.

The type of the **S** and **K** operations is, for some choice of types A, B(x) and C(x) and D(x,y):

$$\mathbf{K}: x \in A \rightarrow (B(x) \rightarrow A)$$
$$\mathbf{S}: (x \in A \rightarrow (y \in B(x) \rightarrow D(x,y))) \rightarrow g \in (x \in A \rightarrow C(x)) \rightarrow (x \in A \rightarrow (B(x)=C(x))) \rightarrow x \in A \rightarrow D(x,g(x))$$

Many of the properties of untyped combinators carry over to these typed combinators, although the types do introduce more complexity. In untyped combinators, the identity combinator can be defined in terms of **S** and **K** by I=**SKK**. Using these typed combinators, we can construct an identity function for any type T by: replacing A by

T and B(x) by $\Pi(A)(\lambda x \in A.T)$ in the type of the first **K**; replacing A by T and B(x) by A in the type of the second **K**; and replacing A by T, B(x) and C(x) by $\Pi(A)(\lambda x \in A.T)$, and D(w,z) by T in the type of **S**. For untyped combinators, given an expression involving a variable x, we can abstract with respect to x to obtain a combinatory term containing no instances of x, but which when applied to a value v evaluates to the same value as the original expression would if v were substituted for all occurrences of x. Similar transformations are possible with typed combinators, given that we know the type of the variable being abstracted. Thus our intuitive notion of functions denoted by means of λ's can be brought into the theory.

Product elimination

The elimination of elements of **Π** types is carried out by the operation of application. Given an element f of the type $\Pi(A)(B)$, and an element a in A, then f(a) is an element of the type B(a).

Two operations are equal (under $=_{\Pi(A)(B)}$) if and only if they have identical normal forms. This aspect of function equality will be discussed later.

Union Introduction

The introduction of elements of a type formed by the **Σ** operation is done by the **p** (for pair) function. It maps an element t of a type T and an element s of a type S(t) into the type $\Sigma(T)(S)$.

Union Elimination

The elimination of such types corresponds to taking a **p**'ed element apart into the pieces it was formed from. Two projection functions, **p1** (the "first" element) and **p2** (the "second" element) exist to perform that action.

$$\mathbf{p}: t \in T \rightarrow (S(t) \rightarrow \Sigma(T)(S))$$
$$\mathbf{p1}: \Sigma(T)(S) \rightarrow T$$
$$\mathbf{p2}: x \in \Sigma(T)(S) \rightarrow S(\mathbf{p1}(x))$$

Two elements of a union type are equal if the first elements are equal according to their type, and the second elements are equal according to the type that they belong to. In terms of the operations introduced above, we have, for a and b of type $\Sigma(A)(B)$,

$$a =_{\Sigma(A)(B)} b \;\equiv\; (\mathbf{p1}(a) =_A \mathbf{p1}(b) \;\&\; \mathbf{p2}(a) =_{B(\mathbf{p1}(a))} \mathbf{p2}(b))$$

Well-ordering Introduction

Creating elements of **W** types closely corresponds to definition by induction. Given an element x of a type A, and a function from B(x) to the **W** type in question, the function **sup** creates an element of the **W** type.

Well-ordering Elimination

One form of elimination from a well-ordering type is similar to using the **p1** and **p2** operations on elements of a union type. That is, given an element **sup**(a,f), we can operate on it to obtain the a and f objects. **lb**(x) gives as its value the label associated with a node in the tree; **pd** gives the predecessor function for that node. The other form of elimination of **W** types corresponds to the definition of recursive functions on the **W** type. The operation **rec** takes as its argument a function, which on an element x of the **W** type and a function to create elements of the type C(y) for all predecessors y of x produces an element of C(x). **rec** produces as its result a function, which given an element x of the **W** type produces an element of C(x).

sup: x ∈ A → (B(x) → **W**(A)(B)) → **W**(A)(B)
lb: x ∈ **W**(A)(B) → A
pd: x ∈ **W**(A)(B) → (B(**lb**(x)) → **W**(A)(B))
rec: x ∈ WW(A)(B) → (v ∈ B(**lb**(x)) → C(**pd**(x)(v))) → C(x) → **Π**(**W**(A)(B))(C)

Two elements of a **W** type are equal if they have the same label at their root, and the same predecessor function. For the label, "the same" means equal by the equality defined for the type of the label.

$$x =_{\mathbf{W}(A)(B)} y \;\equiv\; (\mathbf{lb}(x) =_A \mathbf{lb}(y) \;\&\; \mathbf{pd}(x) =_{\mathbf{\Pi}(B(\mathbf{lb}(x)))(\mathbf{W}(A)(B))} \mathbf{pd}(y))$$

Quotient Introduction

Elements of **/** types are formed by a "one way" operation; it is one of the few in the theory that is not in some sense "reversible". Consider a quotient type A **/** E. Let the equivalence relation induced by E be F. F(x)(y) is a type which is non-empty if x = y or if there is a chain $x_1, \ldots, x_n$ where $x_1 = x$ and $x_n = y$ and for each x_i, x_{i+1} pair, either $E(x_i)(x_{i+1})$ or $E(x_{i+1})(x_i)$ is non-empty. For a particular function E and element x of a type A, the value **q**(x) is an element of the type A **/** E such that if F(x)(y) is non-empty, then $\mathbf{q}(x) =_{A/E} \mathbf{q}(y)$.

Quotient Elimination

Elimination of quotient types can only be carried out by functions formed in a special way. We say that a function f respects the equivalence relation when F(x)(y) non-empty implies f(x) = f(y). A function f of type x ∈ A → B(x) can be converted into one that maps from elements of the quotient type into the same range as specified by B, if both B and f respect the equivalence relation.

q: A → (A **/** E)
$\overline{\mathbf{q}}$: f ∈ **Π**(A)(B) → **Π**(A **/** E)($\overline{\mathbf{q}}$B)
where f and B both respect F (the equivalence relation induced by E),
such that ($\overline{\mathbf{q}}$(f))(**q**(a)) = f(a)

Note that in this formulation it appears at first glance that the type requirements for $\overline{\mathbf{q}}$ are circular, or at least recursive. But since any B to which $\overline{\mathbf{q}}$ will be applied the second time will have a type such as **Π**(A)(**K**V), the "recursion" stops there, since the constant function **K**V can easily be rewritten to be a function of type **Π**(A **/** E)(V), by changing the type of the **K** combinator used.

Two elements **q**(a) and **q**(b) of a quotient type are equal if and only if F(a)(b) is a non-empty type. Note that this definition of equality is in general undecidable, as it depends on the type F(a)(b) being empty or non-empty.

q(a) $=_{A/E}$ **q**(b) ≡ F(a)(b), where F is the induced equivalence relation

<u>Equality Introduction</u>

Elements are assumed to exist for all equality types of the form =(T)(x)(x). The elements are written $\mathbf{ax}_{T,x,x}$ and can be thought of as primitive proofs or axioms stating that objects are equal to themselves.

<u>Equality Elimination</u>

In order to make an equivalence relation out of equality, we assume operations that modify elements of equality types to give us the properties of symmetry and transitivity.

sym: =(T)(x)(y) → =(T)(y)(x)
tran: =(T)(x)(y) → =(T)(y)(z) → =(T)(x)(z)

So to add to our summary of the theory in figure 1, we can list the functions mentioned above with their types, as in figure 2.

2.4. <u>Typings Within the Theory</u>

The type constructor **Π** is intended to represent the intuitive arrow, →, so that for B of type A→V, **Π**(A)(B) represents x∈A→B(x). Sometimes to show the

---

=: T∈V→(T→(T→V))
sym: T∈V→x∈T→y∈T→=(T)(x)(y)→=(T)(y)(x)
tran: T∈V→x∈T→y∈T→z∈T→=(T)(x)(y)→=(T)(y)(z)→=(T)(x)(z)

z: T∈V→(**I**→T)
if: T∈(**B**→V)→x∈T($0_{\mathbf{B}}$)→(T($1_{\mathbf{B}}$)→(x∈**B**→T(x)))

K: A∈V→B∈(A→V)→x∈A→(y∈B(x)→A)
S: A∈V→B∈(A→V)→C∈(A→V)→D∈(x∈A→B(x)→V)→
        (x∈A→(y∈B(x)→D(x,y)))→g∈(x∈A→y∈C(x))→(x∈A→(B(x)=C(x)))
        →x∈A→D(x,g(x))

p: A∈V→B∈(A→V)→t∈A→(s∈B(t)→BBIG(A)(B))
p1: A∈V→B∈(A→V)→BBIG(A)(B)→A
p2: A∈V→B∈(A→V)→x∈BBIG(A)(B)→B(**p1**(x))

sup: A∈V→B∈(A→V)→x∈A→(B(x)→**W**(A)(B))→**W**(A)(B)
lb: A∈V→B∈(A→V)→x∈**W**(A)(B)→A
pd: A∈V-B∈(A-V)→x∈**W**(A)(B)→(B(**lb**(x))→**W**(A)(B))
rec: A∈V→B∈(A→V)→C∈(**W**(A)(B)→V)
        x∈WW(A)(B)→(v∈B(**lb**(x))→C(**pd**(x)(v)))→C(x)→**Π**(**W**(A)(B))(C)

q: A∈V→E∈(A→A→V)→A→(A/E)
$\overline{\mathbf{q}}$: f∈A∈V→B∈(A→V)→E∈(A→A→V)→**Π**(A)(B)→**Π**(A/E)($\overline{\mathbf{q}}$B)
    where f and B both respect the equivalence relation induced by E

Figure 2

---

correspondence to the intuitive concept we will write **Π**(A)(B) as **Π**x ∈ A.B(x)

Using the correspondences noted above and in the previous section, we can convert the above type specifications to expressions called typings which are written in the notation of the V types themselves. For example, $I \in A \rightarrow A$ can be written $I \in$ **Π**(A)(λx ∈ A.A). This says that **Π**(A)(λx ∈ A.A) represents the intuitive type $A \rightarrow A$. Since $A \in V$ and λx ∈ A.A is a constant operation $A \rightarrow V$, the application of **Π** to A and λx ∈ A.A is type correct.

Once we realize the correspondence between **Π** and →; **K**, **S** and λ-terms, and hence combinators, it is tempting to express the intuitive concepts in the formal system itself. But when doing this, one must be careful about levels. We need the concept of → and λ to define **Π** and **K**. This will be clear from an attempt to define the type **Π**(A)(λx ∈ A.A) entirely within the system. We would expect this to be **Π**(A)(**K**A), but the **K** used here is λy ∈ V.λx ∈ y.y, which has type $v \in V \rightarrow (v \rightarrow V)$, which if written as a typing, **K** ∈ **Π**(V)(λx ∈ V.(x → V)), would be misleading because <u>this</u> **Π** is a more abstract operation mapping from the large type containing V. We would have to distinguish it from the first **Π** by writing the first as Π_1 and the second as Π_2. Then we could say **K** ∈ Π_2(V)(λx ∈ V.(x → V)).

2.5. Large Types

What we have said up to this point effectively describes the collection of small types. But also we can see that the collection itself is a type. We can imagine other objects like it, formed from different base types and closed under different operations. We can grasp the meaning of mappings $V \rightarrow V$ and unions **Σ**(V)(λx ∈ V.V). If there were another large type U, say the type of sets, we could imagine operations between them: $V \rightarrow U$, $U \rightarrow V$.

The particular concept of a large type that we have in mind consists of V as a new primitive, and permits all of the types of V to be "lifted" to large types (but it is not possible to create small types by mapping V_2 into V_1). It is also closed under large versions of **Π**, **Σ**, **W**, and **/**. For example, Π_2 has the type $x \in V_2 \rightarrow (x \rightarrow V_2) \rightarrow V_2$.

2.6. Intensionality

In the theory it is possible to analyse the structure of all objects. The first step in the analysis is to be able to recognize the building blocks out of which they are constructed. In order to build as strong a decidable equality as possible in the face of an open-ended universe, we must ensure that equality on the basic constants of the theory is decidable. We assume that basic constants (the ones mentioned in this paper) are recognizable by the use of the **atom** operation, and that equality of such atoms is decidable by the **eq** operation.

$\mathbf{atom}: T \in V \to x \in T \to \mathbf{B}$
$\mathbf{eq}: T \in V \to \Sigma x \in T.\mathbf{atom}(x) \to \Sigma y \in T.\mathbf{atom}(y) \to \mathbf{B}$

Using these operations, we can construct the operations **isΦ**, **is1** and **isB** which will recognize the basic types from V, and the decidable equality on boolean types comes from **eq**.

We also have a discriminator

$\mathbf{isap}: T \in V \to x \in T \to \mathbf{B}$

which will decide if an object is of the form f(a). Objects of this form arise whenever a primitive function (such as **S** or **K**, for instance) is applied to fewer arguments than is necessary to be able to reduce the application to a simpler form. They also arise in cases where the form of an object is given by the application of one function to some arguments, for example with functions formed by **rec** or $\bar{\mathbf{q}}$.

isap and **atom** are related by the fact that $\mathbf{isap}(T)(t) \Rightarrow \neg\, \mathbf{atom}(T)(t)$, and $\mathbf{atom}(T)(t) \Rightarrow \neg\, \mathbf{isap}(T)(t)$. But the open-ended universe allows the possibility that an object is neither an atom nor formed by application, but is rather imported into the system by some new method of constructing objects.

Given that an object is an application, we want to be able to analyze out the function being applied and the object to which it is being applied. The operation **split** performs this function, returning an element of a union type which contains all the relevant information.

$$\mathbf{split}: T \in V \to x \in T \to \mathbf{isap}(x) \to$$
$$\Sigma S \in V.\Sigma B \in S \to V.\Sigma f \in \mathbf{\Pi}(S)(B).\Sigma s \in S.\Sigma p \in S(s) =_V T.f(s) =_T x$$

Using these operations, we can build operations which analyze the intensional structure of V_1 objects. Each such operation maps V_1 into $\mathbf{B}$.

$\mathbf{is\Sigma}: V \to \mathbf{B}$ $\qquad \mathbf{isW}: V \to \mathbf{B}$
$\mathbf{is/}: V \to \mathbf{B}$ $\qquad \mathbf{is\Pi}: V \to \mathbf{B}$

We can construct decomposition operations that allow us to analyze an element of a function type that is not a single primitive combinator, and in particular to obtain information about its domain and range.

$\mathbf{optype}: \Sigma y \in \mathbf{\Pi}(T)(F).\mathbf{isap}(y) \to V$
$\mathbf{argtype}: \Sigma y \in \mathbf{\Pi}(T)(F).\mathbf{isap}(y) \to V$
$\mathbf{op}: x \in \Sigma y \in \mathbf{\Pi}(T)(F).\mathbf{isap}(y) \to \mathbf{optype}(x)$
$\mathbf{arg}: x \in \Sigma y \in \mathbf{\Pi}(T)(F).\mathbf{isap}(y) \to \mathbf{argtype}(x)$

We can also construct combinators to decompose the types. For **Π**, **Σ**, and **W** combinators, one can obtain the type over which the quantification is being performed, and the function mapping the type to V. For quotient types, one can obtain the base type and the equivalence relation being used.

$\mathbf{index}: \Sigma y \in V.(\mathbf{is\Pi}(y) \vee \mathbf{is\Sigma}(y) \vee \mathbf{isW}(y)) \to V$
$\mathbf{family}: x \in \Sigma y \in V.(\mathbf{is\Pi}(y) \vee \mathbf{is\Sigma}(y) \vee \mathbf{isW}(y)) \to (\mathbf{index}(x) \to V)$
$\mathbf{base}: \Sigma y \in V.\mathbf{is/}(y) \to V$
$\mathbf{rel}: x \in \Sigma y \in V.\mathbf{is/}(y) \to (\mathbf{base}(x) \to \mathbf{base}(x) \to V)$

```
where
index(Π(A)(F)) = A
family(Π(A)(F)) = F
base(A / E) = A
rel(A / E) = E
```

The strength of allowing intensionality lies in the ability to completely break down an object and build a new one from its components. This is accomplished in informal reasoning by a form of structural induction on the expression representing the object. To mirror that in the theory, we must have as a primitive a combinator allowing recursion on the form of an object, with appropriate typing to ensure the recursion terminates.

```
RV: C(∅) → C(1) → C(B) →
    (x ∈ Σy ∈ V.isΠ(y) → C(index(x)) →
                      f ∈ Π(index(x))(C(family(x))) → C(x)) →
    (x ∈ Σy ∈ V.isΣ(y) → C(index(x)) →
                      f ∈ Π(index(x))(C(family(x))) → C(x)) →
    (x ∈ Σy ∈ V.isW(y) → C(index(x)) →
                      f ∈ Π(index(x))(C(family(x))) → C(x)) →
    (x ∈ Σy ∈ V.is / (y) → C(base(x)) →
                      f ∈ Π(base(x))(Π(base(x))(C(rel(x)(y)))) → C(x)) →
    (x ∈ V → C(x)) → (x ∈ V → C(x))
```

The eight operands are functions which return a result under the assumption that the argument is the type ∅, the type 1, the type B, formed from a Π operation, etc. It reduces in the "obvious" manner:

```
RV(f1,...,f8)(x) =
     if x = ∅ then f1
else if x = 1 then f2
else if x = B then f3
else if x = Π(T)(F) then f4(x, RV(f1,...,f8)(index(x)),
                                λx ∈ T.(RV(f1,...,f8)(family(x))))
else if x = Σ(T)(F) then f5(x, RV(f1,...,f8)(index(x)),
                                λx ∈ T.(RV(f1,...,f8)(family(x))))
else if x = W(T)(F) then f6(x, RV(f1,...,f8)(index(x)),
                                λx ∈ T.(RV(f1,...,f8)(family(x))))
else if x = T / E then f7(x, RV(f1,...,f8)(base(x)),
                                λx ∈ T.λy ∈ T.RV(f1,...,f8)(E(x)(y)))
else f8(x)
```

In a similar manner, we want to break apart operations into their components. There is a structural recursion combinator on the Π(T)(F) types similar to RV that makes this possible.

```
Rf: T ∈ V → x ∈ T → (T → C(op(x)) → C(arg(x)) → C(x))
         → (T → C(x)) → (T → C(x)) → C(x)
```

The combinator acts as

```
Rf(T)(f1,f2,f3)(x) =
     if T = Π(T)(F)
     then if isap(x)
          then f1(x, Rf(optype(x))(f1,f2,f3)(op(x)),
                     Rf(argtype(x))(f1,f2,f3)(arg(x)))
          else f2(x)
     else f3(x)
```

We can summarize these intensionality functions as is done in figure 3.

Using V_2 concepts and functions, we can formalize the informal notions used to define V_1. For example, Π_1 has the type

$$\Pi_1 \in \Pi_2(V_1)(\lambda x \in V_1.(x \to V_1) \to V_1).$$

But this concept requires the informal concept of a dependent operation. By leaving the level structure open-ended, we create the illusion that the entire system can be formalized within itself.

The theory, although complex and powerful, has been reduced to a simple core of combinators and primitive types. The summarized form in figures 1 through 3 presents all the information necessary to describe level 1 of the theory.

```
atom: T ∈ V → x ∈ T → B
eq: T ∈ V → Σx ∈ T.atom(x) → Σy ∈ T.BATOM(y) → B
isap: T ∈ V → x ∈ T → B
split: T ∈ V → x ∈ T → isap(x) →
        ΣS ∈ V.ΣB ∈ S → V.Σf ∈ Π(S)(B).Σs ∈ S.Σp ∈ S(s) =_V T.f(s) =_T x

is∅: V → B                     isΣ: V → B
is1: V → B                     isW: V → B
isB: V → B                     is / : V → B
isΠ: V → B

index: Σy ∈ V.(isΠ(y) ∨ isΣ(y) ∨ isW(y)) → V
family: x ∈ Σy ∈ V.(isΠ(y) ∨ isΣ(y) ∨ isW(y)) → (index(x) → V)
base: Σy ∈ V.is / (y) → V
rel: x ∈ Σy ∈ V.is / (y) → (base(x) → base(x) → V)

RV: C(∅) → C(1) → C(B) →
    (x ∈ Σy ∈ V.isΠ(y) → C(index(x)) →
                f ∈ Π(index(x))(C(family(x))) → C(x)) →
    (x ∈ Σy ∈ V.isΣ(y) → C(index(x)) →
                f ∈ Π(index(x))(C(family(x))) → C(x)) →
    (x ∈ Σy ∈ V.isW(y) → C(index(x)) →
                f ∈ Π(index(x))(C(family(x))) → C(x)) →
    (x ∈ Σy ∈ V.is / (y) → C(base(x)) →
                f ∈ Π(base(x))(Π(base(x))(C(rel(x)(y)))) → C(x)) →
    (x ∈ V → C(x)) → (x ∈ V → C(x))

optype: Σy ∈ Π(T)(F).isap(y) → V
argtype: Σy ∈ Π(T)(F).isap(y) → V
op: x ∈ Σy ∈ Π(T)(F).isap(y) → (Bopdom(x) → Boprng(x))
arg: x ∈ Σy ∈ Π(T)(F).isap(y) → T

Rf: T ∈ V → x ∈ T → (T → C(op(x)) → C(arg(x)) → C(x))
        → (T → C(x)) → (T → C(x)) → C(x)
```

Figure 3

2.7. Definitional Equality

In practice, one wants to introduce various definitions. For example, one might want to define the binary disjoint union, say, as

S+T = **Σ**(**B**)(**if**(S)(T))

This form of definition and the notion of equality used in it is a linquistic matter. That is, S+T is not a new canonical form of the theory, it is merely an abbreviation of existing forms. The equality S+T = **Σ**(**B**)(**if**(S)(T)) is not a new mathematical identity over V, it simply relates expressions.

We adopt the approach to definitional equality taken in [Martin-Löf 75]. The form of definitions is

<u>for</u> $x_1 \in A_1,\ldots,x_n \in A_n(x_1,\ldots,x_{n-1})$
<u>define</u> $f(x_1)\cdots(x_n)$ = exp

where exp cannot refer to f.

The rules of definitional equality are standard and the relation is decidable in time n·log(n) [Johnson 80; Constable, Johnson, Eichenlaub 81].

2.8. Equality and Normal Forms

The normal form of an expression is obtained by performing all substitutions for definitional equalities, and then performing all the reductions given by the equalities in Figure 4 below. The resulting expression will have no occurrences of applications which could be simplified by substituting arguments for parameters, or by applying the "obvious" simplification rules.

We can now discuss function and type equality in more detail. Two types or functions are equal if their normal forms are the same. With the intensionality functions described in an earlier section, we can almost write a function of level V_2 which would decide equality for types (or functions) of level V_1. Such a decision procedure does not handle types and functions allowed into the universe by the open-ended nature of the constructive theory. We can agree that a type which is from outside the theory and one constructed with **Σ**, for example, are different types; but there is no obvious answer in the case of two un-analyzable objects.

2.9. Working at Higher Levels

One simplifying restriction made on functions is that one is not able to build a function which maps from a V_2 type to create new V_1 types. In order to be able to work at higher levels using concepts from lower levels, we include the **up** combinator. This combinator raises elements of V_1 to be elements of V_2, and similarly transforms elements of those types to be elements of the newly created

$\mathbf{if}(x)(y)(0_B) = x$
$\mathbf{if}(x)(y)(1_B) = y$

$\mathbf{p}(\mathbf{p1}(x))(\mathbf{p2}(x)) = x$
$\mathbf{p1}(\mathbf{p}(x)(y)) = x$
$\mathbf{p2}(\mathbf{p}(x)(y)) = y$

$\bar{\mathbf{q}}(f)(\mathbf{q}(x)) = f(x)$

$\mathbf{is\Pi}(\mathbf{\Pi}(A)(B)) = 1_B$
$\mathbf{is\Pi}(T) = 0_B$ otherwise
$\mathbf{is\Sigma}(\mathbf{\Sigma}(A)(B)) = 1_B$
$\mathbf{is\Sigma}(T) = 0_B$ otherwise

$\mathbf{\Pi}(\mathbf{index}(T))(\mathbf{family}(T)) = T$
$\mathbf{index}(\mathbf{\Pi}(A)(B)) = A$
$\mathbf{family}(\mathbf{\Pi}(A)(B)) = B$

$\mathbf{\Sigma}(\mathbf{index}(T))(\mathbf{family}(T)) = T$
$\mathbf{index}(\mathbf{\Sigma}(A)(B)) = A$
$\mathbf{family}(\mathbf{\Sigma}(A)(B)) = B$

$\mathbf{K}(x)(y) = x$
$\mathbf{S}(f)(g)(x) = f(x)(g(x))$

$\mathbf{sup}(\mathbf{lb}(x))(\mathbf{pd}(x)) = x$
$\mathbf{lb}(\mathbf{sup}(x)(f) = x$
$\mathbf{pd}(\mathbf{sup}(x)(f) = f$

$\mathbf{isW}(\mathbf{W}(A)(B)) = 1_B$
$\mathbf{isW}(T) = 0_B$ otherwise
$\mathbf{is\,/}\,(A\,/\,E) = 1_B$
$\mathbf{is\,/}\,(T) = 0_B$ otherwise

$\mathbf{W}(\mathbf{index}(T))(\mathbf{family}(T)) = T$
$\mathbf{index}(\mathbf{W}(A)(B)) = A$
$\mathbf{family}(\mathbf{W}(A)(B)) = B$

$\mathbf{base}(T)\,\mathbf{/}\,\mathbf{rel}(T) = T$
$\mathbf{base}(A\,/\,E) = A$
$\mathbf{rel}(A\,/\,E) = E$

Figure 4

type.

This final combinator, given in figure 5, allows us to "renumber" the levels at which we have constructed objects. All that is necessary to describe any level of the hierarchy are the descriptions in figures 1 to 5.

2.10. Theories

In PL/CV3, a specific theory is an element of a dependent product type, and theories can be parameterized. In this core version, we simply take a theory to be a sequence of typings, definitions and definitional equalities. This is a linquistic notion of theory which we do not attempt to identify with a mathematical object. Typings of the form $x \in T$ for x a variable are assumptions, other typings must follow from previous typings and equations by one of the rules listed in the previous sections.

$\mathbf{up}$: $V_1 \to V_2$
$\mathbf{up}_T$: $T \to \mathbf{up}(T)$ for every type T

Figure 5

3. Applications

In this section we relate the core theory to more familiar concepts, such as the predicate calculus, natural numbers, and a representation of lists. We are not concerned with he pragmatic issues that arise in trying to really use the full type theory to represent these concepts. Such matters will be discussed in the Ph. D. thesis of the second author, in [Constable, Zlatin 81], and in the work of the PRL project at Cornell.

3.1. Embedding Constructive Logic in the Theory

We will demonstrate that higher order constructive logic can be embedded into the type theory. Interpretations are given for the logical connectives in terms of the type operations; the notion of a proposition having a proof corresponds to the non-emptiness of a type. Any deductions that can be carried out in logic (where quantification is over some type) can be carried out in the type theory.

The higher order logic we will embed is modelled after that presented in [Hilbert, Ackermann 50], but with constructive proof rules. We assume the existence of a type T, the type of an individual variable. An n-ary predicate whose arguments are of types $S_1,S_2,\dots,S_n$ is itself of type $[S_1,S_2,\dots,S_n]$. Then the following clauses give the definition of a formula of the system:

(1) If P is a predicate of type $[S_1,S_2,\dots,S_n]$ and $x_1,x_2,\dots,x_n$ are of types $S_1,S_2,\dots,S_n$, respectively, then $P(x_1,x_2,\dots,x_n)$ is a formula.

(2) If P and Q are formulas, then $P \& Q$, $P \vee Q$, $P \Rightarrow Q$, and $\neg P$ are formulas.

(3) If P(x) is any formula in which the variable x occurs as a free variable of type S, then $\forall x \in S.P(x)$ is a formula, and $\exists x \in S.P(x)$ is a formula.

We assume the usual constructive interpretations for the logical connectives &, $\vee$, $\Rightarrow$, $\neg$, $\forall$, and $\exists$. In particular, we assume that proofs are given in an introduction/elimination (or natural deduction) style proof tree. We will use the notation that $\vdash P$ means that the formula P is provable within the logic, and that $H \vdash P$ means that P is provable within the logic under the assumption that the formulas in the set H are valid.

We first create a function which translates propositions from the syntax of the logic to the syntax of types.

$$
\begin{aligned}
&\mathrm{Trans}(\underline{false}) = \Phi \\
&\mathrm{Trans}(\underline{true}) = \mathbb{1} \\
&\mathrm{Trans}(x) = x \text{ for all variables } x \\
&\mathrm{Trans}(T) = T \\
&\mathrm{Trans}([S]) = \Pi x \in \mathrm{Trans}(S).V_1 \\
&\mathrm{Trans}([S_1,S_2,\dots,S_n]) = \Pi x \in \mathrm{Trans}(S_1).\mathrm{Trans}([S_2,\dots,S_n]) \\
&\mathrm{Trans}(f(x)) = \mathrm{Trans}(f)(\mathrm{Trans}(x))
\end{aligned}
$$

$Trans(A \& B) = \Sigma x \in Trans(A).Trans(B)$ where x is a new variable
$Trans(\exists x \in A.B(x)) = \Sigma(Trans(A))(Trans(B))$
$Trans(A \vee B) = \Sigma n \in \mathbb{B}.\mathbf{if}(Trans(A),Trans(B),n)$ where n is a new variable
$Trans(A \Rightarrow B) = \Pi x \in Trans(A).Trans(B)$ where x is a new variable
$Trans(\forall x \in A.B(x)) = \Pi(Trans(A))(Trans(B))$

Note that the **W** and **/** type formation operations are not used in the result of any translation. One can imagine a logic including a form of "recursive proposition" or "infinite proposition" which would be translated into a type involving the **W** operation. However, the inclusion of **W** and **/** in the type theory means that we cannot in general translate from types back into propositions.

To complete the proof that logic is embedded in the type theory, we should show that the proof rules for the logic have corresponding operations in the type theory that preserve the notion of truth. This is equivalent to showing that for all propositions P,

$\vdash P$ implies there is an element of the type Trans(P).

We will sketch the proof of a slightly stronger statement.

<u>Theorem</u>:

$H \vdash P$ implies that assuming there are elements of the types Trans(h) for all h in H, then we can construct an element of Trans(P) using the combinators given in the preceeding section.

<u>Proof</u>:

Proof is by induction on the height of the proof tree for $H \vdash P$.

<u>Base case</u>:

The height of the tree is 0. Then the proposition to be proven is one of the hypotheses h from H. Assuming there is an element of all the Trans(h), then since P is one of the h's, there is an element of Trans(P); no combinators are necessary.

<u>Inductive step</u>:

The height of the tree is k, and we can assume the theorem for all propositions and proof trees of height < k. We must show the theorem holds for height k as well, and will do so by cases on the rule being applied at the root of the proof tree.

& <u>Intro</u>:

Let the propositions proven in the left and right subtrees be A and B, repectively. The left and right subtrees are of height less than k, so by the induction hypothesis (working with $H \vdash A$ and $H \vdash B$), the types Trans(A) and Trans(B) can be shown non-empty. Let the elements of those types be "a" and "b". Then the element **p**(a)(b) is of type $\Sigma x \in A.B$ where B does not depend on x. But this is exactly an element of Trans(A & B).

& **Elim**:

By the induction hypothesis, we have an element of the type corresponding to the proposiion proven at the root of the subtree, which is of the form A & B. Let the element be "a", an element of the type Trans(A & B), that is, an element of **Σ**x ∈ Trans(A).Trans(B). Then **p2**(a) is an element of the type Trans(B), or **p1**(a) is an element of the type Trans(A), whichever was required.

∨ **Intro**:

We are attempting to prove a proposition of the form A ∨ B, and have proven either A or B in the subtree below the root. By the induction hypothsesis, we can construct an element "a" of the type Trans(A) (or Trans(B), as the case may be), and then **p**(0)(a) (or, respectively, **p**(1)(a)) will be a member of the type **Σ**n ∈ **B**.**if**(Trans(A),Trans(B),n), which is exactly Trans(A ∨ B).

∨ **Elim**:

The first subtree below the root proves a proposition of the form A ∨ B, the second proves a proposition of the form A ⇒ C, and the third proves one of the form B ⇒ C. By the induction hypothesis applied to the first subtree, we can find an element "a" of the type Trans(A ∨ B). Applying the induction hypothesis to the second subtree gives a function f_a of the type Trans(A ⇒ C). Similarly, from the third subtree, we obtain a function f_b of the type Trans(B ⇒ C). Then the element **if**(f_a(**p2**(a)),f_b(**p2**(a)),**p1**(a)) is an element of C.

⇒ **Intro**:

Given a proof tree of a proposition of the form A ⇒ B from hypotheses H, we can obtain, by the induction hypothesis, an element "b" (expressed using combinators) of the type Trans(B) from the proof tree (minus the root node) that corresponds to the proof H ∪ {A}⊢B. Abstracting "b" with respect to the element of A assumed in its creation gives a function "f_b" which maps elements of A to elements of B. This abstraction can be performed using the combinators provided, leaving us with a function expressed as a sequence of combinators.

⇒ **Elim**:

The subtrees provide proofs of a proposition of the form A ⇒ B, and of the proposition A. By the induction hypothesis, we can obtain from the proof of A ⇒ B a function f mapping elements of Trans(A) to elements of Trans(B), and from the proof of A an element a of Trans(A). Applying the function to the element of Trans(A) gives an element f(a) of Trans(B), as is required.

∀ **Intro**:

The subtree provides a proof of a proposition of the form B(x) for an arbitrary x drawn from some type, say A, from a set of hypotheses H. Applying the induction hypothesis to the proof of H ∪ {x ∈ A}⊢B, we obtain an element of B expressed in combinators, depending on the element of Trans(A) chosen. Abstracting with respect to this element gives the function we want to interpret as a proof of the proposition $\forall x \in A.B(x)$, which is a member, as required, of $\mathbf{\Pi}$(Trans(A))(Trans(B)).

$\forall$ Elim:

Similar to the $\Rightarrow$ elimination case. Note that since all objects are represented as combinators, we do not need to worry about capture of bound variables -- there are none to be captured.

$\exists$ Intro:

The subtree of the proof is a proof of a proposition of the form B(x) where x is a particular element of some type, say A. By the induction hypothesis, we can build an element "b" of Trans(B(x)). So the element **p**(x)(b) is an element of $\mathbf{\Sigma}$(Trans(A))(Trans(B)), which is Trans($\exists x \in A.B$), as was to be proven.

$\exists$ Elim:

Similar to the & elimination case.

QED.

So any proposition in this extended logic can be modeled by a type, and if the proposition is true, possibly under some hypotheses, then the translated type is non-empty. Furthermore, all the proof rules of this extended constructive logic correspond to some action on types.

3.2. Building the Integers

We have not assumed the existence of the type of non-negative integers in the core theory because they can be built as a well-ordered type. Thinking again of elements of a $\mathbf{W}$ type as trees, the integer 0 will be represented as a tree of exactly one node labelled with $0_{\mathbf{B}}$; the successor of an integer n will be represented as a tree with a root labelled by $1_{\mathbf{B}}$, and a single outward edge to the tree which represents n. So labels come from the type $\mathbf{B}$, and there are either no edges out of a node if the label is $0_{\mathbf{B}}$, or one edge if the label is $1_{\mathbf{B}}$. So the number of outward edges corresponds to elements of $\mathbf{0}$ and $\mathbf{1}$, respectively. In order to build such a $\mathbf{W}$ type, we need a function f of type $\mathbf{B} \to V$ such that $f(0_{\mathbf{B}}) = \mathbf{0}$, and $f(1_{\mathbf{B}}) = \mathbf{1}$. Such function is $\lambda x \in \mathbf{B}$.**if**($\mathbf{0}$)($\mathbf{1}$)(x), or, using combinators, **if**($\mathbf{0}$)($\mathbf{1}$). So the type

Int = $\mathbf{W}$($\mathbf{B}$)(**if**($\mathbf{0}$)($\mathbf{1}$))

describes the type of non-negative integers.

3.3. An Iteration Function

Preliminary to defining lists in the theory, we define an iteration operation. Using the non-negative integers just built, we construct an operation which takes as input a type T, a function f of type T→T, and an integer n, and returns as output the function of type T→T produced by composing f with itself n times (f^n). The function we are looking for is thus of type $T \in V \to f \in \Pi(T)(K(T)) \to Int \to \Pi(T)(K(T))$.

Since it is built as a recursive function, it must be constructed as a consequence of **W** elimination; specifically, elimination on the non-negative integers as defined above. In order to build a recursive function, we need a function which, given

(1) an integer, or, more specifically, the label and predecessor function which determine the integer, and

(2) a function, which given an element labeling one of the out-edges from the root node of the given integer, yields an element of the desired type; in this case, T→T,

returns an element of the desired type, again, namely T→T.

A function with these objects as arguments has type

$n \in Int \to (\Pi m \in \mathbf{if}(\mathbf{I},\mathbf{1},n).(T \to T)) \to (T \to T)$

Intuitively, it is putting together an answer for the integer from an answer for the previous integer. If the integer was 0, we want the identity function on T to be returned. Otherwise, we want to compose the function whose power we are taking with the answer obtained from the predecessor. By the above definition of Int, the integer is 0 if its label is 0. So part of the answer is $\mathbf{if}(Id_T, \ldots, \mathbf{lb}(n))$. What goes into the ... must be the composition of the given function, f, together with the predecessor's answer. Let g be the function to produce the answer for the predecessor; then the function to operate on with the **rec** combinator is

$$\lambda n \in Int.\lambda g \in (\mathbf{if}(\mathbf{I},\mathbf{1},\mathbf{lb}(n)) \to (T \to T)).$$
$$(\mathbf{if}(Id_T, \mathbf{S}(\mathbf{K}(f))(g(0_1)), \mathbf{lb}(n))).$$

Abstracting with respect to f and T, we obtain the real definition of the exponentiation function:

$$expon = \lambda T \in V.\lambda f \in T \to T.$$
$$\mathbf{rec}(\lambda n \in Int.\lambda g \in (\mathbf{if}(\mathbf{I},\mathbf{1},\mathbf{lb}(n)) \to (T \to T)).$$
$$(\mathbf{if}(Id_T, \mathbf{S}(\mathbf{K}(f))(g(0_1)), \mathbf{lb}(n)))).$$

This can be rewritten completely in combinators, but would be even more unpalatable than the above notation. In a user-pleasant system, it would be specifiable as

```
expon = λT ∈ V.λf ∈ T→T.λn ∈ Int.
            if n = 0
            then Id_T
            else expon(T)(f)(n-1)
```

with automatic translation to the internal form. Research is currently being done into the efficiency of such automatic tranformations.

3.4. Implementing Lists

A list of elements of a specified type is either a marker indicating the end of the list, or it is an element of the type followed by a list.

Consider a fixed type T. Using the type **1** as the type containing our marker, we would like to say that the type of lists of elements of T is given by the disjoint union of **1** and the product of T and the list type. This method of definition can be used to define recursive types [Constable, Zlatin 81], but introduces complications that are better left out of a core theory. In this presentation, we will build lists by using the exponentiation operation defined in the previous section to build the type of lists of length up to n for all integers n; these types can then be united by using the **Σ** operation to form the type of all finite length lists.

We will use the shorthand notation A+B for **Σ**n ∈ **B**.**if**(A,B,n), representing the disjoint union of two types; similarly A×B will be shorthand for **Σ**x ∈ A.B, the cartesian product of two types.

Define the function LL(S) = **1**+T×S. Note that LL(**Φ**) is the type of all empty lists; LL(LL(**Φ**)) is the type of all lists with one or zero elements, and so on. In particular, expon(V)(LL)(n)(**Φ**) (for expon redefined to take large types as a first argument) is the type of all lists of length less than or equal to n. So the union of these types over all integers n is the type we are looking for.

List = λT ∈ V.**Σ**n ∈ Int.expon(V)(LL)(n)(**Φ**)

So List is a function which on an arbitrary type returns the type of lists over that type.

3.5. Further Use of the Theory

Data structures common to computer programs can be written as types in the type theory; most, except for those that themselves have types as components, will lie in V_1. Because of the intensionality of the theory, we can reason about implementations of these data structures with the theory, as well as proving theorems concerning the complexity of functions which operate on these types.

4. Acknowledgements

We would like to thank all our associates whose conversation and criticism have helped us shape the theory. In particular, Per Martin-Löf, Mike O'Donnell, Stuart Allen, Joe Bates, Alan Demers, Paul Dietz, Carl Eichenlaub, Bob Harper, and Daniel Leivant have given their time and thought to the project.

5. References

Aczel, Peter, The Type Theoretic Interpretation of Constructive Set Theory, in Logic Colloquium '77, eds. A. Macintyre, L. Pacholaki, J. Paris; North-Holland Publishing Co., Amsterdam, 1978, pp. 55-66.

Cartwright, R., A Constructive Alternative to Axiomatic Data Type Definitions, Computer Science Department TR 80-427, Cornell University, 1980.

Constable, R.L., Programs and Types, in Proceedings of the 21st Annual Symposium on Foundations of Computer Science, Syracuse, N. Y., 1980.

Constable, R.L. and D. Zlatin, Report on the Type Theory (V3) of the Programming Logic PL/CV3, Technical Report TR 81-454, Computer Science Department, Cornell University.

Constable, R.L., S.D. Johnson, and C.D. Eichenlaub, Introduction to the PL/CV2 Programming Logic, Department of Computer Science, Cornell University, January 1981.

de Bruijn, N.G., A Survey of the Project AUTOMATH, in Essays on Combinatory Logic, Lambda Calculus and Formalism, Academic Press, 1980, pp. 579-606.

Feferman, S., Constructive Theories of Functions and Classes, Logic Colloquium 78, North-Holland, Amsterdam, 1979, pp. 159-224.

Gordon, M., R. Milner, and C. Wadsworth, Edinburgh LCF, A Mechanized Logic of Computation, Lecture Notes in Computer Science, Springer-Verlag, 1979.

Hilbert, D., and W. Ackermann, Mathematical Logic, 2nd edition, trans. Robert E. Luce, Chelsea Pub. Co., New York, 1950.

Hoare, C.A.R., Recursive Data Structures, International Journal of Computer and Information Sciences, Vol. 4, 2, June, 1975, pp. 105-132.

Johnson, S., A Computer System for Checking Proofs, Ph.D. thesis, Department of Computer Science, Cornell University, Ithaca, New York, November 1980.

Martin-Löf, P., An Intuitionistic Theory of Types: Predicative Part, Logic Colloquium '73, ed. H.E. Rose, J.C. Shepherdson, North-Holland, Amsterdam, 1975, pp. 73-118.

Martin-Löf, P., Constructive Mathematics and Computer Programming, 6th International Congress for Logic, Method. and Phil. of Science, Hannover, August, 1979.

Prawitz, D., Natural Deduction, Almqvist and Wiksell, Stokholm, 1965.

Scott, D., Data Types as Lattices, SIAM Journal on Computing, 5, 3, September, 1976.

Stenlund, S., Combinators, Lambda-terms, and Proof-Theory, D. Reidel, Dordrecht, 1972, 183 pp.

CORRECTNESS OF PROGRAMS
WITH FUNCTION PROCEDURES

(extended abstract)

J.W. de Bakker
Mathematical Centre, Kruislaan 413, 1098SJ Amsterdam
Free University, Amsterdam
J.W. Klop
Mathematical Centre, Amsterdam
J.-J.Ch. Meyer
Free University, Amsterdam

ABSTRACT

The correctness of programs with programmer-declared functions is investigated. We use the framework of the typed lambda calculus with explicit declaration of (possibly recursive) functions. Its expressions occur in the statements of a simple language with assignment, composition and conditionals. A denotational and an operational semantics for this language are provided, and their equivalence is proved. Next, a proof system for partial correctness is presented, and its soundness is shown. Completeness is then established for the case that only call-by-value is allowed. Allowing call-by-name as well, completeness is shown only for the case that the type structure is restricted, and at the cost of extending the language of the proof system. The completeness problem for the general case remains open. In the technical considerations, an important role is played by a reduction system which essentially allows us to reduce expression evaluation to systematic execution of auxiliary assignments. Termination of this reduction system is shown using Tait's computability technique. Complete proofs will appear in the full version of the paper.

1. INTRODUCTION

We present a study of partial correctness of programs with programmer-declared functions. Typically, if "fac" is declared as the factorial function, we want to be able to derive formulae such as {x=3} y := fac(x){y=6}. For this purpose, we use a functional language with an interesting structure, viz. the typed lambda calculus together with explicit declaration of (possibly recursive) functions - rather than using the fixed point combinator - and then consider a simple imperative language the expressions of which are taken from this functional language. The reader who is not familiar with the typed lambda calculus may think of function procedures as appearing in ALGOL 68, provided only finite (not recursively declared) modes are used.

Section 2 first introduces the syntax of our language(s). As to the functional language, besides constants and variables it contains *application*, two forms of *abstraction*, viz. with call-by-value and call-by-name parameters, and conditional expressions. The imperative language has assignment, composition and conditional statements. A program consists of a statement accompanied by a list of function declarations. The assignment statement constitutes our main tool in applying a formalism in the style of Hoare to an analysis of correctness of programs with function procedures. A central theme of the paper is the reduction of expression evaluation to execution of a sequence of assignment statements, thus allowing the application of the well-known partial correctness formalism for imperative languages. Some further features of our language are: function evaluation has no side-effects, the bodies of function declarations may contain global variables, and the static scope rule is applied. Section 2 also provides a denotational semantics for the language, with a few variations on the usual roles of environments and states, and applying the familiar least fixed point technique to deal with recursion.

Section 3 presents an important technical idea. A system of *simplification rules* is given for the statements of our language allowing the reduction of each statement to an equivalent *simple* one. These rules embody the above-mentioned imperative treatment of expression evaluation, and play a crucial role both in the definition of the operational semantics to be given in Section 4, and in the proof systems to be studied in Sections 5 to 7. The proof that the reduction always terminates is non-trivial. Details are given in the Appendix; the proof relies on the introduction of a *norm* for each expression. The existence of this norm is proved using an auxiliary reduction system. Reduction in this auxiliary system always terminates as is shown using the "computability" technique of Tait [22]. In Section 4 we define an operational semantics for our language and prove its equivalence with the denotational one.

In Section 5 the notion of partial correctness formula is introduced, and a sound proof system for partial correctness is proposed. The techniques used in the soundness proof rely partly on the equivalence result of Section 4, partly follow the lines of De Bakker [4]. In Section 6 we show that a slight modification of the proof system is complete for a language with only call-by-value abstraction. This is shown by appropriate use of the technique of Gorelick [11], described also e.g. in Apt [1] and De Bakker [4]. Section 7 discusses completeness when call-by-value and call-by-name are combined, but only for the case that all arguments of functions are of ground type (no functions with functions as arguments). We present a complete proof system for this case, albeit at the cost of extending the language of the proof system with an auxiliary type of assignment, allowing the undefined constant in assertions, and adding to the proof system a number of proof rules exploiting the auxiliary assignment. The completeness problem for the general case (functions with functions as arguments) remains open. In the Appendix we give some details on the proof of termination of the simplification system of Section 3.

Partial correctness of programs with function procedures has not yet been investigated extensively in the literature. Clint & Hoare [8] (see also Ashcroft, Clint & Hoare [2], O'Donnell [19]) propose a rule which involves the appearance of calls of programmer-declared functions within assertions. The proof system we shall propose avoids this. A general reference for the (typed) lambda calculus is Barendregt [5]. The semantics of the typed lambda calculus has been thoroughly investigated e.g. by Plotkin [20] and - extended with nondeterminacy, by Hennessy & Ashcroft [12,13]. However, correctness issues in our sense are not addressed in these papers. (LCF [10] *is* a logical system for function procedures, but not the one of partial correctness.) The operational semantics of Section 4 follows the general pattern as proposed by Cook [9] and further analyzed by De Bruin [6]. The partial correctness formalism was introduced by Hoare [13]; many details on further developments can be found in e.g. Apt [1] or De Bakker [4]. Completeness is always taken in the sense of Cook's *relative* completeness [9]. Related work on (in)completeness of partial correctness for procedures is described in Clarke [7]; a survey paper on this topic is Langmaack & Olderog [17].

Acknowledgements. We are grateful for a number of helpful discussions with K.R. Apt, H.P. Barendregt, A. de Bruin, E.M. Clarke, H. Langmaack and E.R. Olderog. Arie de Bruin has in particular clarified some problems we had with the definition of the denotational semantics, and Ed Clarke did the same for the (in)completeness problem.

2. SYNTAX AND DENOTATIONAL SEMANTICS

Notation. For any set M, the phrase "let (m∈)M be such that ..." defines M by ..., and simultaneously introduces m as typical element of M.

We first present the syntax of our language. It uses a typed lambda calculus with programmer-declared functions allowing (explicit) recursion, embedded into a simple imperative language.

The set $(\tau\in)$ *Type* is defined by $\tau ::= \omega \mid (\tau_1 \to \tau_2)$. A type τ is either *ground* $(\tau=\omega)$, *functional* ($\tau \neq \omega$, this abbreviates that $\tau = \tau_1 \to \tau_2$ for some types τ_1, τ_2), or arbitrary. Type $(\omega \to (\omega \to \ldots \to (\omega\to\omega)\ldots))$ is usually abbreviated to $\omega^n \to \omega$, $n \geq 0$.

The set (c∈) *Cons* is that of the *constants*, which are always of the type $\omega^n \to \omega$, $n \geq 0$. We use the letters x, y, z, u for variables of ground type, f, g for variables of functional type, and v, w for variables of arbitrary type. For later use, we assume the respective sets of variables to be well-ordered. In the intended meaning, (function) constants are given initially (as part of some given signature, if one prefers) and assigned values - by some interpretation - in a set $V_\omega^n \to V_\omega$, V_ω the set of ground values. For example, taking V_ω as the set of integers, "+" might be the interpretation of a constant of type $\omega^2 \to \omega$. Function variables are to be programmer-declared ("fac" above is an example). Note that, contrary to the situation for constants, their arguments may themselves be functions (type $((\omega\to\omega)\to\omega)$ is an example).

The set of expressions is defined as follows: First we give the syntax for the untyped expressions (s,t∈) *Uexp*. After that, we present the typing rules which determine the subset *Exp* consisting of all expressions which can be typed according to these rules. From that moment on, s,t always stand for typed expressions.

$$s ::= c \mid v \mid s_1(s_2) \mid \langle \underline{\text{val}}\ x{:}s\rangle \mid \langle \underline{\text{name}}\ v{:}s\rangle \mid \underline{\text{if}}\ b\ \underline{\text{then}}\ s_1\ \underline{\text{else}}\ s_2\ \underline{\text{fi}}$$

(We take this syntax in the sense that wherever an arbitrary variable v may appear, also x,... or f,... may appear). The following formulae suggest the typing rules (s^τ is to be read here as: s is of type τ): (i) c^τ, where $\tau = \omega^n \to \omega$, $n \geq 0$ (ii) x^ω, v^τ for any τ), f^τ for $\tau \neq \omega$ (iii) $(s_1^{\tau_1\to\tau_2}(s_2^{\tau_1}))^{\tau_2}$ (iv) $\langle \underline{\text{val}}\ x^\omega{:}\ s^\tau\rangle^{\omega\to\tau}$ (v) $\langle \underline{\text{name}}\ v^{\tau_1}{:}\ s^{\tau_2}\rangle^{\tau_1\to\tau_2}$ (vi) $(\underline{\text{if}}\ b\ \underline{\text{then}}\ s_1^\tau\ \underline{\text{else}}\ s_2^\tau\ \underline{\text{fi}})^\tau$.

Examples

1. Expressions which cannot be typed:
   x(y), v(v), c(x)(f), <val x:s>(f)
2. Expressions which can be typed:
   f(y), c(x)(y), <val x:c>(y), <val x: <name f: f(x)>>(c)(g), $\underline{\text{if}}\ b\ \underline{\text{then}}\ c_0\ \underline{\text{else}}\ c_1(x)(f(c_2(x)))\ \underline{\text{fi}}$

For simplicity's sake, we only treat call-by-value parameters of *ground* type in our language (whereas call-by-name parameters are arbitrary). When confusion is unlikely, we simply use s instead of s^τ.

As further syntactic categories we introduce (b∈) *Bexp* (boolean expressions), (S∈) *Stat* (statements), (D∈) *Decl* (declarations), (P∈) *Prog* (programs), and (e∈) *Sexp* (simple expressions) as follows:

$$b ::= \underline{\text{true}} \mid s_1^\omega = s_2^\omega \mid \neg b \mid b_1 \supset b_2$$

$$S ::= x{:=}s \mid S_1;S_2 \mid \underline{\text{if}}\ b\ \underline{\text{then}}\ S_1\ \underline{\text{else}}\ S_2\ \underline{\text{fi}}$$

$$D ::= f_1^{\tau_1} \Leftarrow t_1^{\tau_1}, \ldots, f_n^{\tau_n} \Leftarrow t_n^{\tau_n}, \quad n \geq 0$$

$$P ::= \langle D{:}S\rangle$$

$$e ::= x \mid c(e_1)\ldots(e_n), \quad n \geq 0$$

Some further terminology and explanation about syntax is provided in the

Remarks

1. "≡" will denote syntactic identity
2. <D:S> is usually written as <D|S>
3. An example of a program (for suitably chosen constants) is
   <f ⇐ <<u>val</u> x: <u>if</u> x=0 <u>then</u> y <u>else</u> x*f(x-1) <u>fi</u> | y:=1; z:=f(2)>
4. A variable v^τ is *bound* in a program either by abstraction or (for $\tau \neq \omega$) by appearing on the left-hand side of a function declaration. Var_τ is the set of all variables of type τ. $var_\omega(s)$ denotes the set of all free ground variables of s. $x \in var_\omega(s)$ will sometimes be abbreviated to $x \in s$. Similar notations such as $var_\omega(D,S)$, $var_\tau(s)$, $f \in s$, etc. should be clear. A program $P \equiv \langle D|S\rangle$ is called *closed* whenever $var_\tau(P) = \emptyset$ for $\tau \neq \omega$.
5. In a closed program <D|S>, the only free variables are of ground type. In programming terminology, these are the *globals* of the program. They appear either in the body of function declarations (in t_j, where $D \equiv \langle f_i \Leftarrow t_i\rangle_i$) or in S (e.g., in x := <<u>val</u> u: c(u)(y)>(z), the globals are x, y, z).
6. *Substitution* of t for v in s is denoted by s[t/v]. The usual precautions to avoid clashes between free and bound variables apply.
7. An n-tuple $(s_1)\ldots(s_n)$, $n \geq 0$, is often abbreviated to $\vec{s}_{1:n}$ or to $\vec{s}$. $\vec{s}_{2:n}$ denotes $(s_2)\ldots(s_n)$; also, a notation such as $(y:=s)^{\rightarrow}$ is short for $y_1:=s_1;\ldots;y_n:=s_n$, $n \geq 0$.
8. *Simple* expressions e (are always of ground type and) have no function calls or abstraction; they are therefore essentially simpler than arbitrary expressions, and play a certain "atomic" role in the subsequent considerations.

In the *semantics* we introduce domains $(\phi^\tau \in)\ V_\tau$, for each τ, as follows: let V_0 be some arbitrary set, and let $(\alpha\in)V_\omega = V_0 \cup \{\bot_\omega\}$ be the *flat* cpo of ground values over V_0 (i.e., $\alpha_1 \sqsubseteq \alpha_2$ iff $\alpha_1 = \bot_\omega$ or $\alpha_1 = \alpha_2$). Let $V_{\tau_1\to\tau_2} = [V_{\tau_1} \to V_{\tau_2}]$, i.e., all *continuous* functions $V_{\tau_1} \to V_{\tau_2}$, and let $\bot_\tau$ denote the least element of V_τ (i.e., for $\tau = \tau_1 \to \tau_2$, $\bot_\tau = \lambda\phi^{\tau_1}\cdot\bot_{\tau_2}$). Let $(\beta\in)W = \{ff,tt\} \cup \{\bot_W\}$ be the flat cpo of *truth-values*. Let $\Sigma_0 = Var_\omega \to V_0$, and let $(\sigma\in)\Sigma = \Sigma_0 \cup \{\bot_\Sigma\}$ be the flat cpo of *states*. Let $(\eta^\tau\in)N_\tau = \Sigma \to_s V_\tau$, $\to_s$ denoting *strict* functions, be the cpo ordered by $\eta_1^\tau \sqsubseteq \eta_2^\tau$ iff $\eta_1^\tau(\sigma) \sqsubseteq \eta_2^\tau(\sigma)$ for all σ. Let $(\eta\in)N = \cup_\tau N_\tau$, and let $Var = \cup_\tau Var_\tau$. *Environments* ε are functions: $Var \to N$ which are used primarily to assign meanings either to the variables appearing as parameters in abstraction, or to declared function variables. (Note that $\varepsilon(f) \in N$ in general depends on the state since the meaning of f may be changed by assignment to some global variable, such as "y:=1" in the example of remark 3 above.) For technical reasons, it is convenient to address *all* ground variables through ε. This is achieved by the following definitions:

1. ε is called *normal in* x iff $\varepsilon(x) = \lambda\sigma\cdot\sigma(x)$ (i.e., $\varepsilon(x)(\sigma) = \sigma(x)$: normally, the value of a variable is obtained by applying the state to it)

2. ε is said to *store* x iff $\varepsilon(x) = \lambda\sigma\cdot\alpha$, for some α (i.e., $\varepsilon(x)(\sigma) = \alpha$: α is the value - which may be $\perp_\omega$ - stored for the formal parameter x (see Def. 2.1) and is independent of the state)
3. The set *Env* of environments is defined as
$Env = \{\varepsilon \in Var \to N \mid \varepsilon(Var_\tau) \subseteq N_\tau$, and $\forall x[\varepsilon$ is normal in x or ε stores x$]\}$.
4. ε is called *normal* iff $\varepsilon(x) = \lambda\sigma\cdot\sigma(x)$ for *all* x.

We note that, for ε normal in x, $\varepsilon(x)(\sigma)(= \sigma(x)) \neq \perp_\omega$ is always satisfied for $\sigma \neq \perp_\Sigma$, whereas, if ε stores x, we may have that $\varepsilon(x)(\sigma) = \perp_\omega$, for $\sigma \neq \perp_\Sigma$.

Two further pieces of notation are needed:
1. We shall use $\bar{\lambda}\alpha\cdot\phi^{\omega\to\tau}(\alpha)$ as notation for the *strict* function defined by $\lambda\alpha\cdot$ <u>if</u> $\alpha = \perp_\omega$ <u>then</u> $\perp_\tau$ <u>else</u> $\phi^{\omega\to\tau}(\alpha)$ <u>fi</u>
2. For $\alpha \neq \perp_\omega$ and $\sigma \neq \perp_\Sigma$, $\sigma\{\alpha/x\}$ denotes the state such that

$$\sigma\{\alpha/x\}(y) = \begin{cases}\alpha, & \text{if } x \equiv y\\ \sigma(y), & \text{if } x \not\equiv y\end{cases}$$

. Similarly for $\varepsilon\{\eta/v\}$ etc.

In the denotational semantics we first fix an interpretation J for all c: J: *Cons* $\to (V_\omega \to_s (V_\omega \to_s \dots \to_s (V_\omega \to_s V_\omega)\dots))$. Note that the meaning of a constant is always a *strict* function. As valuation functions for the various syntactic classes we introduce

V: *Exp* $\to$ (*Env* $\to (\Sigma \to_s V))$
W: *Bexp* $\to$ (*Env* $\to (\Sigma \to_s W))$
M: *Stat* $\to$ (*Env* $\to (\Sigma \to_s \Sigma))$
N: *Prog* $\to$ (*Env* $\to (\Sigma \to_s \Sigma))$

(E for *Sexp* is given later). They are defined in

DEFINITION 2.1. (denotational semantics)

a. $V(s^\tau)(\varepsilon)(\perp_\Sigma) = \perp_\tau$, and for $\sigma \neq \perp_\Sigma$,
$V(v)(\varepsilon)(\sigma) = \varepsilon(v)(\sigma)$
$V(c)(\varepsilon)(\sigma) = J(c)$
$V(s_1(s_2))(\varepsilon)(\sigma) = V(s_1)(\varepsilon)(\sigma)(V(s_2)(\varepsilon)(\sigma))$
V(<<u>val</u> x:s>)$(\varepsilon)(\sigma) = \bar{\lambda}\alpha\cdot V(s)(\varepsilon\{\lambda\tilde{\sigma}\cdot\alpha/x\})(\sigma)$
V(<<u>name</u> v:s>)$(\varepsilon)(\sigma) = \lambda\phi\cdot V(s)(\varepsilon\{\lambda\tilde{\sigma}\cdot\phi/v\})(\sigma)$
V(<u>if</u> b <u>then</u> s_1 <u>else</u> s_2 <u>fi</u>)$(\varepsilon)(\sigma) =$
    <u>if</u> $W(b)(\varepsilon)(\sigma)$ <u>then</u> $V(s_1)(\varepsilon)(\sigma)$ <u>else</u> $V(s_2)(\varepsilon)(\sigma)$ <u>fi</u>

b. $W(b)(\varepsilon)(\perp_\Sigma) = \perp_W$, and, for $\sigma \neq \perp_\Sigma$,

$$W(s_1=s_2)(\varepsilon)(\sigma) = \begin{cases}\perp_W, & \text{if } V(s_1)(\varepsilon)(\sigma) = \perp_\omega \text{ or } V(s_2)(\varepsilon)(\sigma) = \perp_\omega\\ V(s_1)(\varepsilon)(\sigma) = V(s_2)(\varepsilon)(\sigma), & \text{otherwise}\end{cases}$$

(other clauses are simple and omitted)

c. $M(x{:=}s)(\varepsilon)(\sigma) =$ <u>if</u> $V(s)(\varepsilon)(\sigma) = \perp_\omega$ <u>then</u> $\perp_\Sigma$ <u>else</u> $\sigma\{V(s)(\varepsilon)(\sigma)/x\}$ <u>fi</u>
$M(S_1;S_2)(\varepsilon)(\sigma) = M(S_2)(\varepsilon)(M(S_1)(\varepsilon)(\sigma))$

$M(\underline{\text{if}}\ b\ \underline{\text{then}}\ S_1\ \underline{\text{else}}\ S_2\ \underline{\text{fi}})(\varepsilon)(\sigma) =$

$\underline{\text{if}}\ W(b)(\varepsilon)(\sigma)\ \underline{\text{then}}\ M(S_1)(\varepsilon)(\sigma)\ \underline{\text{else}}\ M(S_2)(\varepsilon)(\sigma)\ \underline{\text{fi}}$

d. $N(<<f_i \Leftarrow t_i>_i \mid S>)(\varepsilon)(\sigma) = M(S)(\varepsilon\{\eta_i/f_i\}_i)(\sigma)$, where $<\eta_1,\ldots,\eta_n> = \mu[H_1,\ldots,H_n]$, and $H_j = \lambda\eta_1'\cdot\ldots\cdot\lambda\eta_n'\cdot V(t_j)(\varepsilon\{\eta_i'/f_i\}_i)$, $j = 1,\ldots,n$.

Remarks.

1. Note that the assignment is strict in the value of its right-hand side. Call-by-value abstraction is strict as well; this observation forms the starting point for the simplification of the next section.
2. It can be shown that $V(s^\tau)(\varepsilon)(\sigma) \in V_\tau$.
3. $\mu[H_1,\ldots,H_n]$ in clause d denotes the simultaneous least fixed point of the operators $H_1,\ldots,H_n$; its existence follows from the continuity of each of the H_j, $j = 1,\ldots,n$.

3. SIMPLIFICATION

We first observe that an analysis of the structure of the expressions s^ω yields that each assignment $x := s^\omega$ is one of the following forms.

1. $x := e$
2. $x := c\vec{s}_{1:n}$ $(n\geq 1)$, not all s_i simple
3. $x := f\vec{s}_{1:n}$ $(n\geq 1)$,
4. $x :=$ <u><val</u> $x':s_0>\vec{s}_{1:n}$ $(n\geq 1)$,
5. $x :=$ <u><name</u> $v:s_0>\vec{s}_{1:n}$ $(n\geq 1)$,
6. $x :=$ <u>if</u> b <u>then</u> s' <u>else</u> s" <u>fi</u> $\vec{s}_{1:n}$ $(n\geq 0)$.

Moreover, we recall that, in 2, all the s_i are of ground type, and in 4 s_1 is of ground type.

We next define the notion of a *simple* statement T by:

$$T ::= x{:=}e \mid x{:=}f\vec{s} \mid T_1;T_2 \mid \underline{\text{if}}\ e_1{=}e_2\ \underline{\text{then}}\ T_1\ \underline{\text{else}}\ T_2\ \underline{\text{fi}}$$

(Essentially, in a simple statement we have eliminated abstraction outside the arguments of function variables.) We now present a system of reduction rules allowing us to reduce each statement to an equivalent (but for the values of certain auxiliary variables) simple statement. Let us call the reduction system RS_1. It has the rules

1. $x{:=}c\vec{s} \rightsquigarrow (y{:=}s)^{\to}; x{:=}c\vec{y}$, not all s_i simple
2. $x{:=}$<u><val</u> $x':s_0>\vec{s} \rightsquigarrow y{:=}s;\ x{:=}s_0[y/x']\vec{s}_{2:n}$
3. $x{:=}$<u><name</u> $v:s_0>\vec{s} \rightsquigarrow x{:=}s_0[s_1/v]\vec{s}_{2:n}$
4. $x{:=}$<u>if</u> b <u>then</u> s' <u>else</u> s" <u>fi</u> $\vec{s} \rightsquigarrow$ <u>if</u> b <u>then</u> $x{:=}s'\vec{s}$ <u>else</u> $x{:=}s''\vec{s}$ <u>fi</u>
5. <u>if</u> <u>true</u> <u>then</u> S_1 <u>else</u> S_2 <u>fi</u> $\rightsquigarrow S_1$
6. <u>if</u> $\neg b$ <u>then</u> S_1 <u>else</u> S_2 <u>fi</u> $\rightsquigarrow$ <u>if</u> b <u>then</u> S_2 <u>else</u> S_1 <u>fi</u>
7. <u>if</u> $b_1 \supset b_2$ <u>then</u> S_1 <u>else</u> S_2 <u>fi</u> $\rightsquigarrow$
   <u>if</u> b_1 <u>then</u> <u>if</u> b_2 <u>then</u> S_1 <u>else</u> S_2 <u>fi</u> <u>else</u> S_1 <u>fi</u>

8. $\underline{\text{if}}\ s_1=s_2\ \underline{\text{then}}\ S_1\ \underline{\text{else}}\ S_2\ \underline{\text{fi}} \rightsquigarrow$
$y_1:=s_1;\ y_2:=s_2;\ \underline{\text{if}}\ y_1=y_2\ \underline{\text{then}}\ S_1\ \underline{\text{else}}\ S_2\ \underline{\text{fi}}$, not all s_i simple

In rule 1 all (ground) arguments of a function constant are evaluated and stored in auxiliary variables. $x:=c\vec{y}$ is an assignment with a *simple* right-hand side, and the s_i are to be subjected to further reduction. Rule 2 expresses call-by-value through assignment. Rule 3 deals with call-by-name through substitution (it is the rule of β- conversion of the lambda calculus). Rules 4 to 8 are self-explanatory. In subsequent applications of RS_1, we shall employ it in the context of a declaration D. We shall then impose upon the y_i the constraints that, in each of the rules 1, 2, and 8 we have:

(i) all y_i are different and do not appear free on the left-hand side of the rule.
(ii) none of the y_i appears free in D.

THEOREM 3.1.

a. The reduction system RS_1 always terminates transforming each statement S to some simple T.
b. In case restrictions (i), (ii) on the choice of the y_i are imposed, T is equivalent to S, but for the values of the auxiliary variables.

Proof. An outline of the proof of part a can be found in the Appendix. The problem is nontrivial since induction on the syntactic complexity of s (in x:=s) does not work directly (because of rule 3), and a suitable means for bringing the type structure into the picture has to be found. The proof of part b is implicit in the considerations of Section 4. □

4. OPERATIONAL SEMANTICS AND THE EQUIVALENCE THEOREM

In the operational semantics we start from the evaluation of simple expressions through the valuation function E: $Sexp \to (\Sigma_0 \to V_0)$ defined by $E(x)(\sigma) = \sigma(x)$, $E(c(e_1)\ldots(e_n))(\sigma) = J(c)(E(e_1)(\sigma))\ldots(E(e_n)(\sigma))$. Next, following the approach of Cook [9], we define a (partial) function C: $Prog \to_{part} (\Sigma \to \Sigma^\infty)$, where $\Sigma^\infty = \Sigma^* \cup \Sigma^\omega$, the set of all finite or infinite sequences of states. In the definition we use "$^\frown$" for concatenation of sequences (on the right-hand side of an infinite sequence it has no effect) and κ: $\Sigma^\infty \to \Sigma$ for the function yielding the last element of a sequence if it exists and $\bot_\Sigma$ otherwise. For ρ a sequence in Σ^∞, if $\rho = \langle\sigma_1,\ldots,\sigma_n\rangle \in \Sigma$, then $\rho\{\alpha/y\}$ denotes $\langle\sigma_1,\ldots,\sigma_{n-1}, \sigma_n\{\alpha/y\}\rangle$, and if $\rho \in \Sigma^\omega$ then $\rho\{\alpha/y\} = \rho$.

We now give the rules for $C(\langle D|S\rangle)$. For brevity, we rather write $C_D(S)$:

DEFINITION 4.1. (computation sequences)

1. $C_D(S)(\bot_\Sigma) = \langle\bot_\Sigma\rangle$, and, for $\sigma \neq \bot_\Sigma$,

2a. $C_D(x:=e)(\sigma) = \langle\sigma\{E(e)(\sigma)/x\}\rangle$

b. $C_D(x:=f\vec{s})(\sigma) = \langle\sigma\rangle ^\frown C_D(x:=t\vec{s})(\sigma)$, if $f \Leftarrow t$ occurs in D (otherwise $C_D(x:=f\vec{s})(\sigma)$ is undefined)

c. $C_D(T_1;T_2)(\sigma) = \langle\sigma\rangle^\frown C_D(T_1)(\sigma)^\frown C_D(T_2)(\kappa(C_D(T_1)(\sigma)))$

d. $C_D(\underline{\text{if}}\ e_1{=}e_2\ \underline{\text{then}}\ T_1\ \underline{\text{else}}\ T_2\ \underline{\text{fi}})(\sigma) = \begin{cases} \langle\sigma\rangle^\frown C_D(T_1)(\sigma), & \text{if } E(e_1)(\sigma) = E(e_2)(\sigma) \\ \langle\sigma\rangle^\frown C_D(T_2)(\sigma), & \text{if } E(e_1)(\sigma) \neq E(e_2)(\sigma) \end{cases}$

3. $C_D(S)(\sigma) = \langle\sigma\rangle^\frown C_D(S')(\sigma)\{\sigma(y_i)/y_i\}_i$, for each rule $S \rightsquigarrow S'$ of the system RS_1, where $y_1,\ldots,y_n$, $n \geq 0$, are the auxiliary variables introduced in that rule (for uniqueness, we assume that the first y_i satisfying restrictions (i), (ii) are chosen).

Remark. In clause 3, the auxiliary variables - after having served their purpose as temporary storage - are reset to their original values by the modification $\{\sigma(y_i)/y_i\}_{i=1}^n$.

LEMMA 4.2. The system of equations for C_D given in Definition 4.1 has a unique solution.

Proof. The proof combines the techniques as described in De Bruin [6] with some ideas from the termination proof for RS_1. □

DEFINITION 4.3. The operational semantics O: $Prog \to_{part} (\Sigma \to_s \Sigma)$ is defined by $O(\langle D|S\rangle) = \kappa \circ C_D(S)$.

Again, we shall often write $O_D(S)$ for $O(\langle D|S\rangle)$. The denotational and operational semantics for closed programs coincide. In order to prove this, some auxiliary notions and results are necessary, some of which also play a part in subsequent sections. (For some background concerning the notion "does not use" see De Bakker [4].)

LEMMA 4.4. (first substitution lemma)

a. $V(s[t/f])(\varepsilon) = V(s)(\varepsilon\{V(t)(\varepsilon)/f\})$

b. $V(s[t/v])(\varepsilon) = \lambda\sigma\cdot V(s)(\varepsilon\{\lambda\tilde{\sigma}\cdot V(t)(\varepsilon)(\sigma)/v\})(\sigma)$

Remark. Note that using v instead of f in part a would (for v of ground type) not be well-formed because of the definition of *Env*.

DEFINITION 4.5.

a. A function η *does not use* x iff for all σ, $\alpha \neq \bot_\omega$, $\eta(\sigma\{\alpha/x\}) = \eta(\sigma)$

b. ε does not use x iff $\varepsilon(f)$ does not use x for all f.

LEMMA 4.6. Let $D = \langle f_i \Leftarrow t_i\rangle_i$, and let η_i be as in Def. 2.1.

a. If $x \notin D$, s and ε does not use x then $V(s)(\varepsilon\{\eta_i/f_i\}_i)$ does not use x.

b. Let $\langle D|s\rangle$ be closed. If $x \notin D$, s then $V(s)(\varepsilon\{\eta_i/f_i\}_i)$ does not use x.

Remark. By way of explanation of clause b we observe that a function which is the meaning of an expression *uses* a variable only if it occurs in the expression directly or indirectly (i.e., as a global of a function procedure called in the expression).

LEMMA 4.7. (second substitution lemma)

a. $V(s[y/x])(\varepsilon)(\sigma\{\alpha/y\}) = V(s)(\varepsilon\{\lambda\tilde{\sigma}\cdot\alpha/x\})(\sigma)$, provided that $y \notin var_\omega(s)\setminus\{x\}$, ε is *normal* in x, y and ε does not use y.

b. $V(s[t/x])(\varepsilon)(\sigma) = V(s)(\varepsilon)(\sigma\{V(t)(\varepsilon)(\sigma)/x\})$ provided that ε is normal in x and ε does not use x.

We now exhibit a series of facts leading to the equivalence theorem. We always assume that $D \equiv \langle f_i \Leftarrow t_i\rangle_i$.

LEMMA 4.8. For $\langle D|S\rangle$ closed and ε normal, $O_D(S) \sqsubseteq N_D(S)(\varepsilon)$.

Proof. Induction on the length of the computation sequence used (by $C_D(S)$) to determine $O_D(S)$.

The reverse inclusion takes more effort and is proved in a number of steps. Assume again that $\langle D|S\rangle$ is closed and ε normal. We introduce some auxiliary syntax. For each τ, let Ω^τ be the nowhere defined expression (i.e., $V(\Omega^\tau)(\varepsilon)(\sigma) = \bot_\tau$, and $C_D(x{:=}\Omega^{\tau\to}s)(\sigma) = \langle\bot_\Sigma\rangle$). With respect to D we define $S^{(j)}$ and $S^{[j]}$, $j = 0,1,\ldots$:
Notation. $S^{(0)} \equiv S$, $S^{(j+1)} \equiv S^{(j)}[t_i/f_i]_i$, $S^{[j]} \equiv S^{(j)}[\Omega/f_i]_i$, $j = 0,1,\ldots$. Let $\varepsilon_k = \varepsilon\{\eta_i^k/f_i\}_i$, $k = 0,1,\ldots$, where $\eta_i^0 = \bot$, $\eta_j^{k+1} = V(t_j)(\varepsilon\{\eta_i^k/f_i\}_i)$, $j = 1,\ldots,n$. For η_i as in Def. 2.1, by continuity we have that $\eta_i = \bigsqcup_k \eta_i^k$, $i = 1,\ldots,n$.

Step

1. $N_D(S)(\varepsilon) = M(S)(\varepsilon\{\eta_i/f_i\}_i)$ (def. 2.1)
2. $M(S)(\varepsilon\{\eta_i/f_i\}_i) = \bigsqcup_k M(S)(\varepsilon_k)$ (continuity)
3. $M(S)(\varepsilon_k) = M(S^{[k]})(\varepsilon)$ (lemma 4.4)
4. $M(S^{[k]})(\varepsilon) \sqsubseteq O_D(S^{[k]})$
   This uses induction on the norm of $S^{[k]}$ as introduced in the Appendix, and the requirement that ε be normal. Note that, since $\langle D|S\rangle$ is closed, $S^{[k]}$ does not contain free function variables (for $\tau \neq \omega$, $var_\tau(S) \subseteq \{f_1,\ldots,f_n\}$; hence, $var_\tau(S^{[k]}) = \emptyset$).
5. If $O_D(S^{[k]})(\sigma) = \sigma' \neq \bot_\Sigma$, then $O_D(S^{(k)})(\sigma) = \sigma'$.
   This is a familiar argument, cf. the "genericity" result of Barendregt [5]. E.g., if $x{:=}s[\Omega/f] \equiv x{:=}\ldots\Omega\ldots$, for input σ yields output $\sigma' \neq \bot_\Sigma$, then Ω is not encountered during execution of s (it never appears in the head position), and execution of $x{:=}\ldots\Omega\ldots$may just as well be replaced by execution of $x{:=}s \equiv x{:=}\ldots f\ldots$
6. $O_D(S^{(k)}) = O_D(S)$.
   This is the fixed point property of (recursively declared) function procedures. A special case is that $O_D(x{:=}s[t/f]) = O_D(x{:=}s)$, for $f \Leftarrow t$ in D.

Combining steps 1 to 6 we obtain that $N_D(S)(\varepsilon) \sqsubseteq O_D(S)$; together with Lemma 4.8 this yields

THEOREM 4.9. For $\langle D|S\rangle$ closed and ε normal, $N_D(S)(\varepsilon) = O_D(S)$.

5. CORRECTNESS AND A SOUND PROOF SYSTEM

We are interested in proving facts such as

$$\models \langle f \Leftarrow \underline{val}\ x\colon \underline{if}\ x=0\ \underline{then}\ 1\ \underline{else}\ x*f(x-1)\ \underline{fi} \mid \{x=3\}y:=f(x)\{y=6\}\rangle.$$

Note that in this example a postcondition $y = f(3)$, though trivially true, would not be particularly helpful. In order to avoid this phenomenon (assertions with unevaluated function calls), we restrict ourselves to assertions with only *simple* expressions (no function calls, and no abstraction either). The class $(p,q,r\in)$ *Assn* is defined by

$$p ::= \underline{true}\ |e_1=e_2|\neg p|p_1\supset p_2|\exists x[p]$$

The valuation T: *Assn* $\to (\Sigma\to_s\{tt,ff\})$ is defined by $T(p)(\bot_\Sigma) = ff$, and, for $\sigma \neq \bot_\Sigma$, $T(e_1=e_2)(\sigma) = (E(e_1)(\sigma) = E(e_2)(\sigma)),\ldots$ (the other clauses are obvious). A *correctness formula* is a construct of the form $\langle D|F_1\Rightarrow F_2\rangle$, where F_1, F_2 are conjunctions of assertions and triples $\{p\}S\{q\}$. An example is the rule of consequence $\langle D|(p\supset p_1)\wedge\{p_1\}S\{q_1\}\wedge \wedge(q_1\supset q)\Rightarrow\{p\}S\{q\}\rangle$. $\langle D|F\rangle$ abbreviates $\langle D|\underline{true}\Rightarrow F\rangle$. Correctness formulae contain D to provide declarations for the (functions called in the) S appearing in them. The "$\Rightarrow$" formalism leads to a system in the style of Gentzen's "sequent calculus" (rather than Gentzen's natural deduction) to deal with recursion. Further explanation of this can be found e.g. in Apt [1] or De Bakker [4]. For the definition of validity we first provide a valuation F, assigning meaning to $\{p\}S\{q\}$ in the usual manner:

$$F(\{p\}S\{q\})(\varepsilon)(\sigma) = \forall\sigma'[T(p)(\sigma) \wedge \sigma' = M(S)(\varepsilon)(\sigma) \wedge \sigma' \neq \bot_\Sigma \Rightarrow T(q)(\sigma')].$$

In case we want to stress that F depends on J (the interpretation of the constants), we write F_J. We then put $\models_J \langle D|F_1\Rightarrow F_2\rangle$ iff for all normal ε such that ε uses no (ground) variables not in D.

$$\forall\sigma \neq \bot[F_J(F_1)(\varepsilon\{\eta_i/f_i\}_i)(\sigma)] \Rightarrow \forall\sigma \neq \bot[F_J(F_2)(\varepsilon\{\eta_i/f_i\}_i)(\sigma)],$$

where the η_i are as in Def. 2.1.

The restrictions on ε firstly imply that all free ground variables of D, F_1, F_2 are treated as normal variables ($\varepsilon(x)(\sigma) = \sigma(x)$, for all x); moreover, for all f, $\varepsilon(f)$ uses only variables in D. For f declared in D, this is to be expected; for f undeclared (a situation stemming from the proof rule for recursion) it has to be postulated for reasons explained in Chapter 5 of De Bakker [4].

Usually, J is understood, and we simply write $\models$ instead of $\models_J$. For simplicity's sake, in the remainder of the paper we always assume $D \equiv f \Leftarrow t$ to consist of the declaration of only one function procedure.

The proof system for partial correctness has three groups of rules. Group I has the obvious rules for "$\Rightarrow$" such as, e.g., transitivity of "$\Rightarrow$" or the fact that $\langle D|F\Rightarrow F_1\rangle$ and $\langle D|F\Rightarrow F_2\rangle$ imply that $\langle D|F\Rightarrow F_1\wedge F_2\rangle$. Group II is the central one. It has two subgroups, one providing a rule for each simple statement, one based on the simplification rules:

II a.1. $\langle D|\{p[e/x]\}x:=e\{p\}\rangle$ (assignment)

2. $\dfrac{\langle D \mid \{p\}x:=g\vec{s}\{q\} \Rightarrow \{p\}x:=t[g/f]\vec{s}\{q\}\rangle}{\langle D \mid \{p\}x:=f\vec{s}\{q\}\rangle}$ with $g \notin D, \vec{s}$. (recursion)

3. $\langle D \mid \{p\}S_1\{q\} \wedge \{q\}S_2\{r\} \Rightarrow \{p\}S_1;S_2\{r\}\rangle$ (composition)

4. $\langle D \mid \{p\wedge(e_1=e_2)\}S_1\{q\} \wedge \{p\wedge(e_1\neq e_2)\}S_2\{q\}$
$\Rightarrow \{p\}$ <u>if</u> $e_1=e_2$ <u>then</u> S_1 <u>else</u> S_2 <u>fi</u> $\{q\}\rangle$ (conditionals)

b. $\langle D \mid \{p\}S'\{q\} \Rightarrow \{p\}S\{q\}\rangle$ (simplification)

where $S \rightsquigarrow S'$ is one of the rules of the system RS_1, and the choice of the auxiliary $\vec{y}$ is further restricted by (iii) none of the $\vec{y}$ occurs free in p or q.

III In the third group, we find a number of auxiliary rules. Besides the already mentioned rule of consequence, it consists of

$\langle D \mid \{p\}S\{q_1\} \wedge \{p\}S\{q_2\} \Rightarrow \{p\}S\{q_1;q_2\}\rangle$ (conjunction)

$\langle D \mid \{p\}x:=s\{p\}\rangle$, provided that $x \notin p$ (invariance)

$\langle D \mid \{p\}x:=s\{q\} \Rightarrow \{p[z/y]\}x:=s\{q\}\rangle$ (substitution, I)
provided that $y \equiv z$ or $y \notin D,s,q$

$\langle D \mid \{p\}x:=s\{q\} \Rightarrow \{p[y/x]\}y:=s[y/x]\{q[y/x]\}\rangle$ (substitution, II)
provided that $x \equiv y$ or $x \notin D$, $y \notin q$

$\langle D \mid \{p\}x:=s\{q\} \Rightarrow \{p[e/y]\}x:=s[e/y]\{q[e/y]\}\rangle$ (substitution, III)
provided $y \not\equiv x$, $y \notin D$, $x \notin e$.

Remark. Note that, in IIa.1, $\langle D \mid \{p[s/x]\}x:=s\{p\}\rangle$ would not work since, in general, $p[s/x]$ is not a well-formed assertion.

THEOREM 5.1. The proof system is sound.

Proof. For the rules of group I this is obvious. For IIa, the assignment axiom follows from $T(p[e/x])(\sigma) = T(p)(\sigma\{E(e)(\sigma)/x\})$, together with $V(e)(\varepsilon)(\sigma) = E(e)(\sigma)$, for ε normal. The recursion rule is a form of Scott's induction (see, e.g., [4]). The composition and conditionals rules are clear. As to group IIb, if $S \rightsquigarrow S'$ is in RS_1, then, by the definition of O_D, we have that $O_D(S) = O_D(S')$, but for the values of $\vec{y}$; hence, for all normal ε, $N_D(S)(\varepsilon) = N_D(S')(\varepsilon)$ (but for ...) and, since the $\vec{y}$ do not occur in p, q, the desired result follows. The rules of group III are partly easy, partly require somewhat tedious manipulations with the substitution lemmas of Section 4 (for related - though not identical - techniques we refer again to De Bakker [4]).

6. COMPLETENESS FOR CALL-BY-VALUE

We consider the language as introduced in Section 2, but restricted by omitting the clause s::=...|<<u>name</u> v:s>|..., i.e., we now only allow call-by-value abstraction, and accordingly restrict the type of all expressions s^τ to $\tau = \omega^n \rightarrow \omega$, $n \geq 0$. The proof system of the previous section - with a few small modifications - can then be shown to be *complete* without too much effort. We first remark that when call-by-value is the only abstraction mechanisms all functions $V(s)(\varepsilon)(\sigma)$ are strict (i.e., $V(s^{\tau})(\varepsilon)(\sigma)(\vec{\alpha}) = \bot_{\tau}$ as soon as any of the α_i equals $\bot_{\omega}$), provided $\varepsilon(g)(\sigma)$ is strict for all free g. We omit the easy proof of this. We now consider the proof system of Section 5, modified as follows:

1. We first replace reduction system RS_1 by RS_{cbv}:
   (i) remove the rule dealing with call-by-name
   (ii) add a rule
   $x{:=}f\vec{s} \rightsquigarrow (y{:=}s)^{\rightarrow};\ x{:=}f\vec{y}$, not all $\vec{s}$ simple, where the $\vec{y}$ satisfy the restrictions (i), (ii) and (iii) mentioned before.

   After a corresponding adaptation of the notion of simple statement:

   $T ::= x{:=}e \mid x{:=}f\vec{e} \mid T_1;T_2 \mid$ <u>if</u> $e_1{=}e_2$ <u>then</u> T_1 <u>else</u> T_2 <u>fi</u>

   it can be shown that, with the use of RS_{cbv}, each statement (with only call-by-value) can be reduced to an equivalent (but for the values of the $\vec{y}$) simple statement (see the Appendix).
2. Rule IIa.2 (recursion) is simplified to

   $$\frac{\langle D \mid \{p\}x{:=}g\vec{e}\{q\} \Rightarrow \{p\}x{:=}t[g/f]\vec{e}\{q\}\rangle}{\langle D \mid \{p\}x{:=}f\vec{e}\{q\}\rangle},\quad g \notin D$$

   Also, rules IIb now refer to the reduction system RS_{cbv}.

Before we can state the completeness theorem, we have to introduce the usual expressibility notion: The interpretation J is *expressive* with respect to the languages *Prog* and *Assn*, provided that for each closed program $P \equiv \langle D|S\rangle$, each p, and each normal ε the following holds:

1. There exists an assertion q (the *weakest precondition* wp(P,p)) such that, for all σ,
   $T(q)(\sigma) \iff \forall\sigma'[\sigma'{=}N(P)(\varepsilon)(\sigma) \wedge \sigma' \neq \bot_{\Sigma} \Rightarrow T(p)(\sigma')]$
2. There exists an assertion r (the *strongest postcondition* sp(p,P)) such that, for all σ,
   $T(r)(\sigma) \iff \exists\sigma'[T(p)(\sigma') \wedge \sigma{=}N(P)(\varepsilon)(\sigma')]$

(By a remark of Olderog, it is actually sufficient to postulate either 1 or 2.)

The following lemma on sp will be needed below:

LEMMA 6.1. For all σ

a. $T(sp(p,\langle D|x{:=}s\rangle)[y/x])(\sigma) = T(sp(p[y/x],\langle D|y{:=}s[y/x]\rangle)(\sigma)$,
   provided that $x \equiv y$ or $x \notin D$, $y \notin p,D,s$.
b. $T(sp(p,\langle D|x{:=}s\rangle)[e/y])(\sigma) = T(sp(p[e/y],\langle D|x{:=}s[e/y]\rangle)(\sigma)$,
   provided that $y \not\equiv x$, $y \notin D$, $x \notin e$.

Now let us extend the proof system described above with all formulae $\langle D|p\rangle$ such that $\models_J \langle D|p\rangle$ (i.e., all J-valid assertions are taken as axioms), and let $\vdash_J$ denote provability in this extended system. We then have

THEOREM 6.2. (completeness theorem for call-by-value) For each closed $\langle D|S\rangle$, and expressive J, if $\models_J \langle D|\{p\}S\{q\}\rangle$ then $\vdash_J \langle D|\{p\}S\{q\}\rangle$.

The proof uses the notion of most general formula of Gorelick [11]. Let $D \equiv f \Leftarrow t$, let $u, u_0, \vec{u}_{1:n}$ be different ground variables not appearing in D, and let $r(u,u_0,\vec{u}) \overset{df.}{\equiv} sp\ (u=u_0, \langle D|u:=f\vec{u}\rangle)$. Next, let $F_0 \overset{df.}{\equiv} \{u=u_0\}u:=g\vec{u}\{r(u,u_0,\vec{u})\}$ for some arbitrary g. We first assert the

LEMMA 6.3. If $\models \langle D|\{p\}S\{q\}\rangle$, and g arbitrary, then $\vdash \langle D|F_0 \Rightarrow \{p\}S[g/f]\{q\}\rangle$.

Proof. Assume $\models \langle D|\{p\}S\{q\}\rangle$.

a. By Section 3 and the definition of the proof system there exists some simple T such that $\models \langle D|\{p\}T\{q\}\rangle$ and $\vdash \langle D|\{p\}T[g/f]\{q\} \Rightarrow \{p\}S[g/f]\{q\}\rangle$.

b. We now prove that (*): for all simple T, if $\models \langle D|\{p\}T\{q\}\rangle$ then $\vdash \langle D|F_0 \Rightarrow \{p\}T[g/f]\{q\}\rangle$. Together with part a, this will establish the desired result. The proof of (*) is by induction the complexity of T. If T is not of the form $x:=f\vec{e}$, the result is easy. Otherwise, we follow the argument as described in [1,4]. □

We now finish the proof of the completeness theorem as follows: By the definition of $r(u,u_0,\vec{u})$ we have $\models \langle D|\{u=u_0\}u:=f\vec{u}\{r(u,u_0,\vec{u})\}\rangle$. Hence, by the fixed point property, $\models \langle D|\{u=u_0\}u:=t\vec{u}\{r(u,u_0,\vec{u})\}\rangle$. By the lemma, we obtain that $\vdash \langle D|F_0 \Rightarrow \{u=u_0\}u:=t[g/f]\vec{u}\{r(u,u_0,\vec{u})\}\rangle$, and, taking $g \not\equiv f$, the recursion rule yields that (**): $\vdash \langle D|F_0\rangle$. By the lemma, assuming $\models \langle D|\{p\}S\{q\}\rangle$, and taking $g \equiv f$, we also obtain $\vdash \langle D|F_0 \Rightarrow \{p\}S\{q\}\rangle$. Together with (**) this yields the desired result $\vdash \langle D|\{p\}S\{q\}\rangle$.

7. THE COMPLETENESS PROBLEM FOR GENERAL ABSTRACTION

We have not been able to find a completeness proof for general abstraction (see also the remarks at the end of this section). However, if we allow both forms of abstraction but restrict *all* types to $\omega^n \to \omega$ $(n \geq 0)$, then we do have a complete system, albeit at the cost of an extension of the language *of the proof system* (i.e., not of the original programming language). The extension is twofold:

1. We introduce an auxiliary assignment statement $x \leftarrow s$, which may be viewed as "non-strict assignment". We allow the modification $\sigma\{\alpha/x\}$ for *any* $\alpha \in V_\omega$ (contrary to the previous situation where $\alpha \neq \bot_\omega$ was required), and put $M(x\leftarrow s)(\varepsilon)(\sigma) = \sigma\{V(s)(\varepsilon)(\sigma)/x\}$. Note that even if evaluation of s does not terminate, a "normal" state ($\neq \bot_\omega$) is delivered (albeit that its value in x equals $\bot_\omega$). Only if x is used subsequently, nontermination of s is observable. Thus, a natural *operational* semantics of this type of assignment seems not feasible. "$\leftarrow$" will be used below to deal with call-by-name (non-strict abstraction), and ":=" to deal with call-by-value (strict abstraction).
2. The class of simple expressions is extended with $e ::= \ldots | \Omega^\omega$; also, for the assertion $p \equiv (e \neq \Omega^\omega)$ we introduce the notation $e\downarrow$. The valuation E is now extended to

E: $Sexp \to (\Sigma \to_s V)$ (instead of $Sexp \to (\Sigma_0 \to V_0)$, as before). Possible evaluations now are $E(x)(\sigma\{\perp_\omega/x\}) = \perp_\omega$, and $E(y)(\sigma\{\perp_\omega/x\}) = \sigma(y)$ for $x \neq y$.

The proof system is modified in the following way:

1. Statements S are as before (but with all s of type $\omega^n \to \omega$).
2. *Intermediate* statements R are defined by

   $R ::= x{:=}e \mid x{\leftarrow}d \mid R_1;R_2 \mid \underline{\text{if}}\ e_1{=}e_2\ \underline{\text{then}}\ R_1\ \underline{\text{else}}\ R_2\ \underline{\text{fi}}$

   Here d is auxiliary construct defined by

   $d ::= e \mid f\vec{e} \mid (R;d)$
3. *Simple* statements T are now defined by

   $T ::= x{:=}e \mid x{\leftarrow}e \mid x{\leftarrow}f\vec{e} \mid T_1;T_2 \mid \underline{\text{if}}\ e_1{=}e_2\ \underline{\text{then}}\ T_1\ \underline{\text{else}}\ T_2\ \underline{\text{fi}}$

Moreover, we introduce two reduction systems RS_2 and RS_3:

RS_2 has rules to simplify S to R:

$x{:=}s \rightsquigarrow y{\leftarrow}s;\ x{:=}y$	s not simple
$x{\leftarrow}c\vec{s} \rightsquigarrow x{\leftarrow}((\vec{y}{:=}\vec{s});c\vec{y})$	not all $\vec{s}$ simple
$x{\leftarrow}f\vec{s} \rightsquigarrow x{\leftarrow}((\vec{y}{\leftarrow}\vec{s});f\vec{y})$	not all $\vec{s}$ simple
$x \leftarrow \langle\underline{\text{val}}\ x':s_0\rangle\vec{s} \rightsquigarrow x{\leftarrow}(y{:=}s_1;\ s_0[y/x']\vec{s}_{2:n})$	
$x \leftarrow \langle\underline{\text{name}}\ x':s_0\rangle\vec{s} \rightsquigarrow x{\leftarrow}(y{\leftarrow}s_1;\ s_0[y/x']\vec{s}_{2:n})$	
$x \leftarrow \underline{\text{if}}\ b\ \underline{\text{then}}\ s'\ \underline{\text{else}}\ s''\ \underline{\text{fi}}\ \vec{s} \rightsquigarrow \underline{\text{if}}\ b\ \underline{\text{then}}\ x{\leftarrow}s'\vec{s}\ \underline{\text{else}}\ x{\leftarrow}s''\vec{s}\ \underline{\text{fi}}$	
(rules 5, 6, 7 of RS_1)	
$\underline{\text{if}}\ s_1{=}s_2\ \underline{\text{then}}\ S_1\ \underline{\text{else}}\ S_2\ \underline{\text{fi}} \rightsquigarrow y_1{\leftarrow}s_1;\ y_2{\leftarrow}s_2;\ \underline{\text{if}}\ y_1{=}y_2\ \underline{\text{then}}\ S_1\ \underline{\text{else}}\ S_2\ \underline{\text{fi}}$	not all $\vec{s}$ simple

(As before, the $\vec{y}$ are assumed to be fresh and not in D.)

RS_3 has rules to simplify R to T:

$$x \leftarrow (y{\leftarrow}d;d') \rightsquigarrow y{\leftarrow}d;\ x{\leftarrow}d'$$

$$x \leftarrow (y{:=}e;d') \rightsquigarrow \underline{\text{if}}\ e{\downarrow}\ \underline{\text{then}}\ y{\leftarrow}e;\ x{\leftarrow}d'\ \underline{\text{else}}\ x{\leftarrow}\Omega\ \underline{\text{fi}}$$

$$x \leftarrow ((R_1;R_2);d) \rightsquigarrow x{\leftarrow}(R_1;(R_2;d))$$

$$x \leftarrow (\underline{\text{if}}\ e_1{=}e_2\ \underline{\text{then}}\ R_1\ \underline{\text{else}}\ R_2\ \underline{\text{fi}};\ d) \rightsquigarrow \underline{\text{if}}\ e_1{=}e_2\ \underline{\text{then}}\ x{\leftarrow}(R_1;d)\ \underline{\text{else}}\ x{\leftarrow}(R_2;d)\ \underline{\text{fi}}$$

Remark. The complications in the systems RS_2, RS_3 are caused by the following phenomenon: The simplification rule

$$x \leftarrow \langle\underline{\text{val}}\ x':s_0\rangle\vec{s} \rightsquigarrow y{:=}s_1;\ x{\leftarrow}s_0[y/x']\vec{s}_{2:n}$$

is not sound, since the right-hand side might (for nonterminating s_1) transform σ to $\perp_\Sigma$ whereas the left-hand side would yield $\sigma\{\perp_\omega/x\}$. This implies that the assignment $y{:=}s_1$ has to be executed only if x is evaluated, and this motivates the introduction of the intermediate d which are first accumulated and then essentially dealt with through the "$e{\downarrow}$" test in rule RS_3, #2.

LEMMA 7.1. Reduction systems RS_2 and RS_3 always terminate, and yield for each S an equivalent (but for the auxiliary variables) intermediate R, and for each R an equivalent T.

The new proof system now has the following rules:

I' As I (in Section 5).

II' a. $<D|\{p[e/x]\}x\leftarrow e\{p\}>$

$<D|\{e\downarrow \supset p[e/x]\}x:=e\{p\}>$

$$\frac{<D|\{p\}x\leftarrow g\vec{e}\{q\} \Rightarrow \{p\}x\leftarrow t[g/f]\vec{e}\{q\}>}{<D|\{p\}x\leftarrow f\vec{e}\{q\}>}, \; g \notin D$$

Composition and conditionals as before

b. All rules from RS_2 and RS_3 are turned into proof rules (in the same manner as was done for RS_1 in Section 5).

III' Obtained from III by replacing everywhere ":=" by "←".

An interpretation J is called expressive with respect to *Prog* and *Assn'* in the usual way, but observe that *Assn'* now contains assertions involving simple expressions including Ω.

THEOREM 7.2. (soundness and completeness). Let $\vdash_J$ be defined as before.

a. For all J, $\vdash_J <D|\{p\}S\{q\}> \Rightarrow \models_J <D|\{p\}S\{q\}>$

b. For expressive J, $\models_J <D|\{p\}S\{q\}> \Rightarrow \vdash_J <D|\{p\}S\{q\}>$.

Proof. Similar to that of Theorem 6.2, using the first two rules of II'a to deal with the two forms of assignment. □

Remark. We do not know whether a complete proof system exists for the case of arbitrary types. By an argument as used in Clarke [7], if we could prove the undecidability of the halting problem for programs in our language interpreted over some *finite* domain, then we could infer incompleteness. However, no such undecidability result is available at present. (Neither do we know whether our language allows an application of Lipton's theorem [18].) It seems rather likely that, as soon as we would extend the language with function procedures *with* side-effects (essentially by extending the syntax of expressions with the clause s::=...|S;s and extending RS_1 with the rule x:=S;s → S;x:=s) then Clarke's simulation argument (using an idea of Jones and Muchnik [15]) could indeed be used to obtain undecidability, thus yielding incompleteness.

APPENDIX TERMINATION OF THE REDUCTION SYSTEMS RS_1, RS_2, RS_3.

Ad RS_1 (see Section 3).

We will describe a proof that every statement can be simplified, using these rules (which as always may be applied inside a 'context'), to a *simple* statement, defined as in Section 3; in such a statement none of the simplification rules can be applied. It is only shown that '*innermost*' simplification always terminates; but in fact one can show that *all* simplifications must terminate (even in a unique result). The proof that innermost simplifications must terminate, is in two parts.

The first part is as follows: assign to every 'redex' statement R (i.e., a statement as in the LHS of the simplification rules) a norm $\{R\} \in \mathbb{N}$ such that the newly created redex statements R' in the RHS of the rules have a *smaller* norm. (The norm of redex statements occurring in S_1, S_2 (as displayed in the rules) does not change during the simplification step.) Then assign to an arbitrary statement S which one wants to simplify, the norm $\{\{S\}\} = <\{R_1\},\ldots,\{R_n\}>$, the 'multi-set' of the norms of all the occurrences of redex statements in S. Now it is easy to see that for an *innermost* simplification step $S \rightsquigarrow S'$ we have $\{\{S\}\} \succ \{\{S'\}\}$, where '$\succ$' is the well-ordering of multisets of natural numbers. Hence every sequence of innermost simplification steps terminates.

The second and more problematic part is to define $\{R\}$. This is done by defining $\{x{:=}s\} = \|s\|$ and $\{\underline{if}\ b\ \underline{then}\ S_1\ \underline{else}\ S_2\ \underline{fi}\} = \|b\|$, where $\|\ \|: Exp \cup Bexp \rightarrow \mathbb{N}$ is a suitable complexity measure (norm) which is to be defined yet. Obviously, we require e.g.:

(1) $\|<\underline{name}\ v{:}s>\vec{s}_{1:n}\| > \|s[s_1/v]\vec{s}_{2:n}\|$;

(2) $\|\underline{if}\ b\ \underline{then}\ s'\ \underline{else}\ s''\ \underline{fi}\ \vec{s}\| > \|b\|, \|s'\vec{s}\|, \|s''\vec{s}\|$;

(3) $\|\neg b\| > \|b\|$; $\|b_1 \supset b_2\| > \|b_1\|, \|b_2\|$,

to name some of the more important requirements. We will define $\|s\|$ and $\|b\|$ by means of the auxiliary reduction system having as set of 'terms' $Exp \cup Bexp$ and as 'reduction' rules:

(i) (λ-reduction) $<\underline{name}\ v{:}s>(s_1) \rightsquigarrow s[s_1/v]$

$<\underline{val}\ x{:}s>(s_1) \rightsquigarrow s[s_1/x]$

(ii) (parallel reduction) $\underline{if}\ b\ \underline{then}\ s_1\ \underline{else}\ s_2\ \underline{fi} \rightsquigarrow s_1$

$\underline{if}\ b\ \underline{then}\ s_1\ \underline{else}\ s_2\ \underline{fi} \rightsquigarrow s_2$

(These rules may be applied inside a 'context'.)

We claim that every reduction in this auxiliary reduction system terminates. Now for $a \in Exp \cup Bexp$, we define: $\|a\| = \Sigma_{a \rightsquigarrow\!\!\!> a'} |a'|$, where $\rightsquigarrow\!\!\!>$ is the transitive reflexive closure of $\rightsquigarrow$, and $|a'|$ is the length of symbols of a' (counting free variables less than other symbols, for a minor technical reason). The effect is that if $a \rightsquigarrow a'$ then $\|a\| > \|a'\|$, hence we obtain (1) and part of (2) above; and (3) and the remaining part of (2) are obtained since if a is a proper subterm of a', then $\|a\| < \|a'\|$, as the definition of $\|a\|$ readily yields.

Of course, $\|a\|$ is only well-defined as a natural number if there are no infinite reductions $a \rightsquigarrow a' \rightsquigarrow a'' \rightsquigarrow \ldots$, i.e., if our claim holds. To establish this *strong* termination property (i.e. *every* reduction sequence in the auxiliary reduction system terminates) constitutes the main problem. A proof of this property is given by the elegant and powerful method of *computability*, which is often used in logic (Proof Theory) to obtain termination results. The method was developed by Tait [22], and independently by some other authors; for more references and some applications, see Troelstra [23].

The termination of RS_{cbv} (see Section 6) follows by the same arguments as used for RS_1.

Ad RS_2 (see Section 7).
Call the LHS of a simplification rule of RS_2 an A-*redex* if it is an assignment $x \leftarrow s$ or $x := s$, and a B-*redex* if it is a conditional statement <u>if</u> b <u>then</u> S_1 <u>else</u> S_2 <u>fi</u>. Note that an A-redex may 'create' a B-redex, and vice versa.

We will measure the complexity of an A-redex by that of s, and of a B-redex by that of the boolean b. So $\{x \leftarrow s\} = \{x := s\} = |s|$ and $\{\underline{\text{if}}\ b\ \underline{\text{then}}\ S_1\ \underline{\text{else}}\ S_2\ \underline{\text{fi}}\} = |b|$ where $|\ |$ denotes the length in symbols.

Now if S is a statement to be simplified by RS_2, define $\{\{S\}\} = <\{R_i\} \mid$ all occurrences of redexes R_i in S>. (Here < > denotes a multiset.) Then it is easy to see that *innermost* simplifications let $\{\{S\}\}$ decrease; hence they must terminate.

One can also show that *all* simplifications in RS_2 terminate, by recognizing RS_2 as a 'regular non-erasing' reduction system in the sense of Klop [16], for which 'weak' and 'strong' termination are equivalent. An alternative, more direct method would be the construction of a more elaborate counting argument.

Ad RS_3 (see Section 7).
Define $|d|_\ell$ as the 'length' of a construct d such that association to the left (w.r.t.;) counts heavier, and assign to $x \leftarrow d$ the norm $\{x \leftarrow d\} = |d|_\ell$. Termination of RS_3 is now easy to prove.

REFERENCES

1. APT, K.R., *Ten years of Hoare's logic, a survey*, in Proc. 5th Scandinavian Logic Symposium (F.V. Jensen, B.H. Mayoh, K.K. Møller, eds.), pp 1-44, Aalborg University Press, 1979 (revised version to appear in ACM TOPLAS).

2. ASHCROFT, E.A., M. CLINT & C.A.R. HOARE, *Remarks on program proving: jumps and functions*, Acta Informatica, <u>6</u>, p. 317, 1976.

3. DE BAKKER, J.W., *Least fixed points revisited*, Theoretical Computer Science, <u>2</u>, pp. 155-181, 1976.

4. DE BAKKER, J.W., *Mathematical Theory of Program Correctness*, Prentice-Hall International, 1980.

5. BARENDREGT, H.P., *The Lambda Calculus, its Syntax and Semantics*, North-Holland, 1981.

6. DE BRUIN, A., *On the existence of Cook semantics*, Report IW 163/81, Mathematisch Centrum, 1981.

7. CLARKE, E.M., *Programming language constructs for which it is impossible to obtain good Hoare-like axiom systems*, J. ACM, <u>26</u>, pp. 129-147, 1979.

8. CLINT, M. & C.A.R. HOARE, *Program proving: jumps and functions*, Acta Informatica, <u>1</u>, pp. 214-224, 1972.

9. COOK, S.A., *Soundness and completeness of an axiom system for program verification*, SIAM J. on Comp., 7, pp. 70-90, 1978.

10. GORDON, M., R. MILNER & C. WADSWORTH, *Edinburgh LCF*, Lecture Notes in Computer Science 78, Springer, 1979.

11. GORELICK, G.A., *A complete axiomatic system for proving assertions about recursive and non-recursive programs*, Technical Report 75, Dept. of Comp. Science, University of Toronto, 1975.

12. HENNESSY, M.C.B., *The semantics of call-by-value and call-by-name in a nondeterministic environment*, SIAM J. on Comp., 9, pp. 67-84, 1980.

13. HENNESSY, M.C.B. & E.A. ASHCROFT, *A mathematical semantics for a nondeterministic typed lambda calculus*, Theoretical Comp. Science, 11, pp. 227-246, 1980.

14. HOARE, C.A.R., *An axiomatic basis for computer programming*, CACM, 12, pp. 576-580, 1969.

15. JONES, N.D. & S.S. MUCHNIK, *Even simple programs are hard to analyze*, JACM, 24, pp. 338-350, 1977.

16. KLOP, J.W., *Combinatory Reduction Systems*, Mathematical Centre Tracts 127, Mathematisch Centrum, 1980.

17. LANGMAACK, H. & E.R. OLDEROG. *Present-day Hoare-like systems for programming languages with procedures: power, limits, and most likely extensions*, in Proc. 7th Coll. Automata, Languages and Programming (J.W. de Bakker & J. van Leeuwen, eds), Lecture Notes in Computer Scence 85, Springer, 1980.

18. LIPTON, R.J., *A necessary and sufficient condition for the existence of Hoare logics*, in Proc. IEEE Symposium Foundations of Computer Science, pp. 1-6, 1977.

19. O'DONNELL, M., *A critique on the foundations of Hoare-style programming logics*, Technical Report, Purdue University, 1980.

20. PLOTKIN, G.D., LCF *considered as a programming language*, Theoretical Comp. Science, 5, pp. 223-256, 1977.

21. REYNOLDS, J.C., *On the relation between direct and continuation semantics*, in Proc. 2nd Coll. Automata, Languages and Programming (J. Loeckx, ed.), pp. 141-156, Lecture Notes in Computer Science 14, Springer, 1974.

22. TAIT, W.W., *Intentional interpretation of functionals of finite type I*, J. Symbolic Logic, 32, pp. 198-212, 1967.

23. TROELSTRA, A.S. et al., *Metamathematical Investigation of Intuitionistic Arithmetic and Analysis*, Lect. Notes in Mathematics 344, Springer, 1973.

A FORMALISM FOR REASONING ABOUT FAIR TERMINATION

- extended abstract -

by

Willem P. de Roever*,
University of Utrecht

Abstract. Fair termination can be expressed, hence reasoned about, in Park's monotone μ-calculus, and the fair weakest precondition operator for boolean guarded do-loops is expressed.

I. Introduction and preliminary remarks

1. Introduction

The use of well-ordered sets to prove termination of programs originates from [Floyd] and remained prominent ever since. After the appearance of nondeterministic and concurrent programming language constructs, the notion of termination was generalized to the notion of liveness [Lamport], which also covers properties such as eventual occurrence of events during program execution. One way of specifying and proving such properties is by applying temporal reasoning [Francez & Pnueli]. This may be formalized by using Temporal Logic [Pnueli], a tool suitable for expressing such eventualities.

Within this framework, one of the more interesting concepts that can be studied is the concept of fairness [GPSS]. However, application of temporal reasoning does not appeal to a direct use of well-foundedness arguments, see e.g. [Lamport & Owicki]. Recently, there is a revival of the interest in such direct appeals, see, e.g. [Apt & Plotkin], generalizing arguments hitherto involving finite nondeterminism to a context of infinite nondeterminism, and [PSL], generalizing sequential well-foundedness arguments to the context of concurrency (using a shared variable model).

A common property of well-foundedness arguments for more complicated types of termination is the use of higher countably infinite ordinals, which can be traced back to [Hitchcock & Park], this in contrast to the fact that for deterministic programs (or programs displaying finite nondeterminism) natural numbers suffice.

----

* The research reported in this paper originated during a visit to the Technion, Haifa, made possible by a grant from its department of Computer Science.

In [Grümberg, Francez, Markowsky & de Roever] a proof rule is presented for fairly terminating guarded do-loops based on a wellfoundedness argument; the rule is applied to several examples, and proved to be sound and complete w.r.t. an operational semantics of computation trees. The rule is related to another rule suggested by Pnueli, Stavi and Lehmann, by showing that the semantic completeness of the [PSL]-rule follows from the completeness of the [GFMdeR]-rule.

The framework in which the completeness results of [GFMdeR] and of [PSL] are obtained is that of set theory. In the present paper we show that fair termination can be expressed, hence reasoned about, in Park's monotone μ-calculus [H&P,Park 80].

In [PSL] three fairness-like notions are introduced:

1. Impartial execution: along infinite computation sequences all moves appear infinitely often (no reference to being enabled or not).
2. Just execution: if along an infinite computation sequence an enabled move eventually becomes continuously enabled, it will be taken eventually.
3. Fair execution: along infinite computation sequences, moves infinitely often enabled are eventually taken.

With each of these notions of fairness a notion of termination can be associated. A guarded loop $*[B_1 \rightarrow S_1 \square \ldots \square B_n \rightarrow S_n]$ fairly (justly, impartially) terminates iff all its infinite computation sequences are not fair (just, impartial).

By restricting the underlying semantics, i.e., the computation sequences, of guarded loops to finite sequences and fair (just, impartial) infinite ones, one can introduce domains of fair (just, impartial) termination w.r.t. to appropriate underlying semantics which generalize the usual notion of domains of termination of loops.

E.g., Dijkstra's random number generator $*[b \rightarrow x := x+1 \square b \rightarrow b := \neg b]$ nowhere terminates necessarily if precondition {b} holds, but it does terminate justly. More examples, also of fair, and not just, termination, are contained in [GFMdeR] and [PSL].

Now the present paper studies the expressibility of fair termination; David Park [Park 81], after hearing about the result presented here, extended it to express just termination.

2. Preliminaries

2.1. For a description of the monotone μ-calculus the reader might consult [H&P, Park 80]. In these papers it is demonstrated that

(i) to study wellfoundedness and nowhere-foundedness arguments one needs least and greatest fixed points of monotone transformations

(ii) the monotone μ-calculus is a natural framework for this study.

Actually, greatest fixedpoints are only a definitional extension of the framework, since $\nu p[\tau(p)]$, denoting the greatest fixed point of a syntactically monotone transformation τ of predicates p (, i.e., p occurs only under an even number of negation signs in τ) can be defined by $\neg\mu p[\neg\tau(\neg p)]$, where $\mu p[\sigma(p)]$ denotes in general the least fixed point of monotone transformation $\sigma(p)$, and "$\neg$" the negation operator.
We assume the reader to be familiar with these results; another source is chapters 7 and 8 of [de Bakker].

2.2. Next we need several notions of predicate transformers. The diamond operator $R \circ p$ was introduced in [deB&deR] and baptised as such some years later by Pratt; let R denote a relation and p a predicate, then $R \circ p(\xi)$ holds iff $\exists \xi'.(\xi,\xi') \in R \wedge p(\xi')$. Its dual, the boxoperator, $R \rightarrow p$, is defined by $\neg R \circ \neg p$. $R \rightarrow p(\xi)$ holds iff $\forall \xi'.(\xi,\xi') \in$ $\in R \Rightarrow p(\xi')$. Also $wp[\![S]\!]q$ will be needed, the weakest precondition operator of statement S w.r.t. postcondition q; $(wp[\![S]\!]q)(\xi)$ holds in some interpretation of S and q iff every computation sequence of S (in that interpretation) starting in ξ, terminates with output satisfying q.
All these notions are described in [de Bakker].

Another convention we assume the reader to be familiar with is that we shall express predicates as "filters", i.e., pairs of subsets of the identity relation Id. That is, with pred: States $\rightarrow$ {true, false} we associate a pair (p,p') with $p(\xi) = \xi$ iff $pred(\xi)$ holds, and $p'(\xi) = \xi$ iff $\neg pred(\xi)$ holds. Let B denote a boolean-expression, and S a relation. Then B; S makes sense as follows: $(B;\ S)(\xi) = \xi'$ iff $B(\xi)$ holds and $S(\xi) = \xi'$. Notice that true $\leftrightarrow (Id,\Omega)$, and false $\leftrightarrow (\Omega,Id)$, with Ω denoting the empty relation; also we shall write true in stead of Id itself.
When occuring in formulae, box and diamond operations have lowest syntactical priority, e.g., $R_1;\ R_2 \Rightarrow p \vee R_3 \circ q$ reads as $(R_1;\ R_2) \Rightarrow (p \vee (R_3 \circ q))$.

2.3. We shall need the language FGC (fair guarded commands), with a similar syntax as ordinary guarded commands, but for <guarded loop> :: = fair *<guarded selection>. The semantics of FGC programs, however, differs from the usual semantics in that only fair execution sequences are considered.

We shall also need ordinary (i.e., not fair) guarded loops $*[B_1 \rightarrow S_1 \square \ldots \square B_n \rightarrow S_n]$.

S_i is enabled in ξ iff $B_i(\xi)$ holds; in the present presentation we assume that $B_i(\xi)$ implies that $S_i(\xi)$ terminates (; in a more general setting we need that $B_i(\xi)$ implies that $S_i(\xi)$ terminates fairly).

Thus, a fairly terminating program has finite computation sequences (terminating ones), and unfair infinite computation sequences, which are excluded using FGC semantics, but may not have infinite fair computation sequences.

II. Expressing fair termination in the monotone μ-calculus

3. Let R_1 and R_2 denote moves (to be interpreted shortly), and R_1^∞ and R_2^∞ denote infinite sequences of these moves. An impartial merge of these two infinite sequences is another infinite sequence consisting of occurrences of R_1 and R_2 s.t. both R_1 and R_2 occur infinitely often in this sequence. Next we interpret R_1 and R_2 as binary relations over some fixed domain D, and ask the question how to characterize those elements ξ of D which serve as inputs to some infinite computation sequence $\xi S_0 \xi_1 S_1 \xi_2 S_2 \ldots \xi_n S_n \ldots$ s.t. $<S_i>_{i=0}^\infty$ is an impartial merge of R_1^∞ and R_2^∞.
This characterization, inspired by David Park, is given by

$$Imp(R_1,R_2) \underset{DEF}{=} \nu p[\mu X[R_1; X \cup Id]\circ R_2 \circ \mu X[R_2; X \cup Id]\circ R_1 \circ p].$$

Here "ν" denotes the greatest fixed point operator of the associated (syntactically monotone) transformation of predicates, and "∘" the diamond operator.

$Imp(R_1,R_2)$ describes the domain of definition of sequences of moves contained in $(R_1^+; R_2^+)^\infty \cup (R_2^+; R_1^+)^\infty$.
Here $\mu X[R_i; X \cup Id]\circ q$ describes the domain of definition of (finite) sequences contained in R_i^*, ending in q. The main technical point in this definition is that $\nu p[R\circ p]$ denotes the domain of definition of infinite repetition of R, cf. [de Bakker].

Now suppose that one starts in state ξ, and that after applying, say, R_1 a finite number of times, possibly finitely often merged with R_2, R_2 is never defined anymore, no matter how many moves R_1 follow. Then $\xi \notin Imp(R_1,R_2)$.

Yet there are conceptions of fairness s.t. ξ would still be contained in the infinite fair merge of R_1 and R_2, namely the notion from [PSL] and defined in §1 by: if π is a (not necessarily infinite) sequence of moves R_1 and R_2, then π is fair iff once move R_i is infinitely often enabled in π, it occurs infinitely often in π, i = 1,2. This conception of fairness is required when reasoning about P- and V-operations and other higher level synchronization constructs s.a. those of Hoare's CSP, cf. [PSL]. We shall express this notion below in the μ-calculus.

First we introduce an auxiliary expression $fair(R_1)\ fin(R_2)$ for the domain of definition of infinite computation sequences of the following kind:

> First R_1 is zero or more times executed, possibly finitely often merged with a finite number of moves R_2. Then a infinite sequence of moves $(R_1;\neg R_2)$ follows, where $\neg R_2$ stands for $\neg(R_2\circ \underline{true})$, i.e. only transitions $\xi\ R_1;\neg R_2\ \eta$ occur s.t. R_1 transforms state ξ into η with R_2 not defined in η.

These sequences are fair since R_2 is only finitely often enabled in the resulting infinite sequences. Their sequences of moves are from $(R_1 \cup R_2)^*\ (R_1\neg R_2)^\infty$.

Let from now on (by abuse of notation) $R^* \underset{DEF}{\equiv} \mu X[R; X \cup Id]$, $R^+ \underset{DEF}{\equiv} \mu X[R; X \cup R]$, $\neg R \underset{DEF}{\equiv} \neg(R \circ \underline{true})$. Then fair (R_1) fin(R_2) is defined by

$$fair(R_1)\ fin(R_2) \underset{DEF}{\equiv} (R_1 \cup R_2)^* \circ \nu p[R_1 \circ \neg R_2 \circ p]$$

Observe that fair(R_1) fin(R_2) is invariant under R_i, $i = 1,2$ (, and hence under $(R_1{}^*R_2{}^*)^*$), i.e.

$$fair(R_1)\ fin(R_2);\ R_i \subseteq R_i;\ fair(R_1)\ fin(R_2).$$

Using the notion of fairness of §1, the domain of definition Fair(R_1,R_2) of the infinite fair merge of R_1 and R_2 is expressed by

$$Fair(R_1,R_2) \underset{DEF}{\equiv} Imp(R_1,R_2) \vee fair(R_1)\ fin(R_2) \vee fair(R_2)\ fin(R_1)$$

i.e., either 1) R_1 and R_2 are both infinitely often enabled and taken,

or 2) after a finite merge of R_1 and R_2, R_2 is never enabled anymore in the remaining computation sequence of R_1 moves,

or 3) after a finite merge of R_1 and R_2, R_1 is never enabled anymore in the remaining computation sequence of R_2 moves.

4. Why are we interested in Fair(R_1,R_2)? Because its complement,

$$\neg Imp(R_1,R_2) \wedge \neg fair(R_1)\ fin(R_2) \wedge \neg fair(R_2)\ fin(R_1)$$

denotes the domain of all finite and unfair infinite computations (as if it where) of the do-loop $*[R_1 \circ \underline{true} \rightarrow R_1 \,\square\, R_2 \circ \underline{true} \rightarrow R_2]$, where unfair means not fair.

In the remainder of this article, when dealing with any kind of boolean guarded loops, i.e. both the fair and the usual kind, resp. $*[\underset{i=1}{\overset{n}{\square}} B_i \rightarrow S_i]$ or $\underline{fair}*[\underset{i=1}{\overset{n}{\square}} B_i \rightarrow S_i]$, we shall assume that $B_i(\xi)$ implies that $S_i(\xi)$ terminates, for simplicity.

Also we use the fact that

$$\nu p[\tau(p)] = \neg \mu p[\neg \tau(\neg p)], \text{ as applied to } \neg Imp(R_1,R_2).$$

Then the domain of all inputs to finite and unfair infinite computations of $*[B_1 \rightarrow S_1 \,\square\, B_2 \rightarrow S_2]$ satisfying predicate q upon output (in case of termination), is expressed by

$$\neg fair(B_1;\ S_1)\ fin(B_2;\ S_2) \wedge \neg fair(B_2;\ S_2)\ fin(B_1;\ S_1) \wedge$$
$$\mu p[(B_1;\ S_1)^* \rightarrow (\neg B_1 \wedge \neg B_2 \rightarrow q) \wedge ((B_2;\ S_2)^+ \rightarrow (\neg B_1 \wedge \neg B_2 \rightarrow q) \wedge (B_1;\ S_1 \rightarrow p))] \quad \ldots (*)$$

This will be proved below. (By abuse of notation, S_i stands for the relation R_i

computed by it.)
Next we remind that the underlying semantics of $\underline{fair}*[\overset{n}{\underset{i=1}{\Box}} B_i \rightarrow S_i]$ is the set of all finite and fair infinite computation sequences of moves $B_1; S_1, \ldots, B_n; S_n$.

The main question now is: How to express $wp[\![\underline{fair}*[B_1 \rightarrow S_1 \Box B_2 \rightarrow S_2]]\!]q$, i.e., the weakest predicate upon inputs guaranteeing that $\underline{fair}*[B_1 \rightarrow S_1 \Box B_2 \rightarrow S_2]$ terminates and all its outputs satisfy q?

__Theorem__ $wp[\![\underline{fair}*[B_1 \rightarrow S_1 \Box B_2 \rightarrow S_2]]\!]q = (*)$

__Proof__

Let us first introduce some abbreviations

$$\begin{aligned}
f_1 &\underset{DEF}{\equiv} fair(B_1; S_1)\ fin(B_2; S_2),\\
f_2 &\underset{DEF}{\equiv} fair(B_2; S_2)\ fin(B_1; S_1),\\
LHS &\underset{DEF}{\equiv} wp[\![\underline{fair}*[B_1 \rightarrow S_1 \Box B_2 \rightarrow S_2]]\!]q\\
RHS &\underset{DEF}{\equiv} \neg f_1 \wedge \neg f_2 \wedge \mu p[(B_1; S_1)* \rightarrow (\neg B_1 \wedge \neg B_2 \rightarrow q) \wedge ((B_2; S_2)^+ \rightarrow\\
&\qquad (\neg B_1 \wedge \neg B_2 \rightarrow q) \wedge (B_1; S_1 \rightarrow p))]
\end{aligned}$$

1) LHS ⇒ RHS should be clear, since our definitions have been set up so as to imply ¬RHS ⇒ ¬LHS.

2) RHS ⇒ LHS

We need some auxiliary results.

As remarked previously, $\neg f_1$ and $\neg f_2$ are invariant under $B_1; S_1$ and $B_2; S_2$.

Hence RHS = RHS_1, where

$$\begin{aligned}
RHS_1 \underset{DEF}{\equiv} \mu p[\neg f_1 \wedge \neg f_2 \wedge ((B_1; S_1)* \rightarrow (\neg B_1 \wedge \neg B_2 \rightarrow q) \wedge \neg f_2 \wedge ((B_2; S_2)^+ \rightarrow\\
(\neg B_1 \wedge \neg B_2 \rightarrow q) \wedge (B_1; S_1 \rightarrow p)))]
\end{aligned}$$

Secondly, let $x(B_1; S_1)*y$ and $(B_1 \wedge \neg B_2)y$ hold. Then $((B_2; S_2)^+ \rightarrow \ldots)y$ and $(\neg B_1 \wedge \neg B_2 \rightarrow q)y$ trivially hold. Hence we restrict ourselves to outputs y of $(B_1; S_1)*$ for which $(\neg B_1 \vee B_2)y$ holds.

Consequently $RHS_1 = \mu p.[RHS_2(p)]$, where

$$\begin{aligned}
RHS_2(p) \underset{DEF}{\equiv} \neg f_1 \wedge \neg f_2 \wedge ((B_1; S_1)*; (\neg B_1 \vee B_2) \rightarrow (\neg B_1 \wedge \neg B_2 \rightarrow q) \wedge\\
\neg f_2 \wedge ((B_2; S_2)^+; (\neg B_2 \vee B_1) \rightarrow\\
(\neg B_1 \wedge \neg B_2 \rightarrow q) \wedge (B_1; S_1 \rightarrow p)))
\end{aligned}$$

Now $\mu p[RHS_2(p)] \Rightarrow LHS$ follows by the least fixed point principle [Park] from $RHS_2(LHS) \Rightarrow LHS$.

We prove the latter by showing that $RHS_2(LHS)(x)$ implies that there exists no computation sequence of $*[B_1 \rightarrow S_1 \Box B_2 \rightarrow S_2](x)$ which is

$\sim\underbrace{\text{either fair and infinite or finite and satisfying } \neg q \text{ upon output}}_{\equiv \text{ condition(C)}}\sim$

Assume $RHS_2(LHS)(x)$.
We distinguish between the following cases:

i) $\nu p[(B_1; S_1)\circ p](x)$ holds.
That is, there exists an infinite computation sequence π of $B_1; S_1$ moves starting in x. By $RHS_2(LHS)(x)$ we have $\neg f_1(x)$, i.e., this infinite computation sequence is necessarily unfair, since $\neg f_1(x)$ expresses that there exists no infinite computation sequence consisting of $B_1; S_1$ and $B_2; S_2$ moves which starts in x with $B_2; S_2$ only finitely often enabled and taken.
Consequently condition(C) is not satisfied by π.

ii) It follows that the remaining computation sequences (if any) contain y s.t. $x(B_1; S_1)^*; (\neg B_1 \vee B_2)y$, i.e. $(\neg B_1 \vee B_2)y$ holds.
It follows from $RHS_2(LHS)(x)$ that either $(\neg B_1 \wedge \neg B_2 \wedge q)y$ holds, and the resulting computation sequence certainly does not satisfy (C), or $B_2(y)$ holds (the point being that $\neg B_1 \vee B_2$ ensures us that one needn't bother about $(B_1 \wedge \neg B_2)y$ holding).
Assume now that $B_2(y)$ holds. Again we distinguish between 2 cases:

iii) $\nu p[(B_2; S_2)\circ p](y)$ holds. Similarly as in case i) this implies the existence of an unfair computation sequence, and again condition(C) is not satisfied.

iv) It follows that all remaining computation sequences (if any) contain z s.t. $x(B_1; S_1)^*; (\neg B_1 \vee B_2)y\ (B_2; S_2)^+; (\neg B_2 \vee B_1)z$
Similarly as in case ii) either $(\neg B_1 \wedge \neg B_2 \wedge q)z$ (with resulting computation sequence not satisfying condition(C)) or $B_1(z)$ holds. Assume the latter.

v) By assumption $B_1(z)$ implies that $S_1(z)$ terminates. Hence it follows from $RHS_2(LHS)(x)$ that there exists u s.t. $z\ B_1; S_1\ u$ and (LHS)u holds. Since (LHS)u implies by definition that there exists no computation sequence starting in u which satisfies condition(C), certainly all remaining computation sequences starting in x either terminate in q or are unfair.

vi) We conclude that $RHS_2(LHS)(x)$ implies that there exists no fair and infinite computation sequence of $*[B_1 \rightarrow S_1 \square B_2 \rightarrow S_2]$ starting in x, and neither a finite one satisfying $\neg q$ upon termination.
Since the unfair execution sequences are excluded when considering <u>fair</u>$*[B_1 \rightarrow S_1 \square B_2 \rightarrow S_2](x)$, steps i) to v) imply that when $RHS_z(LHS)(x)$ holds all computation sequences of <u>fair</u>$*[B_1 \rightarrow S_1 \square B_2 \rightarrow S_2](x)$ terminate satisfying q.

<u>End of proof</u>.

5. <u>Case n ≥ 2.</u>

Next, how does one express $wp[\![\underline{fair}^*[\square_{i=1}^{n} B_i \to S_i]]\!]q$? We need a recurrent scheme of definitions.

$$Imp(R_1, \ldots, R_n) \underset{DEF}{\equiv} \nu p.[\bigvee_{\substack{(i_1, \ldots, i_n) \text{permutation} \\ \text{of } (1, 2, \ldots, n)}} R_{i_1}^+ \circ \ldots R_{i_n}^+ \circ p]$$

$$fair(R_{i_1}, \ldots, R_{i_{n-1}})\, fin(R_{i_n}) \underset{DEF}{\equiv}$$
$$(R_{i_1} \cup \ldots \cup R_{i_n})^* \circ Fair(R_{i_1}; \neg R_{i_n}, \ldots R_{i_{n-1}}; \neg R_{i_n})$$

$$Fair(R_1, \ldots, R_n) \underset{DEF}{\equiv} Imp(R_1, \ldots, R_n) \vee$$
$$\bigvee_{i=1}^{n} fair(R_1, \ldots, R_{i-1}, R_{i+1}, \ldots, R_n)\, fin(R_i)$$

Consequently,

$$\neg Fair(R_1, \ldots, R_n) = \bigwedge_{i=1}^{n} \neg fair(R_1, \ldots, R_{i-1}, R_{i+1}, \ldots, R_n)\, fin(R_i) \wedge$$
$$\mu p[\bigwedge_{\substack{(i_1, \ldots, i_n) \text{permutation} \\ \text{of } (1, \ldots, n)}} (R_{i_1}^+ \to (R_{i_2}^+ \to \ldots (R_{i_n}^+ \to p) \ldots))]$$

And therefore, by generalization of our previous arguments, one has

$$wp[\![\underline{fair}^*[\square_{i=1}^{n} B_i \to S_i]]\!]q = \bigwedge_{i=1}^{n} \neg fair(R_1, \ldots, R_{i-1}, R_{i+1}, \ldots, R_n)\, fin(R_i) \wedge$$
$$\mu p[\![((\bigwedge_{i=1}^{n} \neg B_i) \to q) \wedge \bigwedge_{\substack{(i_1, \ldots, i_n) \text{permutation} \\ \text{of } (1, \ldots, n)}} ((B_{i_1}; S_{i_1})^+ \to ((\bigwedge_{i=1}^{n} \neg B_i) \to q) \wedge$$
$$((B_{i_2}; S_{i_2})^+ \to ((\bigwedge_{i=1}^{n} \neg B_i) \to q) \wedge \ldots ((B_{i_n}; S_{i_n})^+ \to p))) \ldots))].$$

That is, $\xi \in wp[\![\underline{fair}^*[\square_{i=1}^{n} B_i \to S_i]]\!]q$ iff

(i) Upon projecting the indices of moves of a fair finite computation sequence starting in ξ, another sequence (of move indices) is obtained, which is composed of subsequences $i_1^+ \ldots i_n^+$ with $i_1, \ldots i_n$ a permutation of $1, \ldots, n$ which varies in general along the sequence, ending in a subsequence $i_1^+ \ldots i_k^+$, with $i_1, \ldots, i_k$ all different numbers $\in \{1, \ldots, n\}$, $k \geq 0$, s.t. for the original sequence $\bigwedge_{j=1}^{n} \neg B_j \wedge q$ holds at the end.

(ii) For every permutation $i_1, \ldots, i_n$ of $1, \ldots, n$, there exist no finite merge of $[B_{i_j} \to S_{i_j}]$ moves starting in ξ after which <u>both</u> the fact that $\neg B_{i_n}$ holds is an invariant of $[B_{i_1} \to S_{i_1}], \ldots, [B_{i_{n-1}} \to S_{i_{n-1}}]$, <u>and</u> there exists an infinite fair merge of $[B_{i_1} \to S_{i_1}], \ldots, [B_{i_{n-1}} \to S_{i_{n-1}}]$.

6. References

[Apt & Plotkin]: A Cook's tour of countable nondeterminism, proc. ICALP VIII, LNCS 115, 1981.

[de Bakker]: Mathematical Foundations of Program Correctness, Prentice-Hall, 1980.

[de Bakker & de Roever]: A calculus for recursive program schemes, proc. ICALP I, North-Holland, 1973.

[Floyd] : Assigning meaning to programs, J.T. Schwartz (ed.), Math. Aspects of Computer Science, 1967.

[Francez & Pnueli]: A proof method for cyclic programs, Acta Informatica 9, 1978.

[Grümberg, Francez, Makowski & de Roever]: A proof rule for fair termination of guarded commands, Proc. Symposium on Algorithmic Languages, Amsterdam, 1981, North-Holland.

[Hitchcock & Park]: Induction rules and termination, proc. ICALP I, North-Holland, 1973.

[Lamport]: Proving the correctness of multiprocess programs, IEEE-TSE 3, 2, 1977.

[Lamport & Owicki]: Proving liveness properties of concurrent programs, SRI-TR, 1980.

[Park 80]: On the semantics of fair parallellism, LNCS 86, 1980.

[Park 81]: A predicate transformer for weak fair iteration, proc. 6th IBM Symposium on Math. Found. of Computer Science, Hakone, Japan, 1981.

[Pnueli]: The temporal semantics of concurrent programs, TCS, 13, 1, 1981.

[Pnueli, Stavi & Lehmann]: Impartiality, Justice and Fairness: The Ethics of Concurrent Termination, proc. ICALP VIII, LNCS 115, 1981.

KEEPING A FOOT ON THE GROUND
(A POSITION PAPER)

BRENT HAILPERN
IBM T. J. WATSON RESEARCH CENTER
YORKTOWN HEIGHTS, NEW YORK 10598

Much of the progress in the field of programming logics lies in creating new logic systems. How should new systems be judged? If the work presented at this conference is any indication, then logics should be judged by their power (completeness). For example, logic A is better than logic B if logic A can prove everything that logic B can and more. Comparing logics in this manner yields results that may provide insight into the fundamental aspects of programming---just as the equivalence of Turing machines, Post machines, recursively enumerable sets, etc. is fundamental to the study of mechanical computability. I propose, however, that an additional criteria be used to judge the quality of a new programming logic: how easy is it to prove the correctness of programs with this logic?

In this proposal I echo Pnueli and Ben-Ari's (1) proposal to develop "a corpus of formal proofs that can then serve as a body of experimental data upon which further theorizing can be done". They hope that the comparison of two logics would not be that "our logic is more expressive than your logic", but rather that "our proof of algorithm X is more elegant than yours". In other words, a feature that makes a logic more powerful but that confuses the user (programmer, system designer, logician, etc.) is not desirable.

I am not calling for stopping research into more powerful logics---far from it. I do urge, however, that research projects that have devoted all of their effort to developing new logics, should consider trying to verify some "non-trivial" programs with their logics.

There are many domains in the realm of computer science that need the insight that verification can give: network protocols, resource allocation, hardware, and security are examples. The scientists in these fields are highly intelligent individuals, but we cannot expect them to take their time to learn all of our theories in order to decide which is appropriate to their field. Instead, some of us can look for domains---simple areas at first---that are amenable to our techniques. Not only would this benefit those in the field of application, but it might point out some strengths and weaknesses of our techniques.

REFERENCE

(1) Mordechai Ben-Ari and Amir Pnueli. Temporal logic proofs of concurrent programs. Submitted for publication, November, 1980.

FURTHER RESULTS ON PROPOSITIONAL DYNAMIC LOGIC OF NONREGULAR PROGRAMS

D. Harel[*†], A. Pnueli[*] and J. Stavi[†]

Abstract: The main results of this paper are:

(a) The validity problem for PDL with the single additional context-free program $A^{\Delta}(B)A^{\Delta}$, for atomic programs A,B, defined as $\bigcup_{i \geq 0} A^i;B;A^i$, is Π_1^1-complete.

(b) There exists a recursive (but nonregular) one-letter program $L \subseteq A^*$ such that the validity problem for PDL with the single additional program L is Π_1^1-complete.

---

[*] Department of Applied Mathematics, Weizmann Institute of Science , Rehovot, Israel.

[†] Department of Mathematics and Computer Science, Bar-Ilan University, Ramat-Gan, Israel.

1. Introduction

The work described in this paper and its companion [HPS] is motivated by the following remarks, about which more details can be found in [HPS]. Propositional dynamic logic, henceforth PDL, was defined in [FL] following [Pr1] as a logic for reasoning, on a propositional level, about iterative programs. Programs in PDL are members of the set RG of regular expressions over appropriate atomic programs and tests. Denote this standard version of PDL by PDL_{RG}. The main result in [FL] is the decidability (in exponential time, see [Pr2]) of the validity problem for PDL_{RG}.

We are concerned with the validity problem for PDL in which certain nonregular programs are allowed. One reason for this is the well-known correspondence between context-free languages and programs with recursive procedures. In [HPS] we showed that if context-free programs of the simple form $\alpha^{\Delta}(\beta)\gamma^{\Delta}$, for $\alpha,\beta,\gamma \in RG$, are allowed in PDL, with $\alpha^{\Delta}(\beta)\gamma^{\Delta}$ defined as $\bigcup_{i\geq 0} \alpha^i;\beta;\gamma^i$, then the resulting language PDL_K, has a Π^1_1-complete validity problem, i.e., is highly undecidable.

Some questions arising are the following: can one find a single nonregular program L such that $PDL_{RG+\{L\}}$ is undecidable? Π^1_1-complete? is there a nonregular program L over a one letter alphabet such that $PDL_{RG+\{L\}}$ is undecidable? Π^1_1-complete? Conversely, is there any nonregular program L such that $PDL_{RG+\{L\}}$ remains decidable?

The underlying problem, which indeed is left open here, asks for a satisfactory classification of nonregular programs as to their effect on the validity problem for PDL. While no such general results are known at present, we do, however, answer some of the aforementioned questions in this paper.

In Section 2 we provide definitions and preliminaries. These can be skipped by the reader familiar with [HPS]. In Section 3 the main result of [HPS] is strengthened, using a direct encoding into PDL_K of Turing machine computations, to yield the Π^1_1-completeness of PDL with the single additional program $A^{\Delta}(B)A^{\Delta}$ for atomic A and B. The proof can be slightly modified to yield Π^1_1-completeness of PDL with either the single additional program $L = \{ww^R \mid w \in \{A,B\}^*\}$, or both of $A^{\Delta}B^{\Delta}$ and $B^{\Delta}A^{\Delta}$. Here e.g. $A^{\Delta}B^{\Delta}$ abbreviates $A^{\Delta}(\underline{skip})B^{\Delta}$. It is open as to whether adding $A^{\Delta}B^{\Delta}$ alone destroys decidability.

Section 4 is devoted to one-letter programs, i.e., programs $L \subseteq A^*$. We exhibit a particular such program L and show that the addition to PDL of L results also in a Π^1_1-complete validity problem.

2. Preliminaries

Let Π be a set of atomic programs, with $\theta \in \Pi$ the empty program, and let Φ be a set of atomic propositions.

Let $\Sigma' = \Pi \cup \{ P? \mid P \in \Phi\} \cup \{\sim P? \mid P \in \Phi\}$. Let C be a given set of expressions α called programs, each associated with some subset $L_C(\alpha)$ of Σ^*, or $L(\alpha)$ when the context is clear. Throughout we assume that $L(\theta) = \phi$.

The formulas of the propositional dynamic logic of C, denoted PDL_C, are defined as follows:

1) $\Phi \subseteq PDL_C$,

2) if $p,q \in PDL_C$ then $\sim p$, $p \vee q \in PDL_C$,

3) if $p \in PDL_C$ and $\alpha \in C$ then $<\alpha>p \in PDL_C$.

The abbreviations true, false, $\supset$, $\wedge$, $\equiv$ and $[\alpha]p$ are used as usual.

A structure (or model) is a triple $S = (W^S, \pi^S, \rho^S)$, where W^S is a nonempty set of states, $\pi^S : \Phi \to 2^W$ is a satisfiability relation on Φ, and $\rho^S : \Pi \to 2^{W \times W}$ provides a binary relation on W as the meaning of each atomic program in Π. Most often we will omit the superscript of the components of S.

We extend ρ to strings over Σ' as follows,

1) $\rho(\lambda) = \{(u,u) \mid u \in W\}$ (λ the empty string)

2) $\rho(P?) = \{(u,u) \mid u \in \pi(P)\}$

3) $\rho(\sim P?) = \{(u,u) \mid u \notin \pi(P)\}$

4) $\rho(xy) = \rho(x) \circ \rho(y)$ $x,y \in \Sigma'^*$, $\circ$ is the composition operator on binary relations.

The satisfiability relation is defined for all formulas as follows:

1) $u \models P$ iff $u \in \pi(P)$, for $P \in \Phi$,

2) $u \models \sim p$ iff not $u \models p$,

3) $u \models p \vee q$ iff $u \models p$ or $u \models q$

4) $u \models <\alpha>p$ iff $\exists x \in L(\alpha).\ \exists v \in W.$ $(u,v) \in \rho(x)$ and $v \models p$.

Since all our results are negative in nature, they hold also for the more general case where tests $p?$ are allowed for any $p \in PDL_C$. Let RG be the set of regular expressions over Σ'. The reader can easily check that PDL_{RG} coincides with PDL as defined, say in [FL] with the above restriction on tests.

Sets of strings over Σ' are associated with programs in RG as follows:

$L(x) = \{x\}$, for $x \in \Sigma - \{\theta\}$, $L(\theta) = \phi$,

$L(\alpha \cup \beta) = L(\alpha) \cup L(\beta)$

$L(\alpha;\beta) = \{xy \mid x \in L(\alpha),\ y \in L(\beta)\}$

$L(\alpha^*) = (L(\alpha))^* = \bigcup_{i \geq 0} L(\alpha^i)$, where $L(\alpha^0) = \lambda$, and $L(\alpha^{i+1}) = L(\alpha;\alpha^i)$.

A formula $p \in PDL_C$ is valid, denoted $\models p$ if for every structure S and every $u \in W^S$, $u \models p$; p is satisfiable if $\sim p$ is not valid. Hence p is satisfiable if there is a structure S and a state u such that $u \models p$, which we sometimes write $S,u \models p$.

Theorem (See [FL, Prl]): Validity of formulas of PDL_{RG} can be decided in exponential time.

This result should be contrasted with:

Theorem [HPS]: Let $K = RG \cup \{\alpha^{\Delta}(\beta)\gamma^{\Delta} \mid \alpha,\beta,\gamma \in RG\}$, with $L(\alpha^{\Delta}(\beta)\gamma^{\Delta}) = \bigcup_{i\geq 0} L(\alpha^i;\beta;\gamma^i)$.

The validity problem for PDL_K is Π_1^1-complete.

In [HPS] it was actually shown that programs of the form $A^{\Delta}(B)A^{\Delta}$ and $A^{\Delta}(P?)A^{\Delta}$ for some atomic programs A and B and various atomic tests $P?$, suffice for obtaining Π_1^1-completeness. In the next section we use a different technique to show that the single program $A^{\Delta}(B)A^{\Delta}$ actually suffices.

3. $PDL_{RG+\{A^{\Delta}(B)A^{\Delta}\}}$ is Π_1^1-complete

First we show that the existence of certain infinite computations for nondeterministic Turing machines is a Σ_1^1-complete problem. We then reduce this problem to the satisfiability of formulas in $PDL_{RG+\{A^{\Delta}(B)A^{\Delta}\}}$. Let $\{T_m\}_{m\in N}$ be an enumeration of of the (nondeterministic) Turing machines.

Proposition 3.1: The set $G = \{m \mid T_m$, starting on an empty tape, has an infinite computation which repeats its start state infinitely often$\}$ is Σ_1^1-complete.

Sketch of Proof: (in Σ_1^1): Given m, consider the Σ_1^1-formula:

φ_m: $\exists f\ (f(o) = C \wedge \forall x\ \exists y\ g_m(y, f(x), f(x+1)))$, where C encodes the initial empty-tape configuration of T_m, and $g_m(y,v,w)$ is the (recursive) predicate true if y encodes a legal segment of computation of T_m starting at the configuration encoded by v and ending in that encoded by w, and, moreover, the states in both v and w are the start state of T_m. Clearly, φ_m is true iff $m \in G$.

(Complete in Σ_1^1): Consider formulas of the form

φ: $\exists f(f(o) = 1 \wedge \forall x\ \exists y\ g(y,f(x),f(x+1)))$, for recursive g. That these are universal Σ_1^1-formulas is shown in the Appendix.

For any such φ construct a nondeterministic Turing machine T which, starting on the empty tape, initially writes down $x=o$ and $f(x)=1$, and then keeps indefinitely augmenting x and looking nondeterministically for a new y and new value for $f(x+1)$ satisfying g. Whenever it finds such y and $f(x+1)$ it signals by reentering its start state. Clearly, φ is true iff $T=T_m$ for some $m \in G$. □

Given a nondeterministic Turing machine T we shall now construct a formula $\underline{reduce}_T$ in $PDL_{RG+\{A^\Delta(B)A^\Delta\}}$ and show that T has the property described in Proposition 3.1 iff $\underline{reduce}_T$ is satisfiable; hence satisfiability (respectively, validity) in $PDL_{RG+\{A^\Delta(B)A^\Delta\}}$ is Σ_1^1-complete (respectively, Π_1^1-complete).

Let the tape alphabet Σ of T include the blank symbol $\not{b}$, and let V be the set of states, with q_o the start state. Denote $\Sigma_V = \Sigma \cup V$. A configuration of T can be represented by the nonblank portion of the tape surrounded on either side by at least one $\not{b}$, and with the current state inserted just prior to the letter being read. The initial configuration can thus be represented by $\not{b}\, q_o\, \not{b}$. The transition table is given by a yield function $\delta: \Sigma \times V \times \Sigma \rightarrow 2^{(\Sigma_V)^3}$ such that a configuration $c = x\sigma q\tau z$, for $x,z \in \Sigma^*$, $\sigma,\tau \in \Sigma$ and $q \in V$, can result in a configuration xy^Rz for each $y \in \delta(\sigma,q,\tau)$. Let $\overline{\delta}(\sigma,q,\tau) = \Sigma_V^3 - \delta(\sigma,q,\tau)$. Clearly, for every triple σ,q,τ, both $\delta(\sigma,q,\tau)$ and $\overline{\delta}(\sigma,q,\tau)$ are finite.

Our formula $\underline{reduce}_T$ will involve atomic programs A and B, and atomic propositions P_σ for each $\sigma \in \Sigma$ and P_q for each $q \in V$. We let $C(\sigma)$ stand for the program $A;P_\sigma?$, and similarly for $C(q)$. C is extended to strings over $\Sigma \cup V$, and to sets of such strings by $C(xy) = C(x);C(y)$ and $C(W) = \bigcup_{w \in W} C(w)$.

The idea of the reduction is to force models of $\underline{reduce}_T$ to contain an encoding of the infinite computation of T sought after, in the form of an infinite (possibly cyclic) sequence of executions of A and B of the form $p = A^*BA^*BA^*\ldots$. The odd numbered blocks of A's in p encode successive configurations of the computation, and the even blocks encode the reflections around B of their respective previous blocks. The new program $A^\Delta(B)A^\Delta$ is used to force p to contain correct transitions between successive configurations, correct reflections between reflected configurations, and also to ensure a length increase in the blocks of A's to make possible extension of the nonblank portion of the tape.

Define the program $\underline{config}$ to be

$$C(\not{b})\ ;\ C(\Sigma)^*\ ;\ C(V)\ ;\ C(\Sigma)^*\ ;\ C(\not{b})\ ;\ B$$

The program $\underline{good\text{-}config}$ is defined in the same way but with $C(q_o)$ replacing $C(V)$.

The formula $\underline{reduce}_T$ is taken to be the conjunction of the following formulas:

$\underline{\exists computation}$: $[\underline{config}^*] < \underline{config}^*; \underline{good\text{-}config} > \underline{true}$

$\underline{single\ letter}$: $[(A \cup B)^*\ ;\ A]\ \left(\bigvee_{a \in \Sigma \cup V} \left(P_a \wedge \bigwedge_{\substack{b \in \Sigma \cup V \\ b \neq a}} \sim P_b\right)\right)$

$\underline{start}$: $\bigwedge_{\substack{a \in \Sigma \cup V \\ a \neq \not{b} \\ a \neq q_o}} [A^*\ ;\ C(a)]\ \underline{false}$

lengthen: $[\underline{config}^*]\ ([A^*;A;A^{\Delta}(B)A^{\Delta};A;B]\ \underline{false}$

$\wedge\ [A^{\Delta}(B)A^{\Delta};A;A]\ \underline{false}$

$\wedge\ [A^{\Delta}(B)A^{\Delta};A]\ P_{b\!\!/}$

reflection: $\bigwedge_{a\in\Sigma\cup V} [(\underline{config};\ \underline{config})^*;A^*;C(a);A^{\Delta}(B)A^{\Delta};A]\ P_a$

transition: $\bigwedge_{\sigma,\tau,\sigma'\in\Sigma} [(\underline{config};\ \underline{config})^*;\ \underline{config};\ A^*;\ C(\sigma\tau\sigma');\ A^{\Delta}(B)A^{\Delta};A;A]P_{\tau}$

$\wedge\ \bigwedge_{\substack{\sigma,\tau\in\Sigma\\ q\in V}} [(\underline{config};\ \underline{config})^*;\ \underline{config};\ A^*;\ C(\sigma q\tau);\ A^{\Delta}(B)A^{\Delta};\ C(\overline{\delta}(\sigma,q,\tau))]\ \underline{false}$

Lemma 3.1: The formula $\underline{reduce}_T$ is satisfiable iff there exists an infinite computation of T, starting on the empty tape, which repeats the start state q_o infinitely often.

Proof: (if) Let $c_1, c_2, \ldots$ be a representation of the successive configurations of such a computation of T. Without loss of generality assume that for each i, $|c_{i+1}| = |c_i|+2$, and that the two extra elements in c_{i+1} represent an added $b\!\!/$ on either side of c_i. Let c_i' be $c_i^R\ b\!\!/$. Then clearly $c_{i+1} = b\!\!/\ c_i''\ b\!\!/$ where c_i'' is a direct outcome of c_i by the transition table of T. Construct the model S such that its only executions of A and B are given by an infinite sequence, starting at some state u, of the form $A^{|c_1|}\ B\ A^{|c_1|+1}B\ A^{|c_2|}\ B\ldots$, upon which $c_1, c_1', c_2, c_2', \ldots$ are encoded exclusively by the appropriate atomic propositions. For example, if $c_1 = b\!\!/\ q_o\ b\!\!/$, then we might view the initial part of the model as an execution of $A;P_{b\!\!/}?;A;P_{q_o}?;A;P_{b\!\!/}?;B;A;P_{b\!\!/}?;A;P_{q_o}?;A;P_{b\!\!/}?;A;P_{b\!\!/};B;\ \ldots$ We leave to the reader to check that all conjuncts of $\underline{reduce}_T$ are true in S at state u. In particular, since q_o repeats infinitely often, good-config can be executed infinitely often in the model, contributing to the truth at u of ∃computation. Hence $S,u \models \underline{reduce}_T$.

(only if) Let $S,u \models \underline{reduce}_T$. By ∃computation there is an infinite (possibly cyclic) sequence of executions of A and B, starting at u, of the form $p = A^{i_1}\ B\ A^{i_2}\ B\ldots$ By lengthen we have $i_{j+1} = i_j+1$ for all j. By single-letter there is an element of $\Sigma\cup V$ associated with each execution of A along p, enabling us to think of p as representing a sequence $c_1, c_1', c_2, c_2', \ldots$ of words over $\Sigma \cup V$. Consequently, by ∃computation and the structure of config, each such word contains exactly one state in V and hence actually encodes a configuration of T. By start, the word c_1 must be of the form $\not{b}\not{b}^*q_o\not{b}^*\not{b}$, which represents a start configuration. By reflection we have $c_i' = c_i^R\not{b}$. Now, the first conjunct of transition ensures retainment of those parts of the tape of T untouched by a transition from c_i to c_{i+1}, and the second conjunct ensures that this transition is indeed according to the yield function δ. Finally, ∃computation ensures the occurrence of "good" configurations infinitely often along p, and hence that q_o repeats infinitely often during the computation $c_1, c_2, \ldots$. □

Following immediately from Proposition 3.1 and Lemma 3.1, observing the obvious containment in Π_1^1, we have:

Theorem 3.1: The validity problem for $PDL_{RG+\{A^\Delta(B)A^\Delta\}}$ is Π_1^1-complete.

It is quite straightforward to modify the proof of Theorem 3.1 in such a way that rather than a sequence of executions of the form $A^{|c_1|}B\,A^{|c_1|+1}B\,A^{|c_2|}B \ldots$, we have a sequence of the form $A^{|c_1|}\;B^{|c_1|+1}\;A^{|c_2|}\;B^{|c_2|+1}\;\ldots$, with the configurations encoded using the A's and their reflections encoded using the B's. All occurrences $A^\Delta(B)A^\Delta$ are replaced by the appropriate ones of $A^\Delta B^\Delta$ or $B^\Delta A^\Delta$, where, e.g., $L(A^\Delta B^\Delta) = \bigcup_i L(A^i;B^i)$. Further easy modifications of lengthen are required. In this way one obtains:

Theorem 3.2: The validity problem for $PDL_{RG+\{A^\Delta B^\Delta,\, B^\Delta A^\Delta\}}$ is Π_1^1-complete.

By replacing a single B in the proof of Theorem 3.1 with a double B;B, it is possible to obtain the same result for the additional program $L = \{w;w^R \mid w \in \{A,B\}^*\}$. Each $A^\Delta(B)A^\Delta$ is simply replaced by L, and along the path A...ABBA...ABBA... of interest computations of L coincide with those of $A^\Delta(B;B)A^\Delta$. Various other linear context-free grammars give rise to simple programs whose addition to RG results in Π_1^1-completeness. In particular, one can define infinite classes of such programs each of which has the above Π_1^1 property. For example,

$C = \{\, L \mid L$ is of the form $\{\, A^iBA^{ki} \mid i \geq o,$ fixed $k \,\}\,\}$. In each case the aforementioned proof goes through slightly modified.

In the next Section we discuss one-letter programs.

4. Π_1^1 - completeness over one atomic program

In this section we consider the decision problem for validity in PDL_K where the set K of programs consists of RG(A) (the regular expressions over the single letter A) together with finitely many additional programs denoted by the symbols $\Gamma_1, \ldots, \Gamma_k$, which are interpreted by (not necessarily regular) subsets of A^*. Thus, the semantics of PDL_K is determined by a list $S_1, \ldots, S_k$ of subsets of ω ($\omega = \{0,1,2,\ldots\}$) which serve to interpret the programs Γ_i as follows: $L(\Gamma_i) = \{A^n | n \in S_i\}$. Satisfaction of formulas by states in a given PDL-structure is now defined as in Section 2. To obtain undecidability results we shall assume that the language of PDL_K has as many atomic propositions as needed for the proofs presented below. They will be denoted by $P, P_0, P_1 P_2, \ldots$ etc.

Note that the sets $S_1, \ldots, S_k$ are only needed for specifying the semantics of PDL_K and do not figure in the syntax. Nevertheless, we shall write A^{S_i} instead of Γ_i to emphasize that the interpretation $L(\Gamma_i) = \{A^n | n \in S_i\}$ is being used.

For $S \subseteq \omega$ we denote $\overline{S} = \omega - S$ (the complement of S). For $S_1, S_2 \subseteq \omega$ we write $S_1 \leq_m S_2$ and say that S_1 is many-one reducible to S_2 if there is a total recursive function $f : \omega \to \omega$ such that

$$\forall n \; (n \in S_1 \leftrightarrow f(n) \in S_2) \; .$$

Note that if $S_1 \leq_m S_2$ then clearly S_1 is recursive in S_2, that is - membership in S_1 is decidable using a Turing machine with an oracle from membership in S_2. Sometimes one of the sets S_1, S_2 is a set of strings over some finite alphabet (e.g. formulas of some language) and is identified with the set of Gödel numbers of its members, so that the notation $S_1 \leq_m S_2$ still makes sense.

Given $S_1, \ldots, S_k \subseteq \omega$ we denote by $vld(S_1, \ldots S_k)$ the set of all logically valid PDL_K formulas where $K = RG(A) \cup \{A^{S_1}, \ldots, A^{S_k}\}$, as described above. Similarly $stl(S_1 \ldots, S_k)$ is the set of all satisfiable PDL_K formulas. Clearly a PDL_K formula Q is valid iff $\sim Q$ is unsatisfiable, hence each of the above two sets of formulas is recursive in the other. We shall study the complexity of $vld(S_1, \ldots S_k)$ and especially of $vld(S)$ (the case $k=1$) for a given complexity of $S_1, \ldots, S_k$ or of S.

The main results (some of which are trivial observations) are summarized in the following propositions and Theorem.

<u>Prop. 4.1.</u> For any $S_1, \ldots, S_k \subseteq \omega$ and $1 \leq i \leq k$, $S_i \leq_m vld(S_i) \leq_m vld(S_1, \ldots, S_k)$. Hence, if $vld(S_1, \ldots, S_k)$ is decidable then each set S_i is recursive.

<u>Prop. 4.2.</u> Let $S_1, \ldots, S_k \subseteq \omega$, $k > 1$ and let $S = \{kn - i | 1 \leq i \leq k, 1 \leq n \in S_i\}$. Then $vld(S_1, \ldots, S_k) \leq_m vld(S)$.

<u>Prop. 4.3.</u> If $S_1, \ldots S_k$ are recursive (or even merely Δ_1^1) subsets of ω then $vld(S_1, \ldots, S_k)$ is a Π_1^1 set.

<u>Theorem 4.1</u>: There exists a primitive recursive set $S \subseteq \omega$ such that $vld(S)$ is a complete Π_1^1 set.

Note that Theorem 4.1 shows that for recursive S $vld(S)$ may sometimes be as complex as is allowed for by Prop. 4.3. We do not know whether vld(S) is ever decidable except when S is regular (i.e. when $\{A^n | n\in S\}$ is a regular subset of A^*, in which case $PDL_{RG(A)\cup\{A^S\}}$ is not a proper extension of $PDL_{RG(A)}$) . We also do not know whether vld(S) is decidable for particular choices of S such as $\{n^2 | n\in\omega\}$ or $\{n^3 | n\in\omega\}$, though we conjecture that it is not.

We shall now sketch the proofs of the propositions and Theorem.

Proof of 4.1. Note that $n\in S_i$ iff the formula

$$[A^{S_i}]p \supset [A^n]p$$

is valid, hence $S_i \leq_m vld(S_i)$. The rest of the proposition is obvious. □

Proof of 4.2. It will suffice to prove that $stl(S_1,\ldots,S_k) \leq_m stl(S)$, in view of the connection between validity and satisfiability mentioned earlier. Observe now that if $0\in S_i$ and we let $S_i' = S_i - \{0\}$

then $[A^{S_i}]p \equiv p \wedge [A^{S_i'}]p$

and $\langle A^{S_i}\rangle p \equiv p \vee \langle A^{S_i'}\rangle p$

are valid for any formula p , hence $PDL_{RG(A)\cup\{A^{S_1},\ldots,A^{S_i},\ldots,A^{S_k}\}}$ is translatable to $PDL_{RG(A)\cup\{A^{S_1},\ldots,A^{S_i'},\ldots,A^{S_k}\}}$, and hence $stl(S_1,\ldots,S_k) \leq_m stl(S_1,\ldots S_i',\ldots,S_k)$. Thus, by successive applications of this process, we see that $stl(S_1,\ldots S_k) \leq_m stl(S_1-\{0\},\ldots,S_k-\{0\})$ and since the set S in Prop. 4.2 depends only on the non-zero numbers of $S_1,\ldots,S_k$ there is no loss of generality in assuming that $0\notin S_i$ (for i=1,...,k) from the start.

Suppose now that a formula Q of $PDL_{RG(A)\cup\{A^{S_1},\ldots,A^{S_k}\}}$ is given. We want to associate with Q , in an effective way, a formula $\tilde{Q}$ of $PDL_{RG(A)\cup\{A^S\}}$ so that Q is satisfiable iff $\tilde{Q}$ is satisfiable. To make $\tilde{Q}$ more intelligible we write it as a formula of $PDL_{RG(B)\cup\{B^S\}}$. The idea is that the role of A in Q will be played by B^k in $\tilde{Q}$.

$\tilde{Q}$ is the conjunction of the following formulas, where $P_o,\ldots,P_{k-1}$ are new atomic propositions (not occurring in Q):

(1) P_o ,

(2) $[B^*]\ (P_o \vee \ldots \vee P_{k-1})$,

(3) $[B^*] \bigwedge_{o\leq i<j<k} \sim(P_i \wedge P_j)$,

(4) $[B^*] \bigwedge_{o\leq i<k} (P_i \supset [B]P_{i+1})$ (for i=k-1 P_{i+1} is taken to be P_o) ,

(5) Q_1 .

Here Q_1 is obtained from Q by the following replacements: Substitute B^k for A everywhere in Q . Also, wherever A^{S_i} occurs in Q replace it by: $P_o?;B^S;B^i;P_o?$. Thus, $[A^{S_i}]$ is replaced by $[P_o?][B^S][B^i;P_o?]$ and A^{S_i} is replaced similarly.

[The idea is that to perform B^k n times for some $n\in S_i$ we perform B m+i times for some $m\in S$ such that $m+i \equiv 0 \pmod k$. And indeed by the definition of S and the assumption that $0 \notin S_i$ we have: $\{kn \mid n \in S_i\} = \{m+i \mid m \in S,\ m+i \equiv 0 \pmod k\}$.]

It is easy to see that Q is satisfiable iff $\tilde{Q}$ is satisfiable. For if $\tilde{Q}$ is satisfied by a state u_o in some PDL-structure we obtain a model of Q by restricting attention to the states satisfying P_o and interpreting A by: $\rho(A) = \rho(B)^k$. Conversely, if Q is satisfied by a state u_o in some PDL structure we obtain a model of Q_1 by adding new states, replacing each edge $u \xrightarrow{A} v$ in the graph corresponding to the original structure by a chain $u \xrightarrow{B} o \xrightarrow{B} \dots \to o \xrightarrow{B} v$ involving k-1 new states satisfying $P_1, \dots, P_{k-1}$ respectively (all the old states shall satisfy P_o).

This completes the proof that $stl(S_1,\dots,S_k) \leq_m stl(S)$, hence $vld(S_1,\dots,S_k) \leq_m vld(S)$. □

Proof of 4.3. Let $S_1,\dots,S_k$ be Δ^1_1 subsets of w. If suffices to show that $stl(S_1,\dots,S_k)$ is a Σ^1_1 set. First note that every satisfiable formula is satisfiable in a countable structure, as is seen by a standard Lowenheim-Skolem argument. Thus $Q \in stl(S_1,\dots,S_k)$ iff there exists a set $X \subseteq \omega$ (the set of states) and certain subsets of X (the interpretations of the atomic propositions) and a relation over S (the interpretation of the program A) which together constitute a PDL structure in which Q is satisfied. It is a routine exercise to write this as a Σ^1_1 predicate about Q (see Rogers [R] for the requisite background on the analytical hierarchy). □

Proof of Theorem 4.1. Let $C \subseteq \omega$ be any complete Σ^1_1 set (so that C is Σ^1_1 and if D is any Σ^1_1 set then $D \leq_m C$). We will construct a primitive recursive set $S \subseteq \omega$ such that $C \leq_m stl(S)$. Then stl(S) will be a complete Σ^1_1 set (it is Σ^1_1 by Prop. 4.3) and hence vld(S) will be a complete Π^1_1 set.

We shall make use of the following normal form for Σ^1_1 sets: If $C \subseteq \omega$ is Σ^1_1 then there exists a primitive recursive relation $R \subseteq \omega^3$ such that for all $m \in \omega$:

(A) $m \in C \iff \exists X_1 (\forall x,y \in X_1)[x < y \Rightarrow R(m,x,y)]$.

Here (and throughout this proof) the variables $X_1, X_2, \dots$ range over infinite subsets of ω only. The existence of this normal form is proved in the Appendix.

Now let $S_1 = \{2^n \mid n \in \omega\}$ and let $S_2 = \{2^y - 2^x - 2^m \mid m<x<y \text{ and } R(m,x,y)\}$, where R is chosen to correspond to the particular set C with which we start. Then we have:

(B) $m \in C \iff \exists X_2 [(\forall n \in X_2)(n \in S_1 \wedge n > 2^m) \wedge (\forall n_1, n_2 \in X_2)(n_1 < n_2 \Rightarrow n_2 - n_1 - 2^m \in S_2)]$.

Indeed, if $m \in C$ and X_1 is a set as in the r.h.s. of (A) let $X_2 = \{2^x \mid x \in X_1 \wedge x > m\}$. Then X_2 will clearly satisfy the r.h.s. of (B). Conversely, if X_2 satisfies the r.h.s. of (B) let $X_1 = \{\log_2 n \mid n \in X_2\}$. Then X_1 is infinite and if $x,y \in X_1$, $x<y$ then $m<x<y$ and $2^x, 2^y \in X_2$ and so $2^y - 2^x - 2^m \in S_2$. But the triple (m,x,y) is uniquely determined by the numbers $2^y - 2^x - 2^m$, given that $m<x<y$. Hence, if $2^y - 2^x - 2^m \in S_2$ then R(m,x,y) holds (by definition of S_2). Thus X_1

satisfies the r.h.s. of (A) and it follows that $m \in C$. This proves (B).

We can now effectively associate with every $m \in \omega$ a formula Q_m of $PDL_{RG(A)} \cup \{A^{\bar{S}_1}, A^{\bar{S}_2}\}$ **so that** $m \in C$ iff Q_m is satisfiable. Roughly speaking Q_m describes the r.h.s. of (B) with the atomic proposition P being true at those states whose "distance from the origin" is a member of X_2. Q_m is the conjunction of the following formulas:

(1) $[A^*] < A;A^* > P$ ("X_2 is infinite"),

(2) $[A^{\bar{S}_1}] \sim P$ ("$X_2 \subseteq S_1$"),

(3) $\bigwedge_{i=o}^{2^m} [A^i] \sim P$ ("$(\forall n \in X_2)\, n > 2^m$"),

(4) $[A^*;P?;A^{2^m};A^{\bar{S}_2}] \sim P$ ("if $n_1 \in X_2$ and $z \in \bar{S}_2$ then $n_1 + 2^m + z \notin X_2$").

Note that if $m \in C$ then Q_m is satisfied at the root (0) of the following **"linear"** model:

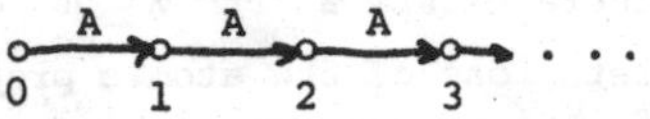

where P is declared true at n iff $n \in X_2$, given a set X_2 as on the r.h.s. of (B). Conversely, given any PDL-structure in which some state u_o satisfies Q_m the conjunct (1) of Q_m guarantees the existence of a sequence of (not necessarily distinct) states

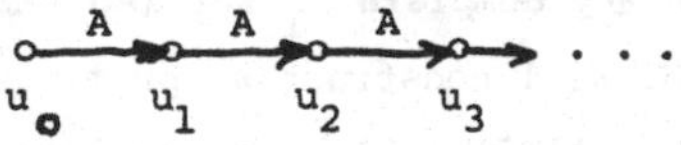

starting from u_o on which P is true infinitely many times. Letting $X_2 = \{n \mid u_n \models P\}$ conjuncts (2), (3) and (4) imply that X_2 satisfies the r.h.s. of (B), hence $m \in C$.

We have thus established that $C \leq_m stl(\bar{S}_1, \bar{S}_2)$ hence by Prop. 4.2 $C \leq_m stl(S)$ where $S = \{2n-1 \mid 1 \leq n \in \bar{S}_1\} \cup \{2n-2 \mid 1 \leq n \in \bar{S}_2\}$. A look at the definitions of S_1 and S_2 shows that they are primitive recursive (note that if $n = 2^y - 2^x - 2^m \in S_2$ then $n > \frac{1}{2} \cdot 2^y$ hence $y < \log_2 2n$ so a bound on m,x,y in terms of n is available) hence so is S. This completes the proof of Theorem 4.1. ▯

Appendix: Normal forms for Σ_1^1 sets.

In this appendix we prove the following two claims, which have been used in Sections 3 and 4 respectively.

Claim 1. If C is a Σ_1^1 subset of ω then there exists a primitive recursive relation $R_1 \subseteq \omega^3$ such that for all $m \in \omega$: $m \in C$ iff $\exists f[f(0)=1 \wedge \forall x R_1(m,f(x),f(x+1)]$.

Claim 2. If C is a Σ_1^1 subset of ω then there exists a primitive recursive relation $R_2 \subseteq \omega^3$ such that for all $m \in C$ iff $\exists X_1 (\forall x,y \in X_1)[x<y \Rightarrow R_2(m,x,y)]$.

In Claim 1 "f" ranges over functions from ω into ω and in Claim 2 "X_1" ranges over infinite subsets of ω. It should be clear that the converses of the two claims are also true (even if R_1, R_2 are merely assumed to be Δ_1^1 rather than primitive recursive) so that we actually have here general normal forms for Σ_1^1 sets. We assume elementary knowledge of the analytical hierarchy (Rogers [R, §16.1] should suffice for this appendix).

To prove both claims we start from the following well known normal form of a Σ_1^1-set C (cf. [R, §16.1, Cor. V]):

(1) $m \in C \Leftrightarrow \exists f_1 \forall x R(m, \overline{f}_1(x))$.

Here R is a primitive-recursive relation (depending on C) and f_1 is the "history function" of f_1, i.e. for each x $\overline{f}_1(x)$ is a number coding the finite sequence $(f_1(0), \ldots, f_1(x-1))$. To be definite we choose the following method of coding finite sequences of numbers by numbers which differs from that of [R]):

$$(x_1,\ldots,x_n) \mapsto \langle x_1,\ldots,x_n \rangle = 2^n \cdot p_1^{x_1} \ldots p_n^{x_n}$$

where $(3=)p_1 < p_2 < \ldots$ are the primes >2 in increasing order. In particular, the empty sequence is coded by $\langle\,\rangle = 2^0 = 1$. Let Seq(x) mean that x codes some finite sequence and let $x \lessdot y$ mean that Seq(x) and Seq(y) and the sequence coded by x is a proper initial segment of the one coded by y . Finally let lh(x) be the length of the sequence coded by x if Seq(x), lh(x) = 0 otherwise. Note that Seq and $\lessdot$ are prim.-rec. relations and lh is a prim.rec. function. Also note that $x \lessdot y \Rightarrow x < y$.

Proof of Claim 1. Given a Σ_1^1 set C choose a prim. rec. $R \subseteq \omega^2$ so that (1) holds for all $m \in \omega$. It clearly follows from (1) that

$m \in C \Leftrightarrow \exists f[f=\overline{f}_1$ for some f_1 and $\forall x R(m,f(x))]$.

But in order for f to be the "history function" of some f_1 it is necessary and sufficient that $\forall x\,[\mathrm{Seq}(f(x) \wedge \mathrm{lh}(f(x))=x]$ and moreover $f(x) \lessdot f(x+1)$ for each x . Equivalently, the condition is that $f(o) = \langle\,\rangle = 1$ and

$\forall x\,[f(x) \lessdot f(x+1) \wedge (\mathrm{lh}(f(x+1)) = \mathrm{lh}(f(x)) + 1)]$. Define $R_1 \subseteq \omega^3$ by

$R_1(m,u,v) \Leftrightarrow R(m,u) \wedge u \lessdot v \wedge \mathrm{lh}(v) = \mathrm{lh}(u)+1$. Then R_1 is prim. rec. and $m \in C \Leftrightarrow \exists f\,[f(o)=1 \wedge \forall x R_1(m,f(x),f(x+1))]$, as required. □

Proof of Claim 2. Start again from the normal form (1) of C. Define $R_2 \subseteq \omega^3$ by $R_2(m,u,v) \Leftrightarrow u \dot{\leq} v \wedge \forall z\,(z \dot{\leq} v \Rightarrow R(m,z))$. Thus $R_2(m,u,v)$ says that v codes some sequence: $v = \langle v_1,\ldots,v_\ell \rangle$, u is of the form $\langle v_1,\ldots,v_k \rangle$ for some $k < \ell$, and $R(m, \langle v_1,\ldots,v_i \rangle)$ holds for every $i < \ell$. Note that R_2 is prim. rec. We claim that

(2) $m \in C \Leftrightarrow \exists X_1\ (\forall x,y \in X_1)\,[x < y \Rightarrow R_2\ (m,x,y)]$.

Suppose that $m \in C$ and let f_1 be as on the r.h.s. of (1). Let $X_1 = \{\overline{f}_1(n) \mid n \in\ \}$. Then X_1 is infinite. If $x,y \in X_1$ and $x < y$ then $x = \langle f_1(o),\ldots,f_1(k-1) \rangle$, $y = \langle f_1(o),\ldots,f_1(\ell-1) \rangle$ where $k < \ell$ and $R_2(m,x,y)$ clearly holds.

Conversely, suppose that X_1 is an infinite set satisfying the r.h.s. of (2). Then for all $x,y \in X_1$ $x < y \Rightarrow x \dot{\leq} y$, hence there exists a unique function $f_1 : \omega \to \omega$ such that $X_1 \subseteq \{\overline{f}_1(n) \mid n \in \omega\}$. For any $k \in \omega$ we can find $n_2 > n_1 > k$ such that $\overline{f}_1(n_1) \in X_1$ and $\overline{f}_1(n_2) \in X_1$, so that $R_2(m,\overline{f}_1(n_1),\overline{f}_1(n_2))$ holds, so the number $z = \overline{f}_1(k)$ satisfies $z \dot{\leq} \overline{f}_1(n_2)$ and hence $R(m,z)$ (by the definition of R_2). Thus $\forall k\, R(m,\overline{f}_1(k))$ so that f_1 satisfies the r.h.s. of (1), whence $m \in C$.

This proves (2) and thereby proves Claim 2. ▯

References

[FL] Fischer, M.J. and R.E. Ladner. Propositional dynamic logic of regular programs. J. Comp. Sys. Sciences, 18 (1979), pp. 194-211.

[HPS] Harel, D., A. Pnueli and J. Stavi. Propositional dynamic logic of context-free programs. 22nd IEEE Symp. on Found. of Comp. Sc., Nashville, Tenn., October 1981.

[Pr1] Pratt, V.R. Semantical considertions on Floyd-Hoare logic. Proc. 17th Symp. on Found. of Comp. Sc., (1976), pp. 109-121.

[Pr2] Pratt, V.R. A near optimal method for reasoning about action. J. Comp. Sys. Sciences, 20, (1980), pp. 231-254.

[R] Rogers, H., Jr., Theory of Recursive Functions and Effective Computability. McGraw-Hill Co., New York, 1967.

SOME OBSERVATIONS ON COMPOSITIONAL SEMANTICS

Theo M.V. Janssen[1]
Dept. Philosophy, Univ. Amsterdam
Roetersstraat 15, 1018 WB Amsterdam

Peter van Emde Boas[2]
Dept. Mathematics, Univ. Amsterdam
Roetersstraat 15, 1018 WB Amsterdam

1 THE PRINCIPLE.

This paper presents an overview of an analysis concerning the so-called *Compositionality principle* which reads:

The meaning of an compound expression is composed from the meanings of its parts .

A complete treatise of this analysis will appear in the forthcoming PhD. thesis of the first author [13] ; for many details we refer to this thesis. A preliminary version of our ideas appeared previously in [9] .

The principle aims at a connection between a language (formal or natural) and its meanings considered as elements in a model. Model theoretic semantics therefore is a necessary presupposition, and consequently the principle seems not to address those people involved with the task of proving programs correct using various syntactic means.

One of the remarkable features is its attractiveness; people from both natural languages, programming languages and mathematical logic are known to refer to this principle while justifying their approach. Frequently the authors are unaware of its outstanding position in contemporary philosophy of language, where it is known as the "Fregean Principle" [21]. A typical quotation from Computer Science (Stoy [24], p 12):

> We give 'Semantic valuation functions', which map syntactic constructs in the program to the abstract values (numbers, truth-values, functions etc.) which they denote. These valuation functions are usually recursively defined: the value denoted by a construct is specified in terms of the values denoted by its syntactic sub components ....

Other quotations provide us with examples where the principle is used as an argument for evaluating proposals (Tennent vs. Apt & de Bakker in [20], p 163) :

> Your first two semantics are not 'denotational' ... because the meaning of the procedure call constructs is not defined in terms of the meanings of its components...

Arguments for adhearing to the principle appear as well: factoring out problems (Milner [17], p 158) : The designer of a computing system should be able to think of his system as a composite of behaviors, in order that he may factor his design problem into smaller problems ... , or naturalness (Mazurkiewics [16], p 75) : One of the most natural methods to assign meanings to programs is to define the meaning of the whole program by the meanings of its constituents .... .

---

[1] Research performed while affiliated to the Math. Centre, Amsterdam, Dept Pure Math.

[2] Partially supported by the dept. Math. Tel Aviv University.

Aim of the analysis is not so much to give a contribution to the huge amount of philosophical writings concerning compositionality and its impacts. Instead we give sufficient and necessary conditions which enable people to develop a model-theoretic semantics for some language, and to decide whether they do so according to the compositionality principle. Finally we explain why it is worthwile to do so. We aim therefore towards a formalization which is liberal in the sence that a great variety of proposals and languages is within the scope of our framework, and restrictive in the sense that it makes possible to decide whether a proposal is compositional or not, and to prove interesting claims about those which are.

2 FORMALIZATION AND FRAMEWORK.

Let L be a language for which we want to develop a model-theoretic semantics with interpretation in a domain D which we leave unspecified for the moment. The principle refers to the fact that elements in L are *composed from parts* , leading to the requirement that L is described by some *syntax* in a meaningfull way ; there are various ways of trivializing the principle by considering each sentence in L as being atomic, or build directly from its atomic parts (the basic symbols). Moreover, the principle requires us also to give meanings to the expressions considered *parts* forming a larger set E . The most general form of a syntactic rule composing a structure out of parts we can imagine will read something like:

From expressions $E_1,\dots,E_k$ *build the composed expression* E *, where* $E=S_j(E_1,\dots,E_k)$.

Here we have to specify which syntactic rule to apply (S_j) , and that the $E_1,\dots,E_k$ are the parts of E . In general one does not want to apply a rule unrestictedly; the domain of expressions E is devided into sections, called *sorts* , *types* or *categories* (depending on the branch of semantics) and one allows the rule to specify the categories for the input parts and the resulting phrase :

From expressions $E_1,\dots,E_k$ *of categories* $C_1,\dots,C_k$ *, respectively, build the expression* E_0 *of category* C_0 *, where* $E_0 = S_j(E_1,\dots,E_k)$.

Some remarks are needed. This format of the rule does not restrict the syntactic operator S_j at all - it may concatenate, substitute, scatter, permute or even delete parts, or add non-part (*syncategorematic*) symbols. As a consequence it is quite conceivable that one has ambiguities of the form $S_j(E_1,\dots,E_k) = S_{j'}(E'_1,\dots,E'_{k'})$, while the intended meanings are not necessarily equal; see E.G. the ambiguity in the sentence John runs or walks and talks , due to the absence of parentheses in English. It is generally accepted that in applying the compositionality principle one should not look at the language L as a collection of strings of symbols, but as a collection of *derivational histories* , whic can be represented by trees or labeled bracketed expressions. See E.G. Schwartz [23], p 2 : Therefore we may take the semantic problem to be that of associating a value .... with each abstract program, i.e. parse tree ... . By looking at these histories the categories moreover become disjoint.

Our analysis thus leads us to considering the syntax to be a set of categories $(C_i)_i$, together with a set of rules $(S_j)_j$ which are operators of the form $S_j: C_1\times\ldots\times C_k \to C_0$. We need moreover basic expressions for starting the construction process. These objects clearly correspond to the *carriers* , *operators* and *generators* of a *many sorted algebra* . Since we consider the elements to be derivational histories rather than generated strings this has the effect that our many sorted algebra becomes *free* (or *initial* in the terminology of ADJ [1]).

Next we turn to the phrase *"composed from the meanings of its constituent parts"*. Consider the same instance of application of a rule: $E = S_j(E_1,\ldots,E_k)$. Suppose the meanings of $E_1,\ldots,E_k$ are given by the semantical objects $D_1,\ldots,D_k$. The principle now states that the meaning of E , denoted D, must be obtained by performing some semantical operator G_j on the meanings D_i : $D = G_j(D_1,\ldots,D_k)$. Note that the semantical operator G_j has full access to the meanings D_i but not to the syntactic structure of the E_i , except for their categories. For if we would allow G_j to use information about the inner structure of the E_i then the principle would not express the whole truth and no longer provide a sufficient condition.

Note that G_j needs to be defined only on those tupples of meanings which arise as meanings of expressions of the proper categories. Writing M(E) for the meaning of expression E and extending this notation to sets of expressions we observe that G_j is an operator $G_j : M(C_1)\times\ldots\times M(C_k) \to M(C_0)$, and that moreover

$$M(S_j(E_1,\ldots,E_k)) = G_j(M(E_1),\ldots,M(E_k)) \quad .$$

The above formula's indicate that we have turned the semantic domain D into a many sorted algebra as well where the sorts are the images under M of the categories (not necessarily disjoint), and were the operators are the semantical operators G_j . The mapping M which transforms derivational histories into their meanings becomes a *homomorfism* .

The formal framework arising out of the above analysis is not new; the two relevant predecessors are R. Montague's *Universal Grammar* [18], and the *Initial algebra semantics* of ADJ [1]. There are some differences. Montague did not use many sorted algebra's, which around 1970 were not yet fashionable among mathematicians. ADJ, working in this spirit, did not refer explicitly to their approach as a framework; furthermore there are some subtle technical differences (E.G. the definition of a homomorfism). The observation that compositionality leads to an algebraic framework can be found in Mazurkiewics [16] and Milner [17]. The connection between the work of ADJ and Montague has been observed by Andreka, Nemeti & Sain [3], and Markusz & Szots [15].

In our framework a many sorted algebra is a collection of sets together with a collection of operators defined on them : $A = \langle (A_s)_{s\in S_A} , F \rangle$, where $f_j \in F$ is an operator $f_j : A_{s_1} \times \ldots \times A_{s_n} \to A_{s_0}$ (all s_i and the number n depending on the operator f_j).

The index set S_A is the set of sorts of A . The set F embodies both the syntactical information about the domains and ranges of the operators (*signature* of the algebra) and the operators themselves, considered both as mappings and operator symbols. We have no further restrictions; the carriers A_s may be non-disjoint, operators may perform any action, and except for the index set S_A the sets involved may be empty. Operators should be, however, total functions.

Consider a pair of algebra's $A = <(A_s)_{s \in S_A}, F>$ and $B = <(B_t)_{t \in T_B}, G>$. Defining a homomorfism $h : A \to B$ presupposes that A and B are *similar* ; I.E., there exists a bijection $\rho : S_A \to T_B$ and $\rho^* : F \to G$ such that for an operator $f : A_{s_1} \times \ldots \times A_{s_k} \to A_{s_0}$ one has $\rho^*(f) : B_{\rho(s_1)} \times \ldots \times B_{\rho(s_k)} \to B_{\rho(s_0)}$.

A homomorfism h then is a mapping $h : \bigcup_{s \in S_A} A_s \to \bigcup_{t \in T_B} B_t$ such that $h(A_s) \subset B_{\rho(s)}$ and $h(f(a_1, \ldots, a_k)) = \rho^*(f)(h(a_1), \ldots, h(a_k))$.

Note that in this definition a homomorfism is not a sorted set of mappings like in ADJ [1,2] ; hence if an element a is of more than one sort its image $h(a)$ is independent of the sort considered.

3 TWO EXAMPLES.

To guide our further discussions we present a pair of simple examples.

Example 1 : Numbers.

We have two categories N and D , and two syntactic operators $S_1 : D \to N$, and $S_2 : N \times D \to N$. D consists of the digits 0,1,2,3,4,5,6,7,8,9 as basic elements; N consists of all strings of digits including strings with leading zero's. The syntactic operators are :

$S_1(d) = d$ (a digit is a one digit number)

$S_2(n,d) = nd$ (concatenation of a number and a digit gives a number)

The semantic domains corresponding to D and N respectively are $\{0,\ldots,9\}$ and $\mathbb{N}$ considered as elements of some model of the natural numbers. The semantic rules are:

$G_1(x) = x$ (the value of a single digit number is the value of its digit)

$G_2(y,x) = 10 \times y + x$.

So the derivational history of the string 237 becomes $S_2(S_2(S_1(2),3),7)$ with meaning $10 \times (10 \times (2) + 3) + 7$.

In the syntax we might as well have asked for concatenation with digits on the left instead of to the right (rule S_2' where $S_2'(d,n) = dn$). This would have made it impossible to define a corresponding semantic rule G_2' . Clearly one has $M(S_2'(0,S_1(7)) = M(S_1(7))$ (since 07 and 7 have the same value) but on the other hand $M(S_2'(1,S_2'(0,S_1(7))) \neq M(S_2'(1,S_1(7)))$ (since 107 and 17 have unequal values). By the homomorfism law this leads to a contradiction:

$$M(S_2'(1,S_2'(0,S_1(7)))) = G_2'(M(1),M(S_2'(0,S_1(7)))) = G_2'(M(1),M(S_1(7))) = M(S_2'(1,S_1(7)))$$

So even in this trivial example the compositionality principle learns us how to organise our syntax.

Example 2 : Strings of length a power of two.

We have a single category A and a single rule S . The unique basic element in A is the string X . The syntactic operator S is a substitution operator : S(w) = [XX/X]w (replace each occurrence of X in w by a pair of X's) . So S(S(S(X))) = S(S(XX)) = S(XXXX) = XXXXXXXX . As domain of meanings we take functions from the set $\mathbb{N}$ to itself ; M(X) is the identity function $\lambda n(n)$. The semantic operator corresponding to S is defined by $G(f) = \lambda n(f(n\times n))$. Hence we have: $M(S(S(S(X)))) = G(G(G(M(X)))) = G(G(G(\lambda n(n)))) = G(G(\lambda n(n\times n))) = G(\lambda n(n\times n\times n\times n)) = \lambda n(n\times n\times n\times n\times n\times n\times n\times n)$.

The same language is also obtained by using a duplication rule S'(w) = ww . A corresponding semantic rule G' is defined by $G'(f) = \lambda n(f(n)\times f(n))$. It would be however an ill designed choice to combine rule S with rule G' ; such a choice prevents a reasonable extension to a fragment where strings involving more than one letter are to be interpreted by polynomials in many variables.

The above example shows us that it is possible to obtain within our framework languages which are not context free, thus rebutting a remark in ADJ [2] . This is due to the fact that we are dealing with a context free set of derivational histories, producing a language which can be arbitrarily complex. Without further restrictions the languages involved even may fail to be recursively enumerable, and in order to exclude these languages various conditions of effectiveness and/or finiteness have to be incorporated in the framework. We observe that, even under the most restrictive conditions of finiteness considered, it remains possible to obtain every recursively enumerable language within our framework ; the proof shows that these languages arise in a rather uninteresting way by simulation of Turing machine computations. We refer the reader to [13] for the details.

4 HOW COMPOSITIONALITY IS ACHIEVED IN PRACTICE - SAFE EXTENSIONS OF ALGEBRA'S

In the above examples we have used tools from various areas of mathematics for describing our sets and operators. Such tools are clearly needed, since otherwise we would be forced to construct our algebra's "from scratch" . On the syntactic level we are working within the algebra of all strings over a given finite alphabet, with operators for concatenation, substitution, copying, permuting and deletion. On the semantic level we have used so far tools from Arithmetic and Lambda Calculus. In particular the operator G_2 in the number example (multiplication by 10 followed by addition) was "created" for this example ; it does not belong to Arithmetic proper. This operator was defined not looking at the domain itself but using the syntactic description of the domain as given by the language of arithmetic.

This analysis draws our attention to the fact that in most cases semantics is not defined directly but by using the intermediate tool of some well understood logical or mathematical language. This mathematical or logical language already has a compositional semantics which is used for obtaining the semantics of the source language.

SOURCE LANGUAGE ↓ translation LOGICAL LANGUAGE ↓ standard interpretation MEANINGS

E.G.

NUMBER DENOTATIONS ↓ ARITHMETIC ↓ MODEL OF NATURAL NUMBERS

This is however not the full picture. The source language and the logical language used are far from similar if considered as many sorted algebra's. In order for the translation to become a homomorfism they first should become similar, and the picture therefore becomes:

SOURCE LANGUAGE ↓ translation T

LOGICAL LANGUAGE — extension E → EXTENDED LOGICAL LANGUAGE

LOGICAL LANGUAGE ↓ standard interpretation M; EXTENDED LOGICAL LANGUAGE ↓ extended interpretation M'

MEANINGS — extension E' → MEANINGS

In practice the extension E is defined by adding new operators and (if necessary) new sorts ; operators in the logical language which are not used in the translation may be omitted. Next one defines the translation T using these new operators, taking for granted that the extension E' at the semantic level, and the extended interpretation M' exist and are well defined. Then the composition M'•T will yield the required interpretation of the source language.

On which grounds one may conclude that M'.exists and is properly defined ? It turns out that it is sometimes not possible to define M' at all. Suppose that in the numbers example we like to define the meaning of a number denotation to be its length rather than its value, disregarding leading zero's. Starting with rule S_2' (prefixing with digits) we might propose a semantic rule G_2'' like $G_2''(d,n)$ = <u>if</u> d=0 <u>then</u> n+1 <u>else</u> n <u>fi</u> . From this formulation, however, we get already an indication of the problem; by referring to the digit d itself, rather than to its semantic meaning (its length) we are using syntactic information about the digit-part. We might take the length of 0 to be 0 , but this would again present problems with 107 obtaining length 2 in stead of 3 . It seems that an operator like G_2'' is not definable in Arithmetic at all.

Remains the problem what kind of extensions are safe in the sense that the interpretation M' exists automatically. As far as creation of new sorts is concerned, introduction of copies of existing types, and of function or product types are safe tools. The corresponding projection operators and operators of functional application are safe as well. Finally we have the possibility of introducing so-called *polynomial operators* - operators which are defined by polynomial terms in the language using the existing operators (E.G. the operator $G_2(y,x) = 10\times y + x$ from the numbers example).

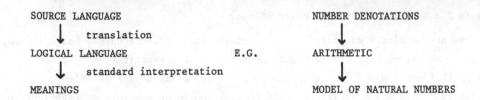

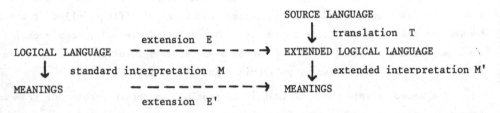

The use of polynomial operators but nothing more describes the position as

explicitly chosen by Montague in Universal Grammar [18] ; the same position seems to have been chosen by ADJ [1,2]. It is definitely a safe position which guarantees the existence of M' , but it leaves open the question whether other constructions of operators are safe as well. The disturbing fact is that they sometimes are. The question requires moreover a much more precise mathematical formulation before an answer can be given.

The results below are due to J. van Benthem [6] . His investigations are resticted to the case of monadic algebra's only. Consider an algebra A with a collection of operators F , and suppose that moreover an equational specification T_A for this algebra is given, which claims for example some operator to be associative etc. . We extend this algebra by some new operator g while simultaneously extending the specification to T . The question is whether some homomorfism h: $\langle A,F\rangle \rightarrow \langle B,F\rangle$ automatically extends to a homomorfism h': $\langle A,F\cup\{g\}\rangle \rightarrow \langle B,F\cup\{g\}\rangle$. This question still allows two distinct interpretations, depending on whether we ask the question for one specific model of the given algebra (*local problem*) or for all models of its theory T_A (*global problem*).

Definitions: The extension $\langle A,F,T_A\rangle \rightarrow \langle A,F\cup\{g\},T\rangle$ is called *safe* provided that for all models A' of T_A and all homomorfisms $h:A'\rightarrow B'$, h extends to a homomorfism $h':\langle A',F\cup\{g\},T\rangle \rightarrow \langle B',F\cup\{g\},T\rangle$. The extension is called *locally safe at A'* if the above extension property holds for the specific model A' . The operator g is called *polynomially definable* if there exists a term t in the specification language for A such that $g(x_1,\ldots,x_k) = t(x_1,\ldots,x_k)$. The operator is called *first order definable* provided $g(x_1,\ldots,x_k) = y \leftrightarrow \varphi(x_1,\ldots,x_k,y)$ is provable for some first order formula φ in T .

Results: g is polynomially definable $\Rightarrow$ g is safe $\Rightarrow$ g is first order definable , but none of these implications can be reversed. The second implication is a corollary to the main characterization result:

Theorem (van Benthem [6]): the operator g is safe iff g is first order definable by a definition of the form $g(x_1,\ldots,x_k) = y \leftrightarrow \varphi(x_1,\ldots,x_k,y)$ for a *positive* first order formula φ provable in T .

As an example consider the case of group theory which can be axiomatized without referring to the inverse operator. Clearly the inverse operator is not polynomially definable over composition and the neutral element only, but extending the language by introducing the inverse operator is globally safe.

The corresponding characterization for polynomially definability reads:

Theorem (van Benthem [6]): the operator g is polynomially definable iff every F-subalgebra of a model of T is closed under g .

It seems that Montague's position is more closely reflected by the local problem in the (usual) case that the model considered of the algebra A is a free term algebra with infinetely many generators:

Theorem (van Benthem [6]): Let <A,F> be an algebra which is freely generated by an infinite set of generators; then the operator g is locally safe at A iff g is polynomially definable.

This theorem extends to the many sorted case as well (F. Wiedijk, personal com.). An example, due to W. Peremans (see [13]) shows that the existence of an infinite set of generators is a necessary condition; consider the extension of the algebra of the natural numbers with successor by the operator addition. The local problem for finitely generated free algebra's is still open.

It should be observed that the above problems in universal algebra seem connected to problems in the theory of algebraic specifications of abstract data types (see Ehrig e.a. [7,8]).

5 REQUIREMENTS ON MEANINGS - INTENSIONS.

According to our interpretation of the compositionality principle the meaning of some expression ultimately depends on the meaning of its atomic parts and its derivational history. Consequently all factors which influence the meaning of some expression should find their way into this history, or into the meanings of the atomic parts otherwise. There is no other place for these factors to go.

There exist a number of factors like points in time, possible worlds, or, in the case of computer languages, computer states, which traditionally are considered as part of a context description influencing the meaning of some expression. A neutral name for those factors, used in philosophy, is *indices*. How to incorporate the dependence of the meaning of expressions on the values of indices into our framework ?

Consider for example the sentence:

The mother of the queen of Holland was in 1970 the queen of Holland

In the above sentence the phrase the queen of Holland occurrs twice with two different meanings, referring to queen Beatrix and queen Juliana respectively. Accordingly in designing a meaning for this phrase we must take into account that its meaning may refer to different royal personages. On the other hand, assuming that both occurrences of the phrase the queen of Holland have the same inner syntactic structure (which seems reasonable) by the compositionality principle their meanings become equal. The solution is given by selecting as meaning for this phrase not the person referred to but a function from points in time to the persons referred to at such a point in time. The global syntactic structure of the sentence then may indicate that such a function has to be evaluated, and the tense operator in 1970 indicates that the evaluation of the second occurrence is performed at another point in time than the first one. In this way a strict interpretation of compositionality can be brought in accordance to our intuition about the meaning of the above sentence.

An example from computer languages is given by the concept of a programming variable, whose value is different at different states - its meaning should be a function from states to values rather than the value at the state considered itself.

Generalising the above examples we observe that frequently the proper meaning of basic terms of some type t should be a function from indices to values of type t rather than an object of type t itself. The indices represent the context dependent information to determine the meaning of the term involved in the sentence under consideration, and the specific values of the indices with repect to which the term is to be evaluated is obtained using the syntactic structure of the context in which the term occurrs within the sentence.

This approach to semantics, the use of functions with indices as arguments, called *intensions* is not new (see E.G. Lewis [14]). It forms the basis for Montague's treatment of a fragment of English in [19] . It is interesting, however, to observe that this approach follows naturally from the compositionality principle.

Interesting in this light is a discussion in Pratt [22]. He considers two notions of meaning: a *static* one (where some expression obtains a meaning once and for all, E.G. an integer expression like 5+13), and a *dynamic* meaning (where the meaning of an expression varies). Next he developes a special logic, called *dynamic logic*, directed at the treatment of programming languages, arguing that a static meaning will not work in practice since the meaning of the relevant expressions in his language varies with time. Our opinion is that a static meaning remains possible, provided an intensional interpretation is chosen at the proper places. Intensional logic becomes in this way a static variant of dynamic logic. Both logics moreover satisfy the practical purpose that they prevent the user from talking about the machine states the user wants to abstract away from; in this regard these treatments differ from the intensional framework proposed by Andreka, Nemeti & Sain [4] , whose logic seems to talk about points in time explicitly, thus making a complete Gödelisation of computations possible.

We also should compare our intensional approach to the methods used in denotational semantics. In denotational semantics program variables are linked to abstract *storage locations* by the use of an *environment*; their value is obtained using the concept of a *store*, which formally is a function from locations to values which models the state. Expressions are evaluated with respect to an environment and a store, and both the environment and the store behaves like an index for the semantic interpretation. Our framework leads us to considering program variables to be interpreted by intensions of the type of values they store. So an integer variable is interpreted by an intension of an integer, which is a semantic value like an integer. The only index is the state of the computer.

In [11,12] we have developpped a semantics for a small fragment of ALGOL 68 based upon this idea. We use an extension of the language of intensional logic as described by R. Montague [19] . We need for this fragment no environments, and the semantics fits well in to the Tarskian framework. Since intensions of integers are values like integers themselves we can consider intensions of intensions, thus obtaining a satisfactory treatment for higher order references or pointers in ALGOL 68. The fragment includes also arrays which are interpreted by functions, in this way providing for a meaning for the array identifier itself, rather than for each of its array elements only. The resulting treatment of assignment, dereferencing, pointers and arrays is simple and elegant.

We conjecture that, by strictly adhering to the compositionality principle, the above fragment can be extended to one which includes declarations of variables, procedure declarations, and procedure calls, without being forced to use an environment as an index. The proof of this conjecture requires however the construction of such a treatment, something we have not yet done.

A final inspiration which might lead to the intensionalising of meanings can be found in the heuristic advice as given by Lewis [14]: In order to say what a meaning is, we may first ask what a meaning does, and then find something that does it. Intensions do what we want them to do; so why not use them as meanings.

6 MOTIVATION.

In this concluding section we list a number of arguments in defence of adhearing to the compositionality principle.

a) *It yields a uniform mathematical framework for semantics.*

Nobody forces you to present some proposal for the semantics of some language within a fixed framework. However, if each proposal uses a new set of concepts and/or a new terminology, your readers will be required to absorb your new system before they can understand your proposal. A standard framework for semantics will make it easier to exchange ideas, to extend work done by others and to combine treatments of language fragments, provided the formalism used is not unnecessary restrictive.

It is interesting to observe at this point that the original motivation which lead the first author to this project was the wish to design a computer program for simulating existing proposals for extensions of Montague's grammar in [19]. It turned out that each proposal would require an entirely new program unless all proposals would fit into a single framework. The resulting analysis and the applications are contained in the forthcomming thesis of the first author [13]; the computer program still has to be written.

Argument a) clearly calls for some framework for semantics, but not necessarily for the present one. Other arguments are required for convincing the reader that, among all possible systems for doing semantics, our algebraic framework should be considered to be the right one. Below we list a number of these arguments - for detailed examples substantiating these arguments the reader is referred to [13].

b) *Elegancy.*

De gustibus non est disputandum (elegancy is a matter of taste) . Our framework is based upon a few simple concepts: many sorted algebra's and homomorfism, which are combined with the tool of a logical language in a convenient way. The system is highly abstract but the abstract insights enable us to solve practical problems.

c) *Generality.*

Our framework applies to natural, mathematical and programming languages alike (as long as a model-theoretic semantics is looked for).

d) *Restrictiveness.*

The framework, by emphasing the use of polynomial operators, gives strong restrictions on the organisation of both the syntax and the semantics for a language. Frequently the syntax and/or semantics have to be reorganised in order to satisfy the requirements of compositionality, and the new syntax and semantics is an improvement over the original one.

e) *Understandable.*

The framework, being a formalization of compositionality, serves the purpose of "factoring out problems" which is used as an argument for compositionality in general.

f) *Power.*

Since the framework is based upon the use of free term algebra's, induction on the structure of an expression is an available tool for proving assertions concerning language and semantics.

g) *Heuristic tools.*

It is our experience that by looking for deviations against the framework, problems can be isolated, analysed and sometimes solved. The following quotation from ADJ [2] shows that this opinion is shared:

The believe that the ideas presented here are key, comes from our experience in the last eight years in developing and applying these concepts.

Next we mention two arguments which we feel to be not convincing.

h) *There is no alternative.*

Excercise: produce one !

i) *The principle is widespread.*

So is a lot of human evil.

Two more arguments concern the principle itself:

j) *Psychology.*

It is sometimes claimed that the principle reflects the process by which human beings understand language. How can we explain that a human being, using a finite brain, manages to understand a potentially infinite set of sentences. As formulated in Frege's words (transl. by Geach & Stoothof [10], p 55):

... even a thought grasped by a terrestrial being for the first time can be put in a form of words which will be understood by someone to whom it is entirely new. This would be impossible, were we not able to distinguish parts in the thought corresponding to the parts of a sentence ...

Not being psychologists we rather abstain from this piece of ontology. In any case the framework was not designed for the purpose of modelling the brain processes.

k) *The fact expressed by the principle is true.*

This claim seems hardly falsifiable since it presupposes an absolute concept of meaning. We don't want to get involved with this type of ontology. The principle has been used as a guiding tool for defining syntax and semantics. For a meaning concept arising out of such an analysis the principle becomes valid. Our experience shows that this can be done for any language. So if we first model the concept of meaning according to the principle and next ask whether the principle is "true" for this concept of meaning the resulting interpretation of the principle becomes circular.

To our opinion argument a) reflects the basic necessity for doing mathematical semantics within a fixed framework, whereas the strong arguments in favour of the compositionality principle are listed under b) ... g).

Our paper by now has become rather philosophical. This is not due to the fact that the research reported here does not contain hard mathematics; several remarks and claims in the text are based upon mathematical results presented in [13]. We merely have hidden the mathematics by concentrating on the relevant issues, some of which are of philosophical nature, but most of which just arose out of the bare necessities of a uniform methodology for doing model-theoretic semantics.

7 REFERENCES.

1 ADJ (J.A. Goguen, J.W. Thatcher, E.G. Wagner & J.B. Wright), *Initial algebra semantics and continuous algebra's*, J. Assoc. Comput. Mach. 24 (1977) 68-95.

2 ADJ (J.W. Thatcher, E.G. Wagner & J.B. Wright), *Notes on algebraic fundamentals for theoretical computer science*, in [5].

3 Andreka, H., I. Nemeti & I. Sain, *Classical many-sorted model theory to turn negative results on program schemes to positive*, Manuscript, Hungarian Acad. Sci. 1978.

4 Andreka, H., I. Nemeti & I. Sain, *Henkin-type model theory for first order dynamic logic*, this volume.

5 de Bakker, J.W. & J. van Leeuwen (eds.), *Foundations of Computer Science III, part 2: Languages, logic, semantics*, Math. Centre Tracts 109 (1979), Amsterdam.

6 van Benthem, J.F.A.K., *Universal algebra and model theory, two excursions on the border*, rep. ZW 7908 dept. math. Univ. Groningen (1980).

7 Ehrig, H., H.J. Kreowski & P. Padawitz, *Stepwise specification and implementation of abstract data types*, in G. Ausiello & C. Böhm (eds.), Proc. ICALP 5, Udine Jul. 1978, Springer LCS 62 (1978) pp. 205-226.

8 Ehrig, H., H.J. Kreowski, J.W. Thatcher, E. Wagner & J. Wright, *Parameterised data types in algebraic specification languages*, in J.W. de Bakker & J. van Leeuwen (eds.), Proc. ICALP 7, Noordwijkerhout jul. 1980, Springer LCS 85 (1980), pp. 157-168.

9 van Emde Boas, P. & T.M.V. Janssen, *The impact of Frege's Principle of compositionality for the semantics of programming and natural languages*, in "Begriffsschrift" Proc. Jenaer Frege Conferenz Jena May 1979; Fr. Schiller Univ. (1979), pp. 110-129.

10 Frege, G. *Compound thoughts (Gedankefüge)*, in P.T. Geach & R.H. Stoohoff (transl.), Logical Investigations. Gottlob Frege, Basil Blackwell, Oxford 1977, pp. 55-78.

11 Janssen, T.M.V. & P. van Emde Boas, *On the proper treatment of referencing, dereferencing and assignment*, in A. Salomaa & M. Steinby (eds.), Proc. ICALP 4, Turku Jul 1977, Springer LCS 52 (1977) 282-300.

12 Janssen, T.M.V. & P. van Emde Boas, *The Expressive Power of intensional logic in the semantics of programming languages*, in J. Gruska (ed.), Proc. MFCS'77, Tatranska Lomnicka, Sep. 1977, Springer LCS 53 (1977), pp. 303-311.

13 Janssen, T.M.V., *Foundations and applications of Montague Grammar*, Ph.D. Thesis Univ. of Amsterdam, forthcomming, ed. Math. Centre Amsterdam.

14 Lewis, D., *General semantics*, in D. Davidson & G. Herman (eds.), Semantics of natural language, Synthese Library 40, Reidel, Dordrecht (1972), pp. 169-248.

15 Markusz, Z. & M. Szots, *On semantics of programming languages defined by universal algebraic tools*, in Proc. Coll. Math. Logic in programming, Coll. Math. Soc. Janos Bolyai, North Holl. Publ. Co. , to appear.

16 Mazurkiewicz, A., *Parallel recursive program schemes*, in J. Becvar (ed.), Proc. MFCS'75, Marianske Lazne, Sep 1975, Springer LCS 32 (1975) pp. 75-87.

17 Milner, R., *Processes: a mathematical model of computing agents*, in H.E. Rose & J.C. Shepherdson (eds.), Logic Colloquium '73 (Bristol), North. Holl. Publ. Co. Amsterdam, 1975, pp. 157-173.

18 Montague, R., *Universal Grammar*, Theoria 36 (1970) 373-398; reprinted in [25].

19 Montague, R., *The proper treatment of quantification in ordinar English*, in K.J.J. Hintikka, J.M.E. Moravcsik & P. Suppes (eds.), Approaches to Natural Language, Synthese Library 49, Reidel, Dordrecht (1973), pp. 221-242; reprinted in [25].

20 Neuholt, E.J. (ed.), *Formal description of programming concepts, Proc. IFIP working conference on formal description of programming concepts, St. Andrews, Canada 1977*, North Holl. Publ. Co., Amsterdam 1978.

21 Partee, B., *Montague grammar and transformational grammar*, Linguistic Enquiry 6 (1975) 203-300.

22 Pratt, V.R., *Dynamic Logic*, in [5].

23 Schwartz, J.T., *Semantic definition methods and the evolution of programming languages*, in R. Rustin (ed.), Formal semantics of programming languages, Courant Comp. Sci. Symp. 2 , Prentice Hall, Englewood Cliffs NJ. 1972, pp. 1-24.

24 Stoy, J.E., *Denotational semantics: the Scott-Strachey approach to programming language theory*, MIT press, Cambridge Mass 1977.

25 Thomason, R.H., (ed.), *Formal Philosophy. Selected papers of Richard Montague*, Yale Univ. Press, New Haven Conn. 1974.

SOME CONNECTIONS BETWEEN ITERATIVE PROGRAMS, RECURSIVE PROGRAMS, AND FIRST-ORDER LOGIC

A.J. Kfoury
Mathematics Department
Boston University
Boston, Mass. 02215

Contrary to the current tendency to define new and more powerful logics than first-order, we continue in this paper the investigation of the relationship between conventional first-order logic and programming formalisms.

We prove algebraic characterizations of the so-called "unwind property" for recursive and iterative programs. These allow us to establish the existence of data types over which: the functions computed by iterative programs are a proper subset of the first-order definable functions, and the first-order definable functions are a proper subset of the functions computed by recursive programs. Our proof techniques are a mixture of first-order model theory, elementary recursion theory, and a new version of the "pebble game".

§ 1. BACKGROUND

The general setting of this paper is defined by the following concepts.

1.1 DATA TYPES: We take a data type $\mathfrak{A}$ to be an object of the form

$$\mathfrak{A} = (\mathbb{A}; \doteq, r_1^A,\ldots,r_m^A ; f_1^A,\ldots,f_n^A)$$

where $\mathbb{A}$ is a set of individual elements, $\doteq$ is the equality relation (different from the metatheoretic =), and $r_1^A ,\ldots, r_m^A; f_1^A ,\ldots, f_n^A$ are primitive relations and functions on $\mathbb{A}$, each with a fixed arity ≥ 0. A data type $\mathfrak{A}$ as just defined may be viewed as a one-sorted (first-order) structure. The sequence τ of primitive relation and function symbols, namely $\tau = (r_1 ,\ldots, r_m; f_1,\ldots,f_n)$, is the similarity type of $\mathfrak{A}$.

For the sake of simplicity (in the formulation of some of the results below), we also require that the universe $\mathbb{A}$ of any structure be countable. Hence when $\mathbb{A}$ is infinite we shall write $\mathbb{A} = \{ a_i \mid i \in \omega \}$, or sometimes identify $\mathbb{A}$ with the set of $\mathbb{N}$ of natural numbers. This restriction has the added benefit of making our results "more relevant" to computer science, where data types are always of countable size.

1.2 PROGRAMS AND PROGRAM SCHEMES: Given a similarity type τ, associated with some structure $\mathfrak{A}$, we consider two classes of program schemes: iterative program schemes and recursive program schemes. An "iterative program scheme" can be drawn as a flow-chart which only mentions relation and function names from τ; whereas a "recursive program scheme" can be drawn as a flow-chart which may also mention in its instructions names of program schemes (including itself).

Although program schemes can be with or without counters, we assume throughout this paper that all program schemes are equipped with counters, i.e. that elementary arithmetic is part of their control structure. We make this assumption primarily for the sake of simplicity. Indeed most structures $\mathfrak{A}$ considered in this paper have enough "structure" so that we can program -- either iteratively or recursively but without counters -- all the computable functions over a subset $\mathbb{N} \subseteq \mathbb{A}$; and therefore, in the case of such structures $\mathfrak{A}$, the presence of counters does not add to the power of a programming language.

We can formally define an iterative (or flow-chart) program scheme S -- with input variables $\{x_1,x_2,\ldots,x_k\}$, $k \geq 0$, and over similarity type $\tau = (r_1,\ldots,r_m;$ $f_1,\ldots,f_n)$ -- to be a finite flow-diagram built up from two kinds of instructions: assignments and tests. In the following definitions we assume we have an infinite supply of program variables $\{y_i \mid i \in \omega\}$ and counters $\{c_i \mid i \in \omega\}$. Input and program variables are assigned values from the universe $\mathbb{A}$ of a structure $\mathfrak{A}$, whereas counters are assigned values from $\mathbb{N}$.

(1) An assignment instruction can take one of the following forms:

(1.1) $\boxed{y_i := v}$ where $v \in \{x_1,\ldots,x_k\} \cup \{y_i \mid i \in \omega\}$;

(1.2) $\boxed{y_i := f(v_1,v_2,\ldots,v_j)}$ where $f \in \{f_1,\ldots,f_m\}$,

$j \geq 0$ is the arity of f, and

$v_1,\ldots,v_j \in \{x_1,\ldots,x_k\} \cup \{y_1 \mid i \in \omega\}$;

(1.3) $\boxed{c_i := c_j}$

(1.4) $\boxed{c_i : 0}$ or $\boxed{c_i := c_i + 1}$ or $\boxed{c_i := c_i \dot{-} 1}$

Note that counters do not "communicate" with input and program variables. Also assignment instructions do not change the values of input variables, only the values of program variables and counters.

(2) A test instruction can take one of the following forms:

(2.1) 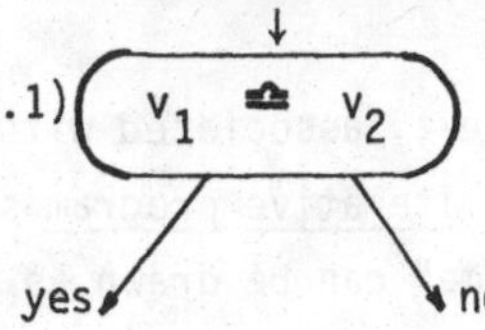

where $v_1, v_2 \in \{x_1, \ldots, x_k\} \cup \{y_i \mid i \in \omega\}$

(2.2) 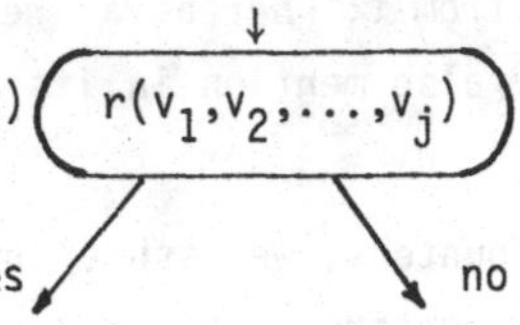

where $v_1, \ldots, v_j \in \{x_1, \ldots, x_k\} \cup \{y_i \mid i \in \omega\}$,

$r \in \{r_1, \ldots, r_m\}$ and $j \geq 1$ is the arity of r ;

(2.3) 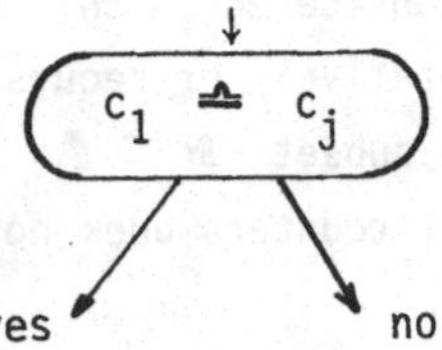

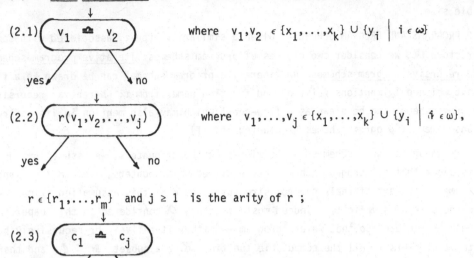

To complete the specification of program scheme S we require that it (as a flow-diagram) have exactly one entry point labelled with input variables $x_1, \ldots, x_k$; and each of the exit points of S be labelled with a variable in $\{x_1, \ldots, x_k\} \cup \{y_i \mid i \in \omega\}$ from which an output value is to be read off.

If we give to each relation and function symbol appearing in S its proper meaning in structure $\mathfrak{A}$, we obtain an iterative program over $\mathfrak{A}$ (or more simply, an iterative $\mathfrak{A}$-program) denoted by $S^{\mathfrak{A}}$. Clearly $S^{\mathfrak{A}}$ defines a k-ary (partial) function on $\mathbb{A}$. We denote the computation of $S^{\mathfrak{A}}$ on input $(a_1, \ldots, a_k) \in \mathbb{A}^k$ by $S^{\mathfrak{A}}(a_1, \ldots, a_k)$. The computation $S^{\mathfrak{A}}(a_1, \ldots, a_k)$ corresponds to a unique path, possibly infinite, through the flow-diagram of S; and a step in the computation is any instruction along the path thus determined. (The results of this paper apply only to deterministic programs.)

Sometimes we want program $S^{\mathfrak{A}}$ to define a k-ary predicate on $\mathbb{A}$. In this case we do not need to label each of the exit points of S with an output variable, the predicate thus defined by $S^{\mathfrak{A}}$ being $\{\vec{a} \in \mathbb{A}^k \mid S^{\mathfrak{A}}(\vec{a})$ converges$\}$.

A recursive program scheme S -- with input variables $\{x_1, x_2, \ldots, x_k\}$ and over similarity type $\tau = (r_1, \ldots, r_m; f_1, \ldots, f_n)$ -- is more general than an iterative program scheme in that it allows in an assignment instruction of the form (1.2) the function symbol f to be also the name of a program scheme (possibly S itself). An apparently more general notion of "recursive program scheme" also allows in a test instruction of the form (2.2) the relation symbol r to be the name of a program scheme (possibly S itself) with each of its exit points having a label from {yes, no}; however, in the presence of the equality relation $\doteq$ and two distinguished elements (identified with "yes" and "no" respectively), there is no loss of generality in restricting recursive calls to appear in assignment instructions only.

More on the classical theory of program schemes can be found in [BGS], [CG],[GL], and [LPP].

Remarks on terminology:

(1) For clarity in the text we try to reserve the word "recursive" to qualify program schemes and programs. A "partial recursive function" on $\mathbb{N}$ will be called a computable function on $\mathbb{N}$, which may or may not be total.

(2) Also, somewhat unconventional, we take the word "partial" to mean "non-total". So that when we talk about a "function" without further qualification, the function is either "total" or "partial" but not both.

1.3 PROGRAMS WITH PARAMETERS: The collection of all program schemes, whether iterative or recursive, in a fixed similarity type is recursively enumerable. When we talk about "all iterative (recursive) $\mathfrak{A}$-programs", we thus talk about the countability infinite set of all iterative (recursive) program schemes S interpreted in $\mathfrak{A}$. As in common programming practice however, we would like to allow finitely many parameters from the universe $\mathbb{A}$ of $\mathfrak{A}$ to appear in a program, in addition to those included as zeroary functions in the similarity type.

To write programs over $\mathfrak{A}$ with parameters from a finite subset $X = \{a_1,\ldots,a_p\} \subseteq \mathbb{A}$, we have to consider the similarity type of the following structure:

$$(\mathfrak{A},X) = (\mathbb{A}; \doteq, r_1^A,\ldots,r_m^A ; f_1^A,\ldots, f_n^A , a_1,\ldots,a_p)$$

where $a_1,\ldots,a_p$ are viewed as constant primitive functions in $(\mathfrak{A},X)$. The similarity type of $(\mathfrak{A},X)$ is denoted by

$$\tau_X = (r_1,\ldots,r_m; f_1,\ldots,f_n, \underline{a}_1,\ldots,\underline{a}_p)$$

where $\underline{a}_i$ is a zeroary function symbol corresponding to constant function a_i. If S is a program scheme in similarity type τ_X, then $S^{(\mathfrak{A},X)}$ is a program over $\mathfrak{A}$ with parameters from X, or more simply a $(\mathfrak{A},X)$ - program. The set of all iterative (recursive) programs over $\mathfrak{A}$ with finitely many parameters is then:

$$\{ S^{(\mathfrak{A},X)} \mid S \text{ is an iterative (recursive) program scheme in similarity type } \tau_X \text{ of } (\mathfrak{A},X) \text{ for some finite } X \subseteq \mathbb{A} \},$$

which we shall also call the set of all iterative (recursive) $(\mathfrak{A}, \mathbb{A})$-programs, A $(\mathfrak{A}, \mathbb{A})$-program is thus a $(\mathfrak{A},X)$-program for some finite $X \subseteq \mathbb{A}$.

§ 2. AN ALGEBRAIC CHARACTERIZATION OF THE UNWIND PROPERTY

A loop in an iterative program scheme S is a cycle (i.e. a simple closed path) in the finite flow-diagram of S. As usual we define a loop-free program scheme to be an iterative program scheme where each of the loops (if any) is of length = 1, i.e. it is a self loop of the form:

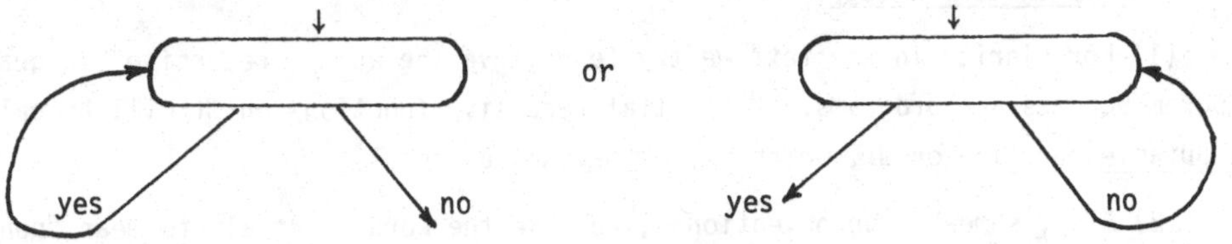

The domain of a program $S^{\mathfrak{A}}$ with input variables $x_1, x_2, \ldots, x_k$, denoted domain ($S^{\mathfrak{A}}$), is the set of all input vectors $\vec{a} \in \mathbb{A}^k$ for which $S^{\mathfrak{A}}(\vec{a})$ converges. We say that $S^{\mathfrak{A}}$ is total if domain($S^{\mathfrak{A}}$) = $\mathbb{A}^k$. Note that domain($S^{\mathfrak{A}}$) is none other than the predicate computed by $S^{\mathfrak{A}}$, as defined in 1.2.

According to our definition here, a loop-free program is not necessarily total. (This is different from our convention in [K] where we distinguished between "loop-free" programs, which are always total, and "quasi-loop-free" programs, which may or may not be total because of the presence of self loops.)

2.1 THE UNWIND PROPERTY: An iterative (or recursive) program $S^{\mathfrak{A}}$ with $k \geq 1$ input variables unwinds -- or equivalently, program scheme S unwinds over structure $\mathfrak{A}$ -- if there is a $n \in \mathbb{N}$ such that for all input values $\vec{a} \in \mathbb{A}^k$, if $S^{\mathfrak{A}}(\vec{a})$ converges then it converges in fewer than n steps.

If $\mathcal{P}$ is a class of $\mathfrak{A}$-programs and every program $S^{\mathfrak{A}} \in \mathcal{P}$ unwinds, we say that $\mathfrak{A}$ has the unwind property for $\mathcal{P}$.

Two programs $S_1^{\mathfrak{A}}$ and $S_2^{\mathfrak{A}}$ are equivalent -- or equivalently, program schemes S_1 and S_2 are $\mathfrak{A}$-equivalent -- if $S_1^{\mathfrak{A}}$ and $S_2^{\mathfrak{A}}$ compute the same function over the universe $\mathbb{A}$ of $\mathfrak{A}$.

2.2 PROPOSITION: If an iterative or recursive program $S^{\mathfrak{A}}$ unwinds then $S^{\mathfrak{A}}$ is equivalent to a loop-free $\mathfrak{A}$-program $\bar{S}^{\mathfrak{A}}$.

The converse of 2.2 is not generally true; that is, there is a structure $\mathfrak{A}$ and a $\mathfrak{A}$-program $S^{\mathfrak{A}}$ such that $S^{\mathfrak{A}}$ is equivalent to a loop-free $\mathfrak{A}$-program, but $S^{\mathfrak{A}}$ does not unwind. We shall specify conditions under which the converse of 2.2 does hold.

Forthcoming results are stated in terms of the following concepts.

2.3 DEFINITION:

(a) Structure $\mathfrak{A}$ is locally finite if every non-empty finite subset of $\mathbb{A}$ generates a finite substructure of $\mathfrak{A}$.

(b) Structure $\mathfrak{A}$ is uniformly locally finite if for every $k \geq 1$ there is a $n \in \mathbb{N}$ (possibly depending on k) such that every k-generated substructure of $\mathfrak{A}$ has at most n elements. ("k-generated" means finitely generated from k distinct elements.)

2.4 THEOREM: The following are equivalent statements:

(a) Structure $\mathfrak{A}$ is uniformly locally finite;

(b) Every recursive program over $\mathfrak{A}$ unwinds;

(c) Every recursive program over $\mathfrak{A}$ with parameters unwinds.

Proof. This is Theorem 3.7 in [K] (with a slight difference in terminology). □

A k-ary predicate X on $\mathbb{A}$, $X \subseteq \mathbb{A}^k$, is parametrically definable in $\mathfrak{A}$ if there is a first-order formula $\psi(x_1,\ldots,x_k,y_1,\ldots,y_\ell)$ and parameters $\vec{b} = (b_1,\ldots,b_\ell) \in \mathbb{A}^\ell$ such that:

$$X = \{\vec{a} \mid \vec{a} \in \mathbb{A}^k \text{ and } \mathfrak{A} \models \psi[\vec{a},\vec{b}]\}$$

If $\ell=0$ we say that X is definable in $\mathfrak{A}$, i.e., without parameters. A k-ary function Y from $\mathbb{A}^k$ to $\mathbb{A}$ is (parametrically) definable in $\mathfrak{A}$ if Y, as a (k+1)-ary relation, is (parametrically) definable in $\mathfrak{A}$.

2.5 COROLLARY: Structure $\mathfrak{A}$ is uniformly locally finite. Then any function or predicate X on $\mathbb{A}$ is computed by a recursive program over $\mathfrak{A}$ (respectively, a recursive program over $\mathfrak{A}$ with parameters) $\Longleftrightarrow$ X is definable (respectively, parametrically definable) in $\mathfrak{A}$ by a quantifier-free formula.

Proof. ($\Leftarrow$) This is true whether or not $\mathfrak{A}$ is uniformly locally finite, and the $\mathfrak{A}$-program computing X can always be written as a loop-free program. Details omitted.

($\Rightarrow$) Since $\mathfrak{A}$ is uniformly locally finite, the recursive $\mathfrak{A}$-program (respec., $(\mathfrak{A},\mathbb{A})$-program) computing X unwinds, by 2.4. By unwinding this program we obtain a loop-free $\mathfrak{A}$-program (respec., $(\mathfrak{A},\mathbb{A})$-program), which can be transformed into an "equivalent" quantifier-free formula. Details omitted. □

To prove the counterpart of 2.4 and 2.5 relative to iterative programs, we need the following series of definitions and results.

Given similarity type $\tau = (r_1,\ldots,r_m; f_1,\ldots,f_n)$ and input variables $\vec{x} = (x_1,\ldots,x_k)$, we define the set of all $\vec{x}$-terms inductively as follows:

(1) $x_1,x_2,\ldots,x_k$ are all $\vec{x}$-terms;

(2) if $f \in \{f_1,\ldots,f_n\}$ is a j-ary function symbol, $j \geq 0$, and $t_1,\ldots,t_j$ are $\vec{x}$-terms, then so too is $f(t_1,\ldots,t_j)$.

A subterm of a term t is one produced in the course of constructing t inductively using rules (1) and (2) above.

We define in a natural way a function <u>rank</u> from the set of $\vec{x}$-terms to $\mathbb{N}$:

(1) if t is a variable or a o-ary function symbol then
$\underline{rank}(t):=0$;

(2) if t is of the form $f(t_1,\ldots,t_j)$, $j \geq 1$, then $\underline{rank}(t):= \max\{\underline{rank}(t_1),\ldots,\underline{rank}(t_j)\}+1$.

It is easy to check that <u>rank</u> is onto $\mathbb{N}$.

Given an $\vec{x}$-term t we shall sometimes exhibit explicitly the variables by writing $t(\vec{x})$ or $t(x_1,\ldots,x_k)$. And if $\mathfrak{A}$ is a structure with similarity type τ, the interpretation of t in $\mathfrak{A}$ will be denoted t^A or $t^A(x_1,\ldots,x_k)$.

With every $\vec{x}$-term t we can associate a finite dag (directed acyclic graph) G_t, with as many input nodes as there are variables and o-ary function symbols in t, and with exactly one output node labelled with the full expression for t.
For example, if c and g are 0-ary and 2-ary function symbols, respectively, then we can represent the (x_1,x_2)-term $g(c,g(g(c,x_1),x_1))$ by the following dag:

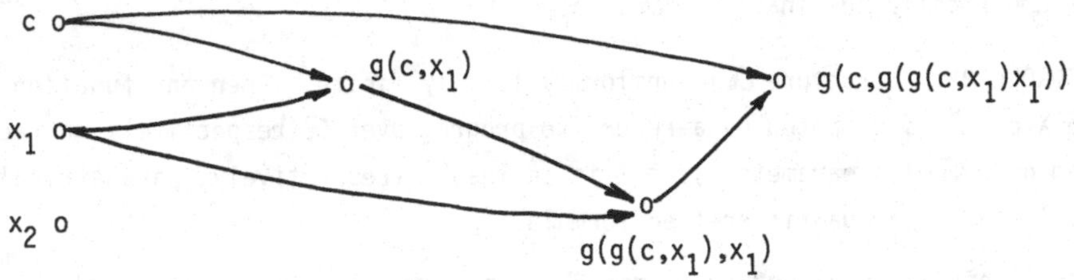

Strictly speaking if nodes u_1 and u_2 are incident to node v in this dag -- and u_1,u_2, v are associated with terms t_1,t_2, $g(t_1,t_2)$ respectively -- we should label the edges (u_1,v) and (u_2,v) with 1 and 2, respectively, corresponding to the order of the two arguments in $g(t_1,t_2)$. For our present purposes however, we may ignore the ordering of edges incident to the same node in G_t.
We define then <u>pebble complexity</u> of t as follows:

$\underline{pebble}(t)$:= minimum # of pebbles required to pebble G_t,
i.e. to reach the output node of G_t.

We shall later consider subsets of the set of all $\vec{x}$-terms according to the number of program variables (corresponding to "pebbles") used by an iterative program scheme. We thus define for each $\ell \geq 0$ the set of all <u>ℓ-$\vec{x}$-terms</u> as follows:

$$\{\, t \mid t \text{ is a } \vec{x}\text{-term and } \underline{pebble}(t) \leq \ell \,\}.$$

The correspondence we assume throughout this paper, except in the Appendix, is between pebbles and program variables only, excluding input variables. In the Appendix, the proper correspondence is between the number of pebbles and the total number of input + program variables. Each of these two correspondences is adopted for convenience in each case. The results are not affected by the difference between the two.

The following are basic definitions for this paper, formulated in terms of the syntactic notions introduced above. We also repeat the definitions of 2.3 but differently.

2.6 DEFINITION:

(a) Structure $\mathfrak{A}$ is <u>locally finite</u> if for all k and all $\vec{a} \in \mathbb{A}^k$ the following set is finite: $\{t^A(\vec{a}) \mid t \text{ is a } \vec{x}\text{-term}\}$.

(b) Structure $\mathfrak{A}$ is <u>locally finite w.r.t.</u>(with respect to) <u>bounded space</u> if for all k, for all ℓ and for all $\vec{a} \in \mathbb{A}^k$ the following set is finite: $\{ t^A(\vec{a}) \mid t \text{ is a } \ell\text{-}\vec{x}\text{-term}\}$.

(c) Structure $\mathfrak{A}$ is <u>uniformly locally finite</u> if for all k there is a $n \in \mathbb{N}$, and for all $\vec{a} \in \mathbb{A}^k$ the following set has at most n elements: $\{ t^A(\vec{a}) \mid t \text{ is a } \vec{x}\text{-term}\}$.

(d) Structure $\mathfrak{A}$ is <u>uniformly locally finite w.r.t. bounded space</u> if for all k and for all ℓ there is a $n \in \mathbb{N}$, and for all $\vec{a} \in \mathbb{A}^k$ the following set has at most n elements: $\{ t^A(\vec{a}) \mid t \text{ is a } \ell\text{-}\vec{x}\text{-term}\}$.

For convenience in the next and later proofs, we define the "distance" from an arbitrary $\vec{a} \in \mathbb{A}^k$ to an arbitrary $b \in \mathbb{A}$. If b is not accessible from $\vec{a}$, then <u>distance</u>$(\vec{a},b)$ is undefined, otherwise:

$$\underline{\text{distance}}(\vec{a},b) := \underline{\inf}\ \{ \underline{\text{rank}}(t) \mid t \text{ is a } \vec{x}\text{-term and } t^A(\vec{a}) = b\}.$$

(Warning: the definition of <u>distance</u> here differs from that in [K], because the definition of <u>rank</u> here is also different from that in [K].)

2.7 LEMMA: If structure $\mathfrak{A}$ is not uniformly locally finite w.r.t. bounded space, then there is an iterative program over $\mathfrak{A}$ which does <u>not</u> unwind.

<u>Proof</u> (outlined). First, by 2.6 part (d), we have the following fact about $\mathfrak{A}$:

$$\exists k\ \exists \ell\ \forall n\ \exists \vec{a} \in \mathbb{A}^k \quad \left| \{t^A(\vec{a}) \mid t \text{ is a } \ell\text{-}\vec{x}\text{-term}\} \right| > n.$$

We construct an iterative program P over $\mathfrak{A}$ with (k+1) input variables $x_1, x_2, \ldots, x_k$, y, and with ℓ program variables, which does not unwind. The action of P is defined by the following steps:

(1) The input to P is arbitrary $\vec{a} \in \mathbb{A}^k$ and $b \in \mathbb{A}$.

(2) P effectively enumerates all ℓ-$\vec{x}$-terms in order of non-decreasing ranks

-- say $t_0, t_1, \ldots, t_i, \ldots$, $i \in \omega$. All that is required in this step is iterative programming over the counters of P, based on some appropriate arithmetization of the ℓ-$\vec{x}$-terms (syntactic objects).

(3) Using the ℓ program variables, and every time a new ℓ-$\vec{x}$-term t_i is generated in step (2), P computes the value of $t_i^A(\vec{a})$ and compares it with b. If $t_i^A(\vec{a}) \not\triangleq b$, P proceeds to generate ℓ-$\vec{x}$-term t_{i+1} in step (2); if $t_i^A(\vec{a}) \triangleq b$, P computes rank($t_i$) which is exactly distance($\vec{a}$,b) and stores rank(t_i) in counter c -- then goes to step (4).

(If b is not accessible from $\vec{a}$, then distance($\vec{a}$,b) is undefined and P will diverge. Because $\mathfrak{A}$ is not uniformly locally finite w.r.t. bounded space, however, it is easy to check that for all $d \in \mathbb{N}$ there are $\vec{a} \in \mathbb{A}^k$ and $b \in \mathbb{A}$ such that distance ($\vec{a}$,b) = d.)

(4) P enters a subroutine Q using counters only, c holding the input to Q. Q can be chosen to be any iterative program computing a number-theoretic predicate not computable by a loop-free program, using "successor", "predecessor", and "zero" (the operations allowed on counters). P converges if and when Q converges. □

Let $\mathfrak{A}$ be an arbitrary structure with similarity type τ. Let T be a subset of the set of all $(x_1, \ldots, x_k)$-terms. The substructure generated by $\vec{a} \in \mathbb{A}^k$ relative to T is a partial substructure $\mathfrak{B}$ of $\mathfrak{A}$ -- defined as follows:

(1) The universe $\mathbb{B}$ of $\mathfrak{B}$ is $\{t^A(\vec{a}) \mid t(\vec{x}) \in T\}$.

(2) For every relation symbol $r \in \tau$, r^B is the restriction of r^A to $\mathbb{B} \subseteq \mathbb{A}$, i.e. $r^B = r^A \upharpoonright \mathbb{B}$.

(3) For every function symbol $f \in \tau$ of arity $j \geq 0$, and every $t_1^A(\vec{a}), \ldots, t_j^A(\vec{a}) \in \mathbb{B}$:

$$f^B(t_1^A(\vec{a}), \ldots, t_j^A(\vec{a})) = \begin{cases} f^A(t_1^A(\vec{a}), \ldots, t_j^A(\vec{a})), & \text{if } f(t_1(\vec{x}), \ldots, t_j(\vec{x})) \in T; \\ \bot, & \text{otherwise.} \end{cases}$$

Let us denote the substructure $\mathfrak{B}$ generated by $\vec{a}$ relative to T by sub($\vec{a}$,T). Note that sub($\vec{a}$,T) is a substructure of $\mathfrak{A}$ in the usual sense, i.e. sub($\vec{a}$,T) is not partial, if T is the set of all $(x_1, \ldots, x_k)$-terms.

We now define an equivalence relation $\sim_T$ on $\mathbb{A}^k$ relative to T; namely for all $\vec{a}$, $\vec{b} \in \mathbb{A}^k$:

$$\vec{a} \sim_T \vec{b} \iff \text{sub}(\vec{a},T) \text{ isomorphic to } \text{sub}(\vec{b},T).$$

We denote the equivalence class of $\vec{a} \in \mathbb{A}^k$ with respect to $\sim_T$ by $[\vec{a}]_T$, so that $\mathbb{A}^k/\sim_T = \{[\vec{a}]_T \mid \vec{a} \in \mathbb{A}^k\}$.

If $\mathfrak{A}$ is locally finite and T arbitrary, or if $\mathfrak{A}$ is locally finite w.r.t. bounded space and T a subset of ℓ-$\vec{x}$-terms for some ℓ, then $\underline{sub}(\vec{a},T)$ is finite for every $\vec{a} \in \mathbb{A}^k$.

If $\mathfrak{A}$ is uniformly locally finite and T arbitrary, or if $\mathfrak{A}$ is uniformly locally finite w.r.t. bounded space and T is a subset of ℓ-$\vec{x}$-terms for some ℓ, then there is an upper bound n such that $\left|\underline{sub}(\vec{a},T)\right| \leq n$ for every $\vec{a} \in \mathbb{A}^k$. This means that the equivalence relation $\sim_T$ has finite index in this case -- a fact we use in the next lemma.

2.8 LEMMA: If $\mathfrak{A}$ is uniformly locally finite w.r.t. bounded space then every iterative program over $\mathfrak{A}$ unwinds.

Proof. We consider an iterative $\mathfrak{A}$-program $S^{\mathfrak{A}}$ computing a k-ary predicate on $\mathbb{A}$. We can transform S into an equivalent red (relational effective definition) as shown in [K]:

$$\underline{red}(S) \;:=\; (\sigma_i(\vec{x}) \mid i \in \omega) ,$$

where each $\sigma_i(\vec{x})$ is a finite conjunction of atomic and negated atomic formulas in variables $\vec{x} = (x_1,\ldots,x_k)$. We also assume that $\underline{red}(S)$ is infinite; when $\underline{red}(S)$ is finite, the proof to follow becomes trivial.

The effective enumeration of $\underline{red}(S)$ corresponds to the effective enumeration of all finite paths (not necessarily consistent) in S, say: $\pi_0,\pi_1,\ldots,\pi_i,\ldots,i \in \omega$. So that computation $S^{\mathfrak{A}}(\vec{a})$ follows path π_i and converges iff $\mathfrak{A} \models \sigma_i[\vec{a}]$. We can always assume that for $i \neq j$, $\sigma_i(\vec{x})$ is not consistent with $\sigma_j(\vec{x})$, i.e. $\exists \vec{x}[\sigma_i(\vec{x}) \wedge \sigma_j(\vec{x})]$ is a contradiction.

It is easily seen that $S^{\mathfrak{A}}$ unwinds iff there is a $n \in \omega$, such that for all $\vec{a} \in \mathbb{A}^k$: if $\mathfrak{A} \models \sigma_i[\vec{a}]$ then $i < n$.

Since S is iterative, all terms appearing in $\underline{red}(S)$ are ℓ-$\vec{x}$-terms for some fixed ℓ; more specifically, the set

$$U := \{ u \mid u \text{ is a } \vec{x}\text{-term which appears as an argument of an atomic or negated atomic formula in } \underline{red}(S) \}$$

is a subset of the set T of all ℓ-$\vec{x}$-terms.

$\mathfrak{A}$ being uniformly locally finite w.r.t. bounded space, $\mathbb{A}^k/\sim_T$ has finitely many equivalence classes. To complete the proof it suffices to show that $S^{\mathfrak{A}}$ unwinds when input vectors are restricted to any one of these equivalence classes $X \in \mathbb{A}^k/\sim_T$. This is easily verified since for all $\vec{a}, \vec{b} \in X$, $\underline{sub}(\vec{a},T)$ and $\underline{sub}(\vec{b},T)$ are isomorphic finite substructures. □

2.9 THEOREM: The following are equivalent statements:

(a) Structure $\mathfrak{A}$ is uniformly locally finite w.r.t. bounded space;
(b) Every iterative program over $\mathfrak{A}$ unwinds;
(c) Every iterative program over $\mathfrak{A}$ with parameters unwinds.

Proof. (a) $\Leftrightarrow$ (b): This double implication follows from 2.7 and 2.8.

(b) $\Leftrightarrow$ (c): Trivial. □

2.10 COROLLARY: Structure $\mathfrak{A}$ is uniformly locally finite w.r.t. bounded space. Then any function or predicate X on $\mathbb{A}$ is computed by an iterative program over $\mathfrak{A}$ (respectively, iterative program over $\mathfrak{A}$ with parameters) $\Leftrightarrow$ X is definable (respectively, parametrically definable) in $\mathfrak{A}$ by a quantifier-free formula.

Proof. This follows the proof of 2.5, and is a direct consequence of 2.9. □

In the next section we give an example of a structure which is uniformly locally finite w.r.t. bounded space -- but not uniformly locally finite, or even locally finite, w.r.t. unbounded space.

In a later paper we show that the converse of 2.5 is also true -- namely, that if the set of functions and predicates computable by recursive programs over structure $\mathfrak{A}$ is identical to the set of functions and predicates definable by quantifier-free formulas in $\mathfrak{A}$, then $\mathfrak{A}$ is uniformly locally finite; on the other hand, we also show that the converse of 2.10 does not hold in general.

§ 3. A STRUCTURE WITH THE UNWIND PROPERTY FOR EVERY ITERATIVE (BUT NOT EVERY RECURSIVE) PROGRAM

The structure $\mathfrak{N} = (\mathbb{N} ; \doteq ; g, 0)$ we now define is not locally finite, but is nonetheless uniformly locally finite w.r.t. bounded space. Hence this is an example of a structure $\mathfrak{N}$ for which every iterative $\mathfrak{N}$-program unwinds, but not every recursive $\mathfrak{N}$-program does.

The universe $\mathbb{N}$ of $\mathfrak{N}$ is the set of all natural numbers. The function $g: \mathbb{N} \times \mathbb{N} \rightarrow \mathbb{N}$ is defined by:

$$g(i,j) = \begin{cases} j+1, & \text{if } i = \lfloor j/2 \rfloor ; \\ 0 , & \text{otherwise.} \end{cases}$$

The structure $\mathfrak{N}$ is essentially the "ω-chained complete binary tree" $\mathbb{D}$ defined in the Appendix. The function g relative to $\mathbb{D}$ is the following map: Given two nodes x and y, if there is a node z with a plain edge from x to z, and with a dashed edge from y to z, then g(x,y)=z -- otherwise g(x,y)=0.

The Proposition in the Appendix shows that $\mathfrak{N}$ is uniformly locally finite w.r.t. bounded space. Thus any iterative $\mathfrak{N}$-program whether total or not, unwinds.

It is easy to see, however, that $\mathfrak{N}$ is not locally finite (w.r.t. unbounded space). There are therefore recursive $\mathfrak{N}$-programs which do not unwind, by 2.4. We can say more about the structure $\mathfrak{N}$.

3.1 LEMMA: There is a recursive $\mathfrak{N}$-program SUCC which computes the successor function on $\mathbb{N}$.

Proof. The recursive $\mathfrak{N}$-program SUCC is given below

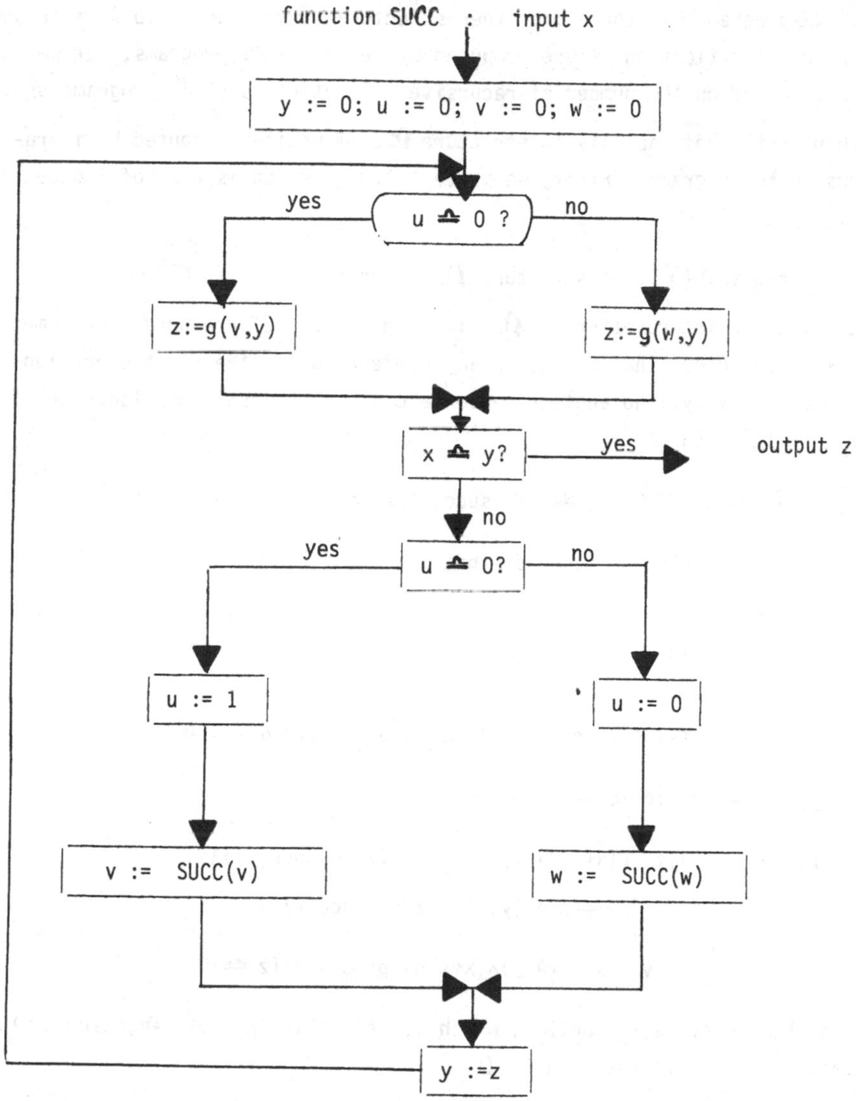

It is not difficult to verify that the above recursive $\mathfrak{N}$-program defines the successor function SUCC: $\mathbb{N} \to \mathbb{N}$. □

Since iterative programs using "successor" and "constant 0" (in assignments) and "equality" (in tests) suffice to define all the computable functions on $\mathbb{N}$, we now have the following result.

3.2 PROPOSITION: Every computable function on $\mathbb{N}$ is computed by some iterative program over the structure ($\mathbb{N}$; ≙; SUCC, g, 0) ; put differently, every computable function on $\mathbb{N}$ is computed by some $\mathfrak{N}$-program with at most one recursive subroutine. □

The preceding result is not true in general. That is, there are structures $\mathfrak{A}$ with universe $\mathbb{A} = \mathbb{N}$ such that not every computable function on $\mathbb{N}$ is computed by some recursive $\mathfrak{A}$-program; and there are other structures $\mathfrak{B}$ with universe $\mathbb{B} = \mathbb{N}$ such that all computable functions on $\mathbb{N}$ are computed by recursive $\mathfrak{B}$-programs, but we cannot put a uniform bound on the number of recursive subroutines such $\mathfrak{B}$-programs use.

We now turn to the definability in structure $\mathfrak{N}$ of functions computed by iterative and recursive $\mathfrak{N}$-programs. First, we prove a lemma, which is also of independent interest.

3.3 LEMMA: The theory Th($\mathfrak{N}$) of structure $\mathfrak{N}$ is decidable.

Proof. This consists in interpreting Th($\mathfrak{N}$) into the theory of Presburger arithmetic, Th $(\langle \mathbb{N}; \simeq; +, \text{succ}, 0 \rangle)$. That is, given any sentence σ (in the first-order language of $\mathfrak{N}$) we effectively find another sentence $\hat{\sigma}$ (in the first-order language of Presburger arithmetic) such that:

$$\mathfrak{N} \models \sigma \text{ iff } \langle \mathbb{N}; \simeq; +, \text{succ}, 0 \rangle \models \hat{\sigma} .$$

Since the latter is decidable, we conclude that Th($\mathfrak{N}$) is too.

To establish the interpretation of Th($\mathfrak{N}$) into Th$(\langle \mathbb{N}; \simeq; +,\text{succ}, 0 \rangle)$, it suffices to construct a formula $\sigma_g(x,y,z)$ in the language of the latter such that for all $a,b,c \in \mathbb{N}$

$$\langle \mathbb{N}; \simeq; +, \text{succ}, 0 \rangle \models \sigma_g[a,b,c] \text{ iff } g(a,b) \simeq c.$$

We can rewrite $g(x,y) \simeq z$ as follows:

$$\begin{aligned} g(z,y) \simeq z \quad \text{iff } & [(x+x \simeq y) \wedge (z \simeq \text{succ}(y))] \\ & \vee [(x+x \simeq \text{pred}(y)) \wedge (z \simeq \text{succ}(y))] \\ & \vee [(x+x \not\simeq y) \wedge (x+x \not\simeq \text{pred}(y)) \wedge (z \simeq 0)] \end{aligned}$$

where "pred" is the predecessor function, which is definable in $\langle \mathbb{N}; \simeq; +, \text{succ}, 0 \rangle$. Remaining details are left to the reader. $\square$

It is worth noting that Th($\mathfrak{N}$) does not admit elimination of quantifiers. Indeed, the set of even numbers is definable in $\mathfrak{N}$ by the following formula $\varphi(y)$:

$$\exists x[g(x,y) \not\simeq 0 \wedge g(x,g(x,y)) \not\simeq 0].$$

$\varphi(y)$ is not equivalent to any quantifier-free formula. That Th($\mathfrak{N}$) does not admit elimination of quantifiers is also a consequence of the next result.

3.4 PROPOSITION:

(a) A function (or a predicate) on $\mathbb{N}$ is computed by an iterative $\mathfrak{N}$-program iff it is definable in $\mathfrak{N}$ by a quantifier-free formula.

(b) There are functions (and predicates) on $\mathbb{N}$ computed by recursive $\mathfrak{N}$-programs which are not definable in $\mathfrak{N}$ by any first-order formulas.

Proof. (a) This follows from the fact that $\mathfrak{N}$ is uniformly locally finite w.r.t. bounded space and 2.10.

(b) Suppose that every predicate computed by a recursive $\mathfrak{N}$-program is definable in $\mathfrak{N}$ by a first-order formula -- and we shall get a contradiction.

Let X be a r.e. but not decidable subset of $\mathbb{N}$. By 3.2, X = domain($S^{\mathfrak{N}}$) for some recursive $\mathfrak{N}$-program $S^{\mathfrak{N}}$ with one input variable. Let $\psi(x)$ be the formula which defines X in $\mathfrak{N}$, so that for all $n \in \mathbb{N}$:

$$\mathfrak{N} \models \psi[n] \quad \text{iff} \quad S^{\mathfrak{N}}(n) \text{ converges.}$$

Since $n \in \mathbb{N}$ is accessible from 0 by finitely many applications of the function g, $\psi[n]$ can be replaced by a closed formula ψ_n in the language of $\mathfrak{N}$. Hence $\psi_n \in Th(\mathfrak{N})$ iff $S^{\mathfrak{N}}(n)$ converges, but the former is decidable while the latter is not -- a contradiction. □

In view of the preceding result, it remains to investigate the class of partial functions and predicates computed by recursive $\mathfrak{N}$-programs which are also definable in $\mathfrak{N}$ by first-order formulas with quantifiers (not done in this paper).

What we have now established is the following proper inclusions:

{functions computed by iterative programs over $\mathfrak{N}$} $\subsetneq$

{functions first-order definable in $\mathfrak{N}$} $\subsetneq$

{functions computed by recursive programs over $\mathfrak{N}$}.

If we denote by $\mathfrak{N}_0$ the structure ($\mathbb{N}$; $\triangleq$; succ, 0) and by $\mathfrak{N}_1$ the standard model of arithmetic ($\mathbb{N}$; $\triangleq$; x,+,0,1), we then have by contrast the following (known) results:

{functions first-order definable in $\mathfrak{N}_0$} $\subsetneq$

{functions computed by iterative programs over $\mathfrak{N}_0$} =

{functions computed by recursive programs over $\mathfrak{N}_0$}.

{functions computed by iterative programs over $\mathfrak{N}_1$} =

{functions computed by recursive programs over $\mathfrak{N}_1$} $\subsetneq$

{functions first-order definable in $\mathfrak{N}_1$}.

APPENDIX: THE PEBBLE GAME ON AN INFINITE DAG

Some of our results depend on certain properties of the pebble game on infinite dags (directed acyclic graphs). We consider a particular infinite dag first, called $\mathbb{D}$, which is best described by the diagram of Figure 1.

The elements of $\mathbb{D}$ are indexed with the natural numbers, $\mathbb{D} = \{ d_i \mid i \in \omega \}$. $\mathbb{D}$ has two distinct intertwined "structures": the structure of an infinite complete binary tree (the plain edges in the diagram), and the structure of a ω-chain (the dashed edges). It is thus helpful to think of $\mathbb{D}$ as being an infinite complete binary tree, whose nodes have been ω-chained by traversing them left-to-right, top-down.

The pebble game on $\mathbb{D}$ is defined as follows. Given a supply of $\ell \geq 1$ pebbles and an initial k-configuration C with $k \leq \ell$, we want to determine the elements of $\mathbb{D}$ accessible from C using no more than the ℓ available pebbles. The initial k-configuration C is a selection of k nodes in $\mathbb{D}$ (the "input values") on which k of the ℓ pebbles are placed. As usual a legal <u>move</u> consists in placing a pebble π on a node x such that all the nodes incident to x have each a pebble already on it; pebble π is not necessarily a fresh pebble, i.e. π may be a pebble we remove from some node, including possibly from one of the nodes incident to x.

If the result of such a move is to go from a k-configuration C to a k'-configuration C', $1 \leq k \leq k' \leq \ell$, we say that C <u>moves</u> to C' -- and we write $C \vdash C'$.

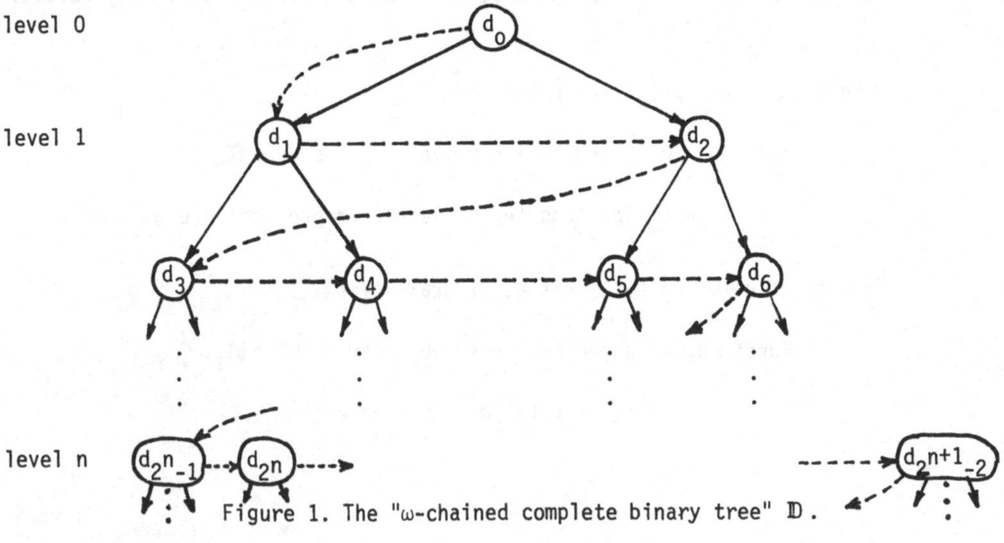

Figure 1. The "ω-chained complete binary tree" $\mathbb{D}$.

A node x is accessible from a configuration C if there is a configuration C' such that $x \in C'$ and $C \vdash\!\overset{*}{\text{---}} C'$, where $\vdash\!\overset{*}{\text{---}}$ is the reflexive transitive closure of $\vdash\!\text{---}$.

A k-configuration C being a selection of k nodes in $\mathbb{D}$, we can intersect C with an arbitrary subset $X \subseteq \mathbb{D}$; the size $|C \cap X|$ of $C \cap X$ can be any value in the set $\{0,1,\ldots,k\}$.

We shall call a (possibly infinite) sequence of configurations $\mathcal{C}=(C_0,C_1,C_2,\ldots)$ a legal sequence if for every $C_i \in \mathcal{C}$ we have $C_i \vdash\!\text{---} C_{i+1}$. The number of pebbles used by $\mathcal{C}$, denoted by $\#(\mathcal{C})$, is defined as follows:

$$\#(\mathcal{C}) := \sup \{ |C| \mid C \in \mathcal{C}\}.$$

We also say that the legal sequence $\mathcal{C}$ reaches a node x if there is a configuration $C_i \in \mathcal{C}$ which contains x; this is equivalent to saying that x is accessible from the initial configuration C_0 of $\mathcal{C}$.

For the purposes of this paper we only need the following result, which we state without its (lengthy technical) proof.

PROPOSITION: Given a supply of ℓ pebbles and a k-configuration C on $\mathbb{D}$, with $k \leq \ell$, the maximum number of nodes accessible from C does not exceed

$$\mu(\ell) = \lfloor 7 \cdot 2^{(\ell-1)} - (\ell+3) \rfloor.$$

This upper bound is tight in that there are k-configurations, $k \leq \ell$, which reach exactly $\mu(\ell)$ nodes.

REMARK: The correspondence we have adopted in this Appendix, between pebbles and variables in an iterative program, is the following one. An initial k-configuration C_0 on the dag $\mathbb{D}$, $k \geq 1$, represents k input values stored in k input variables; and if the supply of pebbles is of size $\ell \geq k$, this means that there are $(\ell-k)$ program variables not used for input. In the course of a computation from C_0, corresponding to a legal sequence $\mathcal{C}=(C_0,C_1,C_2,\ldots)$, the k pebbles initially placed on the nodes in C_0 are also allowed to move.

In the main part of this paper we adopted a slightly different convention, for the sake of convenience. The proper correspondence between pebbles and variables in an iterative program, as discussed before Definition 2.6, is the following one. The pebbles used in a computation represent program variables only, excluding input variables. With this convention, the number ℓ of pebbles required to reach a node in a dag may be less than the number k of input nodes.

Had we followed this convention in this Appendix, we would require that the k pebbles of an initial configuration C_0 not be allowed to move in the course of a computation. The supply of ℓ pebbles would then be independent of k in this case.

REFERENCES

[BGS] Brown, Gries, and Szymanski, "Program schemes with pushdown stores", SIAM J. Comput. 1, 1972.

[CG] Constable and Gries, "On classes of program schemata," SIAM J. Computing,1, 1972.

[GL] Garland and Luckham, "Program schemes, recursion schemes, and formal languages", JCSS, 7, 1973.

[K] Kfoury, "Loop elimination and loop reduction", Proceedings of 21st Symposium on FOCS, 1980.

[LPP] Luckham, Park, and Paterson, "On formalized computer programs", JCSS, 4, 1970.

ON INDUCTION VS. *-CONTINUITY

Dexter Kozen

IBM Thomas J. Watson Research Center
Yorktown Heights, New York 10598

Abstract. In this paper we study the relative expressibility of the infinitary **-continuity condition*

(*-cont) $<\alpha^*>X \equiv \vee_n <\alpha^n>X$

and the equational but weaker *induction axiom*

(ind) $X \wedge [\alpha^*](X \supset [\alpha]X) \equiv [\alpha^*]X$

in Propositional Dynamic Logic. We show: (1) under **ind** only, there is a first-order sentence distinguishing separable dynamic algebras from standard Kripke models; whereas (2) under the stronger axiom ***-cont**, the class of separable dynamic algebras and the class of standard Kripke models are indistinguishable by any sentence of infinitary first-order logic.

1. Introduction

Propositional Dynamic Logic (PDL), introduced by Fischer and Ladner [FL], is the propositional version of Dynamic Logic [Pr1, see also H]. It is a maximally succinct vehicle for the illustration of fundamental principles of program/assertion interaction, since all but the absolutely essential structure is excluded (in particular any structure on the domain of computation). The theory is captured axiomatically in the deductive system of Segerberg [Se], proved complete by Parikh [Pa, see also KP]. PDL combines and generalizes classical propositional logic (for the assertions), the calculus of regular events (for the programs), and modal logic (for their interaction). The three components fit together neatly into a simple but mathematically rich system. Results of a fundamental nature have been established which perhaps would not have been apparent in a more powerful system [K1-4,Pr3-5,KP].

This paper deals with a fundamental principle of looping, namely that *looping is inherently infinitary.* Simpler programming language constructs, such as composition and conditional tests, are captured up to isomorphism by their equations [K1], whereas looping cannot be so captured [RT,K3,K4]. This principle is quite evident in programming language semantics and data type specification (see for example [Sa]). In this paper we illustrate this principle in the context of PDL with two results comparing the expressive power of the familiar PDL induction axiom

(ind) $X \wedge [\alpha^*](X \supset [\alpha]X) \equiv [\alpha^*]X$

and the stronger **-continuity condition*

(*-cont) $<\alpha^*>X \equiv \vee_n <\alpha^n>X$.

The *-continuity condition says that $<\alpha^*>X$ is the join or least upper bound of the propositions $<\alpha^n>X$ with respect to implication. A proof that ***-cont** implies **ind** can be found in [K1]. The axiom ***-cont** appeared in the original definition of dynamic algebras [K1], but later V. Pratt recommended dropping it in favor of **ind**, allowing more models. We shall adopt Pratt's more general definition and call dynamic algebras **-continuous* if they satisfy ***-cont**. All dynamic algebras arising in practice, including and especially the standard Kripke models, are *-continuous.

In [K1] it was shown that any separable dynamic algebra is represented by a (possibly nonstandard) Kripke model. (A dynamic algebra is called *separable* [K1] if $<\alpha>X = <\beta>X$ for all X implies $\alpha = \beta$. A Kripke model is *standard* if α^* is the reflexive transitive closure of binary relation α, otherwise it is *nonstandard*.) In [K3,RT,K4] it was shown that there exist separable *-continuous dynamic algebras that are not represented by any standard Kripke model.

Pratt [Pr1] used universal algebraic techniques to show that dynamic algebras and standard Kripke models share the same equational theory, giving an alternative proof to the completeness of the Segerberg axioms. In this paper we prove the following two results, which compare the expressive power of the two axioms **ind** and ***-cont**: (1) *there is a first-order sentence that distinguishes separable dynamic algebras from standard Kripke models;* but (2) *the class of separable *-continuous dynamic algebras and the class of standard Kripke models agree on all sentences of the infinitary language* $L_{\omega_1\omega}$. These two results are proved in sections 2 and 3, respectively. In section 4 we discuss the effect of allowing an equality symbol between elements of the Kleene (or regular) sort of a dynamic algebra. We show in that section that the infinitary condition $\alpha\beta^*\gamma = \bigvee_n \alpha\beta^n\gamma$ allows a natural axiomatization of the equational theory of regular events. It is known that no purely equational axiomatization exists [R].

It is assumed the reader is familiar with PDL and dynamic algebra. PDL was first defined in [FL], and this reference remains the best introduction. Definitions, basic properties, and examples of dynamic algebras can be found in [K1-4,Pr1-3].

Let L be the usual two-sorted language for PDL and dynamic algebra, consisting of primitive symbols a, b,... (for the Kleene or program sort) and P, Q,... (for the Boolean sort). Terms α, β,... for the Kleene sort and X, Y,... for the Boolean sort are built up using the usual Boolean operators $\wedge$, $\vee$, $\neg$, 0, and 1, the binary Kleene operators $\cup$ (choice) and ; (composition), the unary operators $^-$ (reverse) and * (iteration), and the nullary operators λ (identity) and 0. In addition there are the modal operators $< >$ and $[\ ]$ by which the two sorts interact.

If the defined Boolean operator $\equiv$ is considered an equality, then L can be considered an equational language. Any PDL formula X has an equivalent equational formula $X \equiv 1$, and each equation $X \equiv Y$ is a PDL formula. Thus with no loss of generality we can assume L contains an explicit symbol = for $\equiv$ and insist that all atomic formulas are equations. L then extends naturally to the first-order language $L_{\omega\omega}$ by adding propositional connectives, countably many variables ranging over Kleene elements, countably many variables ranging over Boolean elements, and quantifiers $\forall$, $\exists$ which can be applied to variables of either sort. $L_{\omega\omega}$ can be extended to the infinitary language $L_{\omega_1\omega}$ by allowing countable conjunctions and disjunctions.

The symbols $\vee$, $\wedge$, and $\neg$ will refer to both the Boolean algebra operators and the first-order logical connectives; the intent will always be clear from context.

Since well-formed expressions allow the equality symbol between Boolean elements only, there is no direct way to express identity between Kleene elements. The closest $L_{\omega\omega}$ can come to this is the functional equivalence of α and β, via the relation $\approx$ of *inseparability*:

$$\alpha \approx \beta \text{ iff } \forall X\ \langle\alpha\rangle X = \langle\beta\rangle X .$$

Thus to say that the dynamic algebra $(\mathbf{K},\mathbf{B},\langle\rangle)$ is separable is the same as saying that $\mathbf{K}$ does not contain two distinct inseparable elements. The property of separability is not first-order expressible, as Lemma 3.1 below shows, but it would be if there were an equality symbol for Kleene elements.

2. A first-order sentence that distinguishes separable dynamic algebras from standard Kripke models

In this section we show that, in the absence of the *-continuity condition, there is a first-order sentence that distinguishes separable dynamic algebras from standard Kripke models. Thus, without ***-cont**, standard Kripke models and separable dynamic algebras can agree only on first-order sentences involving at most a few alternations of quantifiers. The entire construction is an implementation of the following idea: An *atom* of a Boolean algebra is a minimal nonzero element. An element X of a Boolean algebra is said to be *atomless* if there does not exist an atom $Y \leq X$. An element X is said to be *atomic* if no nonzero $Y \leq X$ is atomless, or in other words, if every nonzero $Y \leq X$ has an atom $Z \leq Y$. The properties of being an atom, atomless, or atomic are first-order expressible. We construct an dynamic algebra $(\mathbf{K},\mathbf{B},\langle\rangle)$ whose Boolean algebra $\mathbf{B}$ is a subalgebra of the direct product of an atomic Boolean algebra and an atomless Boolean algebra. $\mathbf{K}$ has a program δ such that both the atomic part and the atomless part of $\mathbf{B}$ are preserved under application of $\langle\delta\rangle$, but the neither part is preserved under $\langle\delta^*\rangle$. The structure $(\mathbf{K},\mathbf{B},\langle\rangle)$ therefore violates the first-order property "for any α, if $\langle\alpha\rangle X$ is atomless whenever X is, then $\langle\alpha^*\rangle X$ is atomless whenever X is." On the other hand, any standard Kripke model has this property, since $\langle\alpha^*\rangle X = \cup_n\langle\alpha^n\rangle X$, and if all elements of a family of sets are atomless, then their union is.

Now we give the explicit construction of the dynamic algebra $(\mathbf{K},\mathbf{B},\langle\rangle)$. Let ω be a copy of the natural numbers and let $\mathbf{R}^+$ be a copy of the nonnegative real numbers disjoint from ω. Let S be the disjoint union $\omega \cup \mathbf{R}^+$ Points of S will be denoted x,y,... .

Let $\mathbf{B}_\omega$ be the Boolean algebra of finite and cofinite subsets of ω, and let $\mathbf{B}_{\mathbf{R}^+}$ be the Boolean algebra of subsets of $\mathbf{R}^+$ consisting of finite unions of intervals $[x,y)$ or $[x,\infty)$. Note that $\mathbf{B}_\omega$ is atomic and $\mathbf{B}_{\mathbf{R}^+}$ is atomless. The Boolean algebra $\mathbf{B}$ is the following family of subsets of S:

$$\mathbf{B} = \{\ U \cup V \mid U \in \mathbf{B}_\omega,\ V \in \mathbf{B}_{\mathbf{R}^+}, \text{ and U is bounded iff V is bounded}\ \} .$$

The atoms of $\mathbf{B}$ are the singleton subsets of ω. Thus if $X \in \mathbf{B}$, then X is atomic iff $X \subseteq \omega$, and X is atomless iff $X \subseteq \mathbf{R}^+$. Note that neither ω nor $\mathbf{R}^+$ is an element of $\mathbf{B}$.

Now we define a Kleene algebra $\mathbf{K}$ of binary relations on S. Let δ be the following binary relation:

$$\delta = \{\ (x,y) \mid x,y \in \omega \text{ and } |y-x| \leq 1\ \} \cup \{\ (x,y) \mid x,y \in \mathbf{R}^+ \text{ and } |y-x| \leq 1\ \} .$$

Note that $\delta = \delta^-$, since the definition is symmetric in x and y.

Let **K** be the set of binary relations generated by δ, the zero relation 0, the identity relation λ, and the total relation $S^2 = S \times S$ under the standard operations $\cup$ (set union), ; (relational composition), and $^-$ (reverse).

Lemma 2.1. $\mathbf{K} = \{ 0, \delta^0, \delta^1, \delta^2, ..., S^2 \}$.

Proof. Clearly everything on the right side of the equation is in **K**. For the reverse inclusion, since the set on the right contains the generators 0, δ, $\lambda = \delta^0$, and S^2 of **K**, it remains to show that it is closed under the operations $\cup$, ; , and $^-$. Suppose α, β are of the form 0, S^2, or δ^n. Then so are $\alpha;\beta$ and α^- (recall $\delta = \delta^-$ and therefore $\delta^n = (\delta^n)^-$). Also, $\alpha \cup \beta$ is easily seen to be of this form if either α or β is either 0 or S^2. Finally, if $\alpha = \delta^m$, $\beta = \delta^n$ for some m, n, then since δ is reflexive (i.e. $\lambda \subseteq \delta$), $\delta^m \cup \delta^n$ is either δ^m if $m \geq n$, or δ^n if $m \leq n$. □

In order to make (**K**,**B**,<>) into an dynamic algebra, we need to define the Kleene algebra operations $\cup$, ; , $^-$, and $*$ on **K** and the scalar multiplication <> on **K** × **B**. The operations $\cup$, ; , and $^-$ will have their standard interpretations. For 0 and λ, define $\lambda^* = 0^* = \lambda$, and for any other $\alpha \in$ K, define α^* to be the total relation S^2. We can give <> its standard interpretation, since in light of Lemma 2.1 it is easy to see that if $X \in \mathbf{B}$ then $<\alpha>X \in \mathbf{B}$ for any $\alpha \in \mathbf{K}$.

We claim now that (**K**,**B**,<>) is a separable dynamic algebra. It is certainly separable, since it is clear from Lemma 2.1 that if $\alpha \neq \beta$ then $<\alpha>\{0\} \neq <\beta>\{0\}$. All axioms for dynamic algebras not involving $*$ must hold, since all operators other than $*$ have their standard interpretation. Therefore it remains to show

$$<\alpha^*>X = X \vee <\alpha><\alpha^*>X ,$$
$$<\alpha^*>X = X \vee <\alpha^*>(\neg X \wedge <\alpha>X) .$$

A simple calculation suffices for each case: If X = 0 then both sides of both equations are 0. If $\alpha = 0$ or λ, then $\alpha^* = \lambda$, so both sides of both equations are X. Finally, if $X \neq 0$ and $\alpha = S^2$ or $\alpha = \delta^n$, $n \geq 1$, then both sides of the first equation and the left side of the second are S, thus it remains to show that the right side of the second is S. This is true if X = S; if $X \neq S$, then $<\alpha>X$ is strictly larger than X, so $\neg X \wedge <\alpha>X$ is nonempty, and therefore $<\alpha^*>(\neg X \wedge <\alpha>X) = S$. We have proved

Lemma 2.2. (**K**,**B**,<>) is a separable dynamic algebra. □

Now we construct a sentence σ of $L_{\omega\omega}$ satisfied by every standard Kripke model but violated by (**K**,**B**,<>). A Kleene element α is said to *preserve atomless elements* if $<\alpha>X$ is atomless whenever X is. Define

$$\mathrm{atom}(X) \;=\; X \neq 0 \;\wedge\; \forall Y \;(0 \leq Y \leq X \rightarrow (0 = Y \vee Y = X))$$
$$\mathrm{atomless}(X) \;=\; \forall Y \leq X \;\; \neg\mathrm{atom}(Y)$$
$$\mathrm{pres}(\alpha) \;=\; \forall X \;\; \mathrm{atomless}(X) \rightarrow \mathrm{atomless}(<\alpha>X)$$
$$\sigma \;=\; \forall \alpha \;\; \mathrm{pres}(\alpha) \rightarrow \mathrm{pres}(\alpha^*) .$$

The formulas **atom**(X) and **atomless**(X) say that X is an atom and atomless, respectively; **pres**(α) says that α preserves atomless elements; and the sentence σ says that for any α, if α preserves atomless elements then so does α^*.

Theorem 2.3. Let (**K**,**B**,<>) be the dynamic algebra constructed in Lemma 2.2. Then (**K**,**B**,<>) $\models \neg\sigma$ but $A \models \sigma$ for all standard Kripke models A.

Proof. (**K**,**B**,<>) violates σ since X $\in$ **B** is atomless iff X $\subseteq$ $\mathbf{R}^+$, and δ preserves such sets, whereas δ^* does not, since $<\delta^*>X = S$ for any nonzero X.

On the other hand, for any standard Kripke model A, if β preserves atomless elements, then for any atomless X, $<\beta^n>X$ is atomless for all n. Since A is standard, $<\beta^*>X = \bigcup_n <\beta^n>X$, thus if $<\beta^*>X$ were to contain an atom Y, then Y must intersect some $<\beta^n>X$, and thus $Y \leq <\beta^n>X$ since Y is an atom, contradicting the fact that $<\beta^n>X$ is atomless. Therefore $<\beta^*>X$ must be atomless. Since X was arbitrary, β^* preserves atomless elements. □

3. The power of *-continuity

In this section we show that the class of *-continuous dynamic algebras and the class of standard Kripke models share the same $L_{\omega_1\omega}$ theory. The proof uses the Löwenheim-Skolem theorem for infinitary logic [Ke] in conjuction with results obtained in [K4].

Let A = (**K**,**B**,<>) be a *-continuous dynamic algebra. Recall the definition that $\alpha \approx \beta$ iff $<\alpha>X = <\beta>X$ for all X, and that A is called *separable* if $\alpha \approx \beta$ implies $\alpha = \beta$ for any α, β. This property cannot be expressed by any infinitary sentence over the language L, as Lemma 3.1 below shows.

The relation $\approx$ is a dynamic algebra congruence. Moreover, it is easily checked that $\approx$ respects *-continuity. This allows us to construct the quotient algebra $A/\approx$ = (**K**/$\approx$,**B**,<>), where

$$\mathbf{K}/\approx \; = \{ \alpha/\approx \mid \alpha \in \mathbf{K} \}$$

and $\alpha/\approx$ is the $\approx$-class of α. Thus $A/\approx$ is a *-continuous and separable, and A is separable iff A and $A/\approx$ are isomorphic.

Lemma 3.1. A and $A/\approx$ are equivalent with respect to all $L_{\omega_1\omega}$ sentences.

Proof. Let $f:A \rightarrow A/\approx$ be the canonical homomorphism which takes α to $\alpha/\approx$ and X to X. We show by induction on formula structure that for any $L_{\omega_1\omega}$ formula $\phi(\alpha_1,\ldots,\alpha_k,X_1,\ldots,X_m)$ with parameters $\alpha_1,\ldots,\alpha_k \in \mathbf{K}$, $X_1,\ldots,X_m \in \mathbf{B}$,

$$A \models \phi(\alpha_1,\ldots,\alpha_k,X_1,\ldots,X_m)$$
$$\text{iff } A/\approx \; \models \phi(f(\alpha_1),\ldots,f(\alpha_k),X_1,\ldots,X_m) .$$

If ϕ is atomic, then it is an equation between elements of **B**; since $<\alpha>X = <f(\alpha)>X$ for any α and X, the two statements $\phi(\alpha_1,\ldots,\alpha_k,X_1,\ldots,X_m)$ and $\phi(f(\alpha_1),\ldots,f(\alpha_k),X_1,\ldots,X_m)$ express the same property of **B**. If ϕ is a negation or a finite or countable join or meet, then the induction step is immediate. If ϕ is of the form $\exists$X

$\psi(\alpha_1,\ldots,\alpha_k,X_1,\ldots,X_m,X)$, then

$$A \models \phi \text{ iff } A \models \psi(\alpha_1,\ldots,\alpha_k,X_1,\ldots,X_m,X) \text{ for some } X \in \mathbf{B}$$
$$\text{iff (by the induction hypothesis) there is an } X \in \mathbf{B} \text{ such that}$$
$$A/{\approx} \models \psi(f(\alpha_1),\ldots,f(\alpha_k),X_1,\ldots,X_m,X)$$
$$\text{iff } A/{\approx} \models \exists X\, \psi(f(\alpha_1),\ldots,f(\alpha_k),X_1,\ldots,X_m,X) .$$

Finally, suppose ϕ is of the form $\exists\alpha\, \psi(\alpha_1,\ldots,\alpha_k,\alpha,X_1,\ldots,X_m)$. Then

$$A \models \phi \text{ iff for some } \alpha \in \mathbf{K},\, A \models \psi(\alpha_1,\ldots,\alpha_k,\alpha,X_1,\ldots,X_m)$$
$$\text{iff (by induction hypothesis) for some } f(\alpha) \in \mathbf{K}/{\approx},$$
$$A/{\approx} \models \psi(f(\alpha_1),\ldots,f(\alpha_k),f(\alpha),X_1,\ldots,X_m)$$
$$\text{iff } A/{\approx} \models \exists\alpha\, \psi(f(\alpha_1),\ldots,f(\alpha_k),\alpha,X_1,\ldots,X_m) . \ \Box$$

Lemma 3.2. Any countable separable *-continuous dynamic algebra is isomorphic to $A/{\approx}$ for some standard Kripke model A.

Proof. This was proved in detail in [K4, Theorem 5]. We outline the proof here for the sake of completeness, and to give an idea of the techniques involved.

Let (K,B,<>) be a separable *-continuous dynamic algebra. If the construction of the representation theorem of [K1] is carried out, the result is a (possibly nonstandard) Kripke model with the same dynamic algebra (K,B,<>). Elements of **B** are now subsets of a set S of states, elements of **K** are binary relations on S, and all the operations have their standard Kripke model interpretations with the possible exception of *.

In spite of the fact that $\langle\alpha^*\rangle X$ need not be $\cup_n\langle\alpha^n\rangle X$, the *-continuity condition guarantees that $\langle\alpha^*\rangle X$ is the least element of **B** containing $\cup_n\langle\alpha^n\rangle X$. In the topology on S generated by the elements of **B**, this says that sets of the form $\langle\alpha^*\rangle X - \cup_n\langle\alpha^n\rangle X$ are nowhere dense. Therefore, if **K** and **B** are both countable, then the union of all such sets, call it M, is meager. The Baire Category Theorem then implies that every nonnull $X \in \mathbf{B}$ intersects $S - M$; using this fact, it can be shown [K4, Theorem 4] that all points of M can be dropped from the Kripke model without changing the dynamic algebra.

The resulting Kripke model B may still be nonstandard, for although now $\langle\alpha^*\rangle X = \cup_n\langle\alpha^n\rangle X$, it is still not necessary that α^* be the reflexive transitive closure of α. However, the elements of **K**, taken as primitive, generate a standard Kripke model A, using reflexive transitive closure instead of *. Since $\langle\alpha^*\rangle X = \cup_n\langle\alpha^n\rangle X$, this process introduces no new Boolean elements. Using this and the fact that B is separable, it is then easy to show that $B \cong A/{\approx}$, thus A is the desired standard model. □

We are now ready to prove the main theorem of this section.

Theorem 3.3. The class of standard Kripke models and the class of *-continuous dynamic algebras share the same $L_{\omega_1\omega}$ theory.

Proof. Let ϕ be any sentence of $L_{\omega_1\omega}$. We wish to show that ϕ is satisfied by some standard Kripke model iff ϕ is satisfied by some *-continuous dynamic algebra.

($\rightarrow$) This direction is trivial, since every standard Kripke model is a *-continuous dynamic algebra.

($\leftarrow$) Suppose ϕ is satisfied by some *-continuous dynamic algebra. By the downward Löwenheim-Skolem theorem for infinitary logic [Ke], ϕ is satisfied by a countable *-continuous dynamic algebra B. By Lemma 3.1, ϕ is also satisfied by the countable *-continuous dynamic algebra $B/\approx$, and $B/\approx$ is separable, thus by Lemma 3.2, $B/\approx \;\cong A/\approx$ for some standard Kripke model A. Again by Lemma 3.1, $A \models \phi$. □

4. Equality between Kleene elements

The results of the previous section depend heavily on the fact that equality between Kleene elements cannot be expressed. Thus a natural question at this point is how the $L^=$, $L^=_{\omega\omega}$, and $L^=_{\omega_1\omega}$ theories of dynamic algebras, *-continuous dynamic algebras, and standard Kripke models relate, where $L^=$ is L is augmented with an equality symbol $=$ for Kleene elements.

Separability is expressible in $L^=_{\omega\omega}$, so the analog of Lemma 3.1 fails, since non-separable standard Kripke models exist. However, this condition can be weakened without affecting the main results of [K1-4,Pr1-3]. Let us call a Kleene algebra **K** *inherently separable* if there exists a separable dynamic algebra over **K**. We shall call a dynamic algebra (**K**,**B**,<>) *inherently separable* if its Kleene algebra **K** is. Then every standard Kripke model is inherently separable, since the Boolean algebra can be extended to the full power set. This says that inherent separability is necessary for representation by a standard Kripke model; in [K1] it was shown to be sufficient for representation by a nonstandard Kripke model. Non-inherently separable dynamic algebras have been shown to exist [K1, ex. 2.5]. A problem posed in [K1], still open, is whether every nonstandard Kripke model is inherently separable; this problem is interesting because a positive answer would say that inherent separability is necessary and sufficient for representation by a nonstandard Kripke model.

It follows from the completeness of the Segerberg axioms for PDL that the class of all dynamic algebras and the class of standard Kripke models have the same L equational theory. Pratt proved that separable dynamic algebras and standard Kripke models have the same $L^=$ equational theory [Pr1]. It is an easy observation that this theory is shared by the inherently separable dynamic algebras as well. However, as Pratt observed, the class of all dynamic algebras satisfies strictly fewer equations $\alpha = \beta$ than the class of standard Kripke models. In fact, since there is no finite equational axiomatization of the equational theory of regular events [R], it follows that even with the addition of finitely many equational axioms $\alpha = \beta$, there is always an equation true in all standard Kripke models and false in some (non-inherently separable) dynamic algebra. Thus pure equational logic, although adequate for the L theory of dynamic algebras, fails in $L^=$.

In [K1] a finite set of axiom schemata for Kleene algebras was given, all of which were equations of the form $\alpha = \beta$, except for the infinitary **-continuity condition*

$$\alpha\beta^*\gamma = \bigvee_n \alpha\beta^n\gamma \,.$$

([K1] omitted one equational axiom for the reverse operator $^-$, which we postulate here: $\alpha \leq \alpha\alpha^-\alpha$.) In contrast to the failure of pure equational logic, this simple infinitary extension completely characterizes the $L^=$ equational theory of the standard Kripke models, as Theorem 4.1 below shows. Moreover, it does so in a very natural and intuitive way, since no reference is made to the Boolean part of dynamic algebra.

Theorem 4.1. The *-continuous Kleene algebras and the algebras of binary relations satisfy the same set of equations $\alpha = \beta$.

Proof. One direction is trivial. For the other direction, let X be the set of primitive symbols and let $X^- = \{ a^- \mid a \in X \}$. Strings x, $y \in (X \cup X^-)^*$ are just terms α without $\cup$ or * and with $^-$ applied only to primitive symbols. For $y \in (X \cup X^-)^*$, let $|y|$ denote the length of y, and let y^- denote the string obtained by reversing the order of the symbols in y and changing all the signs. Write $y \rightarrow x$ if x can be obtained from y via repeated application of the rule $\alpha\alpha^-\alpha \rightarrow \alpha$. For example, $ab^-c^-cbb^-c^-a \rightarrow ab^-c^-a$ in one step. For any $x \in (X \cup X^-)^*$, let M_x be the binary relation algebra consisting of $|x|+1$ states $s_0,\ldots,s_{|x|}$ and relations $(s_{i-1},s_i) \in a$ iff the ith symbol of x is a, and $(s_i,s_{i-1}) \in a$ iff the ith symbol of x is a^-. Certainly $(s_0,s_{|x|}) \in x$ in M_x.

We claim that the following four statements are equivalent:

(i) $x \leq y$ in all *-continuous Kleene algebras
(ii) $x \leq y$ in all binary relation algebras
(iii) $(s_0,s_{|x|}) \in y$ in M_x
(iv) $y \rightarrow x$.

The implications (i) $\rightarrow$ (ii) $\rightarrow$ (iii) are trivial. (iii) $\rightarrow$ (iv) follows from the observation that if y describes a path from s_0 to $s_{|x|}$, and if $|y| > |x|$, then there must be a zigzag in y of the form zz^-z for some substring z of x. (iv) $\rightarrow$ (i) is proved by repeated application of the Kleene algebra axiom $\alpha \leq \alpha\alpha^-\alpha$.

Let α be a Kleene term with k occurrences of *. The *-continuity condition implies that in all *-continuous Kleene algebras,

$$\alpha = \bigvee \alpha(m_1,\ldots,m_k) ,$$

where $\alpha(m_1,\ldots,m_k)$ denotes the *-free term obtained by replacing the ith occurrence of * in α by $m_i \in \omega$, and the join is taken over all k-tuples $(m_1,\ldots,m_k) \in \omega^k$. But the Kleene algebra axioms allow any *-free term to be written as a finite join of strings in $(X \cup X^-)^*$, thus there is a countable set $I_\alpha \subseteq (X \cup X^-)^*$ such that $\alpha = \bigvee I_\alpha$ in any *-continuous Kleene algebra.

Now suppose that $\alpha = \beta$ in all binary relation algebras. Then $\bigvee I_\alpha = \bigvee I_\beta$ in all binary relation algebras, and we need only show that this implies that $\bigvee I_\alpha = \bigvee I_\beta$ in all *-continuous Kleene algebras as well. For any $x \in I_\alpha$, since $x \leq \bigvee I_\beta$ in all binary relation algebras, it certainly holds in the algebra M_x constructed above. Since $(s_0,s_{|x|}) \in x$ and since join is set union in M_x, $(s_0,s_{|x|}) \in y$ for some $y \in I_\beta$. By (iii) $\rightarrow$ (i) above, $x \leq y$ and thus $x \leq \bigvee I_\beta$ in all *-continuous Kleene algebras. Since $x \in I_\alpha$ was arbitrary, $\bigvee I_\alpha \leq \bigvee I_\beta$ in all *-continuous Kleene algebras. The reverse inequality holds by a symmetric argument. □

Without the assumption of inherent separability, *-continuity does not go much farther:

Theorem 4.2. There is a universal Horn sentence of $L^{=}_{\omega\omega}$ true in all standard Kripke models but violated in a (non-inherently separable) *-continuous dynamic algebra.

Proof. The property "if $\alpha \leq \lambda$ then $\alpha^2 = \alpha$" is clearly valid in all standard Kripke models. In [K1] an example was given of a Kleene algebra violating this property [K1, ex. 2.5]. This Kleene algebra can be made into a dynamic algebra over the two-element Boolean algebra in a straightforward way. □

Even with the assumption of inherent separability, the $L^{=}_{\omega_1\omega}$ analogy of Theorem 3.3 fails:

Theorem 4.3. There is an $L^{=}_{\omega_1\omega}$ sentence true in all standard Kripke models but false in some inherently separable *-continuous dynamic algebra.

Proof. In [K4], a countable separable *-continuous dynamic algebra (**K**,**B**,<>) was constructed such that (**K**,**B**,<>) is not isomorphic to any standard Kripke model. By Scott's theorem [Ke], there is a sentence σ of $L^{=}_{\omega_1\omega}$ that characterizes (**K**,**B**,<>) up to isomorphism on countable models, thus (**K**,**B**,<>) $\models \sigma$ but no countable standard Kripke model satisfies σ. Therefore no standard Kripke model of any cardinality can satisfy σ, since the downward Löwenheim-Skolem theorem would give a countable subalgebra satisfying σ, and such a subalgebra would still be representable as a standard Kripke model. □

Thus the question remains: for what fragments of $L^{=}_{\omega_1\omega}$ do inherently separable *-continuous dynamic algebras and standard Kripke models agree? In particular, do they agree on all sentences of $L^{=}_{\omega\omega}$?

5. Conclusion

A disadvantage of the *-continuity axiom is that, unlike the induction axiom, it is not equational, and therefore is not expressible within the language of PDL. However the emphasis on equational specifications and finitary deductive systems is in a way unrealistic. Looping is inherently infinitary and nonequational; simpler programming language constructs, such as composition and conditional tests, are captured up to isomorphism by their equations [K1], whereas looping cannot be so captured [K3,RT,K4]. Thus the equational approach must eventually be given up if we are ever to bridge the gap between algebraic and operational semantics. The *-continuity condition is an example of how to do this without sacrificing algebraic elegance.

Besides the theoretical advantage of descriptive precision, the *-continuity condition has a practical advantage as well: it is easier to use, since it is simpler in form than the PDL induction axiom. We have found that it is often easier to start a PDL proof with ***-cont**, using induction informally on the n appearing in the definition of ***-cont**, and then later massage the proof to replace applications of ***-cont** with applications of **ind**.

References

[FL] Fischer, M.J. and R.E.Ladner, "Propositional dynamic logic of regular programs," *J. Comput. Syst. Sci.* 18:2 (1979).

[Ke] Keisler, H.J. *Model Theory for Infinitary Logic.* North Holland, Amsterdam, 1971.

[K1] Kozen, D., "A representation theorem for models of *-free PDL," *Proc. 7th Int. Colloq. on Automata, Languages, and Programming*, Lecture Notes in Computer Science 85, ed. Goos and Hartmanis, Springer-Verlag, Berlin, 1980, 351-362. Also Report RC7864, IBM Research, Yorktown Heights, New York, Sept. 1979.

[K2] -------, "On the duality of dynamic algebras and Kripke models," Report RC7893, IBM Research, Yorktown Heights, New York, Oct. 1979.

[K3] -------, "On the representation of dynamic algebras," Report RC7898, IBM Research, Yorktown Heights, New York, Oct. 1979.

[K4] -------, "On the representation of dynamic algebras II," Report RC8290, IBM Research, Yorktown Heights, New York, May 1980.

[KP] -------, and R. Parikh, "An elementary proof of the completeness of PDL," *TCS*, to appear; also IBM Report RC8097, Jan. 1980.

[Pa] Parikh, R., "A completeness result for PDL," *Symp. on Math. Found. of Comp. Sci.*, Zakopane, Springer-Verlag, May 1978, 403-415.

[Pr1] Pratt, V.R., "Dynamic Algebras: Examples, Constructions, Applications," MIT/LCS Report TM-138, July 1979.

[Pr2] -------, "Models of program logics," *Proc. 20th IEEE Symp. on Foundations of Comp. Sci.* (Oct. 1979), 115-122.

[Pr3] -------, "Dynamic algebras and the nature of induction," *Proc. 12th ACM Symp. on Theory of Computing* (May 1980), 22-28.

[R] Redko, V.N., "On defining relations for the algebra of regular events," (Russian), *Ukrain. Math. Z.* 16 (1964), 120-126.

[RT] Reiterman, J. and V. Trnková, "Dynamic algebras which are not Kripke structures," *Proc. 9th Symp. on Math. Found. of Computer Science* (Aug. 1980), 528-538.

[Sa] Salomaa, A., "Two complete axiom systems for the algebra of regular events," *J. ACM* 13:1 (1966), 158-169.

[Se] Segerberg, K., "A completeness theorem in the modal logic of programs," *Not. AMS* 24:6 (1977), A-552.

TIMESETS

A New Method for Temporal Reasoning About Programs

Leslie Lamport[1]
Computer Science Laboratory
SRI International
Menlo Park, CA 94025, USA

1. INTRODUCTION

The use of temporal logic for reasoning about programs seems to have first appeared in [1], and was developed by Pnueli in [7]. It involves the use of the temporal operator $\Box$, where $\Box A$ means that A is true for all times during the program execution. (Precise definitions for all the temporal operators will be given in Section 4.) The unary operator $\Box$ cannot express all the interesting temporal assertions about a program -- for example, it cannot express the statement that one thing happens before another. It is therefore necessary to generalize it to a binary operator, where $A \Box B$ means that B is true at all times up to but not including the first time that A is false.

The unary $\Box$ operator is sufficient for proving most properties of programs when given the whole program. (See [4], [6].) However, this is not true when treating parts of a program separately. As an example, we consider the program of Figure 1. This is a two-process program containing a mutual exclusion algorithm. The angle brackets enclose atomic operations. If we assume that x_i is changed only by process i (i = 1, 2), and is not changed during the critical section, then both processes cannot be in their critical sections at the same time. Given the entire program, this can be shown by proving $\Box I$ (which means that I is always true), where I is the following assertion:

$$\bigwedge_{i=1,2} [\underline{at}\ w_i \supset x_i] \wedge [\underline{in}\ cs_i \supset (x_i \wedge \neg x_{i+1})] ,$$

where "$\underline{at}\ w_i$" means that process i's program counter value indicates that it is right before the test in the while loop, and "$\underline{in}\ cs_i$" indicates that it is at the beginning of or inside the critical section. (The addition is modulo 2, so 2+1 = 1.)

---

[1]This work was supported in part by the National Science Foundation under grant number MCS-7816783.

Process 1:

```
        .
        .
        .

s1: begin
      <x1 := true>
  w1: while <x2>  do  ... ;
                  <x1 := true>
              od  ;

  cs1: critical section;
            <x1 := false>
      end ;
        .
        .
        .
```

Process 2:

```
        .
        .
        .

s2: begin
      <x2 := true>
  w1: while <x1>  do  ... ;
                  <x2 := true>
              od  ;

  cs2: critical section;
            <x2 := false>
      end ;
        .
        .
        .
```

Figure 1: Program implementing mutual exclusion.

Now suppose we want to reason about the two processes separately. We ask the question: what property of Process 2 is used to guarantee that Process 1 is never in its critical section while Process 2 is? The answer is the following:

A. Whenever $(\neg x_2) \wedge x_1$ is true, Process 2 will not enter its critical section until x_1 becomes false.

We want to show that Property A together with the code of Process 1 implies that the two processes are never in their critical sections at the same time. To do this, we ask what property of Process 1 insures this. The answer is the following:

B. If Process 1 is in its critical section at some time t, then:

1. It was previously at w_1, and
2. At the last time t' when it was at w_1 (just before doing the test):
   (a) x_2 was false (otherwise it would have remained in the while loop), and
   (b) x_1 was true from time t' through time t.

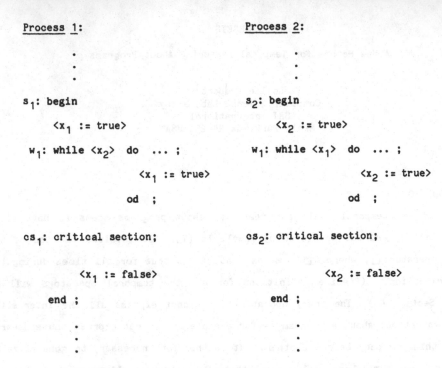

To prove mutual exclusion, we want to show that Properties A and B together imply that for any time t : if Process 1 is in its critical section then Process 2 is not in its critical section. Informally, this is can be shown as follows. Suppose Process 1 is in its critical section at time t. Property B implies that there was some time $t' < t$ such that x_2 was false at time t' and x_1 was true from time t' through time t. Property A states that Process 2 will not be in its critical section from time t' until the first time x_1 becomes false, which is later than time t. Hence, Process 2 is not in its critical section at time t, which is what we had to show.

Now suppose we want to formalize this informal argument. The most obvious way is to introduce some kind of assertion language that includes explicit reference to a time variable, and then apply first order predicate calculus to these assertions. Such an approach was used by Francez and Pnueli in [2]. However, the particular values of the times t and t' used in the above reasoning were irrelevant. All that mattered was the fact that t' was earlier than t. In order to avoid mentioning explicit times, temporal logic introduces the temporal operator $\square$. Using this single operator together with ordinary predicates (boolean functions of the program state), we can formalize the above reasoning.

Temporal logic is a formal deductive system. For such a formal system to be useful, we feel that it must be easy to use it informally (after a reasonable amount of practice). If it is to help us avoid logical errors, then it must provide simple formal statements of simple informal arguments. A good example of such a useful system is first order predicate logic. It provides a very useful aid for informal mathematical reasoning, and can help us to avoid mistakes in proofs involving quantification.

We have found temporal logic to be such a useful system when one needs only the unary $\square$ operator. With practice, one can reason informally using this operator with the same ease that one reasons about quantifiers in predicate logic. However, this does not seem to be the case for the binary $\square$ operator. Properties A and B are expressed formally in terms of this operator as follows. (The reader need not try to understand these expressions.)

$A'.\ \Box\ (\neg x_2 \supset (x_1\ \Box\ \neg\ \underline{in}\ cs_2))$

$B'.\ \Box\ [\ (\underline{in}\ cs_1\ \Box\ x_1) \wedge$

$(\neg(\underline{at}\ w_1 \wedge (\neg x_2) \wedge ((\neg\ \underline{in}\ cs_1) \Box x_1))\ )\ \Box\ (\neg\ \underline{in}\ cs_1)\ )\ ].$

Even with our experience in using temporal logic, it is not obvious to us that the formula B' really expresses the assertion stated informally by Property B. Moreover, we have been unable to find any simple way to derive the desired mutual exclusion property from these formulas. It has been our experience that the unary $\Box$ operator allows one to reason "forward in time" quite easily, and the binary $\Box$ operator allows one to reason "backwards in time" without much difficulty. However, our informal proof required reasoning backwards from time t to time t', and then forward again from time t'. Ordinary temporal logic does not seem capable of handling this reasoning easily. Of course, it should be possible to give a complete axiomatization of this temporal logic in which a proof can be constructed. However, our concern is not whether a proof exists, but rather whether it can be found easily.

This paper describes a new method of temporal reasoning that we feel is more convenient than using the binary $\Box$ of temporal logic. We will give a formal semantics for the method, so we can verify the validity of our reasoning, but we will not give axioms and proof rules.

The paper is organized as follows. Section 2 gives an informal exposition of the method, and Section 3 shows how it can be used to prove the correctness of our example program. In Section 4, we give a formal semantics for the system, providing a rigorous justification for the informal reasoning used in Sections 2 and 3. Section 5 discusses the expressiveness of our method and of a simple generalization. We conclude with a brief discussion of how timesets fit into a general framework for proving properties of programs.

2. AN INFORMAL DESCRIPTION

We now give an informal, intuitive description of our logical system. Readers who are more comfortable with precise formalism are advised to read Section 4 before reading this section.

We assume that an execution of a program consists of a sequence of discrete atomic program steps. (Thus, our model for concurrent programs assumes some interleaving of the actions from different processes.) Executing the program from a starting state σ_0 thus produces a sequence of states $\sigma_0, \sigma_1, \sigma_2, \ldots$, where σ_t is the state after the t<u>th</u> program step. We call σ_t the state "at time t " during the execution, so our "times" are just non-negative integers. We think of time 0 as representing the present, so we are always talking about the present and the future. For simplicity, we assume that an execution sequence is infinite, and let $\sigma_n = \sigma_{n+1} = \ldots$ if the program halts after n steps. Thus, a program that halts after n steps is in the same state from time n onward.

An <u>assertion</u> is a statement about a single execution of the program. Hence, we are always referring to some specific execution sequence. A deterministic program has only one possible execution sequence for a given initial state. For a nondeterministic program, there are many possible sequences beginning with the same initial state. However, it is important to remember that even for nondeterministic programs, we are always referring to one single execution sequence. Since we make no assumptions about which one of the possible sequences it is, anything we can prove about it must be true for any possible execution sequence of the program.

A <u>predicate</u> is a boolean-valued function of the program state. For the program of Figure 1, $\neg x_1$ is the predicate that has the value "true" for those program states in which the variable x_1 has the value "false", and <u>at</u> w_2 is the predicate that has the value "true" for those states in which process 2's "program counter" indicates that it is about to perform the while test in statement w_2. A predicate is said to be true at time t if it is true for the t<u>th</u> state of the program execution sequence.

Our assertions will be based upon sets of "times". Since times are just natural numbers, these sets are all subsets of **N** -- the set of all natural numbers. We will describe subsets of **N** in terms of the interval notation ordinarily used for describing subsets of the real line. For example, for natural numbers m and n we have:

$$[m, n] \stackrel{\text{def}}{=} \{ i \in \mathbf{N} : m \leq i \leq n \}$$

$$[m, n) \stackrel{\text{def}}{=} \{ i \in \mathbf{N} : m \leq i < n \}$$

$$[m, \infty) \stackrel{\text{def}}{=} \{ i \in \mathbf{N} : m \leq i \} .$$

A <u>timeset</u> is a set of natural numbers. For any predicates P and Q, we define the timeset [P ⟶ Q) to consist of the union of all intervals [p, r] such that P is true at time p and Q is false during the entire interval [p, r]. In other words, a time t is in [P ⟶ Q) if and only if there is some time $p \leq t$ such that P is true at time t and Q is false from time p through time t. Thus, all the elements of [P ⟶ Q) are obtained by starting at any time p when $P \wedge \neg Q$ is true, and continuing up to but excluding the first time at which Q is true. If Q is false from time p on, then the entire infinite interval $[p, \infty)$ is a subset of [P ⟶ Q).

The definition of [P ⟶ Q) is illustrated in Figure 2. The rows labeled P and Q show the assumed truth values of those predicates at times 0 - 15, and the X's in the row labeled [P ⟶ Q) indicates the times that are in that set.

For any predicate P, the timeset [P ⟶ ¬P) is just the set of all times at which P is true. We denote this set by [P]. Note that [<u>false</u>] is the empty set, and [<u>true</u>] is the entire set **N**.

The timeset [P ⟶ <u>false</u>) is composed of the union of all intervals $[p, \infty)$ such that P is true at time p. In other words, [P ⟶ <u>false</u>) is the set of all

time :	0	1	2	3	4	5	6	7	8	9	10	11	12	13	14	15	...
P :	F	F	T	F	F	T	F	F	T	F	T	F	F	T	F	F	...
Q :	F	F	F	F	T	F	F	F	T	F	F	T	F	F	F	F	...
[P ⟶ Q) :			X	X		X	X	X			X			X	X	X	...
(Q ⟵ P] :	X	X	X			X				X	X		X	X			...

Figure 2: Example of timesets.

times t such that P is true at some time less than or equal to t. This timeset is denoted $[P \rightarrow \infty)$.

For predicates P and Q, we define the timeset (Q ⟵ P] to be the union of all intervals of the form [r, p] such that P is true at time p and Q is false during the entire interval [r, p]. In other words, (Q ⟵ P] consists of all times obtained by starting at any time p at which $P \wedge \neg Q$ is true, and moving backwards in time up to but excluding the first time at which Q is true. If Q is false at all times earlier than p, then the entire interval [0, p] is a subset of (Q ⟵ P]. This definition is illustrated by the example in Figure 2. Note that (¬P ⟵ P] equals [P].

The timeset (<u>false</u> $\leftarrow$ P] consists of the union of all intervals of the form [0, p] such that P is true at time p -- i.e., the set of all times t such that P is true at some time greater than or equal to t . This timeset is denoted [0 $\leftarrow$ P] .

Timesets of the form [P $\rightarrow$ Q) and (Q $\leftarrow$ P] are called <u>meta-intervals</u>. All the timesets we use are constructed from meta-intervals by the usual set operations of union ($\cup$), intersection ($\cap$) and complementation. With a little practice, it becomes easy to reason about these timesets. For example, the following are true for any predicates P, Q and R and any program execution sequence.

If $[R] \subseteq [Q]$ then

$$[P \rightarrow Q) \subseteq [P \rightarrow R) \quad \text{and} \quad (Q \leftarrow P] \subseteq (R \leftarrow P] \tag{2-1}$$

If $[P] \subseteq [R]$ then

$$[P \rightarrow Q) \subseteq [R \rightarrow Q) \quad \text{and} \quad (Q \leftarrow P] \subseteq (R \leftarrow P] \tag{2-2}$$

To verify 2-1, recall that [P $\rightarrow$ Q) is the union of intervals obtained by starting at a time p when $P \wedge \neg Q$ is true and continuing forward in time until Q becomes true. But $[R] \subseteq [Q]$ means that Q is true whenever R is, so R is false whenever Q is. Hence, such an interval must be contained in the interval obtained by starting at time p and continuing until R is true, which is in the meta-interval [P $\rightarrow$ R) . This shows that [P $\rightarrow$ Q) is the union of intervals, each of which is a subset of [P $\rightarrow$ R) , proving that [P $\rightarrow$ Q) $\subseteq$ [P $\rightarrow$ R) . The argument that (Q $\leftarrow$ R] $\subseteq$ (R $\leftarrow$ P] is obtained by replacing "forward in time" by "backward in time". The verification of the remaining formulas is left to the reader.

The reader may have noticed a certain symmetry between the two parts of relations 2-1 and 2-2. Given any formula, we can form its <u>mirror image</u> by replacing every meta-interval of the form [P $\rightarrow$ Q) by the meta-interval (Q $\leftarrow$ P] , and vice-versa. Since [P] = [P $\rightarrow$ $\neg$P) = ($\neg$P $\leftarrow$ P] , the timeset [P] is its own mirror image. Thus, relation 2-1 combines the relation

if $[R] \subseteq [Q]$ then $[P \rightarrow Q) \subseteq [P \rightarrow R)$

with its mirror image, and similarly for 2-2.

It is often the case that if a relation is true for all program executions then its mirror image is also true for all program executions. However, the fact that there is an earliest time (time zero) but no latest time introduces an asymmetry into our timesets, so the mirror image of a true formula is not necessarily true.

As our example indicated, it is sometimes necessary to be able to "switch directions" -- reasoning forward up to a point and then reasoning backward from there, or vice-versa. For this, we need some way of asserting that going forward (or backward) from some time we reach some desired condition. In particular, we need the following two assertions:

$P \rightsquigarrow Q$: for every time at which P is true, Q is either true then or else will be true some time in the future.

$Q \leftsquigarrow P$: for every time at which P is true, Q must be true then or else have been true some time before then.

These relations are defined formally in terms of timesets as follows.[2]

$$P \rightsquigarrow Q \stackrel{\text{def}}{=} [P] \sqsubseteq [0 \leftarrow Q]$$

$$Q \leftsquigarrow P \stackrel{\text{def}}{=} [P] \sqsubseteq [Q \rightarrow \infty)$$

Note that $P \rightsquigarrow Q$ and $Q \leftsquigarrow P$ are mirror images of one another, since $[0 \leftarrow Q]$ and $[Q \rightarrow \infty)$ are.

The following formulas, which are mirror images of each other, allow us to "switch directions" in our temporal reasoning.

If $[P \rightarrow Q \wedge R) \sqsubseteq [R]$ and $P \rightsquigarrow Q$ then $[P \rightarrow Q) \sqsubseteq (\neg R \leftarrow Q]$ (2-3)

If $(Q \wedge R \leftarrow P] \sqsubseteq [R]$ and $Q \leftsquigarrow P$ then $(Q \leftarrow P] \sqsubseteq [Q \rightarrow \neg R)$ (2-4)

To see that 2-3 is valid, observe that $[P \rightarrow Q \wedge R) \sqsubseteq [R]$ means that starting at any time p when $P \wedge \neg(Q \wedge R)$ is true and going forward in time, R is true until the first time that $Q \wedge R$ is true. This implies that starting at any time

---

[2]The relation $\rightsquigarrow$ is defined somewhat differently than in [5]. In terms of the linear time $\Box$ and $\Diamond$ operators, we are here defining $P \rightsquigarrow Q$ to be $\Box(P \supset \Diamond Q)$.

p when $P \wedge \neg Q$ is true and moving forward in time, R will be true up to and including the first time q when Q is true. The hypothesis $P \leadsto Q$ implies that such a time q does exist. Hence, $[P \rightarrow Q)$ is the union of intervals of the form $[p, q)$ such that Q is true at time q and R is true during the entire interval $[p, q]$. But the interval $[p, q]$ is clearly contained in the meta-interval $(\neg R \leftarrow Q]$. Hence, $[P \rightarrow Q)$ is the union of intervals each of which is contained in $(\neg R \leftarrow Q]$, which demonstrates the required set inclusion. The proof of 2-4 is similar.

3. THE MUTUAL EXCLUSION EXAMPLE

We now reconsider our mutual exclusion example in terms of timesets. First of all, we can restate Properties A and B formally as follows.

A. $[\neg x_2 \rightarrow \neg x_1) \subseteq [\neg \underline{in}\ cs_2]$

B. 1. $\underline{at}\ w_1 \leftarrow \underline{in}\ cs_1$

2.(a) $(\underline{at}\ w_1 \leftarrow \underline{in}\ cs_1] = (\underline{at}\ w_1 \wedge \neg x_2 \leftarrow \underline{in}\ cs_1]$

(b) $(\underline{at}\ w_1 \leftarrow \underline{in}\ cs_1] \subseteq [x_1]$

The reader should not have too much difficulty determining that the above are formalizations of the original informal properties. The desired mutual exclusion property, that both processes are never both in their critical section, is expressed formally by

$$[\underline{in}\ cs_1] \subseteq [\neg \underline{in}\ cs_2] .$$

The formal proof of this property is given below.

1. $(\underline{at}\ w_1 \wedge \neg x_2 \leftarrow \underline{in}\ cs_1] \subseteq [x_1]$: from B2(a) and (b).

2. $\underline{at}\ w_1 \wedge \neg x_2 \leftarrow \underline{in}\ cs_1$:

   from B_1 and B2(a), using the general result that $Q \leftarrow P$ and $(R \leftarrow P] \subseteq (Q \leftarrow P]$ imply $R \leftarrow P$.

3. $(\underline{at}\ w_1 \wedge \neg x_2 \leftarrow \underline{in}\ cs_1] \subseteq [\underline{at}\ w_1 \wedge \neg x_2 \rightarrow \neg x_1)$:

   from 1, 2 and 2-4.

4. $[\underline{at}\ w_1 \wedge \neg x_2 \rightarrow \neg x_1) \subseteq [\neg x_2 \rightarrow \neg x_1)$: by 2-2.

5. $(\underline{at}\ w_1 \wedge \neg x_2 \leftarrow \underline{in}\ cs_1] \subseteq [\neg \underline{in}\ cs_2]$: from 3, 4 and A.

6. $[\underline{in}\ cs_1] \sqsubseteq (\underline{at}\ w_1 \wedge \neg x_2 \leftarrow \underline{in}\ cs_1]$:

from the general result that $[P] \sqsubseteq (Q \rightarrow P]$.

7. $[\underline{in}\ cs_1] \sqsubseteq [\neg\, \underline{in}\ cs_2]$: from 5 and 6.

In all of our reasoning about the mutual exclusion algorithm, we have tacitly assumed that the program starts with Process 1 outside statement s_1 (the **begin/end** that encloses the critical section and its entry protocol). In reasoning about programs with ordinary temporal logic, we have found it convenient not to assume any preferred starting state, but rather to explicitly include any necessary hypotheses about the starting state in the theorems to be proved. Thus, all the results to be proved about the program have the form "if some initial predicate is true at time zero, then ... ".

The algorithm of Figure 1 does not guarantee mutual exclusion unless started in a state in which $\neg\, \underline{in}\ s_1$ is true. For example, if we start in a state in which Process 1 is in its critical section, then Property A does not prevent Process 2 from entering its critical section cs_2 before Process 1 exits from cs_1 . The above proof breaks down because Property B1 is not true in this case.

There are two ways to introduce the explicit hypothesis that Process 1 starts outside its critical section. The first is to say that the conclusion that both processes are not simultaneously in their critical sections need only hold from the first time that Process 1 is outside statement s_1 . In other words, the conclusion need only hold during the times in the meta-interval $[\neg\, \underline{in}\ s_1 \rightarrow \infty)$. Thus, what we must prove is:

$$[\underline{in}\ cs_1] \cap [\neg\, \underline{in}\ s_1 \rightarrow \infty) \sqsubseteq [\neg\, \underline{in}\ cs_2] \cap [\neg\, \underline{in}\ s_1 \rightarrow \infty) . \qquad (3\text{-}1)$$

To correct Property B1, for any timeset T we let "$Q \leftarrow P$ $\underline{during}$ T" mean that any time in T at which P is true is preceded by (or is) a time in T at which Q is true. This is defined formally by:

$$Q \leftarrow P\ \underline{during}\ T \overset{def}{=} [P] \cap T \sqsubseteq [Q \rightarrow \infty) \cap T .$$

Property B1 can then be modified to:

B1'. $\underline{at}\ w_1 \leftarrow \underline{in}\ cs_1\ \underline{during}\ [\neg\, \underline{in}\ s_1 \rightarrow \infty)$.

Using B1' instead of B1, we can proceed pretty much as we did in the previous proof to derive the desired conclusion 3-1. However, at various places in this proof, sets must be replaced by their intersection with $[\neg \underline{in}\ s_1 \rightarrow \infty)$, and we need generalizations of the theorems that were used (such as 2-4).

The second approach is to say that mutual exclusion only needs to hold if the execution sequence has the property that Process 1 is not in statement s_1 at time zero. The assertion "<u>initially</u> P" which asserts that the predicate P is true at time zero is defined formally by:

$$\underline{\text{initially}}\ P \overset{\text{def}}{=} [P \rightarrow \infty) = N .$$

We then express the desired conclusion as:

$$\underline{\text{initially}}\ \neg\ \underline{\text{in}}\ s_1 \supset [\underline{\text{in}}\ cs_1] \subseteq [\neg\ \underline{\text{in}}\ cs_2] , \qquad (3\text{-}2)$$

where $\supset$ denotes logical implication.

Property B1 is modified to:

B1". $(\underline{\text{initially}}\ \neg\ \underline{\text{in}}\ s_1) \supset (\underline{\text{at}}\ w_1 \leftarrow \underline{\text{in}}\ cs_1)$

The proof of 3-2 is identical to the original proof, except for the addition of a few "$\underline{\text{initially}}\ \neg\ \underline{\text{in}}\ s_1 \supset$" terms to the assertions.

It is interesting to compare these two approaches. It may appear that we have proved two different theorems with them. However, we will see later on that 3-1 and 3-2 are completely equivalent because of the quantification over all possible program execution sequences implicit in them.

The first method, involving the proof of 3-1, might be called "pure timeset logic". In pure timeset logic, the only theorems that are used are assertions of the form $S \subseteq T$ for timesets S and T.[3]

The second approach, in which we proved 3-2, might be called a "mixed logic". In this approach, we combined timeset assertions with logical operators to form theorems such as 3-2. However, the only timesets that were used were meta-intervals. We did not have to take unions, intersections or complements of timesets.

---

[3]Any theorem of the form $S = T$ can be replaced by the two theorems $S \subseteq T$ and $T \subseteq S$. We did not need a rule of substitution of equals; the transitivity of $\subseteq$ sufficed.

The pure timeset logic seems to be theoretically more elegant, since the theorems have a simpler structure. However, as this example indicates, the use of the mixed logic seems to result in simpler proofs. Further experience is needed before we can reach any conclusions about the relative merits of these two approaches.

4. A FORMAL SEMANTICS

We now define a formal semantics for our timeset assertions, as well as for ordinary temporal logic assertions. We regard our assertions formally to be strings of symbols. To define a semantics for them, we must specify a class of models and a relation $\models$ between models and assertions, where $\Sigma \models A$ means that the formula A is valid (true) for the model Σ. We then say that an assertion A is valid, written $\models A$, if $\Sigma \models A$ holds for every model Σ.

To reason formally, one needs a logical system with formal inference rules and axioms. However, for the informal reasoning that we have been using -- which is the kind of reasoning mathematicians usually employ — a semantics for the assertions suffices. With such a semantics, we can check that our reasoning is valid -- i.e., that we only derive valid assertions. The construction of a logical system for formalizing this reasoning is an interesting problem, but is beyond the scope of this paper.

We begin with a BNF grammar for the assertions. Assertions are built starting from a set **AP** of atomic predicate symbols. For simplicity, we will formally define our assertions to be completely parenthesized, and will not worry about defining any operator precedence. To define logical operations on assertions, it suffices to define negation and disjunction, since the other operations can be defined in terms of them. Similarly, we need only define complementation and union for timesets.

```
<assertion>  ::=  <pure timeset assertion> | <predicate> |
                   ¬(<assertion>) | (<assertion>) ∨ (<assertion>) |
                   (<assertion>) □ (<assertion>)

<predicate>  ::=  <atomic predicate> | ¬(<predicate>) |
                   (<predicate>) ∨ (<predicate>)

<atomic predicate>  ::=  any element of AP
```

<pure timeset assertion> ::= <timeset> $\sqsubseteq$ <timeset>

<timeset> ::= <meta-interval> | **N** - (<timeset>) | (<timeset>) **U** (<timeset>)

<meta-interval> ::= (<predicate> $\rightarrow$ <predicate>) |
(<predicate> $\leftarrow$ <predicate>)

The unary temporal logic operators $\Box$ and $\Diamond$ are defined in terms of the binary $\Box$ operator as follows:

$\Box\ A \overset{def}{=} (true)\ \Box\ (A)$

$\Diamond\ A \overset{def}{=} \neg(\ \Box\ \neg(A)\ )$

We now define a semantics for these assertions. This exposition will be brief, and we will leave it to the reader to verify that our definitions are complete.

A <u>state</u> is defined to be a boolean valued function on the set **AP** of atomic predicates. If s is a state and P a predicate, then we write $s \models P$ to denote the value of s applied to P. This function is extended to a function on arbitrary predicates by:

$s \models \neg(P) \overset{def}{=} \neg(s \models P)$

$s \models (P \vee Q) \overset{def}{=} (s \models P) \vee (s \models Q)$

For any infinite sequence of states $\sigma = \sigma_0, \sigma_1, \ldots$, and any timeset T, we define T^σ to be a subset of the set **N** of natural numbers as follows:

$[P \rightarrow Q)^\sigma \overset{def}{=} \{\ n : \exists\ m \leq n$ such that $\sigma_m \models P$
and $\forall\ t$ with $m \leq t \leq n : \sigma_t \models \neg Q\ \}$

$(Q \leftarrow P]^\sigma \overset{def}{=} \{\ n : \exists\ m \geq n$ such that $\sigma_m \models P$
and $\forall\ t$ with $m \geq t \geq n : \sigma_t \models \neg Q\ \}$

$(\mathbf{N} - T)^\sigma \overset{def}{=} \mathbf{N} - T^\sigma$

$((S)\ \mathbf{U}\ (T))^\sigma \overset{def}{=} S^\sigma \cup T^\sigma$

For any infinite sequence of states $\sigma = \sigma_0, \sigma_1, \ldots$ and any assertion A, we define $\sigma \models A$ as follows, where σ^{+n} is defined to equal $\sigma_n, \sigma_{n+1}, \ldots$ for any natural number n.

$\sigma \models S \sqsubseteq T \overset{def}{=} \models S^{\sigma} \sqsubseteq T^{\sigma}$

$\sigma \models P \overset{def}{=} \sigma_0 \models P$, for any predicate P

$\sigma \models \neg(A) \overset{def}{=} \neg(\sigma \models A)$

$\sigma \models (A) \vee (B) \overset{def}{=} (\sigma \models A) \vee (\sigma \models B)$

$\sigma \models (A) \Box (B) \overset{def}{=} \forall n : [(\forall m \leq n : \sigma^{+m} \models A) \supset \sigma^{+n} \models B]$

Finally, for we define a model Σ to consist of a set of infinite sequences of states having the property that for every element σ of Σ, σ^{+1} is also an element of Σ. For any assertion A we define:

$\Sigma \models A \overset{def}{=} \forall \sigma \in \Sigma : \sigma \models A$.

A program is represented by a model Σ consisting of the set of all possible execution sequences of that program. Intuitively, $\Sigma \models A$ means that A is a true assertion about the program represented by Σ, while $\models A$ means that A is a tautology that is true for all programs. The assumption that if σ is in Σ then σ^{+1} must also be in Σ implies implies two things:

- Execution may begin anywhere within the program.
- At any instant, the possible future behaviors of the program are completely determined by its current state, and do not depend upon how it reached that state.

It is this assumption that implies the equivalence of 3-1 and 3-2.

5. EXPRESSIVENESS AND EXTENSIONS

In discussing the expressiveness of timesets, two questions naturally arise:

- Do timesets give us all the expressive power of the ordinary temporal operators?
- Do timesets give us any new expressive power?

We define two assertions A and B to be <u>semantically equivalent</u> if for every model Σ: $\Sigma \models A$ holds if and only if $\Sigma \models B$ does. Note that semantic equivalence is weaker than ordinary logical equivalence, which means that $\Sigma \models A \equiv B$ holds for every model Σ. For example, any assertion A is semantically equivalent to the assertion $\Box A$, but the two need not be logically equivalent.

Recall that a pure timeset assertion has the form $S \sqsubseteq T$, where S and T are timesets. Let us define a timeset assertion to be one formed from pure timeset assertions with the ordinary logical operations of negation and disjunction, and an ordinary temporal logic assertion to be one formed from predicates with the ordinary logical operations and the binary $\Box$ operator. The above questions can then be stated more precisely as:

- Is every ordinary temporal logic assertion semantically equivalent to some timeset assertion?
- Is there a timeset assertion that is not semantically equivalent to any ordinary temporal logic assertion?

We conjecture that the answer to both of these questions is "no", so that timeset assertions are strictly less expressive than ordinary temporal logic assertions, but we have been unable to prove either of these results. We can, however, show this to be the case for a restricted class of timesets. We define a meta-interval assertion to be a logical combination of assertions of the form <meta-interval> $\sqsubseteq$ <meta-interval> . We will show that the answer to these two questions is "no" if we replace "timeset assertion" by "meta-interval assertion".

To prove that the answer to the second question is "no" for meta-interval assertions, it suffices to show that every such assertion is logically equivalent to an ordinary temporal logic assertion.[4] Since there are two kinds of meta-intervals, there are four types of meta-interval assertion to consider:

$$
\begin{aligned}
&[P \rightarrow Q) \sqsubseteq [R \rightarrow S) \\
&[P \rightarrow Q) \sqsubseteq (S \leftarrow R] \\
&(Q \leftarrow P] \sqsubseteq [R \rightarrow S) \\
&(Q \leftarrow P] \sqsubseteq (S \leftarrow R] \qquad (5\text{-}1)
\end{aligned}
$$

All we need to do is write ordinary temporal logic assertions that are equivalent to these four timeset assertions. The required temporal logic assertions are rather complex, and are given in the Appendix. Indeed, timesets are useful because these timeset assertions are so much simpler than the equivalent temporal logic assertions.

---

[4]Showing semantic equivalence is not enough, since the negations of semantically equivalent assertions need not be semantically equivalent.

To prove that the answer to the first question is "no" for meta-interval assertions, we simply observe that any of these assertions can be formed from the ones given in the Appendix by using ordinary logical operations. Hence, they can be expressed as ordinary temporal logic assertions having a fixed maximum nesting depth of the $\Box$ operator. However, it can be shown that for any n there exists a temporal logic assertion that is not semantically equivalent to any assertion having a nesting depth less than n.

If our conjectures are correct, and timeset assertions are less expressive than ordinary temporal logic assertions, then it is tempting to try to extend our method of forming timesets to increase the expressive power of the timeset assertions. The simplest way is to generalize the definition of the meta-intervals $[P \rightarrow Q)$ and $(Q \leftarrow P]$ to allow P and Q to be arbitrary timesets. The definition is quite easy: we merely replace "P true at time t" by "t an element of P", and likewise for Q. Formally, we define the semantics of the meta-interval $[S \rightarrow T)$, where S and T are timesets by:

$$[S \rightarrow T)^{\sigma} \stackrel{\text{def}}{=} \{ n : \exists\, m \leq n \text{ such that } m \in S^{\sigma} \text{ and } \forall\, t \text{ with } m \leq t \leq n : t \in T^{\sigma} \}.$$

If we let P denote the timeset $[P]$ for any predicate P, then this subsumes the previous definition. The definition of $(T \leftarrow S]$ is analogous.

With this more general type of timeset, every ordinary temporal logic assertion is logically equivalent to a timeset assertion. To prove this, we first define for every ordinary temporal logic assertion A the timeset $[A]$. If A is a predicate, then the timeset $[A]$ has already been defined. For an arbitrary assertion, $[A]$ is defined inductively as follows:

$$[\neg A] \stackrel{\text{def}}{=} \mathbf{N} - [A]$$

$$[A \vee B] \stackrel{\text{def}}{=} [A] \cup [B]$$

$$[A \Box B] \stackrel{\text{def}}{=} \mathbf{N} - ([\neg A] \leftarrow [\neg B]]$$

We leave it as an exercise for the reader to verify that for any sequence σ of states and any assertion A: $\sigma \models A$ if and only if $0 \in [A]$. The assertion A is then logically equivalent to the timeset assertion $\mathbf{N} \subseteq [A]$.

There are many other ways one might extend these assertion languages. However, we have been guided by one fundamental principle: every assertion should be invariant under finite repetition of states. This means that given any sequence, if we form a new sequence by repeating some of its states a finite number of times -- e.g., turning the sequence a, b, c, d, ... into the sequence a, b, b, b, c, d, d, ... — then no assertion should be able to distinguish between the two sequences. More precisely, if σ' is obtained from σ by a finite repetition of states, then for any assertion A we must have $\sigma' \models A$ if and only if $\sigma \models A$.

This principle is based upon the idea that the only thing that should be observable about the execution of the program is its state changes. For example, we could model a process executing a P operation to a semaphore as either passively waiting for the semaphore to become positive or else repeatedly testing its value, doing something (changing the program state) only when it finds the value positive. These two models should be equivalent, and we should not be able to observe any difference between them.

It is easy to verify that all the assertions we have constructed are invariant under finite repetition of states. For our timeset assertions, this follows from the fact that for any timeset T and any sequence $\sigma = \sigma_0, \sigma_1, \ldots$: if $\sigma_i = \sigma_{i+1}$ then $i \in T^\sigma$ if and only if $i+1 \in T^\sigma$.

The desire to maintain invariance under finite repetition of states has led us to reject several extensions, both to ordinary temporal logic and to timeset logic. The "next state" operator used by Pnueli [3] is one extension to ordinary temporal logic that we have eschewed for this reason.

6. CONCLUSION

Temporal logic is a useful tool for proving properties about programs. There are two kinds of properties one wants to prove:

- Safety properties, which usually have the form $P \supset \Box Q$. Partial correctness is such a property, because it can be stated as "(control at beginning of program $\wedge$ initial condition) $\supset$ $\Box$ (control at end of program $\supset$ termination condition)".

- Liveness properties, which have the form $P \supset (Q \rightsquigarrow R)$. (This is the "$\rightsquigarrow$" operator defined in Section 2.) Termination of a subroutine is such a property, since it can be stated as "(control at beginning of program $\wedge$ initial condition) $\supset$ $\Box$ (control at beginning of subroutine $\rightsquigarrow$ control at end of subroutine)".

When given the entire program, one can usually prove these properties using only the unary temporal operator $\Box$. This operator gives us a type of ordinary modal logic in which informal reasoning is fairly easy.

There are more general safety properties having the form

$$P \supset \Box(Q \supset (R \,\Box\, S)) .$$

This kind of more general safety property arises quite naturally when reasoning about individual parts of a program. Properties A and B of our example program were of this form.

The binary $\Box$ operator takes us outside the realm of ordinary modal logic, and we have found it very difficult to reason informally with it. This has led us to introduce a new method of temporal reasoning based upon timesets. We feel that this method will be helpful in reasoning about these more general safety properties.

We have found that the difficult part of proving a liveness property is proving a number of safety properties as lemmas. The actual temporal logic reasoning used in the proof, involving the $\rightsquigarrow$ and unary $\Box$ operators, is simple. Moreover, this reasoning does not seem to be conveniently expressible in terms of timesets. We therefore feel that timesets will be most useful in proving safety properties of programs, while ordinary temporal logic should be used to derive liveness properties from these safety properties.

One might expect there to be a more general type of liveness property as well. However, this does not seem to be the case for the following reason. Liveness properties differ from safety properties in requiring the use of the $\Diamond$ operator, defined by $\Diamond A \equiv \neg(\Box \neg A)$. (We can define $\rightsquigarrow$ by $A \rightsquigarrow B \equiv \Box(A \supset \Diamond B)$.) A more general liveness property would be formed by taking a negation of the binary $\Box$ operator. However, the equivalence:

$$\neg(A \,\Box\, B) \;\equiv\; (\Diamond \neg B) \wedge ((B \vee \neg A) \,\Box\, A)$$

shows that such a dual can be expressed in terms of the binary $\Box$ and the unary $\Diamond$.

We have seen that we can use ordinary temporal logic to prove liveness properties, but timesets are more convenient for proving at least some safety properties. We believe that all safety proofs can be expressed in terms of pure timeset logic, but that simpler proofs can be written with a mixed logic using timeset assertions and ordinary logical operators -- and perhaps also the unary temporal operator $\Box$. However, more experience is needed to determine the best practical approach to concurrent program verification.

REFERENCES

1. R.M. Burstall. Program Proving as Hand Simulation with a Little Induction. Information Processing 74, 1974, pp. 308-312.

2. N. Francez and A. Pnueli. A Proof Method for Cyclic Programs. Acta Informatica 9, 2 (1978), 133-158.

3. D. Gabbay, A. Pnueli, S. Shelah and Y. Stavi. On the Temporal Analysis of Fairness. Seventh Annual ACM Symposium on Principles of Programming Languages, ACM, Las Vegas, Nevada, January, 1980, pp. 163-173.

4. L. Lamport. The 'Hoare Logic' of Concurrent Programs. Acta Informatica 14 (1980), 21-37.

5. L. Lamport. 'Sometime' is Sometimes 'Not Never': A Tutorial on the Temporal Logic of Programs. Proceedings of the Seventh Annual Symposium on Principles of Programming Languages, ACM SIGACT-SIGPLAN, January, 1980.

6. S. Owicki and L. Lamport. Proving Livness Properties of Concurrent Programs. submitted for publication

7. A. Pnueli. The Temporal Logic of Programs. Proc. of the 18th Symposium on the Foundations of Computer Science, ACM, November, 1977.

APPENDIX: EXPRESSING META-INTERVAL ASSERTIONS

We now construct temporal logic assertions that are logically equivalent to the four meta-interval assertions of 5-1. Our exposition will be informal -- e.g., we say that an assertion is "true at time t " instead of the more formal statement that it is valid for the subsequence σ^{+t} of the sequence σ under consideration. The reader who is uncomfortable with such informal reasoning can translate everything into the precise formal notation of Section 4.

First, we define the temporal operators BF (for "Before") and NB (for "Not Before") by:

$$A \text{ BF } B \overset{\text{def}}{=} \neg ((\neg B) \Box (\neg A))$$

$$A \text{ NB } B \overset{\text{def}}{=} (\neg A) \Box (\neg B) \ .$$

The assertion A BF B means that A must eventually become true, and that it must become true strictly before the first time that B becomes true. The assertion A NB B means that A cannot become true before the first time that B becomes true.

The meta-interval $[P \rightarrow Q)$ is the union of intervals beginning at a time when $P \wedge \neg Q$ is true and continuing up to but excluding the next time that Q is true. The complement of the meta-interval $[R \rightarrow S)$ consists of the union of the following types of intervals.

1. The interval from time 0 up to but excluding the first time that $R \wedge \neg S$ is true, and
2. Any interval starting at a time when S is true up to but excluding the next time that $R \wedge \neg S$ is true.

The meta-interval $[P \rightarrow Q)$ is contained in the meta-interval $[R \rightarrow S)$ if and only if the following two conditions are satisfied.

(a) The beginning of any interval in $[P \rightarrow Q)$ is in some interval in $[R \rightarrow S)$.

(b) The end of any interval in $[R \rightarrow S)$ does not come before the end of any interval in $[P \rightarrow Q)$ beginning inside it.

Condition (a) is equivalent to saying that no interval in $[P \rightarrow Q)$ begins in the complement of $[R \rightarrow S)$. Remembering the above characterization of this complement, we can write conditions (a) and (b) as follows.

(a) 1. $(P \wedge \neg Q)$ NB $(R \wedge \neg S)$

2. $\Box\ (S \supset ((P \wedge \neg Q)$ NB $(R \wedge \neg S)))$

(b) $\Box\ ((P \wedge \neg Q) \supset (S$ NB $Q))$

It then follows that $[P \rightarrow Q) \subseteq [R \rightarrow S)$ is equivalent to the conjunction of the above three assertions.

The meta-interval $(Q \leftarrow P]$ consists of all times at which P BF Q is true. By the above reasoning, it is easy to see that $(Q \leftarrow P] \subseteq [R \rightarrow S)$ is equivalent to the conjunction of the following three assertions.

(a) 1. (P BF Q) NB $(R \wedge \neg S)$

2. $\Box\ (S \supset ((P$ BF $Q)$ NB $(R \wedge \neg S)))$

(b) $\Box\ ((P$ BF $Q) \supset (S$ NB $Q))$

The reader should now have little trouble verifying the following two equivalences.

$$([P \rightarrow Q) \subseteq (S \leftarrow R]) \equiv \Box\ ((P \wedge \neg Q) \supset ((\neg Q) \Box (S \text{ BF } R)))$$

$$((Q \leftarrow P] \subseteq (S \leftarrow R]) \equiv \Box\ ((Q \text{ BF } P) \supset (S \text{ BF } R))$$

PROGRAM LOGICS AND PROGRAM VERIFICATION

Leslie Lamport and Susan Owicki

Our work on program logics began with generalizations of Hoare's axiomatic method to concurrent programs [1], [4]. Pnueli's work suggested an investigation of temporal logics [2] and their application to proving properties of concurrent programs [3]. We are now (intermittently) working on a single program logic for describing the semantics of concurrent programming languages, which will generalize our earlier work.

Our entire approach to program semantics seems to be very different from that of most people working on program logics. These people, whom we will simplistically label "logicians", are concerned primarily with proving properties of classes of programs -- properties such as the computational complexity of deciding if a program will terminate. We will simplistically label ourselves "verifiers", as our chief concern is proving properties of individual programs --e.g., proving that a particular program will terminate. The world needs both logicians and verifiers, and we need one another. Logicians need verifiers to keep their work relevant, and verifiers need logicians to keep them honest. (In typical human fashion, most logicians think they know all they need to about real verification problems for developing theories, and most verifiers think they know enough about logic to verify programs. They're probably both wrong.)

This difference in approach leads us to be interested in different kinds of program logics than logicians. Logicians seem to be looking for the most powerful logic they can find. (One can almost sense a "my logic can express everything yours can -- nyah, nyah!" attitude among them.) We, on the other hand, only require a logic that can express the kinds of properties we want to prove about individual programs.

There are two basic kinds of properties one wants to prove about a program:

The program doesn't do something it shouldn't.

The program does do something it should.

These are called "safety" and "liveness" properties, respectively. We want a program logic for concurrent programs that can express these properties <u>and only these properties</u>. In particular, we don't need to be able to express the following two kinds of properties.

It is possible for the program to do something.

The program is equivalent to some other program.

Since logicians are looking for very powerful logics that can express things about all kinds of nondeterminism, they usually construct logics that can express at least the first kind of property. On the other hand, when one is verifying a program, one wants to use only assertions that are true for any reasonable implementation, unless assumptions about the implementation are made explicit. The assertion that a particular outcome is possible on a non-deterministic program, even when theoretically justified, is likely to be false for some implementations (for example, because the relative speeds of processes is bounded). We do not want this sort of property to be expressible within the logic, because it is not meaningful in the context of verification.

Another major difference between the logics we are interested in and many that have been constructed is that we do not want to use a "next state" operator -- an operator that allows one to construct expressions relating the state at some instant with the state after the next computation step. There are two reasons for this:

Experience has shown that one wants to reason about concurrent programs in terms of assertions, not in terms of sequences of events, and this has been the prime motivation for our work. A next state operator permits one to sneak reasoning about sequences of events into an assertional method.

A next state operator implies a knowledge of what the individual computational steps are. This precludes higher-level reasoning about a program, where one uses properties of subprograms without knowing anything about how they are implemented.

The following example illustrates this latter point. Using Lamport's generalization of Hoare's logic, one can specify an "increment x" operation having the following two properties, where x is of type "real".

1. If the operation is begun with x having the value a, then upon termination x will have the value a + 1.
2. During the operation, the value of x is monotonically nondecreasing. (The value can be read by concurrent operations while the "increment x" is being executed.)

Just using this specification, with no further information about any implementation or underlying model, one should be able to prove properties of programs using this "increment x" operation. Of course, this operation could be implemented by an arbitrary number of computation steps, each adding some quantity less than 1 to the value of x . More significantly, one can construct a computational model in which x is incremented continuously -- i.e., in which there is a time variation t that assumes all real values, and the value of x is a continuous function of t. This seems like a perfectly reasonable model/implementation for our specification of the "increment x" operation so the proof of any property of a program using the "increment x" operation should be valid under this model/implementation. However, one cannot define a "next state" operator with this underlying computational model, which means that the "next state" operator must not be used when reasoning about any program that uses the "increment x" operator. Although continuously increasing variables may be of little practical significance, it appears that operations which update variables monotonically will be an important tool in structuring distributed computations, and we want to be able to reason about them effectively.

There is no reason to expect that a "verifier" should use the same kind of the program logic as a "logician". Logicians don't prove theorems about classes of Cobol programs, and programmers don't write payroll programs in dynamic logic -- all for good reason. One hopes that logicians and verifiers will appreciate each other's aims, and be able to help one another.

REFERENCES

[1] L. Lamport
The 'Hoare Logic' of Concurrent Programs.
Acta Informatica to appear, 1980.

[2] L. Lamport
'Sometime" is Sometimes 'Not Never': A Tutorial on the Temporal Logic of Programs.
In Proceedings of the Seventh Annual Symposium on Principles of Programming Languages.
ACM SIGACT-SIGPLAN, January, 1980.

[3] S. Owicki and L. Lamport
Proving Livness Properties of Programs.
Submitted for publication.

[4] S. Owicki and D. Gries.
An Axiomatic Proof Technique for Parallel Programs.
Acta Informatica 6(4):319-340, 1976.

VERIFICATION OF CONCURRENT PROGRAMS: TEMPORAL PROOF PRINCIPLES

by

ZOHAR MANNA
Computer Science Department
Stanford University
Stanford, CA
and
Applied Mathematics Department
The Weizmann Institute
Rehovot, Israel

AMIR PNUELI
Applied Mathematics Department
The Weizmann Institute
Rehovot, Israel

Abstract

In this paper, the second of a series on the application of temporal logic to concurrent programs, we present proof methods for establishing *invariance* (*safety*) and *eventuality* (*liveness*) properties.

The proof principle for establishing invariance properties is based on computational induction, and is a generalization of the *inductive assertion* method. For a restricted class of concurrent programs we present an algorithm for the automatic derivation of invariant assertions.

In order to establish eventuality properties we present several proof principles that translate the structure of the program into basic temporal statements about its behavior. These principles can be viewed as providing the temporal semantics of the program. The basic statements thus derived are then combined into temporal proofs for the establishment of eventuality properties. This method generalizes the *intermittent assertion* method.

The proof principles are amply illustrated by examples.

The first paper in this series, the *temporal framework* part, appears in *The Correctness Problem in Computer Science* (R. S. Boyer aod J S. Moore, eds.), International Lecture Series in Computer Science, Academic Press, London, 1981.

This research was supported in part by the National Science Foundation under grants MCS79-09495 and MCS80-06930, by the Office of Naval Research under Contract N00014-76-C-0687, and by the United States Air Force Office of Scientific Research under Grant AFOSR-81-0014.

INTRODUCTION

In a previous report [MP2] we introduced the temporal framework for reasoning about concurrent programs. We described the model of concurrent programs that we study which is based on interaction via shared variables and defined the concept of fair execution of such programs. We then demonstrated the application of the temporal logic formalism to the *expression* of properties of concurrent programs. Program properties of interest can be classified according to the syntactic form of the temporal formula expressing them; we studied three classes of properties: invariance properties, eventuality properties and precedence properties. We have shown that almost all of the program properties that were ever considered or studied for either sequential or concurrent programs fall into one of these three categories. These include properties such as partial correctness, clean behavior, global invariants, mutual exclusion, safety, deadlock absence, output integrity – in the invariance category; total correctness, intermittent assertion realization, accessibility, liveness, responsiveness – in the eventualities category; and safe liveness, absence of unsolicited response, FIFO responsiveness and general precedence – in the precedence category.

In this paper, a sequel to [MP2], we concentrate on the application of the temporal logic formalism to *proving* these properties. We would thus present methods for establishing that a given program indeed possesses a certain property. In principle, once a property has been expressed within the temporal logic formalism, and an appropriate temporal characterization of the behavior of the given program derived ([MAN1], [MP1], [PNU1], [PNU2]), the task of proving that the property holds for this program reduces to proving the validity of a certain temporal implication. This implication states that every sequence of states, if it is a fair computation of the given program, has the desired property.

These principles can be justified by the general temporal formalism, and once justified, provide direct, simple, and intuitive rules for the establishment of these properties. They usually replace long but repetitively similar chains of primitive steps in more detailed proofs, and help us focus on the higher level overview of the proof while retaining the necessary standard of rigor.

Previous attempts to develop proof techniques for concurrent programs include [KEL], [LAM] and [OG].

In our exposition, we assume that the reader is familiar with the concepts and definitions introduced in our first paper of this series – [MP2].

THE INVARIANCE PRINCIPLE

Consider a typical concurrent program P of form

$$(\overline{y} := f_0(\overline{x}));\ [P_1 || \ldots || P_m]$$

with input parameters $\overline{x} = (x_1, \ldots, x_k)$ and shared program variables $\overline{y} = (y_1, \ldots, y_n)$ over a domain D. Let ψ be a classical formula, *i.e.*, a formula with no modal operators.

The basic idea in proving that the formula ψ is an invariant of the program P, *i.e.*

$$\models \quad \varphi(\overline{x}) \supset \Box\psi,$$

is to show that:

(*a*) the precondition $\varphi(\overline{x})$ implies that ψ is true initially.

(*b*) ψ is preserved by any possible transition of the program P; that is, if it were true before the transition then it also will be true after the transition.

We can then infer the invariance of ψ under the precondition $\varphi(\overline{x})$.

To state the result more precisely, let $Q(\overline{\pi};\overline{y})$ be a "state property", *i.e.*, it is expressed by a classical formula with no temporal operators, which may refer to the location variables $\overline{\pi}$, the program variables $\overline{y}$, and possibly some global variables.

Let

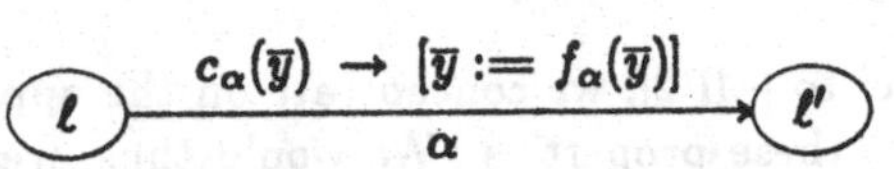

be a transition in process P_j for some $j = 1, \ldots, m$. With each such transition we associate the location transformation function r_α given by:

$$r_\alpha(\pi_1, \ldots, \pi_j, \ldots, \pi_m) = (\pi_1, \ldots, \ell', \ldots, \pi_m),$$

i.e., the value of π_j is replaced by ℓ', while the value of each π_i, $i \neq j$, is unchanged. This transformation denotes the change in the vector $\overline{\pi}$ when transition α is taken, much in the same way that f_α denotes the change in $\overline{y}$ when α is taken.

The notation we use to express the location change as a transformation underlines the similarity between the location and program variables. This leads to the possible description of a transition as:

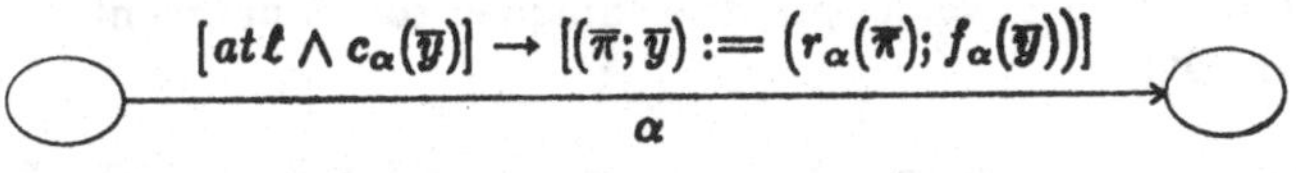

A property $Q(\overline{\pi};\overline{y})$ is said to be *inductive* for P if the following *verification condition* holds for each transition α in P:

$$V_\alpha : \quad [at\,\ell \wedge c_\alpha(\overline{y}) \wedge Q(\overline{\pi};\overline{y})] \quad \supset \quad Q(r_\alpha(\overline{\pi}); f_\alpha(\overline{y})).$$

Intuitively, Q is inductive if it is inherited along every transition *i.e.*, if it was true before the transition and the transition was enabled, it will necessarily be true after the transition. Note that the verification condition is classical, in the sense that it contains no temporal operators, and can therefore be established using classical proof techniques.

Our proof rule for invariance may now be formulated as follows:

The Invariance Principle

Let $Q(\overline{\pi};\overline{y})$ be a state property of a program P such that:

1. Q is true initially; *i.e.*,

$$I:\quad [at\,\overline{\ell_0} \wedge \varphi(\overline{x})] \supset Q(\overline{\pi}; f_0(\overline{x}))$$

holds, where $\overline{\ell_0} = (\ell_0^1, \ldots, \ell_0^m)$ the vector of initial locations.

2. Q is inductive for P; *i.e.*, the verification condition

$$V_\alpha:\qquad [at\,\ell \wedge c_\alpha(\overline{y}) \wedge Q(\overline{\pi};\overline{y})] \supset Q\big(r_\alpha(\overline{\pi}); f_\alpha(\overline{\pi})\big)$$

holds for every transition α in P.

Then we may deduce

$$\vDash\ [at\,\overline{\ell_0} \wedge \varphi(\overline{x})] \supset \Box Q(\overline{\pi};\overline{y}).$$

Condition 1 ensures that Q is true initially, provided we restrict ourselves to inputs $\overline{x}$ satisfying φ and condition 2 ensures that once Q is true it remains so. The conclusion is that Q is invariantly true for all (P,φ)-computations.

Note that this proof principle reduces the proof of a temporal formula of the invariance class into a classical proof of a set of formulas, namely the initial condition I and the verification conditions V_α.

The principle of invariance described here is the most general method known for proving invariance properties of concurrent programs. It can be shown to underlie all other proposed proof methods for invariance properties.

PRAGMATIC CONSIDERATIONS IN CHECKING FOR INDUCTIVENESS

In principle, when checking for the inductiveness of an assertion Q one has to check the verification condition V_α for all transitions α in the program. However, in practice, we can immediately discard many transitions as automatically preserving Q, based on syntactic considerations alone.

If the property Q does not contain any of the location variables $\overline{\pi}$, then the required verification conditions V_α are reduced to

$$V'_\alpha:\ [c_\alpha(\overline{y}) \wedge Q(\overline{y})] \supset Q\big(f_\alpha(\overline{y})\big).$$

In particular, V'_α is trivially true for any transition α where f_α does not modify the variables on which Q actually depends.

A typical case is that of semaphores. We have the following property:

The Semaphore Variable Rule: For a semaphore variable y,

if its initial value is a nonnegative integer
  and if it is modified only by *request* and *release* instructions,
then

$$\models \ \Box(y \geq 0).$$

The only two instructions that may modify the value of a semaphore variable are:

request(y), which is equivalent to

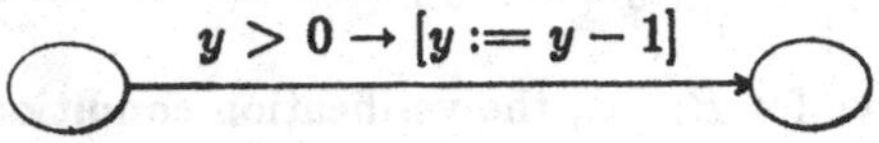

and *release*(y), which is equivalent to

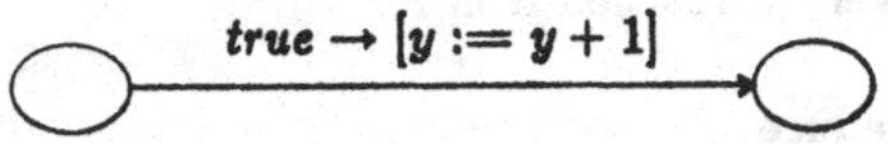

For the *request* case the verification condition is

$$[(y > 0) \ \wedge \ (y \geq 0)] \ \supset \ (y - 1 \geq 0).$$

For the *release* transition the verification condition is

$$[\mathit{true} \ \wedge \ (y \geq 0)] \ \supset \ (y + 1 \geq 0).$$

Both conditions are trivially true. Thus, since the initial value of the semaphore variable y is nonnegative and it is modified only through the semaphore instructions *request*(y) and *release*(y), it follows, by the Invariance Principle, that y is invariantly nonnegative, *i.e.* $\models \Box(y \geq 0)$.

For another example, let us consider a typical assertion of the form:

$$Q(\overline{\pi}; \overline{y}) : \quad at\, L \ \supset \ \phi(\overline{y}),$$

where L is a set of locations in P and ϕ does not depend on the location variables. For an arbitrary transition α of the form

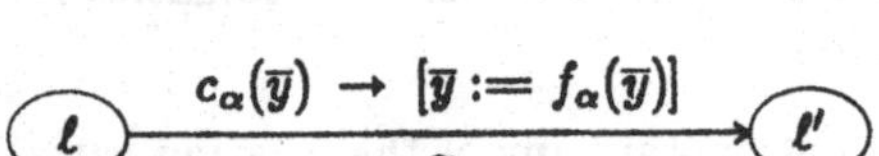

the verification condition is

$$V_\alpha : \quad \{c_\alpha(\overline{y}) \ \wedge \ [(\ell \in L) \ \supset \ \phi(\overline{y})]\} \ \supset \ [(\ell' \in L) \ \supset \ \phi(f_\alpha(\overline{y}))],$$

or equivalently,

$$\{c_\alpha(\overline{y}) \ \wedge \ [(\ell \not\in L) \ \vee \ \phi(\overline{y})] \ \wedge \ (\ell' \in L)\} \ \supset \ \phi(f_\alpha(\overline{y})).$$

There are three cases to consider.

Case: $\ell' \notin L$ (outside or leaving L). Then V_α is trivially true, since the antecedent of the implication is false.

Case: $\ell \notin L$, $\ell' \in L$ (entering L). Then V_α is reduced to

$$c_\alpha(\bar{y}) \supset \phi(f_\alpha(\bar{y})).$$

Case: $\ell, \ell' \in L$ (within L). Then V_α is reduced to

$$[c_\alpha(\bar{y}) \wedge \phi(\bar{y})] \supset \phi(f_\alpha(\bar{y})).$$

Thus, we only have to consider α's which fall into the two latter cases.

EXAMPLE: CONSUMER-PRODUCER

Let us illustrate an application of the invariance principle to the Consumer-Producer program (program *CP* of [MP2]).

$$b := \Lambda, \quad s := 1, \quad cf := 0, \quad ce := N$$

ℓ_0 : *compute* y_1	m_0 : *request*(cf)
ℓ_1 : *request*(ce)	m_1 : *request*(s)
ℓ_2 : *request*(s)	m_2 : $y_2 := head(b)$
ℓ_3 : $t_1 := b \circ y_1$	m_3 : $t_2 := tail(b)$
ℓ_4 : $b := t_1$	m_4 : $b := t_2$
ℓ_5 : *release*(s)	m_5 : *release*(s)
ℓ_6 : *release*(cf)	m_6 : *release*(ce)
ℓ_7 : *go to* ℓ_0	m_7 : *compute using* y_2
	m_8 : *go to* m_0
— P_1 : Producer —	— P_2 : Consumer —

The producer P_1 computes a value into y_1 without using any other program variables; the computation details being irrelevant. It then adds y_1 to the end of the buffer b. The consumer P_2 removes the first element of the buffer into y_2 and then uses this value for its own purposes (at m_7). It is assumed that the maximal capacity of the buffer b is $N > 0$. The '*compute using* y_2' instruction references y_2 but does not modify any of the shared program variables.

In order to ensure the correct synchronization between the processes we use three semaphore variables: The variable s ensures that the accesses to the buffer are protected and provides exclusion between the sections (ℓ_3, ℓ_4, ℓ_5) and (m_2, m_3, m_4, m_5). The variable ce ("count of empties") counts the number of free available slots in the buffer b. The variable cf ("count of fulls") counts how many items the buffer currently holds.

The initial condition is given by:

$$at\,\ell_0 \;\wedge\; at\,m_0 \;\wedge\; (b = \Lambda) \;\wedge\; (s = 1) \;\wedge\; (cf = 0) \;\wedge\; (ce = N).$$

We will use invariances to prove several properties of this program.

First, we observe that due to the semaphore variable rule

(1) $\quad \models \; \Box[(s \geq 0) \wedge (cf \geq 0) \wedge (ce \geq 0)].$

Mutual Exclusion

The exclusive access to the critical sections

$$L = \{\ell_3, \ell_4, \ell_5\}$$

$$M = \{m_2, m_3, m_4, m_5\}$$

can be expressed as:

$$\models \; \Box{\sim}(at\,L \wedge at\,M),$$

i.e., it is never the case that $\pi_1 \in L$ and $\pi_2 \in M$ simultaneously.

Since only one $at\,\ell_i$ and only one $at\,m_i$ can be true at a given instant it is sufficient to prove:

(2) $\quad \models \; \Box[(at\,L + at\,M) \leq 1].$

Note the mixed notation that treats propositions as numerically valued with $true = 1$, $false = 0$.

Formula (2) states an invariance property. It will be proved by showing the invariance of the assertion:

$$Q_1: \quad at\,L + at\,M + s = 1.$$

By the invariance principle we have to show that Q_1 is true initially and that Q_1 is inductive for P.

Initially, we have that $s = 1$ and that $at\,\ell_0 = at\,m_0 = 1$ which implies that $at\,L = at\,M = 0$. Thus the left-hand side of the equality in Q_1 evaluates to 1 and we have that Q_1 holds initially.

Next, we have to check that Q_1 is inductive, *i.e.*, preserved by every transition in P. From inspection of the variables on which Q_1 depends, it is clear that it is sufficient to check the transitions that either modify s or modify the $at\,L$ or $at\,M$ propositions. The only candidates for modifying Q_1 are therefore the transitions $\ell_2 \to \ell_3$, $\ell_5 \to \ell_6$, $m_1 \to m_2$, and $m_5 \to m_6$.

Take, for example, the transition $\ell_2 \to \ell_3$. Going through this transition changes $at\,L$ from 0 to 1 increasing the sum by 1. But, as s is decremented by 1, the sum remains constant. Similar checks of the other transitions will show that they all leave the sum invariant. This establishes the inductiveness of Q_1.

We may therefore conclude by the Invariance Principle that

$$\models \ \Box Q_1$$

i.e., Q_1 is an invariant of the program P.

The combination of $\Box Q_1$ and the semaphore property $\Box(s \geq 0)$ implies property (2) that proves mutual exclusion.

Proper Management of the Buffer

Here we would like to show that

(3) $$\models \ \Box(0 \leq |b| \leq N),$$

i.e., the buffer's maximum capacity is never exceeded throughout the execution and no attempt is made to remove an element from an empty buffer.

We first establish the invariance of the following inductive assertion:

$$Q_2: \qquad cf + ce + at\,\ell_{2..6} + at\,m_{1..6} \ = \ N$$

We use here our abbreviated notation, where $at\,\ell_{2..6}$ stands for $at\{\ell_2, \ldots, \ell_6\}$, *i.e.*, $\pi_1 \in \{\ell_2, \ldots, \ell_6\}$, and $at\,m_{1..6}$ stands for $at\{m_1, \ldots, m_6\}$, *i.e.*, $\pi_2 \in \{m_1, \ldots, m_6\}$. As before, the whole conjunction is interpreted arithmetically: 1 standing for *true* and 0 for *false*. By inspection of the relevant transitions we verify that Q_2 is indeed inductive and initially true, and thus is invariant, *i.e.*,

$$\models \ \Box Q_2.$$

Next consider another necessary invariant assertion:

$$Q_3: \qquad cf + at\,\ell_{5,6} + at\,m_{1..4} \ = \ |b|,$$

where $|b|$ is the size of the buffer b. To establish the invariance of Q_3 we have to also establish the invariance of

$$Q_4: \qquad at\,\ell_4 \ \supset \ \big(|t_1| = |b| + 1\big)$$

and

$$Q_5: \quad at\,m_4 \supset (|t_2| + 1 = |b|).$$

We will check for the joint invariance of Q_3, Q_4, and Q_5 and establish $\models. \Box(Q_3 \wedge Q_4 \wedge Q_5)$.

The conjunction $Q_3 \wedge Q_4 \wedge Q_5$ is initially of the form $(0 = 0) \wedge (false \supset ...) \wedge (false \supset ...)$ which is clearly true.

In order to check the inductiveness of $Q_3 \wedge Q_4 \wedge Q_5$ we must check every relevant transition of the program CP. Let us consider two typical transitions:

$\ell_3 \rightarrow \ell_4$:

Q_3 and Q_5 are not affected at all. In Q_4, both $at\,\ell_4$ and $|t_1| = |b| + 1$ become true on this transition, so that Q_4 is true after the transition.

$\ell_4 \rightarrow \ell_5$:

Here, Q_3, Q_4, and Q_5 are all affected by the transition and we would like, therefore, to illustrate the proof of a verification condition along this transition in greater detail. The verification condition is:

$$[\, at\,\ell_4 \;\wedge\; Q_3(\overline{\pi};\overline{y}) \;\wedge\; Q_4(\overline{\pi};\overline{y}) \;\wedge\; Q_5(\overline{\pi};\overline{y})\,]$$
$$\supset \;[\, Q_3(r(\overline{\pi}); f(\overline{y})) \wedge Q_4(r(\overline{\pi}); f(\overline{y})) \wedge Q_5(r(\overline{\pi}); f(\overline{y}))\,]$$

where

$$r(\pi_1, \pi_2) = (\ell_5, \pi_2)$$

$$f(b, s, cf, ce, t_1, t_2) = (t_1, s, cf, ce, t_1, t_2).$$

The proof proceeds in the following steps:

1.	$at\,\ell_4$	given
2.	$at\,\ell_{5,6} = 0$	from 1
3.	$cf + at\,m_{1..4} = \lvert b\rvert$	by Q_3
4.	$\lvert t_1\rvert = \lvert b\rvert + 1$	by Q_4 using 1
5.	$cf + 1 + at\,m_{1..4} = \lvert b\rvert + 1$	by adding 1 to both sides of 3
6.	$cf + (\ell_5 \in \{\ell_5, \ell_6\}) + at\,m_{1..4} = \lvert t_1\rvert$	from 5 using 4
7.	$Q_3(r(\overline{\pi}); f(\overline{y}))$	by definition of r and f using Q_3

Consider next $Q_4(r(\overline{\pi}); f(\overline{y}))$:

8.	$(\ell_5 = \ell_4) \supset (\lvert t_1\rvert = \lvert t_1\rvert + 1)$	tautology

9. $Q_4(r(\overline{\pi}); f(\overline{y}))$ by definition of r and f using Q_4

As for $Q_5(r(\overline{\pi}); f(\overline{y}))$:

10. $\sim at\, m_4$ by 1 and mutual exclusion (2)

11. $at\, m_4 \supset (|t_2| + 1 = |t_1|)$ from 12

12. $Q_5(r(\overline{\pi}); f(\overline{y}))$ by definition of r and f using Q_5

This concludes the proof of the verification condition for transition $\ell_4 \to \ell_5$. Therefore $Q_3 \wedge Q_4 \wedge Q_5$ is inductive along the transition $\ell_4 \to \ell_5$. We can similarly check that it is inductive along all the other transitions.

Thus we have established:

$$\models \Box(Q_3 \wedge Q_4 \wedge Q_5).$$

Let us now proceed to infer the proper management of the buffer b, *i.e.*, $\Box(0 \leq |b| \leq N)$.

First observe that by Q_3, $|b|$ is equal to a sum of variables all of which are nonnegative. Thus we have

$$\models \Box(|b| \geq 0).$$

On the other hand we have by Q_3 and Q_2 that

$$\begin{aligned} & |b| - cf \\ = \;& at\,\ell_{5,6} + at\,m_{1..4} \\ \leq \;& at\,\ell_{2..6} + at\,m_{1..6} \\ = \;& N - (cf + ce) \end{aligned}$$

The first equality is a direct consequent of Q_3. The inequality results from the fact that $\{\ell_5, \ell_6\}$ is a subset of $\{\ell_2, \ldots, \ell_6\}$ and $\{m_1, \ldots, m_4\}$ is a subset of $\{m_1, \ldots, m_6\}$. The second equality is a direct consequence of Q_2.

Thus, we have

$$|b| - cf \leq N - (cf + ce)$$

which simplifies to

$$|b| \leq N - ce.$$

Since ce is a semaphore variable we have $ce \geq 0$ which gives

$$\models \Box(|b| \leq N).$$

Thus we conclude that property (3),

$$\models \ \Box(0 \leq |b| \leq N),$$

holds.

Comments

• ***Modifying the program***

The need for the auxiliary invariants Q_4 and Q_5 resulted from the splitting of the statements concerning b into several statements according to the single-access rule.

Having first established the mutual exclusion of the regions $L = \{\ell_3, \ell_4, \ell_5\}$ and $M = \{m_2, \ldots, m_5\}$ we can observe that b is not really a shared variable, in that only one process at a time can access it. Correspondingly, we could transform the program, after having established exclusion, by replacing

$$\begin{aligned} \ell_3 &: \ t_1 := b \circ y_1 \\ \ell_4 &: \ b := t_1 \end{aligned}$$

by

$$\ell_3' : \ b := b \circ y_1$$

and

$$\begin{aligned} m_2 &: \ y_2 := head(b) \\ m_3 &: \ t_2 := tail(b) \\ m_4 &: \ b := t_2 \end{aligned}$$

by

$$m_2' : \ (y_2, b) := (head(b),\ tail(b)).$$

This would greatly simplify the subsequent analysis by making Q_3 directly verifiable without using Q_4 and Q_5.

• ***Using virtual variables***

Instead of introducing the auxiliary invariants Q_4, Q_5 it is possible to define a virtual variable b^* by:

$$b^* \quad = \quad \textit{if} \ \ at\,\ell_4 \ \ \textit{then} \ \ t_1 \ \ \textit{else} \ \ (\textit{if} \ \ at\,m_4 \ \ \textit{then} \ \ t_2 \ \ \textit{else} \ \ b)$$

and then directly prove a modified version of Q_3:

$$Q_3^* : \quad cf + at\,\ell_{4..6} + at\,m_{1..3} \ = \ |b^*|.$$

The variable b^* represents the intended value of b, where we use t_i ($i = 1, 2$) instead of b if b is about to be changed to t_i. Because we are focusing our attention on the value as soon as it is obtained, we have modified Q_3 by extending the region $\{\ell_5, \ell_6\}$ into $\{\ell_4, \ell_5, \ell_6\}$ and contracting $\{m_1, m_2, m_3, m_4\}$ into $\{m_1, m_2, m_3\}$.

A SYSTEMATIC SEARCH FOR LINEAR INVARIANTS

In order to dispel the illusion of "magically" drawing the invariants Q_1, Q_2, Q_3 out of thin air, let us describe a method for a systematic search for such invariants. (See also [FRA], [CLA].)

An invariant of the form discussed here is composed of three parts, such that the sum of the first two is equal to the third. We represent such an invariant by:

$$(B + Z) = C.$$

(a) B is the *body* of the invariant and is a linear expression in the semaphore variables and other variables which are incremented by constants (linearly) during cycles in the program.

(b) Z is a sum of expressions of the form $\pi_j \in L$ for some region $L \subseteq L_j$ and will be called a *compensation expression.*

(c) C is a constant.

We start constructing such an invariant by finding an appropriate body.

(a) In the body we look for a linear combination of variables $E = \sum a_i y_i$ such that the net change in each cycle of each process is 0. Obviously, we restrict ourselves to cyclic programs, *i.e.*, non-terminating programs, in which each process eventually returns to its initial location ℓ_0 and to variables whose change along a cycle is constant and independent of the program flow. Semaphore variables usually have this property.

Let us denote for these variables the net change in y_i resulting from a full cycle in process P_j by Δ_i^j. Then our combination $E = \sum a_i y_i$ should satisfy

$$\Delta^j E \;=\; \Sigma a_i \Delta_i^j \;=\; 0$$

for j, $0 \le j \le m$. That is, we require that the value of the expression remains unchanged as a result of a complete cycle of each of the processes.

In our consumer-producer example all our variables are linearly incremented and we have the following table:

$\Delta_s^1 = 0$	$\Delta_s^2 = 0$
$\Delta_{\lvert b \rvert}^1 = 1$	$\Delta_{\lvert b \rvert}^2 = -1$
$\Delta_{cf}^1 = 1$	$\Delta_{cf}^2 = -1$

$\Delta^1_{ce} = -1 \qquad \Delta^2_{ce} = 1.$

We look for a combination

$$E \quad = \quad a_1 \cdot s + a_2 \cdot |b| + a_3 \cdot cf + a_4 \cdot ce$$

such that $\sum a_i \Delta^j_i = 0$ for $j = 1, 2$. This yields the set of equations

$$\begin{aligned} a_1 \cdot 0 + a_2 + a_3 - a_4 &= 0 \\ a_1 \cdot 0 - a_2 - a_3 + a_4 &= 0. \end{aligned}$$

We will be interested in a nontrivial set of independent solutions to these equations.

In this case the equations possess three degrees of freedom, and hence three linearly independent solutions are possible. The exact choice is irrelevant and we pick the following:

1. $a_1 = 1 \qquad a_2 = a_3 = a_4 = 0$
2. $a_3 = a_4 = 1 \qquad a_1 = a_2 = 0$
3. $a_2 = a_4 = 1 \qquad a_1 = a_3 = 0.$

Thus for the following independent linear combinations, the net change in each cycle of each process is 0:

$B_1 : \ s$

$B_2 : \ cf + ce.$

$B_3 : \ |b| + ce.$

Note that B_1 and B_2 correspond to the bodies of Q_1 and Q_2 respectively, while B_3 is a different invariant which will enable us to derive the same conclusion as the combination of Q_2 and Q_3. For the choice $a_1 = a_4 = 0$, $a_2 = -1$ and $a_3 = 1$, we could get $B'_3 : cf - |b|$ which corresponds to Q_3 itself.

(*b*) Having a body B, to derive the right-hand side C of the invariant, we only have to substitute the initial values implied by $\varphi(\overline{x})$ into the body. Doing this for our three invariants we obtain:

$C_1 : \ 1$

$C_2 : \ N$

$C_3 : \ N.$

(*c*) Next, we determine the compensation expressions. Consider a given C and $B(\overline{y})$ and a process P_j with locations $\{\ell_0, \ldots, \ell_e\}$. Since we assume cycling, ℓ_e is not a terminal location but branches back to ℓ_0. By our assumption, the changes in $B(\overline{y})$ can be traced and are constant. Denote by $B_i(\bar{y})$ the value of B at location ℓ_i, $i = 0, 1, \ldots e$ in the process, and let

$$\delta_i = B_0(\bar{y}) - B_i(\bar{y}).$$

Then the compensating expression for process P_j is given by

$$Z_j = \sum_{i=0}^{e} \delta_i \cdot (at\,\ell_i).$$

For example, to evaluate δ_i for $B_1 = s$ in P_1 above we have to compute:

$$s|_{at\,\ell_0} - s|_{at\,\ell_i}.$$

Assuming that P_1 is operating alone, (which is the basic assumption in the computation of the δ_i,) we take the difference between the value of s at ℓ_i and its initial value at ℓ_0. Thus, we have

$$\delta_0 = \delta_1 = \delta_2 = \delta_6 = \delta_7 = 0,$$

since when P_1 is being executed alone the value of s at locations $\ell_0, \ell_1, \ell_2, \ell_6, \ell_7$ is equal to the value of s at ℓ_0, *i.e.*, $s = 1$. Moreover,

$$\delta_3 = \delta_4 = \delta_5 = 1;$$

since when P_1 is executing alone, the value of s at locations ℓ_3, ℓ_4, ℓ_5 is smaller by 1 than the value of s at ℓ_0. Hence, the compensation expression for the body s in P_1 is

$$Z_1 = at\,\ell_3 + at\,\ell_4 + at\,\ell_5.$$

Computing the compensation expression Z_j for the body B for each process P_j we form the full invariant:

$$B + \sum_{j=1}^{m} Z_j = C.$$

For the three bodies we considered, we obtain the following three invariants:

$$I_1: \quad s + at\,\ell_{3..5} + at\,m_{2..5} = 1$$

$$I_2: \quad cf + ce + at\,\ell_{2..6} + at\,m_{1..6} = N$$

$$I_3: \quad |b| + ce + at\,\ell_{2..4} + at\,m_{5,6} = N.$$

Note that Q_3 can be obtained by forming the difference $I_2 - I_3$.

This method of deriving invariants has the advantage that no further proof is needed; indeed, any invariant derived by the method is automatically a true invariant of the program. But it may only be applied to variables which are modified by a constant in atomic instructions, or to programs which can be transformed so as to satisfy this restriction.

EXAMPLE: BINOMIAL COEFFICIENT

Consider next the program BC ([MP2]) for the distributed computation of the binomial coefficient $\binom{n}{k}$ for input parameters $n \geq k \geq 0$.

Program BC_1 (Binomial Coefficient – first version)

$$y_1 := n, \quad y_2 := 0, \quad y_3 := 1, \quad y_4 := 1$$

P_1	P_2
ℓ_0: *if* $y_1 = (n-k)$ *then go to* ℓ_e	m_0: *if* $y_2 = k$ *then go to* m_e
ℓ_1: *request*(y_4)	m_1: $y_2 := y_2 + 1$
ℓ_2: $t_1 := y_3 \cdot y_1$	m_2: *loop until* $y_1 + y_2 \leq n$
ℓ_3: $y_3 := t_1$	m_3: *request*(y_4)
ℓ_4: *release*(y_4)	m_4: $t_2 := y_3/y_2$
ℓ_5: $y_1 := y_1 - 1$	m_5: $y_3 := t_2$
ℓ_6: *go to* ℓ_0	m_6: *release*(y_4)
ℓ_e: *halt*	m_7: *go to* m_0
	m_e: *halt*
— P_1 —	— P_2 —

The task of computing the binomial coefficient

$$\binom{n}{k} = \frac{n \cdot (n-1) \cdot \cdots \cdot (n-k+1)}{1 \cdot 2 \cdot \cdots \cdot k}$$

is distributed between the two processes by having P_1 perform all the multiplications while P_2 is in charge of the divisions. The values of y_1, *i.e.*, $n, n-1, \ldots, n-k+1$, are used to compute the numerator in P_1 (the last value of y_1, $n-k$, is not used), and the values of y_2, *i.e.*, $1, 2, \ldots, k$, are used to compute the denominator (the first value of y_2, 0, is not used). The two processes must synchronize in order that the accumulated product be evenly divisible by the divisors used at m_4 by P_2. This synchronization is realized by the waiting loop at m_2 which essentially ensures that execution will proceed to m_3 only when at least y_2 factors have been multiplied into y_3. We rely here on the mathematical theorem that the product of i consecutive positive integers: $k \cdot (k+1) \cdot \cdots \cdot (k+i-1)$ is always divisible by $i!$. For, consider the intermediate expression at m_2:

$$y_3 = \frac{n \cdot (n-1) \cdot \cdots \cdot (n-j+1)}{1 \cdot 2 \cdot \cdots \cdot (i-1)},$$

where $1 \leq i \leq j \leq n$, $y_1 = n-j$ and $y_2 = i$. The numerator consists of a multiplication of i consecutive positive integers and it is therefore divisible by i. If $j = i$, we have to wait until y_1 is decremented by the instruction in ℓ_5 from $n-i+1$ to $n-i$ before we can be absolutely sure that $(n-i+1)$ has been multiplied into y_3. Thus, Process P_2 waits at m_2 until y_1+y_2 drops to a value less than or equal to n.

The critical sections $L = \{\ell_2, \ell_3, \ell_4\}$ and $M = \{m_4, m_5, m_6\}$, protected by the semaphore variable y_4, ensure exclusive access to the shared variable y_3. Note that this program satisfies the single critical access rule ([MP2]) since for example in the expression $y_1 + y_2$ appearing at m_2 only y_1 is critically accessed.

The invariant

$$I_0: \quad at\,\ell_{2..4} + at\,m_{4..6} + y_4 = 1$$

ensures the mutual exclusion of the critical sections. It is verifiable by the invariance principle in the usual way.

Once this exclusion is established we can transform this program to a simpler program BC_2 such that there is a faithful correspondence between executions of BC_1 and executions of BC_2. This implies that the correctness of BC_1 will follow from that of BC_2.

Program BC_2 (Binomial Coefficient – second version)

$$y_1 := n, \quad y_2 := 0, \quad y_3 := 1$$

ℓ_0: *if* $y_1 = (n-k)$ *then go to* ℓ_e	m_0: *if* $y_2 = k$ *then go to* m_e
ℓ_1: $y_3 := y_3 \cdot y_1$	m_1: $y_2 := y_2 + 1$
ℓ_2: $y_1 := y_1 - 1$	m_2: *loop until* $y_1 + y_2 \le n$
ℓ_3: *go to* ℓ_0	m_3: $y_3 := y_3 / y_2$
ℓ_e: *halt*	m_4: *go to* m_0
	m_e: *halt*
— P_1 —	— P_2 —

Next we introduce two virtual variables:

$$y_1^* = \textit{if } at\,\ell_2 \textit{ then } y_1 - 1 \textit{ else } y_1$$

$$y_2^* = \textit{if } at\,m_{2,3} \textit{ then } y_2 - 1 \textit{ else } y_2.$$

The need for the virtual variables is similar to that of the compensation expressions discussed above. The main invariant on which the correctness of the program is based is I_3 below

$$y_3 = [n \cdot (n-1) \cdots (y_1^* + 1)] \;/\; [1 \cdot 2 \cdots y_2^*]$$

which ties together y_1, y_2 and y_3 (or their virtual versions). It is invariant in the sense that it is preserved after y_1, y_2 and y_3 has each been properly updated. However since the updating of y_1 and y_3 in P_1 for example cannot occur simultaneously, we define y_1^*

which is the anticipated updated value of y_1 as soon as y_3 is updated at ℓ_1. Similarly, y_2^* differs from y_2 between the updating of y_2 and the updating of y_3 in P_2.

We use the following invariants:

$$I_1: \quad [(n-k+at\ell_{1,2}) \leq y_1 \leq n] \ \wedge \ [0 \leq y_2 \leq (k - at\,m_1)]$$

$$I_2: \quad at\,m_3 \supset (y_1 + y_2) \leq n$$

$$I_3: \quad y_3 = [n \cdot (n-1) \cdots (y_1^* + 1)] \,/\, [1 \cdot 2 \cdots y_2^*]$$

In I_3, the product of a zero number of terms evaluates to 1.

The initiality of I_1 to I_3 is easily verifiable.

The two parts of I_1 can be verified separately by considering the transitions $\ell_0 \to \ell_1$, $\ell_2 \to \ell_3$ and $m_0 \to m_1$, $m_1 \to m_2$ respectively.

To verify I_2 we observe that on entering m_3, $y_1 + y_2 \leq n$ holds true. Any possible P_1 transition while P_2 is at m_3 can only decrease the value of $y_1 + y_2$.

Consider now the verification of I_3. The only relevant transitions are $\ell_1 \to \ell_2$ and $m_3 \to m_4$. Denoting the values of the variables after the transition by $y_1^{*\prime}$, $y_2^{*\prime}$, y_3' respectively, we obtain for $\ell_1 \to \ell_2$:

$$y_3 = [n \cdot (n-1) \cdots (y_1^* + 1)] \,/\, [1 \cdot 2 \cdots y_2^*]$$

$$\Rightarrow \quad y_3 \cdot y_1 = [n \cdot (n-1) \cdots (y_1^* + 1) \cdot y_1^*] \,/\, [1 \cdot 2 \cdots y_2^*]$$

as at $\ell_1, y_1 = y_1^*$

$$\Rightarrow \quad y_3' = [n \cdot (n-1) \cdots (y_1^{*\prime} + 1)] \,/\, [1 \cdot 2 \cdots y_2^*].$$

Similarly for the $m_3 \to m_4$ transition:

$$y_3 = [n \cdot (n-1) \cdots (y_1^* + 1)] \,/\, [1 \cdot 2 \cdots y_2^*]$$

$$\Rightarrow \quad y_3 \,/\, y_2 = [n \cdot (n-1) \cdots (y_1^* + 1)] \,/\, [1 \cdot 2 \cdots (y_2^* + 1)]$$

as at $m_3, y_2 = y_2^* + 1$

$$\Rightarrow \quad y_3' = [n \cdot (n-1) \cdots (y_1^* + 1)] \,/\, [1 \cdot 2 \cdots y_2^{*\prime}].$$

The even divisibility of y_3 by y_2 at m_3 is ensured by the fact that by I_2 we have that

$$y_1^* \leq y_1 \leq n - y_2.$$

Thus the number of consecutive factors in the numerator of y_3 is at least y_2 which is evenly divisible by $y_2!$

Here we will consider general methodologies for proving properties of the form

$$\models P \supset \Diamond Q.$$

Many of the cases that we will study focus on a special kind of eventualities called *accessibility statement.* Its characteristic form is

$$at\,\ell \supset \Diamond\, at\,\ell'$$

guaranteeing that being at ℓ we will eventually reach ℓ'. In more general form it can appear as:

$$(at\,\ell \wedge \phi) \supset \Diamond(at\,\ell' \wedge \phi'),$$

where we associate a pre-condition ϕ with the visit at ℓ and a post-condition ϕ' with the visit at ℓ'. The Intermittent-Assertion Method (see [BUR], [MW]) uses this implication as the basic statement for reasoning. Many useful eventuality properties are representable in this form. In this discussion we assume that ℓ and ℓ' belong to the same process. It is however possible to consider generalizations in which this assumption may be relaxed.

Our approach for proving eventuality properties, called *proof by eventuality chains,* is based on establishing a chain of eventualities that by transitivity leads to the ultimate establishing of the desired goal (see also [OL]). The main transitivity argument used here is:

$$\models \phi_1 \supset \Diamond \phi_2 \text{ and } \models \phi_2 \supset \Diamond \phi_3 \quad \Rightarrow \quad \models \phi_1 \supset \Diamond \phi_3.$$

Some common techniques that we use in our proofs are:

- We split a situation into several subcases and pursue each case to its conclusion.
- To establish implications of the form

  $$\models \; (\exists k.\phi(k)) \supset \Diamond \phi'$$

  we use induction

  $$\models \phi(0) \supset \phi' \quad \text{and} \quad \models \forall n.[\phi(n) \supset \Diamond(\phi(n-1) \vee \phi')]$$
  $$\Rightarrow \; \models (\exists k.\phi(k)) \supset \Diamond \phi'.$$

- We frequently establish $\models \phi \supset \Diamond \phi'$ by contradiction: we assume $\phi \wedge \Box \sim\phi'$ and pursue the consequences of this assumption. If we succeed in showing

  $$\models \; [\phi \wedge \Box \sim\phi'] \supset \mathit{false},$$

  then we will have established our desired result. This technique is particularly useful in the verification of a statement of the form

  $$at\,\ell \supset \Diamond \sim at\,\ell$$

in concurrent systems. The reason for that is that by assuming $\Box\, at\,\ell$ we are momentarily (for the duration of the analysis) halting one of the processes at ℓ and have only to analyze the possible movements of the other processes. This usually results in a significant simplification.

We start by presenting an example with an informal proof of its correctness relative to accessibility.

EXAMPLE: MUTUAL EXCLUSION (DEKKER) – INFORMAL PROOFS

As a first example, consider the solution to the mutual exclusion problem that was first given by Dekker and described in ([DIJ]). Here, we assume a shared variable t that may be modified by both processes and two private boolean variables y_1 and y_2, each being set only by its owning process but may be examined by the other.

Program DK (Mutual Exclusion – Dekker's Solution):

$$t := 1,\ y_1 := y_2 := F$$

— P_1 —	— P_2 —
ℓ_0 : *execute*	m_0 : *execute*
ℓ_1 : $y_1 := T$	m_1 : $y_2 := T$
ℓ_2 : *if* $(y_2 = F)$ *then go to* ℓ_7	m_2 : *if* $(y_1 = F)$ *then go to* m_7
ℓ_3 : *if* $(t = 1)$ *then go to* ℓ_2	m_3 : *if* $(t = 2)$ *then go to* m_2
ℓ_4 : $y_1 := F$	m_4 : $y_2 := F$
ℓ_5 : *loop until* $(t = 1)$	m_5 : *loop until* $(t = 2)$
ℓ_6 : *go to* ℓ_1	m_6 : *go to* m_1
ℓ_7 : $t := 2$	m_7 : $t := 1$
ℓ_8 : $y_1 := F$	m_8 : $y_2 := F$
ℓ_9 : *go to* ℓ_0	m_9 : *go to* m_0

The variable y_1 in process P_1 (and y_2 for P_2 respectively) is set to T at ℓ_1 to signal the intention of P_1 to enter its critical section at ℓ_7. Next P_1 tests at ℓ_2 if P_2 has any interest in entering its own critical section. This is tested by checking if $y_2 = T$. If $y_2 = F$, P_1 proceeds immediately to its critical section. If $y_2 = T$ we have a competition between the two processes on the access right to their critical sections. This competition is resolved by using the variable t (turn) that has the value 1 if in case of conflict P_1 has the higher priority and the value 2 if P_2 has the higher priority. If P_1 finds that $t = 1$ it knows it is its turn to insist and it leaves y_1 on and just loops between ℓ_2 and ℓ_3 waiting for y_2 to drop to F. If it finds that $t = 2$ it realizes it should yield to the other and consequently it turns y_1 off and enters a loop at ℓ_5, waiting for t to change to 1. It knows that as soon as P_2 exits its critical section it will set t to 1 so it will not be waiting forever. Once t has been detected to be 1, P_1 returns to the active competition at ℓ_2.

We will proceed to prove for this program both mutual exclusion and accessiblity.

They are complementary properties in this case. The first assures that the two processes cannot simultaneously enter their respective critical sections. The second assures that once a process wishes to enter its critical section it will eventually get there.

Mutual exclusion

To prove mutual exclusion we show the joint invariance of the following three assertions:

$$Q_1: \quad (y_1 = T) \;\equiv\; at\{\ell_2, \ell_3, \ell_4, \ell_7, \ell_8\}$$

$$Q_2: \quad (y_2 = T) \;\equiv\; at\{m_2, m_3, m_4, m_7, m_8\}$$

$$Q_3: \quad \sim at\{\ell_7, \ell_8\} \;\vee\; \sim at\{m_7, m_8\}.$$

That is,

$$\models \;\; \Box(Q_1 \wedge Q_2 \wedge Q_3),$$

where the initial condition is given by

$$at\,\ell_0 \;\wedge\; at\,m_0 \;\wedge\; (t = 1) \;\wedge\; (y_1 = y_2 = F).$$

The inductiveness of the first two assertions is easily checked by considering the different transitions in each of the processes. They certainly hold initially.

To show the invariance of Q_3 which is the statement of mutual exclusion consider the possible transitions that could potentially falsify this assertion.

One such transition is $\ell_2 \rightarrow \ell_7$ while $at\{m_7, m_8\}$. However by Q_2, $at\{m_7, m_8\}$ implies $y_2 = T$ so that the transition $\ell_2 \rightarrow \ell_7$ is disabled. Similarly for the transition $m_2 \rightarrow m_7$ while $at\{\ell_7, \ell_8\}$.

Accessibility

Accessibility in this program is given for P_1 (the case for P_2 is similar) by

$$\models \;\; at\,\ell_1 \supset \Diamond\, at\,\ell_7.$$

The process P_1 signals its wish to enter the critical section by moving from ℓ_0 to ℓ_1. We then would like to prove that it eventually reaches the critical section at ℓ_7.

In analyzing this program we have to interpret the *execute* instructions at ℓ_0 and m_0 as a non-critical section. Consequently we cannot assume that being at ℓ_0 we will eventually get to ℓ_1. Hence the transition graph representation of the *execute* instruction at ℓ_0 (and similarly at m_0) should be represented as:

That is, there is a nondeterministic choice between staying at ℓ_0 and proceeding to ℓ_1.

We will proceed to prove

Theorem: $\models at\,\ell_1 \supset \Diamond at\,\ell_7$.

Here we will present an informal proof of the statement, followed by the justification of some of the steps used in the proof. Motivated by recurrent patterns in the informal proof we will then introduce proof principles that could be used to construct a formal version of the same proof.

The proof of the theorem consists of a sequence of lemmas.

Lemma A: $\models \quad [at\,\ell_3 \wedge (t=1)] \quad \supset \quad \Diamond at\,\ell_7$

proof of Lemma A:

Assume to the contrary that P_1 never takes the $\ell_2 \rightarrow \ell_7$ transition; then henceforth

$$\Box[(at\,\ell_2 \vee at\,\ell_3) \wedge (t=1)]$$

since the only instruction assigning to t a value different from 1 is at ℓ_7 and as long as $t=1$ and the transition $\ell_2 \rightarrow \ell_7$ is not taken, P_1 is restricted to $\{\ell_2, \ell_3\}$.

Under this invariance assumption $at\{\ell_2, \ell_3\} \wedge (t=1)$, let us check the locations of P_2.

case a: P_2 is at m_5. Then $y_2 = F$ and will stay so. By fairness P_1 must eventually get to ℓ_2 and in the next transition out of ℓ_2 must go to ℓ_7 (y_2 being F). Thus

$$\models \quad at\,m_5 \supset \Diamond at\,\ell_7.$$

case b: P_2 is at m_4. Then by the fairness requirement it will eventually reach m_5 so that by case *a*

$$\models \quad at\,m_4 \supset \Diamond at\,\ell_7.$$

case c: P_2 is at m_3. Then in the next transition out of m_3, t is still 1 so the m_4 branch must be taken. Consequently by case *b*

$$\models \quad at\,m_3 \supset \Diamond at\,\ell_7.$$

case d: P_2 is at m_2. Then since, by Q_1, $(at\,\ell_2 \vee at\,\ell_3) \supset y_1 = T$, and since we assumed that P_1 is restricted to $\{\ell_2, \ell_3\}$, the next transition of P_2 will take us to m_3. Thus by case c also have

$$\models \quad at\, m_2 \supset \Diamond\, at\, \ell_7.$$

case e: P_2 is at m_1. Then obviously eventually P_2 will reach m_2 so that by case d we have

$$\models \quad at\, m_1 \supset \Diamond\, at\, \ell_7.$$

case f: P_2 is at m_6. Then eventually P_2 will get to m_1, so by case e

$$\models \quad at\, m_6 \supset \Diamond\, at\, \ell_7.$$

case g: P_2 is at m_0. Then either it will stay in m_0 forever or eventually exit to m_1. In the case that it stays in m_0 forever we have by Q_2, $\Box(y_2 = F)$. Thus in the next transition out of ℓ_2 we must proceed to ℓ_7. Otherwise P_2 will eventually get to m_1 which by case f leads again to $at\, \ell_7$. Thus in any case

$$\models \quad at\, m_0 \supset \Diamond\, at\, \ell_7.$$

case h: Obviously by fairness

$$\models \quad (at\, m_7 \vee at\, m_8 \vee at\, m_9) \supset \Diamond\, at\, m_0,$$

so that by case g, any of these cases also leads to the eventual realization of $at\, \ell_7$.

Thus by analyzing all the possible values of π_2 in P_2 we showed that $at\, \ell_7$ is eventually realized in any of them. Consequently we have that

$$\models \quad [at\, \ell_3 \wedge (t = 1)] \supset \Diamond\, at\, \ell_7.$$

which is the desired result of Lemma A. ∎

Lemma B: $\models \quad [at\{\ell_3, \ldots, \ell_6\} \wedge (t = 2)] \supset \sim at\{m_8, m_9, m_0\}$

proof of Lemma B:

Consider first the invariance of the following statement:

$$Q_4: \quad (t = 2) \supset \sim at\, m_8.$$

The transitions which may possibly falsify this statement are:

- $\ell_7 \to \ell_8$ while P_2 is at m_8. However, due to Q_3, $at\, \ell_7 \wedge at\, m_8$ is an impossible situation.

- $m_7 \to m_8$ while $t = 2$, but the transition sets $t = 1$, so that Q_4 does hold after the transition.

Having established $\models \Box Q_4$ we proceed to establish $\models \Box Q_5$ where

$$Q_5: \ [at\{\ell_3, \ldots, \ell_6\} \wedge (t = 2)] \ \supset \ \sim at\{m_9, m_0\}.$$

Let us investigate the transitions that could possibly falsify Q_5. The relevant transitions are:

- $\ell_2 \to \ell_3$ while $at\{m_9, m_0\}$. However by Q_2, $at\{m_9, m_0\}$ implies that $y_2 = F$ which disables this transition.
- $m_8 \to m_9$ while $t = 2$. However in view of Q_4 the situation $(t = 2) \wedge at\, m_8$ is impossible so that the transition is also impossible.

Taking the conjunction of Q_4 and Q_5 we can infer the result of Lemma B. ∎

Lemma C: $\models \quad at\,\ell_5 \supset \Diamond\, at\,\ell_7$.

proof of Lemma C:

If we are at ℓ_5 there are two possibilities. Either we will eventually get to ℓ_6 with $t = 1$ or we will stay forever in ℓ_5 with $t = 2$ continuously.

In the first case we proceed to ℓ_1 and reach ℓ_2. There we either enter ℓ_7 immediately or get to ℓ_3 with $t = 1$. The value of t will not change on the way since the only possible change of t from 1 to 2 is performed by P_1 at $\ell_7 \to \ell_8$. By lemma A, being at ℓ_3 with $t = 1$ ultimately leads to ℓ_7.

The other case is in which $\Box(t = 2 \wedge at\,\ell_5)$. By lemma B we have that $\Box(\sim at\{m_8, m_9, m_0\})$. Since $at\,\ell_5$ is permanently true so will be $y_1 = F$ by Q_1.

Consider now all the possible locations of π_2 in P_2 excluding m_8, m_9, and m_0:

$at\,m_7$ will eventually lead us to m_8 and turn t to 1.

$at\,m_2$ will lead us to m_7 since $y_1 = F$ and then to m_8.

$at\,m_3$ will lead us to m_2 since $t = 2$.

$at\,m_1$ leads to m_2.

$at\,m_6$ leads to m_1.

$at\,m_5$ will eventually lead to m_6, having $t = 2$.

$at\,m_4$ leads to m_5.

Consequently all the locations in P_2 eventually cause t to turn to 1 and P_1 will eventually get out of ℓ_5 and proceed to ℓ_3 with $t = 1$. Lemma A then establishes the desired result. ∎

We are ready now to prove the desired accessibility theorem, that $\models at\,\ell_1 \supset \Diamond\, at\,\ell_7$.

proof of Theorem:

Proceed with P_1 from ℓ_1 to ℓ_2. There we either immediately enter ℓ_7 or arrive at ℓ_3. Consider the next instant in which P_1 is scheduled. If $t = 1$ we are assured by lemma

A that we will ultimately get to ℓ_7. If $t = 2$ we proceed to ℓ_4 and ℓ_5 from which we are assured by lemma C of eventually getting to ℓ_7. Thus we will get to ℓ_7 in all cases. ∎

PROOF PRINCIPLES FOR EVENTUALITIES

In order to present proofs such as the above in a more rigorous – perhaps even machine checkable – style, we proceed to develop several proof principles. These will enable us to establish the basic accessibility steps ensuring the eventual passage from a location to its successor under the assumption of fairness.

All predicates below are "state predicates" expressed by classical formulas, and will generally depend on the location variables $\overline{\pi}$ as well as on the program variables $\overline{y}$.

A predicate $\phi = \phi(\overline{\pi};\overline{y})$ is said to be *χ-invariant*, where $\chi = \chi(\overline{\pi};\overline{y})$, if for every transition

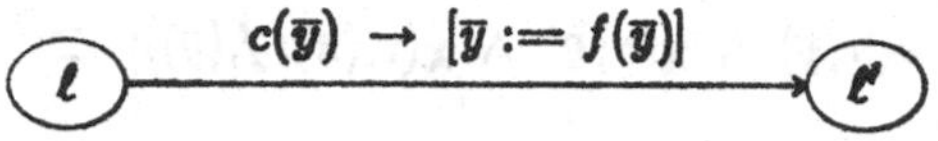

the following formula holds:

$$[at\,\ell \wedge c(\overline{y}) \wedge \chi(\overline{\pi};\overline{y}) \wedge \chi(r(\overline{\pi}); f(\overline{y})) \wedge \phi(\overline{\pi};\overline{y})] \supset \phi(r(\overline{\pi}); f(\overline{y})).$$

That is, ϕ is preserved by any transition which preserves χ.

In all the following we will use $\Box\chi$ to denote that χ is an invariant externally given and guaranteed to be continuously true. It will be useful in conducting conditional proofs.

The Escape Principle for Single Location

Consider a location ℓ in process P_j. Let $\Sigma = \{\alpha_1, \ldots, \alpha_k\}$ be a set of transitions originating in ℓ. Let $\ell^1, \ldots, \ell^k$ be the locations to which the transitions $\alpha_1, \ldots, \alpha_k$ lead and $c_1, \ldots, c_k$ the enabling conditions associated with $\alpha_1, \ldots, \alpha_k$, respectively. We do not require that Σ be the set of all transitions originating in ℓ.

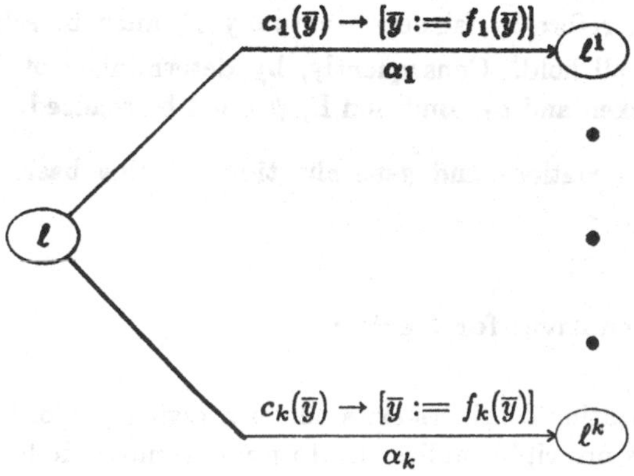

We require that location ℓ be *deterministic*, that is, the conditions c and c' on any two distinct transitions α and α' (not necessarily in Σ) originating in ℓ must be disjoint, *i.e.* $\sim c \vee \sim c'$. In all the programs that we will study all locations would be deterministic except for those that contain an *execute* instruction. We will never apply the escape rule to these locations.

The Rule of Escape (ESC):

Let ϕ, χ, and ψ be predicates such that:

A: ϕ is $(at\,\ell \wedge \chi)$-invariant.
This means that as long as we stay at ℓ and χ is preserved, so is ϕ.

B: Any of the α_i, $i = 1, \ldots, k$, transitions of Σ that preserves χ and is initiated with ϕ true, achieves ψ, *i.e.*, ψ will hold after the transition. This is expressed by

$$[at\,\ell \wedge c_i(\bar{y}) \wedge \phi(\bar{\pi};\bar{y}) \wedge \chi(\bar{\pi};\bar{y}) \wedge \chi(r_i(\bar{\pi}); f_i(\bar{y}))] \supset \psi(r_i(\bar{\pi}); f_i(\bar{y}))$$

for every $i = 1, \ldots, k$.

C: $\phi \wedge \chi$ at ℓ ensures that at least one c_i, $i = 1, \ldots, k$, is true (the transition is enabled), *i.e.*,

$$[at\,\ell \wedge \phi(\bar{\pi};\bar{y}) \wedge \chi(\bar{\pi};\bar{y})] \supset \bigvee_{i=1}^{k} c_i(\bar{y}).$$

Then under these three conditions we may conclude

$$\models [at\,\ell \wedge \phi \wedge \Box\chi] \supset \Diamond\psi.$$

That is, being at ℓ with ϕ true and being assured of the continuous holding of χ guarantees eventual realization of ψ.

To justify the principle consider an execution which starts at ℓ with ϕ true and continuous assurance of χ. By condition A as long as P_j is not scheduled we remain at ℓ with $\phi \wedge \chi$ true. By condition C this implies that all that time $\bigvee_{i=1}^{k} c_i$ is also continuously true. Therefore by fairness eventually P_j must be scheduled in a state in which ϕ, χ, $\bigvee_{i=1}^{k} c_i$ all hold. Consequently, by determinism of ℓ one of the $\alpha_i \in \Sigma$ transitions must be taken and by condition B, ψ must be realized.

There are some variations and generalizations of this basic principle which are discussed next.

The Rule of Alernatives for Regions

The first generalization considers exits out of a region (set of locations) rather than a single location. This principle applies also to nondeterministic locations.

Let $L \subseteq L_j$ be a set of locations in the process P_j and $\Sigma = \{\alpha_1, \ldots, \alpha_k\}$ the set of *all* transitions originating in L and leading to locations $\ell^1, \ldots, \ell^k$ outside of L, *i.e.*, $\ell^i \notin L$.

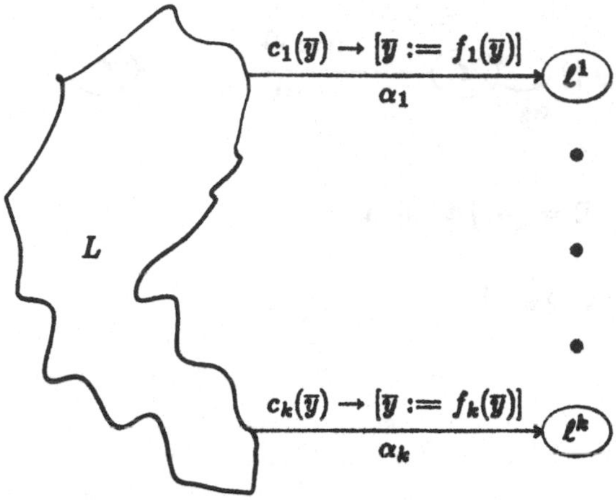

The Rule of Alternatives (ALT):

Let ϕ, χ, ψ be predicates such that:

A: **ϕ is $(at\,L \wedge \chi)$–invariant.**
This means that as long as we stay in L and χ is preserved so is ϕ.

B: **Any of the $\alpha_i, i = 1, \ldots, k$, transitions of Σ that preserves χ and is initiated with ϕ true, achieves ψ, *i.e.*, ψ will hold after the transition. This is expressed by:**

$$[at\,L \wedge c_i(\bar{y}) \wedge \phi(\bar{\pi}; \bar{y}) \wedge \chi(\bar{\pi}; \bar{y}) \wedge \chi(r_i(\bar{\pi}); f_i(\bar{y}))] \supset \psi(r_i(\bar{\pi}); f_i(\bar{y}))$$

for every $i = 1, \ldots, k$.

Then under these conditions we may conclude:

$$\models [at\,L \wedge \phi \wedge \Box\chi] \supset [\Box(at\,L \wedge \phi) \vee \Diamond\psi].$$

That is, being initially in L with ϕ true and being assured of the continuous holding of χ guarantees that we have two alternatives: either we stay in L with ϕ permanently true, or achieve ψ.

Note that since we do not have any condition similar to C above that guarantees the eventual realization of ψ, we must also consider the possibility of remaining in L and satisfying ϕ forever.

To justify the principle, consider an execution which starts in L with ϕ true and continuous assurance of χ. By condition A as long as we stay in L, ϕ will remain true. By condition B once we take any of the α_i transitions in this situation ψ will be realized. Hence the conclusion follows.

Note that the ALT rule can be applied to a region consisting of a single location. Thus for an *execute* instruction:

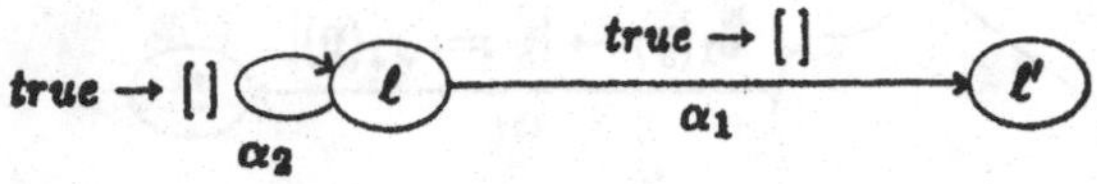

we may take $L = \{\ell\}$ and $\Sigma = \{\alpha_1\}$ to obtain

$$\models \; at\,\ell \supset [\Box\, at\,\ell \vee \Diamond\, at\,\ell'].$$

The Semaphore Rule

Rule ESC above is adequate for dealing with locations for which the disjunction of all their exit conditions (on all the outgoing transitions) is identically true. A location which does not satisfy this requirement is called a *semaphore location* since in a semaphore *request* instruction, represented by

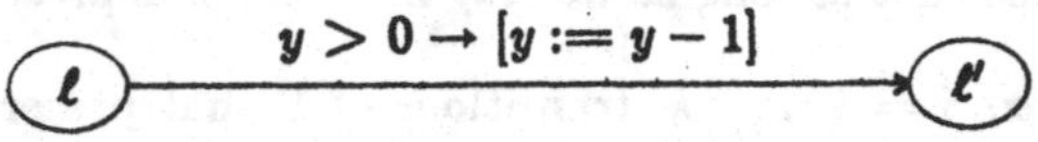

the exit condition E_ℓ is $y > 0$ and is not identically true, nor is it necessarily continuously enabled. Consequently rules ESC and ALT are only sufficient for reasoning about programs that contain no sempahore locations. Once we have semaphore locations we need a stronger rule.

Let ℓ be a (possibly semaphore) location and $\Sigma = \{\alpha_1, \ldots, \alpha_k\}$ the set of *all* the transitions originating in ℓ. Let ℓ^i and c_i, for $i = 1, \ldots, k$, be respectively the location to which α_i leads and the condition enabling it.

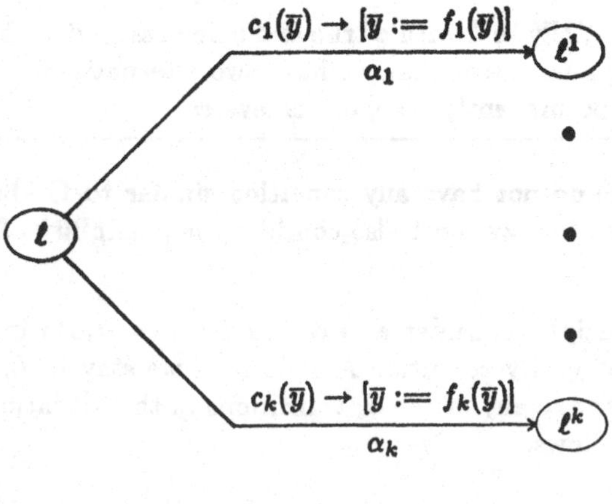

The Semaphore Rule (SEM):

Let ϕ, χ and ψ be state predicates such that:

A: ϕ is $(at\,\ell \wedge \chi)$-invariant.
This means that as long as we stay at ℓ and χ is preserved, so is ϕ.

B: Any of the α_i, $i = 1, \ldots, k$, transitions of Σ, which preserves χ and is initiated with ϕ true, achieves ψ, *i.e.*, ψ will hold after the transition. This is expressed by:

$$[at\,\ell \;\wedge\; c_i(\overline{y}) \;\wedge\; \phi(\overline{\pi};\overline{y}) \;\wedge\; \chi(\overline{\pi};\overline{y}) \;\wedge\; \chi(r_i(\overline{\pi}); f_i(\overline{y}))] \;\supset\; \psi(r_i(\overline{\pi}); f_i(\overline{y}))$$

for every $i = 1, \ldots, k$.

C: If $(\phi \wedge \chi)$ holds permanently at ℓ then *eventually* one of the c_i, $i = 1, \ldots, k$, will be true. That is

$$\models \;\; \Box(at\,\ell \;\wedge\; \phi \;\wedge\; \chi) \;\supset\; \Diamond \bigvee_{i=1}^{k} c_i.$$

Then under these conditions we may conclude:

$$\models \;\; (at\,\ell \;\wedge\; \phi \;\wedge\; \Box\chi) \;\supset\; \Diamond\psi.$$

That is, being at ℓ with ϕ true and being assured of the continuous holding of χ guarantees the eventual realization of ψ.

Note that condition C of SEM is weaker than condition C of ESC in that it does not require $E_\ell = \bigvee_{i=1}^{k} c_i$ to be true whenever $at\,\ell \wedge \phi \wedge \chi$ holds but only requires it to be eventually realized. However, condition C here is a temporal statement and requires temporal reasoning for its justification, while condition C of ESC is static and requires only classical justification.

To justify this rule consider an execution which starts at ℓ with ϕ true and χ continuously maintained. Condition A ensures that as long as we stay at ℓ, $\phi \wedge \chi$ will be preserved. It is impossible that we stay at ℓ forever because by condition C this would imply that $E_\ell = \bigvee_{i=1}^{k} c_i$, which is the full exit condition of node ℓ, is enabled infinitely often while process P_j is never scheduled. By fairness we must have P_j scheduled at least once while E_ℓ is true. This, by condition B and the permanence until this moment of $\phi \wedge at\,\ell \wedge \chi$, will cause ψ to be realized.

It is important to realize the differences between a "semaphore location" and a "busy waiting" location. For comparison consider the following two simplified cases:

(a) *Semaphore location:*

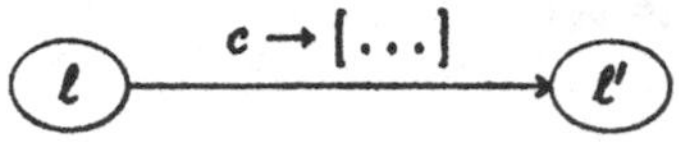

(b) *Busy waiting location:*

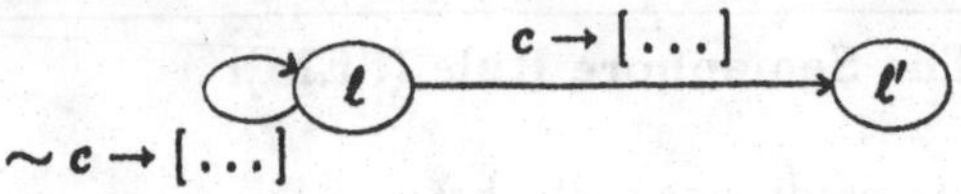

(*a*) **In the semaphore location case the fairness requirement demands that the scheduler will schedule this process at least once while its *c* condition is true provided the condition is true infinitely often. Thus for the SEM principle which is appropriate to this case we only require that *c* is realized infinitely often. This is exactly condition C which in this case is**

$$\models \ \Box(at\,\ell \wedge \phi \wedge \chi) \supset \Diamond c,$$

or is equivalently

$$\models \ \Box(at\,\ell \wedge \phi \wedge \chi) \supset \Box\Diamond c.$$

(*b*) **For the "busy waiting" situation, since the exit condition is $c \vee \sim c = true$, the only obligation that the scheduler has is to eventually schedule this process. There is however nothing to prevent the process from being scheduled at exactly these instants in which *c* is false. Consequently, an infinitely often true *c* is not sufficient to ensure an exit to ℓ'. Instead we must require a stronger guarantee, that *c* be permanently true. Therefore, the corresponding condition C for the "busy waiting" situation for this case is**

$$\models \ (at\,\ell \wedge \phi \wedge \chi) \supset c,$$

which is equivalent to

$$\models \ \Box(at\,\ell \wedge \phi \wedge \chi) \supset \Box c.$$

That is, if staying forever at ℓ guarantees the permanence of *c* then we will eventually exit from ℓ to ℓ'. This can be derived from the ESC rule.

Since $\models \Box c \supset \Diamond c$ we have the following *robustness metatheorem*:

> **A program that has been proven correct for an interpretation of its semaphores as "busy waiting" locations, is automatically correct for the implementation of these locations as true "semaphore" locations.**

Consider, for example, the problem of accessibility of critical sections for the mutual exclusion program *ME*. In the proof to be given later we will reach the conclusion

$$\models \ \Box\, at\,\ell_5 \supset \Diamond\Box(y_1 \neq y_2),$$

where the instruction at ℓ_5 is

$$\ell_5: \quad loop\ while\ y_1 = y_2.$$

Thus, this proof is sound for the interpretation of the *loop* primitive as "busy waiting". By the robustness metatheorem any more efficient implementation of the *loop* primitive, in fact any implementation at all which is "just", *i.e.*, eventually schedules each process, will also cause the program to behave correctly.

The Single Path Rule

In this derived rule we repetitively apply the ESC rule to a chain of locations.

Let $\ell_1, \ell_2, \ldots, \ell_{k+1}$ be a path of *deterministic* locations in P_j with an immediate transition α_i from every ℓ_i to ℓ_{i+1}, $i = 1, \ldots, k$.

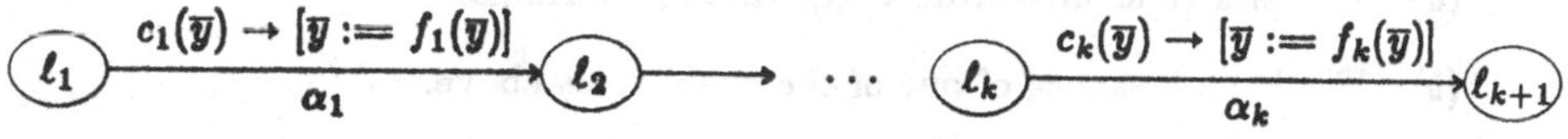

The Single Path Rule (SP):

Let χ, $\phi_1, \ldots, \phi_k$, and $\phi_{k+1} = \psi$ be predicates such that:

A: Each ϕ_i is $(at\,\ell_i \wedge \chi)$-invariant, $i = 1, \ldots, k$.
This means that as long as we stay at ℓ_i and χ is preserved so is ϕ_i.

B: Each transition α_i, $i = 1, \ldots, k$, which preserves χ and is initiated with ϕ_i true achieves ϕ_{i+1}, that is

$$[at\,\ell_i \wedge c_i(\bar{y}) \wedge \phi_i(\bar{\pi}; \bar{y}) \wedge \chi(\bar{\pi}; \bar{y}) \wedge \chi(r_i(\bar{\pi}); f_i(\bar{y}))] \supset \phi_{i+1}(r_i(\bar{\pi}); f_i(\bar{\pi})).$$

C: $(\phi_i \wedge \chi)$ at ℓ_i ensures that c_i is true, *i.e.*,

$$[at\,\ell_i \wedge \phi_i \wedge \chi] \supset c_i.$$

Then under these three conditions we may conclude

$$\vDash\ [\bigvee_{i=1}^{k}(at\,\ell_i \wedge \phi_i) \wedge \Box\chi] \supset \Diamond\psi.$$

That is, if we start anywhere in the path with the appropriate ϕ_i true and χ continuously maintained we eventually wind up having ψ.

This rule is obviously a generalization of ESC and is justified by a repeated application of ESC to $\ell_1, \ldots, \ell_k$ (with $\Sigma_i = \{\alpha_i\}$) respectively.

This rule can be somewhat generalized to a more general graph than a path. The SP principle also applies instead to a tree in which every node has an edge directed towards its ancestor.

This concludes the list of semantic proof rules reflecting the structure of the program and its influence on the possible execution sequences.

* * * * *

In the following "formal" proofs of eventuality properties, we will intentionally omit manipulations which are pure temporal logic deductions, since we have not included an axiomatic system for temporal logic in this paper. Instead we will justify these deductions by saying "temporal reasoning" or "temporal deduction." The reader is invited to convince himself semantically that these deductions are indeed sound, that is, any sequence that satisfies the premises must also satisfy the consequence. Thus our *proofs* will consist, similarly to regular proofs, of a sequence of temporal formulas with a justification for each line in the sequence. A line in a proof may be justified in one of the following ways:

(*a*) If it is a valid first-order temporal logic formula.

(*b*) If it is an instance of one of the proof rules above.

(*c*) If it is a logical or temporal consequence of some preceding lines.

Given a deductive system for our logic (see [MAN2]) we will be able to justify steps of the form *b* and *c* using the axioms and rules of inference. Alternatively, *c*–steps can be justified using a decision procedure for validity in (propositional) temporal logic ([BMP]). For our purpose of presenting proofs at a level which is not too formal, yet displays sufficient detail to be convincing, the style of semantic proofs seems most appropriate.

Note that our only reference to the program itself is through the proof principles ESC, ALT, SEM and SP.

In presenting formal (semantic) proofs we will work our way gradually through examples that use only the ESC and SP rules first, then examples that use also the ALT rule and finally examples using semaphores and the corresponding SEM rule.

EXAMPLE: COUNTING TREE NODES

Consider first the use of eventuality chains in proving the total correctness of the sequential program TN for counting the nodes of a binary tree.

Program TN (Counting the nodes of a tree):

$S := (X),\ C := 0$

$\ell_0:$ *if* $S = ()$ *then goto* ℓ_e
$\ell_1:$ $(T, S) := (hd(S),\ tl(S))$
$\ell_2:$ *if* $T = \Lambda$ *then goto* ℓ_0
$\ell_3:$ $C := C + 1$
$\ell_4:$ $S := \ell(T) \cdot r(T) \cdot S$
$\ell_5:$ *goto* ℓ_0
$\ell_e:$ *halt.*

The program operates on a tree variable T and a variable S which is a stack of trees. The input variable X is a tree. The output is the value of the counter C. Each node in a tree may have zero, one or two descendants.

The available operations on trees are the functions $\ell(T)$ and $r(T)$ that yield the left and right subtrees of a tree T respectively. If the tree does not possess one of these subtrees the functions return the value Λ.

The stack S is initialized to contain the tree X. Taking the head and tail of a stack (functions hd and tl respectively) yields the top element and rest of the stack respectively. The operation in ℓ_1 pops the top of the stack into the variable T. The operation at ℓ_4 pushes both the right subtree and the left subtree of T onto the top of the stack.

At any iteration of the program, the stack S contains the list of subtrees of X whose nodes have not yet been counted. Each iteration removes one such subtree from the stack. If it is the empty subtree, $T = \Lambda$, we proceed to examine the next subtree on the stack. If it is not the empty subtree we add one to the counter C and pushes the left and right subtrees of T to the stack. When the stack is empty, $S = ()$, the program halts.

Denoting by $|X|$ the number of nodes in the tree X, the statement to be proved is formulated as

Theorem: $\models \; at\,\ell_0 \supset \Diamond(at\,\ell_e \wedge C = |X|)$.

In order to prove the theorem we first prove a lemma:

Lemma: $\models \; [at\,\ell_0 \;\wedge\; S = t \cdot s \;\wedge\; C = c] \;\supset\; \Diamond[at\,\ell_0 \;\wedge\; S = s \;\wedge\; C = c + |t|]$.

The lemma states that being at ℓ_0 with a tree t at the top of the stack S, we are assured of a later visit at ℓ_0 where t has been removed from the stack and its node count $|t|$ has been added to C.

Denote by $E(n)$ the statement:

$$E(n): \quad \forall t, s, c\,\{[at\,\ell_0 \;\wedge\; S = t \cdot s \;\wedge\; C = c \;\wedge\; |t| \leq n] \;\supset$$
$$\Diamond[at\,\ell_0 \;\wedge\; S = s \;\wedge\; C = c + |t|]\}.$$

This statement is the restriction of the lemma to trees with node count not exceeding n for some natural number $n \geq 0$.

proof of Lemma:

The lemma can then be stated as $\models \forall n.\; E(n)$; it is proved by induction. We have to show

(a) $\models E(0)$

(b) $\models E(n) \supset E(n+1)$.

(*a*) Since $t \cdot s \neq ()$ and $|t| = 0 \supset t = \Lambda$ we may apply the SP rule to the path $\ell_0 \to \ell_1 \to \ell_2 \to \ell_0$ and obtain

$$1. \quad \models \ [at\,\ell_0 \ \land \ S = t \cdot s \ \land \ C = c \ \land \ |t| = 0] \ \supset \ \Diamond[at\,\ell_0 \ \land \ S = s \ \land \ C = c].$$

This establishes $\models E(0)$.

(*b*) To show $\models E(n) \supset E(n+1)$, consider an arbitrary $n, n \geq 0$, and assume

$$2. \quad \models E(n).$$

Then

$$3. \quad \models \ [at\,\ell_0 \ \land \ S = t' \cdot s' \ \land \ C = c' \ \land \ |t'| = n+1] \ \supset \ \Diamond[at\,\ell_0 \ \land \ S = \ell(t') \cdot r(t') \cdot s' \ \land \ C = c' + 1 \ \land \ |t'| = n+1]$$

by the SP rule applied to the path $\ell_0 \to \ell_1 \to \ell_2 \to \ell_3 \to \ell_4 \to \ell_5 \to \ell_0$, using $|t'| = n+1 \supset t' \neq \Lambda$.

We now use an instantiation of $E(n)$ with $t = \ell(t')$, $s = r(t') \cdot s'$, and $c = c' + 1$ (which is justified since $|t| = |\ell(t')| < n+1$) to obtain

$$4. \quad \models \ [at\,\ell_0 \land S = \ell(t') \cdot r(t') \cdot s' \land C = c' + 1] \ \supset \ \Diamond[at\,\ell_0 \land S = r(t') \cdot s' \land C = c' + 1 + |\ell(t')|].$$

By 3 and 4 we have

$$5. \quad \models [at\,\ell_0 \ \land \ S = t' \cdot s' \ \land \ C = c' \ \land \ |t'| = n+1] \ \supset \ \Diamond[at\,\ell_0 \ \land \ S = r(t') \cdot s' \ \land \ C = c' + 1 + |\ell(t')| \ \land \ |t'| = n+1].$$

We now apply an instance of $E(n)$ again, this time with $t = r(t')$, $s = s'$, and $c = c' + 1 + |\ell(t')|$ (which is justified since $|t| = |r(t')| < n+1$) to obtain

$$6. \quad \models [at\,\ell_0 \land S = r(t') \cdot s' \land C = c' + 1 + |\ell(t')|] \ \supset \ \Diamond[at\,\ell_0 \land S = s' \land C = c' + 1 + |\ell(t')| + |r(t')|].$$

By 5 and 6 we have

$$7. \quad \models [at\,\ell_0 \ \land \ S = t' \cdot s' \ \land \ C = c' \ \land \ |t'| = n+1] \ \supset \ \Diamond[at\,\ell_0 \ \land \ S = s' \ \land \ C = c' + 1 + |\ell(t')| + |r(t')|].$$

Using the property

$$|t| > 0 \ \Rightarrow \ |t| = 1 + |\ell(t)| + |r(t)|$$

we obtain:

$$8. \quad \models [at\,\ell_0 \wedge S = t' \cdot s' \wedge C = c' \wedge |t'| = n+1] \supset \Diamond[at\,\ell_0 \wedge S = s' \wedge C = c' + |t'|].$$

Universally quantifying over the variables t', s' and c' and then renaming them to t, s and c, respectively, we obtain

$$9. \quad \models \forall t, s, c\{[at\,\ell_0 \wedge S = t \cdot s \wedge C = c \wedge |t| = n+1] \supset \Diamond[at\,\ell_0 \wedge S = s \wedge C = c + |t|]\}.$$

Line 9 holds under assumption 2 for every $n, n \geq 0$. Combined with 1 this gives

$$10. \quad E(n) \models E(n+1).$$

Therefore, by the deduction theorem we have

$$11. \quad \models E(n) \supset E(n+1).$$

This concludes the proof of the lemma.

proof of theorem:

To prove the theorem we observe that

$$12. \quad \models [at\,\ell_0 \wedge S = (X) \wedge C = 0] \supset \Diamond[at\,\ell_0 \wedge S = () \wedge C = |X|]$$

by the lemma with $t = X$, $s = ()$, and $c = 0$. But

$$13. \quad \models [at\,\ell_0 \wedge S = () \wedge C = |X|] \supset \Diamond[at\,\ell_e \wedge C = |X|]$$

by SP applied to $\ell_0 \rightarrow \ell_e$. Therefore, by combining 12 and 13, we have

$$14. \quad \models [at\,\ell_0 \wedge S = (X) \wedge C = 0] \supset \Diamond[at\,\ell_e \wedge C = |X|]$$

i.e.,

$$15. \quad \models \Diamond[at\,\ell_e \wedge C = |X|]. \quad \blacksquare$$

One cannot fail to see the close resemblance between the temporal proof presented here and the informal inermittent-assertion proof conducted in [BUR] and [MW]. Our SP principle replaces the "little hand simulation" of [BUR].

EXAMPLE: MUTUAL EXCLUSION (DEKKER) – FORMAL PROOFS

We will now present a formal proof of the accessibility proof of the program DK. An informal proof of this was presented before and we advise the reader to refer to it while reading the following proof. The accessibility statement to be proved is

Theorem: $\models\ at\,\ell_1 \supset \Diamond\, at\,\ell_7$.

We will make use of the invariants derived before, namely:

$$\models\ \Box(Q_1 \wedge Q_2 \wedge Q_3 \wedge Q_4)$$

where

$$Q_1:\quad (y_1 = T)\ \equiv\ at\{\ell_2, \ell_3, \ell_4, \ell_7, \ell_8\}$$

$$Q_2:\quad (y_2 = T)\ \equiv\ at\{m_2, m_3, m_4, m_7, m_8\}$$

$$Q_3:\quad \sim at\{\ell_7, \ell_8\} \vee \sim at\{m_7, m_8\}$$

and

$$Q_4:\quad [at\{\ell_3, \ldots, \ell_6\} \wedge (t = 2)]\ \supset\ \sim at\{m_8, m_9, m_0\}.$$

Q_4 was proved by the standard invariance rule in Lemma B and will not be reproven here.

The proof of the theorem consists of a sequence of lemmas.

Lemma A: $\models\ [at\,\ell_{2,3} \wedge (t = 1)]\ \supset\ \Diamond\, at\,\ell_7$

proof of Lemma A:

1. $\models\ [at\,\ell_{2,3} \wedge (t = 1)]\ \supset\ \{\Box[at\,\ell_{2,3} \wedge (t = 1)] \vee \Diamond\, at\,\ell_7\}$

by the ALT rule at $\ell_{2,3}$ where ϕ is $t = 1$. Note that by $t = 1$, the $\ell_3 \rightarrow \ell_4$ transition is never possible.

2. $\models\ [at\,\ell_{2,3} \wedge (t = 1) \wedge at\,m_5]\ \supset\ [at\,\ell_{2,3} \wedge (t = 1) \wedge at\,m_5 \wedge (y_2 = F)]$

by Q_2.

3. $\models\ [at\,\ell_{2,3} \wedge (t = 1) \wedge at\,m_5 \wedge (y_2 = F)]\ \supset\ \Diamond\, at\,\ell_7$

by SP applied to the path $\ell_3 \rightarrow \ell_2 \rightarrow \ell_7$ where $\phi_3 = \phi_2$ is $(t = 1) \wedge at\,m_5 \wedge (y_2 = F)$ and ψ is $at\,\ell_7$.

4. $\models\ \{\Box[at\,\ell_{2,3} \wedge (t = 1)] \wedge at\,m_5\}\ \supset\ \Diamond\, at\,\ell_7$

is a temporal conclusion of 2 and 3.

This corresponds to case a of Lemma A in the informal proof.

Next we have

5. $\models\ \Box[at\,\ell_{2;3} \wedge (t = 1)]\ \supset\ \Box[at\,\ell_{2,3} \wedge (t = 1) \wedge (y_1 = T)]$

by Q_1.

6. $\models \{\Box[at\,\ell_{2,3} \wedge (t=1) \wedge (y_1 = T)] \wedge at\{m_{1..4}; m_6\}\} \supset \Diamond\, at\, m_5$

by the SP rule applied to the path $m_6 \to m_1 \to m_2 \to m_3 \to m_4 \to m_5$ where χ is $at\,\ell_{2,3} \wedge (t=1) \wedge (y_1 = T)$.

7. $\models \{\Box[at\,\ell_{2,3} \wedge (t=1)] \wedge at\{m_{1..4}, m_6\}\} \supset \Diamond\, at\, m_5$

by 5 and 6.

8. $\models \{\Box[at\,\ell_{2,3} \wedge (t=1)] \wedge at\, m_{1..6}\} \supset \Diamond\, at\,\ell_7$

by 7 and 4.

This covers cases *b, c, d, e, f* of the informal Lemma *A*.

We have

9. $\models at\, m_0 \supset [at\, m_0 \wedge (y_2 = F)]$

by Q_2.

10. $\models [at\, m_0 \wedge (y_2 = F)] \supset \{\Box[at\, m_0 \wedge (y_2 = F)] \vee \Diamond\, at\, m_1\}$

by ALT at m_0 where ϕ is $y_2 = F$. Therefore

11. $\models at\, m_0 \supset [\Box(y_2 = F) \vee \Diamond\, at\, m_1]$

by 9 and 10.

12. $\models [\Box(y_2 = F) \wedge at\,\ell_{2,3} \wedge (t=1)] \supset \Diamond\, at\,\ell_7$

by the SP rule applied to $\ell_3 \to \ell_2 \to \ell_7$ where $\phi_3 = \phi_2$ is $t = 1$ and χ is $y_2 = F$.

13. $\models \{\Box[at\,\ell_{2,3} \wedge (t=1)] \wedge \Box(y_2 = F)\} \supset \Diamond\, at\,\ell_7$

is a consequence of 12. By taking the disjunction of 13 and 8 we get

14. $\models \{\Box[at\,\ell_{2,3} \wedge (t=1)] \wedge (\Box(y_2 = F) \vee at\, m_{1..6})\} \supset \Diamond\, at\,\ell_7$

and then

15. $\models \{\Box[at\,\ell_{2,3} \wedge (t=1)] \wedge at\, m_0\} \supset \Diamond\, at\,\ell_7$

is a consequence of 11 and 14.

This covers case *g* of the informal Lemma *A*.

We also have

16. $\models \{\Box[at\,\ell_{2,3} \wedge (t=1)] \wedge at\, m_{7..9}\} \supset \Diamond\, at\, m_0$

by the SP rule applied to the path $m_7 \rightarrow m_8 \rightarrow m_9 \rightarrow m_0$.

17. $\models \{\Box[at\,\ell_{2,3} \wedge (t=1)] \wedge at\,m_{7..9}\} \supset \Diamond\, at\,\ell_7$

by 15 and 16.

This covers case h of the proof.

Taking the disjunction of 8, 15 and 17 we obtain

18. $\models \Box[at\,\ell_{2,3} \wedge (t=1)] \supset \Diamond\, at\,\ell_7.$

Taking together 1 and 18 yields

19. $\models [at\,\ell_{2,3} \wedge (t=1)] \supset \Diamond\, at\,\ell_7$

which is the result of Lemma A.

Lemma B is an invariance property $\models Q_4$ and is proved using the invariance principle.

Lemma C: $\models at\,\ell_5 \supset \Diamond\, at\,\ell_7$

proof of Lemma C:

1. $\models at\,\ell_5 \supset \{\Box\, at\,\ell_5 \vee \Diamond[at\,\ell_6 \wedge (t=1)]\}$

by the ALT rule at ℓ_5.

2. $\models \Box(t=2) \vee \Diamond(t=1)$

is a temporal tautology using the obvious invariance $(t=1) \vee (t=2)$.

3. $\models \Box\, at\,\ell_5 \supset \{\Box[at\,\ell_5 \wedge (t=2)] \vee \Diamond[at\,\ell_5 \wedge (t=1)]\}$

is a temporal consequence of 2.

4. $\models [at\,\ell_5 \wedge (t=1)] \supset \Diamond[at\,\ell_6 \wedge (t=1)]$

by the ESC rule at ℓ_5 where ϕ is $t=1$.

5. $\models \Box\, at\,\ell_5 \supset \{\Box[at\,\ell_5 \wedge (t=2)] \vee \Diamond[at\,\ell_6 \wedge (t=1)]\}$

is a temporal consequence of 3 and 4.

6. $\models at\,\ell_5 \supset \{\Box[at\,\ell_5 \wedge (t=2)] \vee \Diamond[at\,\ell_6 \wedge (t=1)]\}$

by 1 and 5.

7. $\models \Box[at\,\ell_5 \wedge (t=2)] \supset \Box[at\,\ell_5 \wedge (t=2) \wedge (y_1 = F) \wedge at\,m_{1..7}]$

by Q_1 and Q_4.

We have

$$8. \quad \vDash \quad \{\Box[at\,\ell_5 \wedge (t=2)] \wedge at\,m_7\} \supset \Diamond[at\,\ell_5 \wedge (t=1)]$$

by the ESC rule at m_7 where χ is $at\,\ell_5 \wedge (t=2)$, ψ is $at\,\ell_5 \wedge (t=1)$.

$$9. \quad \vDash \quad \{\Box[at\,\ell_5 \wedge (t=2)] \wedge at\,m_7\} \supset \Diamond[at\,\ell_6 \wedge (t=1)]$$

by 8 and 4.

This covers case a of the informal Lemma C.

Denoting

$$\chi_0: \quad at\,\ell_5 \wedge (t_2=2) \wedge (y_1=F) \wedge at\,m_{1..7}$$

we have

$$10. \quad \vDash \quad [\Box\chi_0 \wedge at\{m_{1,2}, m_{4..7}\}] \supset \Diamond[\chi_0 \wedge at\,m_7]$$

by the SP rule applied to the path $m_4 \rightarrow m_5 \rightarrow m_6 \rightarrow m_1 \rightarrow m_2 \rightarrow m_7$.

$$11. \quad \vDash \quad [\Box\chi_0 \wedge at\{m_{1,2}, m_{4..7}\}] \supset \Diamond[at\,\ell_6 \wedge (t=1)]$$

by 10 and 9.

This covers cases b, d, e, f, g of the informal Lemma C.

We have

$$12. \quad \vDash \quad [\Box\chi_0 \wedge at\,m_3] \supset \Diamond\, at\,m_2$$

by the ESC rule at m_3. Thus

$$13. \quad \vDash \quad [\Box\chi_0 \wedge at\,m_3] \supset \Diamond[at\,\ell_6 \wedge (t=1)]$$

by 11 and 12.

This covers case c of the informal Lemma C.

Taking the disjunction of 11 and 13 and noting that $\chi_0 \supset at\,m_{1..7}$ we obtain

$$14. \quad \vDash \quad \Box\chi_0 \supset \Diamond[at\,\ell_6 \wedge (t=1)].$$

Combined with 7 this gives

$$15. \quad \vDash \quad \Box[at\,\ell_5 \wedge (t=2)] \supset \Diamond[at\,\ell_6 \wedge (t=1)].$$

Combined with 6 we obtain

$$16. \quad \vDash \quad at\,\ell_5 \supset \Diamond[at\,\ell_6 \wedge (t=1)].$$

Now we can derive

$$17.\quad \models\ [at\,\ell_{1,6} \wedge (t=1)] \supset \Diamond[at\,\ell_{2,3} \wedge (t=1)]$$

by the SP rule applied to the path $\ell_6 \to \ell_1 \to \ell_2$ where $\phi_6 = \phi_1$ is $(t = 1)$, ψ is $at\,\ell_{2,3} \wedge (t = 1)$. Using now Lemma A we obtain

$$18.\quad \models\ [at\,\ell_{1,6} \wedge (t=1)] \supset \Diamond\, at\,\ell_7$$

which together with 16 gives

$$19.\quad \models\ at\,\ell_5 \supset \Diamond\, at\,\ell_7.$$

proof of theorem:

Consider now the final proof of the theorem

1. $\models\ at\,\ell_1 \supset \Diamond\, at\,\ell_2$ — by ESC rule at ℓ_1
2. $\models\ at\,\ell_2 \supset \Diamond[at\,\ell_7 \vee at\,\ell_3]$ — by the ESC rule at ℓ_2
3. $\models\ at\,\ell_2 \supset [\Diamond\, at\,\ell_7 \vee \Diamond\, at\,\ell_3]$ — which is temporally equivalent to 2
4. $\models\ at\,\ell_3 \supset \{\Diamond[at\,\ell_2 \wedge (t=1)] \vee \Diamond\, at\,\ell_4\}$ — by the ESC rule at ℓ_3
5. $\models\ [at\,\ell_2 \wedge (t=1)] \supset \Diamond\, at\,\ell_7$ — by Lemma *A*
6. $\models\ at\,\ell_4 \supset \Diamond\, at\,\ell_5$ — by ESC rule at ℓ_4
7. $\models\ at\,\ell_4 \supset \Diamond\, at\,\ell_7$ — by Lemma *C* and 6
8. $\models\ at\,\ell_3 \supset \Diamond\, at\,\ell_7$ — by 4, 5, and 7
9. $\models\ at\,\ell_2 \supset \Diamond\, at\,\ell_7$ — by 3 and 8
10. $\models\ at\,\ell_1 \supset \Diamond\, at\,\ell_7$ — by 1 and 9

This concludes the proof of the theorem.

Consider next proving accessibility for the Consumer-Producer program (program CP). We assume that the computations at ℓ_0 and at m_7 eventually terminate. The statement to be proved is:

Theorem: $\models \; at\,\ell_0 \supset \Diamond\, at\,\ell_3$

We will use in our proof the invariants which were established before

$$\models \; \Box(Q_0 \wedge Q_1 \wedge Q_2)$$

where

$$Q_0: \; (cf \geq 0) \wedge (ce \geq 0) \wedge (s \geq 0)$$

$$Q_1: \; at\,\ell_{3..5} + at\,m_{2..5} + s \; = \; 1$$

$$Q_2: \; cf + ce + at\,\ell_{2..6} + at\,m_{1..6} \; = \; N$$

Note that this is the first example that uses semaphores.

Assuming that the computation of y_1 at ℓ_0 eventually terminates we may conclude

$$\models \; at\,\ell_0 \supset \Diamond\, at\,\ell_1.$$

The rest of the theorem is proved by two lemmas. Lemma A ensures that we get from ℓ_1 to ℓ_2 and Lemma B ensures that we get from ℓ_2 to ℓ_3.

Lemma A: $\models \; at\,\ell_1 \supset \Diamond\, at\,\ell_2$

proof of Lemma A:

Since location ℓ_1 contains a semaphore *request* instruction we will use the semaphore rule SEM to show that eventually P_1 will be granted access to ℓ_2. The premise needed for the SEM rule is $\Box\, at\,\ell_1 \supset \Diamond(ce > 0)$. An intuitive interpretation of this premise is that if we wait long enough at ℓ_1, ce will eventually turn positive. To show this, we give first an informal exposition inspecting the different locations in which P_2 may currently be.

case a: P_2 is at m_6. Then eventually it will execute the *release*(ce) instruction to get $ce > 0$ as required.

case b: P_2 is at m_2, m_3, m_4 or m_5. Then it will eventually get to m_6 which by case a will cause ce to turn positive.

case c: P_2 is at m_1. Then since P_1 is at ℓ_1, $s = 1$ by Q_1. Since we assume that P_1 is waiting at ℓ_1, s will remain 1 as long as P_2 stays at m_2. By the semaphore axiom applied at m_1, P_2 will eventually proceed to m_2 and by case b, ce will eventually turn positive.

case d: P_2 is at m_0. Then since P_1 is at ℓ_1, $cf + ce = N > 0$ by Q_2. If $ce > 0$ we have proven our claim. Otherwise $cf > 0$ and will remain so as long as P_2 stays at m_0. Again by the semaphore axiom P_2 must eventually advance to m_1 and then by case *c*, *ce* will eventually turn positive.

case e: P_2 is at m_7 or m_8. It will eventually get to m_0 and then by case *d*, *ce* will eventually turn positive.

Let us now proceed with the more formal proof:

$$\textbf{1.} \quad \vDash \quad [\Box\, at\,\ell_1 \wedge at\,m_6] \supset [\Box\, at\,\ell_1 \wedge at\,m_6 \wedge (ce \geq 0)]$$

by Q_0.

$$\textbf{2.} \quad \vDash \quad [\Box\, at\,\ell_1 \wedge at\,m_6 \wedge (ce \geq 0)] \supset \Diamond(ce > 0)$$

by ESC applied at m_6 where ϕ is $ce \geq 0$, χ is $at\,\ell_1$, ψ is $ce > 0$.

$$\textbf{3.} \quad \vDash \quad [\Box\, at\,\ell_1 \wedge at\,m_6] \supset \Diamond(ce > 0)$$

is a conclusion of 1 and 2.

This corresponds to case *a* above.

We have

$$\textbf{4.} \quad \vDash \quad [\Box\, at\,\ell_1 \wedge at\,m_{2..5}] \supset \Diamond\, at\,m_6$$

by the SP rule applied to the path $m_2 \rightarrow m_3 \rightarrow m_4 \rightarrow m_5 \rightarrow m_6$.

$$\textbf{5.} \quad \vDash \quad [\Box\, at\,\ell_1 \wedge at\,m_{2..5}] \supset \Diamond(ce > 0)$$

is a conclusion of 4 and 3.

This covers case *b* above.

We have

$$\textbf{6.} \quad \vDash \quad [at\,\ell_1 \wedge at\,m_1] \supset (s = 1)$$

by Q_1.

$$\textbf{7.} \quad \vDash \quad [\Box\, at\,\ell_1 \wedge \Box\, at\,m_1] \supset \Diamond(s = 1)$$

is a temporal consequence of 6.

$$\textbf{8.} \quad \vDash \quad [\Box\, at\,\ell_1 \wedge at\,m_1] \supset \Diamond\, at\,m_2$$

by the SEM rule at m_1 where χ is $at\,\ell_1$.

$$\textbf{9.} \quad \vDash \quad [\Box\, at\,\ell_1 \wedge at\,m_1] \supset \Diamond(ce > 0)$$

is a conclusion of 8 and 5.

This covers case c.

We have

10. $\models$ $[\Box\, at\,\ell_1 \wedge at\,m_0] \supset [(cf > 0) \vee (ce > 0)]$

by Q_2.

11. $\models$ $\Box(at\,\ell_1 \wedge at\,m_0 \wedge (cf > 0)) \supset \Diamond(cf > 0)$

is a trivial temporal tautology.

12. $\models$ $[\Box\, at\,\ell_1 \wedge at\,m_0 \wedge (cf > 0)] \supset \Diamond\, at\,m_1$

by the SEM rule at m_0, where ϕ is $cf > 0$, χ is $at\,\ell_1$.

13. $\models$ $[\Box\, at\,\ell_1 \wedge at\,m_0 \wedge (cf > 0)] \supset \Diamond(ce > 0)$

is a conclusion of 12 and 9.

14. $\models$ $[\Box\, at\,\ell_1 \wedge at\,m_0] \supset \Diamond(ce > 0)$

by a disjunction of 10 and 13.

This corresponds to case d.

We have

15. $\models$ $[\Box\, at\,\ell_1 \wedge at\,m_{7,8}] \supset \Diamond\, at\,m_0$

by the SP rule applied to the path $\ell_7 \rightarrow \ell_8 \rightarrow \ell_0$.

16. $\models$ $[\Box\, at\,\ell_1 \wedge at\,m_{7,8}] \supset \Diamond(ce > 0)$

by 15 and 14.

This covers case e.

By taking the disjunction of 3, 5, 9, 14 and 16 we obtain

17. $\models$ $\Box\, at\,\ell_1 \supset \Diamond(ce > 0)$.

By applying the SEM rule at ℓ_1 we obtain

18. $\models$ $at\,\ell_1 \supset \Diamond\, at\,\ell_2$. ∎

Lemma B: $\models$ $at\,\ell_2 \supset \Diamond\, at\,\ell_3$

proof of Lemma B:

Here again we will apply the SEM rule, this time at ℓ_2. The needed premise for its application is:

$$\models \; \Box\, at\,\ell_2 \supset \Diamond(s > 0).$$

By inspecting the current location of P_2 we distinguish three cases:

case a: P_2 is at m_5. It will eventually advance to m_6 and turn s positive.

case b: P_2 is somewhere in $\{m_2, m_3, m_4\}$. It will eventually get to m_5 and then by case a will turn s positive.

case c: P_2 is somewhere in $\{m_0, m_1, m_6, m_7, m_8\}$. By Q_1, since P_1 is at ℓ_1, s is currently equal to 1.

Thus the more formal proof is given by:

$$1. \quad \models \; [\Box\, at\,\ell_2 \wedge at\,m_5] \supset [\Box\, at\,\ell_2 \wedge at\,m_5 \wedge (s \geq 0)]$$

by Q_0.

$$2. \quad \models \; [\Box\, at\,\ell_2 \wedge at\,m_5 \wedge (s \geq 0)] \supset \Diamond(s > 0)$$

by ESC applied at m_5 where ϕ is $s \geq 0$, χ is $at\,\ell_2$, ψ is $s > 0$

$$3. \quad \models \; [\Box\, at\,\ell_2 \wedge at\,m_5] \supset \Diamond(s > 0)$$

is a conclusion of 1 and 2.

This covers case a.

We have

$$4. \quad \models \; [\Box\, at\,\ell_2 \wedge at\,m_{2..4}] \supset \Diamond(at\,m_5)$$

by the SP rule applied to the path $m_2 \rightarrow m_3 \rightarrow m_4 \rightarrow m_5$.

$$5. \quad \models \; [\Box\, at\,\ell_2 \wedge at\,m_{2..4}] \supset \Diamond(s > 0)$$

by 4 and 3.

This covers case b.

We have

$$6. \quad \models \; [\Box\, at\,\ell_2 \wedge \sim at\,m_{2..5}] \supset (s = 1)$$

by Q_1.

$$7. \quad \models \; [\Box\, at\,\ell_2 \wedge \sim at\,m_{2..5}] \supset \Diamond(s > 0)$$

by 6.

This covers case *c*.

By taking the disjunction of 3, 5, and 7 we obtain

8. $\models \Box\, at\,\ell_2 \supset \Diamond(s > 0)$.

Applying the SEM rule at ℓ_2 yields

9. $\models at\,\ell_2 \supset \Diamond\, at\,\ell_3$,

which is the desired Lemma *B*. ∎

EXAMPLE: BINOMIAL COEFFICIENT

We will now establish the termination of the program BC_1 for the distributed evaluation of a binomial coefficient. Since we have already proved the partial correctness of this program, termination will guarantee total correctness.

The statement to be proved is:

Theorem: $\models \Diamond(at\,\ell_e \wedge at\,m_e)$

The initial condition associated with the proper computation of the program is

$$at\,\ell_0 \wedge at\,m_0 \wedge (y_1 = n) \wedge (y_2 = 0) \wedge (y_3 = 1) \wedge (y_4 = 1) \wedge (0 \le k \le n).$$

We will use in our proof the following invariants that were established above:

$$\models \Box(Q_0 \wedge Q_1 \wedge Q_2),$$

where

Q_0 is $at\,\ell_{2..4} + at\,m_{4..6} + y_4 = 1$

Q_1 is $((n-k) \le y_1 \le n) \wedge (0 \le y_2 \le k)$

Q_2 is $at\,\ell_e \supset (y_1 = n-k)$.

We start by proving a sequence of lemmas:

Lemma A1: $\models [at\,\ell_1 \wedge (y_1 = u)] \supset \Diamond[at\,\ell_2 \wedge (y_1 = u)]$

This lemma ensures that we never get stuck at ℓ_1 which is a semaphore instruction.

proof of Lemma A1:

The proof distinguishes three cases according to the current location of P_2. In all cases we assume that P_1 is waiting at ℓ_1.

case a: P_2 is at m_6. The next time it will be scheduled will increment y_4, making it positive.

case b: P_2 is in $\{m_4, m_5\}$. Eventually it will get to m_6 and increment y_4.

case c: P_2 is in $\{m_0, m_1, m_2, m_3, m_7, m_e\}$. By Q_0 and the fact that P_1 is at ℓ_1, y_4 is currently positive.

In all three cases we can show that the value of y_1 never changes.

Thus we have:

$$1. \quad \models \quad [\Box\, at\,\ell_1 \wedge at\,m_6] \supset [\Box\, at\,\ell_1 \wedge at\,m_6 \wedge (y_4 \geq 0)]$$

by Q_0.

$$2. \quad \models \quad [\Box\, at\,\ell_1 \wedge at\,m_6 \wedge (y_4 \geq 0)] \supset \Diamond(y_4 > 0)$$

by the ESC rule at m_6 where ϕ is $y_4 \geq 0$, χ is $at\,\ell_1$.

$$3. \quad \models \quad [\Box\, at\,\ell_1 \wedge at\,m_6] \supset \Diamond(y_4 > 0)$$

by 2 and 1.

This covers case *a*.

We have

$$4. \quad \models \quad [\Box\, at\,\ell_1 \wedge at\,m_{4,5}] \supset \Diamond\, at\,m_6$$

by the SP rule applied to the path $m_4 \rightarrow m_5 \rightarrow m_6$.

$$5. \quad \models \quad [\Box\, at\,\ell_1 \wedge at\,m_{4,5}] \supset \Diamond(y_4 > 0)$$

by 4 and 3.

This covers case *b*.

We have

$$6. \quad \models \quad [\Box\, at\,\ell_1 \wedge \sim at\,m_{4..6}] \supset (y_4 > 0)$$

by Q_0. Therefore

$$7. \quad \models \quad [\Box\, at\,\ell_1 \wedge \sim at\,m_{4..6}] \supset \Diamond(y_4 > 0)$$

This covers case *c*.

By taking the disjunction of 3, 5 and 7 we obtain

$$8. \quad \models \quad \Box\, at\,\ell_1 \supset \Diamond(y_4 > 0).$$

Applying the SEM rule at ℓ_1 where ϕ is $y_1 = u$ we obtain

9. $\models$ $[at\,\ell_1 \wedge (y_1 = u)] \supset \Diamond[at\,\ell_2 \wedge (y_1 = u)]$. ∎

Lemma A2: $\models$ $\{[at\,\ell_{1..5} \wedge (y_1 = u+1)] \vee [at\,\ell_6 \wedge (y_1 = u)]\} \supset \Diamond[at\,\ell_0 \wedge (y_1 = u)]$

This lemma ensures that being anywhere in ℓ_1 to ℓ_5 we return to ℓ_0 with the value of y_1 smaller by 1 than the original and being at ℓ_6 we return to ℓ_0 with the value of y_1 unchanged.

proof of Lemma A2:

After being ensured by Lemma *A1* of not being blocked at ℓ_1 all that remains is to trace the value of y_1. Indeed:

1. $\models$ $[at\,\ell_1 \wedge (y_1 = u+1)] \supset \Diamond[at\,\ell_2 \wedge (y_1 = u+1)]$

by Lemma *A1*.

2. $\models$ $\{[at\,\ell_{2..5} \wedge (y_1 = u+1] \vee [at\,\ell_6 \wedge (y_1 = u)]\} \supset \Diamond[at\,\ell_0 \wedge (y_1 = u)]$

by applying the SP rule to the path $\ell_2 \to \ell_3 \to \ell_5 \to \ell_6 \to \ell_0$ where $\phi_2 = \phi_3 = \phi_4 = \phi_5$ is $y_1 = (u+1)$, ϕ_6 is $y_1 = u$, and ψ is $at\,\ell_0 \wedge (y_1 = u)$.

3. $\models$ $[at\,\ell_1 \wedge (y_1 = u+1)] \supset \Diamond[at\,\ell_0 \wedge (y_1 = u)]$

by 1 and 2.

4. $\models$ $\{[at\,\ell_{1..5} \wedge (y_1 = u+1)] \vee [at\,\ell_6 \wedge (y_1 = u)]\} \supset \Diamond[at\,\ell_0 \wedge (y_1 = u)]$

by 2 and 3.

This establishes Lemma *A2*. ∎

Lemma A3: $\models$ $[at\,\ell_0 \wedge (y_1 \geq n-k)] \supset \Diamond[at\,\ell_e \wedge (y_1 = n-k)]$.

This lemma establishes the termination of P_1 if started at ℓ_0 with $y_1 \geq n-k$.

proof of Lemma A3:

Define the auxiliary assertion:

$$E_1(u):\ [at\,\ell_0 \wedge (y_1 = u)] \supset \Diamond[at\,\ell_e \wedge (y_1 = n-k)].$$

We will establish the lemma by showing that

$$\models\ (u \geq n-k) \supset E_1(u).$$

This will be established by induction on $u \geq n-k$. We will have to show first

(a) $\models \; E_1(n-k)$

and then

(b) $\models \; [(u \geq n-k) \wedge E_1(u)] \supset E_1(u+1).$

(a) To prove part a we observe that $E_1(n-k)$ just says that if we are at ℓ_0 with $y_1 = n-k$ we will eventually get to ℓ_e with $y_1 = n-k$. This is obvious since when $y_1 = n-k$, P_1 proceeds directly from ℓ_0 to ℓ_e. Indeed:

1. $\models \; [at\,\ell_0 \wedge (y_1 = n-k)] \supset \Diamond[at\,\ell_e \wedge (y_1 = n-k)]$

by the ESC rule applied at ℓ_0 where ϕ is $y_1 = n-k$ considering just the exit $\ell_0 \to \ell_e$ whose enabling condition c is $y_1 = n-k$. In other words,

1'. $\models \; E_1(n-k)$

(b) To prove part b we assume that $u \geq n-k$ and $E_1(u)$ is true and consider an execution that starts at ℓ_0 with $y_1 = u+1$. Since $u+1 > n-k$ we will proceed to ℓ_1 with $y_1 = u+1$. By Lemma $A2$ we will return to ℓ_0 with $y_1 = u$. Now by the assumption of $E_1(u)$ we will eventually get to ℓ_e with $y_1 = n-k$.

For the formal proof, we assume:

2. $\models \; u \geq n-k$

and

3. $\models \; E_1(u),$

i.e.,

3'. $\models \; [at\,\ell_0 \wedge (y_1 = u)] \supset \Diamond[at\,\ell_e \wedge (y_1 = n-k)].$

Then

4. $\models \; [at\,\ell_0 \wedge (y_1 = u+1)]$
$$\supset [at\,\ell_0 \wedge (y_1 = u+1) \wedge (y_1 > n-k)]$$

by 2.

5. $\models \; [at\,\ell_0 \wedge (y_1 = u+1) \wedge (y_1 > n-k)]$
$$\supset \Diamond[at\,\ell_1 \wedge (y_1 = u+1)]$$

by the ESC rule at ℓ_0 using only the $\ell_0 \to \ell_1$ exit where ϕ is $y_1 > n-k$.

6. $\models \; [at\,\ell_0 \wedge (y_1 = u+1)] \supset \Diamond[at\,\ell_1 \wedge (y_1 = u+1)]$

by 4 and 5.

7. $\models \; [at\,\ell_0 \wedge (y_1 = u+1)] \supset \Diamond[at\,\ell_0 \wedge (y_1 = u)]$

by 6 and Lemma $A2$.

$$8. \quad \models \quad [at\,\ell_0 \wedge (y_1 = u+1)] \supset \Diamond[at\,\ell_e \wedge (y_1 = n-k)]$$

by 7 and 3′; *i.e.*, by the definition of E_1,

$$8'. \quad \models \quad E_1(u+1).$$

Applying the deduction theorem to 2, 3, and 8′, we obtain

$$9. \quad \models \quad (u \geq n-k) \supset [E_1(u) \supset E_1(u+1)].$$

Now we may combine parts *a* and *b* (*i.e.*, 1′ and 9) to deduce the lemma using the induction principle. ∎

Lemma A4: $\models \quad \Diamond[at\,\ell_e \wedge (y_1 = n-k)]$

This states that no matter where we are in a properly initialized execution of the program, we will eventually wind up at ℓ_e with $y_1 = n-k$.

proof of Lemma A4:

There are three cases to be considered according to the current location of P_1.

case a: P_1 is already at ℓ_e. Then we have by Q_2 that $y_1 = n-k$.

case b: P_1 is at ℓ_0. Then we are assured by Q_1 that $y_1 \geq n-k$; hence, by Lemma $A3$, we will wind up at ℓ_e with $y_1 = (n-k)$.

case c: P_1 is anywhere else, that is in $\{\ell_1, \ldots, \ell_6\}$. Then we will eventually get to ℓ_0 by Lemma $A2$, which is already covered by case *b*.

We proceed with the formal proof. We have

$$1. \quad \models \quad at\,\ell_e \supset [at\,\ell_e \wedge (y_1 = n-k)]$$

by Q_2.

This corresponds to case *a*.

We have

$$2. \quad \models \quad at\,\ell_0 \supset [at\,\ell_0 \wedge (y_1 \geq n-k)]$$

by Q_1.

$$3. \quad \models \quad at\,\ell_0 \supset \Diamond[at\,\ell_e \wedge (y_1 = n-k)]$$

by Lemma $A3$.

This covers case b.

We have

$$4. \models at\,\ell_{1..6} \supset \Diamond\, at\,\ell_0$$

by Lemma $A2$.

$$5. \models at\,\ell_{1..6} \supset \Diamond[at\,\ell_e \wedge (y_1 = n-k)]$$

by 4 and 3.

This covers case c.

Taking the disjunction of 1, 3 and 5 we obtain

$$6. \models \Diamond[at\,\ell_e \wedge (y_1 = n-k)]$$

which establishes the lemma. ∎

We now turn to the termination of P_2.

Lemma B0: $\models [at\,m_2 \wedge (y_2 = u)] \supset \Diamond[at\,m_3 \wedge (y_2 = u)]$

This lemma states that we can never get blocked at m_2.

proof of Lemma B0:

By Lemma $A4$ we are guaranteed that P_1 will eventually get to ℓ_e with $y_1 = n-k$. In the worst case, by the time P_1 gets to ℓ_e, P_2 is still waiting at m_2. But then by Q_1, $y_2 \leq k$ and $y_1 = n-k$ so that $y_1 + y_2 \leq n$ which enables the exit condition and leaves it enabled until P_2 moves. This proof should not be considered as saying that P_2 will indeed wait at m_2 until P_1 terminates, but this approach provides the easiest proof.

Proceeding with more formal proof we have

$$1. \models [at\,m_2 \wedge (y_2 = u)] \supset \{\Box[at\,m_2 \wedge (y_2 = u)] \vee \Diamond[at\,m_3 \wedge (y_2 = u)]\}$$

by the ALT rule at m_2 where ϕ is $y_2 = u$.

$$2. \models \Box[at\,m_2 \wedge (y_2 = u)] \supset \Diamond[at\,m_2 \wedge (y_2 = u) \wedge at\,\ell_e \wedge (y_1 = n-k)]$$

by Lemma $A4$.

$$3. \models [at\,m_2 \wedge (y_2 = u) \wedge at\,\ell_e \wedge (y_1 = n-k)] \supset [at\,m_2 \wedge (y_2 = u) \wedge at\,\ell_e \wedge (y_1 + y_2 \leq n)]$$

using $y_2 \leq k$ given by Q_1.

$$4. \models [at\,m_2 \wedge (y_2 = u) \wedge at\,\ell_e \wedge (y_1 + y_2 \leq n)] \supset \Diamond[at\,m_3 \wedge (y_2 = u)]$$

by ESC at m_2 considering only the exit $m_2 \to m_3$ where ϕ is $(y_2 = u) \wedge at\,\ell_e \wedge (y_1 + y_2 \leq n)$.

$$5. \quad \models \quad \Box[at\,m_2 \wedge (y_2 = u)] \quad \supset \quad \Diamond[at\,m_3 \wedge (y_2 = u)]$$

by 2, 3, and 4.

$$6. \quad \models \quad [at\,m_2 \wedge (y_2 = u)] \quad \supset \quad \Diamond[at\,m_3 \wedge (y_2 = u)]$$

by 1 and 5. ∎

Lemma B1: $\models \quad [at\,m_3 \wedge (y_2 = u)] \quad \supset \quad \Diamond[at\,m_4 \wedge (y_2 = u)]$

This lemma states that P_2 does not get blocked at m_3 but eventually proceeds to m_4 with an unchanged value of y_2.

It is analogous to Lemma $A1$ and has a very similar proof. In that proof we distinguish three cases according to the location of P_1. They are: P_1 at ℓ_4, P_2 in $\{\ell_2, \ell_3\}$, and P_2 elsewhere. Their analysis is identical to that of Lemma $A1$.

Lemma B2: $\models \quad \{[at\,m_1 \wedge (y_2 = u)] \vee [at\,m_{2..7} \wedge (y_2 = u + 1)]\}$
$$\supset \quad \Diamond[at\,m_0 \wedge (y_2 = u + 1)]$$

This lemma states that if we are anywhere in m_1 to m_7 we will eventually return to m_0 with y_2 properly adjusted.

proof of Lemma B2:

$$1. \quad \models \quad [at\,m_{4..7} \wedge (y_2 = u + 1)] \quad \supset \quad \Diamond[at\,m_0 \wedge (y_2 = u + 1)]$$

by the SP rule applied to the path $m_4 \to m_5 \to m_6 \to m_7 \to m_0$ where $\phi_4 = \phi_5 = \phi_6 = \phi_7$ is $y_2 = u + 1$ and ψ is $at\,m_0 \wedge (y_2 = u + 1)$.

$$2. \quad \models \quad [at\,m_3 \wedge (y_2 = u + 1)] \quad \supset \quad \Diamond[at\,m_0 \wedge (y_2 = u + 1)]$$

by Lemma $B1$ and 1.

$$3. \quad \models \quad [at\,m_2 \wedge (y_2 = u + 1)] \quad \supset \quad \Diamond[at\,m_0 \wedge (y_2 = u + 1)]$$

by Lemma $B0$ and 2.

$$4. \quad \models \quad [at\,m_1 \wedge (y_2 = u)] \quad \supset \quad \Diamond[at\,m_2 \wedge (y_2 = u + 1)]$$

by the ESC rule at m_1 where ϕ is $y_2 = u$ and ψ is $at\,m_2 \wedge (y_2 = u + 1)$.

$$5. \quad \models \quad [at\,m_1 \wedge (y_2 = u)] \quad \supset \quad \Diamond[at\,m_0 \wedge (y_2 = u + 1)]$$

by 4 and 3.

By taking the disjunction of 1, 2, 3 and 5 we obtain:

6. $\models \{[at\,m_1 \wedge (y_2 = u)] \vee [at\,m_{2..7} \wedge (y_2 = u+1)]\} \supset \Diamond[at\,m_0 \wedge (y_2 = u+1)]$.

Lemma B3: $\models [at\,m_0 \wedge (y_2 \leq k)] \supset \Diamond[at\,m_e \wedge (y = k)]$

This lemma establishes the termination of P_2 if started at m_0 with $y_2 \leq k$.

proof of Lemma B3:

Similarly to the proof of Lemma *A3* we define the auxiliary assertion

$$E_2(u): \; [at\,m_0 \wedge (y_2 = u)] \supset \Diamond[at\,m_e \wedge (y_2 = k)].$$

The lemma is established by showing that

$$\models (u \leq k) \supset E_2(u).$$

Analogously to A3 this is proven by descending induction on $u \leq k$. We show the two clauses:

$$(a) \; \models \; E_2(k)$$

and

$$(b) \; \models \; [(u < k) \wedge E_2(u+1)] \supset E_2(u).$$

Part a is proved by observing the direct path from m_0 to m_e in the case that $y_2 = k$. Part b is proved by tracing the execution from m_0 with $y_2 = u < k$ to m_1 with $y_2 = u + 1$ and use the induction hypothesis to finally guarantee $at\,m_e \wedge (y_2 = k)$.

The details of the formal proof are very similar to those of *A3*. ∎

Lemma B4: $\models \Diamond\, at\,m_e$

This statement says that regardless of where we are in a properly initialized execution of the program, we eventually wind up at m_e.

proof of Lemma B4:

Similarly to the proof of Lemma *A4* there are three cases to be considered:

case a: P_2 already at m_e.

case b: P_2 currently at m_0. Then we have by Q_1 that $y_2 \leq k$ and hence by Lemma *B3* we will eventually reach m_e.

case c: P_2 is elsewhere. Then we will eventually get to m_0 by Lemma *B2*.

The formal details are similar to those of Lemma $A4$. ∎

proof of theorem:

To conclude the proof of the theorem we observe that:

$$1. \quad \models \ \ell_e \supset \Box at \ell_e$$

by the ALT rule since ℓ_e has no exits.

$$2. \quad \models \ \Diamond \Box at \ell_e$$

by Lemma $A4$ and 1. Similarly,

$$3. \quad \models \ \Diamond \Box at m_e$$

using Lemma $B4$ and the ALT rule at m_e.

A temporal consequence of 2 and 3 is

$$\models \ \Diamond [at \ell_e \wedge at m_e]. \ ∎$$

Acknowledgement

We thankfully acknowledge the help extended to us by Yoni Malachi, Pierre Wolper, Frank Yellin, Joe Weening, and Rivi Zarhi in reading the earlier drafts of the manuscript. Special thanks are due to Evelyn Eldridge-Diaz for TEXing the manuscript.

REFERENCES

[BMP] Ben-Ari, M., Z. Manna and A. Pnueli, "The temporal logic of branching time," Proceedings of the Eighth ACM Symposium on Principles of Programming Languages, Williamsburg, VA, Jan. 1981, pp. 169-176.

[BUR] Burstall, R.M., "Program proving as hand simulation with a little induction," Proc. IFIP Congress, Amsterdam, The Netherlands (1974), North Holland, pp. 308-312.

[CLA] Clarke, E.M., "Synthesis of resource invariants for concurrent programs," ACM Trans. on Programming Languages and Systems, Vol. 2, No. 3 (July 1980), pp. 338-358.

[DIJ] Dijkstra, E.W., "Cooperating sequential processes", in *Programming Languages and Systems* (F. Genvys ed.), Academic Press, New York, NY, 1968, pp. 43–112.

[FRA] Francez, N., "The analysis of cyclic programs," Ph.D. Thesis, Applied Mathematics Dept., The Weizmann Institute of Science, Rehovot, Israel, July 1976.

[KEL] Keller, R.M., "Formal verification of parallel programs," CACM, Vol.19, No. 7 (July 1976), pp. 371-384.

[LAM] Lamport, L., "Proving the correctness of multiprocess programs," IEEE Transactions on Software Engineering, Vol. SE-3, No. 7 (March 1977), pp. 125-143.

[MAN1] Manna, Z., "Logics of programs," Proc. IFIP Congress, Tokyo and Melbourne (October 1980), North Holland, pp. 41-51.

[MAN2] Manna, Z., "Verification of sequential programs: Temporal axiomatization" in *Theoretical Foundations of Programming Methodology* (F.L. Bauer, ed.), NATO Scientific Series, D. Riedel Pub. Co., Dordrecht, Holland, 1981.

[MP1] Manna, Z. and A. Pnueli, "The modal logic of programs," Proc. 6th International Colloquium on Automata, Languages and Programming, Graz, Austria (July 1979). Lecture Notes in Computer Science, Vol. 71, Springer Verlag, pp. 385-409.

[MP2] Manna, Z. and A. Pnueli, "Verification of concurrent programs: The temporal framework," in *The Correctness Problem in Computer Science* (R.S. Boyer and J S. Moore, eds.), International Lecture Series in Computer Science, Academic Press, London, 1981.

[MW] Manna, Z. and R. Waldinger, "Is 'sometime' sometimes better than 'Always'?: Intermittent assertions in proving program correctness," CACM, Vol. 21, No. 2, pp. 159-172 (February 1978), pp. 159-172.

[OG] Owicki, S. and D. Gries, "An axiomatic proof technique for parallel programs," Acta Informatica, Vol. 6 (1976), pp. 319-340.

[OL] Owicki, S. and L. Lamport, "Proving liveness properties of concurrent programs," unpublished report (october 1980).

[PNU1] Pnueli, A., "The temporal logic of programs," Proc. 18th FOCS, Providence, RI (November 1977), pp. 46-57.

[PNU2] Pnueli, A., "The temporal semantics of concurrent programs," Proc. Symposium on Semantics of Concurrent Computations, Evian, France (July 1979), Lecture Notes in Computer Science,Vol. 70, Springer Verlag, pp. 1-20.

SYNTHESIS OF COMMUNICATING PROCESSES FROM TEMPORAL LOGIC SPECIFICATIONS

Zohar Manna
Computer Science Department
Stanford University
Stanford, CA
and
Applied Mathematics Department
The Weizmann Institute
Rehovot, Israel

Pierre Wolper
Computer Science Department
Stanford University
Stanford, CA

Abstract: In this paper, we apply Propositional Temporal Logic (PTL) to the specification and synthesis of the synchronization part of communicating processes. To specify a process, we give a PTL formula that describes its sequence of communications. The synthesis is done by constructing a model of the given specifications using a tableau-like satisfiability algorithm for PTL. This model can then be interpreted as a program.

1. Introduction

Most concurrent programs can easily be separated into two parts: a *synchronization* part that enforces the necessary constraints on the relative timing of the execution of the different processes and a *functional* part that actually manipulates the data and performs the computation required of the program. For example, the part of a concurrent program that ensures mutual exclusion between sections of code is in the "synchronization part" of that program whereas the code that is made mutually exclusive is in the "functional part".

The synchronization part of a concurrent program is rarely deep, but it is nevertheless frequently complicated. That is, writing it requires a lot of attention to intricate details but does not require insight into a variety of underlying mathematical theories. These characteristics make the development of tools for specifying and automatically synthesizing synchronization code a highly desirable and yet manageable task.

In this paper, we propose to use Propositional Temporal Logic (PTL) as a specification language for the synchronization part of CSP-like programs and we present a corresponding synthesis algorithm based on the decision procedure for PTL.

This research was supported in part by the National Science Foundation under grant MCS80-06930, by the Office of Naval Research under Contract N00014-76-C-0687, by the United States Air Force Office of Scientific Research under Grant AFSOR-81-0014 and by an IBM Predoctoral Fellowship.

CSP, the language of Communicating Sequential Processes, was developed by Hoare [Ho78] as a tool for describing distributed processes. It views distributed processes as interacting exclusively through well defined inter-process input/output (I/O) operations. This makes it quite easy to separate the "synchronization part" of a CSP program from its "functional part". Indeed, the "synchronization part" can be viewed as the program abstracted to its I/O operations. To describe the synchronization part of a CSP program it is then usually sufficient to give the temporal relations that have to exist between the execution of specific I/O operations.

Propositional Temporal Logic ([Pr67], [RU71]) is especially well suited for this task. Indeed, it is an extension of classical propositional logic geared towards the description of *sequences*. Moreover, PTL is decidable and has the finite model property. That is, given a PTL formula it is decidable if that formula is satisfiable, and if it is satisfiable, it has a finite model. This will be the basis of our synthesis method. Indeed, given specifications in PTL, we will use a tableau-like method ([Sm68], [BMP81]) to test for satisfiability and construct a model of the specifying formula. We then extract from that model the synchronization part of a CSP-like program.

2. The CSP Framework

The framework in which we specify and synthesize synchronization problems is that of Hoare's language of Communicating Sequential Processes (CSP) [Ho78]. A program in that language is a collection of (possibly nondeterministic) sequential processes each of which can include inter-process I/O operations. These I/O operations are the only interaction between the processes. Syntactically, an inter-process I/O operation names the source (input) or destination (output) process and gives the information to be transmitted. In Hoare's notation, the operation "output s to process P" is written

$$P!s$$

and the operation "input s from process P" is

$$P?s$$

Semantically, when a process reaches an input (output) operation, it waits for the corresponding process to reach the matching output (input) operation. At that point, the operation is performed and both processes resume their execution. There is no queuing or buffering of messages.

We will use CSP with the following modifications:

a) We consider systems of non-terminating processes. Terminating processes can be accomodated if they are considered to end with a dummy I/O operation that is repeated forever.

b) As we are interested in pure synchronization problems, we will assume that the only information exchanged between processes is a finite set of signals s_i.

c) We assume that when several I/O operations are possible, the one to be executed is chosen fairly. More specifically, we assume that if an I/O operation is infinitely often enabled (both sender and receiver are ready to perform it) it will eventually be executed.

We will specify systems of processes where one process, the synchronizer S, communicates with a set of other processes P_i, $1 \leq i \leq n$.

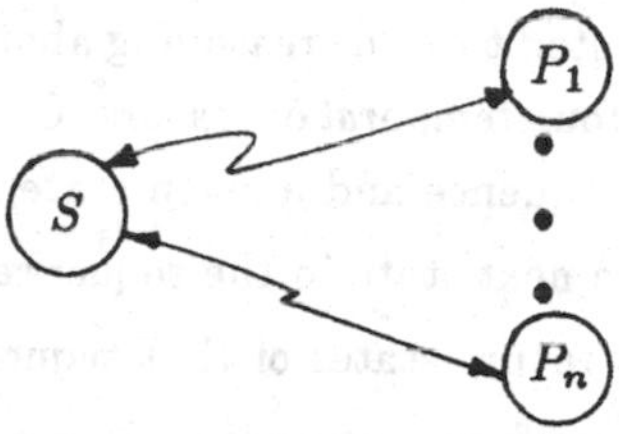

Thus, the only communications taking place are between the synchronizer S and each of the processes P_i.

To specify the synchronization part of such a system, we will look at the infinite *sequence* of I/O operations executed by each of the processes (S and P_i's) that we assume to be non-terminating.

Example: Consider the following system:

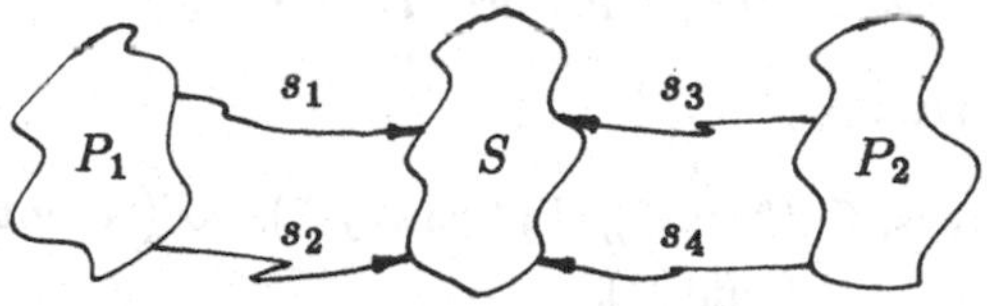

where S receives signals s_1 and s_2 from P_1 and signals s_3 and s_4 from P_2. The sequence of I/O operations executed by S will be some interleaving of the four operations $P_1?s_1$, $P_1?s_2$, $P_2?s_3$, $P_2?s_4$. For instance it could be

$$P_1?s_1 \quad P_2?s_4 \quad P_2?s_3 \quad P_1?s_1 \quad . \; . \; .$$

Similarly, the sequence of I/O operations executed by P_1 will be some interleaving of $S!s_1$, $S!s_2$. ∎

The specifications will, for each process independently, characterize those sequences of I/O operations that are acceptable. The synthesis algorithm will then generate a program that when executed generates a sequence of I/O operations satisfying the specifications.

3. The Specification Language

As a specification language, we use Propositional Temporal Logic (PTL). Temporal Logic was initially developed as a branch of philosophical logic dealing with the nature of time and of temporal concepts ([Pr67], [RU71]). Recently it has been adapted to the task of reasoning about the execution sequences of programs and was found especially useful in proving properties of concurrent programs ([Pn77], [MP81]). Here, we use Temporal Logic in a similar framework; the specific formal PTL system we use is a variant of the one appearing in [GPSS80].

Intuitively, PTL is a logic oriented towards reasoning about sequences. It is a classical propositional logic extended with four *temporal* operators: $\bigcirc$, $\Diamond$, $\Box$ and U; the first three are unary, the last binary. For a sequence and a given state in that sequence,

$\bigcirc f$ is true iff f is true in the next state in the sequence;

$\Box f$ is true iff f is true in all future states of that sequence;

$\Diamond f$ is true iff f is true in some future state (i.e., it is eventually true); and

$f_1 \, U \, f_2$ is true iff f_1 is true for all states until the first state where f_2 is true.

More formally, PTL has the following syntax and semantics:

Syntax:

PTL *formulas* are built from

- A set $\mathcal{P}$ of atomic propositions: $p_1, \; p_2, \; p_3, \ldots$
- Boolean connectives: $\wedge$, $\neg$.
- Temporal operators: $\bigcirc$ ("next"), $\Box$ ("always"), $\Diamond$ ("eventually"), U ("until").

The formation rules are:

- An atomic proposition $p \in \mathcal{P}$ is a formula.
- If f_1 and f_2 are formulas, so are
$$f_1 \wedge f_2, \;\; \neg f_1, \;\; \bigcirc f_1, \;\; \Box f_1, \;\; \Diamond f_1, \;\; f_1 \, U \, f_2.$$

We will also use $\vee$ and $\supset$ as the usual abreviations.

Semantics:

A *structure* for a PTL formula (with set $\mathcal{P}$ of atómic propositions) is a triple $\mathcal{A} = (S, N, \pi)$ where

- S is an enumerable set of states.

• N: $(S \to S)$ is an accessibility function that for each state gives a unique next state.

• π: $(S \to 2^P)$ assigns truth values to the atomic propositions of the language in each state.

For a structure $\mathcal{A}$ and a state $s \in S$ we have

$$\langle \mathcal{A}, s\rangle \models p \quad \text{iff} \quad p \in \pi(s)$$

$$\langle \mathcal{A}, s\rangle \models f_1 \wedge f_2 \quad \text{iff} \quad \langle \mathcal{A}, s\rangle \models f_1 \text{ and } \langle \mathcal{A}, s\rangle \models f_2$$

$$\langle \mathcal{A}, s\rangle \models \neg f \quad \text{iff} \quad \text{not } \langle \mathcal{A}, s\rangle \models f$$

$$\langle \mathcal{A}, s\rangle \models \bigcirc f \quad \text{iff} \quad \langle \mathcal{A}, N(s)\rangle \models f$$

In the following definitions, we denote by $N^i(s)$ the ith state in the sequence

$$s,\ N(s),\ N(N(s)),\ N(N(N(s))),\ \ldots$$

of successsors of a state s.

$$\langle \mathcal{A}, s\rangle \models \Box f \quad \text{iff} \quad (\forall i \geq 0)(\langle \mathcal{A}, N^i(s)\rangle \models f)$$

$$\langle \mathcal{A}, s\rangle \models \Diamond f \quad \text{iff} \quad (\exists i \geq 0)(\langle \mathcal{A}, N^i(s)\rangle \models f)$$

$$\begin{aligned}\langle \mathcal{A}, s\rangle \models f_1\, U\, f_2 \quad \text{iff} \quad & (\forall i \geq 0)(\langle \mathcal{A}, N^i(s)\rangle \models f_1) \text{ or} \\ & (\exists i \geq 0)(\langle \mathcal{A}, N^i(s)\rangle \models f_2 \wedge \\ & \qquad \forall j(0 \leq j < i \supset \langle \mathcal{A}, N^j(s)\rangle \models f_1))\end{aligned}$$

An *interpretation* $I = \langle \mathcal{A}, s_0\rangle$ for PTL consists of a structure $\mathcal{A}$ and an initial state $s_0 \in S$. We will say that an interpretation $I = \langle \mathcal{A}, s_0\rangle$ *satisfies* a formula f iff $\langle \mathcal{A}, s_0\rangle \models f$. Since an interpretation I uniquely determines a sequence

$$\sigma = s_0,\ N(s_0),\ N^2(s_0),\ N^3(s_0),\ \ldots$$

we will often say "the sequence σ satisfies a formula" instead of "the interpretation I satisfies a formula".

Note: The temporal operators we have defined differ from those in [GPSS80] in the following way:

• They are reflexive. That is, a state is included in its own sequence of successors.

• The Until operator does not have an "eventuality component". That is, according to our definitions, $f_1\, U\, f_2$ does not imply $\Diamond f_2$.

Our purpose in using PTL is to describe processes by specifying their allowable sequences of I/O operations. To do this, we consider PTL formulas where the atomic propositions stand for I/O operations. And, to reflect the fact that we are looking at sequences where only one I/O operation occurs at a time, we systematically add to our specifications for each process the following *single event condition*:

$$\Box\Big(\big(\bigvee_{1\le i\le n} p_i\big) \wedge \big(\bigwedge_{1\le i<j\le n} \neg(p_i \wedge p_j)\big)\Big) \tag{3.1}$$

where $p_1, \ldots, p_n$ are all the atomic propositions (I/O operations) appearing in the specifications of that process. In other words, a state of our temporal logic corresponds to the execution of exactly one I/O operation (the atomic proposition true in that state) and the "next" state corresponds to the execution of the next I/O operation.

Example:

For a process P that sends signals s_1 and s_2 to a process S,

$S!s_1$

specifies that all its sequences of I/O operations start with $S!s_1$. And,

$\Box(S!s_1 \supset \bigcirc\, S!s_2)$

specifies that $S!s_1$ is always immediately followed by $S!s_2$, with no other I/O operation being performed by P in between.

4. Examples of Specifications

Let us first recall that when we give the specifications for a synchronization problem, we independently give the specifications for each of the processes involved (the synchronizer S and synchronized processes P_i). That means that for each process we give a PTL formula that, in conjunction with the single event condition (3.1), has to be satisfied by the sequences of I/O operations executed by *that* process. Thus, for instance, $\bigcirc$ means "next" in the particular process we are specifying.

Example 1: Mutual Exclusion

Suppose we have two processes, P_1 and P_2, that communicate with a synchronizer S. The signals sent to the synchronizer by P_i ($i = 1,2$) are $S!begin_i$ (begin critical section) and $S!end_i$ (end critical section). The synchronizer should ensure that processes P_1 and P_2 are never simultaneously in their respective critical sections that start with $S!begin_i$ and end with $S!end_i$. What the specifications for a process P_i should say is that P_i alternately sends $begin_i$ and end_i signals, starting with a $begin_i$. This is expressed by the conjunction of the following formulas:

$S!begin_i$

(the first signal sent is *begin critical section*)

$$\Box(S!begin_i \supset \bigcirc\, S!end_i)$$

(after a *begin critical section* signal, the next signal sent is *end critical section*)

$$\Box(S!end_i \supset \bigcirc\, S!begin_i)$$

(after an *end critical section* signal, the next signal sent is *begin critical section*).

The specifications for the synchronizer are:

$$\Box(P_1?begin_1 \supset ((\neg P_2?begin_2)\ U (P_1?end_1)))$$

(after letting P_1 proceed into its critical section by accepting a $begin_1$ signal, do not let P_2 enter its own critical section until P_1 has finished)

$$\Box(P_2?begin_2 \supset ((\neg P_1?begin_1)\ U (P_2?end_2)))$$

(after letting P_2 proceed into its critical section by accepting a $begin_2$ signal, do not let P_1 enter its own critical section until P_2 has finished).

One would expect that it is also necessary to specify absence of starvation:

$$\Box(\Diamond\, P_1?begin_1 \vee \Diamond\, P_1?end_1)$$

(do not neglect P_1 indefinitely)

$$\Box(\Diamond\, P_2?begin_2 \vee \Diamond\, P_1?end_2)$$

(do not neglect P_2 indefinitely). But as we will see later, in section 6, we do not have to write these conditions explicitly since they will always be systematically introduced during the synthesis. ∎

Example 2: Dining Philosophers

We specify the classical dining philosophers problem for three philosophers. Three philosophers are sitting at a round table in a Chinese restaurant alternatively thinking and eating. Between two philosophers there is only one chop stick and a philosopher needs to pick up both the chop stick at his left and the one at his right before he can eat.

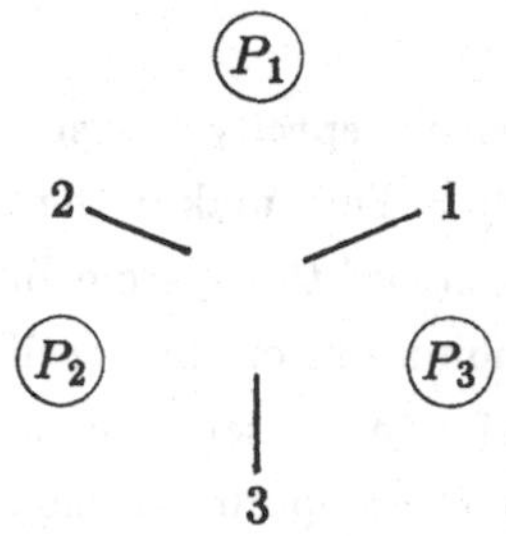

The problem is to synchronize the eating of the philosophers. We have a process P_i per philosopher and a synchronizer (or "chop sticks" process) S. Each philosopher P_i communicates with the synchronizer S by four operations:

$S!pick_i$	pick up chop stick i
$S!pick_{i\oplus 1}$	pick up chop stick $i \oplus 1$
$S!put_{i\oplus 1}$	put down chop stick $i \oplus 1$
$S!put_i$	put down chop stick i

($\oplus$ designates addition modulo 3; we will also use $\ominus$ for subtraction modulo 3).

The specifications for each philosopher P_i, $i = 1, 2, 3$ are:

$$S!pick_i$$

(the first signal sent is $pick_i$)

$$\Box(S!pick_i \supset \bigcirc\, S!pick_{i\oplus 1})$$

$$\Box(S!pick_{i\oplus 1} \supset \bigcirc\, S!put_{i\oplus 1})$$

$$\Box(S!put_{i\oplus 1} \supset \bigcirc\, S!put_i)$$

$$\Box(S!put_i \supset \bigcirc\, S!pick_i)$$

Again, these specifications say that each philosopher repeatedly picks up one chop stick, picks up the second, puts the second chop stick down and puts the first chop stick down.

The specifications for the synchronizer are

$$\Box(P_i?pick_i \supset ((\neg P_{i\ominus 1}?pick_i)\ U (P_i?put_i)))$$

$$\Box(P_i?pick_{i\oplus 1} \supset ((\neg P_{i\oplus 1}?pick_{i\oplus 1})\ U (P_i?put_{i\oplus 1})))$$

for $i = 1, 2, 3$. These essentially say that a chop stick cannot be picked up by two philosophers simultaneously.

5. Overview of the Synthesis

As described in Section 3, when we specify a system of processes, we specify each of the processes involved separately. This makes the specification task much easier. However, to deal with some properties of the system like absence of deadlock or starvation, we have to look at the combination of the specifications of all the processes involved. But, as the specifications refer to the sequence of I/O operations of each process separately, we first have to modify these specifications so that they refer to the global sequence of I/O operations, that is the merge of the sequences of I/O operations of the individual processes.

Thus, the first step of our synthesis is the *relativization procedure* that takes the specifications of each process (the *local specifications*) and transforms them into specifications for the global system of processes (the *global specifications*). After the relativization, we proceed to do the synthesis with the global specifications of the system of processes.

The second step is then to apply a tableau-like satisfiability algorithm for PTL to these global specifications. The tableau decision procedure we use is essentially the one described in [BMP81] restricted to linear time and modified to use our assumption that exactly one atomic proposition is true in each state.

The decision procedure can have two possible outcomes: either it declares that the specifications are unsatisfiable and in that case it means that there is no program that can satisfy the synchronization problem as specified. Or, it produces a *model graph* from which all possible models of the specifications can be extracted.

This model graph could almost be transformed into the programs we are synthesizing except for the fact that there could be some paths in the graph that never satisfy some eventualities (properties of the form $\Diamond f$). In other words, though all models of the specifications can be generated from that graph, not all paths generated by the graph are models of the specifications. Our next step will thus be to unwind the graph to obtain an actual model of the specifications. Unfortunately, this unwinding usually gives a graph that, though it generates only models of the specifications, generates only one or a few of the possible models. In programming terms, this means that our processes will be restricted to only a few of the possible execution sequences satisfying the specifications, which clearly is undesirable.

In the special case where the eventualities are "non temporal" (*i.e.*, of the form $\Diamond f$ where f does not contain temporal operators) we are able to avoid unwinding by relying on our fairness hypothesis on the execution of CSP programs. We then synthesize our programs from a model graph that not only generates only models of the specifications (given the fairness hypothesis) but also can generate all possible models.

The final step in the synthesis will be to extract the processes from the model graph. This is rather straightforward as the model graph itself can be viewed as the synchronizer process and the other processes can be obtained as restrictions of that graph.

In summary, the steps of our synthesis will be

1) relativize the specifications (to obtain the global specifications).

2) apply the satisfiability algorithm (to obtain the model graph).

3) unwind if necessary (to satisfy eventualities).

4) generate the individual processes.

6. Relativization

Our purpose here is to take the local specifications of the processes and transform them into global specifications for the sequence of I/O operations executed by the whole system of processes. At first glance it might seem that the global specifications would simply be the conjunction of the specifications of all the processes involved. However before taking that conjunction there are three problems that have to be dealt with:

(1) At the global level, the sending and receiving of a given message is a single action. Thus, we have to make explicit the correspondence between pairs of matching I/O operations; that is, pairs of operations consisting of an output operation that sends a given message (*e.g.* $S!s$ appearing in P_i) and the corresponding operation that receives that message(*e.g.* $P_i?s$ appearing in S).

(2) The local specifications for a process describe its sequence of I/O operations. But, that sequence is only a subsequence of the global sequence of I/O operations. The local specifications have to be modified to reflect this fact. *Note:* we are reasoning under our assumption that only one I/O operation happens at a time (locally and globally).

(3) The subsequence of the global sequence corresponding to each process is infinite. This has to be made explicit in the global specifications.

These considerations lead us to the following three steps of our relativization procedure.

(1) Rename matching I/O operations to a unique new appellation. For example we would, in our preceeding example, rename $S!begin_1$ and $P_1?begin_1$ to $begin_1$..

(2) Define inP_i to be $p_1 \vee \ldots \vee p_n$ where $p_1, \ldots, p_n$ are the I/O operations appearing in P_i. Then, to refelect the fact that the specifications for P_i concern a subsequence of the global sequence, we transform these specifications using the two following rules:

$$p \rightarrow (\neg inP_i \; U \; p) \tag{6.1}$$

where p is an atomic proposition, and

$$\bigcirc f \rightarrow (\neg inP_i \; U (inP_i \wedge \bigcirc f)) \tag{6.2}$$

That is, the right-hand side of (6.1) is substituted for all the atomic propositions in the specifications of P_i and the right-hand side of (6.2) for all occurences of $\bigcirc$.

Note: in our specific framework, all I/O operations occur between the synchronizer S and some other process P_i. Thus for the synchronizer $inS = true$ and its specifications need not be modified.

(3) For each process P_i we add the following *infinite subsequence requirement.*

$$\Box \Diamond (inP_i) \tag{6.3}$$

That is, some operation of process P_i has to occur infinitely often in the global sequence.

The global specifications are then the conjunction of the specification for the synchronizer, the specification for the processes P_i modified using (6.1) and (6.2) and the requirements (6.3).

The only non-trivial step is step (2). Let us call the local specifications for a process P_i transformed by using rules (6.1) and (6.2) the *modified specifications* for P_i. We have the following result:

Proposition 6.1: A sequence satisfies the modified specifications for P_i if and only if its subsequence consisting of all the I/O operations of P_i satisfies the original specifications for P_i.

The proposition can be easily proved by induction on the structure of the specifications for P_i.

Before we give an example, let us first note that for a formula relative to a process P_i that is of the form

$$\Box(p \supset \bigcirc q)$$

(*i.e.*, if p then q in the next state) the relativized version is

$$\Box((\neg inP_i \; U \; p) \supset (\neg inP_i \; U (inP_i \wedge \bigcirc(\neg inP_i \; U \; q))))$$

This can be simplified, using PTL equivalences to

$$\Box(p \supset \bigcirc(\neg inP_i \; U \; q))$$

(*i.e.*, if p then, from the next state on, we are not in P_i until q).

Example: Mutual exclusion problem

Let us recall that the specifications for the mutual exclusion problem are:

For the processes P_i, $i = 1, 2$:

$S!begin_i$

$$\Box(S!begin_i \supset \bigcirc\, S!end_i)$$

$$\Box(S!end_i \supset \bigcirc\, S!begin_i)$$

For the synchronizer S:

$$\Box(P_1?begin_1 \supset ((\neg P_2?begin_2)\; U(P_1?end_1)))$$

$$\Box(P_2?begin_2 \supset ((\neg P_1?begin_1)\; U(P_2?end_2)))$$

Then, if

$$inP_1 \equiv begin_1 \vee end_1$$

$$inP_2 \equiv begin_2 \vee end_2,$$

the global specifications for the mutual exclusion problem are:

From the specifications of P_1:

$$\neg inP_1\; U\; begin_1$$

$$\Box(begin_1 \supset \bigcirc(\neg inP_1\; U\; end_1))$$

$$\Box(end_1 \supset \bigcirc(\neg inP_1\; U\; begin_1))$$

From the specifications of P_2:

$$\neg inP_2\; U\; begin_2$$

$$\Box(begin_2 \supset \bigcirc(\neg inP_2\; U\; end_2))$$

$$\Box(end_2 \supset \bigcirc(\neg inP_2\; U\; begin_2))$$

From the specifications of S:

$$\Box(begin_1 \supset \neg begin_2\; U\; end_1)$$

$$\Box(begin_2 \supset \neg begin_1\; U\; end_2)$$

The infinite subsequence requirements:

$$\Box \Diamond\, inP_1$$

$$\Box \Diamond\, inP_2$$

Remark: The relativization procedure can be viewed as a semantic rule for the execution in parallel of communicating processes. Indeed, if we view the meaning of a communicating process as its possible sequences of I/O operations as described by a PTL formula, then the relativization procedure gives the meaning of the concurrent execution of the processes.

7. The Satisfiability Algorithm

In this section we will describe the tableau method we use to test for satisfiability and construct a model of the global specifications. We will first briefly review the tableau method for propositional calculus, then indicate how it can be extended to handle temporal logic and finally give in detail the exact algorithm we have developed for our specific purpose.

A set of formulas $\{f_1, \ldots, f_n\}$ is satisfiable if there is an interpretation that simultaneously satisfies all the formulas in that set. The tableau method for propositional calculus is based on the following relations between satisfiablility of sets of formulas:

T1: A set of formulas $\{f_1, \ldots, f_{i_1} \wedge f_{i_2}, \ldots, f_n\}$ is satisfiable if and only if the set of formulas $\{f_1, \ldots, f_{i_1}, f_{i_2}, \ldots, f_n\}$ is satisfiable

T2: A set of formulas $\{f_1, \ldots, \neg(f_{i_1} \wedge f_{i_2}), \ldots, f_n\}$ is satisfiable if and only if the set $\{f_1, \ldots, \neg f_{i_1}, \ldots, f_n\}$ or the set $\{f_1, \ldots, \neg f_{i_2}, \ldots, f_n\}$ is satisfiable

T3: A set of formulas $\{f_1, \ldots, \neg\neg f_i, \ldots, f_n\}$ is 'satisfiable if and only if the set $\{f_1, \ldots, f_i, \ldots, f_n\}$ is satisfiable

To test a formula f for satisfiability, one thus starts with the singleton $\{f\}$ and uses rules T1–T3 to decompose f into sets of its subformulas. If the decomposition is carried on until the sets contain only atomic formulas (atomic propositions or their negation), satisfiability can easily be decided. Indeed, a set of atomic formulas is satisfiable if and only if it does not contain a proposition and its negation. This procedure actually corresponds to transforming the formula into disjunctive normal form. An extensive study of tableau methods for propositional and predicate calculus appears in [Sm68].

For PTL we also have to deal with the temporal operators. This can be done with the following three identities

$$\Box f \equiv f \wedge \bigcirc \Box f \tag{7.1}$$

$$\Diamond f \equiv f \vee \bigcirc \Diamond f \tag{7.2}$$

$$f_1 U f_2 \equiv f_2 \vee (f_1 \wedge \bigcirc(f_1 U f_2)) \tag{7.3}$$

These identities will enable us to decompose a formula into sets containing atomic formulas (atomic propositions and their negation) and PTL O-formulas (formulas having O as their main connective). The achievement of such a decomposition is to separate the requirements expressed by the formula into a requirement on the "current state" (the atomic formulas) and into a requirement on "the rest of the sequence" (the O-formulas). One then checks that the set of formulas concerning the "current state" is satisfiable and then repeats the whole process with the O-formulas, after having removed their outermost O operator. In other words, one tests for satisfiability by trying to build a model state by state. As all the formulas appearing in the process are subformulas of the initial formula, one will eventually reach a state that has already occurred, thus the process terminates.

There is, however, at that point one more step to do. The identity (7.2) allows us to satisfy $\Diamond f$ by always postponing it ($\bigcirc \Diamond f$). Thus, before declaring a formula satisfiable, we have to check that all the formulas of the form $\Diamond f$ can be effectively satisfied; that is, that there is a possible future state in which f is true.

Let us now describe our algorithm in more detail. The central part of the algorithm is the *decomposition procedure* that separates the requirements expressed by a set of formulas S into requirements on the "current state" and on the "rest of the sequence". In that procedure, we use our assumption that exactly one atomic proposition is true in each state. That assumption makes it much more efficient to check all possible assignments of truth values to the atomic propositions in the current state (the number of such assignments is the same as the number of atomic propositions in the language) than to brutally apply the decomposition to a set of formulas including the single event condition (3.1). Indeed, the latter could lead to examining a number of cases that is exponential in the number of atomic propositions, but that would eventualy be restricted to a linear number.

To do this, we decompose the set of formulas S separately for each atomic proposition in the language. That is, for each proposition p, we decompose the set of formulas under the assumption that p is true and the other atomic propositions false. The decomposition procedure thus takes as inputs a set of PTL formulas S and a proposition p. It outputs a set Σ_p of sets S_i of formulas f_{ij}, *i.e.* $\Sigma_p = \{S_i\}$ where each $S_i = \{f_{ij}\}$. Each formula $f_{ij} \in S_i$ either is a O-formula or is "marked", *i.e.* it is a formula that already has been used in the decomposition and is only kept for reference. Under the assumption that p is true, the original set of formulas S is satisfiable if and only if, for some i, all the unmarked formulas in S_i are satisfiable. In other words, the O-formulas in each set S_i give one of the possible requirements on the "rest of the sequence" if p is the proposition true in the current state.

The decomposition procedure initializes Σ_p with the set of sets of formulas $\{S\}$ and then repeatedly transforms it until all the elements S_i of Σ_p contain only marked formulas or O-formulas. It is the following:

(1) (Initialize): start with $\Sigma_p = \{S\}$.

(2) (Expand): repeat steps (3)–(5) until for all $S_i \in \Sigma_p$, all the formulas $f_{ij} \in S_i$ are marked formulas or O-formulas.

(3) Pick a formula $f_{ij} \in S_i \in \Sigma_p$ that is not marked and not a $\bigcirc$-formula.

(4)(Simplify): In the formula f_{ij}, replace all the occurrences of p that are not in the scope of a temporal operator by *true* and all similar occurrences of the other atomic propositions by *false*. Perform boolean simplification. This yields a formula f'_{ij}, called "f_{ij} simplified for p".

(5) (a) if $f'_{ij} \equiv true$ replace S_i by $S_i - \{f_{ij}\}$. Given that p is true, f_{ij} is identically true and can thus be removed from S_i.

(b) if $f'_{ij} \equiv false$ replace Σ_p by $\Sigma_p - \{S_i\}$. In this case, f_{ij} is false and the set S_i is unsatisfiable. It can thus be removed.

(c) if f'_{ij} is a $\bigcirc$-formula, replace S_i by $(S_i - \{f_{ij}\}) \cup \{f'_{ij}\}$. As we have obtained a $\bigcirc$-formula, no more decomposition is necessary.

(d) if f'_{ij} is of type α (see table below), replace S_i by

$$(S_i - \{f_{ij}\}) \cup \{f'_{ij}*, \alpha_1, \alpha_2\}$$

where $f'_{ij}*$ is f'_{ij} marked. Since a formula of type α is satisfiable iff both α_1 and α_2 are satisfiable, we replace f_{ij} by α_1 and α_2. We also keep a record of f'_{ij} by marking it.

(e) if f'_{ij} is of type β (see table below), replace S_i by the two following sets:

$$(S_i - \{f_{ij}\}) \cup \{f'_{ij}*, \beta_1\}, \quad (S_i - \{f_{ij}\}) \cup \{f'_{ij}*, \beta_2\}$$

where $f'_{ij}*$ is f'_{ij} marked. Since a formula of type β is satisfiable iff either β_1 or β_2 are satisfiable, we replace S_i by two sets: one containing β_1 and one containing β_2.

The formulas of type α and β are given in the following two tables. Notice the correspondence between the entries in the tables concerning temporal operators and the identities (7.1)–(7.3).

α	α_1	α_2
$f_1 \wedge f_2$	f_1	f_2
$\neg\neg f_1$	f_1	f_1
$\neg \bigcirc f_1$	$\bigcirc \neg f_1$	$\bigcirc \neg f_1$
$\Box f_1$	f_1	$\bigcirc \Box f_1$
$\neg(f_1 \; U \; f_2)$	$\neg f_2$	$\neg f_1 \vee \bigcirc \neg(f_1 \; U \; f_2)$
$\neg \Diamond f_1$	$\neg f_1$	$\bigcirc \neg \Diamond f_1$

β	β_1	β_2
$\neg(f_1 \wedge f_2)$	$\neg f_1$	$\neg f_2$
$\Diamond f_1$	f_1	$\bigcirc \Diamond f_1$
$(f_1\, U\, f_2)$	f_2	$f_1 \wedge \bigcirc(f_1\, U\, f_2)$
$\neg \Box f_1$	$\neg f_1$	$\bigcirc \neg \Box f_1$

Example: Let us apply the decomposition procedure for q to the set of formulas

$$S = \{\Box(q \supset \neg(p\, U\, r))\}$$

Σ_q first gets initialized to

$$\Sigma_q = \{\{\Box(q \supset (\neg p\, U\, r))\}\}$$

At that point, the only formula we can choose in step (3) is $\Box(q \supset (\neg p\, U\, r))$. As all its atomic propositions occur within the scope of a temporal opeartor ($\Box$), step (4) does not modify it. Step (5d) splits $\Box(q \supset (\neg p\, U\, r))$ into $q \supset (\neg p\, U\, r)$ and $\bigcirc\Box(q \supset (\neg p\, U\, r))$, therefore, we get

$$\Sigma_q = \{\{q \supset (\neg p\, U\, r),\quad \bigcirc\Box(q \supset (\neg p\, U\, r)),\quad \Box(q \supset (\neg p\, U\, r))*\}\}.$$

Step (3) then chooses $q \supset (\neg p\, U\, r)$ which is simplified by step (4), after replacing q by *true*, to $(\neg p\, U\, r)$. This is a formula of type β, we thus split the set that contains it into two sets: one containing r and the other containing $\neg p \wedge \bigcirc(\neg p\, U\, r)$.

$$\begin{aligned}\Sigma_q = \{&\{r,\quad (\neg p\, U\, r)*,\quad \bigcirc\Box(q \supset (\neg p\, U\, r)),\quad \Box(q \supset (\neg p\, U\, r))*\},\\ &\{\neg p \wedge \bigcirc(\neg p\, U\, r),\quad (\neg p\, U\, r)*,\quad \bigcirc\Box(q \supset (\neg p\, U\, r)),\quad \Box(q \supset (\neg p\, U\, r))*\}\}.\end{aligned}$$

Then, as r simplified for q is false, by (5b) the first set is removed and we get

$$\Sigma_q = \{\{\neg p \wedge \bigcirc(\neg p\, U\, r),\quad (\neg p\, U\, r)*,\quad \bigcirc\Box(q \supset (\neg p\, U\, r)),\quad \Box(q \supset (\neg p\, U\, r))*\}\}.$$

And, finally, as $\neg p \wedge \bigcirc(\neg p\, U\, r)$ simplified for q is $\bigcirc(\neg p\, U\, r)$ (p is replaced by *false*), we get by (5c)

$$\Sigma_q = \{\{\bigcirc(\neg p\, U\, r),\quad (\neg p\, U\, r)*,\quad \bigcirc\Box(q \supset (\neg p\, U\, r)),\quad \Box(q \supset (\neg p\, U\, r))*\}\}.$$

∎

We can now proceed to describe the *satisfiability algorithm*. This algorithm uses the decomposition procedure to build a *model graph* that is a search for all potential models of the formula. From that graph, we will be able to decide satisfiability and to construct a model. Each node and edge in the graph is labeled with a set of formulas. The sets of formulas labeling an edge always contain exactly one of the atomic propositions of the language. The edges of the graph will correspond to the "states" of the interpretation of PTL.

The graph is constructed as follows:

(1) Start with a graph containing just one node labeled by a set S containing the formulas f_i to be tested (the *initial formulas*), *i.e.* $S = \{f_i\}$.

(2) Repeatedly apply step (3) to the nodes of the graph until it has been applied to all nodes.

(3) For every atomic proposition p in the language:

   (a) Apply the decomposition procedure for p to the set S of formulas labeling the current node.

   (b) For each set S_i in the set Σ_p generated by the decomposition procedure, create an edge labeled by $\{p\} \cup S_i$ leading to a node labeled by the set of all formulas f such that $\bigcirc f \in S_i$ or to a node that can be determined to be labeled by an equivalent set of formulas. If there is no such node, create one.

Example 1: For the formula

$$f_0 = \Box(q \supset (\neg p \; U \; r)),$$

the graph is:

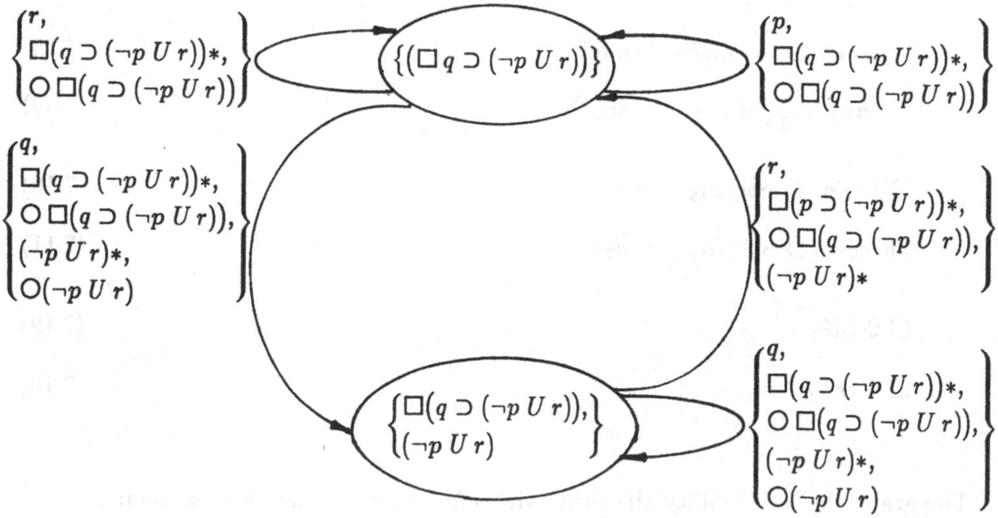

This graph was constructed by starting with a node labeled by $\{\Box(q \supset (\neg p\ U\ r))\}$. Then, applying the decomposition procedure for q to that set of formulas we obtain, as described previously

$$\Sigma_q = \{\{\bigcirc(\neg p\ U\ r),\quad (\neg p\ U\ r)*,\quad \bigcirc\Box(q \supset (\neg p\ U\ r)),\quad \Box(q \supset (\neg p\ U\ r))*\}\}.$$

Thus we create an edge labeled by

$$\{q,\quad \bigcirc(\neg p\ U\ r),\quad (\neg p\ U\ r)*,\quad \bigcirc\Box(q \supset (\neg p\ U\ r)),\quad \Box(q \supset (\neg p\ U\ r))*\}.$$

Since this set contains two $\bigcirc$-formulas ($\bigcirc(\neg p\ U\ r)$ and $\bigcirc\Box(q \supset (\neg p\ U\ r))$), the edge leads to a node labeled by

$$\{(\neg p\ U\ r),\quad \Box(q \supset (\neg p\ U\ r))\}.$$

The other edges are constructed similarly. ∎

Example 2: Mutual exclusion problem.

Let us recall that the global specifications for the mutual exclusion problem are:

$$\neg inP_1\ U\ begin_1 \tag{7.4}$$

$$\Box(begin_1 \supset \bigcirc(\neg inP_1\ U\ end_1)) \tag{7.5}$$

$$\Box(end_1 \supset \bigcirc(\neg inP_1\ U\ begin_1)) \tag{7.6}$$

$$\neg inP_2\ U\ begin_2 \tag{7.7}$$

$$\Box(begin_2 \supset \bigcirc(\neg inP_2\ U\ end_2)) \tag{7.8}$$

$$\Box(end_2 \supset \bigcirc(\neg inP_2\ U\ begin_2)) \tag{7.9}$$

$$\Box(begin_1 \supset \neg begin_2\ U\ end_1) \tag{7.10}$$

$$\Box(begin_2 \supset \neg begin_1\ U\ end_2) \tag{7.11}$$

$$\Box\Diamond\ inP_1 \tag{7.12}$$

$$\Box\Diamond\ inP_2 \tag{7.13}$$

The graph the satisfiability algorithm yields for these specifications is then:

n_1 $\{(7.4), \ldots, (7.13)\}$

$$\left\{ \begin{array}{l} begin_1, \\ (7.4)*, \ldots, (7.13)*, \\ (\neg begin_2 \ U \ end_1)*, \\ \Diamond inP_1*, \quad \Diamond inP_2*, \\ \bigcirc(7.5), \ldots, \bigcirc(7.13), \\ \bigcirc(\neg inP_1 \ U \ end_1), \\ \bigcirc(\neg begin_2 \ U \ end_1), \\ \bigcirc \Diamond inP_2 \end{array} \right.$$

$$\left\{ \begin{array}{l} begin_2, \\ (7.4)*, \ldots, (7.13)*, \\ (\neg begin_1 \ U \ end_2)*, \\ \Diamond inP_1*, \quad \Diamond inP_2*, \\ \bigcirc(7.4), \ldots, \bigcirc(7.6), \bigcirc(7.8), \ldots, \bigcirc(7.13), \\ \bigcirc(\neg inP_2 \ U \ end_2), \\ \bigcirc(\neg begin_1 \ U \ end_2), \\ \bigcirc \Diamond inP_1 \end{array} \right.$$

$$\left\{ \begin{array}{l} (7.5), \ldots, (7.13), \\ (\neg inP_1 \ U \ end_1), \\ (\neg begin_2 \ U \ end_1), \\ \Diamond inP_2 \end{array} \right.$$ n_2

n_3 $$\left\{ \begin{array}{l} (7.4), \ldots, (7.6), (7.8), \ldots, (7.13), \\ (\neg inP_2 \ U \ end_2), \\ (\neg begin_1 \ U \ end_2), \\ \Diamond inP_1 \end{array} \right.$$

$$\left\{ \begin{array}{l} end_1, \\ (7.5)*, \ldots, (7.13)*, \\ \Diamond inP_1*, \quad \Diamond inP_2*, \\ (\neg inP_1 \ U \ end_1)*, \\ (\neg begin_2 \ U \ end_1)*, \\ \bigcirc(7.4), \ldots, \bigcirc(7.13), \\ \bigcirc \Diamond inP_2 \end{array} \right.$$

$$\left\{ \begin{array}{l} end_2, \\ (7.4)*, \ldots, (7.6)*, (7.8)*, \ldots, (7.13)*, \\ \Diamond inP_1*, \quad \Diamond inP_2*, \\ (\neg inP_2 \ U \ end_2)*, \\ (\neg begin_1 \ U \ end_2)*, \\ \bigcirc(7.4), \ldots, \bigcirc(7.13), \\ \bigcirc \Diamond inP_1 \end{array} \right.$$

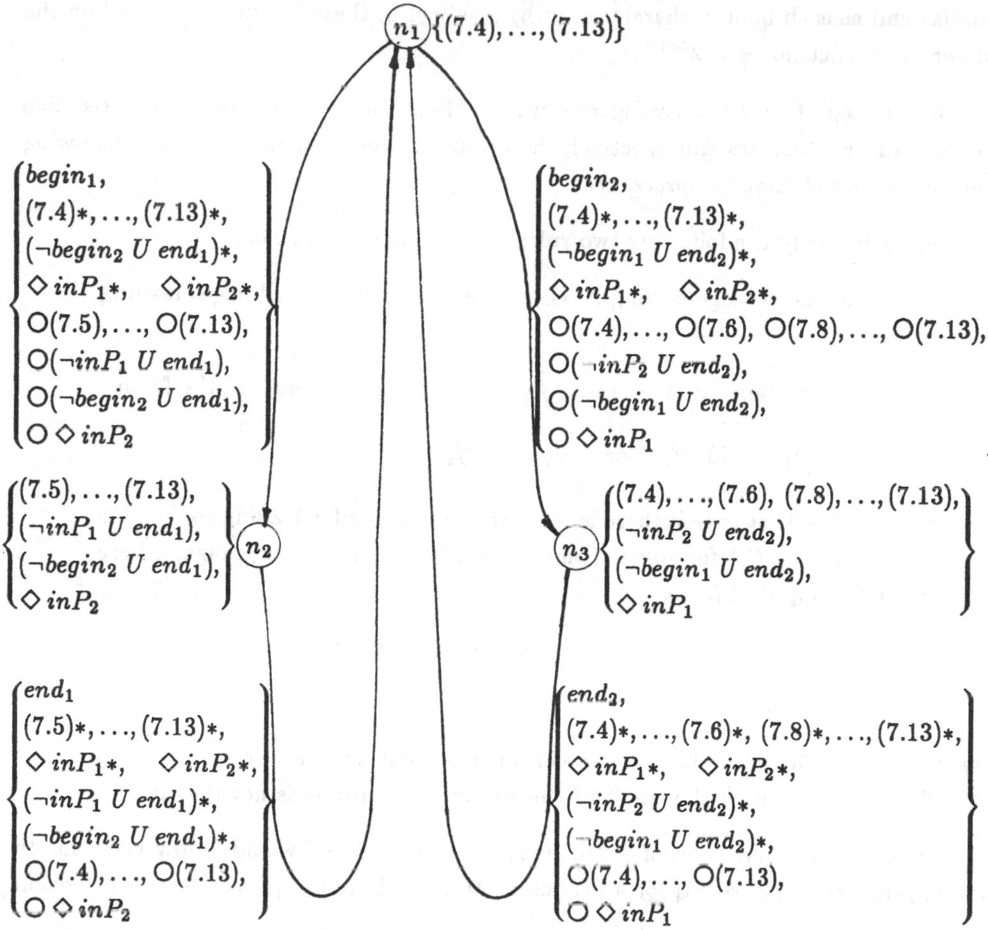

Note that the end_1 edge from n_2 is supposed to lead to a node labeled by

$$\{(7.4), \ldots, (7.13), \quad \Diamond inP_2\}.$$

But, as (7.13) is $\Box \Diamond inP_2$ and as $\Box \Diamond p \equiv \Box \Diamond p \wedge \Diamond p$, this set is equivalent to

$$\{(7.4), \ldots, (7.13)\}$$

and the edge can lead to n_1. Similarly, the end_2 edge from n_3 also leads to n_1. ∎

It is straightforward to give an upper bound on the size of the graph. The number of nodes in the graph is at most 2^{4c+2} where c is the number of temporal operators in the formula to be tested. Indeed, given the α and β rules, the formulas appearing in a node are either the initial formula, a subformula of the initial formula with a temporal operator as its main connective (there are exactly c such formulas), a subformula of the initial formula appearing in the immediate scope of a $\bigcirc$ operator (there are at most c such formulas) or the negation of any of the above. There are clearly at most $4c + 2$ such formulas and as each node is characterized by a subset of these formulas, a bound on the number of distinct nodes is 2^{4c+2}.

The last step of satisfiability algorithm is to check that all the nodes are satisfiable and that all eventualities can effectively be realized. For this, we apply the following nodes and edges *elimination procedure*:

Repeatedly apply the following two rules until no longer possible.

(1) If a node has no edge leaving it, eliminate that node and all edges leading to it.

(2) If an edge contains an *eventuality formula*, that is a formula of the form

$$\Diamond f_1, \quad \neg\Box\neg f_1 \quad \text{or} \quad \neg(\neg f_1\ U\ f_2)$$

then, delete that edge if there is no path from that edge leading to an edge containing $\{p, f'_1\}$ for some atomic proposition p in the language, where f'_1 is f_1 simplified for p.

Note: In the preceeding examples, no elimination is necessary.

We have the following result:

Proposition 7.1: The initial formula, in conjunction with the single event condition (3.1), is satisfiable if and only if the result of the elimination process is not the empty graph.

We will not give here a proof of this result as such a proof would follow very closely the one presented in [BMP81] for a branching time PTL and in [Wo81] for an extension to PTL.

8. Eventualities and Unwinding

If the specifications are satisfiable, the decision procedure described in the previous section has provided us with a non-empty graph. This graph describes the models of the specifications in the sense that every sequence that is a model is a path in the graph and that every finite path obtained from the graph is the prefix of some model. This latter property simply follows from the fact that the decision procedure ensures that the sets of formulas associated with each edge or node of the graph are indeed satisfiable. Unfortunately, it is not always the case that all *infinite paths* obtainable from the graph satisfy the specifications. Indeed, some of these paths could leave some eventuality formula unsatisfied. However, it is always possible to modify the graph so that every infinite path satisfies the specifications.

The construction basically proceeds by *unwinding* the graph up to states where the eventualities are actually realized. The new graph is finite and can be used to generate the program we are trying to synthesize. This unwinding has the disadvantage that it forces the processes to execute one specific path among all those that satisfy the specifications; clearly, this can lead to undesirable inefficiencies.

Example: If the specifications are

$$\Box \Diamond a \wedge \Box \Diamond b, \tag{8.1}$$

the unwinding algorithm could, for instance, give the sequence $a, b, a, b, a, b, \ldots$ as a model. In other words it would require that in order to satisfy (8.1) we alternatively execute a and b. This is correct but could be unacceptable in a situation where a can be repeated substantially faster than b. ∎

In the next section, we will see that under some conditions, the unwinding can be avoided. In the meantime, let us examine the unwinding procedure we use.

Given a graph $G = (N, E)$ with nodes N and edges E, produced by the satisfiability algorithm, we build a new graph $G' = (N', E')$ as follows.

(1) Initially G' consists of a set $N'_0 = N$ of nodes. We will call N'_0 the *initial nodes*.

(2) For each node $n'_0 \in N'_0$ do the following:

(a) Select an edge $e \in E$ leaving the node $n \in N$ corresponding to n'_0.

(b) Build a path starting with $e'_0 = e$ such that all eventualities in e'_0 are satisfied on that path. Given the fact that in the decision procedure we have eliminated all edges containing eventualities that could not be satisfied, we are guaranteed that such a path always exists.

(c) Let e'_f be the last edge in the path built in (b). If the corresponding edge $e_f \in E$ leads to a node $n \in N$ then connect e'_f to the corresponding $n'_0 \in N'_0$.

The result of the construction is a structure that satisfies the specifications.

Example:

For the mutual exclusion problem we specified earlier, the graph G we obtained from the decision procedure is of the form:

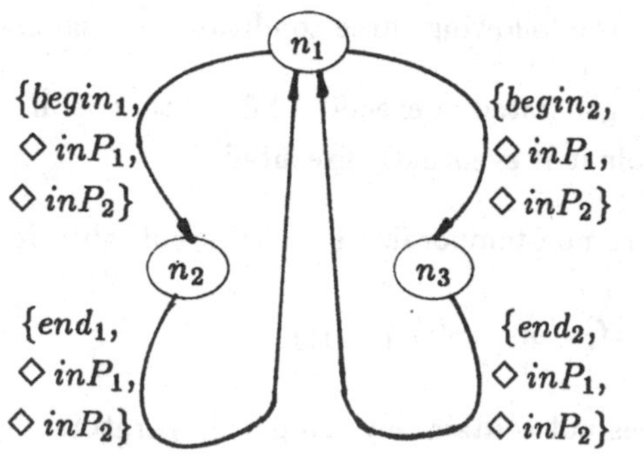

For the sake of simplicity we have only annoted the edges with atomic propositions and eventuality properties. If we apply the unwinding algorithm to this graph, we get the following graph G' where $N'_0 = \{n'_1, n'_2, n'_3\}$:

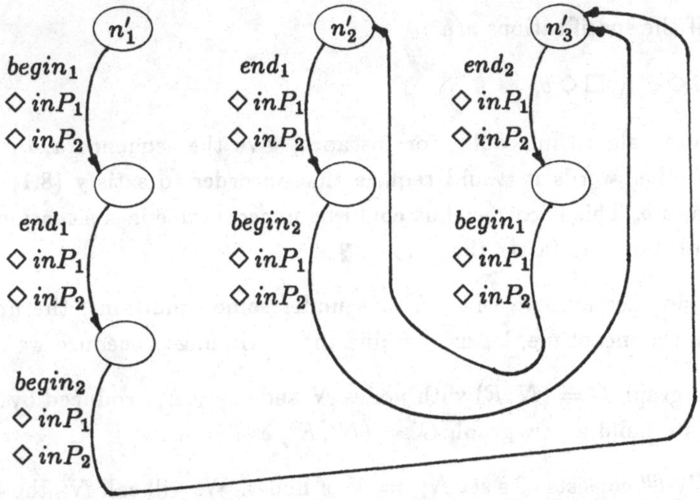

To build the path starting from n'_1, we select the $begin_1$ edge leaving n_1 in G. This edge contains two eventualities: $\Diamond inP_1$ and $\Diamond inP_2$. A path that satisfies both these eventualities is

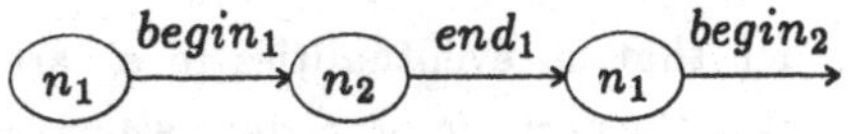

as $begin_1$ satisfies $\Diamond inP_1$ and $begin_2$ satisfies $\Diamond inP_2$. We thus incorparate this path into G' and connect its last edge to n'_3. ∎

9. Dynamic Satisfiability

As we pointed out in the last section, unwinding can lead to very inefficient programs. What we would really like is to be able to avoid the unwinding and decide dynamically, during the execution, which path through the graph we are going to take, but still do this in a way that satisfies the eventualities.

This is possible when the following three conditions are satisfied.

(1) the CSP program generated is executed fairly; that is, if a communication is infinitely often possible it is eventually executed.

(2) all eventualities are non-temporal, *i.e.* in all eventuality formulas

$$\Diamond f_1, \quad \neg\Box\neg f_1 \quad \text{or} \quad \neg(\neg f_1 \; U \; f_2)$$

labeling edges, f_1 does not contain any temporal operators.

(3) The graph satisfies the following dynamic satisfiability criterion.

Dynamic Satisfiability Criterion:

Let us denote by Π_i the set of atomic propositions corresponding to the I/O operations performed between the scheduler S and a process P_i. A model graph is said to satisfy the *dynamic satisfiability criterion* if for each edge containing an eventuality formula of the form

$$\Diamond f_1, \quad \neg\Box\neg f_1 \quad \text{or} \quad \neg(\neg f_1 \; U \; f_2)$$

(where f_1 is non-temporal) all maximum acyclic paths starting from that edge either

(1) contain an edge labeled by a proposition p that satisfies f_1

or

(2) contain a node that has an outgoing edge labeled by a proposition $p \in \Pi_i$ satisfying f_1, provided that either

(a) the edge leaving that node and included in the path is labeled by an atomic proposition $q \in \Pi_i$, *i.e.* an atomic proposition representing an I/O operation performed by the same process P_i as the one performing p

or

(b) No atomic proposition q labeling an edge of that path or any other maximum acyclic path on which f_1 has to be satisfied and conditions (1) or (2a) do not hold is in Π_i.

Essentially, the criterion checks that on *all* infinite paths, either the eventuality is realized or it is infinitely often "possible" and thus will be realized due to the fairness assumption. That means that any "fair" path in the graph is a model of the specifications and, as we will see, will be a potential execution sequence of the synthesized programs. The precise justification of the criterion involves the way we obtain the individual processes and the assumptions we make about their execution. We will discuss these issues in the next section and thus postpone our proof of the criterion until then.

Note: In the mutual exclusion example the three conditions are satisfied. We therefore do not need to unwind that graph. ∎

10. Generating the processes

The processe we generate will look very much like the model graphs we have been dealing with in the preceeding sections. If one takes such a graph and eliminates all the labeling except for the I/O operations labeling edges, the result can be interpreted as a CSP-like program. Indeed, executing such a program is traversing the graph while performing the I/O operations on the edges. A node with several outgoing edges is viewed as a guarded command that has as guards the I/O operations appearing on those edges. Thus, according to the definition of CSP, when such a node is reached, one of the operations that is enabled (*i.e.*, such that the matching process is also ready to execute it) is chosen and the corresponding edge is followed.

The easiest process to obtain is the one for the synchronizer S. As we explained in section 2, all I/O operations are between the synchronizer and some other process P_i. This implies that the model graph we have obtained from the global specifications can be taken as the program for the synchronizer. The only (trivial) transformation that needs to be done is to rename the I/O operations back to their local name (*e.g.*, $begin_1$ becomes $P_1?begin_1$).

Each of the other processes will be obtained by restricting the model graph to the I/O operations of that process.

For a model graph $G = (N, E)$ and a process P_i, we thus build a ***restricted graph*** $G_i = (N_i, E_i)$. Each node of G_i ($n_i \in N_i$) corresponds to sets of nodes of the graph G. For a node n_i, we denote its corresponding set of nodes of G as $\mathcal{N}_{n_i} \subset N$. If the I/O operations of P_i are $\Pi_i = \{p_1, \ldots, p_n\}$, the construction proceeds as follows:

(1) Initially, G_i contains one node; this node corresponds to an initial node of G and all nodes accessible from that node in G through a path containing no edge labeled by a proposition $p \in \Pi_i$.

(2) Repeat step (3) until it has been applied to all nodes in G_i.

(3) Select an unprocessed node $n_i \in N_i$. For all propositions $p \in \Pi_i$ create an edge from n_i to a node $n'_i \in N_i$ such that the set $\mathcal{N}_{n'_i}$ is the set of all nodes accessible in G from any node in $\mathcal{N}_{n_i}$ through a path containing exactly one occurrence of p and no occurrence of any other member of Π_i (we call such a path a p-path). A new node n'_i is created only when G_i does not already contain a node characterized by the set $\mathcal{N}_{n'_i}$. If $\mathcal{N}_{n'_i} = \phi$ no edge is added.

We then just have to rename the I/O operations back to their local name to obtain the process P_i.

Example:

For the mutual exclusion problem specified in section 4, the program for S is:

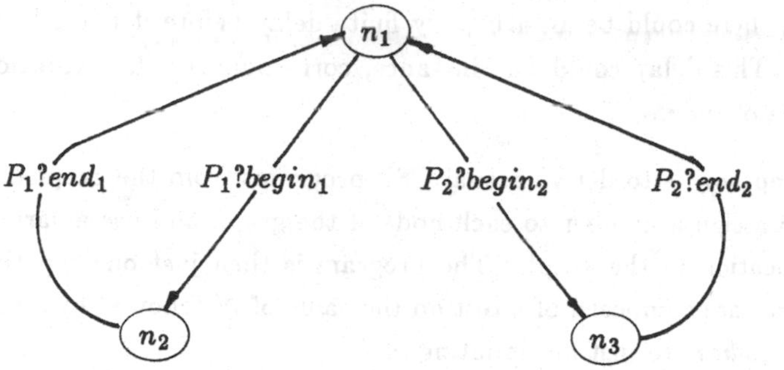

for the processes P_1 we have

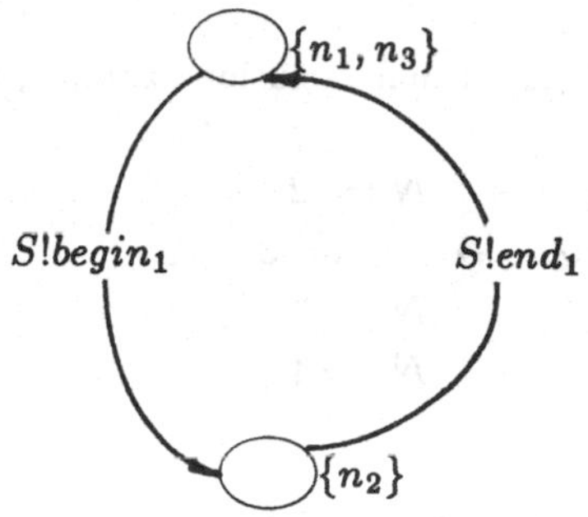

and for the process P_2

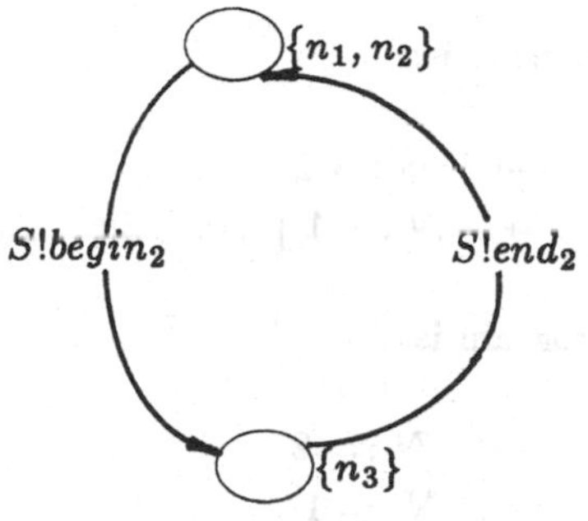

To obtain the graph for P_1, we start with the set of nodes in the model graph accessible from n_1 by a path not labeled by any operation of process P_1. This set is $\{n_1, n_3\}$. The only node accessible from either n_1 or n_3 through a $begin_1$-path is n_2. Thus we have a path labeled by $begin_1$ leading to a node labeled by $\{n_2\}$. There are no nodes accessible from either n_1 or n_3 through an end_1-path, thus no edge labeled by end_1 will leave the node $\{n_1, n_3\}$ of the graph for process P_1. The edges leaving $\{n_2\}$ are constructed similarly. ∎

We view the execution of such a system of processes as it is defined in CSP. That is, the processes have to execute matching I/O operations simultaneously. Note that even though our processes consist solely of I/O operations, we do not assume anything about the relative speed of their execution. This means that after a process executes an

I/O operation, there could be an arbitrary finite delay before it is ready to execute the following one. This delay could for, instance, correspond to the execution of a purely sequential piece of code.

The last step now is to derive actual CSP programs from the graphs. A simple way to do this is to assign a number to each node of the graph and use a variable N to keep track of the location in the graph. The program is then just one repetitive command where the *guards* are composed of a test on the value of N followed by an I/O operation, and where the *bodies* are just an updating of N.

Example:

For the synchronizer S in the mutual exclusion example, the CSP program is:

$$\begin{array}{llll} *[& N=1; P_1?begin_1 & \rightarrow & N:=2 \\ \mathbin{[\!]} & N=1; P_2?begin_2 & \rightarrow & N:=3 \\ \mathbin{[\!]} & N=2; P_1?end_1 & \rightarrow & N:=1 \\ \mathbin{[\!]} & N=3; P_2?end_2 & \rightarrow & N:=1\ ] \end{array}$$

The program repeatedly checks at which location in the graph it is, then waits for the corresponding inputs and finally updates its location variable.

For the process P_1, the program is:

$$\begin{array}{llll} *[& N=1; S!begin_1 & \rightarrow & N:=2 \\ \mathbin{[\!]} & N=2; S!end_1 & \rightarrow & N:=1\ ] \end{array}$$

and for the process P_2, the program is:

$$\begin{array}{llll} *[& N=1; S!begin_2 & \rightarrow & N:=2 \\ \mathbin{[\!]} & N=2; S!end_2 & \rightarrow & N:=1\ ] \end{array}$$

In these programs a purely sequential piece of code can be inserted immediately after the updating of the location variable N. ∎

From the way the processes were obtained, it is clear that any concurrent execution of the system of processes (more precisely the sequence of I/O operations performed during the execution) will correspond to a path through the global graph. Thus in the case where we have unwound the graph, the synthesized processes satisfy the specifications. However, we still have to prove that if the global graph satisfies the dynamic satisfiability criterion, then any fair execution of the extracted program will satisfy all eventualities. Recall that in a fair execution every I/O operation that is infinitely often possible (both sender and receiver are ready to perform it) will eventually be executed.

Proposition 9.1: If the model graph satisfies the dynamic satisfiability criterion, then every fair execution of the extracted programs satisfies the specifications.

Proof: In view of the preceeding remarks, it is sufficient to show that all eventualities are satisfied. Let us assume that there is some eventuality formula $(\Diamond f)$ that is not satisfied for some fair computation. We will show that some operation that realizes the eventuality (satisfies f) is infinitely often possible during that computation. Hence, due to our fairness assumption that operation will be executed, and we have a contradiction. Actually, all we need to show is that for such a computation, some operation satisfying the eventuality will be possible in a finite number of steps. Indeed, the same argument can then inductively be applied to the computation starting after the point where the operation was possible. And, as we only have a finite number of possible I/O operations, one of those satisfying f will be infinitely often possible.

Let us consider the path through the global graph corresponding to our computation. Clearly, no operation p satisfying f appears on that path. Thus either condition (2a) or (2b) of the dynamic satisfiability criterion is satisfied on every maximal acyclic part of the path.

(1) If condition (2a) is satisfied somewhere on the path we have a node on the path that has an outgoing edge labeled by an operation p satisfying f. Thus, at that point the synchronizer S is ready to perform p. As the operation on the path is in the same process P_i as p, that process must also be ready to perform p. Thus p is possible.

(2) If condition (2a) is never satisfied, then (2b) has to be satisfied on every maximum acyclic part of the path. Thus some operation p will repeatedly appear as an alternative branch on the path. As no operation in the process P_i containing p appears on the path, when P_i becomes ready to execute p it will remain in that state. Then, when the synchronizer reaches the next node where p is an alternative, p will be possible. ∎

12. Conclusions and Comparison with Other Work

We have shown how the "synchronization part" of processes could be specified and synthesized. The main techniques we have used are:

(1) abstracting concurrent computations to sequences of "events" (in our case I/O operations)

(2) describing these sequences using Propositional Temporal Logic

(3) using the tableau decision procedure for PTL to synthesize the processes.

Clearly there are some limitations to our approach. The most fundamental one is that the synthesized processes are intrinsically finite state. However, this does not exclude practical use of the method since many synchronization problems have finite state solutions. Getting rid of this limitation would most likely eliminate the decidability property of our specification language. We would then no longer be able to guarantee a correct solution to the problem whenever the specifications are satisfiable.

The PTL we have used in this paper, though it has been called *expressively complete* since it is as expressive as the first order theory of linear order [GPSS80] cannot describe all finite-state behaviors. However, an extension to PTL that would allow the description of all such behaviors has been recently developed [Wo81]. Incorporating it in our specification language would let us describe a wider class of synchronization problems. We also plan to apply the techniques we developed here to the synthesis of network protocols and sequential digital circuits.

Among related work, we should first mention that Clarke and Emerson [CE81] have been independently investigating the use of similar model building techniques for synchronization code synthesis. Their approach is, however, based on a branching time temporal logic and is oriented towards the synthesis of shared memory programs.

Earlier work on the synthesis of synchronization code includes that of Griffiths [Gr75] and Habermann [Ha75]. Griffiths' specification language is rather low-level in the sense that it is procedural in nature. In Habermann's "path expressions", the specification language is regular expressions. This has the disadvantage of requiring a global description instead of a collection of independent requirements, as in PTL. Also, regular expressions cannot describe eventualities explicitly and in [Ha75] no attention is given to the problems of deadlock and starvation.

Among later work on the subject one finds the work of Laventhal [La78], and the one of Ramamritham and Keller [RK81]. Here, the specification language is quite expresssive. In the former approach it is based on first-order predicate calculus with an ordering relation and in the latter on Temporal Logic. However, in both cases the synthesis method is rather informal and does not rely on a precise underlying theory.

Acknowledgements: We wish to thank Yoni Malachi, Joe Weening and Frank Yellin for a careful reading of a draft of this paper.

13. References

[BMP81] M. Ben-Ari, Z. Manna, A. Pnueli, "The Logic of Nexttime", *Eighth ACM Symposium on Principles of Programming Languages*, Williamsburg, VA, January 1981, pp. 164–176.

[CE81] E. M. Clarke, E. A. Emerson, "Synthesis of Synchronization Skeletons from Branching Time Temporal Logic", *Proceedings of the Workshop on Logics of Programs*, Yorktown-Heights, NY, Springer-Verlag Lecture Notes in Computer Science, 1981

[GPSS80] D. Gabbay, A. Pnueli, S. Shelah and J. Stavi, "The Temporal Analysis of Fairness", *Seventh ACM Symposium on Principles of Programming Languages*, Las Vegas, NV, January 1980, pp. 163–173.

[Gr75] P. Griffiths, "SYNVER: A System for the Automatic Synthesis and Verification and Synthesis of Synchronization Processes", Ph. D. Thesis, Harvard University, June 1975.

[Ha75] A. N. Habermann, "Path Expressions", Computer Science Report, Carnegie-Mellon University, 1975.

[Ho78] C. A. R. Hoare, "Communicating Sequential Processes", *Communications of the ACM*, Vol. 21, No 8 (August 1978), pp. 666–677.

[La78] M. Laventhal, "Synthesis of Synchronization Code for Data Abstractions", Ph. D. Thesis, MIT, June 1978.

[MP81] Z. Manna, A. Pnueli, "Verification of Concurrent Programs: the Temporal Framework", *The Correctness Problem in Computer Science* (R. S. Boyer and J S. Moore, eds.), International Lecture Series in Computer Science, Academic Press, London, 1981.

[Pn77] A. Pnueli, "The Temporal Logic of Programs", *Proceedings of the Eighteenth Symposium on Foundations of Computer Science*, Providence, RI, November 1977, pp. 46–57.

[Pr67] A. Prior, **Past, Present and Future**, Oxford University Press, 1967.

[RU71] N. Rescher, A. Urquart, **Temporal Logic**, Springer-Verlag, 1971

[RK81] K. Ramamritham, R. M. Keller, "Specification and Synthesis of Synchronizers", *Proceedings International Symposium on Parallel Processing*, August 1980, pp. 311–321.

[Sm68] R. M. Smullyan, **First Order Logic**, Springer-Verlag, Berlin, 1968.

[Wo81] P. Wolper, "Temporal Logic Can Be More Expressive", *Proceedings of the Twenty-Second Symposium on Foundations of Computer Science*, Nashville, TN, October 1981.

A Note On Equivalences Among Logics Of Programs

25 November 1981

Albert R. Meyer
Massachusetts Institute of Technology[1]

Jerzy Tiuryn
Massachusetts Institute of Technology and Warsaw University

This work was supported in part by The National Science Foundation, Grant Nos. MCS 7719754 and MCS 8010707, and by a grant to the M.I.T. Laboratory for Computer Science by the IBM Corporation.

---

[1]Laboratory for Computer Science, Cambridge, Massachusetts 02139, USA

Abstract

Several different first order formal logics of programs-- Algorithmic Logic, Dynamic Logic, and Logic of Effective Definitions -- are compared and shown to be equivalent to a fragment of constructive $L_{\omega_1\omega}$. When programs are modelled as effective flowcharts, the logics of deterministic and nondeterministic programs are equivalent.

1 Introduction

A number of systems of formal logics which extend predicate calculus have been proposed for reasoning about sequential and nondeterministic programs. These include in rough chronological order

1. The infinitary logic $L_{\omega_1\omega}$ -- suggested by ENGELER 67 as a logic for programming,

2. Algorithmic Logic (AL) -- defined and developed by SALWICKI, *et.al.* 70,

3. μ-calculus -- defined by HITCHCOCK and PARK 73; extended by DE BAKKER 80,

4. Dynamic Logic (DL) -- PRATT 76,

5. Programming Logic (PL) -- CONSTABLE and O'DONNELL 78,

6. Logic of Effective Definitions (LED) -- TIURYN 80.

Each of these logical systems actually represents a family of formal logics, instances of the family being determined by the choice of a few parameters. The principal parameter is the class of programs allowed in formulas. For example, in the case of DL some variants which have been considered are

- *regular* DL, in which programs are taken essentially to be finite, possibly nondeterministic, flowchart schemes with atomic formulas as tests and with *simple assignment statements* of the form x: $=\tau$ where τ is a term,

- *regular-array* DL in which *array assignments* of the form $\tau_1 = \tau_2$ may also occur (cf. MEYER and WINKLMANN 80),

- *regular* DL$^+$ in which for every finite flowchart α, the predicate $LOOPS_\alpha$, which asserts that α has an infinite computation, is included as an extra atomic formula (cf. MEYER and WINKLMANN 80).[2]

- *recursive-call* DL in which programs are taken to be flowchart schemes containing recursive calls with arguments (cf. GREIBACH 75, DE BAKKER 80).

In general, such different choices of the parameters lead to logics which differ in expressive power. For example, TIURYN 81 has recently shown that there is a formula of recursive-call DL, as well as one of regular-array DL, which is not equivalent to any formula of regular DL. On the other hand, MEYER and WINKLMANN 80 have shown that regular DL and regular DL$^+$ are equivalent in expressive power. MEYER and PARIKH 81 have also demonstrated distinctions among the expressive powers of several other versions of DL and $L_{\omega_1\omega}$.

Thus there are genuine distinctions in the expressive, and also model theoretic and undecidability properties among the various instances of DL. These distinctions complicate the problem of comparing the six systems of programming logics listed above. For example, the bulk of the literature on AL defined that system in the particular version where programs are deterministic **while** schemes.[3] Since the original DL allowed nondeterministic schemes, it appeared that DL and AL represented genuinely distinct conceptions of programming logic.

Nevertheless, we claim that with appropriately matched parameters, DL, AL, and LED,

---

[2]However, $LOOPS_\alpha$ may not occur as a test in a program.

[3]Only recently has an AL with nondeterministic schemes been considered by MIRKOWSKA 80.

are actually equivalent systems. We believe that PL can be incorporated into this common framework as well, although its numerous "practical" features make it harder to grasp theoretically.

These systems can be described in more classical terminology as fragments of the constructive portion of $L_{\omega_1\omega}$, with the different instances of the systems characterized by various simple syntactic conditions on infinitary formulas. Thus, we argue that there is a common intuition which leads to the DL-AL-LED-PL framework for programming logic. In what follows we focus on this framework.[4]

In order to compare the DL-AL-LED-PL frameworks, we restrict ourselves to instances of these systems using what we regard as the mathematically most natural and robust notion of *computability* over arbitrary structures, namely computability by *effective flowcharts.* Effective flowcharts may be described informally as generally infinite, nondeterministic, uninterpreted flowchart schemes whose basic instructions are assignment statements and whose basic tests consist of atomic formulas (including equations). Moreover, given a box of the flowchart, one can effectively find the instruction in that box, the number of edges leaving the box, and the endpoints of those edges. For technical convenience we require that the *signature* (i.e., set of symbols occurring, including variables) of any flowchart is *finite.*

A *state* provides an interpretation for all function, predicate, and variable symbols. Given a state, a nondeterministic flowchart defines a set of executable instruction sequences. The set of states in which execution of these instruction sequences can finally terminate is the set of *output states* for the given input state. Thus, any flowchart α defines

---

[4] Technical results of PARK 76 for μ-calculus, and MEYER and PARIKH 81 for the constructive fragment of $L_{\omega_1\omega}$, show that these latter logics are incomparable in expressive power, and both are strictly greater in expressive power than logics in the DL-AL-LED-PL framework unless the notion of program scheme is stretched unreasonably.

a binary *input-output* relation R_α on states where

R_α = {(s,t)| starting in state s, there is an executable sequence of instructions in α which finishes in output state t}.

If there is an infinite executable sequence starting in state s, then α is said to *loop from state* s. Formal definitions are available in MEYER and WINKLMANN 80, MEYER and HALPERN 80, MEYER and PARIKH 80, TIURYN 80.

Friedman, cf. SHEPHERDSON 73, proposed a notion of *effective definitional scheme* as the most general model of effective computability in arbitrary structures. These may be described as the special case of effective flowcharts which are of the form

if P_1 **then** $ASSIGN_1$ **else**
if P_2 **then** $ASSIGN_2$ **else**
if P_3 ...

where P_i is a finite conjunction of atomic formulas or their negations, and $ASSIGN_i$ is a sequence of assignment statements of the form $x := \tau$ with distinct variables x on the lefthand side of each statement in the sequence.

We can generalize effective definitional schemes to be nondeterministic. These nondeterministic effective definitional schemes can be informally described as the infinite parallel OR of statements of the form

if P_i **then** $ASSIGN_i$ **else** ABORT **fi**,

where ABORT is a program with empty input-output relation, e.g., **while** *true* **do** *anything* **od**. Equivalent notions of universal classes of effective procedures on arbitrary structures have been proposed by many other researchers. In particular, it is easy to show

Lemma 1: The following classes of program schemes define the same class of input-output relations:

1. (Non)Deterministic effective flowcharts without array assignments (i.e., simple assignments only),

2. (Nondeterministic) Effective definitional schemes,

3. (Non)Deterministic *finite* flowcharts without array assignments but with stacks.

Similar definitions and lemma can be given for the case that array assignments are allowed. These results indicate the invariance of the class of *computable input-output relations* between states defined by effective flowcharts.

Our main observation is that when effective flowcharts are taken as the notion of program in the programming logics listed above, then all can be reduced to a simple fragment of constructive $L_{\omega_1\omega}$ which we define next.

Definition 2: Let L_{re} be the class of infinitary first order formulas defined inductively as follows:

(a).if P_1, P_2,... is a recursively enumerable sequence of quantifier-free formulas of predicate calculus among which there are only finitely many free variables, then $\vee\{P_i | i \leq 1\}$ is a basic formula of L_{re},

(b).if p,q are formulas of L_{re}, then so are $\neg p$, $p \wedge q$, $p \vee q$, $\exists x[p]$, $\forall x[p]$.

Theorem 3: There is an effective procedure to translate a formula of any one of the following formal logics into an equivalent formula of any of the others:

1. L_{re},

2. DL of deterministic effective flowcharts without array assignments (i.e., only simple assignments occur), henceforth called *DDL-w/o-array*

3. DL of deterministic effective flowcharts (i.e., array assignments may occur) henceforth called *DDL*,

4. DL^+ of nondeterministic effective flowcharts without array assignments, henceforth called *DL^+-w/o-array*,

5. LED,

6. Logic of nondeterministic effective definitional schemes (without array assignments),

7. AL of deterministic effective flowcharts without array assignments,

8. AL of nondeterministic effective flowcharts without array assignments and without the iteration quantifier $\cap$.

We would like to emphasize that according to Theorem 3, DDL-w/o-array and DL^+-w/o-array are equivalent, viz., *adding nondeterminism to effective flowcharts does not increase the expressive power of the dynamic logic.*

Although in many programming situations nondeterminism is a significant addition, we can explain informally why it adds nothing to the logic of deterministic effective schemes: the rich control structure provided by arbitrary effective flowcharts enables a deterministic scheme α_d to "check the results" of any nondeterministic scheme α by carrying out a backtracking search. In particular, suppose α is a nondeterministic effective flowchart without array assignments whose registers, i.e., free variables, are $x = x_0,...,x_{n-1}$. Then there is a deterministic effective flowchart α_d such that $\alpha_d(x,y)$ halts iff $\alpha(x)$ can halt with the final contents of registers x set to y. Thus the assertion that after $\alpha(x)$ halts, it is possible that some property p(x) holds, is equivalent to the assertion that *there exist* y such that $\alpha_d(x,y)$ halts and p(y) holds. In this way, an existentially quantified assertion about a deterministic flowchart has the same expressive power as an assertion about a nondeterministic flowchart.

For more restricted control structures which cannot carry out the backtrack search, nondeterminism indeed makes a difference: P. Berman, J. Halpern, and J. Tiuryn have recently shown that for *regular* programs, DDL is strictly less expressive than DL.

In the case that array assignments do occur in nondeterministic programs, our proof of Theorem 3 breaks down. The nondeterministic flowchart α may have registers x and also assignable arrays, i.e., function symbols f. Again, there is a deterministic "checking" flowchart α_d such that $\alpha_d(x,f,y,g)$ halts iff $\alpha(x,f)$ can halt with the final values of registers x and arrays f equal to y,g. Now, however, in order to reduce an assertion about α to one about α_d as above, it is necessary to existentially bind not only the y variables by also the function symbols g. This second order quantification exceeds the power of DL. But because the values of the arrays g differ only finitely from the values of the f, the full power of second order quantification is not necessary. If there are elements in the domain of interpretation which can serve to represent finite sets, it is possible to simulate this weak second order quantification by first order quantifiers. Any infinite set of finitely generated elements will serve to represent finite sets, so, aside from the pathological case of (essentially) finite domains, we can extend the theorem to nondeterministic effective flowcharts even with array assignments.

Namely, let Σ be some finite set of function symbols. A state is n,Σ-*infinite* iff there are n elements of the domain of the state such that the set of elements generated by applying the functions (which are the interpretations in the state of the symbols) in Σ to these n elements is infinite.

Theorem 4: For any n>0 and finite set Σ of function symbols, there is an effective procedure to translate any formula p of the logics 9.-11. below, into a formula p' of L_{re} such that for every n,Σ-infinite state s,

$$s \models p \text{ iff } s \models p'.$$

9. DL^+ of nondeterministic effective flowcharts,

10. Logic of nondeterministic effective definitional schemes (with array assignments),

11. AL of nondeterministic effective flowcharts without the iteration quantifier $\cap$.

It remains an interesting open question whether the hypothesis of n, Σ-infinity can be eliminated from Theorem 4. Whether the iteration quantifier $\cap$ makes a difference in the presence of nondeterministic programs is also open, but appears to be of technical interest only.

In the next section we present the main definitions among the logics 1.-11., and prove Theorems 3 and 4.

2 Definitions and Proofs

All of the logics 1.-11. are subsets of the following class L_{univ} of formulas which is obtained by combining the features of all the languages.

Definition 5: L_{univ} is defined inductively as follows:

(a).Any atomic formula of predicate calculus with equality is a formula of L_{univ},

(b).if α is an effective flowchart, then $LOOPS_\alpha$ is a formula of L_{univ},

(c).if p,q are formulas of L_{univ}, then so are $\neg p$, $p \wedge q$, $p \vee q$, $\exists x[p]$, $\forall x[p]$,

(d).if $P_1, P_2, \ldots$, is an r.e. sequence of formulas of L_{univ}, then so are $\vee\{P_i | i \geq 1\}$ and $\wedge\{P_i | i \geq 1\}$,

(e).if α is an effective flowchart and p is a formula of L_{univ}, then so are $\langle\alpha\rangle p$ and $[\alpha]p$,

(f).if α is an effective flowchart and p is a formula of L_{univ}, then so are $(\cap\alpha)p$ and $(\cup\alpha)p$.

Whether a state s *satisfies* a formula p of L_{univ}, denoted $s \models p$, is defined in the usual way for p of the form (a), (c), or (d) above.

For case (b), $s \models LOOPS_\alpha$ iff α loops from state s.

For case (e), $s \models \langle\alpha\rangle p$ iff $t \models p$ for *some* state t such that $(s,t) \in R_\alpha$; $s \models [\alpha]p$ iff $t \models p$ for *all* states t such that $(s,t) \in R_\alpha$.

Case (f) covers the *iteration quantifiers* of AL. $s \models (\cup\alpha)p$ iff $s \models \langle\alpha^*\rangle p$, where α^* is an effective flowchart such that R_{α^*} is the reflexive transitive closure of R_α. $s \models (\cap\alpha)p$ iff

$s \models \langle\alpha^n\rangle p$ for *all* $n \geq 0$, where α^n is an effective flowchart such that R_{α^n} = the relational composition of R_α with itself n times.

This defines the *semantics* of L_{univ}.

L_{re} is easily embeddable in all of the logics of Theorem 3, and all are obviously embeddable into one of DDL or DL^+-w/o-array, so we give precise definitions and proofs only for these latter two logics.

Definition 6: *DDL* is the class of formulas defined by rules (a,c,e) of Definition 5 such that the flowcharts α of rule (e) are deterministic. *DL^+-w/o-array* is the class of formulas defined by rules (a,b,c,e) such that the flowcharts α of rule (e) do not contain array assignments.

To prove Theorem 3, we describe translations between L_{re} and DDL, and between L_{re} and DL^+-w/o-array.

The translation from L_{re} actually takes formulas of L_{re} into the intersection of DDL and DL^+-w/o-array. It is obtained trivially from the observation that the atomic formula $\vee\{P_i | i \geq 1\}$ of L_{re} is equivalent to $\langle\alpha\rangle$*true* where α is the effective flowchart

if P_1 **then** x:=x **else**
if P_2 **then** x:=x **else**
if P_3 **then** x:=x **else**....

The translation from DDL to L_{re} is based on

Lemma 7: The following formulas are valid for any flowchart α and formula p of L_{univ}:

1. $\langle\alpha\rangle(p \vee q) \equiv (\langle\alpha\rangle p \vee \langle\alpha\rangle q)$,

2. $\langle\alpha\rangle\exists x[p] \equiv \exists z[\langle\alpha\rangle(p[z/x])]$, where z does not occur in α or p, and p[z/x] is the result of substituting z for x in p.

In addition, the following formula is valid for any *deterministic* flowchart α and formula p of L_{univ}:

3. $\langle\alpha\rangle\neg p \equiv (\langle\alpha\rangle true \wedge \neg\langle\alpha\rangle p)$.

The equivalences of Lemma 7 allow one to "move the <>'s in" thereby converting an arbitrary formula of DDL into an equivalent formula built solely by first order constructs, i.e., the rules of Definition 5.(c), starting from formulas of the form $\langle\beta_1\rangle...\langle\beta_n\rangle P$ where P is an atomic formula of predicate calculus. But a formula of the form $\langle\beta_1\rangle...\langle\beta_n\rangle P$ is equivalent to an r.e. disjunction of formulas $\langle\alpha_i\rangle P$ where α_i ranges over the terminating instruction sequences of the program $\beta_1;...;\beta_n$. Each formula $\langle\alpha_i\rangle P$, where α_i is a finite sequence of assignments and atomic tests and P is quantifier free, is equivalent to a quantifier free formula of predicate calculus, cf. PRATT 76, MEYER and PARIKH 80. In this way DDL translates into L_{re}.

The translation from DL^+-w/o-array into L_{re} proceeds by induction on the definition of DL^+. The only interesting case in the basis of the induction is for formulas of the form $LOOPS_\alpha$. These are obviously equivalent to the r.e. conjunction of the quantifier-free first order formulas which assert that a terminating instruction sequence in α is not executable.

The essential step in the inductive definition of the translation is $\langle\rangle$- elimination. Let α be a nondeterministic effective flowchart without array assignments and let p be a formula of DL^+-w/o-array. By induction, we may assume there is a formula q of L_{re} equivalent to p. Let $x_0,...,x_{n-1}$ be all the variables occurring in flowchart α. It is easy to define an r.e. set of quantifier-free first order formulas $\{P_i | i \geq 0\}$ and an r.e. set of terms $\{\tau_{i,j} | i \geq 0, j<n\}$ such that for all j<n and states s, $s \models P_i$ iff it is possible for α, started in state s, to terminate with the terminal value of x_j equal to the value of $\tau_{i,j}$ in state s.

Let $y_0,...,y_{n-1}$ be new variables which occur neither in α nor in q. The reader can easily check that

$$\exists y_0...\exists y_{n-1}[\ \vee_i\{P_i \wedge (\wedge_{j<n}\ y_j = \tau_{i,j})\} \wedge q[y_0,...,y_{n-1}/x_0,...,x_{n-1}]\ ] \qquad (1)$$

is equivalent in all states to $\langle\alpha\rangle p$.

We remark that introducing quantifiers in formula (1), or indeed any such formula which accomplishes $\langle\rangle$-elimination, is unavoidable. This follows from the fact that the quantifier-free fragment of Deterministic DL^+-w/o-array, which is equivalent to quantifier-free L_{re}, is strictly weaker than the quantifier-free fragment of DL^+-w/o-array, (cf. MEYER and WINKLMANN 80).

This completes the proof of Theorem 3.

In proving Theorem 4, we note that all of the logics 9.-11. are no more expressive that DL^+. We therefore only describe the translation of DL^+ into L_{re}.

As in the proof of Theorem 3, the translation is given inductively. The only interesting case is $\diamond$-elimination.

Let p be a formula of DL^+ and let α be a nondeterministic effective flowchart. By induction, let q be an L_{re} formula equivalent over all n,Σ-infinite states to p. According to Lemma 1 we can find a nondeterministic effective definitional scheme which defines the same input-output relation as α. This effective definitional scheme is an infinite parallel OR of finite deterministic programs α_i of the form

if P_i then $ASSIGN_i$ else ABORT fi

where $ASSIGN_i$ is a finite sequence of assignments.

Obviously $\langle\alpha\rangle p$ is equivalent to the L_{univ} formula

$$V_i\langle\alpha_i\rangle q. \tag{2}$$

It is not hard to show that any formula $\langle\alpha_i\rangle q$ is equivalent to a formula of L_{re}, but this still leaves the difficulty that (2) is an infinite disjunction of L_{re}, not first order, formulas, and L_{re} is not closed under infinite disjunctions. We could eliminate this difficulty if the integer variable i in $\langle\alpha_i\rangle q$ could somehow be taken as a variable of DL, for then the infinite disjunction over i in (2) could simply be replaced by an existential quantification of i. With the aid of the hypothesis of n,Σ-infinity, we will accomplish this as follows.

Each formula $\langle\alpha_i\rangle q$ can be transformed using the equivalences of Lemma 7 so that all the occurrences of $\langle\alpha_i\rangle$ appear in the context

$$\langle\alpha_i\rangle \vee_m G_m \tag{3}$$

where the G_m are quantifier-free formulas of predicate calculus. Let the formula obtained in this way be denoted q_i, so that formula (2) is equivalent to $\vee_i q_i$. (The transformation is uniform in i, so the same set of disjunctions $\vee_m G_m$ occur in each q_i.) In order to eliminate the outermost disjunction in (2) we use the assumption of n,Σ-infinity of states.

Let $y = y_0,\ldots,y_{n-1}$, and z be n+1 individual variables which occur neither in α nor in q_i, and choose some effective enumeration $\tau_1(y)$, $\tau_2(y)$,... of all the terms over y ∪ (signature(α) - variables(α)), i.e., the terms with function symbols from α whose only variables are from **y**.

For $k,i \geq 1$, let $D_{k,i}(y,z)$ be a quantifier-free formula of predicate calculus which expresses the following property: "z is the value of the kth term (in the above enumeration), there are exactly i distinct values among those first k terms, and k is the least integer with the above two properties".

Let q' be a formula obtained from q_i by replacing every subformula of the form (3) by the r.e. disjunction

$$\vee\{D_{k,j}(y,z) \wedge G_{mj} \mid j,k,m \geq 1\}$$

where G_{mj} is a quantifier free first order formula equivalent to $\langle\alpha_j\rangle G_m$. Note that by the uniformity in i of the definition of q_i, it follows that the same q' is obtained for all i.

In q' we have apparently eliminated the index i, but it will be coded in the values of variables y and z. This coding is possible because, by definition of $D_{k,j}$, for every state s there is *at most* one pair of integers $k,j \geq 1$ such that $s \models D_{k,j}$. Moreover, for every n,Σ-infinite state s and for arbitrary $k,j \geq 1$, $s \models \exists y \exists z[D_{k,j}(y,z)]$. Thus in n,Σ-infinite states we can code any pair of integers by using the formulas $D_{k,j}$.

We use the above observation to code the value of index i. Let q" be the formula

$\exists y \exists z[\vee\{P_i \wedge D_{k,i}(y,z) | k,i \geq 1\} \wedge q']$

where P_i is the test portion of α_i.

We claim that for every n,Σ-infinite state s,

$$s \models \vee_i \langle\alpha_i\rangle q \equiv q". \tag{4}$$

In order to prove the claim (4), let us assume that $s \models \langle\alpha_i\rangle q$ for a certain $i \geq 1$. Let $\mathbf{a} = a_0,\ldots,a_{n-1}$ be the generators of an infinite substructure in s, let b be the i-th distinct value in the sequence $\tau_1(\mathbf{a}), \tau_2(\mathbf{a}),\ldots$ and let $k \geq 1$ be the least integer such that $b = \tau_k(\mathbf{a})$. Let s_i be the state in which **y** has the value **a**, z has the value b, and all other symbols have the same interpretation as in s. We have $s_i \models P_i \wedge D_{k,i}(y,z)$ because $s \models P_i$ and y,z do not occur in P_i.

In order to see that $s_i \models q'$, it is enough to observe that for any r.e. set of formulas $\{G_m | m \geq 1\}$,

$$s_i \models \vee\{D_{k,j}(y,z) \wedge G_{mj} | j,k,m \geq 1\} \text{ iff } s \models \langle\alpha_i\rangle \vee_m G_m.$$

In this way we have proved $s \models q"$. The other half of the equivalence (4) is proved similarly.

3 Conclusion

Having reduced essentially all the various programming logics to the L_{re} fragment of infinitary logic, it is easy to deduce a body of model theoretic and undecidability results about programming logic from known results for infinitary logic. Moreover, the reduction to L_{re} is sufficiently straightforward that various infinitary proof theoretic results can also be carried over directly to programming logic.

We interpret these results as evidence that no very new model theoretic or recursion theoretic issues arise from logics of programs on first order structures.

Nevertheless, we believe that the problem of developing formal systems for reasoning about programs offers significant challenges in at least two directions First, to be true to the purpose for which high level programming languages were originally developed and continue to be developed -- namely for economy and ease in the expression of algorithms -- it is important to develop proof methods for dealing with high level programs as textual objects. This has in fact been the focus of the bulk of the literature on program correctness, although many of the complex features of modern programming languages have yet to be adequately addressed. (In our treatment we assumed in effect that the high level programs had already been transformed into effective flowcharts, and thereby we avoided the challenge of developing a proof theory.) A second challenge involves programs operating on higher-type domains which are often assumed to satisfy "domain equations" which appear inconsistent with standard set theory. Development of appropriate logics for reasoning about such domains has just begun, cf. SCOTT 80, and seems an intriguing subject for further research.

4 REFERENCES

1. BANACHOWSKI, L. *et al.* An Introduction to Algorithmic Logic; Metamathematical Investigations in the Theory of Programs, *Mathematical Foundations of Computer Science*, Banach Center Publications, vol. 2, (ed A. Mazurkiewicz and Z. Pawlak), Polish Scientific Publishers, Warsaw, 1977, 7-100.

2. BERGSTRA, J., TIURYN, J. and TUCKER, J., Floyd's Principle, Correctness Theories and Program Equivalence, *Mathematisch Centrum*, IW145/80. To appear in *Theoretical Computer Science*, 1981.

3. CONSTABLE, R.L., and O'DONNELL, M.J., *A Programming Logic*, Winthrop Publishers, 1978.

4. DE BAKKER, J., *Mathematical Theory of Program Correctness*, Prentice-Hall, 1980.

5. ENGELER, E. Algorithmic Properties of Structures, *Mathematical Systems Theory*, 1, 1967, 183-195.

6. ENGELER, E., Algorithmic Logic. In de Bakker (ed.) *Mathematical Centre Tracts* (63) Amsterdam 1975, 57-85.

7. GALLIER, J. H. Nondeterministic flowchart programs with recursive procedures: semantics and correctness, *Theoretical Computer Science*, 13, 2(1981), 193-224.

8. GREIBACH, S. *Theory of Program Structures: Schemes, Semantics, Verification*, Lecture Notes in Computer Science, 36, Springer Verlag, 1975.

9. HAREL, D., *First-Order Dynamic Logic*, Lecture Notes in Computer Science 68, Springer-Verlag, 1979.

10. HAREL, D., A.R. MEYER and V. PRATT, Computability and Completeness in Logics of Programs: Preliminary Report, *9th ACM Symp. on Theory of Computing*, Boulder, Colorado, (May, 1977), 261-268. Revised version, M.I.T. Lab. for Computer Science TM-97, (Feb. 1978), 16 pp.

11. HAREL, D., and PRATT, V. Nondeterminism in logics of programs, *5th Annual Symposium on Principles of Programming Languages*, January 1978, 203-213.

12. HITCHCOCK, P. AND PARK, D. Induction Rules and Termination Proofs, *Automata, Languages and Programming*, (ed M. Nivat), American Elsevier, New York, 1973, 225-251.

13. KEISLER, H.J., *Model Theory for Infinitary Logic*. North-Holland Publ. Co., Amsterdam 1972.

14. KFOURY, D.J., Comparing Algebraic Structures up to Algorithmic Equivalence. In Nivat (ed.) *Automata, Languages and Programming*. North-Holland Publ. Co., Amsterdam 1972, 253-264.

15. KFOURY, D.J., Translatability of schemes over restricted interpretations. *Journal of Comp. and Syst. Sc. 8* (1974), 387-408.

16. MEYER, A.R., Ten thousand and one logics of programming. *EATCS Bulletin*, 11-29; M.I.T. LCS TM 150, MIT Laboratory for Computer Science, Cambridge, Ma., February 1980.

17. MEYER, A.R. and J. Y. HALPERN, Axiomatic Definitions of Programming Languages: A Theoretical Assessment, (Preliminary Report) *Proc. of Seventh Annual POPL Conf.*, January 1980, 203-212; M.I.T. LCS TM 163, April, 1980, 34 pp.; to appear *JACM* (1981).

18. MEYER, ALBERT R., and ROHIT PARIKH, Definability in Dynamic Logic, *Proc. of ACM Symp. on Theory of Computing*, Los Angeles, Cal., April, 1980, 1-7; to appear *Jour. Computer and System Science* (1981).

19. MEYER, A.R. and K. WINKLMANN, On the Expressive Power of Dynamic Logic, Preliminary Report, *Proc. of the 11th Annual ACM Conf. on Theory of Computing*, Atlanta, Ga., May 1979, 167-175; M.I.T. LCS TM 157, February,1980, 36pp; to appear *Theoretical Computer Science* (1981).

20. MIRKOWSKA, G., Complete Axiomatization of Algorithmic Properties of Program Schemes with Bounded Nondeterministic Interpretations, *12th Annual ACM Symp. on Theory of Computing* (1980), 14-21.

21. D. PARK. Finiteness is mu-ineffable, *Theoretical Computer Science* 3, 1976, 173-181.

22. PRATT, V., Semantical considerations on Floyd-Hoare logic, *Proceedings 17th Symposium on Foundations of Computer Science*, Houston, Texas, October 1976, 109-121.

23. SALWICKI, A. Formalized Algorithmic Languages, *Bull. Acad. Pol. Sci.,Ser. Math. Astr. Phys.* 18, 1970, 227-232.

24. SCOTT, D. S. Relating Theories of the %l-Calculus, in *To H. B. Curry: Essays on Combinatory Logic, Lambda Calculus and Formalism*, eds. Seldin and Hindley, Academic Press, New York, 1980, 403-450.

25. SHEPHERDSON, J.C., Computing over abstract structures: serial and parallel procedures and Friedman's effective definitional schemes, In Shepherdson and Rose (eds.) *Logic Colloquium 73.* North-Holland, Amsterdam, 1973, pp.445-513.

26. TIURYN, J., A Survey of the Logic of Effective Definitions, MIT/LCS/TR-246, MIT, Laboratory For Computer Science, Cambridge, Mass., September

1980.

27. TIURYN, J., Unbounded program memory adds to expressive power of first-order Dynamic Logic, *Proceedings 22nd IEEE Symposium on Foundations of Computer Science*, Nashville, Tennessee, October 1981, to appear.

THE REPRESENTATION THEOREM FOR ALGORITHMIC ALGEBRAS

Grażyna Mirkowska
Institute of Mathematics
University of Warsaw
00-901 Warsaw , Poland

ABSTRACT

Algorithmic algebras form semantical base for semantics of algorithmic logics as Boolean algebras do for propositional calculus.The paper contains the proof of the following statement : every separable algorithmic algebra is representable by an algebra of computations.

INTRODUCTION

In this paper we introduce the notion of algorithmic algebra . Algorithmic algebra is a base for algebraic definition of semantics of propositional algorithmic logic and of algorithmic logic. In this paper we consider the problem of representation of algorithmic algebras.

The name "algorithmic algebra" was first used by Glushkow [1] to denote the pain of algebras : algebra of algorithms and the algebra of formulas. Independently we introduced the notion of convolution which is a pair of algebras one of which constitutes a set of operators for the other. Using this notion we defined the semantics for algorithmic logic [5] . Algorithmic algebra is an example of a convolution.

Algorithmic algebra discussed here is a special kind of convolution or two-sorted algebra defined in an axiomatic way. In this it is similar to the notion of dynamic algebra introduced by D.Kozen [2] and carefully studied by many authors [3,4,7,8] . The problem of representation for dynamic algebras was formulated and discussed by D.Kozen [3,4] . It was proved that every separable dynamic algebra is isomorphic to a possibly nonstandard Kripke model of propositional dynamic logic.

The basic difference between algorithmic and dynamic algebras is the set of convoluted operations and the idea to represent algorithms as sets of computations instead of the input-output relations.

The result reported here is closely related to the completeness property of propositional algorithmic logic [6].

1. ALGORITHMIC ALGEBRAS

By an algorithmic algebra we shall understand a pair of algebras $\langle \mathfrak{I}, \mathfrak{B} \rangle$ such that

(1) $\mathfrak{I} = \langle \Pi, I, o, or, \{\curlyvee_a\}_{a \in B}, \{*_b\}_{b \in B} \rangle$

I is a constant, for every b B, $_b$ is one-argument operation. o, or and for every $b \in B$, $\curlyvee_b$ are two-argument operations in Π

(2) $\mathfrak{B} = \langle B, \cup, \cap, -, \{\Diamond M\}_{M \in \Pi}, \{\Box M\}_{M \in \Pi} \rangle$

$\langle B, \cup, \cap, - \rangle$ is a nondegenerated Boolean algebra and for every $M \in \Pi$, $\Diamond M$ and $\Box M$ are one-argument operations in B,

(3) for every $M, N \in \Pi$ and every $a, b \in B$ the following properties hold

$\Box Ma \leqslant \Diamond Ma$

$\Box M(a \cap b) = \Box Ma \cap \Box Mb$

$\Diamond M(a \cup b) = \Diamond Ma \cup \Diamond Mb$

$\Box(M \text{ or } N)a = \Box Ma \cap \Box Na$

$\Diamond(M \text{ or } N)a = \Diamond Ma \cup \Diamond Na$

$\Box Ia = \Diamond Ia = a$

$\Box M(-a) = \Box M(a \cup -a) \cap -\Diamond Ma$

$\Diamond M(-a) \leqslant M(a \cup -a) \cap -\Box Ma$

$\Box(M \text{ o } N)a = \Box M(\Box Na)$

$\Diamond(M \text{ o } N)a = \Diamond M(\Diamond Na)$

$\Box(M \curlyvee_a N)b = (a \cap \Box Mb) \cup (-a \cap \Box Nb)$

$\Diamond(M \curlyvee_a N)b = (a \cap \Diamond Mb) \cup (-a \cap \Diamond Nb)$

$\Box(*_a M)b = \sup_{i \in \omega} \Box(M \curlyvee_a I)^i (b \cap -a)$

$\Diamond(*_a M)b = \sup_{i \in \omega} \Diamond(M \curlyvee_a I)^i (b \cap -a)$.

LEMMA 1.1

In every algorithmic algebra $\langle \mathfrak{I}, \mathfrak{B} \rangle$ the following property holds : For every $a, b \in \mathfrak{B}$ and every $M \in \mathfrak{I}$, if $a \leqslant b$ then $\Diamond Ma \leqslant \Diamond Mb$ and $\Box Ma \leqslant \Box Mb$. □

We shall say that the algorithmic algebra $\langle \mathfrak{T}, \mathfrak{B} \rangle$ is separable if for all $M, N \in \mathfrak{T}$ we have

$M = N$ if and only if for every $a \in \mathfrak{B}$, $\Diamond Ma = \Diamond Na$.

LEMMA 1.2

In every separable algorithmic algebra $\langle \mathfrak{T}, \mathfrak{B} \rangle$ the following equalities hold for every $M, M', M'' \in \mathfrak{T}$ and for every $a, b \in \mathfrak{B}$:

$$M \circ (M' \circ M'') = (M \circ M') \circ M''$$

$$M \text{ or } M' = M' \text{ or } M$$

$$M \circ (M' \text{ or } M'') = (M \circ M') \text{ or } (M \circ M'')$$

$$M \veebar_b M' = M' \veebar_{-b} M$$

$$(M \veebar_b M') \circ M'' = (M \circ M'') \veebar_b (M' \circ M'')$$

$$M \veebar_{b \cup a} M' = (M \veebar_a (M \veebar_b M')) \text{ or } (M \veebar_b (M \veebar_a M'))$$

$$*_b M = (M \veebar_b I) \circ (*_b M) \quad . \qquad \square$$

EXAMPLE

Algebra of programs and the Lindenbaum algebra of the propositional algorithmic logic create an example of an algorithmic algebra [5]. This algebra is not separable since for example the following program

$$(M \text{ or } (\text{while } (a \cup -a) \text{ do } M))$$

is not identical to the program M and for an arbitrary Boolean element b we have :

$$\Diamond(M \text{ or } (\text{while } (a \cup -a) \text{ do } M))\, b = \Diamond Mb \quad . \qquad \square$$

REMARK

Let $\langle \mathfrak{T}, \mathfrak{B} \rangle$ be an algorithmic algebra and $\approx$ be a relation defined for all $M, M' \in \mathfrak{T}$ as follows : $M \approx M'$ iff $(\forall a \in \mathfrak{B})\ \Diamond Ma = \Diamond M'a$, then $\langle \mathfrak{T}/_{\approx}, \mathfrak{B} \rangle$ is a separable algorithmic algebra . $\square$

In the sequel we shall use the following definition :
An algorithmic algebra $\langle \mathfrak{T}, \mathfrak{B} \rangle$ is said to be n-nondeterministically generated iff there exists a set Π_0 which generates $\mathfrak{T}$ and for all $K \in \Pi_0$ and for all $a_1 \ldots a_m$ the following properties hold

$\Diamond K(a \cup -a) \leq \square K(a \cup -a)$,

$$\bigwedge_{i=(i_1 \ldots i_m)=0}^{n-1} \Diamond K(a_1^{i_1} \cap \ldots \cap a_m^{i_m}) \leq \square K \bigvee_{i=(i_1 \ldots i_m)=0}^{n-1} (a_1^{i_1} \cap \ldots \cap a_m^{i_m})$$

where $(i_1 \ldots i_{m_1})$ is a binary representation of i $, m = \lceil \log_2 n \rceil + 1$ and a^0 denotes a , a^1 denotes -a .

2. THE CHARACTERISTIC EXAMPLE OF ALGORITHMIC ALGEBRA

In this section we present a characteristic example of algorithmic algebra. It is a convolution of an algebra of processes with a field of sets. Let us introduce first auxiliary notions.

For an arbitrary set S let us denote by S^* the set of all finite sequences in S and by S^ω the set of all infinite sequences in S. Let $\bar{S} = S^\omega \cup S^*$.

If X , Y are subsets of S , then XS^*Y denote the set of all sequences with the first element in X and the last element in Y , and XS^ω denote the set of all infinite sequences with the first element in X . I_X denote the set $\{(s,s) : s \in X\}$.

Let $A, B \subset \bar{S}$. then $A \cdot B$ denote the set of all sequences c such that

$$c \in A \cap S^\omega \quad \text{or}$$

$$c \in (S^*\{s\} \cap A) \cdot \{s\}^\omega \quad \text{and} \quad \{s\}\bar{S} \cap B = \emptyset \quad \text{or}$$

$$c = c'sc'' \quad \text{and} \quad c's \in A \cap S^* \quad \text{and} \quad sc'' \in B \cap \{s\}\bar{S} \ .$$

Let S be a nonempty set and Z be a family of subsets of S . By an algebra of processes P(S,Z) we shall mean an abstract algebra

$$\langle P , \{\veebar_X\}_{X \in Z} , o , or , id. \{*_X\}_{X \in Z} \rangle$$

such that

P is a subset of S and for every $p, q \in P$ and for every $X \in Z$ we have

$id = I_S$

$p \text{ o } q = p \cdot q \qquad p \veebar_X q = (X\bar{S} \cap p) \cup ((-X)\bar{S} \cap q)$

$p \text{ or } q = p \cup q \qquad *_X p = I_{-X} \cup (XS^\omega \cap p) \cup (XS^*X \cap p) \cdot (*_X p)$.

LEMMA 2.1

For every $p \in P$ and every set $X \in Z$ in the algebra of processes P(S,Z) the following equivalency hold

$$cs \in (*_X p) \cap S^*\{s\} \quad \text{iff} \quad (\exists j) \ cs \in (p \veebar_X id)^j \ \text{and} \ s \notin X \ .$$

□

By an algebra of computations we shall mean a pair of algebras $\langle P(S,Z), Z\rangle$ where $P(S,Z)$ is an algebra of processes and Z is a field of subsets of the set S with two families of one-argument operations $\{\Diamond p\}_{p\in P}$, $\{\Box p\}_{p\in P}$ such that for every $X,Y \in Z$

$$\Diamond pX = Y \quad \text{iff} \quad \text{for every } y\in Y, \quad p\cap\{y\}S^{*}X \neq \emptyset .$$

$$\Box pX = Y \quad \text{iff} \quad \Diamond pX = Y \text{ and } p\cap YS^{\omega} = \emptyset \text{ and } p\cap YS^{*} \subset YS^{*}X .$$

REMARK

Every semantics of an arbitrary algorithmic logic indicates an algebra of computations . □

Below we shall investigate whether an algebra of computations is an algorithmic algebra .

LEMMA 2.2

In every algebra of computations $\langle P(S,Z), Z\rangle$ the following properties hold : for every $p \in P(S,Z)$ and $X \in Z$

$$\Box p(-X) = \Box pS \cap -\Diamond pX \quad \text{and} \quad \Diamond p(-X) \leq \Diamond pS \cap -\Box pX .$$

The proof is by an easy verification and is omitted . □

REMARK

The equality $-\Diamond pX = \Box p(-X)$ does not hold for every p and X. Indeed , if p contains only infinite sequences or is empty set then $-\Diamond pX = S$ and $\Box p(-X) = \emptyset$. □

LEMMA 2.3

In every algebra of computations $\langle P(S,Z),Z\rangle$ the following equalities hold for every $p,q \in P(S,Z)$ and every $X,Y \in Z$

$$\Box p(X\cap Y) = \Box pX \cap \Box pY \qquad \Box(p \text{ or } q)X = \Box pX \cap \Box qX$$

$$\Diamond p(X\cup Y) = \Diamond pX \cup \Diamond pY \qquad \Diamond(p \text{ or } q)X = \Diamond pX \cup \Diamond qX$$

$$\Box(p \circ q)X = \Box p(\Box qX) \qquad \Box(p \veebar_X q)Y = (X\cap \Box pY) \cup (-X\cap \Box qY)$$

$$\Diamond(p \circ q)X = \Diamond p(\Diamond qX) \qquad \Diamond(p \veebar_X q)Y = (X\cap \Diamond pY) \cup (-X\cap \Diamond qY).$$

PROOF

As an example we shall prove only one from the mentioned above equalities. The remaining ones can be shown analogously .

Let $y \in \Diamond(p \circ q)X$ for some $p,q \in P(S,Z)$ and $X \in Z$. By the definition of the algebra of computation we have

$$(p \circ q) \cap \{y\}S^*X \neq \emptyset .$$

By the definition of the operation $\circ$, there exist finite sequences c, c' and states $s,s' \in S$ such that

$$yc's' \in p \quad , \quad s'cs \in q \quad \text{and} \quad s \in X .$$

Thus there exist finite sequence c' and a state $s' \in S$ such that

$$yc's' \in p \quad \text{and} \quad s' \in \Diamond qX .$$

Hence $y \in \Diamond p(\Diamond qX)$. This proves that $\Diamond(p \circ q)X = \Diamond p(\Diamond qX)$. □

LEMMA 2.4

(1) In every algebra of computations $\langle P(S,Z), Z \rangle$

$$\Diamond(*_X p)Y = \bigcup_{j \in \omega} \Diamond(p \veebar_X id)^j(Y-X)$$

$$\Box(*_X p)Y \supset \bigcup_{j \in \omega} \Box(p \veebar_X id)^j(Y-X)$$

for every $p \in P(S,Z)$ and $X,Y \in Z$.

(2) There exists an algebra of computations such that

$$\Box(*_X p)Y \neq \bigcup_{j \in \omega} \Box(p \veebar_X id)^j(Y-X) \quad \text{for some } p \in P(S,Z) \text{ and } X,Y \in Z.$$

PROOF

(1) If $s \in \Diamond(*_X p)Y$ then there exists a finite sequence $scs' \in *_X p$ such that $s' \in Y$. By lemma 2.1 there exists i_o such that

$$scs' \in (p \veebar_X id)^{i_o} \quad \text{and} \quad s' \in Y-X .$$

Hence $s \in \Diamond(p \veebar_X id)^{i_o}(Y-X)$ and therefore $s \in \bigcup_{j \in \omega} \Diamond(p \veebar_X id)^{i_o}(Y-X)$.
Conversely.
$s \in \bigcup_{j \in \omega} \Diamond(p \veebar_X id)^i(Y-X)$ implies that $s \in \Diamond(p \veebar_X id)^{i_o}(Y-X)$ for some i_o. Hence, there is a finite sequence $scs' \in (p \veebar_X id)^{i_o}$ such that $s' \in Y$ and $s' \notin X$. It means that $scs' \in (*_X p)$ and $s \in Y$ and therefore $s \in \Diamond(*_X p)Y$.

The second part of (1) can be proved analogously.

(2) The proof of (2) is a simple consequence of the remark 2.1 in [6]. □

We shall say that an algebra of computations $P(S,Z),Z$ is n-nondeterministically generated iff there exists a set of binary relations P_o which generates $P(S,Z)$ and for every $p\in P_o$ and every $s\in S$ $\text{card}\{s':(s,s')\in p\} \leq n$.

THEOREM 2.1

Every n-nondeterministically generated algebra of computations is an algorithmic algebra .

PROOF

Let $\langle P(S,Z),Z\rangle$ be an n-nondeterministically generated algebra of computations. By lemmas 2.2, 2.3 and 2.4 it is enough to prove that for every $p\in P$ and every $X,Y\in Z$

$$\Box(*_X p)Y = \bigcup_{j\in\omega}\Box(p \veebar_X \text{id})^j(Y-X) .$$

Let $s\in\Box(*_X p)Y$. It means that all sequences in $(*_X p)$ are finite and for all $scs'\in *_X p$, $s'\in(Y-X)$. Let us consider the set of all sequences of the form $sc\in p$. We can conceive this set as a tree with the ordering relation " to be an initial segment " . The degree of each vertex in this tree is by assumption at most $\max(2,n)$. By König's lemma there exists a common upper bound of the length of all branches. i.e. there exists a natural number m such that all sequences in $(p \veebar_X \text{id})^m$ are finite and all final elements of these sequences are in $(Y-X)$. Hence $s\in\Box(p \veebar_X \text{id})^m(Y-X)$ and therefore

$$s \in \bigcup_{j\in\omega}\Box(p \veebar_X \text{id})^j(Y-X) . \quad \Box$$

3. THE REPRESENTATION THEOREM

In this section we shall consider a class of algorithmic algebras which are n-nondeterministically generated. Our aim is to prove that every separable , enumerable algebra of that class is isomorphic to an n-nondeterministically generated algebra of computations.

We adopt the following definition of isomorphism .

Two algorithmic algebras $\langle\mathfrak{I}_1,\mathfrak{B}_1\rangle$ and $\langle\mathfrak{I}_2,\mathfrak{B}_2\rangle$ are isomorphic iff there exists a pair of functions (h,h') such that

$$h : \mathcal{T}_1 \xrightarrow[\text{onto}]{1-1} \mathcal{T}_2 \qquad h' : \mathcal{B}_1 \xrightarrow[\text{onto}]{1-1} \mathcal{B}_2$$

and for every $a, b \in \mathcal{B}_1$ and for every $M, N \in \mathcal{T}_1$

$$h(M \circ N) = h(M) \circ h(N) \qquad h'(a \cup b) = h'(a) \cup h'(b)$$
$$h(M \text{ or } N) = h(M) \text{ or } h(N) \qquad h'(a \cap b) = h'(a) \cap h'(b)$$
$$h(M \veebar_a N) = h(M) \veebar_{h'(a)} h(N) \qquad h'(-a) = -h'(a)$$
$$h(*_a M) = *_{h'(a)} h(M)$$
$$h'(\Diamond Ma) = \Diamond h(M) h'(a)$$
$$h'(\Box Ma) = \Box h(M) h'(a).$$

Below we shall show the construction of the canonical algebra for a given algorithmic algebra $\langle \mathcal{T}, \mathcal{B} \rangle$. This algebra appears to be an algebra of computations isomorphic to the algebra $\langle \mathcal{T}, \mathcal{B} \rangle$.

Let $\langle \mathcal{T}, \mathcal{B} \rangle$ be an n-nondeterministically generated, enumerable algorithmic algebra and let Π_0 be the set of generators of $\mathcal{T}$. By Q we shall denote the set of all infinite operations in $\mathcal{B}$ of the following form :

$$\sup_{i \in \omega} \Diamond (M \veebar_a I)^i (-a \cap b) \qquad \sup_{i \in \omega} \Box (M \veebar_a I)^i (-a \cap b)$$

where $a, b \in \mathcal{B}$ and $M \in \mathcal{T}$.

Let us denote by S the set of all Q-filters in $\mathcal{B}$ and by Z the family of sets $Z_a = \{ F \in S : a \in F \}$ for $a \in \mathcal{B}$.

By $P_{\mathcal{T}}$ we shall denote the algebra of processes generated by the sets S and Z and such that

$$P_{\mathcal{T}} = \langle \{p_M\}_{M \in \mathcal{T}}, \circ, \text{or}, \{\veebar_X\}_{X \in Z}, \{*_X\}_{X \in Z} \rangle$$

where

$$p_K = \{ (F, F') \in S^2 : \Diamond K (a \cap -a) \in F, (\forall a)(\Box Ka \in F \Rightarrow a \in F') \} \text{ for all } K \in \Pi_0$$

and for all $M, N \in \mathcal{T}$

$$p(M \circ N) = p_M \circ p_N \qquad p(M \text{ or } N) = p_M \text{ or } p_N$$
$$p(M \veebar_a N) = p_M \veebar_{Z_a} p_N \qquad p(*_a M) = *_{Z_a} p_M \quad .$$

LEMMA 3.1

The family Z is a field of sets .

The proof is by an easy verification and is omitted . □

LEMMA 3.2

The system $\langle P_{\mathfrak{T}} , Z_{\mathfrak{B}} \rangle$ creates an n-nondeterministically generated algebra of computations .

PROOF

The proof will consist of two steps :

1°. For every $K \in \Pi_0$ and every $F \in S$, card $\{F' : (F,F') \in p_K\} \leq n$,

2°. For every $M \in \mathfrak{T}$ and every $a \in \mathfrak{B}$

$$\Diamond p_M Z_a = Z_{\Diamond Ma}$$

$$\Box p_M Z_a = Z_{\Box Ma} .$$

Ad 1°. Let us assume that $n = 3$. Suppose that for some $K \in \Pi_0$ and for some Q-filter F there exist four different Q-filters $F_1 \ldots F_4$ such that $(F,F_i) \in p_K$ for $i = 1,\ldots,4$. Thus there exist Boolean elements $b_1,\ldots,b_4$ such that

$$b_i \in F_i - \bigcap_{j \neq i} F_j \qquad i = 1,\ldots,4 .$$

Let us put

$$a_1 = (b_1 \cap -b_2 \cap -b_3 \cap -b_4) \cup (b_2 \cap -b_1 \cap -b_3 \cap -b_4)$$

$$a_2 = (b_1 \cap -b_2 \cap -b_3 \cap -b_4) \cup (-b_1 \cap -b_2 \cap b_3 \cap -b_4) .$$

Then $[\Diamond K(a_1 \cap a_2) \cap \Diamond K(a_1 \cap -a_2) \cap \Diamond K(-a_1 \cap a_2)] \in F$. Since by assumption the algebra $\langle \mathfrak{T} . \mathfrak{B} \rangle$ is 3-nondeterministically generated then

$$\Box K (a_1 \cup a_2) \in F .$$

Hence by the definition of the relation p_K , $(a_1 \cup a_2) \in F_4$, contrary to the definition of this filter .

Analogously we can prove the property 1° for every natural number n .

Ad 2°. The prove of 2° is by induction on the complexity of M .

Let $M \in \Pi_0$ and suppose $F \notin Z_{\Diamond Ma}$ and $F \in \Diamond p_M Z_a$. Hence $-\Diamond Ma \in F$ and there exists F' such that $(F,F') \in p_M$ and $a \in F'$.

By the definition of p_M for $M \in \Pi_0$ we have

(1) $\Diamond M(a \cup -a) \in F$,

(2) for every $a \in \mathfrak{B}$ if $\Box Ma \in F$ then $a \in F'$.

By the properties of algorithmic algebra and by (1) we have $\Box M(-a) \in F$. Thus by (2) $-a \in F'$, contrary to $a \in F'$.

Conversely, let us assume that $F \in Z_{\Diamond Ma}$. By lemma 10.4 in [6] there exists Q-filter F' such that a F' and $(F,F') \in p_M$ .Hence $F \in \Diamond p_M Z_a$.

Assume that property 2° holds for all M', M'' that are of less complexity than M and for all $a \in \mathfrak{B}$.

Let M be of the form $*_a M'$.

$F \in Z_{\Box(*_a M')b}$ iff $\Box(*_a M')b \in F$ iff $\sup_{j\in\omega} \Box(M' \veebar_a id)^j(-a\cap b) \in F$.

Since F is a Q-filter then there exists natural number j such that

$$\Box(M' \veebar_a id)^j\,(-a\cap b) \in F \quad .$$

By inductive assumption , there exists j such that $F \in \Box p_{(M' \veebar_a id)^j}\, Z_{(-a\cap b)}$ and therefore $F \in \Box(p_{M'} \veebar_{Z_a} id)^j(-Z_a \cap Z_b)$.

Thus all sequences of the form Fc which belong to $(p_{M'} \veebar_{Z_a} id)^j$ are finite and all terminal elements of these sequences belong to $(-Z_a \cap Z_b)$. By 1^0 it follows that all sequences in $(*_{Z_a} p_{M'})$ of the form Fc are finite and all its terminal elements belong to Z_b . Hence $F \in \Box(p_{*_a M'})Z_b$.

All the remaining cases can be checked analogously . $\Box$

The algebra of computations $\langle P_{\mathfrak{I}} , Z_{\mathfrak{B}} \rangle$ defined above will be called canonical for the algorithmic algebra $\langle \mathfrak{I}, \mathfrak{B} \rangle$.

THEOREM 3.1

Every separable n-nondeterministically generated, enumerable algorithmic algebra is isomorphic to an algebra of computations .

PROOF

Let $\langle \mathfrak{I}, \mathfrak{B} \rangle$ be a separable, enumerable, n-nondeterministically generated algorithmic algebra and let $\langle P_{\mathfrak{I}} , Z_{\mathfrak{B}} \rangle$ denote its canonical algebra .

We shall prove that the mappings

$$h : \mathfrak{I} \longrightarrow P_{\mathfrak{I}} \quad \text{and} \quad h' : \mathfrak{B} \longrightarrow Z_{\mathfrak{B}}$$

defined for all $M \in \mathfrak{I}$ and $a \in \mathfrak{B}$ as follows

$$h(M) = p_M \qquad h'(a) = Z_a$$

create isomorphism between $\langle \mathfrak{I}, \mathfrak{B} \rangle$ and $\langle P_{\mathfrak{I}} , Z_{\mathfrak{B}} \rangle$.

(a) The function h' is an one-one mapping .

Let $a \neq b$, $a, b \in \mathfrak{B}$. Then $a \cap -b \neq 0$ or $b \cap -a \neq 0$, where 0 is the smallest element of $\mathfrak{B}$. By lemma 9.3 in[9] there exists Q-filter F_0 in $\mathfrak{B}$ such that $a \cap -b \in F_0$ or $b \cap -a \in F_0$. Hence $\{F : a \in F\} \neq \{F : b \in F\}$, i.e. $h'(a) \neq h'(b)$.

(b) The functions h and h′ are homomorphisms.

This follows immediately from the definition of functions h,h′ and from lemma 3.2 .

(c) The function h is an one-one mapping .

Let $M \neq M'$ and $M, M' \in \mathfrak{T}$. Since $\langle \mathfrak{T}, \mathfrak{B} \rangle$ is a separable algorithmic algebra then there exists $b \in \mathfrak{B}$ such that $\Diamond Mb \neq \Diamond M'b$.

By (a) we have $h'(\Diamond Mb) \neq h'(\Diamond M'b)$ and by (b) $\Diamond h(M)h'(b) \neq \Diamond h(M')h'(b)$.

Let $F \in \Diamond h(M)h'(a)$ and $F \notin \Diamond h(M')h'(a)$, Hence there exists a finite sequence of the form FcF' in $h(M)$ such that $c \in S^*$, $a \in F'$.

But $FcF' \notin h(M')$. Thus $h(M) \neq h(M')$. □

REFERENCES

[1] Glushkow W., On the problem of minimalization of programs and schemes of algorithms, Kibiernietika, 1966, 5 ,

[2] Kozen D., On the duality of dynamic algebras and Kripke models, IBM Reports , 10/5/79 ,

[3] Kozen D., On the representation of dynamic algebras, IBM Reports 10 /10/ 79 .

[4] Kozen D.. A representation theorem for models of -free PDL, IBM Reports , 9 /7/ 79 .

[5] Mirkowska G., Algorithmic logic and its applications in the theory of programs , doctoral dissertation ,University of Warsaw 1972 ,

[6] Mirkowska G., PAL - propositional algorithmic logic .Fundamenta Informaticae 1981,

[7] Pratt V., Dynamic algebras : examples, constructions applications , MIT Reports LCS/TM - 138, 1979.

[8] Pratt V., Dynamic algebras and the nature of induction , 12-th Ann, ACM Symp. on Theory of Computing , Los Angeles CA May 1980 .

[9] Rasiowa H..Sikorski R., The Mathematics of metamathematics, PWN Warsaw , 1963 ,

[10] Reiterman J..Trnkova V., Dynamic algebras which are not Kripke structures , MFCS′80, Lecture Notes in Computer Sci., Springer Verlag 1980 .

NONSTANDARD DYNAMIC LOGIC

I. Németi

Math. Inst. Hungar. Acad. Sci. Budapest
Reáltanoda u. 13-15, H-1053 Hungary

There does exist a branch of Dynamic Logic which is called Nonstandard Dynamic Logic. Works in this line are e.g. [4],[3],[22],[23],[1],[11],[9],[13],[18],[5],[14],[21]. A systematic introductory monograph with motivation, examples, overview of the field etc. is [4] which will be sent to anybody on request. A published introduction to Nonstandard DL with at least some of these features is [3]. Intuitive examples, illustrations are in [18],[20],[4]. The first results in this field were proved in [1] in 1977 under the restriction that the data structure satisfies Peano's axioms. This condition was later eliminated by the above quoted works.

In the present paper we give the basic definitions of Nonstandard DL (§1-3). We formulate some fundamental results and indicate that this logic is <u>not so very nonstandard</u> as one might think, see RDL in Def.13 and Prop.2. Then we show how to use this logic to compare methods of program verification. Some well known program verification methods will be characterized, see Fig.2. Some properties of the lattice of logics of programs with decidable proof concepts will be established. §5 contains the detailed proof of Thm.6. This proof uses model theoretic tools (e.g. ultraproducts) to establish properties of program verification methods. The emphasis is on basic definitions and properties of Nonstandard DL, on Fig.2, and on the proof of Thm.6. For intuitive motivation see the very end of the present paper.

Connections with other branches of nonclassical logic and computer science are discussed in §8,9 of [3]Part II and in §6-8 of [4]. Motivation for Nonstandard DL is e.g. in [22],[4],[3].

NOTATIONS

In the following we shall recall some standard notations from textbooks on logic (mainly from [17],[8]).

d   denotes an arbitrary similarity type of classical one-sorted models. I.e. d correlates arities (natural numbers) to function and relation symbols. See Def.1(i) in this paper.

ω denotes the set of natural numbers such that $0 \in \omega$.

Natural numbers are used in the von Neumann sense, i.e.

$n = \{0,1,\ldots,n-1\}$ and in particular

0 is the empty set.

$X = \{x_w : w \in \omega\}$ denotes a set of variables.

F_d is the set of classical first order formulas of type d with variables in X. Cf. e.g. [8]p.22.

τ denotes a term of type d in the usual sense of logic, see [8]p.22 or [17]p.166,Def.10.8(ii).

M_d denotes the class of all classical one-sorted models of type d, see e.g. [8] or [17]Def.11.1, or Def.s 1 and 3 here.

A classical one-sorted model is denoted by an underlined capital like $\underset{\sim}{T}$ or $\underset{\sim}{D}$ and its universe is denoted by the same capital without underlining. E.g. T is the universe of $\underset{\sim}{T}$, and D is that of $\underset{\sim}{D}$.

By a "valuation of the variables" in a model $\underset{\sim}{D}$ a function $g : \omega \to D$ is understood, see [17]p.195.

$\tau[q]_{\underset{\sim}{D}}$ denotes the value of the term τ in the model $\underset{\sim}{D}$ under the valuation q of the variables, see [8]p.27,Def.13.13 or [17] Def.11.2. If τ contains no variable then we write τ instead of $\tau[q]_{\underset{\sim}{D}}$, if $\underset{\sim}{D}$ is understood.

$\underset{\sim}{D} \models \varphi[q]$ denotes that the valuation q satisfies the formula φ in the model $\underset{\sim}{D}$.

$L_d = \langle F_d, M_d, \models \rangle$ is the classical first order language of similarity type d, see [22].

${}^{A}B$ denotes the set of all functions from A into B, i.e. ${}^{A}B = \{f : f \text{ maps } A \text{ into } B\}$, see [17]p.7.

A function is considered to be a set of pairs.

Dom f denotes the domain of the function f, $\text{Dom } f \overset{d}{=} \{a : (\exists b)\langle a,b\rangle \in f\}$.

Rng f denotes the range of the function f, $\text{Rng } f \overset{d}{=} \{b : (\exists a)\langle a,b\rangle \in f\}$.

A sequence s of lenght n is a function with Dom s = n.

$\langle U_s : s \in S\rangle$ denotes the function $\{\langle s,U_s\rangle : s \in S\}$. Moreover for an expression Expr(x) and class S we define

$\langle \text{Expr}(x) : x \in S\rangle$ to be the function $f : S \to \text{Rng } f$ such that $(\forall x \in S)$ $f(x) = \text{Expr}(x)$.

$\text{Sb}(X) \overset{d}{=} \{Y : Y \subseteq X\}$ is the powerset of X.

X^* denotes the set of all finite sequences of elements of X, i.e. $X^* \overset{d}{=} \bigcup\{{}^{m}X : m \in \omega\}$. We shall identify X^* with $\{H : H \subseteq X \text{ and } |H| < \omega\}^*$, and also with $(X^*)^*$. We think of X^* as the set of "words over the alphabet X".

$A \sim B \overset{d}{=} \{a \in A : a \notin B\}$.

§1. SYNTAX of program schemes

Recall d, X, F_d from the list of notations. Now we define the set P_d of program schemes of type d.

The set Lab of "label symbols" is defined to be an arbitrary but fixed subset of the set Tm_d^0 of all constant terms of type d, i.e. d-type terms which do not contain variable symbols. (Lab is chosen this way for technical reasons only. There are many other possible ways for handling labels, see [23].) Logical symbols: $\{\wedge, \neg, \exists, =\}$. Other symbols: $\{\leftarrow$, IF, GOTO, HALT, (,) , : $\}$.

The set U_d of commands of type d is defined as follows:

$(i: x \leftarrow \tau) \in U_d$ if $i \in Lab$, $x \in X$, and τ is a term of type d and with all variables in X.

$(i: \text{IF } \chi \text{ GOTO } v) \in U_d$ if $i, v \in Lab$, $\chi \in F_d$ is a formula without quantifier.

$(i: \text{HALT}) \in U_d$ if $i \in Lab$.

These are the only elements of U_d.

By a program scheme of type d we understand a finite sequence p of commands (elements of U_d) ending with a "HALT", in which no two members have the same label, and in which the only "HALT-command" is the last one. Further, if $(i: \text{IF } \chi \text{ GOTO } v)$ occurs in p then there is u such that the command (v:u) occurs in p. I.e. an element p of P_d is of the form $p = \langle(i_0:u_0),\dots,(i_{n-1}:u_{n-1}),(i_n:\text{HALT})\rangle$ where $n \in \omega$, $(i_m:u_m) \in U_d$ for $m \leq n$ etc.

Convention 1 If a program scheme is denoted by p then its parts are denoted as follows:

$$p = \langle(i_0:u_0),\dots,(i_{n-1}:u_{n-1}),(i_n:\text{HALT})\rangle .$$

Throughout we shall use the definition

$$c \stackrel{d}{=} \min\{w \in \omega \ : \ (\forall v \in \omega \sim w)[x_v \text{ does not occur in p}]\}.$$

I.e. $\{x_w : w < c\}$ contains all the variables occurring in the program scheme p, and if $c > 0$ then x_{c-1} really occurs in p. We shall use x_c as the control variable of p.

An example for a program scheme $p \in P_d$ is found in §5 in the proof of Thm.6 on Fig.3.

§2. SEMANTICS of program schemes

By a language with semantics we understand a triple $L = \langle F , M , \models \rangle$ of classes such that $\models \subseteq M \times F \times Sets$ where Sets is the class of all sets. Here F is called the syntax of L, M the class of models or possible interpretations of L, and $\models$ the satisfaction relation of L. Instead of $\langle a,b,c \rangle \in \models$ we write $a \models b[c]$, and we say "c satisfies b in a". See [22].

Here we try to develop a natural semantic framework for programs and statements about programs. In trying to understand the "Programming Situation", its languages, their meanings etc. the first question is how an interpretation or model of a program or program scheme $p \in P_d$ should look like. The classical approach says that an interpretation or model of a program scheme is a relational structure $\underset{\sim}{D} \in M_d$ consisting of all the possible data values. The program p contains variables, say "x". The classical approach says that x denotes elements of D just as variables in classical first order logic do. Now we argue that x does not denote elements of D but rather x denotes some kind of "locations or "addresses" which may contain different data values (i.e. elements of D) at different points of time. Thus there is a set I of locations, a set T of time points, and a function $ext : I \times T \to D$ which tells for every location $s \in I$ and time point $b \in T$ what the content of location s is at time point b. Of course, this content ext(s,b) is a data value, i.e. it is an element of D. Time has a structure too ("later than" etc.) and data values have structure too, thus we have structures $\underset{\sim}{T}$ and $\underset{\sim}{D}$ over the sets T and D of time points and possible data values respectively. Therefore we shall define a model or interpretation for programs $p \in P_d$ to be a four-tuple $\mathfrak{M} = \langle \underset{\sim}{T} , \underset{\sim}{D} , I , ext \rangle$ where $\underset{\sim}{T}$ and $\underset{\sim}{D}$ are the time structure and data structure resp., I is the set of locations and $ext : I \times T \to D$ is the "content of ... at time ..." function (see Def.4). We shall call the elements of I intensions instead of locations. The reasons for this and for the name "ext" are explained in [3]§9,[4]§8. For a detailed account of the above considerations see also §8,9 of [3] and §7,8 of [4].

Of course when specifying semantics of a programming language P_d we may have ideas about how an interpretation $\mathfrak{M}$ of P_d may look like and how it may not look. These ideas may be expressed in the form of axioms about $\mathfrak{M}$. E.g. we may postulate that $\underset{\sim}{T}$ of $\mathfrak{M}$ has to satisfy the Peano Axioms of arithmetic. For such axioms see Def.s 13-17. These axioms are easy to express since a closer investigation of $\mathfrak{M}$ defined above reveals that it is a model of classical 3-sorted logic (the sorts being "time", "data" and "intensions"). Thus the axioms can be formed in classical 3-sorted logic (Def.5) in a convenient manner to express all our ideas or postulates about the semantics of the programming language P_d under consideration.

Now we turn to work out these ideas in detail.

DEFINITION 1 (one-sorted models)

(i) By a (classical or one-sorted) similarity type d we understand a pair $d = \langle H, d_1 \rangle$ such that d_1 is a function $d_1 : \Sigma \to \omega$ for some set Σ, $H \subseteq \Sigma$ and $(\forall r \in \Sigma) d_1(r) \neq 0$.

The elements of Σ are called the symbols of d and the elements of H are called the operation symbols or function symbols of d. Let $r \in \Sigma$. Then we shall write $d(r)$ instead of $d_1(r)$.

(ii) Let $d = \langle H, d_1 \rangle$ be a similarity type, let $\Sigma = \mathrm{Dom}\, d_1$ as above. By a model of type d we understand a pair $\underset{\sim}{D} = \langle D, R \rangle$ such that R is a function with $\mathrm{Dom}\, R = \Sigma$ and $(\forall r \in \Sigma) R(r) \subseteq {}^{d(r)}D$ and if $r \in H$ then $R(r) : {}^{(d(r)-1)}D \to D$.

Notation: $\langle D, R_r \rangle_{r \in \Sigma} \stackrel{d}{=} \langle D, \langle R_r : r \in \Sigma \rangle \rangle \stackrel{d}{=} \langle D, R \rangle$.

I.e. $\underset{\sim}{D} = \langle D, R_r \rangle_{r \in \Sigma}$ is a model of type d iff R_r is a $d(r)$-ary relation over D and if $r \in H$ then R_r is a $(d(r)-1)$-ary function, for all $r \in \Sigma$.

If $r \in H$ and $d(r)=1$ then there is a unique $b \in D$ such that $R_r = \{\langle b \rangle\}$ and we shall identify R_r with b. If $r \in H$, $d(r)=1$ then r is said to be a constant symbol and $R_r \in D$ is the constant element denoted by r in $\underset{\sim}{D}$.

The set D is called the universe of $\underset{\sim}{D}$.

(iii) $M_d \stackrel{d}{=} \{\underset{\sim}{D} : \underset{\sim}{D} \text{ is a model of type } d\}$.

End of Definition 1

DEFINITION 2 (the similarity type t of arithmetic and its standard model $\underset{\sim}{N}$)

t denotes the similarity type of Peano's arithmetic. In more detail, $t = \langle \{0, sc, +, \cdot\}, t_1 \rangle$ where $\mathrm{Dom}\, t_1 = \{\leq, 0, sc, +, \cdot\}$, $t(\leq)=2$, $t(0)=1$, $t(sc)=2$ and $t(+)=t(\cdot)=3$.

The standard model $\underset{\sim}{N}$ of t will be sloppily denoted as $\langle \omega, \leq, 0, suc, +, \cdot \rangle = \underset{\sim}{N}$ instead of the more precise notation $\underset{\sim}{N} = \langle \omega, R \rangle$ where $R(\leq) = \{\langle n, m \rangle \in {}^2\omega : n \leq m\}, \ldots, R(sc) = \langle n+1 : n \in \omega \rangle$. Note that $\underset{\sim}{N} \in M_t$. End of Definition 2

Throughout the paper t is supposed to be disjoint from any other similarity type, moreover if d is a similarity type then $Dom(d_1) \cap Dom(t_1)=0$ is assumed throughout the paper.

<u>DEFINITION 3</u> (many-sorted models, [17])

(i) By a <u>many-sorted similarity type</u> m we understand a triple $m = \langle S,H,m_2\rangle$ such that m_2 is a function $m_2 : \Sigma \to S^*$ for some set Σ, $H \subseteq \Sigma$ and $(\forall r \in \Sigma) m_2(r) \notin {}^0S$.

The elements of S are called the <u>sorts</u> of m. If $r \in \Sigma$ then we shall write $m(r)$ instead of $m_2(r)$.

(ii) Let m be a many-sorted similarity type and let $\Sigma = Dom\ m_2$ as above. By a <u>(many-sorted) model</u> of type m we understand a pair $\mathfrak{M} = \langle\langle U_s : s \in S\rangle, R\rangle$ such that R is a function with $Dom\ R = \Sigma$ and if $r \in \Sigma$ and $m(r) = \langle s_1,\ldots,s_n\rangle$ then $R(r) \subseteq U_{s_1} \times \ldots \times U_{s_n}$ and if in addition $r \in H$ then $R(r)$ is a function $R(r) : U_{s_1} \times \ldots \times U_{s_{n-1}} \to U_{s_n}$.

U_s is said to be the <u>universe of sort s</u> of $\mathfrak{M}$.

(iii) $M_m \overset{d}{=} \{\mathfrak{M} : \mathfrak{M}$ is a many-sorted model of type $m\}$.

<u>End of Definition 3</u>

<u>DEFINITION 4</u> (the 3-sorted similarity type td)

(i) To any one-sorted similarity type d we associate a 3-sorted similarity type td as follows:

Let $d = \langle H,d_1\rangle$ be any one-sorted similarity type. Recall that t is a fixed similarity type introduced in Def.2 and by our convention $Dom(d_1) \cap Dom(t_1)=0$.

Now we define td to be $td \overset{d}{=} \langle S,K,td_2\rangle$ where

a) $S \overset{d}{=} \{t,d,i\}$, $|S|=3$. (S is the set of sorts of td.) Here the elements of S are used as symbols only; we could have chosen $S = \{0,1,2\}$ as well.

b) $K \overset{d}{=} \{ext,0,sc,+,\cdot\} \cup H$. ($K$ is the set of operation symbols of td.)

c) $td_2 : (Dom(t_1) \cup Dom(d_1) \cup \{ext\}) \to S^*$ such that
$td_2(ext) = \langle i,t,d\rangle$,
$td_2(r) \in {}^n\{t\}$ if $t(r)=n$ and
$td_2(r) \in {}^n\{d\}$ if $d(r)=n$.
E.g. $td_2(\leq)=\langle t,t\rangle$, $td_2(+)=\langle t,t,t\rangle$, etc.

By these the 3-sorted similarity type td is defined.

(ii) Let $\mathfrak{M} = \langle\langle U_t,U_d,U_i\rangle, R_r\rangle_{r\in\Sigma}$ be a td-type model. Then (1)-(3) below hold:

(1) $\langle U_t, R_r \rangle_{r\in Dom(t_1)} \in M_t$.

(2) $\langle U_d, R_r \rangle_{r\in Dom(d_1)} \in M_d$.

(3) $R_{ext} : U_i \times U_t \to U_d$.

Notation: $\langle\langle U_t, R_r \rangle_{r\in Dom(t_1)}, \langle U_d, R_r \rangle_{r\in Dom(d_1)}, U_i, R_{ext}\rangle \overset{d}{=}$
$\overset{d}{=} \langle\langle U_t, U_d, U_i\rangle, R_r\rangle_{r\in\Sigma}$.

We define: $\underset{\sim}{T} \overset{d}{=} \langle U_t, R_r\rangle_{r\in Dom(t_1)}$, $T \overset{d}{=} U_t$,
$\underset{\sim}{D} \overset{d}{=} \langle U_d, R_r\rangle_{r\in Dom(d_1)}$, $D \overset{d}{=} U_d$ and $I \overset{d}{=} U_i$.

The sorts t,d, and i are called time, data and intensions respectively. $\underset{\sim}{T}$ is said to be the time-structure of $\mathfrak{M}$.

End of Definition 4

Convention 2 Whenever an element of M_{td} is denoted by the letter $\mathfrak{M}$ then the parts of $\mathfrak{M}$ are denoted as follows:

$\langle \underset{\sim}{T}, \underset{\sim}{D}, I, ext\rangle \overset{d}{=} \langle\langle U_t^{\mathfrak{M}}, U_d^{\mathfrak{M}}, U_i^{\mathfrak{M}}\rangle, r^{\mathfrak{M}}\rangle_{r\in\Sigma} \overset{d}{=} \mathfrak{M}$.

Note that $\mathfrak{M}\in M_{td}$ iff $[\underset{\sim}{T}\in M_t, \underset{\sim}{D}\in M_d$, and $ext : I\times T \to D]$.

For a more detailed introduction to many-sorted languages, like $L_{td} = \langle F_{td}, M_{td}, \models\rangle$ defined below, the reader is referred e.g. to the textbook [17]. If understanding Def.s 3-6 here is hard for the reader then consulting [17] should help since L_{td} is the most usual classical many-sorted language of similarity type td.

DEFINITION 5 (the first order 3-sorted language $L_{td} = \langle F_{td}, M_{td}, \models\rangle$ of type td, [17])

Let $d = \langle H, d_1\rangle$ be any one-sorted similarity type. Recall from Def.s 3 and 4 that t is a fixed similarity type, and td is a 3-sorted similarity type with sorts {t,d,i}.

(i) We define the set F_{td} of first order 3-sorted formulas of type td.:

Let $X \overset{d}{=} \{x_w : w\in\omega\}$, $Y \overset{d}{=} \{y_w : w\in\omega\}$ and $Z \overset{d}{=} \{z_w : w\in\omega\}$ be three disjoint sets (and $x_w \neq x_j$ if $w\neq j\in\omega$ etc). We define Z, X, and Y to be the sets of variables of sorts t, d, and i respectively.

F_t^Z denotes the set of all first order formulas of type t with variables in Z, F_d denotes the set of all first order formulas of type d with variables in X, and Tm_t^Z denotes the set of all first order terms of type t with variables in Z.

The set $Tm_{td,d}$ of terms of type td and of sort d is defined to be the smallest set satisfying conditions (1)-(3) below.

(1) $X \subseteq Tm_{td,d}$.

(2) $ext(y_w,\tau) \in Tm_{td,d}$ for any $\tau \in Tm_t^Z$ and $w \in \omega$.

(3) $f(\tau_1,\dots,\tau_n) \in Tm_{td,d}$ for any $f \in H$ if $d(f)=n+1$ and $\tau_1,\dots,\tau_n \in Tm_{td,d}$.

The set F_{td} of first order formulas of type td is defined to be the smallest set satisfying conditions (4)-(8) below.

(4) $(\tau_1=\tau_2) \in F_{td}$ for any $\tau_1,\tau_2 \in Tm_{td,d}$.

(5) $r(\tau_1,\dots,\tau_n) \in F_{td}$ for any $\tau_1,\dots,\tau_n \in Tm_{td,d}$ and for any $r \in H$ if $d(r)=n$.

(6) $(y_w=y_j) \in F_{td}$ for any $w,j \in \omega$.

(7) $F_t^Z \subseteq F_{td}$.

(8) $\{\neg\varphi, (\varphi\wedge\psi), (\exists z_w\varphi), (\exists x_w\varphi), (\exists y_w\varphi) : w \in \omega\} \subseteq F_{td}$ for any $\varphi,\psi \in F_{td}$.

By this the set F_{td} has been defined. Note that $F_d \subseteq F_{td}$.

(ii) Now we define the "meanings" of elements of F_{td}.

By a <u>valuation</u> (of the variables) into $\mathfrak{M}$ we understand a triple $v=\langle g,k,r\rangle$ such that $g \in {}^{\omega}T$, $k \in {}^{\omega}D$ and $r \in {}^{\omega}I$. The statement "<u>the valuation</u> $v=\langle g,k,r\rangle$ <u>satisfies</u> φ <u>in</u> $\mathfrak{M}$" is denoted by $\mathfrak{M} \models \varphi[v]$ or equivalently by $\mathfrak{M} \models \varphi[g,k,r]$.

The truth of $\mathfrak{M} \models \varphi[g,k,r]$ is defined the usual way (see [17]) which is completely analogous with the one-sorted case. E.g.

$\mathfrak{M} \models (y_0=y_1)[g,k,r]$ iff $r_0=r_1$,

$\mathfrak{M} \models (x_1=ext(y_2,z_0))[g,k,r]$ iff $k_1=ext^{\mathfrak{M}}(r_2,g_0)$,

$\mathfrak{M} \models \varphi[g,k,r]$ iff $\underset{\sim}{T} \models \varphi[g]$ for $\varphi \in F_t^Z$,

$\mathfrak{M} \models \varphi[g,k,r]$ iff $\underset{\sim}{D} \models \varphi[k]$ for $\varphi \in F_d$ etc.

The formula $\varphi \in F_{td}$ is <u>valid</u> in $\mathfrak{M}$, in symbols $\mathfrak{M} \models \varphi$, iff $(\forall g \in {}^{\omega}T)(\forall k \in {}^{\omega}D)(\forall r \in {}^{\omega}I)\ \mathfrak{M} \models \varphi[g,k,r]$.

(iii) The (3-sorted) language L_{td} of type td is defined to be the triple $L_{td} = \langle F_{td},M_{td},\models\rangle$ where $\models$ is the satisfaction relation defined in (ii) above.

<u>End of Definition 5</u>

<u>DEFINITION 6</u> (the class STM_d of standard models)

Let $\mathfrak{M} = \langle \underset{\sim}{T},\underset{\sim}{D},I,ext\rangle \in M_{td}$. $\mathfrak{M}$ is said to be <u>standard</u> iff conditions (i)-(iii) below hold.

(i) $\underset{\sim}{T} = \underset{\sim}{N}$. (For $\underset{\sim}{N}$ see Def.2.)

(ii) $I = {}^{\omega}D$.

(iii) $(\forall s \in I)(\forall b \in T)\ ext(s,b) = s(b)$.

The class of all standard elements of M_{td} is denoted by STM_d.

<u>End of Definition 6</u>

In this paper we shall define several sets of axioms in the language L_{td}, see Def.s 13-17. Each of them will be valid in the class STM_d of standard models.

Now we define the <u>meanings of program schemes</u> $p \in P_d$ in the 3-sorted models $\mathfrak{M} \in M_{td}$.

<u>Notation</u>: Let $\langle \underset{\sim}{T}, \underset{\sim}{D}, I, ext \rangle \in M_{td}$, see Convention 2. Let $s_0, \dots, s_m \in I$, $\bar{s} \overset{d}{=} \langle s_0, \dots, s_m \rangle$. Let $b \in T$. Then we define

$ext(\bar{s}, b) \overset{d}{=} \langle ext(s_0,b), \dots, ext(s_m,b) \rangle$.

<u>DEFINITION 7</u> (traces of programs in time-models)

Let $p \in P_d$ and $\mathfrak{M} \in M_{td}$. We shall use Conventions 1 and 2. Let $s_0, \dots, s_c \in I$ be arbitrary intensions in $\mathfrak{M}$. Let $\bar{s} = \langle s_0, \dots, s_{c-1} \rangle$. The sequence $\langle s_0, \dots, s_c \rangle$ of intensions is defined to be a <u>trace of p</u> in $\mathfrak{M}$ if the following (i) and (ii) are satisfied.

(i) $ext(s_c, 0) = i_0$ and $ext(s_c, b) \in \{ i_m : m \leq n \}$ for every $b \in T$.

(ii) For every $b \in T$ and for every $j \leq c$ if $ext(s_c, b) = i_m$ then statements (1)-(3) below hold.

(1) If $u_m = "x_w \leftarrow \tau"$ then

$$ext(s_j, b+1) = \begin{cases} i_{m+1} & \text{if } j=c \\ \tau[ext(\bar{s},b)]_{\underset{\sim}{D}} & \text{if } j=w \\ ext(s_j,b) & \text{otherwise} \end{cases} .$$

(2) If $u_m = $ "IF χ GOTO v" then

$$ext(s_j, b+1) = \begin{cases} v & \text{if } j=c \text{ and } \underset{\sim}{D} \models \chi[ext(\bar{s},b)] \\ i_{m+1} & \text{if } j=c \text{ and } D \not\models \chi[ext(\bar{s},b)]. \\ ext(s_j,b) & \text{otherwise} \end{cases}$$

(3) If $u_m = $ "HALT" then $ext(s_j, b+1) = ext(s_j, b)$.

<u>End of Definition 7</u>

<u>DEFINITION 8</u> (possible output)

Let $s = \langle s_0, \dots, s_c \rangle$ be a trace of $p \in P_d$ in $\mathfrak{M} \in M_{td}$.

(i) Let $k \in {}^{\omega}D$. The trace s is said to be <u>of input k</u> iff $(\forall j < c)\ k(j) = ext(s_j, 0)$.

(ii) Recall from Convention 1 that i_n is the label of the HALT-command of p. Let $b \in T$. We say that <u>s terminates at time b in $\mathfrak{M}$</u> iff $ext(s_c, b) = i_n$.

(iii) Let $k, q \in {}^{\omega}D$. We define q to be a <u>possible output</u> of p <u>with input</u> k in $\mathfrak{M}$ iff (a)-(d) below hold for some s.

(a) $s = \langle s_0, \ldots, s_c \rangle$ is a trace of p in $\mathfrak{M}$.

(b) s is of input k.

(c) There is $b \in T$ such that s terminates p at time b and $\langle q_0, \ldots, q_{c-1} \rangle = \langle ext(s_0, b), \ldots, ext(s_{c-1}, b) \rangle$.

(d) $(\forall j \in \omega)[j \geq c \Rightarrow q_j = k_j]$.

If q is a possible output of p with input k in $\mathfrak{M}$ then we shall also say that $\langle q_0, \ldots, q_{c-1} \rangle$ is a possible output of p with input $\langle k_0, \ldots, k_{c-1} \rangle$.

<u>End of Definition 8</u>

By now we have defined a semantics of program schemes.

<u>Remark</u>: A trace $\langle s_0, \ldots, s_c \rangle$ of a program $p \in P_d$ correlates to each variable x_w $(w \leq c)$ occurring in the program p an intension or "<u>history</u>" s_w such that the value $ext(s_w, b)$ can be considered as the "value contained in" or "extension of" x_w at time point $b \in T$. The intension $s_w \in I$ represents a function $ext(s_w, -) : T \to D$ from time points to data values D. This function is the "history" of the variable x_w during an <u>execution of the program p in the model $\mathfrak{M}$</u>. Def.7 ensures that the sequence $\langle ext(s_0, -), \ldots, ext(s_c, -) \rangle$ of functions can be considered as a behaviour or "run" or "trace" of the program p in $\mathfrak{M}$. Here s_c is the intension of the "control variable".

<u>About using Th.</u>: It might look counter-intuitive to execute programs in arbitrary elements of M_{td}. However, we can collect <u>all our postulates about time</u> into a set $Ax \subseteq F_{td}$ of axioms which this way would define the class $Mod(Ax) \subseteq M_{td}$ of all <u>intended interpretations</u> of P_d. Then traces of programs in $Mod(Ax)$ provide an intuitively acceptable semantics of program schemes. Such a set Ax of axioms will be proposed in Def.13. <u>If</u> one wants to define semantics with unusual time structure e.g. parallelism, nondeterminism, interactions etc. then one can choose an Ax different from the one proposed in this paper.

§3. STATEMENTS about programs

We introduce our language DL_d for reasoning about programs or in other words the language DL_d of our first order dynamic logic.

DEFINITION 9 (the language DL_d of first order dynamic logic)

Let d be a (one-sorted) similarity type.

(i) DF_d is defined to be the smallest set satisfying conditions (1)-(3) below.

(1) $F_{td} \subseteq DF_d$.

(2) $(\forall p \in P_d)(\forall \psi \in DF_d)\ \Box(p,\psi) \in DF_d$.

(3) $(\forall \varphi,\psi \in DF_d)(\forall x \in X \cup Y \cup Z)\ \{\neg\varphi, (\varphi \wedge \psi), (\exists x\varphi)\} \subseteq DF_d$.

By this we have defined the set DF_d of dynamic formulas of type d.

(ii) Now we define the meanings of the dynamic formulas in the 3-sorted models $\mathfrak{M} \in M_{td}$. Let $\mathfrak{M} = \langle \underset{\sim}{T}, \underset{\sim}{D}, I, ext \rangle \in M_{td}$. Let v be a valuation of the variables of F_{td} into $\mathfrak{M}$, i.e. let $v = \langle g,k,r \rangle$ where $g \in {}^{\omega}T$, $k \in {}^{\omega}D$, and $r \in {}^{\omega}I$. We shall define $\mathfrak{M} \models \varphi[v]$ for all $\varphi \in DF_d$.

(4) If $\varphi \in F_{td}$ then $\mathfrak{M} \models \varphi[v]$ is already defined in Def.5.

(5) Let $p \in P_d$ and $\psi \in DF_d$ be arbitrary. Assume that $\mathfrak{M} \models \psi[v]$ has already been defined for every valuation v of the variables of F_{td} into $\mathfrak{M}$. Let $g \in {}^{\omega}T$, $k \in {}^{\omega}D$, and $r \in {}^{\omega}I$. Then

$\mathfrak{M} \models \Box(p,\psi)[g,k,r]$ iff $[\mathfrak{M} \models \psi[g,q,r]$ for every possible output q of p with input k in $\mathfrak{M}]$. For "possible output" see Def.8.

(6) Let $\varphi,\psi \in DF_d$ and let $x \in X \cup Y \cup Z$. Then $\mathfrak{M} \models (\neg\varphi)[g,k,r]$, $\mathfrak{M} \models (\varphi \wedge \psi)[g,k,r]$ and $\mathfrak{M} \models (\exists x\varphi)[g,k,r]$ are defined the usual way.

Let e.g. $w \in \omega$. Then $\mathfrak{M} \models (\exists z_w \varphi)[g,k,r]$ iff (there is $h \in {}^{\omega}T$ such that $(\forall j \in \omega)(j \neq w \Rightarrow h_j = g_j)$ and $\mathfrak{M} \models \varphi[h,k,r]$).

(iii) The language DL_d of first order dynamic logic of type d is defined to be the triple $DL_d \overset{d}{=} \langle DF_d\ , M_{td}\ , \models \rangle$ where $\models$ is defined in (ii) above.

End of Definition 9

Notation: Let $p \in P_d$ and $\psi \in DF_d$. Then $\Diamond(p,\psi)$ abbreviates the formula $\neg\Box(p,\neg\psi)$. In our language DF_d we introduced the logical connectives $\neg, \wedge, =, \exists, \Box$ only. However, we shall use the derived logical connectives $\forall, \rightarrow, \leftrightarrow, \vee$, TRUE, FALSE, $\Diamond$ too in the standard sense. E.g. $(\varphi \vee \psi)$ stands for the formula $\neg(\neg\varphi \wedge \neg\psi)$.

Remark: Standard concepts of programming theory can be expressed in DL_d. E.g. $\Box(p,\psi)$ expresses that p is partially correct w.r.t. output condition ψ, and $\Diamond(p,\psi)$ expresses that p is totally correct w.r.t. output condition ψ in the weaker sense.

Convention 3 We shall use the model theoretic consequence relation $\models$ in the usual way. I.e. let $Th \subseteq DF_d$, $\varphi \in DF_d$ and $K \subseteq M_{td}$. Then

$\mathfrak{M} \models \varphi$ iff $(\forall g \in {}^{\omega}T)(\forall k \in {}^{\omega}D)(\forall r \in {}^{\omega}I)$ $\mathfrak{M} \models \varphi[g,k,r]$,

$\mathfrak{M} \models Th$ iff $(\forall \varphi \in Th)$ $\mathfrak{M} \models \varphi$,

$K \models Th$ iff $(\forall \mathfrak{M} \in K)$ $\mathfrak{M} \models Th$,

$Mod(Th) \stackrel{d}{=} Mod_{td}(Th) \stackrel{d}{=} \{\mathfrak{M} \in M_{td} : \mathfrak{M} \models Th\}$, and

$Th \models \varphi$ iff $Mod(Th) \models \varphi$.

Note that $Mod(Th)$ is a sloppy abbreviation of $Mod_{td}(Th)$, we shall use it when context helps the reader to guess which similarity type h such that $Th \subseteq F_h$ is used in $Mod(Th) = Mod_h(Th)$.

DEFINITION 10 (proof concept [17])

Let $L = \langle F,M,\models \rangle$ be a language. By a proof concept on the set F we understand a relation $\vdash \subseteq Sb(F) \times F$ together with a set $Pr \subseteq F^*$ such that $(\forall Th \subseteq F)(\forall \varphi \in F)[Th \vdash \varphi$ iff $(\langle H,w,\varphi \rangle \in Pr$ for some finite $H \subseteq Th$ and for some $w \in F^*)]$. Recall that we identify F^* with $\{H \in Sb(F) : |H| < \omega\}^*$.

The proof concept $(\vdash, Pr)$ is decidable iff the set Pr is a decidable subset of F^* in the usual sense of the theory of algorithms and recursive functions (i.e. if Pr is recursive).

Pr is called the set of proofs, and $\vdash$ is called derivability relation. End of Definition 10

Sometimes we shall sloppily write " $\vdash$ is a decidable proof concept" instead of " $(\vdash, Pr)$ is a decidable proof concept".

Note that the usual proof concept of classical first order logic is a decidable one in the sense of the above definition. As a contrast we note that the so called effective ω-rule is not a decidable proof concept.

THEOREM 1 (strong completeness of DL_d)

There is a decidable proof concept $(\stackrel{N}{\vdash}, Prn)$ for the language DL_d such that for every $Th \subseteq DF_d$ and $\varphi \in DF_d$ we have $[Th \models \varphi$ iff $Th \stackrel{N}{\vdash} \varphi]$.

Proof: can be found in [3], as well as in [4]Thm.2 pp.30-38. QED

DEFINITION 11 (the proof concept $(\overset{N}{\vdash},Prn)$ of DL_d)

By Thm.1 above there exists a decidable set $Prn \subseteq (DF_d)^*$ such that $(\forall Th \subseteq DF_d)(\forall \varphi \in DF_d)[\ Th \overset{N}{\vdash} \varphi$ iff $(\exists$ finite $H \subseteq Th)(\exists w)\ \langle H,w,\varphi\rangle \in Prn\ ]$.

The decision algorithm for Prn is rigorously constructed in [3] Thm.2, and [4]Thm.2,pp.30-38, and in [19].

From now on we shall use Prn as defined in the quoted papers. The only important properties of Prn we shall use are its decidability and its completeness for DL_d. End of Definition 11

By a logic we understand a pair $\langle L,(\vdash,Pr)\rangle$ where $L = \langle F,M,\models\rangle$ is a language in the sense of §2 and $(\vdash,Pr)$ is a proof concept for L in the sense of Def.10. The logic $\langle L,(\vdash,Pr)\rangle$ is said to be complete iff $(\vdash,Pr)$ is a decidable proof concept and for all $Th \subseteq F$ and $\varphi \in F$ we have $[Th \models \varphi$ iff $Th \vdash \varphi]$.

We define First order Dynamic Logic of type d to be the logic $\langle DL_d\ ,\ (\overset{N}{\vdash},Prn)\rangle$ where the proof concept $(\overset{N}{\vdash},Prn)$ is defined in Def. 11. By Theorem 1, First order Dynamic Logic $\langle DL_d,(\overset{N}{\vdash},Prn)\rangle$ is complete.

Given any logic, say $\langle DL_d, \overset{N}{\vdash}\rangle$, decidable sets $Ax \subseteq DF_d$ of formulas (i.e. theories Ax) give rise to new logics. We shall make this precise in Def.12 below.

DEFINITION 12 (new proof concepts $(Ax\overset{N}{\vdash})$ from old $\overset{N}{\vdash}$, $DL_d(Ax)$, $Dlog_d(Ax)$)

Let $Ax \subseteq DF_d$ be decidable but otherwise arbitrary.

(i) Let $Th \subseteq DF_d$ and $\varphi \in DF_d$ be arbitrary. We say that φ is $(Ax\overset{N}{\vdash})$-provable from Th iff $Th \cup Ax \overset{N}{\vdash} \varphi$. That is φ is provable by the proof concept $(Ax\overset{N}{\vdash})$ from Th iff $Th \cup Ax \overset{N}{\vdash} \varphi$. Thus $(Ax\overset{N}{\vdash})$ is a new recursively enumerable "provability" relation.

(ii) $pf(Ax\overset{N}{\vdash}) \overset{d}{=} \{\langle H,\langle L,w\rangle,\varphi\rangle \in (DF_d)^* : \langle H \cup L,w,\varphi\rangle \in Prn$ and $L \subseteq Ax\}$.
Clearly φ is $(Ax\overset{N}{\vdash})$-provable from Th iff $(\exists \langle H,w,\varphi\rangle \in Prn)\ H \subseteq Th \cup Ax$.
Clearly $pf(Ax\overset{N}{\vdash})$ is a decidable subset of $(DF_d)^*$.

(iii) We have defined a new proof concept $\langle (Ax\overset{N}{\vdash})\ ,\ pf(Ax\overset{N}{\vdash})\rangle$ where $pf(Ax\overset{N}{\vdash})$ is the decidable set of all $(Ax\overset{N}{\vdash})$-proofs. We shall always denote this new proof concept by $(Ax\overset{N}{\vdash})$. So whenever we write $(Ax\overset{N}{\vdash})$ we shall mean $\langle (Ax\overset{N}{\vdash}),pf(Ax\overset{N}{\vdash})\rangle$ but we shall not write it out explicitly.

(iv) We define the new language $DL_d(Ax)$ associated to $Ax \subseteq DF_d$ to be $DL_d(Ax) \overset{d}{=} \langle DF_d\ ,\ Mod_{td}(Ax)\ ,\ \models\rangle$.

(v) We define the new dynamic logic $Dlog_d(Ax)$ associated to Ax to be $Dlog_d(Ax) \overset{d}{=} \langle DL_d(Ax), (Ax \overset{N}{\vdash})\rangle$. End of Definition 12

On Figure 2, different proof concepts $(Ax_1 \overset{N}{\vdash})$, $(Ax_2 \overset{N}{\vdash})$ etc. will be compared with each other as well as with such classic proof concepts as Floyd's $\overset{F}{\vdash}$ and Rod Burstall's $\overset{mod}{\vdash}$.

DEFINITION 13 (Dax, Reasonable Dynamic Logic, $\overset{\omega}{\models}$)

In Def.s 14-17 below the axiom systems Ia, Tpa, Ex, $\{Axe\} \subseteq DF_d$ will be defined. We define the logical axioms of Reasonable Dynamic Logic to be $Dax \overset{d}{=} Ia \cup Tpa \cup Ex \cup \{Axe\}$.

We define Reasonable Dynamic Logic to be $Dlog_d(Dax)$. See Def.12 (v) above.

Let $Th \subseteq DF_d$ and $\varphi \in DF_d$. Then we define $[Th \overset{\omega}{\models} \varphi$ iff $(STM_d \cap Mod(Th)) \models \varphi]$. End of Definition 13

Note that $STM_d \models Dax$ is easy to prove.

Is our dynamic logic nihilistic or counterintuitive?:
We claim that the answer is no for our Reasonable Dynamic Logic $Dlog_d(Dax)$. To execute programs in arbitrary elements of M_{td} might look counterintuitive. However $Dlog_d(Dax)$ is a complete logic with decidable proof concept and there is nothing wrong with executing programs in elements of $Mod_{td}(Dax)$. See e.g. Prop.2 below, Thm.7 of [3], Thm.6 of [9]p.34 and Fig.2.

PROPOSITION 2 Let $\mathfrak{M} \models Dax$ and $p \in P_d$. Then (i)-(ii) below hold.

(i) To every input q there is exactly one trace of p in $\mathfrak{M}$ with input q.

(ii) Assume that the trace $s \in {}^m I$ of p in $\mathfrak{M}$ terminates at time $b \in T$. Then $(\forall a \in T)[b \leq a \Rightarrow (\forall i < m) ext(s_i, b) = ext(s_i, a)]$ and $(\exists a \in T)(\forall k \in T)[$(s terminates p at time k) $\Leftrightarrow a \leq k]$.

Proof: Detailed proofs can be found in [3]Thm.s 3-4, [4]Thm.s 3-4, pp. 42-45, except for the existence of traces in (i) which is proved in [20], but the idea of this proof is available in [3]proof of Thm.7.
QED(Proposition 2)

On Fig.2, different dynamic logics $Dlog_d(Ax)$ with various $Ax \subseteq DF_d$ will be compared with each other and with classical logics of programs like Floyd-Hoare Logic, Burstall's modal-dynamic logic etc.

§4. Comparing methods for program verification, the status of some well known ones

We shall show how to use our logic DL_d to compare powers of methods of program verification, as well as to generate new methods for program verification. We shall see that the program verification methods form a lattice, see Fig.2. It might be interesting and also useful to find out about well known program verification methods how they are situated in this lattice.

Three well known program verification methods we shall look at are Floyd's inductive assertions method $\overset{F}{\models}$, Burstall's time modalities method $\overset{mod}{\models}$ [7], and Future-enriched time modalities method $\overset{fum}{\models}$ [12]. Burstall's $\overset{mod}{\models}$ is often called intermittent-assertion method, see e.g. [16]. These methods will be defined rigorously, see Def.20 for $\overset{F}{\models}$, Def.18 for $\overset{mod}{\models}$, and Def.19 for $\overset{fum}{\models}$. The last one, $\overset{fum}{\models}$, is $\overset{mod}{\models}$ enriched with future tense and past tense. By spotting the precise locations of $\overset{F}{\models}$, $\overset{mod}{\models}$ and $\overset{fum}{\models}$ in the lattice of program verification methods we shall find a precise answer to the question asked at SRI in 1976: "Is sometime sometimes better than always?" [16].

We have to fix the criteria to be used when we compare program verification methods. We shall say that one method $\vdash_1$ is stronger than another $\vdash_2$ iff more programs can be proved to be partially correct by $\vdash_1$ than by $\vdash_2$. So we shall consider the reasoning power to prove partial correctness statements $\varphi \rightarrow \Box(p,\psi)$ to be the criterion to compare different methods. This choice has nothing to do with our logic DL_d, namely DL_d is suitable for proving total correctness of programs. It was proved in [3]Thm.7 and in Thm.7 of [4] that the Kfoury-Park[15] negative result on proving total correctness is <u>not</u> true for DL_d.

We shall consider program verification methods only with decidable proof concepts.

About generating new program verification methods by DL_d.: A safe way of dreaming up new sound program verification methods is to define a decidable set $Ax \subseteq DF_d$ of axioms such that $STM_d \models Ax$. Then $(Ax \overset{N}{\models})$ is a sound program verification method. A reasonable axiom system is e.g. Dax introduced in Def.13. Clearly $STM_d \models Dax$. Thus by Thm.1 we can be sure that whenever $Th \cup Dax \overset{N}{\models} \Box(p,\psi)$ then really $Th \overset{\omega}{\models} \Box(p,\psi)$ that is the proof method $(Dax \overset{N}{\models})$ is sound.

Below we shall introduce several such axiom systems Ax, with $STM_d \models Ax$. Later we shall compare them in Fig.2. One can consider these axiom systems as different candidates for being the logical axioms for dynamic logic. Or if we want to imitate what people do in modal logic then we could say that every recursively enumerable $Ax \subseteq DF_d$ such that $STM_d \models Ax$ is a dynamic logic and if $STM_d \models Ax_1$ and $STM_d \models Ax_2$ and $Ax_1 \not\models Ax_2$ then Ax_1 and Ax_2 are two different dynamic logics and if $Ax_2 \models Ax_1$ then Ax_2 is a dynamic logic stronger than Ax_1.

Usually, any axiom system, say Axname, introduced below will consist of two parts Tname and Iname such that Axname = Tname ∪ Iname. Tname consists of postulates about the time structure $\underset{\sim}{T}$ hence Tname $\subseteq F_t^Z$, see Def.16. Iname consists of induction axioms about the intensions, see Def.15. Typical examples are $\forall z(sc(z)\neq 0) \in$ Tname and $(x=ext(y,0) \wedge \forall z[x=ext(y,z) \rightarrow x=ext(y,sc(z))]) \rightarrow \forall z(x=ext(y,z)) \in$ Iname.

<u>DEFINITION 14</u> (ind(φ,z), IA, Ia, Lax)

Let d be a similarity type. Then td, F_{td} and Z were defined in Def.s 4 and 6 in §2. Let $z \in Z$ be arbitrary. Let $\varphi \in F_{td}$. We define the induction formula ind(φ,z) as follows:

$$ind(\varphi,z) \overset{d}{=} ([\varphi(0) \wedge \forall z(\varphi \rightarrow \varphi(sc(z))] \rightarrow \forall z\varphi) ,$$

where φ(0) and φ(sc(z)) denote the formulas obtained from φ by replacing every free occurrence of z in φ by 0 and sc(z) resp.

The induction axioms are:

$IA \overset{d}{=} \{ind(\varphi,z) : \varphi \in F_{td} \text{ and } z \in Z\}$.

$Lax \overset{d}{=} \{(j\neq k) :$ j and k are two different elements of Lab$\}$.

$Ia \overset{d}{=} IA \cup Lax$. <u>End of Definition 14</u>

Clearly $IA \subseteq F_{td}$ since if $\varphi \in F_{td}$ and $z \in Z$ then $\varphi(0), \varphi(sc(z)) \in F_{td}$ because 0 and sc(z) are terms of sort t. It is important to stress here that φ may contain other free variables of all sorts. All the free variables of φ are also free in ind(φ,z) except for z. They are the "<u>parameters</u>" of the induction ind(φ,z).

The theory IA says that if a "property" φ changes during time T then it must change "some time", i.e. there is a time point $b \in T$ when φ is just changing.

Our strongest set of induction axioms is Ia. We shall distinguish various subsets of Ia.

<u>DEFINITION 15</u> (Iq, $I\Sigma_1$, $I\Pi_1$, If, I1, I′, Ict, Imd and Ifm)

$If \overset{d}{=} \{\varphi \in IA :$ φ contains no free variable of sort t or d$\} \cup Lax$.

$I1 \overset{d}{=} \{\varphi \in IA : (\forall i \in \omega)[i > 0 \Rightarrow z_i$ does not occur in φ neither free nor bound$]\} \cup Lax$.

$I' \overset{d}{=} \{ind(\varphi,z_0) \in I1 \ : \ \varphi \in F_{td}$ is such that "+" and "·" do not occur in φ and there is no subformula $\psi \in F_t^Z$ of $\varphi\} \cup Lax$.

$Ict \overset{d}{=} \{ind(\exists x_0 \ldots x_m[(\bigwedge_{i \le m} x_i = ext(y_i, z_0)) \wedge \varphi], z_0) \ : \ m \in \omega$ and $\varphi \in F_d\} \cup Lax$.

Let $(\Sigma_{0,t}F_{td}) \overset{d}{=} \{\varphi \in F_{td} \ : \ \varphi$ contains no quantifier of sort t, that is $(\forall i \in \omega)[$"$\exists z_i$" does not occur in $\varphi]\}$.

$Iq \overset{d}{=} \{ind(\varphi,z_0) \ : \ \varphi \in (\Sigma_{0,t}F_{td})\} \cup Lax$.

$I\Sigma_1 \overset{d}{=} \{ind(\exists z_1 \ldots z_m \varphi, z_0) \ : \ \varphi \in (\Sigma_{0,t}F_{td})$ and $m \in \omega\} \cup Lax$.

$I\Pi_1 \overset{d}{=} \{ind(\forall z_1 \ldots z_m \varphi, z_0) \ : \ \varphi \in (\Sigma_{0,t}F_{td})$ and $m \in \omega\} \cup Lax$.

$Imd \overset{d}{=} \{mod\varphi \ : \ \varphi \in IA^{mod}\}$, where mod and IA^{mod} will be defined in Def.18.

$Ifm \overset{d}{=} \{fum\varphi \ : \ \varphi \in Ifum\}$, where fum and Ifum will be defined in Def.19.

<u>End of Definition 15</u>

On Fig.1 we compare the sets of induction axioms introduced in Def. 15 above. <u>Warning</u>: As opposed to Fig.2, the comparison on Fig.1 is <u>not</u> modulo partial correctness of programs but instead it is absolute. That is, on Fig.1, $[I_1 \geq I_2$ iff $I_1 \models I_2]$ and $I_1 \equiv I_2$ means $(I_1 \leq I_2$ and $I_2 \leq I_1)$. The sign $\not\equiv$ indicates that the inequality in question is known to be proper, that is $I_2 \not\equiv I_1$. We shall discuss Fig.1 after the discussion of Fig.2 in §5.

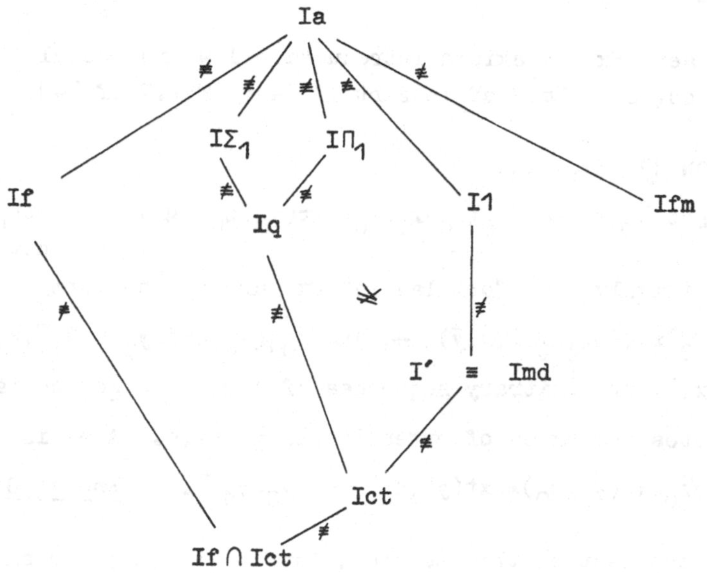

<u>FIGURE 1</u>

DEFINITION 16 ($Ts \subseteq To \subseteq Tpres \subseteq Tpa \subseteq F_t^Z$ and Tfm)

Notation: $sc^0(z_0) \stackrel{d}{=} z_0$ and $(\forall n \in \omega) sc^{n+1}(z_0) \stackrel{d}{=} sc(sc^n(z_0))$.

$Ts \stackrel{d}{=} \{ z_0 \neq 0 \leftrightarrow \exists z_1(z_0 = sc(z_1)),\ sc(z_0) = sc(z_1) \rightarrow z_0 = z_1,\ sc^n(z_0) \neq z_0 : n \in \omega,\ n \neq 0 \}$.

$To \stackrel{d}{=} \{ (z_0 \leq z_1 \wedge z_1 \leq z_2) \rightarrow z_0 \leq z_2,\ (z_0 \leq z_1 \wedge z_1 \leq z_0) \rightarrow z_0 = z_1,$
$z_0 \leq z_1 \vee z_1 \leq z_0,\ 0 \leq z_0,\ (z_0 \leq z_1 \wedge z_0 \neq z_1) \leftrightarrow sc(z_0) \leq z_1,$
$0 = z_0 \vee \exists z_1(z_0 = sc(z_1)) \}$.

Tpres is the decidable set of Presburger's axioms for $\underset{\sim}{N}$:

$Tpres \stackrel{d}{=} To \cup \{ z_0 + 0 = z_0,\ z_0 + sc(z_1) = sc(z_0 + z_1),\ ind(\varphi, z_0) : \varphi \in F_t^Z$ and "$\cdot$" does not occur in $\varphi \}$.

Tpa is the set of Peano's axioms formulated in the language F_t^Z about the similarity type t, see e.g. Example 1.4.11 in [8]p.42.:

$Tpa \stackrel{d}{=} Tpres \cup \{ z_0 \cdot 0 = 0,\ z_0 \cdot sc(z_1) = z_0 \cdot z_1 + z_0,\ ind(\varphi, z_0) : \varphi \in F_t^Z \}$.

$Tfm \stackrel{d}{=} \{ fum\varphi : \varphi \in Tfum \}$, where fum and Tfum will be defined in Def.19. End of Definition 16

Note that $Ts \subseteq To$ is not literally true but $To \models Ts$. We require $To \subseteq Tpa$ because we have the symbol $\leq$ in the similarity type t. We also note that $To \models Tfm$, and, clearly, $STM_d \models Tpa$. I.e. Fact 16.1 below holds.

FACT 16.1 $STM_d \models Tpa \models Tpres \models To \models Tfm$ and $To \models Ts$.

The set Ex of axioms introduced below are useful to prove total correctness, see Thm.7 of [3]Part II, and Thm.7 of [4].

DEFINITION 17 (Ex, Axe)

$Ex \stackrel{d}{=} \{ [\forall z_0 \exists x_0 \varphi \rightarrow \exists y_0 \forall z_0 \exists x_0 (x_0 = ext(y_0, z_0) \wedge \varphi)] : \varphi \in F_{td}$ and y_0 does not occur in $\varphi \}$.

More intuitively, the formulas in Ex are of the form

$\forall \bar{z} \forall \bar{x} \forall \bar{y} [\forall z_0 \exists x_0 \varphi(z_0, x_0, \bar{z}, \bar{x}, \bar{y}) \rightarrow \exists y_0 \forall z_0 \varphi(z_0, ext(y_0, z_0), \bar{z}, \bar{x}, \bar{y})]$

where $\bar{z}, \bar{x}, \bar{y}$ are arbitrary sequences of variables not containing z_0, x_0, y_0.

Axe denotes the axiom of extensionality, i.e. Axe is

$(\forall y_0 \forall y_1 [\forall z_0 ext(y_0, z_0) = ext(y_1, z_0) \rightarrow y_0 = y_1]$. End of Definition 17

For the rest of this section, let $d = \langle H, d_1 \rangle$ be an arbitrary but fixed one-sorted similarity type, see Def.1.

A direct Kripke style semantics for DL_d^{mod} defined below can be found in [23]. Moreover, in [23] a direct Kripke style definition is given for the validity relation $\models^{mod}$ defined indirectly in Def. 18.

DEFINITION 18 (modal dynamic language DL_d^{mod} of type d)

(i) Syntax DF_d^{mod} .:

T_d^{mod} is defined to be the smallest set satisfying (1)-(2) below:

(1) $\{x_n, y_n\} \subseteq T_d^{mod}$ for every $n \in \omega$.

(2) $f(\tau_1,\dots,\tau_n) \in T_d^{mod}$ for every $f \in H$ if $d(f)=n+1$ and $\{\tau_1,\dots,\tau_n\} \subseteq T_d^{mod}$.

DF_d^{mod} is defined to be the smallest set satisfying (3)-(5) below:

(3) $(\tau = \sigma) \in DF_d^{mod}$ for all $\tau, \sigma \in T_d^{mod}$.

(4) $R(\tau_1,\dots,\tau_n) \in DF_d^{mod}$ for every $R \in \mathrm{Dom}\, d_1$ if $R \notin H$, $d(R)=n$ and $\{\tau_1,\dots,\tau_n\} \subseteq T_d^{mod}$.

(5) $\{\mathrm{Alw}\varphi, \mathrm{First}\varphi, \mathrm{Next}\varphi, \exists x_n\varphi, \exists y_n\varphi, \neg\varphi, (\varphi\wedge\psi), \Box(p,\varphi)\} \subseteq DF_d^{mod}$ for all $n \in \omega$ and for all $\varphi,\psi \in DF_d^{mod}$ and all $p \in P_d$.

(ii) Translation function $\mathrm{mod} : DF_d^{mod} \to DF_d$.:

The definition goes by recursion on the structure of DF_d^{mod}. Sometime we write $\mathrm{mod}\varphi$ instead of $\mathrm{mod}(\varphi)$. Let $n \in \omega$, $\tau_1,\dots,\tau_n \in T_d^{mod}$, $\varphi,\psi \in DF_d^{mod}$ and $p \in P_d$. Now

$\mathrm{mod}(y_n) \stackrel{d}{=} \mathrm{ext}(y_n, z_0)$, $\mathrm{mod}(x_n) \stackrel{d}{=} x_n$,

$\mathrm{mod}(\mathrm{Alw}\varphi) \stackrel{d}{=} \forall z_0(\mathrm{mod}\varphi)$,

$\mathrm{mod}(\mathrm{First}\varphi) = \exists z_0(z_0 = 0 \wedge \mathrm{mod}\varphi)$,

$\mathrm{mod}(\mathrm{Next}\varphi) \stackrel{d}{=} \exists z_1(z_1 = sc(z_0) \wedge \exists z_0(z_0 = z_1 \wedge \mathrm{mod}\varphi)$,

$\mathrm{mod}(g(\tau_1,\dots,\tau_n)) \stackrel{d}{=} g(\mathrm{mod}\tau_1,\dots,\mathrm{mod}\tau_n)$ if $g \in \mathrm{Dom}\, d_1$ is such that $d(g)=n+1$ in case $g \in H$ and $d(g)=n$ in case $g \notin H$,

$\mathrm{mod}(\tau_1=\tau_2) \stackrel{d}{=} (\mathrm{mod}\tau_1 = \mathrm{mod}\tau_2)$, $\mathrm{mod}(\exists x_n\varphi) \stackrel{d}{=} \exists x_n \mathrm{mod}\varphi$, $\mathrm{mod}(\exists y_n\varphi) \stackrel{d}{=} \exists y_n \mathrm{mod}\varphi$,

$\mathrm{mod}(\neg\varphi) \stackrel{d}{=} \neg\mathrm{mod}\varphi$, $\mathrm{mod}(\varphi\wedge\psi) \stackrel{d}{=} (\mathrm{mod}\varphi \wedge \mathrm{mod}\psi)$, $\mathrm{mod}(\Box(p,\psi)) \stackrel{d}{=} \Box(p, \mathrm{mod}\psi)$.

By the above, the function $\mathrm{mod} : DF_d^{mod} \to DF_d$ is fully defined.

(iii) Validity relation $\models^{mod} \subseteq M_{td} \times DF_d^{mod}$.:

Let $\mathfrak{M} \in M_{td}$ and $\varphi \in DF_d^{mod}$. Then we define $\mathfrak{M} \models^{mod} \varphi$ iff $\mathfrak{M} \models \mathrm{mod}\,\varphi$.

(iv) Axioms IA^{mod} of modal dynamic logic .:

$IA^{mod} \stackrel{d}{=} \{ ([\mathrm{First}\varphi \wedge \mathrm{Alw}(\varphi \to \mathrm{Next}\varphi)] \to \mathrm{Alw}\varphi) : \varphi \in DF_d^{mod} \} \cup \mathrm{Lax}$.

(v) The language DL_d^{mod} of modal dynamic logic .:

$DL_d^{mod} \stackrel{d}{=} \langle DF_d^{mod}, Mod_{td}(IA^{mod}), \models^{mod} \rangle$, where for any $Th \subseteq DF_d^{mod}$ we define $Mod_{td}(Th) \stackrel{d}{=} \{\mathfrak{M} \in M_{td} : \mathfrak{M} \models^{mod} Th\}$. Let $Th \subseteq DF_d^{mod}$ and $\varphi \in DF_d^{mod}$. Then $Th \models^{mod} \varphi$ is defined to hold iff $Mod_{td}(IA^{mod} \cup Th) \models^{mod} \varphi$, see Convention 3. <u>End of Definition 18</u>

<u>PROPOSITION 3</u> (completeness of DL_d^{mod})

Let $Th \subseteq DF_d^{mod}$ and $\varphi \in DF_d^{mod}$. Then

$Th \models^{mod} \varphi$ iff $\{mod\psi : \psi \in Th \cup IA^{mod}\} \models^{N} mod\varphi$.

<u>The proof</u> of Prop.3 is immediate by the definitions and by the completeness theorem of DL_d, i.e. by Thm.1. <u>QED</u>

The modality symbol Alwfu used below intuitively means "<u>Alw</u>ays in the <u>fu</u>ture". Similarly Alwpaφ intuitively means "<u>Alw</u>ays in the <u>pa</u>st φ". In [12] "Alwfuφ" and "Nextφ" are denoted by "Fφ" and "Xφ" respectively.

<u>DEFINITION 19</u> (future enriched modal dynamic language DL_d^{fum} of type d)

(i) <u>Syntax</u>.: DF_d^{fum} is defined to be the smallest set satisfying (1)-(2) below:

(1) $DF_d^{mod} \subseteq DF_d^{fum}$.

(2) $\{Alwfu\varphi, Alwpa\varphi, Alw\varphi, First\varphi, Next\varphi, \exists x_n\varphi, \exists y_n\varphi, \neg\varphi, (\varphi \wedge \psi), \Box(p,\psi)\} \subseteq DF_d^{fum}$ for all $n \in \omega$, $\varphi,\psi \in DF_d^{fum}$ and all $p \in P_d$.

(ii) <u>Translation function</u> $fum : DF_d^{fum} \to DF_d$.:

The definition of fum goes by recursion on the structure of DF_d^{fum}. Sometime we write fumφ instead of fum(φ), i.e. $fum\varphi \stackrel{d}{=} fum(\varphi)$.

Let $\varphi \in DF_d^{mod}$. Then $fum(\varphi) \stackrel{d}{=} mod(\varphi)$, see Def.18(ii).

Let $n \in \omega$, $\varphi,\psi \in DF_d^{fum}$ and $p \in P_d$. Then

$fum(Alwfu\varphi) \stackrel{d}{=} \forall z_1[z_1 \geq z_0 \to \exists z_0(z_0 = z_1 \wedge fum\varphi)]$,

$fum(Alwpa\varphi) \stackrel{d}{=} \forall z_1[z_1 \leq z_0 \to \exists z_0(z_0 = z_1 \wedge fum\varphi)]$,

$fum(Alw\varphi) \stackrel{d}{=} \forall z_0(fum\varphi)$, $fum(Next\varphi) \stackrel{d}{=} \exists z_1[z_1 = sc(z_0) \wedge \exists z_0(z_0 = z_1 \wedge fum\varphi)]$,

$fum(First\varphi) \stackrel{d}{=} \exists z_0(z_0 = 0 \wedge fum\varphi)$, $fum(\exists x_n\varphi) \stackrel{d}{=} \exists x_n fum\varphi$, $fum(\exists y_n\varphi) \stackrel{d}{=} \exists y_n fum\varphi$

$fum(\neg\varphi) \stackrel{d}{=} \neg fum\varphi$, $fum(\varphi \wedge \psi) \stackrel{d}{=} ((fum\varphi) \wedge (fum\psi))$, $fum(\Box(p,\psi)) \stackrel{d}{=} \Box(p, fum\psi)$.

By the above the function $fum : DF_d^{fum} \to DF_d$ is fully defined.

(iii) <u>Validity relation</u> $\models^{fum} \subseteq M_{td} \times DF_d^{fum}$.:

Let $\mathfrak{M}\in M_{td}$ and $\varphi\in DF_d^{fum}$. Then we define $\mathfrak{M} \overset{fum}{\models} \varphi$ iff $\mathfrak{M} \models fum\varphi$.

(iv) <u>Abbreviations or shorthands</u>: $(Som\varphi) \overset{d}{=} (\neg Alw\neg\varphi)$, $(Somfu\varphi) \overset{d}{=} (\neg Alwfu\neg\varphi)$, $Sompa\varphi \overset{d}{=} (\neg Alwpa\neg\varphi)$, and we use the usual shorthands $\forall x_n$, $\forall y_n$, $\vee$, $\rightarrow$, $\Diamond$, etc. introduced below the definitions of DL_d and DL_d^{mod}.

(v) <u>Axioms</u>. (v)1 Induction axioms:

$$Ifum \overset{d}{=} \{([\varphi\wedge Alwfu(\varphi\rightarrow Next\varphi)] \rightarrow Alwfu\varphi) \ : \ \varphi\in DF_d^{fum}\} \cup Lax.$$

(v)2 Time-structure axioms:

$$\begin{aligned} Tfum \overset{d}{=} \{ & First(Alwfu\varphi\rightarrow Alw\varphi), \ First(\varphi\leftrightarrow Alwpa\varphi), \\ & (\varphi\rightarrow Sompa\varphi\wedge Somfu\varphi), \ ([Alwpa\varphi\wedge Alwfu\varphi]\rightarrow Alw\varphi), \\ & (SomfuSomfu\varphi\rightarrow Somfu\varphi), \ (SompaSompa\varphi\rightarrow Sompa\varphi), \\ & (Alwfu\varphi\leftrightarrow[\varphi\wedge NextAlwfu\varphi]), \ (NextAlwpa\varphi\leftrightarrow[Next\varphi\wedge Alwpa\varphi]) \\ & : \ \varphi\in DF_d^{fum}\}. \end{aligned}$$

(vi) <u>Future enriched modal dynamic language</u> is defined to be $DL_d^{fum} \overset{d}{=} \langle DF_d^{fum}, DM_d^{fum}, \overset{fum}{\models}\rangle$ where $DM_d^{fum} \overset{d}{=} \{\mathfrak{M}\in M_{td} : \mathfrak{M} \overset{fum}{\models} Ifum\cup Tfum\}$. We use $Th \overset{fum}{\models} \varphi$ etc. in accordance with Convention 3, i.e.

$Th \overset{fum}{\models} \varphi$ iff $(\forall\mathfrak{M}\in DM_d^{fum})[\mathfrak{M} \overset{fum}{\models} Th \Rightarrow \mathfrak{M} \overset{fum}{\models} \varphi]$. <u>End of Definition 19</u>

<u>Remark</u>: Note that $\varphi \overset{fum}{\models} Alw\varphi$ for all $\varphi\in DF_d^{fum}$ since $\mathfrak{M} \overset{fum}{\models} \varphi$ implies $\mathfrak{M} \overset{fum}{\models} Alw\varphi$ by definition. Also note that

$$\begin{aligned} Ifum\cup Tfum \overset{fum}{\models} \{ & ([First\varphi\wedge Alw(\varphi\rightarrow Next\varphi)] \rightarrow Alw\varphi), \\ & Alw([First\varphi\wedge Alwpa(\varphi\rightarrow Next\varphi)] \rightarrow NextAlwpa\varphi) \ : \\ & : \ \varphi\in DF_d^{fum}\}. \end{aligned}$$

<u>PROPOSITION 4</u> (completeness of DL_d^{fum})

Let $Th\subseteq DF_d^{fum}$ and $\varphi\in DF_d^{fum}$. Then

$Th \overset{fum}{\models} \varphi$ iff $\{fum\psi : \psi\in Th\cup Ifum\cup Tfum\} \overset{N}{\models} fum\varphi$.

<u>Proof</u>: By Thm.1 and Def.19. <u>QED</u>

<u>COROLLARY 5</u> There are decidable proof concepts $\overset{mod}{\vdash}$ and $\overset{fum}{\vdash}$ such that $\langle DL_d^{mod}, \overset{mod}{\vdash}\rangle$ and $\langle DL_d^{fum}, \overset{fum}{\vdash}\rangle$ are complete logics.

<u>DEFINITION 20</u> (Floyd-Hoare logic $\langle HFL_d , (\overset{F}{\vdash} , Prf)\rangle$)

(i) The set HF_d of <u>Floyd-Hoare statements</u> of type d is an important sublanguage of DF_d.:

$HF_d \overset{d}{=} \{ (\varphi \rightarrow \Box(p,\psi)) \ : \ p \in P_d$ and $\varphi,\psi \in F_d\}$. Clearly $HF_d \subseteq DF_d$.

(ii) <u>Floyd-Hoare language</u> HFL_d is defined to be:

$HFL_d \overset{d}{=} \langle HF_d \cup F_d , Mod_{td}(Iq) , \models\rangle$.

(iii) The relation $\overset{F}{\vdash} \subseteq \{Th : Th \subseteq F_d\} \times HF_d$ was defined in a rigorous manner in [3]Def.17, [4]Def.17,p.55, [6],[2]p.118. We shall use this definition of $\overset{F}{\vdash}$ without reformulating it, but we note that in the quoted papers there is a <u>decidable</u> set $Prf \subseteq (HF_d \cup F_d)^*$ such that $(\forall Th \subseteq F_d)(\forall \varrho \in HF_d)[Th \overset{F}{\vdash} \varrho$ iff $(\exists$ finite $H \subseteq Th)(\exists w)\langle H,w,\varrho\rangle \in Prf]$. Hence Prf is the set of $\overset{F}{\vdash}$-proofs and Prf is decidable. Cf. Def. 10. According to Def.10, $(\overset{F}{\vdash},Prf)$ is a decidable proof concept for the Floyd-Hoare language HFL_d. <u>End of Definition 20</u>

<u>The lattice of proof methods for partial correctness of programs</u>

Instead of "proof method for program verification" we shall simply say "proof method". By a <u>proof method</u> we understand a proof concept $(X \overset{Y}{\vdash})$ in the sense of Def.12 or one in the sense of Def.10. Thus e.g. $\overset{F}{\vdash}$ and $(Dax \overset{N}{\vdash})$ are proof methods. When we call $(X \overset{N}{\vdash})$ a proof method for program verification then what we <u>intuitively</u> have in mind is the proof concept $(X \overset{N}{\vdash})$ as a device for proving properties of programs. We shall concentrate on the powers of proof methods $(X \overset{Y}{\vdash})$ to prove partial correctness of programs.

We define a pre-ordering $\leq$ on the proof methods as follows: $(X \overset{Y}{\vdash}) \leq (Y \overset{Z}{\vdash})$ is defined to hold iff $[(Th \cup X \overset{Y}{\vdash} \varrho) \Rightarrow (Th \cup Y \overset{Z}{\vdash} \varrho)]$ for every similarity type d, $Th \subseteq F_d$ and $\varrho \in HF_d$.

The relation $\leq$ induces an equivalence relation $\equiv$ defined as: $(X \overset{Y}{\vdash}) \equiv (Y \overset{Z}{\vdash})$ iff $[(X \overset{Y}{\vdash}) \leq (Y \overset{Z}{\vdash})$ and $(Y \overset{Z}{\vdash}) \leq (X \overset{Y}{\vdash})]$.

A straight line $X \overset{Y}{\vdash}$ —— $Y \overset{Z}{\vdash}$ on Fig.2 indicates the relation $(X \overset{Y}{\vdash}) \leq (Y \overset{Z}{\vdash})$. A line with $\neq$ added like $X \overset{Y}{\vdash}$ ——$\neq$—— $Y \overset{Z}{\vdash}$ indicates the strict relation $<$ that is $[(X \overset{Y}{\vdash}) \not\geq (Y \overset{Z}{\vdash})$ and $(X \overset{Y}{\vdash}) \leq (Y \overset{Z}{\vdash})]$. A line with =? added like $X \overset{Y}{\vdash}$ ——=?—— $Y \overset{Z}{\vdash}$ indicates that $(X \overset{Y}{\vdash}) \leq (Y \overset{Z}{\vdash})$ but we <u>do not know</u> whether $(X \overset{Y}{\vdash}) \geq (Y \overset{Z}{\vdash})$ holds or not. Broken line $X \overset{Y}{\vdash}$ - - $\not\leq$ - - $Y \overset{Z}{\vdash}$ with $\not\leq$ indicates that $(X \overset{Y}{\vdash}) \not\leq (Y \overset{Z}{\vdash})$ (but we do not know

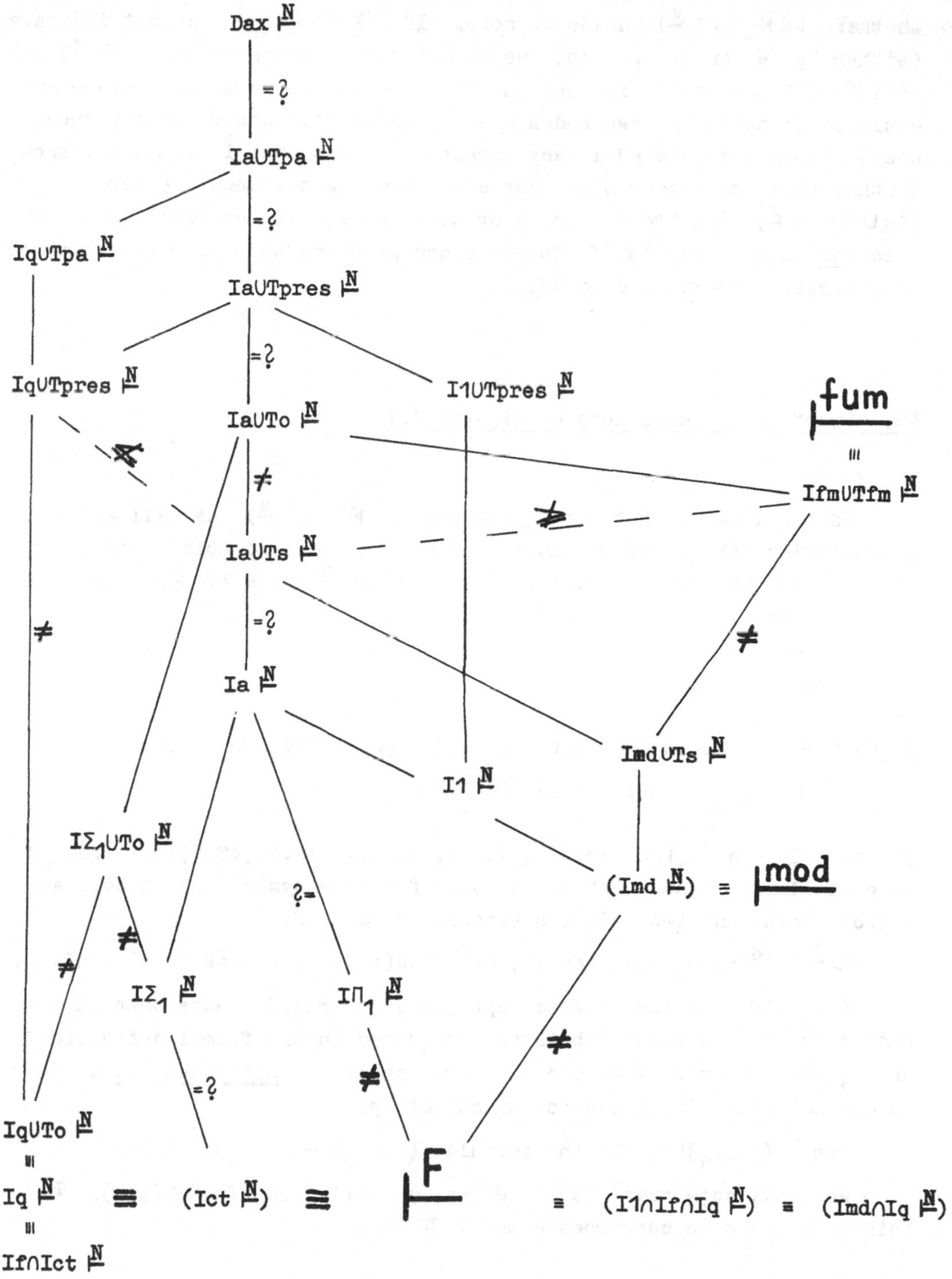
Dax ⊨N
=?
IaUTpa ⊨N
=?
IqUTpa ⊨N
IaUTpres ⊨N
=?
IqUTpres ⊨N
I1UTpres ⊨N
IaUTo ⊨N
fum
IfmUTfm ⊨N
≠
IaUTs ⊨N
=?
Ia ⊨N
ImdUTs ⊨N
I1 ⊨N
IΣ1UTo ⊨N
(Imd ⊨N) ≡ mod
?=
IΣ1 ⊨N
IΠ1 ⊨N
=?
IqUTo ⊨N
Iq ⊨N ≡ (Ict ⊨N) ≡ F ≡ (I1∩If∩Iq ⊨N) ≡ (Imd∩Iq ⊨N)
If∩Ict ⊨N

FIGURE 2

whether $(X \overset{Y}{\models}) \geq (Y \overset{Z}{\models})$ holds or not). If $(X \overset{Y}{\models}) \nleq (Y \overset{Z}{\models})$ is not indicated (either by $\neq$ or by $\nleq$) then we do not know whether or not $(X \overset{Y}{\models}) \leq \leq (Y \overset{Z}{\models})$. Hence "=?" is used only to stress that we do not know whether equivalence holds. If two nodes are not connected then we do not know whether they are related in any direction or not that is we do not know whether they are comparable. For example we do not know whether $(Iq \cup TPres \overset{N}{\models}) \leq (Ia \cup To \overset{N}{\models})$ holds or not. Note that the fact $Iq \not\models Iq \cup To$ does not imply $(Iq \overset{N}{\models}) \nleq (Iq \cup To \overset{N}{\models})$ since proof methods here are compared only w.r.t. $Th \subseteq F_d$ and $\rho \in HF_d$.

§5. Proofs and discussions of Figures 2,1

We shall prove that the inclusions $(X \overset{Y}{\models}) \leq (Y \overset{Z}{\models})$ as well as the inequalities $(X \overset{Y}{\models}) \nleq (Y \overset{Z}{\models})$ indicated on Fig.2 all do hold. First, in Thm.6 below, we prove one inequality $(Ia \cup To \overset{N}{\models}) \nleq (Ia \cup Ts \overset{N}{\models})$ and then after proving Thm.6 we shall proving the rest of Fig.2.

Thm.6 below is in contrast with the result $(Iq \cup To \overset{N}{\models}) \equiv (Iq \cup Ts \overset{N}{\models})$ indicated on Fig.2.

THEOREM 6 There are a finite d and $\Box(p,\psi) \in HF_d$ such that $Ia \cup To \overset{N}{\models} \Box(p,\psi)$ but $Ia \cup Ts \overset{N}{\not\models} \Box(p,\psi)$.

Proof. Let $d \overset{d}{=} \langle \{su, zero\}, \{\langle su,2\rangle, \langle zero,1\rangle, \langle R,1\rangle, \langle S,1\rangle\}\rangle$, i.e. d is a similarity type which has a unary function symbol su, a constant symbol zero and two relation symbols R and S.

Let $0' \overset{d}{=} zero$ and $(\forall n \in \omega)(n+1)' \overset{d}{=} su(n')$. Let $Lab \overset{d}{=} \{n' : n \in \omega\}$.

Let $p \in P_d$ be the program represented on Fig.3. Note that in defining p we use fewer labels than required in the formal definition of P_d, but it is easy to see that this change is not essential while it considerably simplifies the traces of p.

Let $\psi(x_0,x_1) \in F_d$ be the formula $(\neg S(x_0) \rightarrow x_0 = x_1)$.

We shall show that $Ia \cup Ts \not\models \Box(p,\psi)$ while $Ia \cup To \overset{N}{\models} \Box(p,\psi)$. To this end, first we construct a model $\mathfrak{M} \in M_{td}$.

6.0. The definition of $\mathfrak{M} \in M_{td}$.:

Z denotes the set of all integers such that $\omega \subseteq Z$ is the set of nonnegative members of Z.

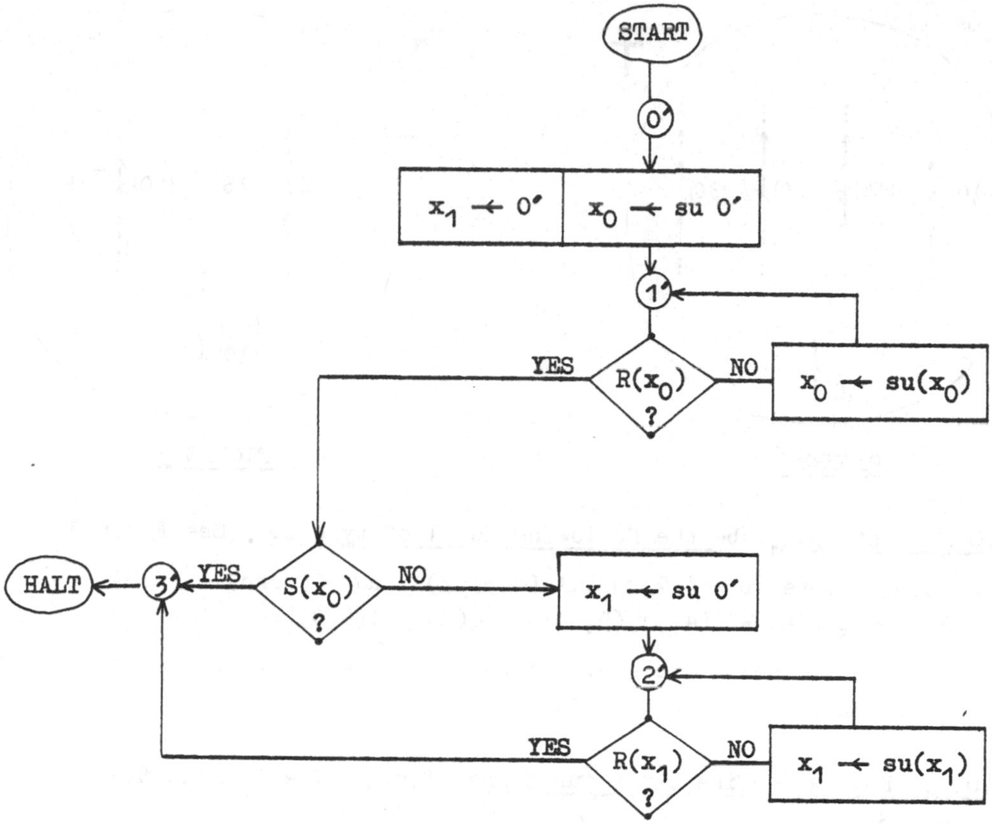

FIGURE 3

Let $A \stackrel{d}{=} (6\times Z) \cup (\{6,7\}\times\omega)$. We often write (i,n) instead of $\langle i,n\rangle$. Note that if $a\in A$ then $a=(i,n)$ for some $i\in 8$ and $n\in Z$. Let suc : $A \to A$ be defined by $suc(i,n) \stackrel{d}{=} (i,n+1)$ for every $(i,n)\in A$.

<u>6.0.1. Let $\underset{\sim}{T}\in M_t$ be the following model of type t.</u> (See Fig.4.)

$\underset{\sim}{T} \stackrel{d}{=} \langle T,Q\rangle$ where $T = (\{6\}\times\omega)\cup(4\times Z)$ and $Q(0) = (6,0) \stackrel{d}{=} 0^T$, $Q(sc) = suc$, $Q(\leq) = 0$ and $Q(+) = Q(\cdot) = T\times T\times\{0^T\}$. See Def.s 1 and 2.

We shall sloppily identify $\underset{\sim}{T}$ with the structure $\langle T,suc,0^T\rangle$. At two places above we should have written $(T\times T)\cap suc$ instead of suc but we hope that context helps to understand that we meant e.g. $Q(sc) \stackrel{d}{=} (T\times T)\cap suc$. We shall commit this kind of sloppiness in the future too.

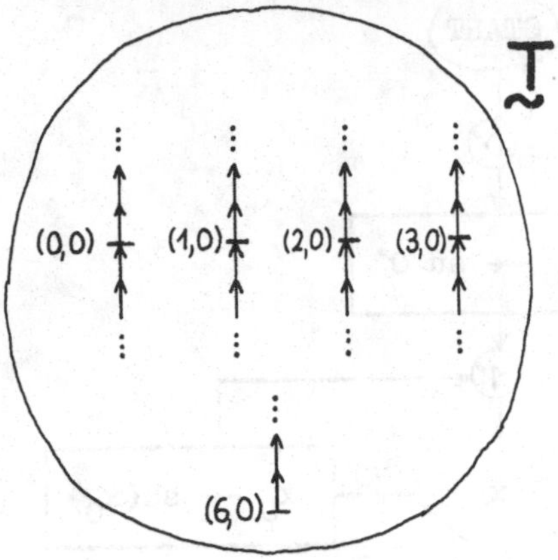

FIGURE 4

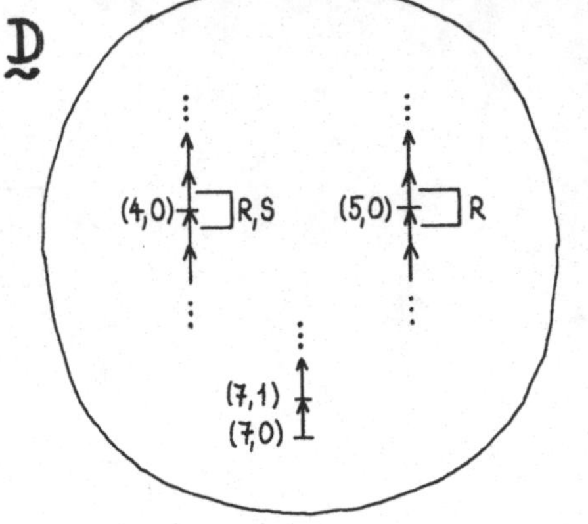

FIGURE 5

6.0.2. Let $\underset{\sim}{D} \in M_d$ be the following model of type d. (See Fig.5.)

$\underset{\sim}{D} \overset{d}{=} \langle D,G\rangle$ where $D = (\{7\}\times\omega)\cup(\{4,5\}\times Z)$ and $G(zero) = (7,0)$, $G(su) = suc$, $G(R) = \{(4,0),(5,0)\}$, $G(S) = \{(4,0)\}$.

Notation: Let $n\in\omega$. We shall identify n' with $(7,n)$ since $(7,n)$ is the value of the term n' in $\underset{\sim}{D}$.

6.0.3. Next we define three functions $f,h,g : T \to D$ illustrated on Fig.s 6-8.

$$f \overset{d}{=} \{\langle(6,n),n'\rangle,\langle(0,-n),(4,-n)\rangle,\langle(0,n),(4,0)\rangle,\langle(1,-n),(5,-n)\rangle, \langle(1,n),(5,0)\rangle,\langle(i,z),(5,0)\rangle \;:\; n\in\omega,\ i\in\{2,3\},\ z\in Z\}.$$

$$h \overset{d}{=} \{\langle(6,n),0'\rangle,\langle(0,z),0'\rangle,\langle(1,-n),0'\rangle,\langle(1,n),n'\rangle,\langle(2,-n),(4,-n)\rangle, \langle(2,n),(4,0)\rangle,\langle(3,-n),(5,-n)\rangle,\langle(3,n),(5,0)\rangle \;:\; n\in\omega,\ z\in Z\}.$$

$$g \overset{d}{=} \{\langle(6,0),0'\rangle,\langle(6,n+1),1'\rangle,\langle(0,-n),1'\rangle,\langle(0,n+1),3'\rangle,\langle(1,-n),1'\rangle, \langle(1,n+1),2'\rangle,\langle(2,-n),2'\rangle,\langle(2,n+1),3'\rangle,\langle(3,-n),2'\rangle,\langle(3,n+1,3'\rangle \;: \;: n\in\omega\}.$$

6.0.4. Let $I \overset{d}{=} \{f,h,g\}$, $valueof \overset{d}{=} \langle k(a) : \langle k,a\rangle\in I\times T\rangle$ and $\mathfrak{M} \overset{d}{=} \langle \underset{\sim}{T}, \underset{\sim}{D}, I, valueof\rangle$. We have defined the model $\mathfrak{M}\in M_{td}$.

CLAIM 6.1. $\mathfrak{M} \models Ia\cup Ts$.

Proof. Clearly, $\mathfrak{M} \models Ts\cup Lax$. To prove $\mathfrak{M} \models IA$ we shall use an ultraproduct construction. Let F be a nonprincipal ultrafilter on ω and let $\mathfrak{M}^+ \overset{d}{=} \langle \underset{\sim}{T}^+,\underset{\sim}{D}^+,I^+,ext\rangle \overset{d}{=} {}^{\omega}\mathfrak{M}/F$ be the usual ultrapower of $\mathfrak{M}$. Let $\delta : \mathfrak{M} \to \mathfrak{M}^+$ be the usual diagonal embedding. For every $i\in\omega$

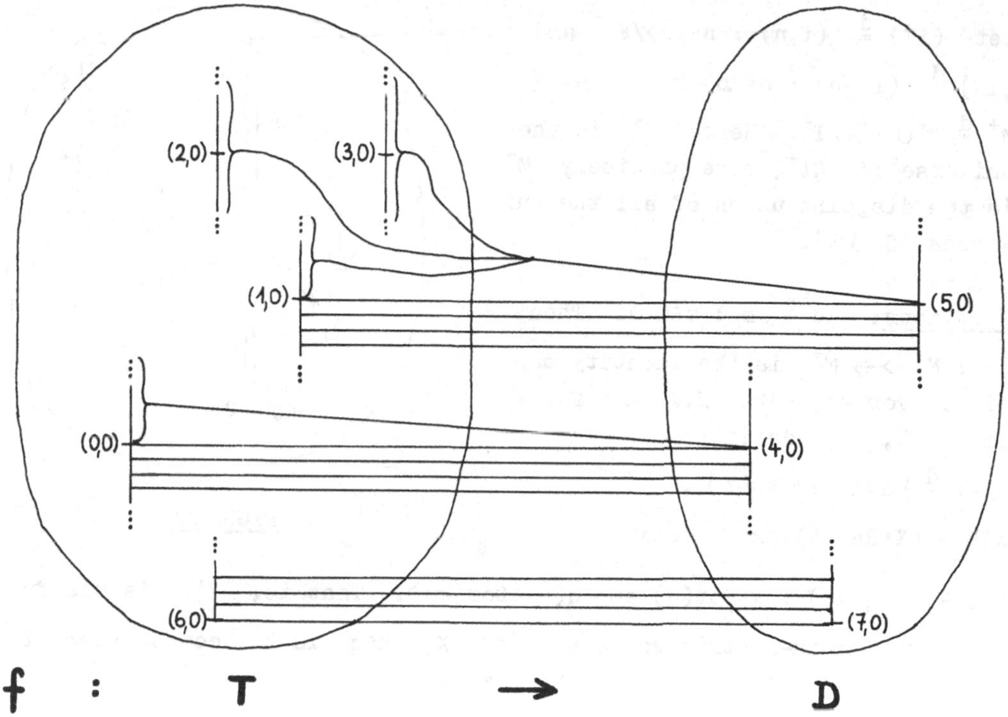

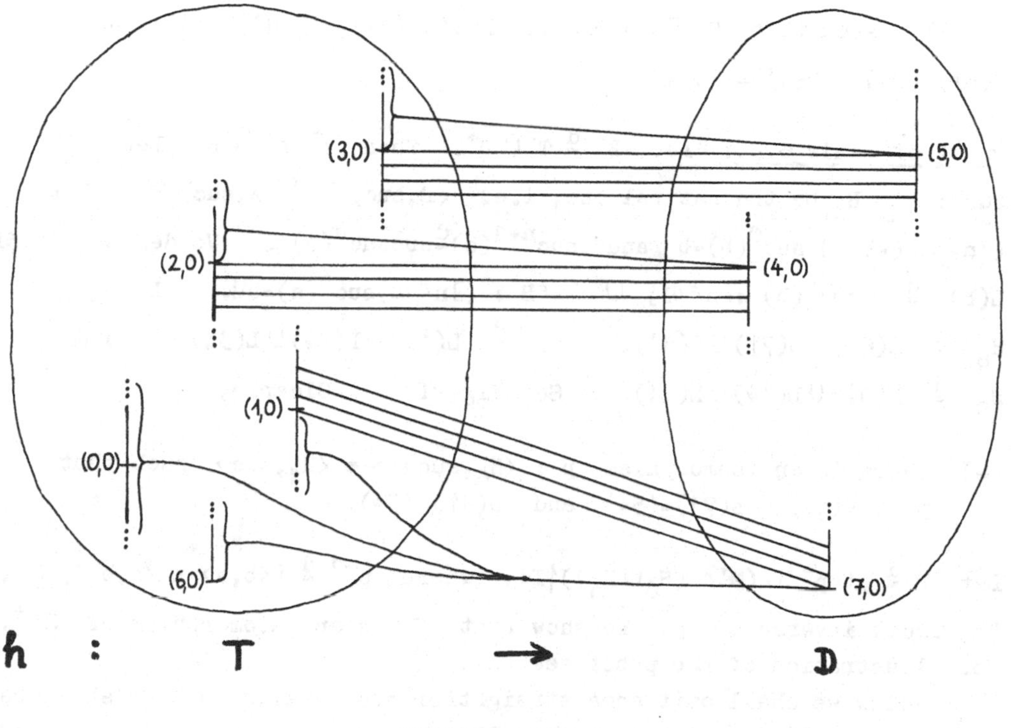

FIGURES 6-7

let $(i\uparrow) \overset{d}{=} \langle (i,n) : n\in\omega \rangle / F$ and $(i\downarrow) \overset{d}{=} \langle (i,-n) : n\in\omega \rangle / F$. Let $M^+ \overset{d}{=} T^+ \cup D^+ \cup I^+$. Hence M^+ is the universe of $\mathfrak{M}^+$, more precisely M^+ is the disjoint union of all the universes of $\mathfrak{M}^+$.

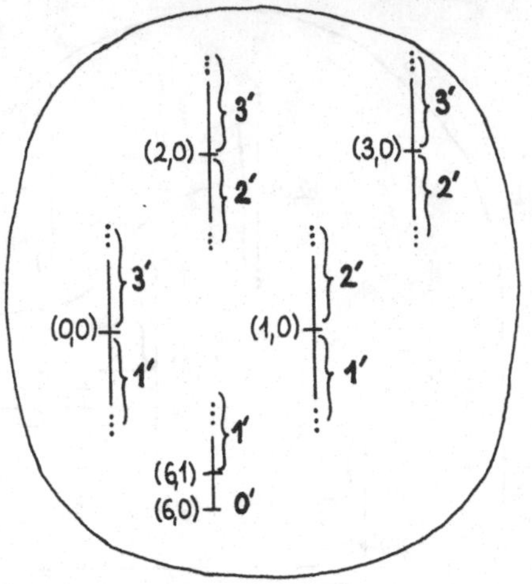

FIGURE 8

Notations: $Id \overset{d}{=} \langle m : m\in M^+ \rangle$. Then $Id : M^+ \rightarrowtail\!\!\!\twoheadrightarrow M^+$ is the identity mapping. For any sets X,Y and functions k,q we define:

$X \sim Y \overset{d}{=} \{a\in X : a \notin Y\}$,

$X \upharpoonright k \overset{d}{=} (X \times Rng\ k) \cap k$ and

$k \circ q \overset{d}{=} \langle k(q(x)) : x\in Dom(q) \text{ and } q(x)\in Dom(k) \rangle$. That is, $X \upharpoonright k$ is the function k domain-restricted to the set X, $k\circ q$ is the composition of k and q. Then $X \upharpoonright Id \subseteq k$ means that k is identity on X.

CLAIM 6.2. There are automorphisms $P : \mathfrak{M}^+ \rightarrowtail\!\!\!\twoheadrightarrow \mathfrak{M}^+$ and $Q : \mathfrak{M}^+ \rightarrowtail\!\!\!\twoheadrightarrow \mathfrak{M}^+$ of $\mathfrak{M}^+$ such that $P \circ \delta = Q \circ \delta = \delta$, $P(6\uparrow) = (1\downarrow)$, $P(1\uparrow) = (3\downarrow)$ and $Q(6\uparrow) = (0\downarrow)$, $Q(1\uparrow) = (2\downarrow)$.

Proof of Claim 6.2.: Let $B \overset{d}{=} T^+ \cup D^+$. Then $\delta : A \rightarrowtail B$. Let $suc : B \to B$ be the natural one, i.e. $\langle B, suc \rangle \overset{d}{=} {}^{\omega}\langle A, suc \rangle / F$. Let $(\forall n\in\omega)(\forall b\in B)\ suc^0(b) \overset{d}{=} b$ and $suc^{n+1}(b) \overset{d}{=} suc\,suc^n(b)$. We define $(\forall b\in B)$ $L(b) \overset{d}{=} \{suc^n(b) : n\in\omega\} \cup \{a\in B : (\exists n\in\omega) suc^n(a) = b\}$. Let $H_6 \overset{d}{=} L(6\uparrow) \cup L(7\uparrow) \cup L(1\uparrow)$, $H_1 \overset{d}{=} L(1\downarrow) \cup L(5\downarrow) \cup L(3\downarrow)$ and $H_0 \overset{d}{=} L(0\downarrow) \cup L(4\downarrow) \cup L(2\downarrow)$. See Fig.9! Clearly,

(*) there is an isomorphism $p : \langle H_6, suc \rangle \rightarrowtail\!\!\!\twoheadrightarrow \langle H_1, suc \rangle$ such that $p(6\uparrow) = (1\downarrow)$, $p(7\uparrow) = (5\downarrow)$ and $p(1\uparrow) = (3\downarrow)$.

Let $P \overset{d}{=} p \cup p^{-1} \cup (M^+ \sim (H_6 \cup H_1)) \upharpoonright Id$, where $p^{-1} \overset{d}{=} \{\langle b,a \rangle : \langle a,b \rangle \in p\}$ is the usual inverse of p. We show that P is an automorphism of $\mathfrak{M}^+$. For illustration of the proof see Fig.9.

Below we shall omit some straightforward details, but we shall be glad to send [20], which contains all the details of the present proof

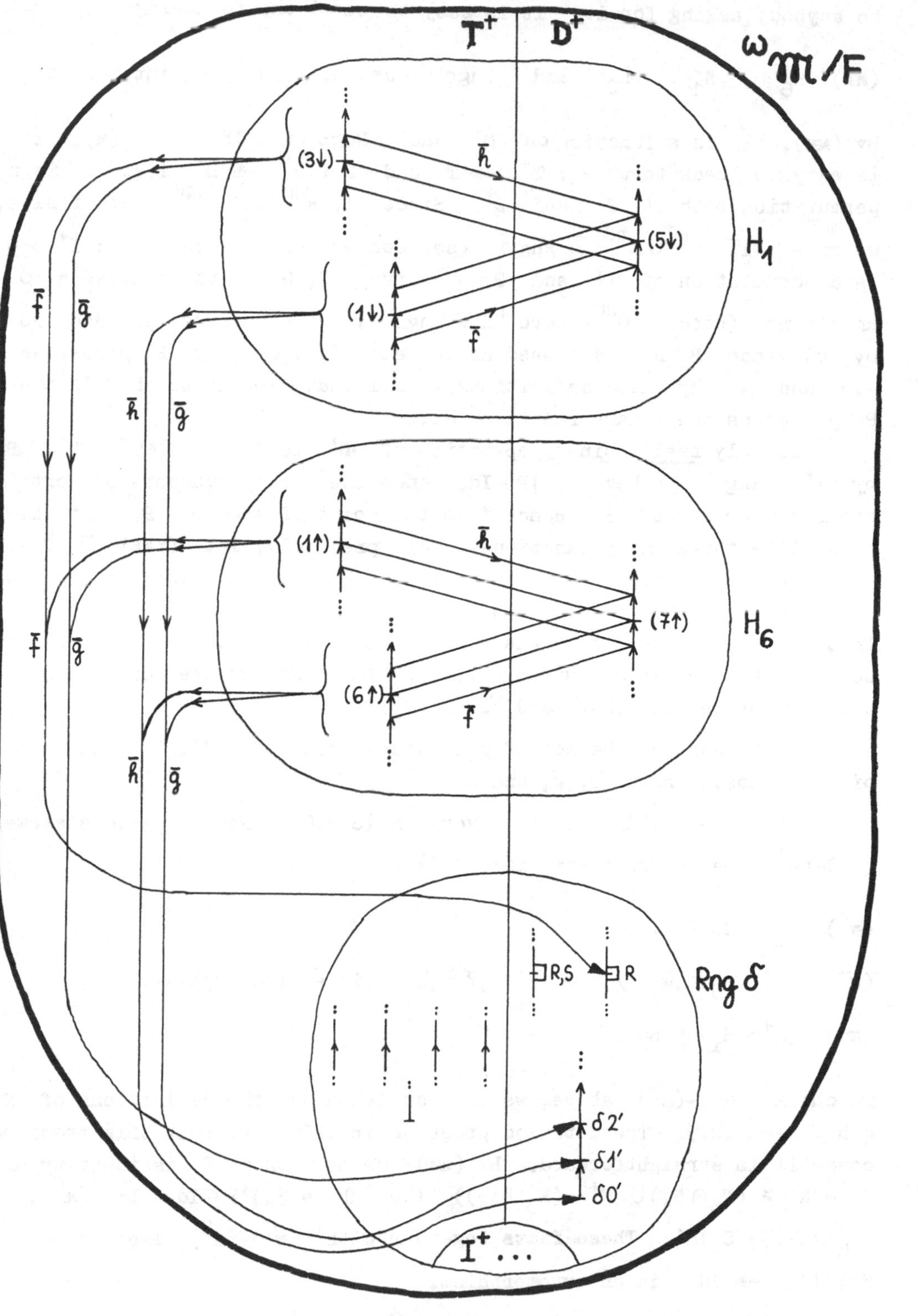

FIGURE 9

to anybody asking for it. It is easy to check the following

(**) H_6 , H_1 , H_0 and $Rng\delta$ are pairwise disjoint.

By (**), P is a function on M^+ and $Rng\delta \upharpoonright P \subseteq Id$. By (*), it is easy to check that $P : T^+ \rightarrowtail\!\!\!\!\twoheadrightarrow T$ and $P : D^+ \rightarrowtail\!\!\!\!\twoheadrightarrow D^+$ i.e. P is a permutation both of T^+ and D^+. Since I, $R^{\mathfrak{M}}$ and $S^{\mathfrak{M}}$ are finite, we have $I^+ \cup R^{\mathfrak{M}^+} \cup S^{\mathfrak{M}^+} \subseteq Rng\,\delta$ (see Convention 2). Thus $P : I^+ \rightarrowtail\!\!\!\!\twoheadrightarrow I^+$ is a permutation of I^+ and P preserves R, S and the constants 0 and zero (since $\{0^{\mathfrak{M}^+}, zero^{\mathfrak{M}^+}\} \subseteq Rng\,\delta$). P preserves sc and su by (*) since $B \sim H_i$ is closed under suc (and clearly P preserves +,· and ≤ by their definitions). All what remains to show is that P preserves the binary function ext.

The only <u>really binary</u> operation of $\mathfrak{M}^+$ is ext : $I^+ \times T^+ \to D^+$. But by $I^+ \subseteq Rng\delta$ we have $I^+ \upharpoonright P \subseteq Id$, hence the first arguments of ext are fixed points of P. Hence from the point of view of P, ext behaves like three unary functions. More precisely, let $(\forall k \in I)\ \bar{k} \overset{d}{=} \langle ext(\delta k, a) : a \in T^+\rangle$. Note that $I^+ = \{\delta f, \delta g, \delta h\}$. Then to see that P preserves ext it <u>is</u> enough to check that $(\forall k \in I)$[P preserves $\bar{k}$]. Thus we reduced $\mathfrak{M}^+$ to a unary model $\mathfrak{M}' = \langle M^+, \bar{f}, \bar{g}, \bar{h}\rangle$ and we have to show that P is an automorphism of $\mathfrak{M}'$. Now we are going to show that P preserves $\bar{f}$, $\bar{g}$, and $\bar{h}$.

$Su\,\mathfrak{M}'$ denotes the set of all subuniverses of $\mathfrak{M}'$, i.e. subsets of M^+ closed under $\bar{f}$, $\bar{g}$, and $\bar{h}$.

Let $N_i \overset{d}{=} H_i \cup Rng\,\delta$, for every $i \in \{6,1,0\}$. Now we claim statements $(*^3)$-$(*^5)$ below for every $i \in \{6,1,0\}$:

$(*^3)$ $N_i \in Su\,\mathfrak{M}'$.

$(*^4)$ $P : \langle N_6, \bar{f}, \bar{g}, \bar{h}\rangle \rightarrowtail\!\!\!\!\twoheadrightarrow \langle N_1, \bar{f}, \bar{g}, \bar{h}\rangle$ is an isomorphism.

$(*^5)$ $(M^+ \sim H_i) \in Su\,\mathfrak{M}'$.

To check $(*^3)$-$(*^5)$ above, we use Los lemma and the definitions of f, g,h , see Fig.9. The detailed proof is in [20]. We omit this proof because it is straightforward. By (**) we have that P is identity on $N_6 \bullet N_1 \overset{d}{=} (N_6 \cap N_1) \cup (M^+ \sim (N_6 \cup N_1))$ i.e. $(N_6 \bullet N_1) \upharpoonright P \subseteq Id$. By $(*^5)$, $(N_6 \bullet N_1) \in Su\,\mathfrak{M}'$. These facts together with $(*^3)$-$(*^5)$ imply that $P : \mathfrak{M}' \rightarrowtail\!\!\!\!\twoheadrightarrow \mathfrak{M}'$ is an automorphism.

So far, we have seen that $P : \mathfrak{M}^+ \rightarrowtail\!\!\!\!\twoheadrightarrow \mathfrak{M}^+$ is an automorphism.

Clearly P satisfies the conditions of Claim 6.2. The construction of Q is obtained from the above proof by substituting Q, H_0, N_0, (2↓), (4↓) and (0↓) into the places of P, H_1, N_1, (3↓), (5↓) and (1↓) respectively, everywhere. QED(Claim 6.2.)

We turn to the proof of $\mathfrak{M} \models IA$. Let $\varphi(z_0) \in F_{td}$ be any formula possibly with parameters from M. More precisely, let $m \in \omega$, $p \in {}^mM$ and let $\varphi(z_0)$ be the formula $\varphi(z_0,p)$ that is $\varphi(z_0,p_0,\dots,p_{m-1})$. We assume that $\varphi(z_0,p)$ is obtained from some $\varphi(z_0,\bar{z},\bar{x},\bar{y}) \in F_{td}$ by substituting p in place of $\langle \bar{z},\bar{x},\bar{y} \rangle$ such that everything belongs to the appropriate sort, e.g. if p_0 is substituted for z_1 then $p_0 \in T$. Assume that $\varphi(z_0,p)$ has no free variable other than z_0. Let $b \in T$ be arbitrary. Then $\mathfrak{M} \models \forall z_0 \varphi(z_0,p)$ and $\mathfrak{M} \models \varphi(b,p)$ have their obvious meanings, see e.g. Def.1.3.14-15 of [8]p.28 where $\varphi(b,p)$ and $\forall z_0 \varphi(z_0,p)$ are denoted by $\varphi[b,p]$ and $(\forall z_0 \varphi)[p]$ respectively.

We want to prove $\mathfrak{M} \models ind(\varphi,z_0)$. Assume

(C1) $\mathfrak{M} \models \varphi(0,p)$ and $\mathfrak{M} \models \forall z_0(\varphi(z_0,p) \rightarrow \varphi(sc(z_0),p))$.

Then $(\forall n \in \omega)\, \mathfrak{M} \models \varphi(\langle 6,n \rangle,p)$ since $\langle 6,n \rangle = sc^n(0)$ in $\mathfrak{M}$. Then

(C2) $\mathfrak{M}^+ \models \varphi((6\uparrow),\delta \circ p)$ holds by Los lemma.

Let P,Q be the automorphisms the existence of which is claimed in 6.2. Since P is an automorphism, by (C2) we have $\mathfrak{M}^+ \models \varphi(P(6\uparrow),P \circ \delta \circ p)$, hence $\mathfrak{M}^+ \models \varphi((1\downarrow),\delta \circ p)$ by $P(6\uparrow)=(1\downarrow)$ and by $P \circ \delta = \delta$. By the Los lemma there is $V \in F$ such that $(\forall n \in V)\, \mathfrak{M} \models \varphi(\langle 1,-n \rangle,p)$. Since F is nonprincipal, V is infinite which implies by (C1) that $(\forall z \in Z)$ $\mathfrak{M} \models \varphi(\langle 1,z \rangle,p)$. Then $\mathfrak{M}^+ \models \varphi((1\uparrow),\delta \circ p)$. Using Claim 6.2, $P(1\uparrow)=(3\downarrow)$, $Q(1\uparrow)=(2\downarrow)$, Los lemma and (C1) as above we obtain $(\forall z \in Z)[\mathfrak{M} \models \varphi(\langle 3,z \rangle,p)$ and $\mathfrak{M} \models \varphi(\langle 2,z \rangle,p)]$. By (C2) and $Q(6\uparrow)=(0\downarrow)$ we have $\mathfrak{M}^+ \models \varphi((0\downarrow),\delta \circ p)$. Then as above, by (C1) we conclude $(\forall z \in Z)\, \mathfrak{M} \models \varphi(\langle 0,z \rangle,p)$. We have proved $(\forall b \in T)\, \mathfrak{M} \models \varphi(b,p)$ which means $\mathfrak{M} \models \forall z_0 \varphi(z_0,p)$. Thus $\mathfrak{M} \models ind(\varphi(z_0,p),z_0)$. Since the choice of p was arbitrary, this means $\mathfrak{M} \models \forall \bar{z} \forall \bar{x} \forall \bar{y}\, ind(\varphi(z_0,\bar{z},\bar{x},\bar{y}),z_0)$. Since $\varphi \in F_{td}$ was chosen arbitrarily, we proved $\mathfrak{M} \models IA$. QED(Claim 6.1.)

CLAIM 6.3. $\mathfrak{M} \not\models \Box(p,\psi)$.

Proof. Let $s \stackrel{d}{=} \langle f,h,g \rangle$. Then s is a trace of p in $\mathfrak{M}$. To see this fact observe that $g=s_2$ is the history of the control variable of p, see Fig.s 6-8. Let $b \stackrel{d}{=} \langle 2,0 \rangle$. Then s terminates p in $\mathfrak{M}$

at time b since $s_2(b) = g(b) = 3'$ is the label of the HALT command of p. The output $\langle s_0(b), s_1(b)\rangle$ of p at time b does not satisfy ψ in $\mathfrak{M}$ since $\neg S(\langle 5,0\rangle)$ and $s_0(b) = f(b) = (5,0) \neq (4,0) = h(b) = s_1(b)$. Thus $\langle(5,0),(4,0)\rangle$ is a possible output of p in $\mathfrak{M}$ but $\underset{\sim}{D} \not\models \psi(x_0,x_1)[(5,0),(4,0)]$. <u>QED(Claim 6.3.)</u>

By Thm.1, 6.1 and 6.3 above we have the following

<u>COROLLARY 6.4.</u> $Ia \cup Ts \not\models^{N} \Box(p,\psi)$.

<u>CLAIM 6.5.</u> $Ia \cup To \models^{N} \Box(p,\psi)$.

<u>Proof.</u> Let $Ax \overset{d}{=} Ia \cup To$. Let "$(\forall z_1 < z_0)\varphi$" stand for the formula $\forall z_1[(z_1 \leq z_0 \wedge z_1 \neq z_0) \rightarrow \varphi]$. Similarly for "$(\forall z_1 \geq z_0)\varphi$" etc. For every $\varphi(z_0) \in F_{td}$ we define first(φ, z_0) to be the formula $[(\forall z_1 < z_0)\neg\varphi(z_1) \wedge \varphi(z_0)]$.

<u>CLAIM 6.6.</u> Let $\varphi \in F_{td}$. Then $Ax \models (\exists z_0\varphi(z_0) \rightarrow \exists z_0 \text{first}(\varphi,z_0))$.

<u>Proof.</u> Let $\psi(z_2)$ be the formula $[(\exists z_0 \leq z_2)\varphi(z_0) \rightarrow (\exists z_0 \leq z_2)\text{first}(\varphi,z_0)]$. Then $To \models \psi(0) \wedge \forall z_2[\psi(z_2) \rightarrow \psi(sc(z_2))]$ is easy to prove. By $\text{ind}(\psi(z_2),z_2) \in Ia$ we conclude $Ax \models \forall z_2\psi(z_2)$. Then obviously $Ax \models [\exists z_0\varphi(z_0) \rightarrow \exists z_0\text{first}(\varphi,z_0)]$. <u>QED(Claim 6.6.)</u>

For any $\varphi(z_0) \in F_{td}$ let hyp(φ,z_2) be the formula $(\varphi(z_2) \wedge (\forall z_0 \geq z_2)[\varphi(z_0) \rightarrow \varphi(sc(z_0))]$.

<u>CLAIM 6.7.</u> Let $\varphi(z_0) \in F_{td}$. Then $Ax \models \forall z_2[\text{hyp}(\varphi,z_2) \rightarrow (\forall z_0 \geq z_2)\varphi(z_0)]$.

<u>Proof.</u> $To \models [\text{hyp}(\varphi,z_2) \rightarrow \neg\exists z_0\text{first}([\neg\varphi(z_0) \wedge z_0 \geq z_2],z_0)$. By 6.6. then $Ax \models (\text{hyp}(\varphi,z_2) \rightarrow \neg\exists z_0[\neg\varphi(z_0) \wedge z_0 \geq z_2])$. <u>QED(Claim 6.7.)</u>

Let $\mathfrak{M} = \langle \underset{\sim}{T}, \underset{\sim}{D}, I, \text{ext}\rangle \in \text{Mod}_{td}(Ax)$ be arbitrary. Let $s \in {}^3I$ be an arbitrary trace of p in $\mathfrak{M}$.

<u>Notations</u>: Throughout, instead of the term $\text{ext}(s_i,z_j)$ we shall write $s_i(z_j)$. Let $b \in T$. Then $\bar{s}(b) \overset{d}{=} \langle s_i(b) : i \in 3\rangle$ and $\bar{\bar{s}}(b) \overset{d}{=} \langle s_0(b), s_1(b)\rangle$.

<u>CLAIM 6.8.</u> (i) $\mathfrak{M} \models [s_2(z_0) \in \{2',3'\} \rightarrow (\forall z_1 \geq z_0)s_0(z_1) = s_0(z_0)]$.
(ii) $\mathfrak{M} \models (s_2(z_0) = 2' \rightarrow (\exists z_1)[z_1 \leq z_0 \wedge s_2(z_1) = 1' \wedge s_0(z_1) = s_1(z_0)])$.

Proof. Proof of (i): Let $b \in T$ be such that $s_2(b) \in \{2', 3'\}$. Let $\gamma(z_1)$ be the formula $[s_2(z_1) \in \{2', 3'\} \wedge s_0(z_1) = s_0(b)]$. Clearly, $\mathfrak{M} \models \gamma(b)$. Also $\mathfrak{M} \models \gamma(z_1) \rightarrow \gamma(sc(z_1))$ because s is a trace of p. Hence $\mathfrak{M} \models (\forall z_1 \geqslant b)\gamma(z_1)$, by 6.7. Thus $\mathfrak{M} \models (\forall z_1 \geqslant b) s_0(z_1) = s_0(b)$.

Proof of (ii): Let $\kappa(z_0, z_1)$ be the formula $[z_1 \leqslant z_0 \wedge s_2(z_1) = 1' \wedge \wedge s_0(z_1) = s_1(z_0)]$ and let $\varphi(z_0)$ be the formula $[s_2(z_0) = 2' \rightarrow \rightarrow \exists z_1 \kappa(z_0, z_1)]$. We have to prove $\mathfrak{M} \models \forall z_0 \varphi(z_0)$.

Let $b \in T$. Assume $\mathfrak{M} \models \varphi(b)$. If $s_2(sc(b)) \neq 2'$ then $\varphi(sc(b))$ is obviously true. Assume therefore $s_2(sc(b)) = 2'$.

Case 1 $s_2(b) \neq 2'$. Then, since s is a trace, $s_2(b) = 1'$. Then $s_2(sc(b)) = 2'$ implies $\kappa(sc(b), sc(0))$. I.e. $\mathfrak{M} \models \varphi(sc(b))$ holds.

Case 2 $s_2(b) = 2'$. Then by $\varphi(b)$, there exists $a \in T$ with $\kappa(b, a)$. Since s is a trace of p and $s_2(b) = s_2(sc(b)) = 2'$ we have $\neg R(s_1(b))$. Hence by $\kappa(b, a)$ we have $s_2(sc(a)) = 1'$ and $s_0(sc(a)) = su(s_0(a)) = = su(s_1(b)) = s_1(sc(b))$. We have $sc(a) \leqslant sc(b)$ since $a \leqslant b$ by $\kappa(b, a)$. Thus $\kappa(sc(b), sc(a))$ proving $\mathfrak{M} \models \varphi(sc(b))$.

We proved $\mathfrak{M} \models \forall z_0(\varphi(z_0) \rightarrow \varphi(sc(z_0)))$. Since $\varphi(0)$ is obviously true, by IA we proved $\mathfrak{M} \models \forall z_0 \varphi(z_0)$. QED(Claim 6.8.)

Now we turn to the proof of $\mathfrak{M} \models \square(p, \psi)$. Let $\langle a, d \rangle \in {}^2D$ be any possible output of p in $\mathfrak{M}$. Then there are a trace $s \in {}^3I$ of p and $e \in T$ such that $\bar{s}(e) = \langle a, d, 3' \rangle$. If $\underset{\sim}{D} \models S(a)$ then $\underset{\sim}{D} \models \psi[a, d]$ is obvious. Assume therefore $\underset{\sim}{D} \models \neg S(a)$. By 6.6. there is $c \in T$ such that $\text{first}(\bar{s}(sc(c)) = \bar{s}(e), c)$ holds (since $e \neq 0$). Let this c be fixed. Then $\bar{s}(c) \neq \bar{s}(sc(c))$, hence $s_2(c) \neq 3'$. Since s is a trace of p, by $s_2(sc(c)) = 3'$ we have $\bar{\bar{s}}(c) = \bar{\bar{s}}(sc(c)) = \langle a, d \rangle$. Then $\neg S(a)$ implies $s_2(c) \neq 1'$ proving $s_2(c) = 2'$. By $s_2(sc(c)) = 3'$ then we have $R(d)$. By 6.8(ii) we have $(\exists b < c)(\exists x \in D)\ \bar{s}(b) = \langle d, x, 1' \rangle$. By $R(d)$ we have $s_2(sc(b)) \in \{2', 3'\}$ and $s_0(sc(b)) = s_0(b)$. Then by 6.8(i) and $sc(b) \leqslant c$ we have $d = s_0(b) = s_0(sc(b)) = s_0(c) = a$. We proved $\underset{\sim}{D} \models \psi[a, d]$. By the choices of e, s, and $\mathfrak{M}$ we proved $Ia \cup To \models \square(p, \psi)$. Then by Thm.1 we have $Ia \cup To \overset{N}{\models} \square(p, \psi)$. QED(Theorem 6.)

PROOF OF THE REST OF FIGURE 2 :

1) Proofs of the inequalities (all these proofs use ultraproducts):

(1.1) Sketchy proofs of $(Iq \cup Tpres \overset{N}{\models}) \nleq (Iq \cup To \overset{N}{\models})$ and $(Iq \cup Tpres \overset{N}{\models}) \nleq \overset{F}{\models}$ are Thm.9(iv $\not\Rightarrow$ i) in Part II of [3] and [4]p.93

together with pp.60-65 Claim 9.1 there. Detailed proof is available from the author.

(1.2) $(Iq \cup Tpres \overset{N}{\models}) \not\equiv (Ia \cup Ts \overset{N}{\models})$ is proved in [20]. The proof is a modification of the above proof of Thm.6: it uses Corollary 6.4 unchanged and the only part that is changed is formulation and proof of Claim 6.5. See also the $Iq \cup Tpres \models \Box(p,\psi)$ part of proof of (1.1) above.

(1.3) $(Ifm \cup Tfm \overset{N}{\models}) \not\leq (Ia \cup Ts \overset{N}{\models})$ is proved in [20]. The proof is a modification of the above proof of Thm.6; it uses Corollary 6.4 unchanged.

(1.4) $(Imd \overset{N}{\models}) \not\leq \overset{F}{\models}$ is proved in detail in Thm.9(v $\not\Rightarrow$ i) of [4]pp. 59-93, see also Thm.s 11/e - 11/g of [4]pp.100-107, and [23].

(1.5) The proof of $(Ia \cup To \overset{N}{\models}) \not\leq \overset{F}{\models}$ is very easy! See Thm.10 in [3]Part II. In the proof of Thm.9(v $\not\Rightarrow$ i) in [3] a partial correctness statement $\rho \in HF_d$ and a finite $Th \subseteq F_d$ are selected and an easy ultraproduct proof is outlined to show $Th \overset{F}{\not\models} \rho$. It is very easy to show $Th \cup Ia \cup To \overset{N}{\models} \rho$ by using the proof methods of Thm.s 3-4 in [3] for that Th and ρ.

(1.6) $(Ia \cup To \overset{N}{\models}) \not\equiv (Ia \cup Ts \overset{N}{\models})$ is Thm.6 proved above in the present paper.

(1.7) $(I\Pi_1 \overset{N}{\models}) \not\leq \overset{F}{\models}$ and $(I\Sigma_1 \cup To \overset{N}{\models}) \not\equiv (I\Sigma_1 \overset{N}{\models})$ are proved in [20]. The proof of the Π_1-part is a modification of the proof of Thm.9 (v $\not\Rightarrow$ i) of [4]pp.59-93 where only Claim 9.4 (and its proof) is modified. For the Σ_1-part, the proofs of Thm.s 3-4 in [3] and in [4]pp.42-45 are also used. Actually using these proofs it is not very hard to modify the present proof of Thm.6 to prove $(I\Sigma_1 \cup To \overset{N}{\models}) \not\equiv (I\Sigma_1 \overset{N}{\models})$.

(1.8) All the other inequalities indicated by $\not\equiv$ or by $\not\leq$ on Fig.2 are immediate consequences of (1.1)-(1.7) above and of the inclusions "$\leq$" and equivalences "$\equiv$" indicated there (which we turn to prove now).

<u>2) Proofs of equivalences</u> $(X \overset{Y}{\models}) \equiv (Y \overset{Z}{\models})$:

(2.1) $(Ict \cap If \overset{N}{\models}) \geq \overset{F}{\models}$ is proved in proofs of Prop.12 and Thm.9 (i $\Rightarrow$ ii) in Part II of [3], and also in [4]pp.57-58 and p.111. The detailed proof is given in proving Thm.9(i $\Rightarrow$ ii) in both quoted papers.

(2.2) By Fig.1, all the induction axiom systems Iname introduced in this paper are $\geq Ict \cap If$. Hence $(Iname \overset{N}{\models}) \geq \overset{F}{\models}$ follows from (2.1) with the only exception of Ifm. It is not hard to check that $(Ifm \overset{N}{\models}) \not\geq \overset{F}{\models}$.

(2.3) A <u>simple proof</u> of all the remaining equivalences $\equiv$ in

Fig.2 under the restriction that Th contains the Peano axioms is found in [6] which was first published in 1977 in Hungarian, see [1]. Even under this strong restriction, the question whether $(\mathrm{Ex} \cup \mathrm{Ia} \cup \mathrm{Tpa} \overset{N}{\models}) \equiv (\mathrm{Ia} \cup \mathrm{Tpa} \overset{N}{\models})$ remains an open problem.

(2.4) $(\mathrm{Iq} \cup \mathrm{To} \overset{N}{\models}) \leq \overset{F}{\models}$ is Thm.9(iii ⇒ i) in Part II of [3] and in [4]p.56. A detailed proof arises if one reads Prop.7 of [9]p.121 together with [10].

(2.5) All the statements $(X \overset{Y}{\models}) \leq (Y \overset{Z}{\models})$ implicit in Fig.2 are easy consequences of (2.4) and (2.1) above. <u>END of proofs of Fig.2.</u>

ON THE INTUITIVE MEANING OF FIGURE 2

One of the central themes of Nonclassical Logic is the study of the lattice of the various modal logics. This activity turned out to be a rather fruitful part of modal logic providing much insight into the nature of modal reasoning. Analogously, on Fig.2, we investigate the lattice of the various dynamic logics $\mathrm{Dlog}_d(\mathrm{Ax})$ for various $\mathrm{Ax} \subseteq F_{td}$. We hope this might provide insight into the nature of reasoning about programs (or more generally, reasoning about consequences of actions).

For example, Thm.6 says that if the set of logical axioms Ax of our Dlog(Ax) contain full induction Ia over time then it does matter whether or not time instances can be compared by the "later than" relation. In this case the dynamic logic $\mathrm{Dlog}(\mathrm{Ia} \cup \mathrm{To})$ in which we can say "z_0 is later than z_1" is stronger (modulo HF_d) than the one $\mathrm{Dlog}(\mathrm{Ia} \cup \mathrm{Ts})$ in which we cannot.

As a contrast, if the logical axioms contain only restricted induction Iq over time then the logic $\mathrm{Dlog}(\mathrm{Iq} \cup \mathrm{To})$ with "later than" is not stronger than the one Dlog(Iq) without it. However, here the logic $\mathrm{Dlog}(\mathrm{Iq} \cup \mathrm{Tpres})$ in which we can perform addition on time is stronger than the one $\mathrm{Dlog}(\mathrm{Iq} \cup \mathrm{To})$ in which we cannot. Intuitively $z_0=z_1+z_2$ means that "z_0 is z_2 time after z_1".

Now we turn to the question "is sometime sometimes better..." in the title of [16]. The formulas in $(\Sigma_{0,t}F_{td})$ can be considered to be the formulas without time modalities "Sometime" and "Always". Hence Iq is time induction over all the formulas <u>without time modalities</u> (time induction over the non-modal formulas). The result $(\mathrm{Imd} \overset{N}{\models}) > (\mathrm{Iq} \cup \mathrm{To} \overset{N}{\models})$ in Fig.2 can be interpreted to say that the logic Dlog(Imd) in which "Sometime" is available is indeed stronger than the one $\mathrm{Dlog}(\mathrm{Iq} \cup \mathrm{To})$ without "Sometime". But this result implies only that "Sometime" is better <u>if</u> we allow arbitrarily complex time-modality prenexes "Sometime$\exists x_0(x_0=y_0 \wedge$ Always$\exists x_1(x_1=y_1 \wedge$ Sometimeφ))" see the definition of DF^{mod} (Def.18). This was not mentioned in the title of [16]. So a finicky interpretation of the quoted question might lead us to the "pure sometime logic" Dlog($I\Sigma_1$) in which we can perform time-induction over Sometimeφ with $\varphi \in (\Sigma_{0,t}F_{td})$ but we cannot do time-induction over "$\neg$Sometimeφ" or over "Sometime$\exists x_0(x_0=y_0 \wedge$ Alwaysφ)". Thus the result $(I\Sigma_1 \cup To \overset{N}{\models}) > (Iq \cup To \overset{N}{\models})$ and the problem whether or not $(I\Sigma_1 \overset{N}{\models}) \equiv (Iq \overset{N}{\models})$ both in Fig.2 are relevant to a more careful analysis of the quoted question.

By another part of Fig.2, future tense "Sometime in the futureφ" as used e.g. in [12] adds to the reasoning power of dynamic logic Dlog($Ia \cup Ts$) with full time-induction. The rest of Fig.2 can be interpreted in this spirit, to investigate what kinds of logical constructs do increase the reasoning power (-s of which versions) of dynamic logic. Such logical constructs are "later than", "at z_0 time after z_1 it is the case that φ", "Sometimeφ" etc. By passing we note that it clearly shows on Fig.2 that the well known dynamic logics $\langle HFL_d, \overset{F}{\models}\rangle$, $\langle DL_d^{mod}, \underline{\models^{mod}}\rangle$, and $\langle DL_d^{fum}, \underline{\models^{fum}}\rangle$ are strictly increasing in this order in reasoning power modulo partial correctness of programs, i.e. modulo HF_d. That is $\overset{F}{\models} < \underline{\models^{mod}} < \underline{\models^{fum}}$.

We believe that Fig.2 is much more important for computer science than Fig.1, therefore we shall be sketchy in proving Fig.1.

<u>ON THE PROOFS OF FIGURE 1</u>

<u>The inclusions</u> indicated on the figure are straghtforward, except for $I' \models Imd$ and $Imd \models I'$. $I' \models Imd$ can be seen by observing that mod(φ) is semantically equivalent to an element of I', for every $\varphi \in DF^{mod}$. The idea of the proof of $Imd \models I'$ is to translate I' into Imd. Instead of giving here the definition, we show the idea on an example. Let $\varphi \overset{d}{=} R(s_0, ext(y_0, sc(0)), ext(y_0, sc(z_0))))$. Then $\varphi' \overset{d}{=} \exists x_1 \exists x_2[FirstNext(x_1=y_0) \wedge NextNext(x_2=y_0) \wedge R(x_0,x_1,x_2)]$. Now the translation of ind(φ, z_0) is defined to be $[First\varphi' \wedge Alw(\varphi' \rightarrow Next\varphi')] \rightarrow \rightarrow Alw\varphi'$.

<u>On the inequalities</u> indicated on Fig.1.: $I' \not\models I1$ can be checked

by showing $I' \not\models ind(R(ext(y_0, z_0+z_0)), z_0)$ or $I' \not\models ind(sc(z_0)\neq 0, z_0)$. (These are proved in detail in [20]. In the proofs, models $\mathfrak{M}$ are constructed such that $\mathfrak{M} \models I'$. The proofs of $\mathfrak{M} \models I'$ are simplified versions of the proof of Claim 6.2 in the present paper.) By Fig.2 we have that $(\exists p \exists \psi)[Imd \models \square(p,\psi)$ but $Iq \cup To \not\models \square(p,\psi)]$. Therefore $Iq \not\models Imd$, that is $Imd \not\leq Iq$ and hence $I1 \not\leq Iq$. An easy argument shows that $I1 \not\models Iq$, i.e. I1 and Iq are not comparable. By Fig.2, $Iq \not\models I\Sigma_1$ and $Iq \not\models I\Pi_1$. $I\Pi_1 \not\models I1$ and $I\Sigma_1 \not\models I1$ can be proved by [20] roughly by considering $\langle \underset{\sim}{T}, \underset{\sim}{T}, \{Id\}, valueof \rangle$ (but we did not check the details carefully). The remaining inequalities on Fig.1 are not hard. $I\Sigma_1 \not\models I\Pi_1$ and $I\Pi_1 \not\models I\Sigma_1$ are in [20]. <u>End of proof of Fig.1.</u>

<u>Intuitive motivation</u> for the second part of the present paper is a section entitled "Intuitive ... of Fig.2" in §5 immediately below the end of proof of Fig.2. To this we add that our Fig.2 is analogous with Fig.1 of the monograph [6 b] on first order modal logic and Kripke models. For the lattice of modal logics see e.g. [6 a], we point out this because the main result proved in the present paper concerns the lattice of dynamic logics.

REFERENCES

[1] Andréka,H. and Németi,I., Completeness of Floyd's program verification method w.r.t. nonstandard time models, Seminar Notes, Math. Inst.H.A.Sci.-SZKI 1977 (in Hungarian). This was abstracted in [2].

[2] Andréka,H. and Németi,I., Completeness of Floyd Logic, Bull. Section of Logic Wroclaw Vol 7, No 3, 1978, pp.115-121.

[3] Andréka,H. Németi,I. and Sain,I., A complete logic for reasoning about programs via nonstandard model theory. Part I, Part II. Theoret.Comput.Sci. 17(1982) no.2 and no.3.

[4] Andréka,H. Németi,I. and Sain,I., A complete first order dynamic logic. Preprint No. 810318, Math.Inst.H.A.S., Budapest, 1980.

[5] Andréka,H. Németi,I. and Sain,I., Henkin-type semantics for program schemes to turn negative results to positive. In: Fundamentals of Computation Theory'79 (Proc.Conf. Berlin 1979), Ed.: L. Budach, Akademie Verlag Berlin 1979. Band 2. pp.18-24.

[6] Andréka,H. Németi,I. and Sain,I., A characterization of Floyd provable programs. In: Mathematical Foundations of Computer Science'81 (Proc.Conf. Strbské Pleso Czechoslovakia 1981)Lecture Notes in Computer Science, Springer Verlag, 1981.

[6 a] Blok,W.J., The lattice of modal logics. J. Symbolic Logic. To appear.

[6 b] Bowen,K.A., Model theory for modal logic. D.Reidel Publ.Co., Boston 1979, x+127 pp.

[7] Burstall,R.M., Program proving as hand simulation with a little induction. IFIP Congress, Stockholm, August 3-10, 1974.

[8] Chang,C.C. and Keisler,H.J., Model Theory. North-Holland, 1973.

[9] Csirmaz,L., A survey of semantics of Floyd-Hoare derivability. CL&CL - Comput.Linguist.Comput.Lang. 14(1980)pp.21-42.

[10] Csirmaz,L., On the completeness of proving partial correctness. Acta Cybernet. To appear.

[11] Csirmaz,L. and Paris,J.B., A property of 2-sorted Peano models and program verification. Preprint Math.Inst.H.A.S. Budapest, 1981.

[12] Gabbay,D. Pnuely,A. Shelah,S. and Stavi,J., On the temporal analysis of fairness. Preprint, Weizmann Inst. of Science, Dept. of Applied Math., May 1981.

[13] Gergely,T. and Úry,L., Time models for programs. In: Mathematical Logic in Computer Science (Proc.Coll.Salgótarján 1978)Colloq.Math. Soc.J.Bolyai 26 Ed.s: Gergely,T. Dömölki,B. North-Holland, 1981. pp.359-427.

[14] Hájek,P., Making dynamic logic first-order. In: Mathematical Foundations of Computer Science'81 (Proc.Conf. Strbské Pleso Czechoslovakia 1981) Lecture Notes in Computer Science, Springer Verlag, 1981.

[15] Kfoury,D.J. and Park,D.M.R., On the termination of program schemas. Information & Control 29(1975),pp.243-251.

[16] Manna,Z. and Waldinger,R., Is "Sometime" sometimes better than "Always"? Intermittent assertions in proving program correctness. Preprint No. Z173, Stanford Research Inst., Menlo Park, June 1976.

[17] Monk,J.D., Mathematical Logic. Springer Verlag, 1976.

[18] Németi,I., Nonstandard runs of Floyd provable programs. Preprint, Math.Inst.H.A.S., Budapest, 1980.

[19] Németi,I., Hilbert style axiomatization of nonstandard dynamic logic. Preprint, Math.Inst.H.A.S., Budapest, 1980.

[20] Németi,I., Results on the lattice of dynamic logics. Preprint, Math.Inst.H.A.S., Budapest, 1981.

[21] Richter,M.M. and Szabo,M.E., Towards a nonstandard analysis of programs. In: Proc. 2nd Victoria Symp. on Nonstandard Analysis (Victoria, British Columbia, June 1980) Lecture Notes in Mathematics, Ed.: A. Hurd, Springer Verlag, 1981.

[22] Sain,I., There are general rules for specifying semantics: Observations on abstract model theory. CL&CL - Comput.Linguist.Comput. Lang. 13(1979),pp.251-282.

[23] Sain,I., First order dynamic logic with decidable proofs and workeable model theory. In: Fundamentals of Computation Theory'81 (Proc. Conf. Szeged 1981)Lecture Notes in Computer Science, Springer Verlag, 1981.

A Critique of the Foundations of Hoare-Style Programming Logics

Michael J. O'Donnell

Purdue University

ABSTRACT

Much recent discussion in computing journals has been devoted to arguments about the feasibility and usefulness of formal verification methods for increasing confidence in computer programs. Too little attention has been given to precise criticism of specific proposed systems for reasoning about programs. Whether such systems are to be used for formal verification, by hand or automatically, or as a rigorous foundation for informal reasoning, it is essential that they be logically sound. Several popular rules in the Hoare language are in fact not sound. These rules have been accepted because they have not been subjected to sufficiently strong standards of correctness. This paper attempts to clarify the different technical definitions of correctness of a logic, to show that only the strongest of these definitions is acceptable for Hoare logic, and to correct some of the unsound rules which have appeared in the literature. The corrected rules are given merely to show that it is possible to do so. Convenient and elegant rules for reasoning about certain programming constructs will probably require a more flexible notation than Hoare's.

Key words and phrases: verification, soundness, partial correctness, defined functions, Goto, logic.

CR categories: 5.21, 5.24, 4.29.

1. Introduction

Logic is the study of the relation between a symbolic language and its meaning, with special emphasis on the legitimate ways of reasoning in the language. A primary accomplishment of Mathematical Logic in the earlier part of this century was the formalization of the First Order Predicate Calculus, a logical language which is generally regarded as sufficient in principle for nearly all mathematical discourse. Formal rules for reasoning in the First Order Predicate Calculus have been shown to be correct and powerful enough to derive all true theorems of this language. In the last decade, new languages and formal rules for reasoning about programs have been proposed, and attempts have been made to justify the correctness of these rules.

A particularly popular language for reasoning about programs is the language of Hoare triples [13]. The Hoare language includes the formulae of the First Order Predicate Calculus, plus triples of the form A{P}B, with A and B Predicate Calculus formulae and P a program or part of a program. Such a triple is intended to mean that, if the initial state of a machine satisfies the assertion A, then after running the program P, B must be true of the final state. Unfortunately, several different definitions of the correctness of a system of reasoning, which are equivalent for the Predicate Calculus, are not equivalent for the Hoare language. So we must be very careful when studying rules for reasoning in the Hoare language to use a criterion for correctness which corresponds to our intuitive idea of legitimate reasoning. Several articles on Hoare logic in the past few years [6,16,19] have attempted to justify rules of reasoning by criteria which are insufficient to give intuitive confidence in the derivations which are carried out by such rules.

There are three main reasons for using a formal presentation of logic instead of relying solely on intuition when reading and writing technical arguments:

[1] A formal presentation provides a uniform standard which may be used as a final authority in disagreements.

[2] Formal presentation makes a system of reasoning into a mathematical object which may be studied objectively to discover its properties.

[3] A formally presented system may be processed automatically by computers.

To be useful for any of these three purposes, a formal system must be intuitively correct. A common enterprise in logic is to formalize the notion of correctness and to prove that a formal system is correct. Along with such a proof, a careful intuitive inspection of the formal definition of correctness is essential, since everything hinges on this definition. Such careful scrutiny has generally been omitted in published work on Hoare logics. The purpose of this paper is to begin such a scrutiny. I will show that several proposed rules for reasoning about programs have been judged by faulty standards of correctness, and are in fact incorrect by the proper standards.

Section 2 describes four different technical definitions of correctness and argues that only the strongest of these definitions is intuitively sufficient. Section 3 introduces the Hoare language and its meaning. Section 4 shows the well-known correct rules for reasoning about programs with assignments, conditionals and while loops. Section 4 extends the rules to handle programs with function definitions. The first two published attempts to give rules for function definitions [6,16,19] were incorrect. Section 5 discusses the problems of reasoning about programs with <u>Goto</u> commands. The best-known rule for reasoning about Gotos [6] is also incorrect, although it satisfies a weaker condition which is sometimes mistaken for correctness.

2. Criteria for correctness of a logical system

Two primary requirements are known for the correctness of a system of reasoning, each with several variations in its technical definitions. Consistency refers to the inability of a system to derive an explicit contradiction, while the stronger notion of soundness says that everything derived in a system is in some sense true. There are two natural definitions of consistency.

Definitions

Assume that a relation contradictory(Φ) has been defined on finite sets Φ of formulae in a language so that contradictory(Φ) captures the intuitive notion that the formulae in Φ are explicitly contradictory.

A logical system of reasoning is strongly consistent if it is not possible to prove all of the formulae in a set Φ such that contradictory(Φ).

A logical system of reasoning is weakly consistent if it is not possible to prove a single formula F such that contradictory({F}).

Strong consistency certainly implies weak consistency.

In the First Order Predicate Calculus, contradictory(Φ) holds whenever Φ contains two formulae of the forms F and ¬F or a single formula of the form (F&¬F), or the formula False. Other sets of formulae may be taken as contradictory as long as it is obviously impossible for all formulae in the set to be true. Since (F&¬F)

(equivalently, False) is provable if and only if F is provable and ¬F is provable, weak and strong consistency are equivalent for the First Order Predicate Calculus with the definition of <u>contradictory</u> above, or with any reasonable more liberal definition. But in Hoare logics, two formulae A{P}B and C{Q}D cannot be combined with a symbol like &. So weak and strong consistency might not be equivalent for systems of reasoning in Hoare languages. I show in Section 5 that a system proposed by Musser [16,19] for reasoning about function definitions in Euclid is weakly consistent but not strongly consistent. The proposed system violates the principle that (F&¬F) is provable if and only if F and ¬F are each provable.

Strong consistency, for some reasonable definition of <u>contradictory</u>, is intuitively a necessary condition for the correctness of a logical system, but it is not in general a sufficient condition, since a system might prove a formula which is false but does not contradict any other provable formula.

<u>Definitions</u>

A set of formulae Φ <u>implies</u> a formula F if F is true in every world in which all the formulae in Φ are true.

A logical system is <u>theorem sound</u> if every provable formula is true.

A logical system is <u>inferentially sound</u> if, for every set of formulae Φ and every formula F, if F can be proved from assumptions in Φ, then Φ implies F.

In any system where contradictory formulae cannot all be true, theorem soundness implies strong consistency. By letting Φ be the empty set, we see that inferential soundness implies theorem soundness.

In the First Order Predicate calculus, F is provable from

assumptions in Φ if and only if there is some finite subset $\{F_1, \ldots, F_n\}$ of Φ such that $((F_1 \& \ldots \& F_n) \Rightarrow F)$ is provable with no assumptions. Since the meaning of the implication symbol is just that the left side implies the right side, theorem and inferential soundness are equivalent for the First Order Predicate Calculus. In Hoare logics, it is not always possible to join two formulae with an implication sign, so theorem soundness may be weaker than inferential soundness.

Although theorem soundness seems at first glance to be enough for an intuitive claim of correctness, this weaker form of soundness only justifies the theorems of a system, not the methods of reasoning. If a formal system is to provide a satisfactory foundation for actual reasoning, the methods of proof should be intuitively correct, not just symbol manipulation tricks which fortuitously produce true theorems at the end. One might argue that certain rules for program verification are intended only for automatic theorem proving, not for human consumption, so that the steps of reasoning are not important as long as the answer is right. Even from such a restricted point of view, theorem soundness is at best not a very robust notion.

Suppose that a certain logical system is incomplete, so that some particular true formula F cannot be proved. Such a system might be theorem sound, even though assuming F would lead to a proof of some false or even contradictory formula G. Any attempt to extend this system by adding true formulae as axioms or by providing additional correct rules of inference would be very dangerous, since once the true formula F became provable, so would the false formula G. In Section 6 I show that the rules for reasoning about Goto commands proposed by Clint and Hoare [6] create a system of reasoning with this dangerous property: because of the lack of inferential soundness, addition of true axioms yields an inconsistency. Arbib and Alagić

[1,3] also noticed a problem with the Clint and Hoare Goto rule. In inferentially sound systems every step of reasoning is correct, so soundness is preserved when additional true axioms or additional sound rules are added.

3. Meanings of formulae in Hoare logics

Recall that a Hoare formula is either a formula of the First Order Predicate Calculus or a triple A{P}B with A and B formulae of the Predicate Calculus and P a program or program segment (some people prefer to write {A}P{B}). Predicate Calculus formulae are built from function, constant and variable symbols, relational symbols, the equality sign, and the usual logical symbols & (and), V (or), ¬ (not), => (implies), ∀x (for all x) and ∃x (there exists x). For example,

∀x ∃y (y>x & Prime(y))

is a Predicate Calculus formula expressing the fact that there exist arbitrarily large primes. Such formulae have the standard meanings, which correspond exactly to the intuition; see [18] for a formal treatment.

Great effort has gone into formalizing the meanings of programs [22,11], but for this discussion I will use only programs whose meanings are intuitively obvious. There are two popular ways to define the meaning of a Hoare triple A{P}B, which differ in their treatments of cases where P fails to halt.

Definitions

A Hoare triple A{P}B is a true partial correctness formula if, whenever the program segment P begins execution with its first command, in a state for which A is true, and P terminates normally by executing its last command, then B is true of the resulting final state.

A{P}B is a true total correctness formula if, whenever P begins execution with its first command, in a state for which A is true, then P terminates normally by executing its last command, and B is true of the resulting final state.

For example,

A{While True do x:=x end}B

is always a true partial correctness formula, independently of A and B. Partial correctness formulae make no distinction between failure to terminate and abnormal or unsuccessful termination due to an error such as division by zero. The formula above is a false total correctness formula as long as there exists a state for which A is true. False{P}B is a true formula for both partial and total correctness. If P always halts when started in a state for which A is true, then the partial and total correctness meanings for A{P}B are the same. For example,

x>0&y>0{z:=1; i:=0; While i<y do z:=z*x; i:=i+1 end} $z=x^{y}$

is a true formula for both partial and total correctness, roughly expressing the fact that the program inside the braces computes x to the y power. To achieve machine independence, programs in Hoare formulae are assumed to be executed on an ideal machine with an arbitrarily large memory capacity, so that there are no overflows.

The partial correctness meaning for Hoare triples is more popular than the total correctness meaning because it is thought to be easier to deal with in formal proofs. Of course a partial correctness proof for a program is only valuable if we convince ourselves by some other means that the program halts. In the rest of this discussion, Hoare triples will always be interpreted as partial correctness formulae unless otherwise stated.

For the Hoare language contradictory(Φ) should hold whenever some Predicate Calculus subset of Φ is contradictory. Also, if Ψ is a contradictory set of Predicate Calculus formulae, and P is a well-formed program which obviously halts (e.g., a program with no loops), and if Φ contains all the formulae True{P}A for A in Ψ, then Φ is contradictory. Any additional intuitively contradictory sets of formulae may be added to the definition of contradictory(Φ) without affecting the following discussion.

4. Proof rules for programs with conditional and while

Consider a programming language with simple assignments

x := E

for expressions E, a command

Null

which does nothing, a command

Fail

which never terminates normally, two-branched conditionals of the form

If A then P else Q end,

and loops of the form

While A do P end.

Commands may be sequenced in the Pascal style with semicolon separators. Of course, Null and Fail are not needed, but they are convenient for discussion.

Assume that we have taken some sufficiently powerful proof rules from Mathematical Logic for all of our Predicate Calculus reasoning. In order to prove theorems in the form A{P}B we need additional rules for reasoning about programs. Such rules are commonly written in the form

$$\frac{F_1, \ldots, F_n}{G}$$

where $F_1, \ldots, F_n$ and G are schematic descriptions of formulae. The meaning of such a rule is that, whenever the hypotheses $F_1, \ldots, F_n$ have already been proved, we may prove the conclusion G in one more step. Sometimes restrictions are also given which limit the allowed applications of the rule. A rule with no hypotheses is often called an axiom or postulate.

The following well-known set of proof rules [13] is inferentially sound [8] for partial correctness Hoare logic with the conditional-while programming language described above:

Empty: $\dfrac{}{A\{\ \}A}$

Null: $\dfrac{}{A\{\underline{\text{Null}}\}A}$

Fail: $\dfrac{}{A\{\underline{\text{Fail}}\}B}$

In the next rule note that A(E/x) means A with the expression E replacing all free occurrences of x. A variable occurrence x is free as long as it is not in a subformula beginning with x or x. In the process of replacing x by E, quantified variables in ∀y and ∃y within

A must be renamed so that all variables in E remain free after substitution.

Assignment: $$\frac{}{A(E/x)\{x:=E\}A}$$

Composition-1: $$\frac{A\{P\}B,\ B\{Q\}C}{A\{P;Q\}C}$$

Conditional: $$\frac{A \& B\{P\}C,\ A \& \neg B\{Q\}C}{A\{\underline{\text{If}}\ B\ \underline{\text{then}}\ P\ \underline{\text{else}}\ Q\ \underline{\text{end}}\}C}$$

While: $$\frac{A \& B\{P\}A}{A\{\underline{\text{While}}\ B\ \underline{\text{do}}\ P\ \underline{\text{end}}\}A \& \neg B}$$

Consequence: $$\frac{A \Rightarrow B,\ B\{P\}C,\ C \Rightarrow D}{A\{P\}D}$$

To see that these rules are inferentially sound, we merely check each rule individually to see that whenever the hypotheses are true, the conclusion must also be true. Since combinations of inferentially sound systems are inferentially sound, we need not consider the possible interactions between rules. Cook [8] has shown that these rules are sufficiently powerful to prove all true statements in the Hoare language of conditional-while programs.

5. Defined functions

Let us add to the conditional-while programming language the ability to define functions by means of subprograms. For simplicity, consider only recursion-free (i.e., noncircular) definitions of unary functions, with no nesting of definitions, no side-effects and no global variables. Such a simple version of function definitions already provides interesting pitfalls for Hoare logic. Function definitions will be written in the form

f: Function(x); local $z_1,\ldots,z_n$; P; return(y) end

$x,y,z_1,\ldots,z_n$ must be distinct and must contain all variables in P. n may be 0, in which case there are no local variables, and the phrase local $z_1,\ldots,z_n$; is omitted. The form return(y) must occur exactly once, at the end, and should be thought of as a punctuation like Function(x) rather than a command. The value of x must not be changed in P. Any changes to the values of $y,z_1,\ldots,z_n$ within P have no effect on the values of these variables outside of the function definition.

Clint and Hoare [6,14] proposed the following rule:

Function-1:

$$\frac{A\{P\}B}{\forall x(A \Rightarrow B(f(x)/y))}$$

where f has been defined as

f:Function(x); local $z_1,\ldots,z_n$; P; return(y) end

and A and B do not contain $z_1,\ldots,z_n$ free.

Ashcroft [4] noticed that adding the rule Function-1 to those of Section 4 yields an inconsistency. Let f be defined as

(*) f: Function(x); Fail; return(y) end.

Consider the following derivation:

1)	True{<u>Fail</u>}False	Fail
2)	∀x True=>False	Function-1, 1)
3)	False	Predicate Calculus

So, the system containing Function-1 is not even weakly consistent.

It may appear that Function-1 only derives contradictions from pathological function definitions which never halt. A similar contradiction arises whenever a defined function fails to halt for some possible argument, even if the value of the function is never computed for that argument. For example, it is very natural to define the factorial function by a program which works correctly for positive arguments, but computes forever on negative arguments. The presence of such a definition leads to a contradiction even if factorial is only computed for positive arguments.

Alagić and Arbib [1] present the rule Function-1 with an informal warning that the function body must halt when A is true initially. For a logical rule to be useful, we must be able to decide when the rule has been applied correctly. Alagić and Arbib's restriction, taken literally, cannot be formalized in an acceptable fashion, since the halting of P is undecidable. One reasonable way to fix the rule Function-1 with such a restriction is to provide means for proving termination, that is, to use a total correctness logic instead of partial correctness. Alternatively, the rule could be restricted to some decidable proper subset of the set of all function bodies which halt.

The inconsistency in Function-1 is essentially Russell's paradox [21] in disguise. Russell's paradox arises from the definition of a set R as the set of all sets which do not contain themselves. Does R contain itself? A set may be represented by a function, called the characteristic function, which returns 1 for inputs in the set and 0 for inputs not in the set. Russell's set R is represented by the defined function

r: <u>Function</u>(g); y:=1-g(g); <u>return</u>(y); <u>end</u>

Now, the following derivation mimics Russell's paradox:

1)	1-g(g)=1-g(g){y:=1-g(g)}y=1-g(g)	Assignment
2)	True => 1-g(g)=1-g(g)	Predicate Calculus
3)	y=1-g(g) => y≠g(g)	Arithmetic
4)	True{y:=1-g(g)}y≠g(g)	Consequence, 1),2),3)
5)	∀g(True => r(g)≠g(g))	Function-1, 4)
6)	r(r)≠r(r)	Predicate Calculus, 5)

Musser [16,19] proposed a modified function rule in Euclid notation. Musser's basic idea is that the paradox of Function-1 arises when formulae A and B are chosen in such a way that there does not exist a function f satisfying ∀x(A=>B(f(x)/y)). The existence of such a function may easily be expressed in the First Order Predicate Calculus as ∀x(A=>∃yB). To avoid the extra step of substituting various values for x, Musser includes the substitution in his rule. Musser's rule covers recursion, a form of data abstraction, and more complicated uses of parameters, but, for my restricted function definitions, the rule is essentially

Function-2:

∃y(A(E/x) => B(E/x)), A{P}B

(A(E/x) => B(E/x,f(E)/y))

where f has been defined as

f:<u>Function</u>(x); <u>local</u> $z_1,\ldots,z_n$;
P; <u>return</u>(y) <u>end</u>

and A and B do not contain $z_1,\ldots,z_n$ free.

This rule may be applied with only one choice of A and B for each function definition.

The additional hypothesis $\exists y(A(E/x) \Rightarrow B(E/x, f(E)/y))$ prevents the simple contradiction which arose from Function-1. Now we need two proofs to derive a contradiction. Let f again be defined by a body which never halts (*).

1)	True{<u>Fail</u>}y=0	Fail
2)	$\exists$y(True => y=0)	Predicate Calculus
3)	True => f(0)=0	Function-2, 1),2)
4)	f(0)=0	Predicate Calculus, 3)

Similarly,

1)	True{<u>Fail</u>}y≠0	Fail
2)	$\exists$y(True => y≠0)	Arithmetic
3)	True => f(0)≠0	Function-2, 1),2)
4)	f(0)≠0	Predicate Calculus, 3)

So, the system containing the rules of Section 4 as well as Function-2 is not strongly consistent. It is weakly consistent only because of the peculiar restriction that Function-2 may be applied to each function for only one choice of A and B. (Musser's rule does not express the restriction so explicitly. In Euclid, the Predicate Calculus formulae A and B in A(E/x) => B(E/x,F(E)/y) must be included in the function definition, so the single allowed application of Function-2 to f is determined by the definition of f.)

A strongly consistent system may be achieved through the following rule. The trick is to allow assertions about expressions f(E) only after f(E) has been computed within an expression G[f(E)]. So, if f(E) is undefined, any attempt to compute G[f(E)] fails, and all partial correctness formulae about z:=G[f(E)] are true. If the expression E does not contain the variable z, the following rule may be used for reasoning about defined functions:

$$\frac{A\{P\}B}{A(E/x)\{z:=G[f(E)]\}B(E/x,f(E)/y)}$$

where f has been defined as

f:<u>Function</u>(x); <u>local</u> z_1, ..., z_n;
P; <u>return</u>(y) <u>end</u>

and A and B do not contain
$z_1,\ldots,z_n$ free,

and z does not occur in E.

If the variable z appears in the expression E in z:=G[f(E)], then the rule above does not work, because the assertion B(E/x,f(E)/y) has a different meaning after the assignment than before the assignment. The following more complicated rule uses the substitution technique from the Assignment rule to keep the assertion B(E/x,f(E)/y) before the assignment:

Function-assignment:

$$\frac{A\{P\}B}{A(E/x)\&(B(E/x,f(E)/y)\Rightarrow C(G[f(E)]/z))\{z:=G[f(E)]\}C}$$

where f has been defined as

f:<u>Function</u>(x); <u>local</u> $z_1,\ldots,z_n$;
P; <u>return</u>(y) <u>end</u>

and A and B do not contain
$z_1,\ldots,z_n$ free.

If defined functions are used in the conditions of conditionals and loops, two more rules are required:

Function-conditional:

$$\frac{A\{P\}B,\ C\&G[f(E)]\&B(f(E)/y)\{Q\}D,\ C\&\neg G[f(E)]\&B(f(E)/y)\{R\}D}{A(E/x)\&C\{\underline{\text{If}}\ G[f(E)]\ \underline{\text{then}}\ Q\ \underline{\text{else}}\ R\}D}$$

where f has been defined as

f:<u>Function</u>(x); <u>local</u> $z_1,\ldots,z_n$;
P; <u>return</u>(y) <u>end</u>

and A and B do not contain $z_1,\ldots,z_n$ free.

Function-while:

$$\frac{A\{P\}B,\ C\&G[f(E)]\{Q\}C}{A(E/x)\&C\{\underline{\text{While}}\ G[f(E)]\ \underline{\text{do}}\ Q\ \underline{\text{end}}\}C\&\neg G[f(E)]}$$

where f has been defined as

f:<u>Function</u>(x); <u>local</u> $z_1,\ldots,z_n$;
P; <u>return</u>(y) <u>end</u>

and A and B do not contain $z_1,\ldots,z_n$ free.

These three rules may be extended in a natural way to handle more than one defined function.

The soundness of rules for function definitions is a slippery issue when function bodies fail, since the normal interpretation of the Predicate Calculus does not allow for partial functions. So, we consider a Predicate Calculus formula containing a program-defined function f to be true when it is true for all total functions f consistent with the values computed by the definition of f [7]. If the definition fails to halt, then every total function is consistent with all the computed values (there are none), so only assertions which hold for all functions, such as $\forall x\ f(x)=f(x)$, are true for f. The assertion $f(0)=0$ is only true when the definition of f actually computes the output value 0 on input 0. Under such an interpretation, Function-assignment, Function-conditional and Function-while are inferentially sound.

Since the systems containing Function-1 or Function-2 are not even strongly consistent, they cannot be sound. Notice that Function-1 is an inferentially sound rule under the total correctness interpretation. For total correctness the rules Fail and While are not sound, so alternate rules must be used for reasoning about these constructs in a total correctness logic [7,10].

The logical system containing the rules of Section 4 plus Function-assignment, Function-conditional and Function-while cannot be relatively complete according to Cook's [8] definition, because there is no way to prove properties of f(x) unless f(x) is actually computed in the program. This system is sufficient to prove all partial correctness properties of programs which only mention values of defined functions when those values have actually been computed.

6. The Goto problem

Since the Hoare language is tailored to the description of exactly two states associated with a program execution -- the normal entry and exit states -- it is not surprising that trouble arises in considering program segments with more than one mode of entry and/or exit. Such multiple entry and exit segments occur when the Goto command is used. It is not obvious how to interpret A{P}B when P may terminate by executing Goto 1, with the label 1 occurring outside of P. The usual solution, proposed by Donahue [11], is to regard such termination as abnormal. So True{Goto 1}False is a true partial correctness formula, and, by itself, Goto 1 is indistinguishable from Fail.

Under this interpretation, the Composition-1 rule is unsound. For example, True{Goto 1}False and False{1: Null}False are true hypotheses for Composition-1, but the associated conclusion True{Goto 1; 1: Null}False is false, since Goto 1; 1: Null is equivalent to Null. No system containing Composition-1 may be inferentially sound for reasoning about programs with Gotos. In [11] Donahue places such strong restrictions on the use of Gotos that it is syntactically impossible to have a program segment P;Q with a jump between P and Q. Composition-1 is sound for Donahue's restricted language.

Clint and Hoare [6] proposed a rule for reasoning about Gotos which may be combined with Composition-1 in a theorem sound system. To understand this rule, consider a programming language with assignment, conditional, while loops, sequencing and Gotos which may branch out of but not into the scopes of conditionals and loops. Without loss of generality, let all labels be attached to Null commands. The Null rule must be expanded to allow labelled Null commands:

$$\text{Null-label:}\quad \frac{}{A\{l\text{: }\underline{\text{Null}}\}A}$$

The Clint-Hoare Goto rule is:

$$\text{Goto-1:}\quad \frac{B\{\underline{\text{Goto}}\ l\}\text{False} \vdash A\{P\}B,\quad B\{\underline{\text{Goto}}\ l\}\text{False} \vdash B\{Q\}C}{A\{P;\ l\text{: }\underline{\text{Null}};\ Q\}C}$$

The following critique also applies to Kowaltowski's variation on the Clint-Hoare Goto rule [15]. The hypothesis

$$B\{\underline{\text{Goto}}\ l\}\text{False} \vdash A\{P\}B$$

is intended to mean that A{P}B has been proved using B{Goto l}False as an assumption (similarly for B{Goto l}False ⊢ B{Q}C).

The system of reasoning using the rules of Section 4 plus Goto-1 is theorem sound. Notice that True{Goto l}False, although true, cannot be proved with these rules, so Composition-1 cannot be used to produce True{Goto l; l: Null}False. Any extension of this system in which True{Goto l}False is provable is theorem unsound, and even inconsistent.

What about the inferential soundness of the Goto-1 rule itself? That depends on how we interpret the truth or falsehood of

B{Goto 1}False ⊢ A{P}B.

If we interpret this hypothesis as true only when there is a proof of A{P}B from B{Goto 1}False in the particular system we are using, then the meaning of this rule depends on the whole system. For example, the rule would be sound within the Clint-Hoare system, but not in a system which proves True{Goto 1}False. Clarke [5] uses this weak interpretation of ⊢ in expressing the soundness of a rule for recursive procedures. A more robust interpretation is that

B{Goto 1}False ⊢ A{P}B

is true whenever there exists an inferentially sound system in which A{P}B may be proved assuming B{Goto 1}False -- equivalently, whenever B{Goto 1}False implies A{P}B. Donahue [11] uses this stronger interpretation of ⊢ in his treatment of recursive procedures. Since B{Goto 1}False is true, the implication reduces to simply A{P}B [3]. Contrary to Donahue's Theorem 5.15 [11], the Goto-1 rule is certainly not sound in the stronger interpretation, since

False{Goto 1}False ⊢ True{Goto 1}False,

False{Goto 1}False ⊢ False{ }False

are true hypotheses, yet the associated conclusion

True{Goto 1; 1: Null}False

is false. Arbib and Alagić noticed this difficulty independently [3].

Pernaps the insistence on inferential soundness and the most liberal possible interpretation of seems too picky. After all, it seems that we only need to be careful about Gotos, which are well-known to be dangerous beasts, and avoid introducing axioms like True{Goto 1}False. Unfortunately, the rule Goto-1 may yield false conclusions in the presence of added rules or axioms which do not appear to have anything to do with Gotos. For example, consider the sound and intuitively attractive rule:

```
Zero:          ----------------
               True{P; x:=0}x=0
```

In the presence of the rule Zero, Goto-1 derives incorrect formulae. For example:

```
1)   1)  x=0{Goto 1}False                       Assumption
     2)  True{x:=1; Goto 1; x:=0}x=0            Zero
2)   1)  x=0{Goto 1}False                       Assumption
     2)  x=0{ }x=0                              Empty
3)  True{x:=1; Goto 1; x:=0; 1: Null}x=0        Goto-1, 1),2)
```

The correct theorem True{x:=1; Goto 1; x:=0; 1: Null}x≠0 is also provable, so the system containing Goto-1 and Zero is not strongly consistent.

How may we reason correctly about Gotos? One way is to return to the Floyd [12] style of proof, in which a proof follows the control flow of a program. Constable and O'Donnell [7] have explored this idea. Manna and Waldinger's intermittent assertions [17] also handle Gotos easily. Even if we insist on using the Hoare language, we may still have a sound system for reasoning about Gotos. First, Composition-1 must be replaced by:

```
                   A{P}B, B{Q}C
Composition-2:     ------------
                      A{P;Q}C

                   where there are no
                   Goto branches from
                   P to Q or Q to P.
```

To understand the rest of the rules, notice that A{P; Fail; 1: Null}B says that if A is true initially, and P terminates by executing Goto 1, then B is true of the final state. Alagić and Arbib [1,3] express the same idea in the more convenient special notation {A}P{1: B}.

```
Goto-2:            ----------
                   A{Goto 1}B


Goto-label-same:   ----------------------
                   A{Goto 1; P; 1: Null}A


Goto-label-other:
                   A{P; Fail; 1: Null}B
               ----------------------------
               A{P; m: Null; Fail; 1: Null}B

               where 1 and m are different labels.


Goto-composition:

         A{P; Fail; 1: Null}C, A{P}B, B{Q; Fail; 1: Null}C
         -------------------------------------------------
                   A{P; Q; Fail; 1: Null}C

         where there are no
         Goto branches from
         P to Q or Q to P.


Goto-conditional:

         A&B{P; Fail; 1: Null}C, A&¬B{Q; Fail; 1: Null}C
         -----------------------------------------------
         A{If B then P else Q end; Fail; 1: Null}C
```

Goto-while:
$$\frac{A\&B\{P\}A,\ A\&B\{P;\underline{Fail};\ 1:\ \underline{Null}\}C}{A\{\underline{While}\ B\ \underline{Do}\ P\ \underline{end};\ \underline{Fail};\ 1:\ \underline{Null}\}C}$$

Combination:
$$\frac{A\{P\}B,\ A\{P;\ \underline{Fail};\ 1:\ \underline{Null}\}B}{A\{P;\ 1:\ \underline{Null}\}B}$$

Alagić and Arbib [1] present the Goto-2, Goto-label and Goto-while rules in a somewhat more powerful notation. They also give the Goto-composition and Composition-1 rules combined into one rule, neglecting to state the restriction that there are no jumps between P and Q. Without such a restriction, the rule becomes unsound. (In private correspondence, Arbib indicates that the rule was only intended to apply to a restricted form of statement, called an L-statement. Arbib and Alagić's rule is sound for L-statements. The restriction is not given explicitly in the statement of the rule.) Combination is strengthened to include one application of Composition-1. Goto-conditional is omitted in [1].

The system consisting of the rules Null, Fail, Assignment, Conditional and While from Section 4, along with Null-label Composition-2, Goto-2, Goto-label, Goto-composition, Goto-conditional, Goto-while and Combination above, is inferentially sound. Cook's techniques for proving relative completeness [8] may be used to show that this system is sufficiently powerful to derive all true partial correctness formulae for our simple programming language with Gotos.

De Bruin [9] proposes an interpretation of A{P}B under which a variant of the Clint-Hoare system is sound. B{P}C is true with respect to a sequence of "label invariants" $A_1, \ldots, A_n$ if, whenever P is executed in a state satisfying B, either P fails to terminate, or P terminates normally in a state satisfying C, or P terminates by branching to the ith label l_i in a state satisfying A_i. Thus,

B{Goto l_i}False is true if and only if $B \Rightarrow A_i$. While de Bruin's technique gives a technically correct support for something very much like the Clint and Hoare Goto rule, the formal justification requires an infinite class of proof systems, one for each different choice of label invariants. Under de Bruin's interpretation, a much simpler Goto rule is the following.

Goto-3: $\dfrac{}{A_i\{\underline{\text{Goto}}\ l_i\}B}$

7. Summary and Conclusions

I have argued that a logical system is only correct when it is inferentially sound, so that every intermediate step in a proof, as well as the final result, is true according to some intuitively meaningful notion of truth. Weaker correctness criteria, such as theorem soundness, which guarantees the truth of final results, but not intermediate steps, are unacceptable because they allow intuitively false reasoning which leads by formal tricks to true results. A logical system which is theorem sound but not inferentially sound is very dangerous because the addition of true axioms may introduce an inconsistency.

Rules proposed for reasoning about defined functions and Gotos in the Hoare style have not always met the standard of inferential soundness. Inferentially sound rules are not hard to find, but they are unsatisfyingly inelegant. The problem seems to be that partial correctness reasoning in the Hoare language is very natural for programs with only conditionals and loops for control structures, but not for programs with defined functions and/or Gotos. Defined functions tangle partial correctness and termination together to such an extent that it is no longer convenient to separate them. Since it is essential to prove termination anyway, we should use total correctness logics for reasoning about function definitions. Goto commands destroy the Hoare-style analysis of programs by structural induction, since the semicolon does not really indicate composition in the presence of Gotos, as it does in their absence. Goto commands are handled very naturally in the Floyd style of reasoning.

Acknowledgements

The presentation of this polemic benefited from the criticisms of Carl Smith, Doug Comer, Dirk Siefkes and Fran Berman.

Bibliography

1. Alagić, S. and Arbib, M.A. The Design of Well-Structured and Correct Programs. Springer-Verlag, New York, (1978).

2. Apt, K.R. A sound and complete Hoare-like system for a fragment of Pascal. Report IW/78, Mathematisch Centrum, Afdeling Informatica, Amsterdam, (1978).

3. Arbib, M.A. and Alagić, S. Proof rules for gotos. Acta Informatica 11.2, (1979), 139-148.

4. Ashcroft, E.A., Clint M. and Hoare, C.A.R. Remarks on program proving: jumps and functions, Acta Informatica 6:3 (1976), 317.

5. Clarke, E.M. Programming language constructs for which it is impossible to obtain good Hoare-like axiom systems, JACM 26:1, (1979), 129-147.

6. Clint, M. and Hoare, C.A.R. Program proving: jumps and functions Acta Informatica 1:3 (1972), 214-224.

7. Constable, R. and O'Donnell, M. A Programming Logic. Winthrop, Cambridge Massachusetts, (1978).

8. Cook, S.A. Soundness and completeness of an axiom system for program verification. SIAM Journal on Computing 7:1 (1978), 70-90.

9. de Bruin, A. Goto Statements. Chapter 10 of Mathematical Theory of Program Correctness by J. de Bakker. Prentice/Hall International, Englewood Cliffs, NJ, (1980).

10. Dijkstra, E.W. Guarded commands, nondeterminacy and formal derivation of programs. CACM 18:8, (1975), 453-457.

11. Donahue, J.E. Complementary Definitions of Programming Language Semantics. Lecture notes in Computer Science 42, Springer-Verlag, New York, (1976).

12. Floyd, R.W. Assigning meanings to programs. Proceedings of symposia in applied mathematics, 19, American Mathematical Society, Providence, (1967).

13. Hoare, C.A.R. An axiomatic basis for computer programming. CACM 12:10, (1969), 576-580.

14. Hoare, C.A.R. and Wirth, N. An axiomatic definition of the programming language PASCAL. Acta Informatica 2:4, (1973), 335-355.

15. Kowaltowski, T. Axiomatic approach to side effects and general jumps. Acta Informatica 7:4, (1977), 357-360.

16. London, R.L., Guttag,J.V., Horning, J.J., Lampson, B.W., Mitchell, J.G., and Popek, G.J. Proof rules for the programming language Euclid. Acta Informatica 10:1, (1978), 1-26.

17. Manna, Z. and Waldinger, R. Is "sometime" sometimes better than "always"? Second international conference on Software Engineering, (1976).

18. Mendelson, E. Introduction to Mathematical Logic. 2nd edition, Van Nostrand, N.Y., (1976).

19. Musser, D. A proof rule for functions. USC information sciences institute technical report ISI/RR-77-62, (1977).

20. Olderog, E. Sound and complete Hoare-like calculi based on copy rules. Technical report 7905, Christian-Albrechts Universitat, Kiel, (1979).

21. Russell, B. Letter to G. Frege, June 16, 1902. From Frege to Godel: A Source Book in Mathematical Logic, 1879-1931. J. van Heijenoort (Ed.), Harvard University Press, Cambridge, (1967), 124-125.

22. Scott, D. and Strachey, C. Towards a mathematical semantics for computer languages. Computers and Automata. J. Fox (Ed.), Wiley, New York, (1972), 19-46.

Some Applications of Topology to Program Semantics

Rohit Parikh[1]

Mathematics Department, Boston University
and
Laboratory for Computer Science, MIT

Abstract: The relationship between programs and the set of partial correctness assertions that they satisfy, constitutes a Galois connection. The topology resulting from this Galois connection is closely related to the Lindenbaum topology for the language in which these partial correctness assertions are stated. This relationship provides us with a tool for understanding the incompleteness of Hoare Logics and for answering certain natural questions about the connection between the relational semantics and the partial correctness assertion semantics for programs.

---

§1. Introduction. Doing program semantics usually involves associating mathematical objects (meanings) with programs in some uniform way. Apart from the extra rigor afforded by the mathematical framework, this association has certain other features of interest. Usually, the mathematical objects in question are simpler than the actual code. Thus it becomes easier to grasp, and prove facts about the mathematical "meaning" of a program than it is to prove them about the program itself. It also becomes posible, to a certain extent, to give some substance to the claim "These two programs are really the same, even though they *look* different". Indeed, two programs are "the same" just when they have the same meaning.

However, since this "the same as" relation is not that of equality but of equivalence, a problem can arise since programs that are equivalent for one purpose, may not be equivalent for another. An obvious example is where two programs exhibit the same input-output behaviour, but have different computational complexities.

Suppose that θ is our meaning function, then two programs α and β are *equivalent* relative to θ iff $\theta(\alpha) = \theta(\beta)$. We can write $\alpha \approx \beta$ to indicate that α and β are equivalent in this sense. Suppose now that # is some operation which yields the more complex program $\alpha\#\beta$ from α and β and which we would like to be able to perform on our programs. Say # is concatenation. We would clearly want that *if* $\alpha \approx \beta$ and $\gamma \approx \delta$ then *also* $\alpha\#\gamma \approx \beta\#\delta$. In other words, $\approx$ is a *congruence relation* for the operation #. If this happens, we shall say that the

---

1. Research supported in part by NSF grant MCS79-10261

meaning function θ *supports* the operation #. Thus, for example, the usual relational semantics associates with a program α the binary relation R_α on the state space W, consisting of all pairs of states (s,t) such that some execution of α beginning at s, terminates at t. This relational semantics for programs supports the sequential operations of *concatenation*, *if then else*, and *while do*. But it does not support the operation // (shuffle) which converts two sequential programs α and β into the concurrent program $\alpha//\beta$. The binary relations associated with α and β do not contain enough information to yield the binary relation for $\alpha//\beta$. Since our primary purpose in this paper is to study sequential (though possibly nondeterministic) programs, the relational semantics will be good enough for us.

Consider now another semantics that has been proposed, for example by Hoare and Lauer [HL], namely the set of partial correctness assertions (PCAs) satisfied by a program α. How does this semantics relate to and compare with the relational semantics? It would seem that the set of PCAs satisfied by a program ought to be enough, at least from the user's point of view, for what else does the user need to know about the program except what the program *accomplishes*? Now we saw above that whatever semantics is used by the user, it ought to support any operations on programs that the user is going to perform. However, now another consideration will enter. The set of PCAs satisfied by a program α is infinite, and a user can know only a finite number (though perhaps an arbitrarily large number) of them. It follows that the the answer to the question "Does $\alpha\#\beta$ satisfy the PCA $\{A\}\alpha\#\beta\{B\}$?" must depend only on a finite number of PCAs satisfied (or not satisfied) by α and similarly for β. In other words the set of PCAs satisfied by $\alpha\#\beta$ must depend "continuously" on the sets for α and β. This continuity condition can be formulated very naturally in terms of the Lindenbaum topology on the state space which is induced by the language L in which the PCAs are stated (i.e. from which the assertions A and B are taken). It turns out that the connection between the topology and the relational semantics yields some useful insights into the relationship between the relational semantics and the PCA semantics and also into the difficulties traceable to the "while do" construct.

§2. Preliminaries. We begin by giving some preliminary facts about Galois connections and closure operators and pointing out their relevance in the present context.

Definition 1: Let W be a set (of states or worlds). $\mathcal{P}(W)$ is the power set of W. A *closure* operation on W is a map J: $\mathcal{P}(W) \dashrightarrow \mathcal{P}(W)$ such that

(i) $X \subseteq Y \Rightarrow J(X) \subseteq J(Y)$
(ii) $X \subseteq J(X)$
(iii) $J(J(X)) = J(X)$

Then by (iii) the sets J(X) for $X \subseteq W$ are just the fixed points of J, and they will be called the *closed* sets of W. It is easily seen that the intersection of a family $\mathcal{F}$ of closed sets is again closed. For let $\mathcal{F}$ be such a family, X_i be the sets in $\mathcal{F}$ and let $X = \bigcap X_i$: $X_i \in \mathcal{F}$. Then since $X \subseteq X_i$ for all these X_i, we have $J(X) \subseteq X_i$ for all i. I.e. $J(X) \subseteq X$. However (ii) tells us that $X \subseteq J(X)$. So the two are equal.

The operator J as defined above need not be a *topological* closure operator. For example if W is a group and J(X) denotes the subgroup generated by X, then J will satisfy (i)-(iii) above but will not be a topological closure operation and will fail to satisfy (iv) and (v) below.

(iv) $J(X \cup Y) = J(X) \cup J(Y)$
(v) $J(\emptyset) = \emptyset$

If J *does* satisfy (iv) and (v), then the empty set is closed and a finite union of closed sets is closed, so J will be a topological closure operator, and the sets J(X) will be the closed sets of a topology on W.

Now we consider Galois connections and how they might give rise to such a topological closure operator.

Definition 2 (Birkhoff-Ore): Let P and Q be two partially ordered sets. Suppose that M and T are two maps M: P --> Q and T: Q --> P satisfying

(α) If $p \leq p'$ then $M(p') \leq M(p)$
If $q \leq q'$ then $T(q') \leq T(q)$

(β) $p \leq T(M(p))$
$q \leq M(T(q))$

then the pair M, T constitute a *Galois connection* between the sets P and Q.

To apply this defintion to a semantic system, let L be some set (a language) and suppose we are given a relation $\models$ (satisfaction) between the elements of W and L. Here $\models \subseteq W \times L$ and instead of writing $(s,A) \in \models$ we shall usually write $s \models A$. Given $\Gamma \subseteq L$ define Mod(Γ), the *models* of Γ, to be the set $\{s \in W \mid \text{for all } A \in \Gamma, s \models A\}$. Similarly, given $X \subseteq W$ define Th(X), the *theory* of X, to be the set $\{A \in L \mid \text{for all } s \in X, s \models A\}$. Then the maps Mod, Th have the properties:

(a) If $\Gamma \subseteq \Gamma'$ then $Mod(\Gamma') \subseteq Mod(\Gamma)$
If $X \subseteq X'$ then $Th(X') \subseteq Th(X)$

(b) $\Gamma \subseteq Th(Mod(\Gamma))$
$X \subseteq Mod(Th(X))$

The conditions (a) (b) make these maps Mod, Th a Galois connection between $\mathcal{P}(L)$ and $\mathcal{P}(W)$. Now we get a closure operator J on W by letting J(X) equal Mod(Th(X)) for all $X \subseteq W$. We shall write Mod(A), Th(s) respectively for Mod({A}) and Th({s}).

So far we have made no assumptions about L. For all we know, L consists of a single statement. Now we impose some conditions on L.

Definition 3: L has *falsehood* if there is an element $\bot \in L$ such that $Mod(\bot) = \emptyset$. L has *disjunction* if for every A, B in L there is a C such that $Mod(C) = Mod(A) \cup Mod(B)$.

The element C above, chosen somehow (usually C will be provided by the syntax of L) will be denoted $A \vee B$. Other operations from the propositional calculus may be introduced with similar notations. However, we are not assuming as yet that these other operations are present in L.

Lemma 1: If L has $\bot$ and $\vee$ then J is a topological closure operator with closed sets Mod(X) for $X \subseteq L$. Moreover the sets Mod(A) for A in L generate the topology. (This topology is of course the Lindenbaum topology on W.)

Proof: We need to check that the conditions (i)-(v) above are satisfied.

Since both the operations Mod and Th reverse set inclusion, their composition restores it, so (i) above follows. (ii) follows from the fact that if $s \in X$ then for all $A \in Th(X)$, $s \models A$. Hence $s \in Mod(Th(X))$. Thus $X \subseteq J(X)$ always and so also $J(X) \subseteq J(J(X))$. However, we can show by a similar argument that for all $\Gamma \subseteq L$, $\Gamma \subseteq Th(Mod(\Gamma))$. Taking Γ to be Th(X) we get $Th(X) \subseteq Th(Mod(Th(X)))$ and since Mod reverses inclusion, we get $Mod(Th(Mod(Th(X)))) \subseteq Mod(Th(X))$, i.e. $J(J(X)) \subseteq J(X)$. Thus (iii) follows.

To see (iv) note that since $X \subseteq X \cup Y$ and $Y \subseteq X \cup Y$, we get $J(X) \subseteq J(X \cup Y)$ and $J(Y) \subseteq J(X \cup Y)$. Hence $J(X) \cup J(Y) \subseteq J(X \cup Y)$. So much follows without assuming anything about L. To see the reverse inclusion suppose that $s \notin J(X) \cup J(Y)$. Then there is an $A \in Th(X)$ such that $s \not\models A$ and a $B \in Th(Y)$ such that $s \not\models B$. Let $C = A \vee B$. Then $s \not\models C$ and $C \in Th(X \cup Y)$, so that $s \notin Mod(Th(X \cup Y)) = J(X \cup Y)$. Finally, to see (v), $Th(\emptyset)$ contains all of L, including $\bot$. But then $J(\emptyset) \subseteq Mod(\bot) = \emptyset$.

To see that the sets Mod(A) are a basis for the topology, we only need to notice that $Mod(A \vee B) = Mod(A) \cup Mod(B)$. Hence the sets Mod(A) are closed under finite unions. Moreover for an arbitrary X, the closed set $J(X) = Mod(Th(X)) = \bigcap Mod(A)$: $A \in Th(X)$, and is therefore in the topology generated by the sets Mod(A). ∎

In case L is countable, the topology on W is a pseudo-metric topology.

Definition 4: A *pseudo-metric* on W is a function d from W×W to the reals, satisfying:

(i) $d(s,t) \geq 0$, $d(s,s) = 0$.
(ii) $d(s,t) = d(t,s)$
(iii) $d(s,u) \leq d(s,t) + d(t,u)$

If $d(s,t) = 0$ implies $s=t$, then d is a *metric.*

Suppose that L is countable and $L = \{B_1,...,B_n,..\}$. Call s and t *indistinguishable*, $s \equiv t$ if for all n, $s \models B_n$ iff $t \models B_n$. It is easily seen that the space $W, \mathcal{T}$ is a pseudo-metric space under the pseudo-metric

$d(s,t) = 0$ if $s \equiv t$.
$d(s,t) = 1/n$ otherwise, where B_n is the first formula satisfying $s \models B_n$ iff $t \not\models B_n$.

Let us say that $s_n \dashrightarrow s$ (s_n *converges* to s) iff $d(s_n,s) \dashrightarrow 0$. Then it is readily verified that a subset X of W is closed iff whenever $\{s_n\} \in X$ and $s_n \dashrightarrow s$, then $s \in X$. Note that $s_n \dashrightarrow s$ and $s_n \dashrightarrow t$ with $s \neq t$ is quite possible, and happens iff $s \equiv t$. If we identify points s, t with $s \equiv t$, then the resulting space has a true distance function on it and is a metric space. Let $\underline{W}$ denote the quotient space of W.

Now we turn to the consideration of partial correctness semantics. Since, as we remarked before, relational semantics is adequate for our purposes, we shall identify programs with binary relations on W, i.e. with subsets of $W \times W$. Given a program α, it satisfies the PCA $\{A\}\alpha\{B\}$ iff for all $(s,t) \in \alpha$, if $s \models A$ then $t \models B$. To connect this up with Galois connections, we consider a new system $(W \times W, L \times L, \models')$ defined by letting $(s,t) \models'(A,B)$ iff $s \models A \Rightarrow t \models B$, i.e. $s \not\models A$ or $t \models B$. Then $\{A\}\alpha\{B\}$ holds iff $\alpha \subseteq Mod'(A,B)$ iff $(A,B) \in Th'(\alpha)$. To emphasise the PCA connection we shall write $Th'(\alpha)$ as $Pca(\alpha)$ and $Mod'(\Gamma)$ as $Rel(\Gamma)$, for $\alpha \subseteq W \times W$ and $\Gamma \subseteq L \times L$.

Lemma 2: If L has $\bot$, $\vee$ and $\wedge$ (conjunction), then $L \times L$ has $\bot'$, $\vee'$ and $\top'$ (truth) and hence the operation J' is a topological closure operation on $W \times W$. Moreover, if L also has $\neg$ (negation) then the topology on $W \times W$ induced by J' is the square of the Lindenbaum topology on W induced by J.

Proof: Note that there is no (s,t) such that $s \not\models \top$ or $t \models \bot$, i.e. such that $(s,t) \models'(\top,\bot)$. Hence $\bot'$ can be $(\top,\bot)$. Similarly, $(\bot,\top)$ can be taken to be $\top'$.

Again, if (A,B), (C,D) are in $L \times L$, then we can take $(A \wedge C, B \vee D)$ to be $(A,B) \vee (C,D)$. For $(s,t) \models'(A \wedge C, B \vee D)$ iff $s \not\models A \wedge C$ or $t \models B \vee D$ iff $s \not\models A$ or $s \not\models C$ or $t \models B$ or $t \models D$ iff ($s \not\models A$ or $t \models B$) or ($s \not\models C$ or $t \models D$) iff $(s,t) \models'(A,B)$ or $(s,t) \models'(C,D)$ as required.

To see the last part of the lemma, let $\mathcal{T}_1$ be the topology on $W \times W$ induced by J', and let $\mathcal{T}_2$ be the square of the Lindenbaum topology on W. Both $\mathcal{T}_1$ and $\mathcal{T}_2$ are topologies on $W \times W$.

Now a basic closed set Mod'(A,B) in $\mathcal{T}_1$ can be written,

$$Mod'(A,B) = (Mod(\neg A)\times Mod(T)) \cup (Mod(T)\times ModB)$$

and is therefore in $\mathcal{T}_2$. Similarly, the basic closed set of $\mathcal{T}_2$ can be written,

$$Mod(A)\times Mod(B) = Mod'(\neg A,\bot) \cap Mod'(T,B)$$

and is in $\mathcal{T}_1$. Hence $\mathcal{T}_1 = \mathcal{T}_2$. ∎

We remark that in general, the language L×L does not have the conjunction operation, nor does it have a negation. Since the union of two sets of formulae acts like the set of their conjunctions, the first deficiency can be avoided somewhat. The second one is, however, essential.

We shall denote the Lindenbaum topology on W as $\mathcal{T}_l$ and the PCA topology on W×W as $\mathcal{T}_p$.

§3. *Semiclosed sets*: In general we do not expect the maps J or J' to be one to one. If this were the case then the topologies in question would be discrete topologies, and this does not happen in most cases. Hence we normally expect that for most X, J(X) properly contains X. However, it will usually also happen that the topology is not even T_0, i.e. that certain elements of W are indistinguishable from each other. We say that two states s and t are *indistinguishable* relative to L, $s \equiv_L t$ iff for all A ∈ L, s⊨A iff t⊨A. Where confusion is unlikely, we shall just write ≡ for $\equiv_L$. If L is a first order language, then the relation ≡ is just elementary equivalence. Given X ⊆ W let X^+ be the set of all t such that s ≡ t for some s ∈ X. Similarly, for X ⊆ W×W, let X^+ be the set of all (s',t') in W×W such that for some (s,t) in X, (s,t) $\equiv_{L\times L}$ (s',t') iff for some (s,t) in W×W, $s \equiv_L s'$ and $t \equiv_L t'$.

Lemma 3: $X \subseteq X^+ \subseteq J(X)$.

Proof: The first inclusion follows from the fact that ≡ is reflexive. As for the second, if s ≡ t, where s ∈ X, then for all A ∈ Th(X), s⊨A and hence t⊨A. Thus t ∈ J(X). Since t was arbitrary in X^+, $X^+ \subseteq J(X)$. ∎

Of course, a similar argument applies also to J' and L×L.

It follows that if X is closed (X = J(X)) then $J(X) = X^+$. The converse need not hold.

Definition 5: X is *semi-closed* if $J(X) = X^+$.

The relevence of the notion of semi-closure is as follows. If α is a real program and L is a first order language, then it is quite unlikely that $\alpha = \alpha^+$ and hence α cannot actually be closed. This happens because an actual program will take us from a structure with some assignment to variables to the *same* structure with a (possibly different) assignment to variables. An actual program cannot take us from one structure to a different, even elementarily equivalent structure. Thus the only actual program that will be closed will be the empty program, which never terminates. However the prospects that α is semi-closed are much better. Moreover, if we identify two states that are L-equivalent, and work in $\underline{W} = W/\equiv$, then the notions of closure and semi-closure coincide. In other words, a program α is semi-closed iff $\underline{\alpha}$ is closed in $\underline{W}\times\underline{W}$, where $\underline{\alpha}$ is the image of α under the quotient map from $W\times W$ to $\underline{W}\times\underline{W}$. Theorems 1 and 2 below show that the topological notion of semi-closure is closely tied to expressiveness.

Definition 6: α is *deterministic* if for all $(s,t), (s,t') \in \alpha$, $t = t'$.
α is *L-deterministic* if for all $(s,t), (s',t')$ in α, if $s \equiv_L s'$, then $t \equiv_L t'$.

Definition 7: Let A be a subset of W and $\alpha \subseteq W\times W$. By $WLP_\alpha(A)$ we shall mean the set $\{s \in W | \forall t \text{ in } W, (s,t) \in \alpha \rightarrow t \models A\}$. By $WP_\alpha(A)$ we shall mean the set $\{s \in W | \forall t \text{ in } W, (s,t) \in \alpha \Rightarrow t \models A \text{ and } \exists t \text{ such that } (s,t) \in \alpha\}$. By $WP_\alpha(A) \in L$ we shall mean that there is a $B \in L$ such that for all $s \in W$, $s \in WP_\alpha(A)$ iff $s \models B$. Similarly for WLP. This small abuse of language should not cause confusion. Notice that in dynamic logic notation, $WLP_\alpha(A)$ is just $[\alpha]A$ and $WP_\alpha(A)$ is $[\alpha]A \wedge \langle\alpha\rangle A$. WP (WLP) stands, of course, for weakest (liberal) precondition.

Throughout the rest of this section we assume that α is deterministic and L-deterministic and that L has all propositional connectives.

Lemma 4: $\forall A \in L$, $WP_\alpha(A) \in L$ iff $\forall A \in L$, $WLP_\alpha(A) \in L$.

Proof: $WLP_\alpha(A) = WP_\alpha(A) \vee \neg WP(T)$
$WP_\alpha(A) = WLP_\alpha(A) \wedge \neg WLP_\alpha(\bot)$ ∎

We shall say that L is *expressive* for α if the conditions of the lemma just above are obeyed. I.e. if $\forall A \in L$, $WP_\alpha(A) \in L$. Note that $WLP_\alpha(\bot) \in L$ iff $WP_\alpha(T) \in L$.

Theorem 1: If L is expressive for α then α is semiclosed.

Proof: Suppose $(s,t) \in J'(\alpha)$. Then every closed set that contains α, contains (s,t). In particular $Rel(WLP_\alpha(\bot),\bot)$ is such a set. Since $t \not\models \bot$, we must have $s \not\models WLP_\alpha(\bot)$, and so $\exists t'$ such that $(s,t') \in \alpha$. Now for all B, if $t' \models B$, then, since $\alpha \subseteq Rel(WP_\alpha(B),B)$, and the latter is closed, $(s,t) \in Rel(WP_\alpha(B),B)$, and also, by determinism, $s \models WP_\alpha(B)$, so $t' \models B$. Thus $t \equiv t'$ and $(s,t) \in \alpha^+$. ∎

Lemma 5: Suppose that L is first order. A subset X of W is clopen iff it is "in" L.

Proof: If $X \in L$, then $\exists A$ such that $X = \{s | s \models A\}$ is closed, and $W-X = \{s | s \models \neg A\}$ is also closed so both are clopen.

Conversely, suppose that X is clopen, and then so is W-X. Then since sets of the form Mod(A) are the basic closed sets, $X = \bigcap Mod(A):Mod(A) \supseteq X$ and $Y =$

$\bigcap$Mod(B):Mod(B) $\supseteq$ W-X. Now there are no s in X$\cap$(W-X) so these A's and B's are inconsistent. By the compactness theorem, some *finite* subset is inconsistent. Hence there are a finite number $A_1,\ldots,A_n$ which are already inconsistent with the B's. Then X, i.e. $\bigcap$Mod(A_i):i$\le$n, is clopen. ∎

Theorem 2: Suppose that L is first order. If α is semi-closed, and $WLP_\alpha(\perp)$ is in L, then L is expressive for α.

Proof: This is equivalent to showing that for all A, $WP_\alpha(A)$ is a clopen subset of W. Now notice that the sets $WLP_\alpha(\perp)$, $WP_\alpha(A)$ and $WP_\alpha(\neg A)$ are all disjoint and cover W. Hence if they are all closed, then they are all clopen.

Now the first set is closed by hypothesis. Consider the second, call it X. If $s_n \in X$, for all n, and s_n --> s, then we have to show that s $\in$ X. Now, we know that since $s_n \in X$, then for all n, there are t_n such that $(s_n,t_n) \in \alpha$. Since W is compact, the t_n have a convergent subsequence converging to some t. So (s,t) $\in$ J'(α). Also, all the t_n satisfy A, since $s_n \in X$, and so t also satisfies A.

Now α is semi-closed, so there is (s',t') $\equiv$ (s,t) and (s',t') $\in \alpha$. Now $WLP_\alpha(\perp)$ is clopen and does not contain the s_n, so it cannot contain s. Hence there is a t", such that (s,t") $\in \alpha$. Then we have (s',t') $\in \alpha$, (s,t") $\in \alpha$ and s $\equiv$ s'. Hence, by L-determinism, t" $\equiv$ t'. Now t $\equiv$ t' $\equiv$ t" and t$\models$A, so t"$\models$A. Thus s $\in$ X, and X is closed.

Similarly the set $WP_\alpha(\neg A)$ is also closed and all sets under consideration are clopen. ∎

The following question arises very naturally. Which programs α are semi-closed? Clearly a program for which the first order language is not expressive, cannot be semi-closed. Also it is useful to know which operations # on programs commute with closure, i.e. satisfy J'(α#β) = J'(J'(α)#J'(β))? The second question is quite important, because if # does not commute with J' then we cannot expect to find out the PCAs satisfied by α#β from those satisfied by α and by β. This is because knowing the PCAs of a program α does not allow us to distinguish between α and J'(α), and hence any sound argument that applies to the PCAs of all binary relations *cannot* give us any elements of Pca(α#β) - Pca(J'(α)#J'(β)).

Our results so far have been rather abstract, albeit rather general. To get our feet back on the ground, we consider some particular classes of programs.

§4. While schemes for a first order language. We consider while schemes, with some fixed finite set u̲ of program variables.

A state s consists of a domain D, an interpretation M for the language L over D, plus a valuation ϕ: program variables --> D.

W = all such states. (We can confine ourselves to countable ones.)
$\models$ = first order satisfaction.

The class of prgrams will include assignments u $\leftarrow$ t, where u is a variable and t is a term, with all variables in t, and u itself, from $\underline{u}$. The programs will be closed under concatenation (;), "if A the α else β" and "while A do α", where A is a first order formula. It is straightforward to show that all these programs are deterministic and also L-deterministic. A program will be called loop-free if it has no while-loops in it.

Since non-open formulae A need not be decidable, people may rebel at calling all these objects "programs". Hence we shall be careful, in actual examples of programs, to use only quantifier-free A. However, our theorems will not need this restriction. Moreover, (2) and (4) below apply to arbitrary binary relations α.

Theorem 3: (1) $\mathcal{T}_p$ is pseudo-metrisable and compact.
(2) If A is in L, then
J'(if A then α else β) = if A then J'(α) else J'(β)
(3) All loop-free programs are semi-closed.
(4) J'(α;β) $\subseteq$ J'(α);J'(β). (But not necessarily vice versa.)

Proof: (1) Pseudo-metrisability follows from the fact that L×L is countable. For convenience, we shall take $d'((s,t),(s't')) = d(s,s') + d(t,t')$. Compactness follows from that the fact the Lindenbaum topology $\mathcal{T}_l$ is compact and $\mathcal{T}_p$ is just the square of $\mathcal{T}_l$.

(2) We assume that L = $\{B_1,...,B_n,..\}$ and that this enumeration is used for defining the pseudo-metric.

Suppose (s,t) belongs to the right hand side. If s$\models$A then (s,t) must be in J'(α). Hence for every n, there is (s_n,t_n) in α such that $d'((s,t),(s_n,t_n)) <$ 1/n. Hence for large n (i.e. for n > m where A is B_m) $s_n\models$A and so $(s_n,t_n) \in$ if A then α else β. Since (s,t) is is a limit point of the (s_n,t_n), (s,t) $\in$ J'(if A then α else β). The case where s$\models\neg$A is similar.

Suppose now that (s,t) is in the left hand side. Suppose that s$\models$A and A = B_n.For $\epsilon > 0$, let m > n be such that $1/m < \epsilon$. There must be (s',t') in α such thatd'((s,t),(s',t')) < 1/m. Hence d(s,s') < 1/m and since m > n, s'$\models$A. So (s',t') $\in$ if Athen α else β, and d'((s,t),(s',t')) < ϵ. So it must be that (s,t) $\in$ J'(if A thena else β).

(3) This follows immediately from theorem 1 of the previous section and the fact that L is expressive for loop-free programs.

(4) Suppose (s,t) $\in$ J'(α;β). Then exists a sequence $\{(s_n,t_n)| n > 0\}$ such that $(s_n,t_n) \in \alpha;\beta$ and (s_n,t_n) --> (s,t). Hence there exist u_n such that

$(s_n,u_n) \in \alpha$ and $(u_n,t_n) \in \beta$. By compactness we can find a subsequence of the u_n which converges to some u. Then $(s,u) \in J'(\alpha)$ and $(u,t) \in J'(\beta)$ and so $(s,t) \in J'(\alpha);J'(\beta)$.

(2) above indicates that we can be optimistic about finding proof rules for "if then else". However, the situation is different for ; .

Lemma 6: Let # be a binary operation on programs. If there is a complete and sound proof system for deriving the PCAs of $\alpha\#\beta$ from those of α and β, then for all α and β, $J'(\alpha\#\beta) = J'(J'(\alpha)\#J'(\beta))$.

Proof: Observe first that $Pca(\alpha) = Pca(\alpha')$ iff $J'(\alpha) = J'(\alpha')$. For if $Pca(\alpha) = Pca(\alpha')$ then $J'(\alpha) = Rel(Pca(\alpha)) = Rel(Pca(\alpha')) = J'(\alpha')$. On the other hand, if $J'(\alpha) = J'(\alpha')$, then $Pca(\alpha) = Pca(Rel(Pca(\alpha))) = Pca(J'(\alpha) = Pca(J'(\alpha') = Pca(Rel(Pca(\alpha'))) = Pca(\alpha')$.

Let us define the meaning function $\theta(\alpha)$ for a program α to be $Pca(\alpha)$. Recall that $\alpha \approx \alpha'$ stands for $\theta(\alpha) = \theta(\alpha')$. I.e. for $Pca(\alpha) = Pca(\alpha')$. Then if θ supports #, then we must have $\alpha \approx \alpha'$ and $\beta \approx \beta'$ implying, $\alpha\#\beta \approx \alpha'\#\beta'$. Now let $\alpha' = J'(\alpha)$ and $\beta' = J'(\beta)$. Then by the previous paragraph, the antecedent holds.
Hence we have $Pca(\alpha\#\beta) = Pca(J'(\alpha)\#J'(\beta))$. Thus $J'(\alpha\#\beta) = J'(J'(\alpha)\#J'(\beta))$. ∎

Lemma 7: If α and β are closed, then so is $\alpha;\beta$.

Proof: Suppose that α and β are closed. We have to show that $J'(\alpha;\beta) = \alpha;\beta$. Clearly $\alpha;\beta \subseteq J'(\alpha;\beta)$. So suppose that $(s,t) \in J'(\alpha;\beta)$. Then there exist $(s_n,t_n) \to (s,t)$ and $(s_n,t_n) \in \alpha;\beta$. Hence there exist u_n such that $(s_n,u_n) \in \alpha$ and $(u_n,t_n) \in \beta$. By compactness we can pick a convergent subsequence converging to some u. Then since α and β are closed, $(s,u) \in \alpha$ and $(u,t) \in \beta$. So $(s,t) \in \alpha;\beta$. ∎

Corollary: $J'(J'(\alpha);J'(\beta)) = J'(\alpha);J'(\beta)$.

We now give an example of two programs α and β such that $J'(\alpha;\beta)$ is properly included in $J'(\alpha);J'(\beta)$. It will follow by lemma 6 and and the corollary to lemma 7 that we cannot, in general, find the PCAs of $\alpha;\beta$ from those of α and β.

Example: The first order language L has function symbols f,g, predicate symbols P,Q, and constants c,d. Let A be the formula which is the conjunction of:

$(\forall x)(f(g(x)) = g(f(x)) = x)$
$(\forall x)((Px \rightarrow Pf(x)) \wedge (Qx \rightarrow Qf(x)))$
$(\forall x)(Px \rightarrow Qx)$
$(\forall x)(Px \wedge \neg Pg(x) \leftrightarrow x=c)$
$(\forall x)(Qx \wedge \neg Qg(x) \leftrightarrow x=d)$

We consider "standard" and "non-standard" models of A. A standard model M_n of A looks like $\mathbb{Z}$ (the integers, including the negative integers), with $c < d$. P holds for all integers ≥ c and Q for all integers ≥ d. d-c is n. f is successor and g is predecessor. The *nonstandard* model M_ω looks like *two* copies of the integers with c in copy 1 and d in copy 2. f and g are as before. P holds throughout copy 2, and in copy 1 for all x ≥ c. Q *fails* throughout copy 1, and in copy 2 for all x < d. For either kind of model, there *may also* be other copies of the integers, some satisfying both P and Q, some neither, and some only P, but these extra copies do not contain c or d. Pictures of both kinds of models are shown at the end of the paper. All models of A look either like M_n or like M_ω.

Lemma 8: For all A with one free variable, either $(M_n,c) \models A$ for all sufficiently large n (including ω) or $(M_n,c) \models \neg A$ for all sufficiently large n. (Similarly for d instead of c).

Proof: The proof uses Ehrenfeucht games and will be omitted here.

Now consider the programs α and β

α: $(x \leftarrow c);(\text{while } x \neq d, \text{ do } x \leftarrow f(f(x)))$

β: $(x \leftarrow f(d));(\text{while } x \neq c, \text{ do } x \leftarrow g(g(x)))$

It is easily seen that for $s = (M_n,c)$ and $t = (M_n,d)$ and for all $n \leq \omega$, $(s,t) \in \alpha$ iff n is finite and even and $(t,s) \in \beta$ iff n is finite and odd. Thus $X \cap (\alpha;\beta)$ is empty where X is the clopen subset of W×W consisting of all (s,t) such that $s \models A$ and $t \models A$. It follows (since X is open) that $X \cap J'(\alpha;\beta)$ is also empty.

However, $X \cap (J'(\alpha);J'(\beta))$ is not empty, for it is easily seen, using the previous lemma that if s is (M_ω,c) and t is (M_ω,d), then $(s,t) \in J'(\alpha)$ and $(t,s) \in J'(\beta)$ and so $(s,s) \in J'(\alpha);J'(\beta)$.

Hence $J'(\alpha;\beta) \neq J'(\alpha);J'(\beta)$.

Conclusion: We conclude that there are no rules which are sound for all binary relations (e.g. the Hoare rules) which will be adequate to prove the PCAs of while programs from the PCAs of their components.

References

[B] G. Birkhoff, *Lattice Theory*, Amer. Math. Soc. Colloq. Publications vol. 25 (1940).

[BTT] J. Bergstra, J. Tiuryn and J. Tucker, Correctness Theories and Program Equivalence, *Stichting Mathematisch Centrum*, Amsterdam (1979)

[C] P. M. Cohn, *Universal Algebra*, Harper and Row (1965).

[GM] I. Greif and A. Meyer, Specifying the Semantics of While Programs, *6th Annual Symposium on Principles of Programming Languages*, ACM (1979), pp. 180-189. To appear in TOPLAS.

[HL] A. Hoare and P. Lauer, Consistent and Complementary Formal Theories of the Semantics of Programming Languages, *Acta Informatica 3* (1974) pp. 135-155.

[LPP] D. Luckham, D. Park and M. Paterson, On Formalised Computer Programs, *JCSS 3* (1970) pp. 220-249.

[MH] A. Meyer and J. Halpern, Axiomatic Definitions of Programming Languages: A Theoretical Assessment, *7th Annual Symposium on Principles of Programming Languages*, ACM (1980), 202-212.

[MP] A. Meyer and R. Parikh, Definability in Dynamic Logic, *Proc 12th Annual ACM Symposium on Theory of Computation* (1980) pp. 1-7. To appear in *JCSS.*

[O] O. Ore, Galois Connexions, *Trans. Amer. Math Soc.* 55 (1944) pp. 493-513.

[Pa] R. Parikh, Propositional Logics of Programs - Systems, Models and Complexity, *7th Annual Symposium on Principles of Programming Languages*, ACM (1980), pp. 186-192.

Figures:

(i) A picture of M_6 (There may be other copies of $\mathbb{Z}$. See text.)

```
. • . . . . . . • . . . . . . . . . .
  c           d
  P→..        Q→...
```

(ii) A picture of M_ω. (There may be more copies of $\mathbb{Z}$. See text.)

copy 1

```
. • . . . . . . . . . . . . . . . . . .
  c
  P→...
```

copy 2

```
. . . . . . . • . . . . . . . . . .
              d
              Q→..
          ←..P..→
```

Using Graphs to Understand PDL

V. R. Pratt
Stanford University

Abstract

This paper begins with the problem of sharpening our understanding of PDL. The position we take here is that PDL, which is ordinarily defined using regular operations on programs, is better understood in terms of finite state automata. Accordingly we rederive some basic PDL results (finite model, deterministic exponential satisfiability) in terms of automata. As corollaries to this we obtain answers to the following open questions. (i) What is the time complexity of satisfiability for propositional flowgraph logic? (ii) Can regular expressions be axiomatized equationally as succinctly as they can be represented with automata? We also show how converse and test relate to flowgraph operations.

The evidence to date strongly suggested that problem (i) should require double exponential time. We give a deterministic one-exponential bound, tight to within a polynomial. Two novel aspects of our algorithm are that it solves the problem by translation to modal logic with minimization, and that the concept of state is abstracted out of the algorithm. The tractability of satisfiability can be traced to two key properties of the definition of flowgraph operations. For (ii) we give for each flowgraph of size n a complete axiomatization of size a polynomial in n, by showing how to axiomatize matrix transitive closure equationally.

Our treatment of converse and test shows that they enjoy the same two key properties as flowgraph operations, permitting a uniform treatment of the bulk of the major flow-of-control constructs.

Introduction

(i) Satisfiability. The first thorough treatment of logics of programs dealt with flowcharts [Flo]. Most subsequent papers have emphasized structured or algebraic programs, justified in part by the existence of translations of flowcharts to structured programs. For most purposes this justification suffices. Recently however, the complexity of some aspects of logics of programs has dropped to the point where the overhead of such translations can no longer be ignored. In particular the deterministic complexity of satisfiability of propositional dynamic logic (PDL) [FL] is one exponential [Pr1], a tight bound [FL]. PDL treats structured programs, whose operations are captured abstractly by the three Kleene operations $\cup$, ;, *. It is natural to ask whether a similar bound is possible for logics of flowcharts.

The two basic techniques for translating flowcharts into structured programs each contribute an exponential overhead to this bound, leading to a two-exponential cost for testing satisfiability. The first technique is to use Kleene's translation from finite state automata to regular expressions [Kle]. This translation unavoidably increases the size of the input by an exponential [EZ]. The second technique is to introduce Boolean variables which can be used to code the identity of flowgraph vertices. This technique has the dual advantage of keeping program size to within a constant factor of input size and permitting translation of deterministic flowgraphs into the deterministic algebraic constructs (**if-then-else, while-do**), not possible with Kleene-like translations alone [AM]. For the purposes of testing satisfiability however, this translation does violence to the language, so that unlike the Kleene translation the complexity of satisfiability must now be addressed anew. K. Abrahamson [Abr] has demonstrated a two-exponential lower bound on the complexity of propositional logics of programs with Boolean variables.

Thus the available methods for reducing the flowgraph logic satisfiability problem to known problems unavoidably lead to double-exponential complexity. One might therefore guess that reasoning about flowgraphs was inherently harder than reasoning about structured programs, for a given size of program.

We shall show that this problem is of complexity one exponential. To do this we shall show how to adapt existing techniques for PDL to flowgraphs. In doing so we shall shed some light on the methods used for PDL. The role of Fischer-Ladner closure [FL] in PDL is somewhat mysterious; it is clear that it works, but it is not clear why that particular notion of closure should be the right one. The rationale for the corresponding concept in flowgraph logic will be seen to be both clear and natural.

(ii) Axiomatization. The equational theory of PDL has recently been shown to be finitely axiomatizable [Seg,Par]. (This is surprising considering the much earlier result that the equational theory of regular algebra, in essence a fragment of PDL, is not finitely axiomatizable [Red].) It follows from Kleene's translation [Kle] that the construct defined by an arbitrary flowgraph is also finitely axiomatizable; the axioms are those of PDL together with an equation $\langle f(\mathbf{a})\rangle p = \langle \varphi(\mathbf{a})\rangle p$ where $\varphi(\mathbf{a})$ is the regular expression for $f(\mathbf{a})$.

Unfortunately $\varphi(\mathbf{a})$ may be of size an exponential in the size of $f(\mathbf{a})$ [EZ]. The question arises as to whether a more succinct but equally precise axiomatization is possible. We give a complete axiomatization of f of length a polynomial in the size of the flowgraph defining f.

(iii) Converse and Test. The converse of a program can be thought of as that program run backwards. Converse provides a convenient way of introducing forwards reasoning into a logic of programs that treats only backwards reasoning (in the sense that a program is treated as transforming a postcondition into a precondition, cf. [Dij]). Parikh [Par] showed that the two axioms $p \rightarrow [a]\langle a^{-}\rangle p$ and $p \rightarrow [a^{-}]\langle a\rangle p$ completely axiomatize converse. In [Pr2] the question was raised as to the mathematical content of these two axioms; in particular was there an algebraic treatment of converse analogous to that given in the same paper for *? There also remains the question of the complexity of satisfiability of PDL with converse, which has not previously been addressed.

We give an analysis of converse, based on Parikh's axioms, that leads directly to answers to these questions. Tests can also be handled with a scaled-down version of the same analysis.

Definitions

Multimodal Logic. Our domain of discourse has two sorts, a Boolean algebra **B** of propositions p,q,r,... and a set R of actions a,b,c,..., together with an operation $\Diamond(a,p)$ (or $\langle a \rangle p$ or just ap) satisfying $a0 = 0$ and $a(p \vee q) = ap \vee aq$. We call such algebras (**B** R $\Diamond$) *multimodal*; they supply the models for multimodal logic. The intuitive meaning of ap is "a can bring about p;" its dual ~a~p, or [a]p, means "a will only bring about p."

Separability. With R we associate the equivalence relation of *inseparability*: $a \approx b$ when $\forall p[ap = bp]$. A *separable* multimodal algebra (SMA) is one in which inseparability is identity. The actions of an SMA may be treated as functions, with $\Diamond$ acting as application.

Flowgraph Logic. Propositional *dynamic* logic (PDL) is the language of multimodal algebras together with the three Kleene operations on R: $a \cup b$, a;b (or just ab), and a^*. PDL with converse admits an additional unary operation, $a^{\smile}$. Propositional *flowgraph* logic (PFL) extends PDL by including all flowgraph operations, defined below. PFL can be thought of as PDL with finite-state automata taking the place of regular expressions. PFL is no more expressive than PDL since every flowgraph operation is a Kleene polynomial (i.e. representable as a composition of Kleene operations). Our primary interest in PFL is its apparent greater succinctness; of secondary interest is the insight that PFL gives into PDL.

Flowgraphs. A k-ary *flow schema* (V,E) is a finite set V of vertices and a set $E \subseteq V \times [1,k] \times V$ of labelled edges (x,i,y). A k-ary *flowgraph* or finite-state automaton $(V,E,\vdash,F)$ is a k-ary flow schema (V,E) together with a start vertex $\vdash \in V$ and a set of final vertices $F \subseteq V$.

Here is an example of a three vertex quaternary flow schema.

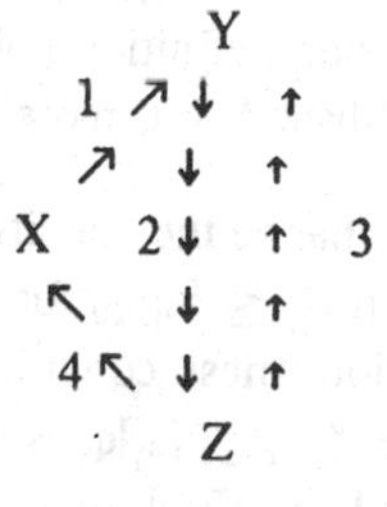

If we take X to be the start vertex and Y and Z to be final vertices, we then have a flowgraph.

Tags. A *tagging* of a flowgraph is an element **q** of the direct power $\mathbf{B}^V$ (itself a Boolean algebra), that is, an assignment of Boolean *tags* to the vertices of the flowgraph. The *start* tag is $\mathbf{q}_{\vdash}$.

Flowgraph Operations. With each k-ary flowgraph we associate some k-ary operation $f: R^k \to R$ such that f(a)p is the start tag of the least tagging **q** for which $\mathbf{q}_x \geq \mathbf{a}_i \mathbf{q}_y$ for each edge (x,i,y) and $\mathbf{q}_x \geq \mathbf{p}$ for each final vertex x. A *flowgraph algebra* (**B** R $\Diamond$) is a multimodal algebra (**B** R $\Diamond$) together with all flowgraph operations.

The question arises as to whether least taggings always exist. This is a good point at which to introduce the two most important properties of this definition.

Lemma 1. The set of solutions in B^V to the inequations defining a flowgraph operation, keeping the actions fixed, forms a sublattice of B^V (i.e. is closed under $\wedge$ and $\vee$).

Proof. Suppose $q_x \geq a_i q_y$ and $q_x' \geq a_i q_y'$. Then $q_x \wedge q_x' \geq a_i q_y \wedge a_i q_y' \geq a_i(q_y \wedge q_y')$ and $q_x \vee q_x' \geq a_i q_y \vee a_i q_y' = a_i(q_y \vee q_y')$. Similarly if $q_x \geq p$ and $q_x' \geq p$ then $q_x \wedge q_x' \geq p$ and $q_x \vee q_x' \geq p$. ∎

Corollary. For finite **B** and fixed **a** the least tagging **q** always exists.

Lemma 2. If R is a semilattice (i.e. is closed) under PDL $\cup$, the set of solutions in R^k to the inequations defining a flowgraph operation, keeping the tags fixed, forms a subsemilattice of R^k (i.e. is closed under $\cup$).

Proof. If $q_x \geq a_i q_y$ and $q_x \geq b_i q_y$ then $q_x \geq a_i q_y \vee b_i q_y = (a_i \cup b_i) q_y$. ∎

Corollary. For finite **B** and fixed **q** a maximal action solution always exists.

Our satisfiability algorithm has two main stages, called pull-up and pull-down. Each corollary shows that one of these stages is possible.

A separable multimodal algebra (SMA) can be expanded to a flowgraph algebra in at most one way, by separability and the uniqueness of least elements of Boolean sets. A finite SMA can always be expanded to a flowgraph algebra, by the corollary to Lemma 1.

It is helpful to compare the definition of * obtained in this way with the definition given by Segerberg's axioms [Seg]. The corresponding flowchart has a single vertex $\vdash$ and a single edge $(\vdash,1,\vdash)$, with $\vdash$ being both the start and the only final vertex. The definition says that a^*p is the least q for which $q \geq aq$ and $p \geq q$. It is shown in [Pr3] that this is precisely the content of the Segerberg axioms. Hence for * at least our definition coincides with Segerberg's axioms. The corresponding agreement may be established yet more easily for $\cup$ and ;.

We may relate our tags to Floyd's tags thus. Change the condition so that $[f(a)]p$ (= $\sim f(a) \sim p$) is the start tag of the *greatest* tagging **q** for which $q_x \leq [a_i]q_y$ for each edge (x,i,y) and $q_x \leq p$ for each final vertex x. Reading $\leq$ as implication, these conditions can be readily recognized as those appropriate for partial correctness. Indeed $q_x \leq [a_i]q_y$ is $q_x\{a_i\}q_y$ in the notation of [Hoa]. These are the partial correctness tags used in [Flo], and are clearly no more than the complements of our tags. Our tags are the natural ones to use from a model-theoretic viewpoint; furthermore if we were to use partial correctness tags the section on axiomatizing flowgraphs would be much more awkward.

The connection between flowgraphs and flowgraph operations is essentially identical to the connection between finite state automata and Type 3 grammars. The nonterminals of grammars correspond to our tags, the terminals to actions. Replacing $\geq$ by $\rightarrow$ and p by λ in our defining inequations yields Type 3 grammar rules. The language defined by a such a grammar is obtained by assigning the least languages to the nonterminals consistent with the conditions obtained by interpreting each rule's $\rightarrow$ as $\supseteq$, and taking the assignment to $Q_\vdash$ (the axiom or sentence nonterminal) to be the language defined. This corresponds exactly to our definition of a flowgraph operation.

Syntax and Semantics. A formula of propositional flowgraph logic (PFL) is a term built up from propositional variables P,Q,... and action variables A,C,... using Boolean, modal, and flowgraph operations. A *model* or *valuation* is a homomorphism from terms (thought of as forming a word algebra) into a flowgraph algebra. A model *of a formula* is one mapping that formula to other than 0. A formula is *satisfiable* when it has a model.

Testing Satisfiability

We present our decision method for satisfiability as an extension of the propositional truth table method to multimodal logic followed by a further extension to flowgraph logic. We also abstract out the state-oriented aspects of the algorithm by first giving concrete data structures and operations for the abstractions **B**, R, and ◇, and then stating the algorithm in terms of the abstractions alone.

Data Structures. As all our constructions are finite we may represent **B** as 2^W, the power set of the set W of its atoms, in the usual way. For the free Boolean algebra G(X) generated by X, W may be taken to be 2^X. Each action a may be represented as that element a of $\mathbf{B}^W$ for which a_w = aw, whence ◇ is interpreted as dot product, actions and propositions both being W-dimensional. At the computer level sets will be bit vectors. Homomorphisms are computed inductively with the usual recursive approach; it is only necessary to compute the homomorphism at subformulas of the input and at any Boolean generators introduced by construction.

Algorithm 1. For propositional logic the algorithm is very simple. Let X be the set of propositional variables in r. Let **B** = G(X), and let h be the Boolean homomorphism from Boolean terms on X into **B** that fixes X. Then r is satisfiable just when $h(r) \neq 0$.

Algorithm 2. For multimodal logic we shall add a pullup and a pulldown stage to Algorithm 1.. Let X be the propositional variables in r together with one generator Q_{Ap} for each subformula Ap of r. Again let **B** = G(X), and let h be the Boolean homomorphism from Boolean terms on X into **B** that fixes X. Extend h to all subformulas of r by letting $h(Ap) = h(Q_{Ap})$.

Pullup: Interpreting ◇ as application, let h(A) be the maximum strict finitely additive function on **B** for which $h(A)h(p) \leq h(Q_{Ap})$ for all Q_{Ap} in X, which exists by the corollary to Lemma 2.

Pulldown: While there exists Q_{Ap} for which $h(A)h(p) < h(Q_{Ap})$ (strict <) subtract $h(Q_{Ap})-h(A)h(p)$ from the elements of **B** (and hence pointwise from the actions).

On termination $h(A)h(p) = h(Q_{Ap}) = h(Ap)$, making h a flowgraph homomorphism, so again r is satisfiable just when $h(r) \neq 0$. This completes algorithm 2.

There is a straightforward way to compute the greatest action a satisfying all inequations $p_i \geq aq_i$, where i indexes the inequations. For each atom u in W take au to be the conjunction of all p_i's for which $u \leq q_i$. There is also an economical way to subtract a constant from all propositions simultaneously. Maintain a "mask," a proposition which is subtracted from each element as it is encountered in the course of the algorithm. To subtract a constant merely replace the mask by its disjunction with the constant. Initially the mask is 0. Thus subtraction itself costs one Boolean operation, at the price of doubling the cost of the whole algorithm.

Algorithm 3. For flowgraph logic the algorithm in its entirety is to translate the flowgraph formula r to the multimodal formula r' and a set of multimodal inequations, then test r' with a modified version of Algorithm 2.

Translation: For each occurrence of $\langle f(a)\rangle p$ in r: (i) for each vertex x of the flowgraph defining f, let Q_x be a new propositional variable, denoting a tag; (ii) replace the occurrence of $\langle f(a)\rangle p$ by $Q_{\vdash}$; (iii) introduce $Q_x \geq a_i Q_y$ for each edge (x,i,y) and $Q_x \geq p$ for each final vertex x; (iv) if any a_i is not a variable, recursively translate $a_i Q_y$ in this way.

Modifications to Algorithm 2: (i) Before the pullup, for each inequation $p \geq q$ produced by translation, subtract q-p from **B**. (ii) In the pulldown, initially and after each subtraction reset each tag $h(Q_x)$ to the least value consistent with the inequations. This may be done iteratively by setting all tags to 0 and then while there exists any failing inequation of the form $Q_x \geq p$ (including the case $p = AQ_y$) adding h(p) to $h(Q_x)$.

Analysis. Let n denote the length of the input r and let $N = 2^n$. It is readily seen that $|X| \leq n$ for all three algorithms, whence $|W| \leq N$, and the longest chain in **B** is also at most N. Thus the cost of a Boolean operation is O(N) while the cost of an action operation is $O(N^2)$.

The first algorithm is of complexity O(nN), since we perform at most n Boolean operations to evaluate r.

The second algorithm spends time O(nN) to evaluate the subformulas. Pullup costs $O(nN^2)$ since there are n inequations each of which is considered once for each of the N atoms at which the values of the actions are determined. Pulldown also costs $O(nN^2)$ since it can reduce the left side of each of n inequations at most N times, this being the length of the longest chain. Thus the algorithm costs $O(nN^2)$ altogether.

The third algorithm pays more for pulldown. Subtraction at $O(nN^2)$ is dominated by tag minimization at $O(nN^3)$. (Tag minimization for the special case of the flowgraph for * gives one familiar way to compute reflexive transitive closure of binary relations. Tag minimization can be reduced to integer matrix multiplication in the same way reflexive transitive closure can, so $O(N^{2.5+})$ is possible.) Pulldown has at most N subtractions (the length of the longest chain) and therefore costs $O(N^4)$, or $O(N^{3.5+})$ using fast matrix multiplication.

Thus our algorithm is of deterministic complexity one exponential in the length of the input, which is within a polynomial of the lower bound on the special case of flowgraph logic consisting of PDL [FL]. (Note that in [FL] length of input was measured in bits, accounting for what might otherwise appear as a log n discrepancy in the exponent.)

Comparison with Dynamic Logic. In the usual algorithms for PDL [FL,Pr1], the set corresponding to the X of our method is the Fischer-Ladner closure of the input, defined to be all subformulas of the input together with a(a*p) if a*p is in the set, a(bp) if (ab)p is in, etc. If each Kleene operation is viewed in terms of its definition by the appropriate flowgraph, the role of these formulas a(a*p), a(bp), etc. can be seen to be the same as that of the introduced variables Q_{Ap} and Q_x. The flowgraph point of view in our opinion gives a simpler perspective on the essential concepts underlying the algorithm, and incidentally demonstrates that at least for testing satisfiability nothing especially distinguishes the Kleene operations from the other flowgraph operations.

Axiomatization

The problem is to supply a succinct complete axiomatization of each flowgraph operation, thereby generalizing to PFL the Segerberg axioms for PDL [Seg], without incurring the necessarily exponential overhead [EZ] of direct translation of flowgraphs to regular expressions. The trick we use here is to equationally axiomatize matrix transitive closure, a problem of interest in its own right.

We start with the Segerberg axiomatization of transitive closure for propositional dyamic logic (PDL), namely $p \vee aa^*p \leq a^*p \leq p \vee a^*(ap\text{-}p)$. One source of dynamic algebras introduced in [Pr1] is the concept of matrices of actions acting on vectors of propositions. The trick is to interpret the above axiomatization of * as being about such matrices.

What we shall axiomatize is not a single flowgraph operation but rather all the single-exit flowgraph operations defined by one flow schema. A V-vertex flow schema f(**a**) may be represented as a V×V matrix **A** of actions: $\mathbf{A}_{xy} = \cup\{\mathbf{a}_i|(x,i,y)\in E\}$. A flowgraph operation defined by this schema with start vertex x and final vertex y corresponds to $\mathbf{A}^*_{xy}$. Thus what we shall define is **A***, using the above axiomatization. The associated Boolean algebra is $\mathbf{B}'^V$ for arbitrary **B**', that is, V-dimensional vectors **P**,**Q**,... over **B**', while **R** consists of matrices of actions **A**,**C**,... drawn from an arbitrary **R**'. ◇ is matrix-vector product, the inner operation being ◇' and the outer operation V'. The axiom for **A*** is of course

$$\mathbf{P} \vee \mathbf{AA^*P} \leq \mathbf{A^*P} \leq \mathbf{P} \vee \mathbf{A^*(AP\text{-}P)}$$

This is not a solution to the original problem because it deals with matrices and vectors. However it is obvious that it can be reduced to a system of 2v inequations involving v Boolean variables in place of the one matrix variable **P** and v^2 action variables, one for each $\mathbf{A}^*_{xy}$, in place of the one matrix expression **A***, where v = |V|. The one problem is that the same variable may appear in more than one inequation. Since each inequation is assumed to be universally quantified over, we lose the connection between variables spread over more than one inequation. To restore the connection it suffices to combine the inequations into one inequation, easily done for Boolean inequations: $p \leq q$ and $p' \leq q'$ combine as $(p\text{-}q)\vee(p'\text{-}q') = 0$.

This may be illustrated with the following flowgraph with start vertex X and final vertices Y,Z, and edges a,b,c,d defining f(a,b,c,d), equivalent to the regular expression (a(bc)*d)*a((bc)*∪b(cb)*).

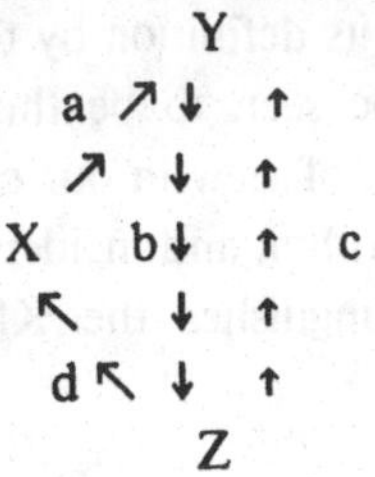

In place of P, A, and A* we shall write

$$P = \begin{bmatrix} p \\ q \\ r \end{bmatrix} \quad A = \begin{bmatrix} \varphi & a & \varphi \\ \varphi & \varphi & b \\ d & c & \varphi \end{bmatrix} \quad A^* = \begin{bmatrix} e & f & g \\ h & i & j \\ k & l & m \end{bmatrix}$$

Writing out the two matrix axioms as two triples of axioms, we get

$$\begin{array}{lcl} p \vee ahp \vee aiq \vee ajr & \leq & ep \vee fq \vee gr \\ q \vee bkp \vee blq \vee bmr & \leq & hp \vee iq \vee jr \\ r \vee dep \vee chp \vee dfq \vee ciq \vee dgr \vee cjr & \leq & kp \vee lq \vee mr \end{array}$$

and the equivalent of the induction axiom for this flowchart

$$\begin{array}{lcl} ep \vee fq \vee gr & \leq & p \vee e(aq\text{-}p) \vee f(br\text{-}q) \vee g(dp \vee cq\text{-}r) \\ hp \vee iq \vee jr & \leq & q \vee h(aq\text{-}p) \vee i(br\text{-}q) \vee j(dp \vee cq\text{-}r) \\ kp \vee lq \vee mr & \leq & r \vee k(aq\text{-}p) \vee l(br\text{-}q) \vee m(dp \vee cq\text{-}r) \end{array}$$

It is now straightforward to combine each triple of inequations into one equation. It should be clear from the example how it is possible for the same variable to appear in more than one inequation if this is not done. Note that the resulting two equations still contain common variables, but each was derived from a separate Segerberg axiom whence they need not themselves be combined into one equation.

When this exercise is performed for the one-vertex flowgraph defining * we obtain exactly the Segerberg axioms.

What keeps the size down to a polynomial in the size of the flowgraph is the fact that we only multiply matrices of expressions in these axioms. In the domain of regular expressions, multiplication of expression matrices is of complexity a polynomial in v whereas reflexive transitive closure of expression matrices is of complexity [EZ] exponential in the dimension v.

Converse and Test

The converses of binary relations and languages are familiar. But what is converse abstractly? A clue is given by Parikh's axiomatization of converse, $p \leq [a]a^- p$ and $p \leq [a^-]ap$. These two axioms look very symmetric; however there is the following remarkable asymmetry: the first converse axiom corresponds to the first Segerberg * axiom ($p \vee aa^*p \leq a^*p$) while the second converse axiom corresponds to the second * axiom ($a^*p \leq p \vee a^*(ap\text{-}p)$). This can be seen in the following theorem, which intimately parallels the corresponding theorem of [Pr3]. Define μS

to be the least element of S.

Theorem 3. The converse axioms express $a^{-}p = \mu\{q|p\leq[a]q\}$.

Proof. Assume the converse axioms. The first says that $a^{-}p \in \{q|p\leq[a]q\}$. Now suppose q is an arbitrary element of that set. Hence $p \leq [a]q$, so $a^{-}p \leq a^{-}[a]q \leq q$ (contrapositive of the second converse axiom), whence $a^{-}p$ must be the least element of $\{q|p\leq[a]q\}$.

Now assume that $a^{-}p = \mu\{q|p\leq[a]q\}$. Then the first converse axiom holds immediately. Since $p \in \{q|[a]p\leq[a]q\}$, we have $a^{-}[a]p \leq p$, whose contrapositive is the second converse axiom.∎

This suggests that we define a^{-} so that $a^{-}p$ is the least q such that $[a]q \geq p$, or $\sim p \geq a\sim q$. *Lemmas 1 and 2 continue to hold for such inequations.* This key fact permits us to apply to converse the techniques we used for flowgraph operations. Each occurrence of $a^{-}p$ is translated to $Q_{\vdash}$ and $\sim p \geq a\sim Q_{\vdash}$ is added to the system of inequations and translated recursively if a is not a variable. The rest is as for flowgraph logic, except that in pulldown, when an inequation of the form $p \geq A\sim Q$ fails during tag minimization where Q is a tag, add to h(Q) the quantity $h(A)^{-}h(p)$ where $h(A)^{-}$ is the transpose of h(A) viewed as a $W\times W$ bit matrix. The complexity of course remains one exponential.

Tests. Abstractly we may define the test p? to be the action satisfying $p?q = p\wedge q$. To put this on a par with flowgraph operations and converse, we may say that p?q is the least r such that $r \geq p\wedge q$. Again we observe that Lemmas 1 and 2 hold, the latter vacuously. Thus tests fit into the method even more easily than does converse. As a practical matter the test p?q should be translated out entirely in the translation stage as $p\wedge q$, introducing no new variables.

Acknowledgments

R. Floyd, E. Dijkstra, and M. Majster respectively persuaded me indirectly to consider flowcharts, suppress explicit reference to states, and replace induction with minimization in the definition. D. Kozen was indispensable as a source of perspective on algebraic program logic.

Bibliography

[Abr] Abrahamson, K., Decidability and Expressiveness of Logics of Processes, Ph.D. Thesis, TR #80-08-01, Dept. of Comp. Sci., U. of Wash., Seattle, 1980.

[AM] Ashcroft, E., and Z. Manna, Translating Program Schemas to While-Schemas, SIAM J. Comput., **4**, 2, 125-146, June, 1975.

[Dij] Dijkstra, E.W., **A Discipline of Programming**, Prentice-Hall. 1976

[EZ] Ehrenfeucht, A., and P. Zeiger, Complexity Measures for Regular Expressions, JCSS, **12.**, 2, 134-146, April, 1976.

[FL] Fischer, M. J., and R. Ladner, Propositional Dynamic Logic of Regular Programs, JCSS, **18**, 2, 194-211, April 1979.

[Flo] Floyd, R. W., Assigning Meanings to Programs, In **Mathematical Aspects of Computer Science** (ed. J.T. Schwartz), 19-32, 1967.

[Hoa] Hoare, C.A.R., An Axiomatic Basis for Computer Programming, CACM **12**, 576-580, 1969.

[Kle] Kleene, S.C., Representation of Events in Nerve Nets, in **Automata Studies**, (eds. Shannon, C.E. and J. McCarthy), 3-40, Princeton University Press, Princeton, NJ, 1956.

[Par] Parikh, R., A Completeness Result for a Propositional Dynamic Logic, Lecture Notes in Computer Science No. 64, 403-415, Springer-Verlag, 1978. Also M.I.T. Laboratory for Computer Science Technical Memorandum No. 106, July 1978.

[Pr1] Pratt, V.R., Models of Program Logics, Proc. 20th IEEE Conference on Foundations of Computer Science, San Juan, PR, Oct. 1979.

[Pr2] Pratt, V.R., Dynamic Algebras: Examples, Constructions, Applications, MIT/LCS/TM-138, M.I.T. Laboratory for Computer Science, May 1979.

[Pr3] Pratt, V.R., Dynamic Algebras and the Nature of Induction, Proc. 12th ACM Symp. on Theory of Computing, 22-28, Los Angeles, CA, May, 1980.

[Red] Redko, V.N., On Defining Relations for the Algebra of Regular Events, (Russian), Ukrain. Mat. Z., **16**, 120-126, 1964.

[Seg] Segerberg, K., A Completeness Theorem in the Modal Logic of Programs, Preliminary report. Notices of the AMS, **24**, 6, A-552. Oct. 1977.

CRITICAL REMARKS ON MAX MODEL OF CONCURRENCY

A.Salwicki
Institute of Informatics
University of Warsaw
PKiN p.o.box 1210
00-901 Warsaw POLAND

ABSTRACT

A few critical remarks on a mathematical model of concurrency are discussed. As the result we were able to improve the model, to state new problems to be studied later on and to remark that the ideas of our model can be applied to the tasking of ADA, CSP and CCS. It means that apart of standard semantics of ADA there is another one and it is not obvious which semantics is more natural.

§1. INTRODUCTION

A new mathematical model of concurrent computations has been invented by T.Müldner, A.Salwicki and L.Stapp in 1976 during the work on design of LOGLAN'77 programming language[14,16,18]. Making use of it we were able to define semantics of concurrent programs in LOGLAN'77 [cf LOGLAN report 3]. moreover T.Müldner defined and studied several synchronization tools ranging from primitive MER's mutual exluding regions to monitors [3,15]. The last case required the full power of LOGLAN with its prefixing on various levels.

The semantics of concurrency most frequently met in the literature is founded on a/ sharing of memory i.e. there are shared variables in various processes that constitute a program, b/ arbitrary interleaving of atomic instructions.

Our model makes use of the assumption a/ i.e. the components of a program that operate concurrently - we shall call them processes - do share memory. However we reject b/. In MAX model of concurrency if there exist a configuration with several nonconflict atomic instructions ready to execution,then any of possible next configurations is a result of a maximal committment of processors. In other words if there is a situation in which there are say three processes ready to execute atoms A_1, A_2, A_3 and any pair A_i, A_j is nonconflict but all three cannot be executed in parallel because of conflict then there are possible three solutions not more that follow from three maximal nonconflict choices A_1 A_2, A_1 A_3 and A_2 A_3. At the first glance we seem to restrict too much. However there is power in this restriction.

First of all consider simple program

K: <u>cobegin</u> b:= <u>false</u> ‖ a:=<u>true</u> ; b:=a <u>coend</u>

while the arbitrary interleaving of atoms brings about b as well as -b i.e.

$\models_{ARB}$ $\Diamond$ K b $\wedge$ $\Diamond$ K-b

i.e. it is possible that after K b holds as well as it is possible that after K -b holds

our principle of maximal committment necessarily brings about b

$\models_{MAX}$ $\Box$ K b

i.e. it is necessary that after K b holds.

The first comment we have heard was "well, this is an example which shows that ARB $\neq$ MAX , however one can think about a transformation T on programs such that for every program P

$$\text{Behaviours}_{MAX}(P) = \text{Behaviours}_{ARB}(P)$$

i.e. the transformation T simulates MAX within ARB.
This conjecture was disproved by H.D.Burkhard. In[4] he proved that in very natural enviromnent of Petri nets MAX semantics can not be simulated by any such transformation. Moreover there exist a program (a Petri net) P such that its MAX behaviour cannot be imitated by the ARB behaviour of any program (Petri net). It means that in general the principle of maximal nonconflict firing induces the semantics which is not subject to simulation by sequences of usual (one-element) firings of transitions. Arbitrary interleaving of atoms is equivalent with multiplexing which in turn if used to simulate real parallelism introduces behaviours (coputations) not occurring in practice.

In this sketch we shall examine further remarks on MAX model.

1. The model of maximal choices might be proper for models with shared memory. However, recent models CSP[7], CCS [11] and ADA[1] reject shared memory and introduce loosely coupled processes or tasks that communicate instead of sharing variables. At the first glance MAX seems artificial and unnecessary in these models. Below, we shall show that a MAX-like semantics can be devised also for these models.

2. Max semantics applied to the case of dining philosophers solves it [20]. This we conceive as unnatural. It is very unlikely that the randomly operating hardware will solve synchronization problem for philosophers. This remark is a challenge to further investigations that should answer the question in which circumstances MAX model of concurrency is a natural and faithful mathematical description of the phenomena happening in hardware.

3. Several authors cf Kwong [9], Lamport [10] are improving the ARB model by the demand of finite delay property [9] or fairness property . We shall argue that MAX has this property. On the other hand we conjecture that the class of fair ARB computations in undecidable one.

4. Patrick Cousot observed that our model has an unpleasant property: an atomic instruction once initiated can remain in the state "under execution" indefinitely long. This is inconsistent with our intuition unless we wish to include situations in which the hardware fails. Below, we indicate how to improve the model.

§2. MAX SEMANTICS OF CONCURRENT PROGRAMS

Here we recall the definition of MAX in a short, informal way [16]. In order to simplify our considerations we shall study a very simple extension of the language of dterministic while programs. Let $K_1 \dots K_n$ be while programs then the expression

$$\underline{\text{cobegin}}\ K_1 \parallel \dots \parallel K_n\ \underline{\text{coend}}$$

is a concurrent program.

By a snapshot of a computation we shall mean a pair consisting of a valuation v of variables and of n-tuple of instructions sequences

$$\left(v,\ m_1 I_1^{(1)} \dots I_{k_1}^{(1)} \quad \dots \quad m_n I_1^{(n)} \dots I_{k_n}^{(n)}\right)$$

where m_i is a mark either $*$ (ready to execute) or o (under execution) indicating the status of the instruction $I_1^{(i)}$ $i = 1, \dots, n$

We shall make use of the notion of relation of nonconflict which holds among certain assignment instructions and tests. We shall not give the definition of this relation here. The reader can conceive the relation of conflict as a family of sets of instructions such that a set is in conflict iff it contains at least two instructions sharing a common variable x and one of them changes the value of the variable x. Now we shall define the tree of possible computations of a program

$$K: \underline{\text{cobegin}}\ K_1 \| \ldots \| K_n\ \underline{\text{coend}}$$

at a valuation v in a given algebraic system data structure $\mathfrak{A}$

We shall define inductively a tree T and a labelling which with every vertex of the tree T associates a snapshot.

1. The root of the tree T is labelled by

   $(v, *K_1 \quad \ldots \quad *K_n)$ - initial snapshot

2. Let κ be a vertex of T with a snapshot associated to it.

   a/ if all n sequences of instructions are empty then the vertex is a leaf of the tree T i.e. it has no sons.

   b/ in the opposite case there exists at least one nonempty sequence.

   Let us denote the snapshot associated with κ by c

   $$c: \left(v', m_1 I_1; rem_1 \ \ldots \ m_n I_n; rem_n\right) \qquad m_i \in \{*, o\} \quad i=1,\ldots,n$$

There is at least one $*$ mark among $m_1, \ldots, m_n$. Now consider the set

$$S = \{I_1 \ \ldots \ I_n\}$$

of the first instructions, we can assume that all these instructions are either assignments or tests.

Let l will be the number of all maximal nonconflict sets S_i which are subsets of S and do include the set E consisting of all instructions marked .

$$E \subset S_i \subset S \qquad i = 1,\ldots,l$$

Next, for every set S_i $(i=1,\ldots,l)$ we shall consider all nonempty subsets of S_i and denote them S_{ij} $(j=1,\ldots,g_i)$

Since instructions of an S_{ij} set are nonconflict we can consider a snapshot c_{ij} resulting from the snapshot c by simultaneous execution of all instructions contained in the set S_{ij}. The valuation (state of memory) changes in accordance with assignments executed, all executed instructions are deleted from their sequences, their successors are marked $*$, all instructions from $S_i - S_{ij}$ are marked o, all other instructions from S keep their marks from the previous snapshot c. Every new snapshot determines a descendant of the vertex κ, let us denote it K_{ij} . We associate the snapshot c_{ij} with the vertex K_{ij}. By an possible computation of the program K a a valuation v in a given data structure $\mathfrak{A}$ we shall mean any path in the tree T.

§3. MAX SEMANTICS FOR ADA, CSP and CCS

C.A.R.Hoare [7] and R.Milner [11] proposed two models of of parallelism CSP and CCS. No shared variable s in these models. Instead, processes communicate via "ports". This sort of concurrency assumes certain rather strong synchronization mechanisms. The advantage of CSP and CCS follows from the fact that the analysis of concurrent programs seems much easier. Processes are looesly coupled and exchange information when needed instead of sharing common variables. Obviously, these models can be reduced to models with shared variables [6] Here, we are going to show that MAX-like semantics can be proposed also for CSP and CCS as well. In fact we shall propose a new semantics for tasking in ADA. The parallelism in ADA is close to CSP and CCS. The differences are less important and are motivated by certain requirements of "real" programmming lang age when CSP and CCS can afford simpler forms.

In ADA tasks do compute independently, in parallel, unless a communication is required. The notion of rendez-vous is introduced and explained. A rendez-vous is asymmetric, a caller names a calleee in a statemant of the form

<u>call</u> B.shakehands (actual param)　　　here B is a name of callee

The callee B shakes hands with the caller by execution of the statement

<u>accept</u> shakehands (statements)

The callee does not know with whom it will communicate. There is a synchronization mechanism assumed in ADA such that the earlier process has to wait for the later indepedently whether it is the caller or callee.

It is implicitly assumed that communications (rendez-vous) can be performed in the arbitrary order.

We are calling the attention of the reader that sometimes communications themselves can take place concurrently and this can completely change the picture of tasking in ADA.

Consider four tasks acting in parallel

<u>task</u> ZERO	<u>task</u> ONE
...	...
Z:<u>call</u> B.send(0)	O:<u>call</u> A.send(1)
...	...

<u>task</u> A	<u>task</u> B
...	...
U:<u>accept</u> send (a:=formal)	F:<u>accept</u> send (b:=formal)
A:<u>call</u>B.send (a)	S:<u>accept</u> send (b:=formal)

Obviously there are two sets of possible rendez-vous

1-st: Z and F, Aand S, O and U

2-nd: Z and S, A and F, O and U.

Suppose, that the initial status of processors is $\{Z,O,U,F\}$. According to the report of ADA one has to consider both sets of rendez-vous as possible behaviours. The resulting values of the variable b are different. We propose another semantics. Skipping all unnecessary details we claim that the maximal communication will take place, namely,

Z will shake hands with F and O with U.

Hence it is impossible to observe the second set of rendez-vous. In MAX semantics it is necessary that the final value of the variable b is one.

This simple observation has deeper consequences. It is not difficult to extend our modest example to a bigger program Pr such that the same program Pr will deadlock in the original semantics of ADA report and will not deadlock in new MAX-like semantics. Another program Π will deadlock in MAX semantics and will avoid deadlock in the original standard semantics. Similarly we can construct examples for all other interesting and important semantical phenomena. Finally it is not clear which semantics is better suited to model computations of ADA programs.

Analogously, one can construct examples showing that similarly CSP and CCS can be equipped with new semantics. This in turn creates new questions to be answered, e.g. how to adjust the calculus given by R.Milner for CCS to CCS with maximal communications?

§4. FAIRNESS

Consider the following program

P_1: cobegin b:=false ∥ while b do x:=x+1 coend.

According to L.Lamport the termination property of this program decides about fairness of semantics (or scheduler or similar thing) Analysing this program with the help of MAX definition we can prove the following property

$$(x = k) \Rightarrow \Box P_1 \left(x = k \vee x = k+1 \right)$$

i.e. the program P_1 always terminates either immediately or after one iteration of the instruction x := x+1. Therefore MAX satisfies the axiom of fairness.

Consider the ARB semantics. For every program K and every initial data there is a tree of possible computations. Now, let us reject all unfair computations. i.e. computations that delay a ready step indefinitely long. The question is whether there exist an algorithm to reject all unfair computations. Our conjecture is that the class of all fair computations is not r.e. set. It would mean that there is no hope for a machine which would filtrate out all unfair computations. D.Kozen [8] conjectures that all fair computations form a Π_2^c set.

We should mention that although the problem of fairness is solved by MAX semantics still there are similar and important phenomena e.g. livelocks.
Consider the following programs

x:=1 ; cobegin x :=0 ∥ while x ≠ 0 do x := x+1 coend

cobegin while x≠0 do x :=x+1 ∥ while y > x do y := y+x coend

Now, we can not guarantee that the programs will terminate, in every step of computations we have to solve conflict and it is possible that an infinite computation will result from the choices. From the earlier considerations one can deduce a method to avoid livelocks in programs like above. The livelock phenomenon is as natural as looping in sequential programs and needs to be treated in a separate way.

§5. FAIRNESS IN TERMINATION OF INITIALIZED ACTIONS IS NEEDED

The following remark was made by P.Cousot [5]. Consider the program

P_2: <u>cobegin</u> y:=2 ; b := <u>false</u> ‖ <u>while</u> b <u>do</u> x := x+1 <u>coend</u>

Now, we can not prove the property

$$\exists n_0 \ (x = k) \Rightarrow \Box P_2 \ (x < k + n_0)$$

since instruction y:=2 once initiated can remain in this state indefinitely long and simultaneously the right process will loop indefinitely.

There is a similarity with the previous examples however everyone will agree with the opinion that any processor operating correctly will finish execution of an assignment in a finite amount of time. Therefore the modifications of our original model are not only necessary but also natural. Depending on the goal (application) we can propose several improvements. The most general one which does not assume anything about speed of processors results in a lengthy .detailed definition. We shall describe it fully elsewhere.
For any snapshot a subsequent snapshot is defined in dependence on two nondeterministic choices. First. we choose nondeterministically a maximal nonconflict set S_i of atomic actions to be initiated. Second we choose a subset S_{ij} of S_i of the terminated actions. In order to improve our model we have to add some information to the snapshots indicating how long an action is under execution. weghts or times One can foresee any finite number of steps as the required time for terminating an action. This would lead to very thick trees ofcomputations.

There is another possibility. Usually. we do have some information about speed of processors. We can axiomatize it by formulas

$$(b \wedge x = k) \Rightarrow \Box \, \underline{\text{cobegin}} \ \ y{:=}\tau; \ \ b{:=}\underline{\text{false}} \,\| \ \underline{\text{while}} \ b \ \underline{\text{do}} \ x{:=}x+1 \ \underline{\text{coend}} \ (x < k + n_0)$$

This formula expresses the fact that the time needed to perform instruction $y{:=}\tau$ is not greater than n_0 additions. It is new that axioms can carry information about hardware and not about data structure or program connectives.

REFERENCES

1 ADA. report on the programming language. DoD Washington, July 1980

2 Arjomandi E..Fischer M., Lynch N.. A difference in Efficiency between Synchronous and Asynchronous Systems. 13-th ACM STOC Symp. Milwaukee,1981

3 Bartol W.M. et al. LOGLAN'79 report on the programming language T.Müldner ed. to appear in Lecture Notes on Computer Science

4 Burkhard H.D.. On priorities of parallelism: Petri nets under the Maximum Firing Strategy. to appear in proceedings of Symp on Algorithmic logic and LOGLAN. Poznań 1980

5 Cousot.P.. personal communication

6 Fischer M.,Lynch N., On describing the behaviour and implementation of distributed systems. Theoretical Computer Science 13 1981 17-43

7 Hoare C.A.R., Communicating systems programming CACM 21 1978 no 8

8 Kozen D., personal communication

9 Kwong Y.S.. On the absence of livelocks in parallel programs in Proc Symp. Semantics Conc. Computations Lecture Notes in Computer Sci. vol. 70 Springer . Berlin. 1979

10 Lamport L., "Sometimes" is sometimes "Not Never" , in Proc 7th ACM POPL Symp. . Las Vegas , 1980

11 Milner R.. A calculus of communicating Systems. Lecture Notes in Computer Science. Springer. Berlin. 1980

12 MirkowskaG.. Complete Axiomatization of Algorithmic Properties of Program Schemes with Bounded Nondezetministic Interpretations 12th ACM STOC Symp. , Los Angeles. 1980

13 Mirkowska g.. Model existence theorem in algorithmic logic with nondeterministic programs. Fundamenta Informaticae 3 1980 157-170

14 Müldner T., On semantics of parallel programs. ICS PAS Reports 323 Warasw . 1979 to appear in Fundamenta Informaticae

15 Müldner T., On properties of certain synchronizing tool for parallel computations. FCT'77 M.Karpiński ed. Lecture Notes on Comp. Science vol 56. Springer .Berlin. 1977. 459-465

16 Müldner T., Salwicki A., On algorithmic properties of concurrent programs to appear in Proc Sem on ALg Logic Zürich 79 E.Engeler ed. Lecture Notes on Computer Science Springer

17 ReifJ., Spirakis P.. Distributed Algorithms for Synchronizing Interprocess Communication Within Real Time. 13th ACM STOC Symp.

18 Salwicki A., Applied Algorithmic Logic in Proc MFCS'77 ed.J. Gruska Lecture Notes on Computer Science vol 53. Springer .Berlin. 1977 352-363

19 Salwicki A.. On algorithmic logic and its applications . to appear

20 Stapp L., On synchronization of philosophers, manuscript, Warsaw Technical University, 1981

II. TRANSCRIPT OF PANEL DISCUSSION

(The following is a transcript of the discussion which took place on Wednesday afternoon. Several participants presented five-minute positions, followed by open discussion. The transcript has been fairly heavily edited to bring out the main points. I apologize to those participants whose voice was not audible enough to transcribe.)

Michael O'Donnell[1]: I'm not going to talk about Dynamic Logic, because I view it mainly as an attempt to nail down fundamental concepts and not to illuminate techniques that we use for reasoning. Instead I'm going to look at attempts more explicitly aimed at giving rituals that a person can invoke. The most visible such attempt is Hoare logic. I think there has been significant success in that area: invariants are important in reasoning about loops. But I claim we haven't been careful enough with results about Hoare logic itself. A lot of people are familiar with the fact that the Hoare induction rule was shown unsound by Ashcroft, corrected by Musser in a way that was unsound, etc. Look at the goto rule: as far as I know, apart from a vague mention of trouble in a paper by Alagić and Arbib, it has been accepted as legitimate, and there is even a proof of correctness. In conjunction with other rules Hoare gives, the goto rule happens to prove true theorems only, but it is not a sound rule. My position is that if we are going to make up rules to help us reason about programs that are going to sit in the literature for eight or nine years, we ought to be more careful with them. We ought to focus on them in terms of a careful definition of soundness. On the whole, we have not done this with the Hoare rules.

Peter van Emde Boas: I think that the problem with the goto rule is really a problem with syntax. There are other constructs, such as exit statements, with perfectly transparent, complete proof systems to deal with things like jumps. Considering a program containing gotos to be just a concatenation of instructions is definitely the wrong syntax because it doesn't correspond to the semantics. This is an example, pure and simple, of why we should allow the semantic principle of compositionality to guide the definition of syntax, rather than force the semantics to conform to a syntax which has come down through history and which is completely wrong.

---

[1] This is an abbreviated version of O'Donnell's remarks. See "A Critique of the Foundations of Hoare-style Programming Logics", this volume, for a more comprehensive exposition.

Barry Rosen: If I could paraphrase, I think Mike's position is that we need to have systems that are rigorous and robust. Correct results should not depend on fifty finicky details and unstated conventions about how proofs are written. The ordinary Hoare-style goto rule does depend on very tricky tacit conventions about how proofs are written. This is not the way to go about setting up a general-purpose logic of programs.

O'Donnell: In fact, the goto rule is the easiest one to shoot down, but the function rules that are still around appear to have the same problems. I would make the stronger point that robustness is not even enough, but also every step in a proof should make intuitive sense.

Edmund Clarke: Maybe the goto statement itself deserves the credit for the pathology here, but I wouldn't want to get rid of functions.

O'Donnell: Except that it's very easy to do the goto correctly. They just didn't.

Willem de Roever: Barry Rosen just mentioned finicky details, but there isn't any Hoare system for recursive procedures which is without those finicky details. As far as I know, nobody is working on that at the moment. There are substitution rules, which you see for example in de Bakker's book, with all kinds of weird axioms. Other people propose alternative systems which are just as weird. We are in a world, as far as recursion and Hoare logic are concerned, in which there is no sound or healthy way, no unfinicky way, to reason about them.

Krzysztof Apt: There are many papers on what problems and details arise when one adds recursive procedures to other systems, and I think that Mike has made a very sound suggestion. He says that a proof rule should be sound, not only in the usual sense, but also in the sense that whenever you add some additional true statements to the theory, it remains sound. I believe that this formulation captures the problems not only with the goto rule but also with recursion. Of course, in the realm of richer programming languages, this formulation might have to be appropriately refined, but I think that this is a very just proposal.

*****

Brent Hailpern: I guess my position could be entitled "A plea for simplicity". I find myself in the verification camp rather than in the logician camp, and I've been feeling outnumbered recently. I've enjoyed the presentations very much, but I'd like to encourage you to try to look closer into real world problems. There are some projects that really need our help with verification, like network protocols, resource allocation hardware, and data base security, because people in the outside world are not doing a very good job with them. There is some work going on, but it's not getting the kind of support from this community that it should. I question whether more powerful proof systems are really what you want for treating these problems. They may be what you want for proving metalogical results like completeness, and I'm not saying that's bad, but when you want to explain something about network protocols to somebody, you don't want to have to explain all of Dynamic Logic. Instead, you want to provide a set of tools that they can use to verify what they put down on a chip. I've been trying to show in my own papers that using Temporal Logic doesn't always give you the simplest proof. It's worthwhile to look at a restricted class of problems, use the tools we've already proposed, prove the thing correct, and then present it to the people who work in that area, and see what they have to say about it. Does your explanation help them or does it make it worse? Do they understand their program better because you've verified it? In network protocols, first you have to explain what an insertion is, and then you have to explain that it's useful to characterize a set of states by some global property and then show that the state transitions really specify what your protocol does and these properties are really the things you want to prove. This is not always easy to do - sometimes your proof techniques don't make things any clearer, especially when your proof is five times as long as the original protocol.

O'Donnell: One problem you pointed out there is the lack of any coherent computer science education protocol. You should not have people in that position who don't know what an insertion is.

Hailpern: The people I've been dealing with all have electrical engineering backgrounds, and when they program protocols, they build them up with actual wires and get voltages to go up and down. Even if we had a better computer science education they probably would not have benefited.

de Roever: My experience has been slightly different. These people by now are willing to start learning things by themselves. They read the articles and say, "Yes, that's a nice model. Why don't we use CSP?" and then they explain their routing algorithms with it. Unfortunately, their correctness proofs are refused by international journals because they are 100 pages long. The journals ask, "Please give us a 25-page proof", but nobody knows how to do it, because of the formalism.

Robert Constable: To raise this to the level of a moral dilemma, consider Hoare's article on ADA. Suppose someone asks you to help verify the tasking processes of ADA. You're telling us when we should to along with them and help out. Hoare's saying, "Whatever you do, don't touch it, don't get near it, don't encourage the language, don't let people build anything critical with ADA. Which of you two should we listen to?

Hailpern: It's hard for one to say, "Listen to me rather than to Hoare", and I don't think I'm willing to say that. But I am willing to say that there are problems that are solved by tools that many people accept, and this verification community should look at some of those that haven't been verified, and maybe use that as part of the standard for comparing logics or determining what is hard to verify.

Clarke: I think that examining some of these issues may also lead to more interesting questions in logic as well. For example, the work on scheduling we heard yesterday, in which we talked about sequential file programs, alone leads to interesting questions.

Hailpern: In particular Ed Clarke and I had some arguments over the uses of history variables. I've taken the approach that maybe it's better to augment the logic with history variables rather than introduce groups; but these are things that I understand and its fairly easy to make other people understand; right now it's a stopgap, but it seems to be useful for the time being.

*****

Albert Meyer: Actually I keep generating more positions as I hear what's going on, but let me try and confine myself to the ones I prepared beforehand. The first position harks back to the topic of my own talk and the line of research that my colleagues and I have been following about Dynamic Logic and these various logics of programs. I think the punch line of the talk that I gave earlier today, that all these logics reduce to a small fragment of infinitary logic, says that there doesn't seem to be anything dynamic about Dynamic Logic anymore, and that somehow or other, doing logics of programs has slipped away from us now. We find ourselves doing what logicians did twenty years ago, when they first got interested in infinitary logic. As long as I'm being negative on this topic that we have devoted quite a few years to recently, let me add that it's not ever clear that one should be looking at these infinitary logics like Dynamic Logic or Algorithmic Logic. I think that the arguments of Andréka/Németi and Cartwright/McCarthy effectively contradict the earlier arguments of Hitchcock and Park, which say that you have to go beyond first-order logic in order to prove very natural basic things about programs. I think you can prove an awful lot, just using first order induction, and it's not clear when we're dealing with the simple class of recursive or iterative programs that one needs anything more than the first-order predicate calculus. I think we've made a lot of progress in this line of research and I think it's clear enough now that I'm inclined to conclude that it may have been a dead end. I would like to be contradicted in that by the audience, but that is now my judgement. We had to do it, but having done it, we now realize that there wasn't anything new there, at least as far as I'm concerned. I think that a direction which now looks exciting to me, where a different kind of thinking may be needed, may arise out of the issue of computability in higher types, and the ideas that Constable was talking about[1] and that Scott has been talking about for a long time now. Now let me change the subject slightly and hark back to what Hailpern and Constable said about raw power. They both concern the practical applications of formal logical systems, I think that most philosophically-minded logicians will be quick to tell you that they never expected the metamathematics of number theory to enable you to prove theorems of number theory more easily. That's an article of faith that we in program logics are operating under now, but I don't know many logicians that would subscribe to it. I'm sympathetic to it, and I think it's worth pursuing metamathematical study in the hope that we may learn something about theorem proving out of it, but logicians certainly don't see that as a justification for logic. Rather, they hope that by studying the modes of reasoning about logic by doing metamathematics, they will be able to learn certain things about structures. For example, some theorems in algebra are obtained by studying the expressible properties of structures in higher order languages. Let me mention what I see as the difficulties of doing what Bob Constable wants, of adding enough raw power to some logical system so that you can mirror the kinds of proofs that you'll find in a logic book. The rigorous but informal proofs that one will find in any paper (except maybe a paper by a logician) cannot be translated directly over into a formal language, preserving the size of the proof. For example, one of my favorite methods of proof begins, "Without loss of generality ...", and I wonder how one would translate that without a significant expansion in some formal system. Related to that is another more concrete principle: "By symmetry ...". Another one is "similarly", which you've all seen. One of the more concrete ones is "By Church's thesis ...", which we use all the time in recursion theory, and I claim in fact that we use it rigorously. There's nothing shaky about those proofs, but the difference between rigor and formality is very huge here, and one of the open problems is to bridge that gulf, I think perhaps by inventing a higher level language that rigorously captures what we do in English, and I don't know how to do that quite yet. Yes, I'll even accept "Clearly ..." as one of my proof principles. Another one is "By a routine application of induction on the definition of ...", etc. My favorite is "As the reader may verify ...". The point is that I think we're very far from being able to take rigorous proofs and formalize them, and it seems to me that those are the serious obstacles.

---

[1] Constable and Zlatin, "The Type Theory of PL/CV3", this volume.

Istvan Németi: I know how a logician does "similarly", by the so-called "theory morphisms". That's something that Burstall and Goguen use for their theory of stepwise refinement. Mathematical logic is a generalization of that. You just look at the category of all theories and all interpretations between theories (nowadays this is the most important subject of mathematical logic, much more important than looking at just one theory). Half of this is just the theory morphisms or pullbacks or pushouts between theory morphisms. This can be represented by cylindric algebras. Suppose you want to express analogy or similarity between two theories, T_1 and T_2, but each contains concepts which cannot be translated into the other, because the connections are vague, not one-one. In cylindric algebra theory, the connection is established by taking a third theory T_3 and interpreting it this way.

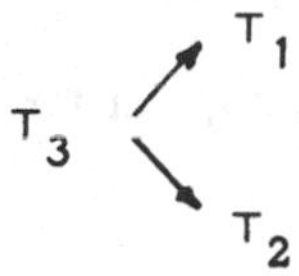

Hailpern: Your goal should not necessarily be to have proof techniques that an automatic theorem prover can use. It's a wonderful goal and I'd love to see it, but it would also be nice if people who did not develop the theory can understand the proofs without too much explanation.

O'Donnell: Forgetting about the jokes, like "clearly ..."

Meyer: It's not a joke. In fact, as any graduate student will tell you, it's absolutely infuriating.

O'Donnell: Yes, it is, and of course the formal equivalent is a fairly powerful decision procedure for a large fragment of whatever logic you're working in. But I would like you to think about all the statements you made, but replace "proof" in all cases by "program". That is, let's go back a few decades before we had computers. People still had to describe algorithms, they had to teach one another how to do long division and so on. They also studied Turing machines. Now it was certainly obvious that the Turing machine was not a very convenient way of doing long division. There was a large gap between discussion of the algorithm for the purpose of carrying it out, and discussion of the algorithm for the purpose of understanding it. Now I wouldn't say that we're totally pleased with the result, but after only a few decades of work, we have PASCAL, ALGOL, etc., which are acceptably useful for the intuitive, understandable description of algorithms and are completely formal.

Meyer: I don't agree with that. I think that they're acceptable because people lowered their tolerance for what they would accept as they got beaten down with time, but if you look at the literature on recursion theory, automata theory, or other areas where there are decision procedures, where you're trying to describe moderately complicated algorithms, the gulf between a perfectly clear rigorous description in English and a PASCAL program is a major one which you'd hire a staff of people to overcome.

O'Donnell: I'm not suggesting that the gulf isn't a major one, but rather that the abutment which has been added to one edge of that gulf in a mere couple of decades is tremendous when you consider the history of science. It's rather silly to conclude from the remaining gulf that it's unbridgeable.

Meyer: I don't say it's unbridgeable, but I'm not willing to say we'll bridge it in the next decade.

O'Donnell: Some people may be foolish enough to say that, but we have gotten it to a level where the abutment is of significant use to us, and there's no reason to think that with the same amount of work we can't get an abutment on the other side of the logic chasm that is of at least as much use to us. We certainly have not put the equivalent effort into logic.

van Emde Boas: I have two points: first, I claim that the method for getting rid of the statement, "By Church's thesis ..." can be found in my thesis from '74. When I used it, I know an editor who flatly asked me to get rid of all the applications of this formalism in the paper before publication.

Meyer: I can't remember - was I the editor?

van Emde Boas: My other comment is, I think that there may be some other content to the Németi/Andreka paper this morning.[1]

I think in this kind of discussion we are missing one of the gists of Temporal and also Intentional Logic. What we saw this morning was not Temporal Logic. Temporal Logic deals with time without being capable of talking explicitly about moments of time. Likewise, Intentional Logic is capable of dealing with states without talking explicitly about them. In the applications of Intentional Logic, states will arise, but the logic itself has no term which refers to a state. This is an inherent weakness of these languages which makes them interesting, much more interesting than type theory, which is essentially first-order over Henkin-like interpretations.

---

[1] I. Németi, "Nonstandard Dynamic Logic", this volume.

Clarke: It's important to be able to specify the correctness of a program even if you can't actually prove that the program meets its specifications. For example, I remember how discouraging it was in an operating systems class to have the teacher assign a mutual exclusion problem without being able to state precisely what we were assuming about fairness. Secondly, if we could get some mechanical assistance, it might be possible to get around these objections to verifying programs. Although we would be unlikely to have that in general, we could hope to get it for very simple classes of programs which are nevertheless very important, for example in network protocols for microcode.

Marek Karpinski: I would like to ask Albert: is your position that of the computer scientist or that of the mathematician?

Meyer: I'm not sure I understand the question, but let me try answering it anyway. I wasn't positioning myself in any particular camp. I was offering two concrete positions. One was that we were trying to find what things might be special about programs that are different from other mathematical objects, and that we haven't found it, at least in the first pass. I don't know if I take that position as a logician, verifier, or person. The other position here is that I see a substantial gulf between what we're doing now and direct practical applications. That doesn't disturb me. I'm happy to continue doing what we're doing now, I think that it's premature to do what Hailpern was asking us to do, about connecting up what we're doing now with the efforts of well-intentioned engineers in VLSI. I think that would be a distraction for us. We're very far removed from such direct applications. It's a different enterprise, and the issues of "Similarly ...", "Clearly ...", "Without loss of generality, ..." are one reflection of that. These are issues of artificial intelligence and knowledge base built into verifiers that are quite apart from the focus of our concerns in this symposium. Important concerns, but ones that frankly cow me, and I'm not about to leap into that until I finish what I do see as our job.

Rohit Parikh: I'd like to address myself to the first of the positions, which is related to the talk we heard this morning.[1] Two historical things came to my mind. One was the period of the early thirties, when various people proposed different technical definitions of "computable function", and then later on it was proved by a series of theorems that these definitions were all equivalent. Now this was a cause for congratulations rather than a cause for sorrow. It meant that we had singled out a very important, lucrative notion. I'm not saying we have done that there, I'm saying that that's one paradigm, which appeared in a paper of Myhill sometime in the late

---

[1] Albert R. Meyer, Jerzy Tiuryn, "A note on equivalences among logics of programs", this volume.

'50s, in which he showed that all creative sets were recursively isomorphic. Now since all non-trivial theories then known were creative, all of them were recursively isomorphic; thus people studying group theory, people studying number theory, and other people studying other kinds of theories, were in fact all studying the same field! Now the second paradigm didn't work that way. So the question is, which of these paradigms applies here? The fact is that these different logics, Algorithmic Logic, Dynamic Logic, etc. are similar, and I think that it's almost nationalistic to have so many different systems rather than a single one. Everyone wants to say "my system is better", and study it, even though it's only a slight variant of someone else's. The result is that we are preventing the rest of the world from appreciating our work, because one person's definitions are useless in reading another person's paper. I would say, on the other hand, that the fact that these are all reducible to infinitary first-order logic, while a very useful and interesting observation, is maybe not germane, because you can make this reduction while having no programs appear on the right hand side, thus the questions that are most interesting to us have disappeared; we have kept expressive power, but we have lost exactly this sense of motion that we wanted in the first place.

David Harel: Yes, you've taken away about 4/5 of my remarks. The little bit that's left is a counter-balance to your [Meyer's] first position. After your talk this morning, at least one person said that if I hadn't made my remark he would have gone away thinking that everything that was done before your talk was all the same, and that's it. Here again I have the feeling that there are people who will go away from this discussion thinking, after your position A now, that we have to leave everything now to logicians, because everything has been reduced to infinitary first-order logic. I'd just like to counterbalance that view maybe a little more extremely than I would have done otherwise, by saying that I don't think that's right. Just because there were simpler programming languages underneath, and that in the lattice of formal systems there is some element up here which is greater than all these logics, doesn't mean you can take this top element instead, since it doesn't show what might have been thought down below, as you say it does. Another point is that some questions which logicians should ask themselves are motivated by computer science. For example, something like dynamic algebras or some aspect of PDL I'm sure are of interest to logicians, as interactions with pure logicians have shown recently. Another example is data base theory, in which for example there is some work by Ashok Chandra and myself that has led to some open questions which turned out to be technically very interesting to logicians, simply because of the fact that they had thought only about infinite model theory, and there came a very simple question about finite models that they couldn't answer immediately. It turned out to be technically very complicated, and we had no idea it would meet with this response. So if we do what you say, and say everything sits there under $L_{\omega_1\omega}$, let's go home and do something else, then logicians won't get a crack at these problems which are useful and interesting.

Meyer: I think I agree with everything you say except for what I hear is an interpretation of my remarks, which were meant to be narrower. I certainly don't want to cut off the whole area. In fact I distinguish in my own mind, and maybe I should say explicitly, between these first order versions of Dynamic and Algorithmic Logic, which I spoke about, and the propositional versions, which are quite different technically, and have a very different theory which does sound really neat and useful, as we saw for example in Ed's talk.[1] So please don't interpret what I'm saying as a blanket criticism that says that the whole subject of logics of programs and program verification reduces to logic and we should give up. Rather, the particular set of questions involving the first-order extensions to Dynamic and Algorithmic Logic, Logic of Effective Definitions, etc., in an effort to capture reasoning about control structure, I believe in fact have reduced to some clear logical questions about $L_{\omega_1 \omega}$, and I would most encourage my own students to pursue those questions further. I'm still happy to have students working on PDL, type theory, and in this area in general, which I think is well worth pursuing.

Németi: Partly I would like to agree with you and partly disagree. First the disagreement: we have shown that the first version of first-order Dynamic Logic can be reduced to classical first-order logic. The reducibility is nothing negative. It is only the beginning of the story, I believe, because we still don't understand first-order dynamic logic. The theory of first-order logic cannot just replace the thing that has been reduced, and that's the disagreement. I completely agree with you that logic should be the fundamental study. It's most useful if there is an understanding of the basic principles; then people can build more reliable systems and so on, but one shouldn't confuse this with fundamental research. In electrical engineering, Maxwell's work is very important. His questions help one understand what electricity is. But when I was an electrical engineer, I never designed a machine by using his equations. Still I wouldn't have been able to do what I did if I hadn't known about them. One other disagreement: I strongly protest against saying that mathematical logic is metamathematics. I think that mathematical logic is a branch of mathematics, the phenomena of the real world, just like the differential equations. Boole published his work under the title "Laws of Thought". The subject of logic is the phenomena of thinking. That's not metamathematics.

---

[1] Clarke and Emerson, "Design and Synthesis of Synchronization Skeletons using Branching Time Temporal Logic", this volume.

Meyer: I don't agree. I don't think that mathematical logic as I know it has anything to do with natural world or social world phenomena. I don't know anybody who thinks the way Gentzen or Hilbert proof rules work. I'm not convinced that mathematical logic really gives any laws of thought. I don't think people think that way.

Németi: So you ought to be telling this to logicians - that's very nice, they should hear that.

Erwin Engeler: This is an idealistic position that people have been convinced of ever since the work of Ianov, Frege, and Whitehead and Russell, namely that in principle it should be possible to translate all of our mathematical reasoning into these formal systems. I don't think anybody in his right mind believes that there are currently proofs or solutions of problems that are done this way.

O'Donnell: I think that the distinction Istvan (Németi) made between giving the laws of thought and studying the laws of thought was missed. If we look at things carefully we would never suggest that the real numbers are the actual things that are in the air when we make measurements in physics - in fact physical measurements don't act like real numbers in many important ways. Nevertheless, we accept real analysis as a study of physical measurement, at least to some extent. You may be admitting that a lot of mathematical logic has been done wrong, but I think we can take certain good hunks of it as studies of particular ways of thought, perhaps not entirely precise, but interesting and valuable nevertheless.

*****

Amir Pnueli: I'm sorry Leslie Lamport couldn't be here today, because he is usually more expressive on this subject than I, but since part of the message I have to say is that expressibility is not of importance, maybe I will be able to state this position. I will go back to the origins - not as far back as the Bible, but only to the Algol 60 report. The specification of this programming language was said to consist of syntax, semantics, and pragmatics. They weren't really very true to form in filling out those three obligations. They were very good with syntax, and we have all been occupied at certain times with semantics since. Pragmatics somehow failed to materialize. What I would like to propose is that in the proper definition, programming logic should be something that should have all those three facets: syntax, semantics, and pragmatics. Those things which consist of only syntax and semantics alone are mathematical systems which may have originally been inspired by programming but have now become quite removed from it. It's not very surprising that those people who deal with only syntax and semantics will sometimes feel that they have reached a dead end, or that they might show that everything under the sun is equivalent. I'm not an expert on the subject, but I somehow have the suspicion that if you ask logicians to estimate the value of the purely logical work in our field, they would say that the results are not very deep. When I was able to attract logicians to do what we have been doing, usually the main thing that attracted them and caused them to cooperate was the pragmatics, the motivation. Of course you may not agree with this definition of programming logic, but if you do, and if you measure the relative efficiency or usefulness of two programming logics, all three aspects should be compared. It is not sufficient just to compare expressibility. If we were just relying on expressibility, we should all be programming with Turing machines, and why should we bother to develop any other language? Restricting expressibility might have some benefits. I want to mention two concrete examples, both having to do the Temporal Logic. Temporal Logic is really a very tiny fragment of Dynamic Logic. It's true that anything I can say by $\Diamond P$, that's "eventually P", can be modeled by a single-letter proposition and a single-letter program in this form: $\langle a^* \rangle P$. The only difference is in the pragmatics. How do we apply those things to programming concepts? This makes a world of difference. In Dynamic Logic, your letters convey elementary programs; in Temporal Logic, they convey the passage of time. If you want to stick to Dynamic Logic, and interpret single elementary programs as the passage of time, that's OK, you have adopted the interpretation of Temporal Logic, and they will then be equivalent under the pragmatic, although the notation might be a little inconvenient. Another criticism was that from the point of view of expressibility, Temporal Logic is equivalent to the first-order theory of linear order, and everything that can be said in Temporal Logic can be said by using explicit time variables. I say again, the semantics is the same, but the syntax is different. If you don't worry at all about syntax, if you don't worry about the difference between a Turing machine and a PASCAL program, then you may not care that these are syntactically different, but if you like a structured representation of the thing you are dealing with, if you would like to study the minimal structure of time that is necessary in order to reason about those things, then perhaps Temporal Logic still has a place under the sun. If you agree that the analogy that I'm drawing between programming logics and programming languages is a valid one, then all three parts are important. A programming logic is not only something to prove metatheorems about, but it is also something to write programming proofs in. In that respect it is very similar to a programming language, and therefore pragmatics should be part of every good specification and design of a programming logic.

Meyer: First, Amir presents his case very well and I agree with him. All three facts make an applicable and useful mathematical theory, both of programming languages and of their logics. The place where I have difficulty is where Amir himself begins by saying that the Algol 60 report did fine on syntax; John Backus promised that in six weeks a comparable report would appear describing the semantics; and nobody really has anything definitive or even terribly lucid to say about the pragmatics. Therefore, while I don't deny its crucial importance, it seems to me unreasonable to put the burden on us to solve that problem, which is not the kind of problem that you come to theoreticians with. The pragmatic problems have to be dealt with by the practitioner, at least to formulate them to the point where they can be studied theoretically. When they're still in this muddy state, we have to change modes and become practitioners in order to participate. The world is divided up into people who are good at different kinds of things, and people narrow their focus of attention for sensible reasons. I don't feel the obligation to change what I'm good at to go do something else. When the pragmatics get clear enough to work on, we'll work on them.

Barry Rosen: On the other hand, I don't think you can expect people who are trying to get something up and running, out the door, selling, etc., to produce clear concepts by themselves and then hand theorists nice clean mathematical problems. There has to be dialog.

Meyer: More than dialog, it's multilog. We've seen this kind of thing happen before. The practitioners knew many years ago how to build very good compilers, even though they didn't know what grammars were. It was taught by an apprentice system. As time went on, the difficulty was not in producing compilers, but rather in teaching the methods. Concepts evolved, grammars developed, and now we're at the stage where we can teach that stuff pretty well, since the theory is much more tractable. I hope that a similar thing will happen here.

Rosen: But still it's very difficult to produce a good compiler for any reasonably expressive programming language. It's not merely difficult to teach it, it's difficult to do it. There has been some success in that area, but it is still a very difficult task.

Meyer: Yes, but although you may run a great risk when you're doing theory in isolation from practice, that doesn't mean that in order to do useful research on theoretical aspects of program semantics and logic, that you in fact have to go into the production compiler business.

Engeler: I submit that theory and practice are not related at all. Most of us are teaching in universities, and most of our students go out into practice. If we can do a good job teaching them theoretical concepts, including things from programming logics, even if they don't use it every day, here is where we will have the most influence. This is perhaps more important than using our little games on the rather large-scale problems that people work on.

Hailpern: I think you're (Meyer) undervaluing your own results when you say that they really aren't ready for practice outside, because we're still working on the theory. In Temporal Logic there are gems that people outside of this auditorium need and really do want. If you never look at that, even if you are a good mathematician, you will never find out that you may have a beautiful concept but nobody in his right mind will ever use it. The better concept is one that is intuitive enough so that one does not have to understand the theory to use the tool. You don't have to understand how Maxwell arrived at his equations to be able to put together something that works with electricity. Maybe these are not the best tools, maybe this is like FORTRAN or assembly language, but until you get feedback from the outside, you'll never converge on something that everybody is going to be able to use. Now maybe that's not your goal, but that's one of mine.

Pnueli: What Albert said was right, but I think there is a confusion here between the muddiness of pragmatics in the programming language constructs (and I agree that it hasn't crystallized very well there) and pragmatics in the programming logic. What I meant was very simple. First I would like every paper on programming logic to say something about how this programming logic is to be applied to proving something about programs. Secondly, I would like to say what pragmatic considerations are: from a pragmatic point of view, one programming logic is better than another if it is easier to prove certain things in it or if the proof comes out more elegant or more natural. To measure this is not very easy, and it's sometimes difficult to prove that proofs in one language will always be easier than another, but at least it's something which is very well defined.

Németi: I'd like to protest a little bit about what you (Pnueli) said about our papers. The structure of our technological society is just not like that. There was a guy called Roentgen. You could have gone to him and said, "What are you doing playing around with these funny things of yours? Why don't you try to heal people who have colds?" There are theoreticians who are doing basic research, and there are less theoretical theoreticians, and there are technologists, so there is a whole spectrum of research in science. The theoreticians doing the basic research are really needed, because the basic ideas, the fundamental ways we look at things, come from there. Now, if you want to restrict them to report each time how this will be used, then it will result in impotence.

Engeler: It also works the other way around. Any practitioner worth his salt will go out and look for things that will be helpful to him.

Vaughan Pratt: When Amir first told me about Temporal Logic at a conference about three years ago or so, he showed me some axioms for it, and he wasn't sure whether he could prove such-and-such from it. I looked at his axioms and showed him how to prove it. The reason I was able to do this was that these axioms were the same as the ones that we had just recently been given by Segerberg for Propositional Dynamic Logic. Now had there been a dearth of PDL axioms or a dearth of understanding of the semantics of PDL, I think I might have been very excited by Temporal Logic, because it seemed to offer some clean description of a programming logic. Since it didn't seem to be telling me anything new, it just seemed to be removing a little bit of the structure of PDL, I was not so excited. My feeling is that unless you can show me a major advance resulting from cutting down on the size of the logic, in other words, an advance that I can actually take advantage of, then I'm not terribly interested in the fact that you've made the logic smaller.

Dexter Kozen: I'd like to know exactly what you (Pnueli) mean by pragmatics. There are a number of papers in Temporal Logic which are supposedly pragmatic, but they all seem to apply nice general proof principles to very simple examples. Five years ago we were proving McCarthy's 91 function correct, now everybody's doing two-processor mutual exclusion. I'd like to know what's pragmatic about that. Dave Luckham spoke yesterday about high level specification languages and indicated that this is the real problem, because these general proof principles don't apply when you get down to the grunge.

Pnueli: First I find it very difficult to define what pragmatic is. On the other hand, I would like to center more on the question that I would know how to identify some pragmatic considerations. For example, questions of complexity of decision procedures is a pragmatic consideration - how fast can you decide something in your theory. Another is the one that I mentioned, namely that in comparing two systems, one is pragmatically better than another if it can be applied to different cases in a more successful way. I'm sure Brent Hailpern can answer about applications which are more than examples, like concurrent problems of more than just two processes. He did this in his thesis and he's doing the same thing here, more realistic things. Now clearly there is a gap. Actually I didn't interpret what David (Luckham) said yesterday that the general principles are invalid. I think that what he said was that there are a lot of things that have to be added to them, and he's concentrating on all those additions. I didn't get the impression that he said that general principles don't apply, but they have to be enriched by a lot of other things. I would say that those are clearly pragmatic considerations. He's starting from the pragmatic side of it. Hopefully we'll meet somewhere in the middle sometime.

van Emde Boas: There is a definition of pragmatics in natural language, and we might try to find out whether it makes sense here. In natural language, pragmatics deals with the question of whether a given correct and meaningful sentence makes sense in a certain situation. In this context you would ask if a given syntactically and semantically correct program makes sense. I'm not sure if that's the pragmatic you had in mind.

Pnueli: It has some bearing on it, because it tells you whether a certain sentence can be applied in a certain situation. If this is the case, then this is identical to what I have in mind. If somebody asks me what Temporal Logic is good for or why is it interesting, I cannot claim that it is interesting because it can express things, or the syntax is more interesting, or the axioms are more interesting. What I can say is that it can be applied to concurrent programs where very few other languages or systems were applicable before. So the pragmatic value of Temporal Logic is high in that sense.

Meyer: I agree with everything except the very last couple of words. The pragmatic value is very high, but it's not the pragmatic value of Temporal Logic. It's the pragmatic value of that study of the applications, which could perfectly well have been done with Dynamic Logic or any of these other systems.

Kozen: You don't like the fact that people are comparing Dynamic Logic and Temporal Logic with respect to expressiveness, bit if it's the case that logic L1 can do everything that logic L2 can do, why is it so bad to go with L1? You claim you need more power, you want to start with Temporal Logic and expand it to handle other situations. Isn't that what Dynamic Logic does?

Pnueli: My own preference is to use the Temporal Logic operators and apply them by considering execution sequences. Now if anyone would like to start with the syntax of Dynamic Logic, interpret a single letter as the transition of time, and adopt all the axioms of Dynamic Logic, and apply it in a similar way to concurrent programs, he is welcome. That's exactly the kind of system I'm interested in, a system that consists of those operators, and can be applied in a particular interpretation, to a particular application. So I have nothing against trying to apply Dynamic Logic in this way, to execution sequences.

Pratt: Then why maintain the distinction?

Pnueli: I don't know, the notation seems a little easier.

Hailpern: I think there is a distinction in there, and I think it's a worthwhile one. There have been a series of operators in Temporal Logic proposed: henceforth, eventually, next, until, while, etc. It's an interesting challenge, at least for me, to use as few as possible and still keep the proof simple. In particular I have avoided using the until operator, and at times had to go through some gyrations to do so. The until operator of Temporal Logic subsumes everything. But there are some very nice properties that you can prove very clearly with simple, intuitive proofs. Similarly with Dynamic Logic: yes, you can prove everything, but having the programs inside the operators just makes me have to type two or three extra characters, and doesn't buy me anything.

Kozen: But that's not why the until operator was introduced. It was introduced to simplify the syntax down to a point where you could prove a hard mathematical result about the expressibility of the language or completeness of a deductive system. It wasn't introduced to make proofs simpler or for any other pragmatic reason. But it is still relevant to what you're doing.

Hailpern: Absolutely, these questions are important and they should be studied. It's just that there's another component there that seems to be slighted a bit in the purely theoretical approach.

van Emde Boas: Considering this pragmatic aspect, take the case of regular programs. There is a clear difference between the Temporal Logic approach and the Dynamic Logic approach. The Dynamic Logic language more or less reflects the structure of programs you are going to consider. Logical formulas decompose according to how the programs are built. In the Temporal Logic machinery you only have this finite automation sitting in there which describes the entire state space. In this case, Dynamic Logic gives you this slight step of compositionality which makes life easier and therefore it should be considered pragmatic. Would you consider such an argument to be valid in comparing these systems?

Pnueli: Yes, and I would say it even more strongly than you: in sequential, well-structured programs, Dynamic Logic is clearly a much better tool than Temporal Logic. I'm sorry that for concurrent programs, we don't know yet how to reason about structured programs in structured ways. Temporal Logic reasons in a non-structured way, so far. That's something I would call to the attention of anyone who's interested in improving the situation.

Parikh: I would like to submit that this whole discussion in a way may be fruitless. First of all there seems to be no argument that Dynamic Logic is more expressive than Temporal Logic. On the other hand, it seems that people like Manna and Pnueli who have been getting down to brass tacks and proving programs correct, have been doing a service to the field which casts a certain amount of credit on Temporal Logic, and by implication also on Dynamic Logic. I don't know if it makes sense for people to confine their areas so narrowly that they say, "I'm interested in Dynamic Logic but not in Temporal Logic", or vice versa. It's more or less the same general area and people should work on whatever interests them.

*****

Németi: One of our (my and Hajnal Andréka's) positions is that there is a lot of work to be done in first-order Dynamic Logic. One problem is the following: Propositional Dynamic Logic is fine, because the set of tautologies is recursively enumerable. In first-order Dynamic Logic, completeness is usually done with the help of supernatural forces: completeness with respect to oracles, arithmetical completeness, things like that. One thing that I really believe is that the set of proofs should be decidable. It may be just a coincidence, but I don't know of any other logic without decidable proofs. I don't care what the set of proofs looks like or what the details are, but it should be decidable. Some people have studied effective ω-rules. Using the effective ω-rule, you can prove that Fermat's conjecture is true, but so far, nobody has had time to check the proof. Now I'd like to say a few words about another thing that bothers me about the present directions of research. One question is, do we want categoricity or not? In other words, do we want our logic to describe our model completely? Do we want to have a logic with infinitely many axioms or a recursively enumerable set of axioms such that the class of models for this theory will be just one? My position is that if we have this property, if we take our definitions so far, then we have lost logic - we are back to the age before modern advances in logic and model theory.

Kozen: I disagree with that in the sense that striving for categoricity can bring operational semantics and algebraic semantics closer together. The operationalist has just one model in mind, and really doesn't care about all these nonstandard models. The algebraist complains that once you try to describe everything that's going on, you're really doing number theory, not logic or universal algebra. Unfortunately, there's a tradeoff between the two, and there are advantages and disadvantages to both. The idea now is to find some happy medium where you can have algebraic elegance and still describe what pragmatists want to describe.

O'Donnell: The problem is not in having categoricity, but in having it in a dishonest way. If you're going to be studying logic, you're going to be working in a fixed formal system, and asking about its stability and power. There have been some technically correct but I think nonsensical results, and I'll get personal here. Albert (Meyer) came the other year and told us that in Dymanic Logic you can say what the integers are. There is a technical interpretation of that which is perfectly true. However, all it really says is that we have declared by fiat that we know what the integers are, because programs can only loop an integer number of times. We have really restricted the models. The claim that we have somehow used the mechanism of Dynamic Logic to say what the integers are, is false. If we want to study the power of a language, we have to allow all reasonable interpretations, so that discovering how much categoricity is achieved by rules of reasoning will actually give some measure of the power of the logic. I think you fail to do that by introducing ω with mad abandon. That's what you (Kozen) did in "*-continuity"[1], didn't you? The interpretation you proposed, if I remember correctly, is that a^* means exactly the union of a^i over all i.

Kozen: No, not at all. Join, - not union - there's a big difference. Join is a purely syntactic concept. Although it's infinitary, it's very useful in informal proofs and comes closer to the standard models, so it's doing just what you (O'Donnell) want.

Parikh: I'd like to respond to Dexter's comments, but say something of a slightly different nature. When we talk about categoricity, in this context, there are two quite different kinds of categoricity which we ought to distinguish, at least at the outset. There is categoricity of structure on the one hand, for example, running a program over the field of real numbers, when in fact we know that there are no real numbers but only some representation of them which isn't really the real numbers at all. At that level, we may not be all that interested in categoricity. In any case, the structure that we are studying is only an approximation to the structures that we are primarily interested in. But there is also the other kind of categoricity, which is the basic use of natural numbers involved in saying that the program terminates. Now one of the reasons why Hoare logic is incomplete is that you have the following situation: there is some model in which, starting in a state satisfying condition P, in an infinite number of steps you can go to condition $\neg Q$, and therefore $\{P\}A\{Q\}$ is not true of that model. It seems to me that to allow these infinite computations is not so wonderful because real computer scientists not only don't want infinite computations, they don't even want ones that are very long.

[1] Kozen, "On induction vs. *-continuity", this volume.

O'Donnell: But you miss the point. The point is not that we are deciding whether to allow these things or not. The point is that we have a logic with certain rules of inference, and an intended interpretation. The intent of that logic may be to talk about real programs which run a finite amount of time, but that is a very slippery concept. We can keep in mind that one standard model over the others, but when we want to analyze the logic, we must ask what it really talks about, not what we wish it talked about, and it really does talk about some infinite computations that halt. We should admit that, and study the extent to which it also talks about those weird things as a measure of how far we are from the ideal. Let me point out though that occasionally we discover suddenly that the nonstandard models are the ones we are interested in. This happened to real analysis; it also happened in trees, when people discovered that in lazy evaluation, nonstandard models of rather anemic theories of trees turned out to be quite implementable and useful. So we do occasionally have the good fortune to make something that looked like an outrageous model reasonable and useful. But the main reason is still to measure the power of logic.

*****

Krzysztof Apt: I just want to sketch a summary of the work that we have heard about in the last few days. I think that what connects us all is the problem of programs, but is it something that connects us or something that divides us? The original goal of all these logics of programs was to prove programs correct, but I think we are quite far from this goal, in the sense that we are now busy with other issues. I would like to present a hierarchy of problems which I think somehow represents work in the last 15 years, so we can find out where we are in this hierarchy, how far we are from practice, and how far we are from logic. At the top of the hierarchy we have the problem of proving programs correct. The next thing would be to devise some systems which allow us to prove programs correct. At the next step we must justify these systems. This involves introducing notions like soundness and completeness. There may be some problems with what completeness really means, so we start to refine these notions or introduce some new notions like expressiveness. The next thing in this hierarchy are theorems of the following kind: you have some notion, suppose expressiveness, and you can now prove that under the assumption of expressiveness you can prove completeness. Every well-versed, mature mathematician will now ask if the implication can be reversed. So what we are doing at this moment is studying the notions from level 4. At a certain moment we are interested in studying models of these logics. I think that this is more or less the spectrum that covers the whole conference.

1) Proving programs correct
2) Design of proof systems
3) Justification of systems
4) Additional notions to study 3)
5) Proving theorems about 4)
6) Model theory

Owicki and Lamport tried to say[1] that we can be divided into logicians and verifiers, but this is too simplistic, because the spectrum is almost continuous in a sense, and it's difficult to say where the divisions are. It's obvious that people who study 6) are logicians, and those who study 1) are verifiers, however there are a lot of us on the border here. I put myself somewhere around 3). I am interested in this direction, because I used to be a logician, and I left logic because the theorems which I really considered interesting and important were not the theorems I was supposed to prove. This spectrum covers our different interests, and if we try to convince one another that we ought to be doing this or that, we should realize that it is definitely only a question of taste, and not whether it is somehow closer to practice. Each level adds yet another theoretical aspect to this hierarchy, and I believe that at a certain moment practice really doesn't matter, and it becomes completely irrelevant what sort of computers or programming languages you use. It worries me to see people comparing tools with complete disregard to what practice has to offer. What particularly worries me is when people still consider <u>while</u> programs exclusively, when the whole theory of programming languages continues to develop, and more and more new interesting programming concepts arise, and they cry out for tools of reasoning. In particular I do not think that the problem of translating one set of notions into another is of any relevance. We have what Amir suggested, a sort of hand-in-hand development of programming concepts and logics which deal with these concepts. That's exactly the thing that I personally like about Hoare logic: there you have a very close correspondence between programming concepts and the deductive system. The fact that this is not a logic in the sense of mathematical logic, because you cannot conjoin or negate formulae, I think has a certain advantage here, because one is barred from considering Hoare algebras or thinking about compactness theorems, and is simply forced to consider devising proof systems which deal with programs. I think that as soon as you make it a program logic in the sense of devising a set of connectives, you start going up in the hierarchy, and I'm convinced that this is not the right direction.

---

[1] Lamport and Owicki, "Program Logics and Program Verification", this volume.

Parikh: I want to respond to the last point. You've got this large area consisting of several quite different levels. The fact that there are so many levels says that in a project of this kind you expect a lot of variety. What is bad is that there is not adequate communication between the different levels, so that ideas from the top level eventually filter down to the bottom level and vice versa. I think that may be due to the fact that people have two different kinds of training: those who are trained in logic gravitate toward 6) and those whose primary training is in programming gravitate towards 1), and even that with difficulty. There aren't sufficiently many people to form links between these various levels.

Apt: I presented this hierarchy just to show what we are doing, and at the very last tried to indicate which level I prefer. I think that the fact that there is a lack of communication is not by chance. This is an indication that these levels are hardly related to each other. From a logical point of view, these things are very closely interrelated, but from a practical point of view, there are very huge gaps.

Parikh: I disagree with you. From my point of view the defect is in lack of communication. For example, yesterday when Dave Luckham gave his talk about ADA, I was very pleased that someone was giving a background talk to which we could relate. But after five minutes I found myself completely unable to follow. It seems to me that we have a desperate need for people who can look at a program and single out features of interest to a mathematician, and conversely someone who will take mathematical results and apply them.

Kozen: One thing that would help is that if people in area 1) would open themselves up to some of the very nice techniques that are available and some of the nice insight that can come from looking at things from a more theoretical perspective. I find it very closed-minded to refuse to add negation or conjunction to Hoare logic because you think it will lead you off in the wrong direction. But then you will spend all your time hacking Hoare logic and never really get the insight that comes from looking at more modern systems like Dynamic and Temporal Logic or the use of the large body of techniques of classical logic available.

Apt: But I think these techniques only apply to the second step of this hierarchy. I cannot imagine that someone on level 1) will ever be bothered by the fact that some notions are needed to study completeness of some systems. The problem is that people from practice are indeed interested in how to prove their programs correct, but they are not interested in any higher levels of this hierarchy. From a certain point on, we are completely, exclusively mathematical logic.

Kozen: On the contrary, I think that a practitioner should be interested in a completeness theorem, knowing that this set of axioms characterizes in a nutshell everything that is true that you might want to prove, and nothing is left out, so that if you can't prove something, either you aren't trying hard enough or it isn't true. It's not the fault of the system.

Hailpern: But does the practitioner have to know the completeness proof from scratch? I agree that completeness is good for a practitioner to know. But human beings can't cover all this range of information. You can't expect the practitioner to go after theory because they're not interested in it, they would rather be content in knowing that someone else has done it. What's important is that there's communication between the various steps. Maybe one thing that could come out of this workshop is more than just a proceedings, but model theorists and ADA provers getting together and saying what they have done, and where it fits in.

van Emde Boas: I'm puzzled whether the system is supposed to function without semantics. Where in this hierarchy is the activity of assigning meanings to programs gone? Does it not show up at all until level 6 ?

Apt: This is a hierarchy about logics of programs, not about semantics. Structures like dynamic algebras, Kripke models, etc., occur only because you have to justify your proof systems. This is an auxiliary notion from outside the hierarchy.

Németi: My feeling is that this hierarchy is a very grave oversimplification. The field is just too complicated to describe in one dimension. But in general I feel that it's much more important to understand what's going on than to be able to prove certain programs correct.

van Emde Boas: I have the impression that level 1) through level 5) all can be done if you only have access to the syntax. If someone comes up with a programming language whose semantics is entirely empty, then you will not know what you are talking about unless you consider level 6).

Hailpern: Isn't there a meaning of programs at each of these levels? One is talking about compiler semantics of PASCAL or ADA. One is talking about linear time or branching time in temporal logic.

Pnueli: Just one nasty remark in response to someone who asked if a verifier would be interested in seeing a proof of completeness. The answer is yes, because a verifier would like to know if the proof of completeness depends on either using oracles or that his program is run on nonstandard models. This tells how to estimate the value of the notion of completeness. In your hierarchy you would like to know, when you say relative completeness, whether you mean relative to something which you have no chance of ever verifying completely.

Apt: Another thing I realize is that if I try to prove some programs correct, the knowledge of how the completeness proof proceeds helps me, because it may give me some heuristic. But I do not want to make any claims that it has some direct impact on practice. There is another point, that this hierarchy should be restricted somehow from growing too big. After level 5), the problems, methods, and results are purely mathematical logic and have been removed from their grass roots in level 1). Our idea now is to get together to have these levels communicate, but I think that in the long run they will just move further away from each other.

Németi: I don't think so, because your view depends on this hierarchy which I don't agree with. Number 3) bothers me a lot. Your way of looking at things is just not the same as mine. For example, in 6), there is dynamic algebra. If University students studying to be programmers were taught dynamic algebra, they would get tremendous insight into the things they will eventually deal with. It's a great problem what to teach programmers. You can tell them about some particular computer system, but they might never use it. It's much better to teach something that will give general insight. You have put dynamic algebras into 6), but I think dynamic algebras should also be in 1) because they deal with phenomena that programmers encounter every day.

Apt: Circuit theory is very closely connected with logical operations, which are very closely connected with Boolean algebras. But do good circuit designers really need to know that two countable atomless Boolean algebras are isomorphic? They could not care less. I think that even if you told them, it wouldn't help them devise better circuits. I think exactly the same thing can be said about dynamic algebra. I cannot imagine a situation where knowledge of dynamic algebra would improve the quality of programs.

Németi: But it would improve the quality of the programmer.

Pnueli: If the problem is really communication among the levels, I think that this conference could be a definite contribution.

Parikh: Many people get their degrees and go into applied areas. If they have theoretical training before they start working in applications, it will be easier for them to keep in touch with theoretical developments that affect their work. Right now I think we have a lot of people who are lacking in this.

*****

Vol. 77: G. V. Bochmann, Architecture of Distributed Computer Systems. VIII, 238 pages. 1979.

Vol. 78: M. Gordon, R. Milner and C. Wadsworth, Edinburgh LCF. VIII, 159 pages. 1979.

Vol. 79: Language Design and Programming Methodology. Proceedings, 1979. Edited by J. Tobias. IX, 255 pages. 1980.

Vol. 80: Pictorial Information Systems. Edited by S. K. Chang and K. S. Fu. IX, 445 pages. 1980.

Vol. 81: Data Base Techniques for Pictorial Applications. Proceedings, 1979. Edited by A. Blaser. XI, 599 pages. 1980.

Vol. 82: J. G. Sanderson, A Relational Theory of Computing. VI, 147 pages. 1980.

Vol. 83: International Symposium Programming. Proceedings, 1980. Edited by B. Robinet. VII, 341 pages. 1980.

Vol. 84: Net Theory and Applications. Proceedings, 1979. Edited by W. Brauer. XIII, 537 Seiten. 1980.

Vol. 85: Automata, Languages and Programming. Proceedings, 1980. Edited by J. de Bakker and J. van Leeuwen. VIII, 671 pages. 1980.

Vol. 86: Abstract Software Specifications. Proceedings, 1979. Edited by D. Bjørner. XIII, 567 pages. 1980

Vol. 87: 5th Conference on Automated Deduction. Proceedings, 1980. Edited by W. Bibel and R. Kowalski. VII, 385 pages. 1980.

Vol. 88: Mathematical Foundations of Computer Science 1980. Proceedings, 1980. Edited by P. Dembiński. VIII, 723 pages. 1980.

Vol. 89: Computer Aided Design - Modelling, Systems Engineering, CAD-Systems. Proceedings, 1980. Edited by J. Encarnacao. XIV, 461 pages. 1980.

Vol. 90: D. M. Sandford, Using Sophisticated Models in Resolution Theorem Proving.
XI, 239 pages. 1980

Vol. 91: D. Wood, Grammar and L Forms: An Introduction. IX, 314 pages. 1980.

Vol. 92: R. Milner, A Calculus of Communication Systems. VI, 171 pages. 1980.

Vol. 93: A. Nijholt, Context-Free Grammars: Covers, Normal Forms, and Parsing. VII, 253 pages. 1980.

Vol. 94: Semantics-Directed Compiler Generation. Proceedings, 1980. Edited by N. D. Jones. V, 489 pages. 1980.

Vol. 95: Ch. D. Marlin, Coroutines. XII, 246 pages. 1980.

Vol. 96: J. L. Peterson, Computer Programs for Spelling Correction: VI, 213 pages. 1980.

Vol. 97: S. Osaki and T. Nishio, Reliability Evaluation of Some Fault-Tolerant Computer Architectures. VI, 129 pages. 1980.

Vol. 98: Towards a Formal Description of Ada. Edited by D. Bjørner and O. N. Oest. XIV, 630 pages. 1980.

Vol. 99: I. Guessarian, Algebraic Semantics. XI, 158 pages. 1981.

Vol. 100: Graphtheoretic Concepts in Computer Science. Edited by H. Noltemeier. X, 403 pages. 1981.

Vol. 101: A. Thayse, Boolean Calculus of Differences. VII, 144 pages. 1981.

Vol. 102: J. H. Davenport, On the Integration of Algebraic Functions. 1–197 pages. 1981.

Vol. 103: H. Ledgard, A. Singer, J. Whiteside, Directions in Human Factors of Interactive Systems. VI, 190 pages. 1981.

Vol. 104: Theoretical Computer Science. Ed. by P. Deussen. VII, 261 pages. 1981.

Vol. 105: B. W. Lampson, M. Paul, H. J. Siegert, Distributed Systems – Architecture and Implementation. XIII, 510 pages. 1981.

Vol. 106: The Programming Language Ada. Reference Manual. X, 243 pages. 1981.

Vol. 107: International Colloquium on Formalization of Programming Concepts. Proceedings. Edited by J. Diaz and I. Ramos. VII, 478 pages. 1981.

Vol. 108: Graph Theory and Algorithms. Edited by N. Saito and T. Nishizeki. VI, 216 pages. 1981.

Vol. 109: Digital Image Processing Systems. Edited by L. Bolc and Zenon Kulpa. V, 353 pages. 1981.

Vol. 110: W. Dehning, H. Essig, S. Maass, The Adaptation of Virtual Man-Computer Interfaces to User Requirements in Dialogs. X, 142 pages. 1981.

Vol. 111: CONPAR 81. Edited by W. Händler. XI, 508 pages. 1981.

Vol. 112: CAAP '81. Proceedings. Edited by G. Astesiano and C. Böhm. VI, 364 pages. 1981.

Vol. 113: E.-E. Doberkat, Stochastic Automata: Stability, Nondeterminism, and Prediction. IX, 135 pages. 1981.

Vol. 114: B. Liskov, CLU, Reference Manual. VIII, 190 pages. 1981.

Vol. 115: Automata, Languages and Programming. Edited by S. Even and O. Kariv. VIII, 552 pages. 1981.

Vol. 116: M. A. Casanova, The Concurrency Control Problem for Database Systems. VII, 175 pages. 1981.

Vol. 117: Fundamentals of Computation Theory. Proceedings, 1981. Edited by F. Gécseg. XI, 471 pages. 1981.

Vol. 118: Mathematical Foundations of Computer Science 1981. Proceedings, 1981. Edited by J. Gruska and M. Chytil. XI, 589 pages. 1981.

Vol. 119: G. Hirst, Anaphora in Natural Language Understanding: A Survey. XIII, 128 pages. 1981.

Vol. 120: L. B. Rall, Automatic Differentiation: Techniques and Applications. VIII, 165 pages. 1981.

Vol. 121: Z. Zlatev, J. Wasniewski, and K. Schaumburg, Y12M Solution of Large and Sparse Systems of Linear Algebraic Equations. IX, 128 pages. 1981.

Vol. 122: Algorithms in Modern Mathematics and Computer Science. Proceedings, 1979. Edited by A. P. Ershov and D. E. Knuth. XI, 487 pages. 1981.

Vol. 123: Trends in Information Processing Systems. Proceedings, 1981. Edited by A. J. W. Duijvestijn and P. C. Lockemann. XI, 349 pages. 1981.

Vol. 124: W. Polak, Compiler Specification and Verification. XIII, 269 pages. 1981.

Vol. 125: Logic of Programs. Proceedings, 1979. Edited by E. Engeler. V, 245 pages. 1981.

Vol. 126: Microcomputer System Design. Proceedings, 1981. Edited by M. J. Flynn, N. R. Harris, and D. P. McCarthy. VII, 397 pages. 1982.

Voll. 127: Y.Wallach, Alternating Sequential/Parallel Processing. X, 329 pages. 1982.

Vol. 128: P. Branquart, G. Louis, P. Wodon, An Analytical Description of CHILL, the CCITT High Level Language. VI, 277 pages. 1982.

Vol. 129: B. T. Hailpern, Verifying Concurrent Processes Using Temporal Logic. VIII, 208 pages. 1982.

Vol. 130: R. Goldblatt, Axiomatising the Logic of Computer Programming. XI, 304 pages. 1982.

Vol. 131: Logics of Programs. Proceedings, 1981. Edited by D. Kozen. VI, 429 pages. 1982.

This series reports new developments in computer science research and teaching – quickly, informally and at a high level. The type of material considered for publication includes:

1. Preliminary drafts of original papers and monographs
2. Lectures on a new field or presentations of a new angle in a classical field
3. Seminar work-outs
4. Reports of meetings, provided they are
   a) of exceptional interest and
   b) devoted to a single topic.

Texts which are out of print but still in demand may also be considered if they fall within these categories.

The timeliness of a manuscript is more important than its form, which may be unfinished or tentative. Thus, in some instances, proofs may be merely outlined and results presented which have been or will later be published elsewhere. If possible, a subject index should be included. Publication of Lecture Notes is intended as a service to the international computer science community, in that a commercial publisher, Springer-Verlag, can offer a wide distribution of documents which would otherwise have a restricted readership. Once published and copyrighted, they can be documented in the scientific literature.

Manuscripts

Manuscripts should be no less than 100 and preferably no more than 500 pages in length.

They are reproduced by a photographic process and therefore must be typed with extreme care. Symbols not on the typewriter should be inserted by hand in indelible black ink. Corrections to the typescript should be made by pasting in the new text or painting out errors with white correction fluid. Authors receive 75 free copies and are free to use the material in other publications. The typescript is reduced slightly in size during reproduction; best results will not be obtained unless the text on any one page is kept within the overall limit of 18 x 26.5 cm (7 x 10½ inches). On request, the publisher will supply special paper with the typing area outlined.

Manuscripts should be sent to Prof. G. Goos, Institut für Informatik, Universität Karlsruhe, Zirkel 2, 7500 Karlsruhe/Germany, Prof. J. Hartmanis, Cornell University, Dept. of Computer-Science, Ithaca, NY/USA 14850, or directly to Springer-Verlag Heidelberg.

Springer-Verlag, Heidelberger Platz 3, D-1000 Berlin 33
Springer-Verlag, Tiergartenstraße 17, D-6900 Heidelberg 1
Springer-Verlag, 175 Fifth Avenue, New York, NJ 10010/USA

ISBN 3-540-11212-X
ISBN 0-387-11212-X